MIKE MENTZER

MIKE MENTZER

AMERICAN ODYSSEUS

JOHN LITTLE

Copyright © John Little, 2025

Published by ECW Press
665 Gerrard Street East
Toronto, Ontario, Canada M4M 1Y2
416-694-3348 / info@ecwpress.com

All rights reserved. No part of this publication may be reproduced, stored in a retrieval system, or transmitted in any form by any process — electronic, mechanical, photocopying, recording, or otherwise — without the prior written permission of the copyright owners and ECW Press. The scanning, uploading, and distribution of this book via the internet or via any other means without the permission of the publisher is illegal and punishable by law. This book may not be used for text and data mining, AI training, and similar technologies. Please purchase only authorized electronic editions, and do not participate in or encourage electronic piracy of copyrighted materials. Your support of the author's rights is appreciated.

Cover design: Ian Sullivan Cant
Cover images: Robert Gardner / Courtesy of Gail Gardner and his estate

LIBRARY AND ARCHIVES CANADA CATALOGUING IN PUBLICATION

Title: Mike Mentzer : American Odysseus / John Little.

Names: Little, John R., 1960- author

Description: Includes bibliographical references.

Identifiers: Canadiana (print) 20250140527 | Canadiana (ebook) 20250140551

ISBN 978-1-77041-784-7 (softcover)
ISBN 978-1-77852-398-4 (ePub)
ISBN 978-1-77852-399-1 (PDF)

Subjects: LCSH: Mentzer, Mike. | LCSH: Bodybuilders—United States—Biography. | LCSH: Weight lifters—United States—Biography. | LCSH: Bodybuilding. | LCGFT: Biographies.

Classification: LCC GV545.52.M46 L58 2025 | DDC 613.7/13092—dc23

This book is funded in part by the Government of Canada. *Ce livre est financé en partie par le gouvernement du Canada.* We also acknowledge the support of the Government of Ontario through the Ontario Book Publishing Tax Credit, and through Ontario Creates.

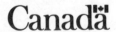  

PRINTED AND BOUND IN CANADA   PRINTING: MARQUIS   5 4 3 2 1

Purchase the print edition and receive the ebook free.
For details, go to ecwpress.com/ebook

To Jack Neary.
The man whose writings introduced Mike Mentzer
not only to me but to the world.

Zeus, who sets mortals on the path to understanding, Zeus, who has established as a fixed law that "wisdom comes by suffering." But even as trouble, bringing memory of pain, drips over the mind in sleep, so wisdom comes to men, whether they want it or not.

— Aeschylus

Pain is the *sine qua non* of creation. In order to create, one must be willing to endure suffering, to endure unspeakable pain.

— Mike Mentzer

TABLE OF CONTENTS

Foreword by Randy Roach   xi
Prologue   xxi

PART ONE: THE CAMEL

Chapter One: Born in the USA   3
Chapter Two: Brave New World   10
Chapter Three: The Dream Merchants   21
Chapter Four: Family Issues   31
Chapter Five: The Will to Power   38
Chapter Six: Mind and Body   48
Chapter Seven: Nautilus Emerges   60
Chapter Eight: Authorities by Proxy   68
Chapter Nine: The Cuban Muscle Crisis   76
Chapter Ten: A New Approach   86
Chapter Eleven: Relationships   98

PART TWO: THE LION

Chapter Twelve: A Man of Science   111
Chapter Thirteen: Muscles, Masculinity, and Mr. America   122
Chapter Fourteen: Destiny Beckons   135
Chapter Fifteen: A Peek Behind the Curtain   148
Chapter Sixteen: The Challenge to the Throne   162

Chapter Seventeen: Betrayals	176
Chapter Eighteen: Perfection in Acapulco	189
Chapter Nineteen: Turning Pro	196
Chapter Twenty: The Blows of Fate	205
Chapter Twenty-One: Playing with Fire	216
Chapter Twenty-Two: Leverage	237

PART THREE: THE CHILD

Chapter Twenty-Three: Preparing for War	253
Chapter Twenty-Four: Flash Point Down Under	269
Chapter Twenty-Five: The Sting	285
Chapter Twenty-Six: Aftermath	300
Chapter Twenty-Seven: Bodybuilding Lost	314
Chapter Twenty-Eight: Winds of Change	322
Chapter Twenty-Nine: Unmoored	336
Chapter Thirty: The Storm and the Light	347
Chapter Thirty-One: Descent into Madness	363
Chapter Thirty-Two: The Ghost in the Machine	376
Chapter Thirty-Three: Redemption	383
Chapter Thirty-Four: Against the Odds	392
Epilogue	411
Notes	425
Bibliography	496
Acknowledgments	522
About the Author	525

FOREWORD

Back in the early summer of 2023, I had been discussing with John Little his latest book on the legendary martial artist, Bruce Lee. *Wrath of the Dragon: The Real Fights of Bruce Lee* (ECW Press) was one of many projects John had published on the late fighting superstar and this one just happened to fall on the 50th anniversary of his death. Knowing John as a prolific writer, I turned the conversation to ask what his next publication would be. He told me he was seriously considering a biography on Mike Mentzer, a bodybuilding star of the late 1970s who had passed away at only age 49 in June 2001.

I was curious as to what drew John to write about him since Mike had been gone and out of competition for so long. When he told me that he initially had over 50,000 subscribers to his YouTube channel dedicated to Mike Mentzer, I was quite surprised. Even more amazing was that, less than a year later, the number of subscribers had grown to over 130,000. However, the success of the channel was not a factor in his decision to write an in-depth book on Mike.

The impetus grew out of a growing concern that no one else was stepping up to the plate to tackle a project of this magnitude. John had grown tired of seeing Mike's life and legacy misrepresented by those who simply didn't know the facts and were not present during the times in question; some were not even born when Mike was competing. John wasn't sure he should be the one to author the book as he felt that he was far too close to the subject matter to remain unbiased. So, he offered me a unique opportunity, which was to come along for the ride and observe his objectivity (this of course was dependent on whether I could keep my own biases in check). John simply wanted to present the truth about Mike — good and bad — as he believed truth was the one virtue that Mike valued above all others, often at his own cost.

Shortly after this conversation, I realized that questioning a biography of a late bodybuilder from decades ago was somewhat foolish given my past experiences. I, too, had been asked several times in interviews over the years about the fascination, often bordering fixation, with 1970s bodybuilding — the era in which Mike Mentzer competed. In fact, during an interview with Shawn Stone on his *Carved Outta Stone* podcast that summer of 2023, he'd asked me: "In a sport continually focused on bigger and more, why is there still so much nostalgia for the golden era of bodybuilding?"

The golden era of bodybuilding is a flexible range of years often defined by the experienced, and often biased, eyes of the beholder. Whatever boundaries are put forth, the 1970s are typically indicated. Why has this span of years fixated so many, not just for those old enough to have lived through it but also for the young who can now experience much of that historical timeframe through today's social media outlets? The decade of the 1970s saw a substantial acceleration in the commercialization of both amateur and especially professional sports. The landscape started to change back in the early 1960s when big-name athletes had begun acquiring representation from agencies such as Mark McCormack's International Management Group (IMG). This coincided with the launch of CBS's *Sports Spectacular* and ABC's *Wide World of Sports*, two of America's major television networks airing athletic competitions. Viewership for sports programming expanded exponentially leading up to the 1970s as more and more television sets began permeating multiple rooms throughout North American households. With this marriage of corporate America and athletics came much larger amounts of money. Inevitably, this proliferation and elevation of the athlete sparked a heightened reframing of the nationwide amateur infrastructure that was the feeding tube for the professional ranks.

With so much more at stake in the fields, arenas, courts, and rings, athletes and coaches were seeking any advantage that would move them into that number one position. Muscular size and strength through progressive resistance training finally shook the long-standing "muscle-bound" myth that had shrouded the lifting of weights for decades. Ironically, the existing tools of the game, such as the barbell, also had to make room for new innovations within this emerging field.

With an innate brilliance, not to mention a knack for physics and an arrogance to match, Arthur Jones landed on the scene in June of 1970 boasting a very contrasting training modality compared to the orthodoxy of that era. Jones anchored his abbreviated, high-intensity training ideology to his revolutionary equipment technology, machines he claimed matched or varied the resistance more closely to the axial movements of the human body. Using a combination of intellect and hyperbole, he cleverly packaged and marketed his new Nautilus-branded equipment to all emerging avenues willing to acknowledge the advantages of increased bodily strength. As you shall see, the industry influence of Arthur Jones is very pertinent to this story. Regardless of any debate over exercise tools and the acceptance of functional muscle by mainstream sports, it was inevitable that the obscure field of bodybuilding would shake its campy, circus stigma and take advantage of this unprecedented media exposure, ready to be leveraged for corporate gain.

Beginning in the late 1960s and through the 1970s, several factors aligned that would shift the sport in public perception and governance. As a result of the elevation of these superior, physically developed athletes, compounded by Hollywood's continual vaporization of the conservative wardrobe, America was rapidly becoming image conscious. This was music to the ears of Joe and Ben Weider. The two brothers moved on this opportune moment and allied themselves with the right personnel who would redefine, restructure, and muscle their fledging International Federation of Body Builders (IFBB) into the reigning authority over the sport by the beginning of the 1980s.

The marketing horse for the Weider publications actually landed on the shores of America in the fall of 1968 in the form of Arnold Schwarzenegger. Arnold would endorse Weider supplements and equipment through the pages of Joe Weider's magazines while reigning as Mr. Olympia (the IFBB professional flagship title) from 1970 through 1975, and then one more time in 1980. Perhaps the most powerful promotion for Arnold, IFBB bodybuilding, and (inevitably) the Weiders in the 1970s came through the efforts of writer Charles Gaines and photographer George Butler. These two men tackled the daunting if not outright daring task of prying bodybuilding from previous comparisons to the likes of the "roller derby" and presenting it to the mainstream as both sport and art. Leveraging success from their July 1972 *Sports Illustrated* feature on bodybuilding, Gaines and Butler set off on a four-year bodybuilding campaign that culminated in the two greatest bodybuilding marketing vehicles under the "Pumping Iron" label. The book was published in late 1974 followed by the movie in early 1977.

The backend of the 1970s was arguably the apex of the sport in terms of visibility and popularity, an era deemed "golden" by those old enough to witness this new cultural acceptance of building muscles come to bear. This was the evolving and exciting atmosphere in which John Little's young and ambitious protagonist, Mike Mentzer, would engage. What exactly differentiated Mike from the rest of the bodybuilding crowd during that period? Mike's competitive bodybuilding career was meteoric in its rise but very abrupt in its closure. His post-competition life was rife with both physical and psychological turbulence. Yet, he still holds a high degree of popularity twenty-plus years after his untimely death just shy of his 50th birthday.

Acknowledging his persistent popularity, it is fair to ask: what qualifies John Little to write such a magnum opus on a long-deceased athlete's rollercoaster odyssey of mind and body? John worked for many years within the industry, writing for several magazines in addition to authoring several books on his own training methods. In addition, he became a close friend of his subject during some very troubling years for Mike Mentzer. After being granted the privilege of reading through the working drafts of this project, it is my honest opinion that only John Little could provide such an in-depth perspective on this often enigmatic, polarizing bodybuilding personality. I can't help but wonder if John subconsciously knew this.

Mike Mentzer wasn't your basic muscle head. He was a grade-A student, active in football as a youth, and still very athletic even years later when carrying close to competition bodyweight (John will reveal just what kind of strength and speed Mike demonstrated during one of the 1981 ABC *Superstars* competitions). During the public's estrangement from bodybuilding in the 1960s, Mike's father was fine with him using weights to build muscular size and strength for football but was very much disappointed when his son abandoned the gridiron for the pursuit of sheer bodybuilding. Mike Mentzer chose his own course in life, always seeming to avoid the path of least resistance. Even when ascending in physique competition just past the mid-1970s, when the atmosphere was becoming much friendlier to bodybuilding, Mike once again chose a direction that most likely cost him his career in the sport.

Foreword

John Little has done a forensic deep dive into this acclaimed "golden era" of bodybuilding, specifically the late 1970s, and exposed an almost incestuous underlying business modality that had existed for years and would continue in ensuing decades. Throughout the history of the sport, skin color, training/diet/supplement preferences, sex appeal, and further carnal availability have all been determinant factors for just who would adorn magazine covers, model for product promotional ads, and perhaps win a contest or two. Joe Weider was as close to an industry megalomaniac as one would ever find. Within the boundaries of his muscle media, everything from supplements, equipment, and (especially) training principles bore his name.

Mike Mentzer caught Joe Weider's eye at the 1975 Mr. America, where he placed third. His placement didn't matter to Joe, it was the "look" that landed Mike the cover shot on Joe's April 1976 issue of *Muscle Builder/Power* magazine before Mike even won the America title later that year. By the summer of 1977, Mike had moved to California and was writing for Joe's magazine, in which he would appear on the cover two more times before the year's end. With Joe and Arnold's relationship being strained at that time, and Frank Zane, the reigning Mr. Olympia, moving up in years, had Joe found his heir apparent for Arnold Schwarzenegger?

Joe was intrigued with Mike beyond his physique. Mike had been a premed student who also studied psychology and philosophy and had been considering a career in psychiatry. He believed in building the mind every bit as much or even more than just building big muscles. Everything was looking very positive with this new relationship except for one minor caveat that would affect the dynamics of the Schwarzenegger/Weider/Mentzer business triangle. After years of proclaiming himself as "the trainer of champions since 1936," and pretty much corralling every exercise technique under the sun as a "Weider Principle," Joe obviously harbored some anxieties that his new protégé was a growing proponent of the high-intensity training protocols of Arthur Jones, a man Joe wished would simply just go away. And that is basically what Arthur did when he took his expanding training technologies into what he believed were more prestigious markets, such as the evolving sports medicine and rehabilitation fields.

Was Mike Mentzer just another of bodybuilding's Nautilus leftovers? Hardly! Arthur did offer his training ideologies to bodybuilding's icon, Bill Pearl, very early upon Arthur's arrival on the Iron Game scene. However, at that time in his early forties, Bill was already comfortable with his bodybuilding ways. So, Arthur Jones simply took the HIT (High-Intensity Training) baton and tossed it out there for any he felt smart enough to pick it up and run with it. Mike Mentzer was in fact intelligent enough to do just that. You will learn when Mike first connected with Arthur and the influence Arthur had on Mike in terms of both exercise and diet for building the body.

Once Mike Mentzer had thoroughly absorbed the principles of intense and abbreviated training, he applied those protocols beyond that of anyone else and took his physique well past any of his previous development benchmarks. It is estimated that he put on almost 30 pounds from his first attempt at the 1975 IFBB Mr. America up to his highly controversial placement at the 1980 Mr. Olympia, a very contentious point in bodybuilding history. The return of a retired Arnold Schwarzenegger to this contest arguably marked a derailment for the sport at the height of its public popularity and acceptance, in addition to representing a drastic turning point in both the career and life of Mike Mentzer.

With much research, thought, and consideration, John Little examines the latter years of the 1970s leading up to this clash of young challenging old —someone new threatening a long-established hierarchical orthodoxy. Why did Arnold really return to bodybuilding at that stage in his life? Just how blatant was the rigging of the 1980 Mr. Olympia in favor of Arnold? Did Joe Weider care, need, or even want Arnold back as champion? Was Mike Mentzer threatening an entrenched training paradigm? What dilemma confronted Joe Weider by giving the young Mike such media attention in his prestigious sales catalogs, *Muscle Builder/Power* and *Muscle & Fitness*? Was Mike already indicted, tried, and convicted in the court of Arnold Schwarzenegger long before their clash in the fall of 1980 at the Sydney Opera House in Australia? And was Weider an active witness for the prosecution?

The revelation that comes from the answers to these questions is mind-boggling to say the least, yet this quagmire represented just the four years leading up to the 1980 Mr. Olympia. It was the final two decades of Mike Mentzer's post-competitive years that brought his deepest valleys and steepest hills, replete with rumors, accusations, and more industry contention. Personally, I knew more than most about those 1970s competitive years because of the extensive research I had conducted for my own publications, but there was still more for me to learn due to John's in-depth focus on Mike's every pertinent contest.

Nonetheless, what was totally new ground for me was learning that Mike's greater challenge was more than he had ever faced on any posing dais, a battle that raged in his own mind, specifically from the mid-1980s until his death just over 15 years later. These were without doubt the most difficult years for John to write about a man whom he initially saw as a mentor and, eventually, a peer and good friend. John pulls no punches when dealing with these controversial periods for Mike Mentzer. Drawing upon this evolved relationship, John examines the potential familial roots of depression in the Mentzer family, along with Mike's admitted drug usage, to see if a rational explanation could be put forth on Mike's challenging emotional journey.

The dark years of the 1980s did yield a much brighter decade for Mike Mentzer through most of the 1990s. The controversies that arose in these years stemmed primarily from Mike's strong convictions and promotion of his Heavy Duty scientific approach to bodybuilding. His resurgence and popularity grew to arguably surpass Arthur Jones, his original inspiration for this style of training. While Arthur Jones was brilliant in his entrepreneurial ventures, his intellect and articulation could be sidetracked by his hyperbole, brazenness, and often crude conduct. Mike Mentzer was also very intelligent and articulate while being much more personable in his manner. Assisting Mentzer's popularity was the fact that a good number of his amazing photos still circulated in magazines (and later, on the Internet) years after he stopped competing. And when it comes to bodybuilding, a picture is worth a thousand words. Strictly from a visual viewpoint, the 25 years younger Mike Mentzer made Arthur Jones look like the proverbial two miles of bad road.

Physiques aside, John Little asserts that, when given a platform, Mike Mentzer was always compelling. And Mike was in fact captivating still when I saw him in the late 1990s, even when his health was in decline. John has a style of writing that combines an underlying, guiding analysis with a knack for allowing his subjects to speak in their own words. This is what you will find in the following pages of this very informative biographical publication: Mike speaking not only on his evolving philosophy and world viewpoint, but also being very candid about bodybuilding in terms of the importance of genetics, the true impact of anabolic steroids, and the sheer insanity that can engulf contest preparation.

Interestingly, Mike did not want his hypertrophied physique to define his life. He had no plans of becoming a multiple Mr. Olympia winner. In fact, his attention to his own physicality began to diminish as he endeavored to learn more about the human mind, an imbalance that no doubt contributed to his decline in health. Due to his close relationship with Mike, John is able to take the reader down the road of Mike's final weeks to the very day of his death. It was at this point in the manuscript that I needed to take a break, sit back in my chair, and absorb what I had just read. I had become so captivated by this revelational material that it dawned on me that I had missed almost the entirety of the 2024 Super Bowl. I had gone through just over 500 pages in a few days, and this was a lot to process.

But in reading this, Mike Mentzer became fully alive again in my mind, and I found myself reminiscing back to 1978 when I saw him score a perfect 300 to win that year's IFBB World Bodybuilding Championships (Mr. Universe) in Acapulco, broadcasted on CBS's *Sports Spectacular*. That year, I remember picking up *Muscle Builder* after a five-year hiatus and seeing Mike in Joe Weider's flagship magazine. At the time, I was following bodybuilder Franco Columbu's regimen of two-hour workouts conducted six days per week, which I had copied from his 1977 publication, *Winning Bodybuilding*. By 1980, Mike Mentzer had become a very positive influence on my training with his own book release, *The Mentzer Method to Fitness*. I could not believe what a difference there was in the training protocols between Franco and Mike! Where Franco advocated up to 12 hours of training per week, Mike was saying I would be pushing the limit at four hours weekly. I was convinced that Mike walked his talk, and from that point on I would watch for anything he put forth.

Looking back at the history of muscle building, I contend that Mike was definitely an impact player, as of course was Arthur Jones, Vince Gironda, and even Joe Weider and Bob Hoffman before him. To carry such a label, one must inculcate some type of lasting change within the culture of the industry, and it is my opinion that Mike Mentzer did just that. Some of course would speak out in defense of Arthur Jones, saying that he launched the high-intensity training counter to conventional training before Mike, and there is truth to this argument. However, Mike took Arthur's principles and tightened them further. Even Arthur would concede to Ellington Darden in 2003, two years after Mike's death, that if he could go back in time, he would also have cut his sets down to what Mike had later recommended.

Mike did in fact have a few factors in his favor by the end of the 1970s. He had a Mr. Olympia–caliber physique, good looks, and timing. The dawning of the 1980s saw an explosion in the proliferation of training facilities across the industrial West. Following on the heels of this expansion was the burgeoning field of personal training, a profession Mike himself would take up in the 1990s. What Mike Mentzer espoused was a potential boon to both industries.

Once upon a time, bodybuilders were the anchors of any gym. However, this new training era was going to cater to the growing image and health-conscious public, and having just a handful of grunting, screaming, odor-emanating bodybuilders slamming and banging weights three hours per day, several times per week, was not a marketing allure for this new target clientele. Mike contended that this simply did not have to be the case. No one needed to be in the gym for that amount of time, not even professional bodybuilders. Decades later, current research vindicates Mike's position, showing that excessive exercise goes beyond diminishing returns and can actually be detrimental to one's health.

Intense, brief, and infrequent were the principles; finding the minimum amount of exercise that imposed the maximum amount of growth stimulation was the goal. Both Arthur Jones and Mike Mentzer believed the principles were immutable, while the application could vary according to a genetic cross-section of the general population. These tenets not only facilitated a significant increase in a gym's membership base but also were highly conducive to success for any personal trainer willing to apply this basic logic. Keeping the above protocols as a foundation, I have maintained loyalty from clients for ten, 15, and even 20 years. These are typically very busy professionals who, when convinced that twice or even once per week training for less than an hour was all that was necessary, found it easy to invest in their health by incorporating such training permanently into their lifestyle.

It was this very rationale of easy lifestyle infusion due to brevity and infrequency of training that led me to become somewhat disillusioned with Mike in the latter 1990s. I had first spoken to him several years earlier when he was making his resurgence in muscle media. He was refreshing to converse with since he was so brutally honest about anything you asked him. It was when I traveled to Mississauga, Ontario, with three friends in 1998 to catch one of Mike's seminars that all four of us were quite surprised at what we witnessed. As mentioned earlier, mentally and verbally he was still captivating, but physically he was not what we expected. It had been 18 years since he last competed, so we certainly did not expect a contest-shape Mike Mentzer. I remember thinking that with such genetics, and so little exercise necessary to maintain even a modicum of conditioning, it just was not there.

I was not at all angry with Mike, nor did I throw him under the bus for any of his newly acquired bad habits, since I was not a bastion of purity myself. I was just disappointed and never really pursued him as much from that point onward. I can't say that I was overly surprised with his death three years later, but I was certainly saddened by the news.

I've only come to understand what was going on in his life at the time through this book. There is a necessity for this to be published, not just for Mike's continuously growing fan base, but for veterans such as myself who needed the full context of his story. I found myself recentered in my feelings towards him, and John's words reminded me why I came to like and admire Mike Mentzer as a teenager in the 1970s. He taught me the principles that would pretty much guarantee my successful training career.

As I stated earlier, it is my opinion that only John Little could have written this book in this manner. I am sure most of Mike Mentzer's fans would feel that John was very fortunate to have known Mike Mentzer in such a personal capacity. However, after extensive correspondence and conversations with John, along with the privilege of having first access to the manuscript, I can safely say that Mike Mentzer was, in turn, very blessed to have known John Little, a man who gave so much time and effort to give such an amazing, everlasting, and rightful legacy to his friend long since passed away.

Randy Roach
author of *Muscle, Smoke & Mirrors, Vol. I–III*

PROLOGUE

"Mike Mentzer died," came the voice at the other end of the phone. The news should have been surprising. In truth, I had been preparing myself for this message for over ten years. I do recall, however, that upon hanging up the phone I told myself that we were lucky to have had him for as long as we did.

The Mike Mentzer I had first become aware of was a sight to behold. He had been described by a female reporter in 1981 as being "a strikingly handsome man who moves with the fluid grace of a panther. A superstar."[1] And this he certainly was. But when I had last visited with him — in the ICU of the West Los Angeles Veterans Affairs Medical Center, some seven months prior to receiving this phone call — he was no longer any of these things. Indeed, he was almost unrecognizable — even to a person who had known him for 21 years.

The physique, of course, was long gone (and that, surprisingly, had been by choice); the face was gaunt, the voice raspy. He was then recovering from having suffered a mild heart attack, but this had been simply the latest in a series of maladies that had afflicted him during the past six years of his life. He had already lived through the neurosis and psychosis, the destitution, the drugs, the torn triceps, the neck surgery, and the blood clotting disorder in his lungs. He had ceased giving a damn many years before this. He had stopped working out, and, apart from walking his personal training clients from machine to machine in Gold's Gym, he lived a sedentary lifestyle. Sometime in the early 1990s he had taken up smoking and was up to two packs of Camel Lights a day. He was drinking more than he should have.

And, in his final year, he was living on some very potent painkillers. Indeed, so frail did he appear during our last get-together at the hospital that I wasn't sure he would survive my visit.

But he did. He actually began to rebound — yet again. He grew healthier and more productive in the months that followed. But "health," a maxim once declared, "is simply the slowest rate at which you can die." Evidently, at a mere 49 years of age, Mike Mentzer's time had run out.

He should have been forgotten shortly thereafter, just like all the other bodybuilding champions from yesteryear who had appeared in the muscle magazines, won a few contests, and then faded from public awareness. Some even endured a living death, surviving long enough to see their relevance slowly turn to mist. At one point in their lives, these men stood just this side of deity, their habits, diets, and muscle-building routines memorized internationally by thousands, their posters hung upon the walls of bedrooms and commercial gymnasiums. But then they were spoken of no more, replaced in the public consciousness by a new crop of physique champions. No more articles were written about them in the bodybuilding press; their posters were taken down and their names no longer mentioned.

Legacies written in the wind.

And yet Mike Mentzer endures. Perhaps, as I had long suspected, there was something more, deeper, to Mike Mentzer than just a suit of muscles. Something relatable, perhaps even noble. If we look beyond the aesthetic that his many images project, we will observe that at one period of his life he was the personification of the ancient ideal of *mens sana in corpore sano* ("a healthy mind in a healthy body"). For certain, there have been aesthetically appealing bodies and philosophical minds, but seldom if ever do they unite in one person.

There were certainly, during his final years, interludes when neither his mind nor the body in which it resided were particularly healthy. But, as Heraclitus pointed out eons ago, "The only thing that is constant is change." Beyond this, Mike Mentzer's story itself is compelling, revealing an honest and sincere man in an industry where deceit and corruption held sway; an intelligent — no, brilliant — mind in a profession where brute muscle ruled. But despite such sapience, he so loved bodybuilding that he was unable to see it for what it truly was: always a business, never a sport. There followed a massive fall and the loss of the body that brought him his fame as he tried unsuccessfully to stave off the inherited mental illness that had stalked him his entire life. And then, in the third and final act to the drama, he rebooted his intellect, which, in turn, brought into being a complete redemption of his legacy — and all of this within the compass of 49 years. Above all, his was a life that experienced every facet of the human experience: love, friendship, benevolence, power, knowledge, celebrity, triumph, and joy, as well as the antipodes of hate, loneliness, cruelty, weakness, anonymity, defeat, and profound grief. It was a wheel that turned, rotating from productivity to destitution; and just as it was turning again, he died.

He started as a bodybuilding hero of mine and ended up a close friend. While it was hard to see the hero become mortal, I must confess that I preferred the friendship — with all the hardships that went with it — to the idolatry. I count myself fortunate to have witnessed many aspects of his story firsthand. And what a ride — and an education — it proved to be.

In looking back, I see that Mike was never more alive than when he had a wrong to right or a cause to champion. When he was a competitive bodybuilder, there were certainly no shortage of dragons to slay. However, when the path to bodybuilding glory was sealed off to him, he tended to create battles to fight within himself: drugs, alcohol, homelessness, madness. Yet when these things set upon him, he ultimately prevailed — if only to create another internal battle that he had to fight all over again.

Calm or stasis, while often the professed goal of one's life, never seemed to satisfy him. He once recounted how the existentialist Jean-Paul Sartre had written that he had never felt more alive than when he was fighting the Nazis via the French underground during World War II. Similar stories have come down to us from soldiers who returned home from the war in Vietnam. Upon returning to our civilized society after having experienced the highs of human focus and awareness, and the kill-or-be-killed experience of jungle warfare, many of these veterans discovered that simply getting a job in an insurance company or some other such profession left them deeply unsatisfied and beckoned problems to enter their lives. Having been exposed to the high of living with every nerve fully exposed, they just couldn't find meaning in a sedate treadmill-type existence. President Andrew Jackson had once said of himself: "I was born for the storm and the calm does not suit me." And so it was, I believe, with Mike Mentzer.

When he was engaged in a project that required his full attention he was, indeed, a genius of sorts; brilliant, with a logic that clamped down upon a subject like a steel trap. When left without such an all-consuming purpose, however, he became his own worst enemy. And, strange to say, that's the way he wanted it. He once told me that "anything I am or am not is a result of the choices I've made or my abdication thereof."

Certainly, Mike's life was one of choices: some good and some bad. And, as his friend, I hope I have presented the choices that came to define his life honestly, which is the only way Mike would have wanted it.

PART ONE
THE CAMEL

He's no mean man, not with a build like that . . . Look at his thighs, his legs, and what a pair of arms — his massive neck, his big, rippling strength!

— Homer, *The Odyssey*

CHAPTER ONE

BORN IN THE USA

The city of Philadelphia was said to be as vital to America as the heart is to the human body. At least, that's what Founding Father Robert Morris believed.[1] There's certainly no disputing that it was a key city in America's fight for freedom and independence. This was particularly true for one of its boroughs: Germantown, which was established in the late 1600s by the Mennonites, Quakers, and various other Dutch and German immigrants to Pennsylvania.

It was within Germantown's parameters that the anti-slavery movement was born,[2] and a revolutionary battle was fought;[3] on two occasions, it was where President George Washington made his home.[4] And somewhere within its 3.327 square miles of real estate, which were still smoldering from the embers of the American War of Independence, Mike Mentzer was born.

Germantown was something of an anomaly for the Mentzer clan, however. For the better part of its American history, the family's roots were planted firmly in the soil of the Lancaster County region of Pennsylvania, some 67.7 miles away to the west. The Pennsylvania Mentzer lineage can be traced back to Johannes Meinzer (1701–81) from Hagsfeld, Karlsruhe, Baden-Württemberg, Germany, who immigrated to America in 1751.[5] Like most immigrants to the new world, Johannes arrived by ship, his port of entry being Philadelphia Harbor.[6] Johannes was 50 years old when he stepped off the gangplank and onto American soil for the first time. But upon his death in 1781, he was buried in Lancaster County.[7]

Mike's paternal grandfather was Samuel Mentzer (1893–1956),[8] who served in World War I,[9] and later found employment as a machinist[10] and horse trainer.[11] His wife Kathryn (née Coldren, 1897–1959)[12] worked part time cleaning homes,[13] but was primarily occupied with raising their six children of whom Mike's father Harry, born on July 12, 1923,[14] was the fifth.[15]

Mike's maternal stock was more recently established. His grandfather on his mother's side, Romolo De Stefano, was born in Abruzzi, Italy, on May 29, 1893, and immigrated to the United States on May 24, 1903.[16] His grandmother, Anna De Stefano (née: Sciossa), was born on November 9, 1895, in San Severo, Foggia, Italy, and arrived in America in March 1907.[17] The couple were married on September 14, 1914,[18] and Maria Elena (Mike's mother) — the third of five children — was born on September 4, 1922, in Atlantic City, New Jersey.[19]

After serving a four-year stint (1942–46)[20] as a drill instructor[21] in the United States Marine Corps during World War II, Harry Mentzer was honorably discharged. How and when he met Marie is unclear, but he clearly fell for her in a big way, as Marie was not without a back story. In June of 1940,[22] at the age of 18, she had married Uno Elmer Mantyla, a 21-year-old employee of the U.S. Hospital Corps. It had evidently been a marriage of necessity, as their first child, a daughter named Marie Ann, was born on October 9, 1940,[23] just four months after their wedding vows were exchanged.[24]

The newlyweds moved around a bit; they were married in Philadelphia, moved to Richmond, Virginia (where their daughter was born), then returned to Philadelphia, where another child, a son, Elmer Jr., was born on April 15, 1945.[25] However, while Uno was traveling alone in his home state of Minnesota in the fall of 1949, tragedy struck that shattered the family. Fifteen miles east of Detroit Lakes, Uno lost control of his car, which overturned, killing him instantly.[26] At 27, with a nine-year-old son and four-year-old daughter to raise, Marie was in a tough spot. Her parents were living in Philadelphia and, fortunately, were happy to have her move back into the family home, alongside her two brothers (Bernard and Carl) and a sister-in-law, Patricia, who worked as a typist at a life insurance company.[27] Marie helped her mother with the housekeeping chores,[28] but with only a limited education, she had no skills that would bring in a decent income. She worked at odd jobs to make ends meet.[29]

Not long after Harry and Marie were dating, she became pregnant, and shortly after the discovery of this fact, Harry proposed. Welcoming the stability and normalcy their union meant to her two young children, Marie accepted. The pair were married on March 5, 1950, a mere six months after Uno had been laid to rest.[30]

Their first child, Michael John Mentzer, was born eight months later, on November 15, 1951.[31] We know nothing of his infancy, save that he was evidently healthy and presumably happy. On August 3, 1953, the new family expanded again when Marie gave birth to Raymond Harry Mentzer.[32] It was around this time that the family, including ten-year-old Marie and six-year-old Elmer, left Germantown and headed west to settle in the town of Ephrata, Pennsylvania, the region where Harry's relatives had settled.

Mike remembered Ephrata as "kind of a farming community, which is where the Pennsylvania Dutch, and the Mennonites, and that culture, sort of predominates."[33] It certainly contained (and maintains to this day) a strong religious presence. Even its name is religious — derived from "Ephrath," the former name of current-day Bethlehem in Palestine.[34]

The region was developed in 1732 by Johann Conrad Beissel, a man who had a falling-out with the German Baptist community over what day the Sabbath was on. Beissel sided with Judaism on that issue, holding that Saturday was the correct day of the Lord. Thereafter, Beissel and his followers were referred to as German Seventh Day Baptists. They established a "Camp of the Solitary" by the banks of Cocalico Creek, and began a life of farming, papermaking, milling, and textiles production, while they collectively looked to the skies and waited for Jesus to return.[35]

Since Beissel's time, the 3.42 square miles that comprise Ephrata saw some 46 houses of worship spring from its soil, making for approximately 13.5 churches every square mile. Surprisingly, given such a spiritually charged environment, the Mentzer household was not a religious one.[36] Harry had moved his family to Ephrata for work, not spiritual sustenance.

The absence of a strong religious influence in the home, however, did not mean that the Mentzer children were lacking in either ethical or behavioral guidance. "We had a fairly solid upbringing," Mike recalled. "We were taught the difference between right and wrong. We were expected to do certain things. My father expected us to maintain a certain level of discipline around the house."[37] It is possible (as it is not uncommon) that Harry favored his own boys over the children from Marie's first marriage. If so, it would explain how a divide of sorts formed within the household. Mike would later confess that he was "never real close to my brother [Elmer] or sister — or even my mother very much. . . . I was a son who was very much influenced by his father, [and who] very much wanted his love. That was a strong impact on my mind."[38]

The earliest photo we have of Mike Mentzer is from his kindergarten class. There, in amongst the carefully arranged images of 43 other students who attended Washington Avenue School, bookended between the photos of fellow classmates Kozette Widder and Connie Good, a five-year-old Mike smiles out at us. It is an image obviously taken long before the muscles arrived, and the storms life would throw at him. Here is a cute, clean-cut, and innocent-looking little boy — and yet there is an unusual confidence in his eyes. We would learn later that it was a confidence that belied an almost crippling shyness. "I spent much of my time alone at home, rather introverted, not accustomed to being around other children," he would later confess.[39] "I had a hard time being focused on; if anybody looked at me, I'd just recede into the background. I just shriveled up."[40] His shyness came to a head when Marie tried to take him to his first day of kindergarten:

> I'll never forget as my mother walked out the door, holding my hand to take me up the street . . . I all of a sudden bolted back inside and locked the door. It never occurred to me that she'd have a key. But my next remembrance of that day was my mother walking into the classroom where all the children were seated, carrying me wailing under her arm.[41]

On another occasion he froze when he was expected to join the other children in the schoolyard:

> I found it almost impossible to go out into the middle of the playground and play baseball. My playmate, a perceptive, bright young kid who in fact ended up going all through high school with me, recognized it and prodded me into playing baseball. And it's funny; ever after that I didn't have a hard time fitting in. It was just that initial reluctance.[42]

While Mike continued to grapple with his shyness (which would plague him throughout his life),[43] his father was grappling with issues of his own. The odd jobs he had accepted since his discharge from the Marines weren't bringing in enough money to support a family of six. "Harry was never far from trouble," recalled Mike's cousin Sid Mentzer. "He would go to [his brother] Charlie for money loans when he was in a bind."[44] While the loans certainly helped, they provided only a temporary solution to an ongoing financial problem. Harry needed something that would bring in consistent money. He opened a small garage on Willow Street in Lancaster County,[45] and, he signed on with the Kenosha Auto Transport Corp. (Wisconsin) to be a long-haul truck driver in his spare hours and weekends (Teamsters Chauffeurs Local Union 771).[46] Occasionally, Harry would bring Mike along with him to the garage and have him do menial tasks. Later, during junior high and high school, Mike worked at the garage and helped his father repair cars and trucks.

If there was one attribute that Harry prized over all others, it was intelligence. Perhaps this was the result of his never having had the luxury of a formal education.[47] Perhaps he simply sought bragging rights amongst his friends and relatives.[48] Whatever the reason, he wanted his sons to do well in school, and even offered material rewards should A's appear on their report cards. With Mike it occurred often — he made the honor roll in grades seven and ten[49] — which saw Harry reward him with a $20 bill on the first occasion, and a new baseball mitt on the second.[50] Ray, sadly, seldom made the cut, which caused some issues to develop between the brothers. "Right from the start our father instilled the masculine qualities of competition in us," Ray recalled. "Mike was leading more of a passive, laid-back life in grade school. I was wilder, a street fighter. Because I was getting bad grades and Mike was doing well, I had an inferiority complex. I felt I had to prove myself, so I was a bit of a bully. Everybody told me to calm down. I used to worry about being perceived as stupid. My parents pushed me. 'Why can't you be like your brother? He gets A's,' they told me. That made me angry, and I would rebel. Mike was getting A's, and I wasn't."[51] When asked if he ever requested help from his more academically inclined brother, Ray shook his head. "Mike never had the patience to help me."[52]

Both boys, however, excelled in athletics, which, being a former Marine drill instructor, Harry encouraged.[53] In 1962, Ray placed third in the 20-yard freestyle in the Ephrata Jaycee Swim Meet.[54] In 1964, by the time Mike entered junior high school, he had acquired a reputation in the neighborhood for his athletic ability.[55] He excelled in track and field[56] and was a standout in football.[57] The coach of the community swim team, hearing of the young phenom, extended a special invitation for Mike to try out, and was left stunned when Mike beat the local champion. He was even more stunned afterward when Mike informed him that he had no interest in being on the swim team.[58]

When not cheering his boys on from the sidelines, Harry received a vicarious thrill by pitting his sons against each other in a variety of athletic feats; he looked on delightedly as they raced against each other along the alleyway at the side of the family home. He even had them don boxing gloves and swap punches with each other, having taught them both the fundamentals of the sweet science.[59]

As was often the case in American families during the 1950s, it was the father who was the primary authority within the home — and this was particularly the case for his two sons. Gradually but consistently, Harry's tough, self-reliant attitude permeated his sons' psyches. Mike would later recall:

> He was a tough-minded individualist, and always seemed to find it easy to stand up for what he believed in. In fact, at times, he revelled in it. Not that his was a crusading spirit, but he was not averse to a fight. And, from time to time, he would even boast about his integrity and strength of conviction, which had a way of irritating some of what I refer to as weak-willed, namby-pamby types around us. My brother Ray and I responded very strongly to my father's self-esteem, which resulted in our becoming staunch individualists.[60]

While Mike inherited a strong sense of individualism from his father, he would inherit something else entirely from his mother: a progressive mental illness that up until his late twenties manifested in periodic bouts of depression.[61] This, at times, threatened to completely overwhelm him, particularly if he had no goal to focus on.[62] Years later, when he was a professional bodybuilder, his training and competitions kept his mind strongly focused, which served to keep the problem somewhat at bay. But when purpose was absent, depression would descend and consume him.[63] During his teenage years, the illness presented itself via profound shyness and anxiety, which the boy alleviated through extensive reading, academic study, and athletic competition. However, Mike's predisposition to this mental health issue, in addition to his mother's, didn't make for a lot of happy times within the Mentzer household.

Matters weren't helped when certain of the Ephrata townspeople spoke derisively of "the Mentzers" (that is, Harry, Mike, and Ray), claiming that the males in the family were arrogant and conceited. But if the negative social statements were intended to humble Mike, they had the opposite effect.

"Such comments only served at the time to fuel my nascent individualism," he said. "Actually, we were not arrogant or conceited. We were just proud of ourselves."[64]

While that may have been true, a schism was forming in the Mentzer triumvirate. For while Ray idolized his older brother, it was clear to him that Mike was favored by their father. Mike's name was the one his father dropped at family gatherings. Mike was the scholar. The brain. The kid was different — better, the implication was — than anybody else's kid, including by inference Ray, and Harry's stepchildren. It was not a good situation.

Marie had to be aware of the pecking order of the children in Harry's eyes. However, she was the biological mother to all four children, and, clearly, loved them all equally. Trying to maintain a loving impartiality that overcompensated for Harry's lack of it couldn't have been easy. While all the children got along well with each other, there was a tension in the house that did little to mitigate Marie's occasional bouts of depression.

CHAPTER TWO

BRAVE NEW WORLD

It was during Marie's attempt to remedy an onset of depression that the course of her young son's life would change. Mike was eleven years old and standing in line with her at an Ephrata pharmacy while she waited for her prescription to be filled. That's when he noticed the magazine rack.

The various colors of the covers beckoned him to take a closer look. Leaving her side, the boy made his way over to the rack and gave it a spin. As he glanced at the merry-go-round of periodicals that came and went before his eyes, he suddenly stopped the rack from spinning. His attention was now focused on the latest edition of *Muscle Builder/Power*,[1] a publication devoted to the fringe activity of bodybuilding. The cover of the magazine featured but a single image: a full body shot of bodybuilder/actor Steve Reeves holding a saber above his head.[2] Reeves may well have been the best-looking, best-built male in the history of bodybuilding. Standing six foot one and weighing 215 pounds, Reeves was something to behold. He competed in an era before steroids were introduced into the sport, and yet claimed to sport a 52-inch chest and 29-inch waist, with arms, calves, and neck that stretched a tape measure to a large but symmetrical 18¼ inches.[3] Mike was riveted: "The moment I set my eyes on that picture on the cover of *Muscle Builder* I knew right then that I was going to be a bodybuilder — a champion bodybuilder like Steve Reeves, whoever he was!"[4] He asked his mother to purchase the magazine, which she did — he couldn't wait to get home to devour its contents. Upon his father's return from work that evening, Mike begged him to buy a set of weights. "Not until Christmas," Harry replied.[5] As weight training would make a person stronger for sports like football, Harry believed a barbell set might be an investment in his son's future, possibly as a fullback in the NFL.[6]

While Mike eagerly counted down the days to Christmas, he discovered that his elder stepbrother, Elmer, had already started lifting weights in a friend's garage just down the street from where they lived. This intrigued Mike further. "A couple of times he allowed me to tag along," he recalled. "And I was just in awe of these bigger guys lifting heavy weights."[7]

Christmas couldn't come fast enough.

In the meantime, Mike continued to train his muscles with calisthenics. He was forever doing push-ups and sit-ups, climbing trees, and jumping over fences to strengthen his (by then) 12-year-old physique.[8] True to his word, Harry saw to it that on Christmas morning the highly coveted barbell set was beneath the tree. "I remember that gleeful morning when I found the weights under the Christmas tree," Mike recalled. "I spent all Christmas down in the basement lifting weights."[9] He was so intensely focused during his first workout that he was oblivious to who was around him — which resulted in an embarrassing accident. "I was at home when Mike got his first barbell set," his stepsister, Marie, recalled. "And I remember him lifting it up the first time and hitting my mother by accident — she got a black eye."[10]

Mike's weight training quickly started paying dividends. Working out alone in the basement of the family home three days a week, using only one exercise per muscle group and only three sets an exercise (per the instruction booklet that came with his Billard Barbell set),[11] Mike went from weighing 95 pounds at the age of 12 to 165 pounds by the age of 15 — an incredible 70-pound bodyweight gain in a mere three years.[12] "In those three years, with some credit to post pubescent development, I made the best progress of my life," Mike would later recall.[13] Anybody with an eye for such things could tell that this kid's genetic endowment for building muscle was off the charts. Harry, seeing the rapid transformation in his son, began to rub his palms in anticipation; his boy — clearly — was on the fast track to the NFL.[14]

To hasten Mike's strength development for the gridiron, Harry introduced his son to a long-time friend of his, John Myers. Myers was a 40-year-old powerlifter of some repute in the community. Myers, in turn, introduced Mike to his training partner, a man in his mid-twenties named Russell Hertzog.

Hertzog, a concrete finisher by trade, also happened to be a competitive weightlifter who specialized in Olympic weightlifting.[15] And within his garage on Cherry Street were some serious pieces of weight training equipment: a power rack, a bench press, squat racks, Olympic barbells, and literally a *ton* of Olympic weights.

The two men took readily to the teenager and brought him under their wing. The trio worked out three days a week in Hertzog's garage. When the bitterly cold Pennsylvania winter arrived, the trainees applied heating liniment to their muscles and donned several sweatshirts and continued to hit the iron. Sometimes it became so cold in the unheated garage that Mike's nostrils would freeze shut.[16] It didn't matter; increased strength and muscle mass was his goal, and these were aims that required consistency in one's training, irrespective of the weather.

Mike's strength exploded under the older men's tutelage. In the Olympic lifts he was soon able to clean and jerk 315 pounds, snatch 225 pounds, and perform a standing press with 250 pounds.[17] "I began working very heavy when I was only fourteen," Mike recalled. "At which time I could quarter squat with more than 700 pounds. At age sixteen, I could full squat with 500 pounds. I believe that the foundation I laid with those early squat workouts contributed to my ability to develop muscle at a rapid rate later as I exited puberty."[18] Both Mike and his father were enjoying the results Mike's workouts had produced. It seemed as if his strength and muscle size were increasing each month. "My father was really delighted," Mike admitted. "Especially after I started playing fullback for the junior high team."[19]

Thirty-eight miles west from Ephrata along Interstate 183 sits the York Barbell Company. During the mid-1960s, York was the hub of strength training in America. Bob Hoffman,[20] the owner of the company (which was then the nation's leading manufacturer and distributor of barbell and dumbbell sets), was the coach of the U.S. Olympic weightlifting team, and had a large office within the building, which also featured a full weight training facility on its main floor. York was nicknamed "Muscle Town," as, apart from Hoffman's coaching pedigree and barbell business, he was also the publisher of two popular strength training and bodybuilding magazines: *Strength and Health* and *Muscular Development*. As Mike recalled:

> As a young teenager... Johnny Myers... would take me on frequent visits to "Muscle Town," as York was called, to watch

the nation's and world's best Olympic lifters, powerlifters and bodybuilders train. I got the opportunity to spend entire Saturday afternoons at the then famous York Barbell Club watching men like Bill March, Tony Garcy, and the precocious Bob Bednarski — our best ever heavyweight Olympic lifter — practice technique, as well as challenge their personal bests in the press, snatch, and clean and jerk. Also, [I watched] Terry Todd and Ernie Pickett, the first official champs in organized powerlifting, train on the bench press squat and deadlift. This had an enormous impact on me as I took up these lifts — the press, snatch, clean and jerk, bench press, squat, and deadlift — early on.[21]

One of the permanent fixtures at York was the legendary bodybuilding champion John Grimek,[22] a two-time Mr. America winner (1940 and 1941), who also had the Mr. Universe (1948) and Mr. USA (1949) titles on his résumé. Even more impressive titles were bestowed upon him by the bodybuilding writers of the period, who dubbed Grimek the "Monarch of Muscledom"[23] and, even more intriguingly, "The Glow."[24] Standing five foot eight and a half and weighing in at rock-solid 195 pounds, Grimek was legendary within bodybuilding circles. Born to Slovakian parents in Perth Amboy, New Jersey, on June 17, 1910, he was phenomenally strong. He performed partial overhead presses in his basement with a barbell he had attached to chains suspended from the ceiling, and got to the point where he could support one thousand pounds in such a fashion.[25] Apart from his bodybuilding laurels, Grimek was strong enough to represent the United States in weightlifting at the 1936 Berlin Olympic Games, where he placed ninth.[26] Moreover, while working as an artist's model at Princeton University in the 1930s, he had met and conversed several times with the Nobel Prize–winning physicist Albert Einstein.[27]

On the occasions when he could screw up the courage, Mike approached Grimek to learn the secrets to his bodybuilding success.[28] He wouldn't have learned much. Not that Grimek wasn't knowledgeable, but his most productive bodybuilding program wasn't all that much different from the original bodybuilding course that came with Mike's first barbell set: three days per week, perhaps a dozen or so exercises, performed for one set each.[29] It's true that Grimek later experimented with different protocols (including daily training), but his competitive days were by this point 24 years in the rearview mirror, and he hadn't put on a pound of muscle since. While Grimek still looked rugged, powerful, and muscular, by the mid-1960s he was an example of bodybuilding's past. Mike's eyes were on the future. Every month, Mike rushed to the newsstands and scooped up the latest muscle magazines. The Hoffman publications, of course, were purchased first. But there were also magazines showing up on newsstands that were published by a man named Joe Weider.

Joe Weider, along with his brother Ben, were born into an impoverished Jewish ghetto in Montreal shortly after World War I.[30] Like many people born into poverty, the Weider brothers obsessed over the prospect of surmounting their lot in life. Unlike many people, however, both men admired dictators; Joe (strangely, given his ancestry) was fascinated with Adolf Hitler,[31] while Ben gravitated to Napoleon Bonaparte.[32] Joe longed for personal power, and when he saw a photograph of John Grimek displaying a tremendously powerful physique that also radiated a certain rugged aesthetic, he took up weight training in an effort to get some of that for himself.[33]

While Joe grew stronger and his physique filled out, he lacked the genetics to become either the next Grimek or a champion bodybuilder. But coming up short on the physique front didn't preclude him from making his passion his career. He copied down names and addresses from a weight training "pen pal" list that appeared at the back of Bob Hoffman's *Strength and Health* magazine, and sent each of them a subscription card for a new publication he intended to create entitled *Your Physique*. In surprisingly short order he had sufficient subscribers to his fledgling publication that he was able to devote himself full time to its creation.[34] However, magazine sales alone did not prove sufficient to pay the bills, as bodybuilding was only a fringe activity at that time.

Joe decided that, like Bob Hoffman, he could supplement his magazine sales by selling barbells. He soon partnered up with a bodybuilder out of New Jersey by the name of Dan Lurie.[35] Joe would publish the magazine and Lurie would manufacture the barbells they would sell through the publication. Joe's magazines eventually diversified; some (such as *Your Physique*) were devoted solely to bodybuilding, while others (such as *Adonis* and *Body Beautiful*) catered to the homosexual community.[36] Joe and Dan eventually had a falling-out and parted ways. But Joe continued on with *Your Physique*.[37] Thenceforth, he dubbed himself "The Trainer of Champions Since 1936." The title wasn't completely without foundation, as, according to Joe, he had once advised an already well-built young man by the name of René Leger on how he could improve his physique by lifting weights. Eleven years later, Leger won the Mr. Canada contest (an event that the Weider brothers would promote). This, to Joe's way of thinking, was directly (if not solely) attributable to the advice he had shared with him over a decade earlier.[38]

Joe would later acquire the handle "The Master Blaster,"[39] which initially was a somewhat sarcastic sobriquet, owing to Joe's penchant for bombastic verbiage when writing about the workout methods the bodybuilders employed ("Zappy," "Whack," "Bomb")[40] as well as his description of the potency of the supplements he sold through his magazines, such as this gem:

> In just 30 days you'll be a new breed of wildcat. You'll be a muscularized "take charge" blaster — full of power and rugged vigor to help you perform like a tiger and drive 'em [the chicks] crazy this summer — from dawn to dusk![41]

By 1964, Joe and Ben were tightening their collective grip on a slowly growing bodybuilding industry. While Hoffman more or less controlled the Amateur Athletic Union's (AAU) sanctioning of competitive weightlifting events in addition to the Mr. America contest, the Weiders, in an attempt to gain a foothold in the industry, had resuscitated a governing body they had created in the 1940s: the International Federation of Bodybuilders (IFBB).[42] The federation had lain dormant for 16 years, but they dusted it off in the 1960s to produce their versions of the Mr. America and Mr. Universe contests. And, by 1965, they were preparing to launch a brand-new competition: the Mr. Olympia.

If things went according to plan, particularly with Joe's magazine to promote it, the Mr. Olympia, the Weider brothers believed, could become the premiere bodybuilding competition in the world. And the best part: the winner of the contest would appear in Joe's magazines advertising Joe's products, giving them the endorsement of a *champion* bodybuilder, a bona fide seal of approval, which, from a marketing standpoint, could potentially result in millions of dollars flowing into the Weider coffers.

Certainly there was considerable buzz within the bodybuilding communities throughout America leading up to the new competition, as the event would also feature two recent IFBB promotions, the IFBB Mr. America and

Mr. Universe contests. Meanwhile, within the York Barbell Company, Bob Hoffmann fumed. He had no use for the Weiders, whom he dismissed as unscrupulous parvenus.[43] Not that Hoffmann had much use for bodybuilding, per se, considering bodybuilding contests little more than male beauty pageants, particularly when compared with the power and glory of Olympic weightlifting. In his eyes, Joe's publications and Ben's sanctioning organization were nothing more than attempts to erode the hard-earned status of the AAU and its Mr. America contest, a venue that was his exclusive domain. Indeed, 17 years previously, when the Weiders' IFBB was in its infancy, Hoffman devoted an entire editorial in his magazine to criticizing it:

> A new organization known as the "International Federation of Body Builders," not affiliated with the A.A.U. or the International Weight Lifting Federation which has controlled International Weight Lifting for many years, not recognizing amateur rules of any sort, is tossing leading professionals and the rankest amateurs into the same competition so that the newcomer has no chance to win. This outfit has been branded an outlaw group by the governing bodies of sport and any athlete who takes part in one of their competitions loses his standing with the A.A.U. and cannot compete in A.A.U. activities, the world's weight lifting championships or the Olympic Games. Literally he becomes a man without a country. The organization we are discussing is backed by Weider, a young fellow who refused to follow the rules of the A.A.U.[44]

But there was nothing Hoffman could do about it; the IFBB Mr. Olympia competition was going to happen.

Mike, of course, was excited at the prospect of such a contest. As he read the promotional articles about it in Weider's magazine, he envisioned how incredible it would be to be sitting in the audience watching champions such as Dave Draper and Larry Scott — bodybuilders whose pictures were all over the ads and articles in Joe's magazines. Scott had been crowned Mr. America in 1962 and was fresh off a Mr. Universe win in 1964. Even more than Draper, Scott was the epitome of what a bodybuilder should look like, at least from a 1960s perspective. At the risk of reading like one of Joe Weider's training articles from the day, the similes a writer can use to describe Scott's physique are of necessity hyperbolic. He did have shoulders that looked like cannonballs and biceps to match. He had a wasp waist and large thighs and calves. These, in combination with a handsome face, perfect teeth, tanned brown skin, and blond hair were unlike anything the bodybuilding world had ever seen before. Scott appeared on no fewer than 12 covers of Joe's magazines leading up to the 1965 Mr. Olympia contest[45] and had moved a ton of protein product for the Master Blaster. Simply put, Larry Scott was lightning in a bottle. And while Mike had heard the scandalous comments about the IFBB's forthcoming contest from within the York compound, this only added intrigue to the event.

It's hard for an outsider to bodybuilding to fathom just how alluring such magazines and contests were (and, in some instances, continue to be) to the psyches of young males. The image that the Weiders, as well as Hoffman and the other publishers in the industry, were painting of bodybuilding represented, to borrow from Huxley, a brave new world, complete with a new image of the masculine ideal; the means of becoming more attractive to the opposite sex, having greater strength, improved appearance and confidence, and a sense that a young person had within him — as an individual — the power to literally shape his own destiny. All this coming at a time when a boy's natural testosterone production was kicking into high gear. It was a high that had no comparison. Indeed, when viewed in this light, getting good grades in school or being part of a "team" was an impotent substitute.

Joe Weider was right; bodybuilders were, indeed, the "new breed"; the Nietzschean concept of the *Übermensch* brought down to earth and made flesh. This was a siren call for a good many young males that was simply too seductive to resist. Weider et al. were offering up a fraternity of iron and muscle that featured its own pantheon of gods, its own ambrosia and dietary laws, its own tithing (in the donations the boy or his parents made each month for the magazines, the barbell sets, gym memberships, and supplements), and a message of transcendence; of striving to overcome one's lowly physical self to ascend to the levels of the gods themselves — as prescribed in the teachings revealed in the pages of the bodybuilding periodicals and training courses. And this, in Joe Weider's case at least, was by design. He had paintings and later bronze busts of himself commissioned in which he appeared as God (Zeus-like, more specifically). Some of these were printed on the labels of his supplement products, which featured Joe's head and heavily muscled shoulders splitting the clouds, with rays of sunlit energy emanating from his image (during the 1970s Joe commissioned paintings of various bodybuilders who endorsed his products; they were depicted as demi-gods and warriors to further drive home the image of the "Weider lifestyle" that the neophyte bodybuilders should look to embrace). Bodybuilding, as it was being presented, was not a fringe activity for the insecure; it was an open sesame to the Elysian Fields.

And so, when John Myers offered to drive Mike to New York to attend the premiere Mr. Olympia contest at the Brooklyn Academy of Music on September 18, 1965,[46] a 14-year-old Mike Mentzer was beside himself with excitement.

The event was officially billed as "the 1965 IFBB Mr. Universe — Mr. America — Mr. Olympia — Miss Americana Muscle/Beauty Show."[47] And as its rather lengthy title indicated, there were no fewer than four separate competitions for the patrons to witness that night. A crowd of 2,100 fans packed the auditorium within the music academy,[48] and many more milled about outside, waiting for a glimpse of the bodybuilding champions they had read about each month in the magazines. "I can recall quite clearly standing outside the Brooklyn Academy of Music amid the throng and seeing Larry Scott arrive, and the people going literally crazy," Mike recalled. "It was almost a religious experience."[49]

The Miss Americana title was won by Vera Ann Schultz of Bellerose, New York.[50] To nobody's surprise, the "Blond Bomber" (as he had been so monikered in the Weider publications), Dave Draper, won the Mr. America contest.[51] He had been in against some seasoned competitors such as Chet Yorton and Zabo Koszewski, but Draper's physique — and the Weider-driven publicity behind it — made the decision in his favor a fait accompli. Even more impressive to Mike, however, had been the appearance of a 15-year-old Massachusetts native, Dave Mastorakis, who, despite being only a year older than Mike, had a physique that was huge, ripped, and staggeringly impressive.[52] He was the youngest person ever granted entry to the Mr. America contest, and, despite his age, he was not at all out of place standing on the same stage as the highly promoted Draper or the other bodybuilding veterans. Mike made a mental note to find out more about this kid.

Next up was the Mr. Universe competition, which was won by Earl Maynard from Manchester, England.[53] This was no small accomplishment, requiring him to defeat the celebrated St. Lucian (recently relocated to London, England) Rick Wayne, who had generated considerable publicity of his own ever since his Mr. Great Britain victory earlier that year.[54] Frank Zane, a future three-time Mr. Olympia, was also left behind in Maynard's wake.

The Mr. Olympia contest was restricted to previous Mr. Universe winners. It was rarified air. And yet, even though many winners of that title had been approached to compete (including the legendary Steve Reeves, who won the title in 1950), only two competitors showed up: Larry Scott and Harold Poole.

Poole had won the Universe title in a fiercely contested battle against Larry Scott two years previously,[55] and he was in excellent condition on this night as well. Given that Maynard had (just) won the Mr. Universe title, he was given a nudge toward the stage so that the number of competitors for the new title could increase by 33.3 percent. It would be to no avail, however, as Larry Scott lived up to his hype and came out on stage looking every bit the superstar he had become. "I took one step out from the side of the stage into view," Scott would later recall, "[and] a wave of sound crashed into me along with an explosion of flash bulbs. It was hard to believe the response was for me."[56]

Larry Scott was the winner long before the judges tallied their scores.[57]

As the victor of the first-ever Mr. Olympia contest, Larry Scott was awarded neither a check nor a trophy, but rather a gaudy crown that Joe had created specifically for the event by George Alagantakis, an employee of the G.A. Novelty Company in New York City.[58] According to the contest report that appeared in Joe's magazine, the crown featured "crystal and ruby on gold, lined with red velvet and trimmed with leopard."[59] Joe placed the crown upon Scott's head, and the fans went wild. According to Rick Wayne, "for six minutes and four encores Larry Scott was hotter than the Beatles — hotter than Cassius Clay — hotter than Jesus."[60]

The Master Blaster was ecstatic: his new contest was a resounding success. Scott for his part, couldn't get the bizarre topping off his dome quick enough. He quickly left the stage and hurried along to an elevator in the company of Dave Draper, where the pair ascended several floors to where their dressing room was. "After his coronation," Rick Wayne recalled, "Larry Scott had to wait two hours before he could safely leave the theater. A party in his honor went on without him."[61] Mike joined the throng waiting to catch a glimpse of the new champion outside the Brooklyn Academy of Music. Growing impatient, he let his hero worship get the best of him:

> After the show I climbed over a high fence to get backstage and up a fire escape and, lo and behold, I walked into this room and there was Larry Scott and Dave Draper! And I just stood there gawking at them, watching Larry wiping the oil off his enormous arms. I clearly recall being even more impressed by his calves. Larry was quite friendly, and I left the building on an elevator with Larry and Dave. It was exciting, and I remember thinking how exciting it must be to be the center of that excitement — to have fans waiting for you.... Seeing Larry Scott take the first Mr. Olympia made an enormous impact. It fuelled my ambition to go further.[62]

Mike wanted to win this new title, but he knew that he would have to travel the same route that Larry Scott had in order to do so. He would first have to win the Mr. America, then the Mr. Universe, before he could compete for bodybuilding's ultimate trophy (or crown, as it were). He went home that night and pulled out his most recent copy of *Muscle Builder/Power* and scribbled in the margins of one of the articles: "Mr. America, Mr. Universe, Mr. Olympia," and, next to these titles, he wrote down the dates that he expected to win them — 1972, 1974, and 1976, respectively.[63]

Everything was different now. Larry Scott was the king — not Steve Reeves; Joe Weider's contests were where the top bodybuilding talent was competing — not Bob Hoffman's. A whole new world had just opened itself to Mike. He was going to be a champion bodybuilder — just like Larry Scott — and have fans lined up outside to see him enter and exit a building. He, too, would possess the ability to bring people to their feet when he posed.

He had joined the fraternity, and everything else was now secondary: sports, school, and, if need be, family.

CHAPTER THREE

THE DREAM MERCHANTS

By the summer of 1966, it was clear to Mike Mentzer's 15-year-old mind that he had to change his training method. Larry Scott, the reigning Mr. Olympia, was training six days a week — performing 12 sets for his biceps alone![1] The old-time bodybuilders might have been content training only three days per week with one or two sets per body part, but that was back in the 1940s. It was now 1966 and a new age had dawned.

Unbeknownst to Mike, it was the age of steroids.

It is not known precisely when steroids entered the bodybuilding world, but certainly the muscle-building benefits of testosterone had been recognized since the 1930s.[2] Gradually, this knowledge found its way into circles in which one of the effects of testosterone — enhanced muscle growth — was highly desired.[3] By the mid-1960s, all of the top bodybuilders were using steroids,[4] some at three times the prescribed dosages.[5] One of the effects of steroid use, quite apart from a dramatic enlargement of the muscles, was a marked enhancement of its user's recovery ability.[6] In the past, those looking to build muscle had to wait at least 48 hours between workout sessions in order for their body's energy and repair systems to have adequate time to make the necessary adaptation that a workout had stimulated. But steroids rapidly accelerated this process. For those who took the drugs there existed no reason to limit their workouts to only three days per week with one to three sets per body part; it was now possible to train daily — and to make progress light years beyond what could be achieved without chemical augmentation.

Just how big a difference synthetic testosterone makes in the development of muscle mass was revealed by Doug McGuff, an ER physician and co-author of the bestselling book *Body by Science*, who brought to light a study that appeared in the *New England Journal of Medicine* in 1996. The study randomly assigned 43 normal men to one of four groups: one that received a placebo injection and performed no exercise, another that received a testosterone injection and performed no exercise; another that received a placebo injection and exercised with weights; and a group that received a testosterone injection and exercises with weights. According to the "Methods" section of the study:

> The men received injections of 600 mg of testosterone enanthate or placebo weekly for 10 weeks. The men in the exercise groups performed standardized weight-lifting exercises three times weekly. Before and after the treatment period, fat-free mass was determined by underwater weighing, muscle size was measured by magnetic resonance imaging, and the strength of the arms and legs was assessed by bench-press and squatting exercises, respectively.[7]

Dr. McGuff summarized the results of the study as follows:

> In terms of lean body mass, naturally, the people that got a placebo injection and did not exercise basically showed no change in their lean body mass whatsoever. The group that got an injection of testosterone but did not weight train or did not exercise, those people got an increase of 3.2 kg of lean body mass. Then the group that got the placebo injection but did resistance exercise, that group got 1.9 kg of increase in lean body mass compared to 3.2 kg in the group that just got the testosterone injection. Stated differently, testosterone in a supraphysiologic dose of 600 mg produced 43% greater gains in lean body mass than training by itself. And then when you looked at the group that got testosterone plus the exercise those people gained 6.1 kg of lean mass — literally triple what someone would get if they trained without the chemical assistance.[8]

Despite the drugs' considerable potency as muscle-building agents, and their use by the top physique champions, anabolic steroids were seldom if ever mentioned within the bodybuilding press. The reason, of course, was simple: the bodybuilding companies didn't sell them. Steroids were medications that were manufactured by drug corporations and distributed solely through pharmacies. Not being part of the science or pharmaceutical industry, Joe Weider, Bob Hoffman, and all of the other publishers who would come into the industry found it far more profitable to promote the idea that the protein supplements they sold were responsible for building the muscle mass that the champions displayed in their magazines. It was the moral equivalent of someone who wanted to sell bicycles telling people that Pablo Escobar earned his massive wealth as a result of the bicycle business he started at 16 years of age, rather than the massive quantities of cocaine he sold.[9]

And it worked. The majority of those who read the ads and articles believed what they were told; that the muscles they saw on bodybuilders such as Larry Scott or Harold Poole were nothing more than the result of these individuals' increased dedication to training — i.e., more hours spent in the gym, and the right brand of protein powder. And so, to duplicate their heroes' success, aspiring bodybuilders fell in line; they performed more sets, hit the gym more days per week, and purchased more protein supplements. Those who published the magazines controlled the industry; they owned the organizations that ran the contests, and they owned the only publications in which information on how to build bigger muscles could be found. Their word on such matters was final.

In truth, however, such subterfuge was not new in bodybuilding. Ever since its inception, the enterprise had been dominated by commercial interests. Young men, wishing they had the strength and muscular development of other young men, were willing to listen to — and pay — anyone who claimed that he could change them from how they were to how they wanted to be.

One of the first to exploit this desire was Eugen Sandow, a German bodybuilder and showman who, in 1901, promoted the first bodybuilding contest (one of the judges at the competition being none other than Sir Arthur Conan Doyle, the author of Sherlock Holmes). Sandow soon began marketing training courses and a supplement called Plasmon (which he stated was "an excellent strength builder").[10] After Sandow, however, the focus of the commercial interests in bodybuilding shifted to selling barbell sets. By the 1940s, bodybuilding magazine publishers were selling training courses along with their barbell sets,[11] which, while profitable unto themselves, were one-off sales; once these were purchased, the retailer would receive no additional money from the consumer. By the 1960s, however, supplements returned to bodybuilding with a vengeance.[12] They were promoted as almost magic elixirs with spectacularly transformative properties. More importantly, supplements were consumables, requiring repeat purchases each month to refill the supply. The most obvious sales pitch was that muscle (what one wanted to build) was made of protein (one of muscle's components). This connection couldn't be played up enough. Witness, for example, the following ad that appeared touting "Joseph Weider, Trainer of Champions" Hi-Protein supplement:

> YOU ARE PROTEIN!
> Not a muscle can be developed — not a single drop of blood can be manufactured — not a tissue can be replaced *without protein*! Protein, combined with heavy exercise, is the secret of muscular growth . . .
>
> WHY YOU NEED EXTRA PROTEIN
> Bodybuilders must have *more* protein than anyone — because the harder they work out, the more tissues must be replaced. Therefore, the *more* protein, they need to *repair* and "*re-proteinize*" their bodies for vigorous, rugged workouts. If you get insufficient protein your muscles *stay small*, regardless of how hard you work them . . .
>
> WEIDER PROTEIN IS TOPS
> Because it is derived from the richest sources of soy protein, Weider HI-PROTEIN is a favorite with bodybuilders everywhere.[13]

And, if the above wasn't sufficient to make people part with their hard-earned dollars, Joe concluded his ad by stating that his Hi-Protein supplement was "Medically Approved."[14] What medical body lent its approval to his product was never indicated.

Joe recognized that most young men became interested in bodybuilding solely to get bigger, and he made sure his supplements catered specifically to that desire. His "Crash Weight Gain Formula #7" supplement was a perfect example of this. Through the pages of his magazines, Joe declared that this product would lead to a 14-pound weight gain in 14 days; it would lead to a fast, healthy weight gain; it would add muscle and strength to the entire body; it would add muscle and strength without the necessity of engaging in exercise programs; a user of this product simply had to drink his way to good health; his product would allow an individual to gain weight in specific areas; and use of the product would allow an individual to control the distribution of the newly gained weight, and that this was a new, "scientifically blended," milkshake-flavored drink.[15]

Joe's ads featured bodybuilding champions such as Dave Draper, Larry Scott, Don Howorth, Frank Zane, and later Arnold Schwarzenegger and Franco Columbu, touting the product along with testimonials.[16] Joe was realistic enough to recognize that his physique, despite his greatest efforts over the decades, was nowhere near impressive enough to cause aspiring bodybuilders to part with their money (he had only once screwed up the courage to enter a bodybuilding competition, the 1951 Mr. Universe contest, only to place fifth in his height class).[17] But the Master Blaster was also savvy enough to recognize that someone who actually had impressive muscles most certainly could — and the bigger his muscles, the better the supplement sales. At least from the prepubescent males who equated their potential attractiveness to the opposite sex with the size of their biceps.

Joe had made extensive and successful use of Dave Draper for this purpose during the early 1960s. Draper was a tall, blond, genetically gifted bodybuilder who had won the Mr. New Jersey contest in 1963, and also happened to sport the most impressive pair of arms the world of bodybuilding had seen at that time. Poor Dave, who was almost as shy as Mike Mentzer, would later claim that he toiled away for $87.50 a week in Joe's warehouse in Santa Monica, while Joe featured him in virtually every one of his product ads — from protein powder to barbell sets — and raked in millions.[18] Dave eventually took Joe to court over his uncompensated exploitation,[19] but by then Joe had Arnold Schwarzenegger to take his place.

The problem for aspiring young bodybuilders was that nutritional science was only (and even then, not uniformly) being taught in high school health classes and universities, and typically by middle-aged teachers who, to the nascent counterculture movement, represented the old ways. More significantly, to Mike and other tyros, these teachers knew nothing about bodybuilding — and they looked like it. By contrast, the bodybuilders advertising Weider's products were young, virile, and hip. And it wasn't just

Joe's magazines that claimed you needed protein supplements, but *all* the bodybuilding magazines. Each periodical sold its own brand of protein, and the common denominator that united them all was the notion that supplemental protein was the key to building bigger muscles. "I was quite young when I first started bodybuilding," Mike would recollect years later. "I, like most people, read muscle magazines as if they were sacred scripture. I fell for their advertising blandishments. I took every protein powder, vitamin you can think of."[20] Having no knowledge that what he was reading in the magazines was simply sales hype, Mike felt compelled — if he was to succeed in his bodybuilding quest — to purchase these products:

> I became deluded from reading all the muscle magazines, especially their seductive advertisements which promised that we all could be Mr. Americas almost overnight if we would only invest our money in a particular product. A good example was one that promised a-pound-a-day muscle gains if we drank a certain drink every day. A very enthusiastic, but admittedly ignorant young bodybuilder, I fell for that one hook, line, and sinker, and went from 180 to 250 pounds (most of the weight gain being bodyfat) in seven months! On top of that, I was becoming rather concerned about the hideous stretch marks that began appearing all over my body, along with the fact that I had outgrown two or three wardrobes. The next six months I spent trying to undo the damage. You see, it was in vogue in those days to "bulk up and then cut down;" i.e., to gain as much weight as possible despite the content, then trim off the fat you gained and be left with just muscle. Well, by the time I was done cutting and trimming more than six months later, I ended up weighing a few pounds less than the 180 pounds I began with. The starvation and overtraining that led to such a weight loss caused me to lose muscle. I actually ended up with less muscle than I had when I started.[21]

Despite what was proclaimed in Weider's ads, it's doubtful that any of the top bodybuilders used his protein products. "It wasn't much of a secret that the top competitive bodybuilders did not use much of the Weider product line even when offered for free," claimed bodybuilding historian and author

Randy Roach. "Weider's primary market was his publications' readership and the general public through the department store chains. Both the profit margins and the gullibility were higher in those realms."[22]

While Joe Weider would eventually be taken to court for his outlandish claims about his Crash Weight Gain Formula #7 product (and later for other products), in 1964 that was still ten years away.[23] In the 1960s his ads ran unchecked, and the money rolled in.

Joe's business rival Bob Hoffman wasn't above getting in on the supplement action either. Indeed, he had been in the protein market since 1952, marketing his Hi-Proteen, a product very similar to Weider's in both name and content.[24] And, in keeping with the tenor of the times, he made sure to mention in his ads that his was a product born of the latest scientific research:

> The production of a "miracle food," such as High-Protein, is not a hit-or-miss affair. A world-famous food research laboratory is put to work. Their chemists and the doctors, who are a part of their organization, work out the product. They profit by their years of study, experience, and research.[25]

This all sounded very advanced, and just what one would expect of such a powerful new supplement. However, the truth was nothing like the ad; Hoffmann was mixing up the ingredients himself with a paddle inside the not-so-sanitary York Barbell Company building.[26]

Hoffman had actually torpedoed a former advertiser in his *Strength and Health* magazine after he saw how profitable the protein supplement business was. He cancelled the ads of advertiser Irvin Johnson's Hi-Protein that were appearing in *Strength and Health* and replaced them with ads for his own Hi-Proteen supplement. The name change was subtle enough that consumers simply assumed it was the same product and continued ordering it from his magazine.[27]

Later, not content with having a product similar to Weider's, Hoffman sought to distance himself from his competitor by coming out with a completely new protein product: "Hoffman's Protein from the Sea." In 1961, he premiered it to the bodybuilding world:

> Fish are considered to be the best fed animals in the world, consuming nutritious, organically-rich vegetation and other

fish, which in turn have eaten the organically-rich foods so abundant in the depths of the sea. The fish protein used in HOFFMAN'S PROTEIN FROM THE SEA is richer than organic meats and many other high protein products in the essential amino acids. It digests well, is almost 100% assimilated and supplies your body with elements it needs for building, maintenance and repair.[28]

The new supplement had one serious flaw, however. It actually made people sick to their stomachs. "That was the most vile stuff I had ever smelled or tasted in my life!" Mike recalled. "And a couple of times I remember my brother regurgitating this stuff after trying to get it down."[29] "Hoffman's Protein from the Sea" did not get a lot of repeat orders and slowly disappeared from Hoffman's supplement line.[30]

His bad experience with the supplement hucksters notwithstanding, Mike's interest in bodybuilding was growing. Apart from Larry Scott, Mike was taken by the appearance of another bodybuilder who appeared frequently in the muscle magazines: Bill Pearl.[31]

Bill Pearl was born on the Warm Springs Indian Reservation in Oregon on October 31, 1930.[32] By the 1940s, he was lifting weights, inspired by his bodybuilding predecessors Eugen Sandow and John Grimek. In 1953, Pearl exploded onto the bodybuilding scene, winning the Mr. Southern California, Mr. California, AAU Mr. America, and National Amateur Body-Builders' Association (NABBA) Mr. Universe (Professional) contests all in the same year. After a three-year break from competition, he returned to win the 1956 Mr. USA (Professional) and, five years later, the 1961 NABBA Mr. Universe (Professional). He repeated this triumph by reclaiming the NABBA Mr. Universe (Professional) title in 1967.[33]

By virtue of winning the Mr. Universe title, Pearl was invited to compete in the first Mr. Olympia contest in 1965, but not being a fan of the Weider brothers, he opted to decline. "I didn't compete in the Olympia because I considered it a Mickey Mouse affair," he said. "I'm not knocking the IFBB, but at the time I thought the Olympia was created to promote the Weiders and their organization."[34]

To Mike, Pearl's physique embodied the very essence of masculinity.[35] Both Mike and Ray (who was now actively pumping iron as well) began to write letters to Pearl, querying him about how best to train.[36] Pearl took the time to answer each letter,[37] and, as a result of his suggestions, Mike gradually swapped out his limited-sets three-day-per-week training routine for a training program that had him performing up to 20 sets a body part and visiting the gym six days a week.[38]

During this transitional period, Mike continued to read every muscle magazine that came out each month.[39] In 1966, that totaled six publications: *Muscle Builder/Power* and *Mr. America* (which were published by Joe Weider and promoted the IFBB contests), *Strength and Health* and *Muscular Development* (which were published by Bob Hoffman and promoted the AAU contests), *Muscle Training Illustrated* (which was published by Joe's former partner in the barbell business, Dan Lurie, and promoted a new organization, the World Bodybuilding Guild, or WBBG, which he had introduced in 1965)[40] and *Iron Man* (which was published by Peary Rader and, to its credit, was more or less neutral regarding the sports' governing bodies).

It was while flipping through the pages of *Iron Man* magazine that Mike happened upon an ad for some gym equipment that had been created by Ed Jubinville, a highly respected bodybuilder, muscle control artist, and equipment designer, who not only promoted very successful bodybuilding contests throughout New England but was also a judge at the 1965 Olympia contest.[41] Mike recognized the model in the ad as Dave Mastorakis, the 15-year-old competitor who had so impressed him at the IFBB Mr. America contest in Brooklyn the previous September. Given what appeared to be their proximity in age, Mike was keen to know what this kid was doing in terms of exercises, sets, reps, and protein supplements to be good enough to be invited to compete in the Mr. America contest.[42] He took note of the mailing address that appeared at the bottom of the ad, and quickly dashed off a letter to Ed Jubinville.[43]

It was something of a Hail Mary on Mike's part, to be certain, but nothing ventured, nothing gained. Mike popped the letter in the post and returned home, hoping that he would receive a reply. By this point in time, Dave Mastorakis was something of a sensation on the east coast. Despite only training for a little over two years, he had already been featured in a three-picture spread in Hoffman's *Strength and Health* magazine, along with the following caption:

> Dave just turned 15 and has been training for two years. He does both lifting and bodybuilding. In addition, he loves to

run and swim. He is 162 pounds at a height of 5'5" and has made a 210-pound clean and jerk and a 250 press. We think Dave has one of the finest builds of any 15-year-old that we have seen.[44]

As far as Dave's training went, his instructor was, in fact, Ed Jubinville, who had his young student working out on a basic three-day-per-week whole-body program, consisting of approximately eight or so exercises performed for three sets each.[45] In truth, the program wasn't much different than the one Mike had been following up until recently. In due course, Mike's letter found its way to Ed's shop in Holyoke, Massachusetts. Ed scanned the letter and discovered that it was written by a 14-year-old who wasn't looking to purchase bodybuilding equipment but wanted to get in touch with Dave Mastorakis. The next time Dave came to the shop, Ed handed him the letter.

"Here is a pen pal for you if you want to write him."[46]

Dave read the letter and wrote Mike back. Their correspondence continued for several months. Soon Dave's parents found themselves comfortable enough to put their boy on a bus in Granby, Massachusetts, bound 307 miles southwest to Ephrata, Pennsylvania, and the Mentzer home, where he would spend half the summer of 1966.[47]

CHAPTER FOUR

FAMILY ISSUES

As the Greyhound bus made it way along Interstate 287 South, the teenager inside it had no idea that he was heading to a house still smoldering from an emotional explosion that had gone off during the fall of 1965.

Not long after watching Dave compete in the 1965 IFBB Mr. America contest, Mike decided that bodybuilding was the only form of competition he was interested in. He told his parents that he was quitting junior high football.[1] "Football just didn't give me the gratification I wanted," Mike recalled. "I wanted something I could pursue myself. I was always something of a rebel. A quiet rebel. I never joined clubs, I didn't like things where I had to share my interests, or my energies."[2] Tim Lutz, Mike's best friend throughout high school, remembered that "he just gave up everything for weightlifting. Basically, once he got hooked, he never strayed from that. He just got into it and was so focused on bodybuilding."[3]

When Harry learned of Mike's decision, he was apoplectic. He "tried to pound some sense into my head,"[4] Mike recalled. "He tried to dissuade me from bodybuilding; in fact, it caused a serious rift for a while."[5] It was at this point that Mike learned that his dreams and ambitions counted for very little in the Mentzer home. It was Harry's edicts that were law within the house on 117 Chestnut Street. Mike's aspirations were fine, so long as they aligned with those of his father. The baseball mitt, $20 bills, and bragging about his son at family gatherings bore testimony to that. But now that the pair were out of sync, Mike experienced a different side of his dad. Where Harry was once Mike's biggest supporter, he was now his biggest critic. While previously

Harry considered lifting weights a great activity for building strength for football, lifting those same weights for bodybuilding purposes he considered nothing more than a fast track to homosexuality. "That's one of the allegations levelled against bodybuilders," Mike said. "That it leads to narcissism, which, in turn, somehow leads to homosexuality. That is utter bullshit.[6] Sure, there are homosexual bodybuilders. You have homosexuals in every area of life. It's no greater or less in bodybuilding. Sexual orientation is determined in the first three to five years of life. Weightlifting is not going to change that."[7]

But from ex-Marine Harry Mentzer's perspective, weight training counted for nothing if its ultimate purpose was to stand on stage in your underwear and strike poses before a roomful of strangers. To set the boy straight, Harry said he would no longer pay for Mike's clothes or protein supplements. If Mike wanted to pursue this ridiculous bodybuilding dream of his, he would be doing it on his own — there would be no support coming from the family. Moreover, Harry declared, the subject was never to be brought up again.[8]

Marie, who never really understood her son's psychology,[9] simply fell in line with her husband. Unlike Harry, however, she at least attempted to put a soft spin on the situation; it wasn't that she disapproved of Mike's bodybuilding per se, it was just that she could no longer afford the milk bill that went with the supplements he was taking.[10] But Mike knew better. A line had been drawn in the sand. And the backlash didn't stop at the Mentzer doorstep. When Mike wasn't receiving verbal disapproval from his father, he was getting it from his friends and football coaches.[11] It was lost on these people why Mike would give up the glory of the gridiron in favor of bodybuilding. What a ludicrous activity! He was a good student — clearly, of above-average intelligence in relation to his peers. How did he develop such a critical blind spot?

Eight months later, the tension in the Mentzer home still hung in the air like smoke. This was the environment that Dave Mastorakis entered. For his part, Mike looked forward to Dave's arrival; he would have someone to talk to who understood his passion for bodybuilding. When Dave's bus pulled into the terminal in Lancaster County, Marie Mentzer was there to meet it.[12] Dave's high school in Massachusetts had already finished for the year, but Mike's hadn't,[13] so both teenagers would have to wait until Mike's school day was over before they could meet face to face for the first time. Marie had no difficulty recognizing the new houseguest as he stepped down from the bus. Mike had already shown her Dave's photos in the magazines. "She was very,

very nice," Dave recalled. "*Very* Italian."[14] After a short drive, during which the pair exchanged small talk, Marie's car finally came to a stop within the family driveway. Dave collected his suitcase from the trunk and followed Marie into the house. He recalled the home being a single-level, modest-sized one; small, but well kept.[15] Marie's oldest son, Elmer, had moved out of the house by this point and was living on his own. Her daughter, Marie Ann, had also left home and recently gotten married, which meant Mike and Ray now had their own bedrooms.[16]

When his school day ended, Mike raced home to greet his friend. He ushered Dave downstairs to the home gym, where the two compared notes on bodybuilding. When Ray got home from school, he asked his mother where Mike and Dave were, and quickly bounded down the stairs to join them. He wanted to ask Dave questions and have him assess his 14-year-old physique. Mike had no interest in having his little brother monopolize the conversation and told Ray to leave. "Ray was just young enough to be a pain in the butt," Dave recalled. "I think Ray was probably a little over 14. I was about 16 and a half, and Mike was going on 16. Ray was very jealous of Mike spending his time with me. But he was just a little kid."[17] Dave tried to be diplomatic and answered Ray's seemingly endless list of questions. Ray then dragged their houseguest upstairs to his bedroom and stripped down to his underwear to show Dave his muscles. Dave told the teenager that he looked good, and even took a photo of Ray flexing his biceps, which he said he would send to him so that Ray could see for himself.

Mike's patience finally ran out. In order to get away from Ray, Mike announced to his mother that he was taking Dave over to Russell Hertzog's garage gym, but that they would be back later that evening for dinner. Ray was told in no uncertain terms that he couldn't tag along. While his younger brother pouted, Mike and Dave made their way over to Russell's residence on Cherry Street. Soon John Myers arrived.[18] Once again, training was discussed, and Dave learned that Mike had incorporated some powerlifting into his program as a result of Myers's influence.[19]

Returning to the Mentzer home later that night, the pair sat down to one of Marie's pasta dinners, which impressed Dave to no end.[20] As bodybuilding was not to be discussed in Harry's presence, Mike and Dave took to playing board games. "We would play Monopoly for days until the game was officially over," Dave recalled.[21] His ten days in Ephrata passed quickly, and when Dave stepped onto the bus to return home to Massachusetts, he did so with the knowledge that an enduring friendship had just been born.[22] The two friends continued to communicate via letters over the next several months, and when Mike got out of school the following summer (1967), he and his dad climbed into Harry's truck and, with a boat hitched onto the back of the rig, drove eight hours northeast to Dave's home in Granby. There Mike was dropped off to stay with the Mastorakis family for a couple of weeks.[23] The next summer (1968), Dave was back in Ephrata for another two-week visit.[24] These back-and-forth visits continued for several years. The two friends wrote to each other constantly[25] — always about bodybuilding: what exercises they found to be most effective, what the latest champion was recommending, and what they knew about the latest nutritional supplement the muscle magazines were promoting.

While Mike was obsessing over bodybuilding, little brother Ray recognized that an opportunity had just presented itself. He had played second fiddle to Mike in Harry's eyes for far too long. With Mike's fall from grace, an opening had now appeared that would allow him to reverse this situation and win his father's favor. Harry wanted a football player — and Ray was determined to give him one. His dedication to his weight training sessions quickly built the five-foot-ten young man up to an impressive 205 pounds by grade ten.[26] Like his brother before him, Ray was a fullback — and a good one. He also played defensive end — whatever position his football coaches wanted. Even 31 years later, his coach, Dick Dean, recalled his prowess on the field:

> When I think of Ray, I remember that day against Warwick.... We were really getting after the quarterback, and he was playing defensive end. They decided to run a pitch play right at him and I think the quarterback saw him and just wanted to get rid of the ball. Well, Ray read the play and intercepted the pitch and went for a touchdown. He was a pretty good athlete and a pretty tough football player.[27]

Ray's devotion to football paid off; he was soon named one of the three captains of the Junior High Mounts football team and went on to set a new scoring record for the squad, racking up 95 points in seven games as the Mounts steamrolled their way to a Junior High record of 6–1 during the season.[28] By 1969, Mike's little brother was not only a star on the gridiron, but he was becoming a force to be reckoned with in junior high school wrestling as well,[29] running up a competitive season record of 15 wins with only one loss.[30] Ray's athletic exploits were written up frequently in the local newspapers.[31] The joy had come back to Harry's life, and Ray was basking in the newfound attention. *He* was the one now receiving special treatment from his father; Mike was ignored. "I was into all the sports: wrestling, football, baseball," Ray recalled. "And I was doing very well. The competitive state between Mike and I eased as I made my mark in sports. Mike wasn't very interested in school sports at that time. He was becoming active in bodybuilding. He spurned team sports, and, in turn, my father spurned him."[32]

Mike gradually ceased working out with his father's friends and signed up at the Lancaster YMCA, which had more specialized bodybuilding equipment.[33] His parents' influence had now been eclipsed by that of his hero, Bill Pearl. "I became an idolater," Mike said. "Bill Pearl became my hero. The thought of getting a physique like his kept me going in bodybuilding."[34] He was on his own with his bodybuilding efforts — and he was okay with that. "I tend to be an individualist, an extreme individualist," he said. "And bodybuilding is an extremely individualistic and even lonely sport. You're there with the barbells all by yourself. It's just you — your mind and your body."[35]

But being an individualist, whose sole interest was lifting weights and building muscle came at a price, Mike's former friends stopped hanging around with him. They weren't into bodybuilding, and no longer had much if anything in common with him. Girls were intimidated by his size (at first, at any rate),[36] and other guys at school were concerned that they suffered by comparison.[37] By now, Mike had grown into a strikingly handsome young man with an extraordinary build. To protect their fragile egos, older teenagers would challenge him to fight quite often.[38] Sometimes there was no challenge at all, just a sucker punch, and then it was on.[39] Mike was typically slow to anger, but if he was attacked, his challenger almost instantly regretted it. "I remember that when Mike was younger, I think he could have stood up to anybody," his friend Roger Schwab recalled.[40] After several of these challenges, Mike was cut a wide berth, which allowed him to go about his business unimpeded.[41] In time, Mike ceased trying to justify his devotion to bodybuilding:

> There was a guy from a TV station who asked me, "How do you respond to those who look on you as a freak?" My response was, "I don't mind being a freak in a world of conformists."

> That's the way I look at my bodybuilding. Most people are so damned preoccupied with what other people think that they're afraid to be themselves. The great fear is the fear of ostracism. People want to meld in with the crowd. I never liked the idea that I had to be like everyone else.[42]

Apart from the gym at the YMCA, Mike was most comfortable in a classroom, and with one teacher who earned his respect:

> My favorite teacher was Elizabeth Schaub, who taught twelfth grade English Literature. Mrs. Schaub was an "old-fashioned" no-nonsense type who expected her students to master what she taught and played a crucial role in developing my appreciation of language, thought and writing. Although I balked at the time, she had us read many of the classics, and write reports, or essays, on them. That was in 1968–69, when times were different, and the schools provided better education than today, though still light-years away from the ideal in education. I did quite well in both grammar and high school, sometimes getting all A's, though mostly A's and B's. Most important, all of my educational experiences described above — starting with Mrs. Schaub — served to fuel the further development of my nascent passion for literature and writing after college. While my high school literature teacher had instilled a certain liking for those intellectual disciplines in high school, I rebelled at having to read so many lengthy books and write the innumerable essays (I was blindly, sophomorically rebellious at the time). Once I left high school and college, free to study on my own, I continued reading the classics along with books on psychology and philosophy.[43]

He was moved by Shakespeare,[44] but American authors left him unimpressed. "I don't like to read American bestsellers," he said. "People like Kurt Vonnegut bore me to death. Writers in America don't write so their books will endure, they write so they can get a movie contract. American everything is so plastic and transient."[45] Although he read voraciously, he never considered himself to be a bookworm,[46] and found that most of the extracurricular activities his fellow students enjoyed held no interest for him.[47] He attached no importance at all to simply becoming popular. "I don't care to have many friends and acquaintances," he said. "But the few good friends I possess are very close to me."[48]

Meanwhile, the pressure continued to build inside the Mentzer home. In late 1968, Mike was involved in a minor traffic accident when a senior citizen failed to stop his car at an intersection.[49] While it wasn't his fault, that didn't make Harry any less livid. The gulf between father and son was growing; Harry didn't care about the "classics" of literature and cared even less about bodybuilding. For Mike's part, he viewed his father as out of step with the times, a vestige from a bygone era, unappreciative of the fact that there existed a big world out there beyond the confines of Lancaster County. He described Harry dismissively to the press as "the prototypical American male — John Wayne, football, bomb them and all that."[50] As for Ray's desire to please his father by jumping through athletic hoops, Mike viewed that as a barrier to his brother's development as an individual. Any type of conformity was anathema to him.[51] One day while driving with his friends, Mike drove right past Ray, who was walking home from school. Ray would never forget this slight (although Mike would insist that it never happened).[52] And while the growing divide between Mike and his father had disordered the Mentzer family, Harry was about to take things to a far more serious level of disruption.

Alta Jean Markley (née McCord), recently divorced,[53] was the new dispatcher at the Kenosha Auto Transport Corp. Harry, of course, was in the dispatch office constantly to pick up boats that he trucked from coast to coast. And when Alta Jean looked his way, Harry did not avert his eyes. Soon they were seeing each other clandestinely.[54] But Marie was no fool; she knew her husband, and quickly grew suspicious that something wasn't right, which caused yet another wave of strain to wash over the Mentzer household. Mike also suspected his father's infidelity, which caused Harry's moral authority within the household to drop even lower in his eyes. Mike couldn't wait to leave home.

Upon graduating high school in 1969, and "being young and restless, and wanting to escape the dominion of my dad,"[55] Mike Mentzer made his move.

He enlisted in the United States Air Force.

CHAPTER FIVE

THE WILL TO POWER

At this point in the narrative, we must break away from Mike's story and travel some 4,200 miles east to Germany. There, sweating and straining within a gymnasium in Munich is a 19-year-old Arnold Schwarzenegger, a young man with big plans. In 10 years' time, he will become Mike's biggest rival, or rather Mike will become his. And in 12 years' time, they will collide in a bodybuilding contest that will launch the film (and later the political) career of one, and all but destroy the career of the other. Because of the significance of Arnold's role in Mike's story, the author must beg the reader's indulgence to explore the young Austrian's entry and experiences in the world of bodybuilding, in order to set the stage contextually for the historical clash that will occur between these two men and alter the course of their respective lives.

Arnold had already garnered a good deal of attention in the European bodybuilding industry by virtue of his winning the Junior Division of the Mr. Europe contest in 1966. A year later he won the NABBA Mr. Universe at only 20 years of age, the youngest winner in the history of the contest.[1] And a year after that, he was brought to the attention of Joe Weider by Albert Busek, a gym manager in Munich, who was also an excellent photographer and would eventually become the editor of the German-language editions of Joe's magazines. Albert had been promoting Arnold everywhere and anywhere he could ever since he had first laid eyes on him at the Mr. Europe contest:

> I told everybody, including Joe, to get ready for the "Schwarzenegger Era." In early 1968, Joe and I met in Dusseldorf,

and I had told him again about the Schwarzenegger Era. I realized immediately that Joe was a true bodybuilding fan. When you sit in front of him, the discussions about bodybuilding go from one aspect to another. I shared that same sort of love, and I think my passion for Arnold's potential made an impact on him.[2]

Indeed. Joe was so impressed shortly thereafter he had signed Arnold to a contract and moved him to Los Angeles. In return, the Master Blaster had training articles written "by Arnold Schwarzenegger" (actually ghostwritten by other writers Joe employed) and Arnold appeared in Joe's ads promoting Weider bodybuilding equipment and nutritional supplements.[3] A year after signing on with Joe, Arnold added the IFBB Mr. Europe, the IFBB Mr. International, the IFBB Mr. Universe, and the NABBA Pro Mr. Universe (all in 1969)[4] to his résumé, and he appeared on the cover of Joe's magazines no fewer than five times between 1968 and 1969.[5] Arnold was clearly the new big thing in bodybuilding.

Arnold was born in Thal, Austria, on July 30, 1947[6] to a doting mother[7] and a stern father.[8] Well, "stern" might be something of an understatement. Arnold's father, Gustav (1907–72),[9] had been a card-carrying member of the Nazi party.[10] After the war ended, Gustav became the chief of county police in Arnold's hometown,[11] drank heavily,[12] and ruled over the Schwarzenegger household with an iron fist. Beatings were not an uncommon occurrence.[13] The environment was such that Arnold knew at a young age that he couldn't live under the same roof as his father for much longer:

> My hair was pulled. I was hit with belts. So was the kid next door, and so was the kid next door. It was just the way it was. Many of the children I've seen were broken by their parents, which was the German-Austrian mentality. Break the will. They didn't want to create an individual. It was all about conforming. . . . I was one who did not conform and whose will could not be broken. Therefore, I became a rebel. Every time I got hit, and every time someone said, "You can't do this," I said, "This is not going to be for much longer, because

I'm going to move out of here. I want to be rich. I want to be somebody."[14]

Like the Weider brothers before him, who likewise had suffered through oppressive childhoods, Arnold became (in the words of his biographer Laurence Leamer) "obsessed with power."[15] Images of conquerors flashed through his mind: "Normal people can be happy with a regular life," he said. "I was different. I felt there was more to life than just plodding through an average existence. I'd always been impressed by stories of greatness and power. Caesar, Charlemagne, Napoleon were names I knew and remembered."[16]

This desire for power would prove to be a strong motivating factor throughout Arnold's life. But certainly, nobody could have predicted that bodybuilding should prove to be the catalyst for his achieving this. For one thing, he hadn't initially appeared to be genetically blessed for the enterprise. Helmut Cernic, a former Mr. Austria who was a trainer at the Graz Athletic Union (the first gym in which Arnold trained) recalled:

> He had very bad posture, a slightly sunken chest, fallen shoulders, very skinny legs, and used to train with his eyes half closed and his mouth half open, so that the whole effect was as if he wasn't all there. Soon after he started his first training session at the [gym] he turned around to another bodybuilder, Johnny Schnetz, who was around his age, and said: "Well, I give myself about five years and I will be Mr. Universe." We all looked at each other as if to say, "This boy is crazy."[17]

The Graz Athletic Union was founded by a bodybuilder named Kurt Marnul, who was then the reigning Mr. Austria.[18] Marnul had been the one who had invited 14-year-old Arnold to train at the gym and devised the teenager's first serious training program:

> He wanted to gain muscle, so he trained biceps, shoulders, and legs on the first day. The next day he trained triceps, calves, and the midsection. And then he would repeat the first program on the third day. He would train every day.[19]

At about the time that Mike Mentzer was discovering Steve Reeves on the cover of *Muscle Builder* magazine in Ephrata, Marnul was giving 15-year-old Arnold Schwarzenegger his first injection of anabolic steroids in Gratz.[20] This he augmented with Dianabol tablets (another steroid).[21] All told, Marnul reported, Arnold was ingesting 310 milligrams of steroids a week at the tender age of 15.[22]

Steroids weren't illegal at this point in time, of course, and those who ingested them did so in the belief that they were simply taking a very potent aid to building muscle, which in bodybuilding was the name of the game after all. The drugs and training proved to be a potent pairing for the young man, as Arnold's physique quickly exploded into growth. Twelve months after coming under Marnul's tutelage, he had gained 22 pounds of muscle, with his arms growing from 13 to 16 inches, and his chest improving from 40½ to 45¾ inches.[23]

Arnold's steroid usage increased, along with the concern of some of his gym-mates. One of his training partners, Helmut Riedmeier, claimed that Arnold "used to inject himself with steroids and took them for breakfast, lunch, and dinner quite openly."[24] He even supplied them to his fellow competitors. Rick Wayne, for example, who competed in the 1966 NABBA Mr. Universe contest in London, England recalled that, "Over tankards of beer Arnold talked with me about steroids. When I told him I'd never used them, he said it might be interesting to find out what would happen if I did. He presented me with a month's supply of Dianabol, just in case I became sufficiently curious."[25] As far as the potential risks of the drugs, who knew anything about that in the 1960s? In any event, it was a risk Arnold was certainly willing to take if it meant that he could build more muscle and win more contests:

> All I needed to know was that the top international champions were taking steroids, something I confirmed by asking the guys in London. I would not go into a competition with a disadvantage. "Leave no stone unturned" was my rule. And while there wasn't any evidence of danger — research into steroids side effects was only getting under way — even if there had been, I'm not sure I would have cared. Downhill ski champions and Formula One race drivers know they can

get killed, but they compete anyway. Because if you don't get killed, you win."[26]

Arnold stated his beliefs about steroids even more succinctly to his gym mate Helmut Cernic: "If you told me that if I ate a kilo of shit I would put on muscles, I would eat it."[27] More steroids, of course, meant faster recovery time from workouts, which, in turn, allowed for more training to take place, and this combination meant faster muscle growth. In an article that Busek wrote in 1967, he stated that Arnold was training seven days a week for up to six hours at a time, performing 60 sets per muscle group.[28] He further proclaimed that Arnold was tipping the scales at a massive 235 pounds, with arms that stretched a tape measure to a stunning 20½ inches.[29] Any bodybuilder who was willing to do anything and everything it took to become as huge as possible was money on the hoof in Joe Weider's eyes. And Arnold was willing to do anything it took.[30]

But Joe wasn't alone in his awe of the Austrian. Other movers and shakers within the bodybuilding industry, such as Bob Hoffman and Dan Lurie, had likewise expressed interest in having Arnold endorse their products.[31] In Europe, Albert Busek was intrigued almost to the point of obsession ("sycophant" was the term Bill Pearl used to describe Busek's relationship to Arnold),[32] bending over backwards to give Arnold publicity that would advance his career, not only in Europe but in the United States as well. During the 1967 Mr. Universe contest in London, Busek, at Arnold's bidding, was quite willing to use his press credentials to spy on Arnold's chief opposition, Dennis Tinerino, and report back to Arnold on his conditioning.[33] There were even judges at bodybuilding competitions, such as Wag Bennett in England, who would drop all pretense of impartiality and objectivity when Arnold competed, and who, in the words of Arnold biographer Laurence Leamer, "actively conspired with Arnold about how he could win."[34] With such a support system in place, it's little wonder how Arnold became successful in competition so early in his career. Everyone within the bodybuilding industry who had products to sell knew what bigger muscles meant in terms of money to be made — and it caused them to almost fall over themselves in an effort to curry favor with bodybuilding's newest star.

Such followers and support were important to Arnold because he had a plan. Just like Mike Mentzer's, Arnold's life had changed when he spotted a bodybuilding magazine in his home village of Thal. The cover featured a photo of the bodybuilding champion Reg Park, who, like Steve Reeves before him, had played the role of Hercules in some low-budget films that were produced in Italy. Again, like Mike, Arnold knew immediately — at 14 years of age — that his future had just been revealed:

> I scraped up the *pfennigs* that I had left and bought that magazine. It turned out that Hercules was an English guy who'd won the Mr. Universe title in bodybuilding and parlayed that into a movie career — then took the money and built a gym empire. Bingo! I had my role model! If he could do it, I could do it! I'd win Mr. Universe. I'd become a movie star. I'd get rich. One, two, three — bing, bang, boom! I found my passion. I got my goal.[35]

For his part, Joe couldn't get Arnold into his publications fast enough. By 1968, sales of his magazine had dropped.[36] Dave Draper had lost his marketing luster; his last contest, the 1967 Mr. Olympia, saw him place a disappointing fourth. Moreover, the ads for Weider products in which he appeared featured the same old photos and evidently had lost some of their impact. After winning two Mr. Olympia titles (1965 and 1966), Larry Scott had retired from professional bodybuilding to devote more time to his family and his Mormon faith, and after two years without steroids or training, his once Herculean physique had rapidly disappeared. No one wanted to buy a protein product advertised by a guy who now weighed 156 pounds.[37] And then there was Joe's current Mr. Olympia (1967–69), Sergio Oliva, who brought his own set of problems to the table. First, despite bolting with the rest of the Cuban weightlifting team to the American embassy in Jamaica during the Central American and Caribbean Games and being granted political asylum in the United States,[38] to most Americans he was still Cuban (read: communist). The American public was then in the middle of the Cold War and not that far removed from the Cuban Missile Crisis and the Bay of Pigs debacle. Having Sergio market Joe's products in his magazine held the same consumer appeal to Americans as having Fidel Castro in his ads. The second problem Sergio had was even more challenging. According to Rick Wayne:

> Oliva suspected that a black Mr. Olympia wasn't nearly as useful to Joe Weider as a white one. It was no secret around

Weider headquarters that whenever the publisher featured a black champion on the cover of *Muscle Builder*, sales plummeted. Surely a champion who couldn't sell magazines was at bottom close to useless as an endorser of food supplements and gym equipment.[39]

But Joe recognized that whatever down times his magazines were experiencing would change dramatically the instant Arnold signed up with him. Surprisingly, it didn't take much to bring Arnold into the fold; Joe offered to pay his way to California, provide a gym membership, an apartment, a car, pay for his food, and promote him "to the whole world."[40] In return, Joe now had a very marketable muscle man to hawk his products. Arnold's arm, according to Weider's *Muscle Builder/Power* magazine, now measured 21½ inches[41] — and Arnold allowed Joe to say in articles and ads that he used Joe's Crash Weight-Gain Formula #7.[42] The money train started up again.

Despite Joe's promotion, when Arnold entered the IFBB Mr. Universe contest in 1968, he was trounced by a considerably smaller and lighter bodybuilder named Frank Zane.[43] This setback stunned the new arrival and put his master plan temporarily on hold. He had thought that simply coming in and overwhelming the opposition with his size would've been sufficient,[44] but, standing next to the highly defined Frank Zane, he looked like the Michelin Man.[45]

Joe Weider quickly hustled his new employee off to the Studio City gym of Vince Gironda, a man who had a knack for sharpening up physiques.[46] As the reader has no doubt observed, while Joe marketed himself as "The Trainer of Champions Since 1936," he was more the "Exploiter of Champions," using the fruits of others — those with great genetics, combined with hard training and steroid ingestion — to sell his products. Vince Gironda, on the other hand, was the real deal, a true trainer of champions, having worked with physique stars such as Larry Scott, Rick Wayne, and Don Howorth. He was further considered the "Trainer to the Stars," and was responsible for putting muscle on movie and television actors such as James Garner, Johnny Carson, Clint Eastwood, Cher, Michael Landon, and, later, Sean Penn, Denzel Washington, and Burt Reynolds.[47] Joe wanted Arnold to be razor-sharp the next time he stepped on stage to compete. Vince did what he could, but it didn't appear to him that Arnold was particularly motivated. "I didn't think he had it because he didn't show the kind of drive I thought was necessary," Vince recalled. "However, he had a slow plodding type of Germanic drive, where he showed up every day and plodded away at it, but he didn't do anything remarkable."[48]

It was while training at Vince's gym, however, that Arnold met two people who would prove to have a dramatic impact on his future. The first was Mits Kawashima, a Hawaiian gym owner, who, wanting to take advantage of Arnold's publicity in Joe's magazines, invited the Austrian to Honolulu for a guest posing exhibition in early 1969.[49] The second person of consequence that Arnold met was Paul Graham, an Australian bodybuilder, strongman, crocodile wrestler, and professional wrestler,[50] who would soon become Arnold's roommate in California.[51] Paul needed a place to stay, and he had a car;[52] Arnold had a place to stay but needed a car. It seemed like a good fit.

Apart from the promotion he received in Joe's magazines, it will be remembered that what had prompted Arnold to come aboard with Joe was the promise of a car, free rent of an apartment, and a weekly paycheck.[53] Joe had delivered on the apartment, but there was no indication of when the car was going to arrive, and, so far, Arnold had only been receiving $65 a week.[54] Arnold needed more money and — great news! — his new roommate, the crocodile wrestler, said he had a job for him. Once again, the stars looked to be aligning. "The crocodile wrestler [Paul Graham] . . . worked for a dealership. . . . In fact, he hired me," Arnold said. "One of the dealer's specialties was exporting used cars and I earned pocket money that fall by driving cars down to Long Beach and onto a freighter headed for Australia."[55] Perhaps unbeknownst to Arnold, the cars Paul had him driving were stolen.[56] And certainly unbeknownst to Paul, the FBI had been keeping a close eye on America's piers for several months.[57] It wasn't long before they were on to him. And when Paul and Arnold flew to Hawaii for Mits Kawashima's guest posing gig, the Feds made their move. The *Honolulu Advertiser* broke the story:

AUSTRALIAN WRESTLER HELD ON CAR CHARGE

An Australian wrestler, here to appear in a physical culture exhibition at McKinley High School, was arrested by FBI agents yesterday on a stolen car charge.

Paul M. Graham, 30, professional wrestler and former holder of the Mr. Sydney title in the Mr. Universe competition, was arrested at a Waikiki hotel.

He was arrested on a warrant from Los Angeles charging him with causing stolen motor vehicles to be transported in interstate and foreign commerce.

Graham told a local acquaintance that he had an auto dealership in Australia.

He is being held in lieu of $25,000 bond after arraignment before U.S. Commissioner Henry. W.C. Wong. Wong set Feb. 7 as the hearing date.

He was to appear at a health and physical culture show Feb. 8 at McKinley High School. The show, sponsored by the Hawaii Athletic and Physical Culture Association, also headlines Mr. Universe, Arnold Schwarzenegger.[58]

Ten days later, Paul Graham waived his right to a preliminary hearing and agreed to voluntarily return to face a federal court charge in Los Angeles. The *Honolulu Star-Bulletin* reported in its February 10, 1969, edition that Paul had been indicted by a federal grand jury in Los Angeles the previous Wednesday (February 5).[59] When interrogated, Paul Graham evidently indicated that he had acted alone in shipping the stolen cars from America to Australia. Consequently, he was the only one charged (and later convicted) of the offense.[60] In truth, the FBI was only concerned about the international transportation of the stolen goods; *who* stole them was a local matter and not within their jurisdiction.[61]

Upon Arnold's return to California, Joe immediately delivered on his promise of a car — a secondhand Volkswagen Beetle.[62] Arnold decided (or perhaps Vince decided for him) that Vince's gym was no longer going to be his training center. Arnold now began training at Gold's Gym in Santa Monica, where he could observe and interact with the veteran bodybuilders who trained there. Joe now promoted Arnold as the man who could knock the great Sergio Oliva from his Mr. Olympia throne. He almost did, losing by a single point to the man bodybuilding fans had dubbed "The Myth" in the 1969 Mr. Olympia contest. And now with a full year to prepare for his next kick at the Mr. Olympia can, Arnold pulled out all the stops, arrived at the contest in top shape, and won the title in 1970. The articles and the ads continued,[63] and the money rolled in. Joe's editor, Gene Mozee, recalled one day at the Weider office when $90,000 in supplement and equipment orders came into the office.[64]

Weider and Schwarzenegger were now a powerful team about to take the 1970s by storm, one that would eventually place an aspiring bodybuilder named Mike Mentzer squarely in its crosshairs.

CHAPTER SIX

MIND AND BODY

A few miles southeast of Washington, DC, near the town of Morningside in Prince George's County, Maryland, sits Andrews Air Force Base. Named after Lieutenant General Frank Maxwell Andrews,[1] the commanding general of the United States Armed Forces in the European Theater of Operations during World War II, the base is also home to two Boeing VCC-25 aircrafts that serve as Air Force One whenever the president of the United States happens to be aboard.[2]

In June 1970, 18-year-old Mike Mentzer stepped off a bus and onto the base.[3] He smiled at the situation he now found himself in. "I had joined the Air Force to see the world," he recalled, "and ended up in Washington DC, only about 150 miles away from my home."[4]

Like most young students, his thinking at this stage of his life was the polar opposite of that of the right-wing jingoists who populated so much of America, but "God and country" hadn't been the reason underlying his enlistment. "Just after I graduated from high school, I didn't know what I wanted to do," he recalled. "I had always entertained the idea of going into medicine, but then I didn't think I was quite ready for it. I really lacked direction. I saw the military as a way of giving me something to get me on the track."[5] Never a conformist, Mike grew his hair longer than regulation allowed and was constantly looking over his shoulder for senior officers who might catch him on it — but they never did. Given his natural athleticism and prodigious strength, he was able to get through boot camp without much difficulty. "In the first two weeks they really work you to see what you're made of," he recalled. "If they see you can handle it — the discipline and all — they start to ease up, and even provide encouragement. And they really respect a guy who is well-built. My first month I was made squad leader, just because I was big and muscular."[6] He was put to work as an orderly at the base hospital.

The gymnasium at the base proved to be a major disappointment to the young man. "You know, when I came down here to Washington, I was disillusioned in a lot of ways. First of all, I lifted weights since I was 11 years old and I expected to find tons of weights down here," Mike recollected. "But the only thing that I found was one dusty looking Universal lifting machine."[7] Despite the lack of training equipment, Mike would state years later that "I had some of the best workouts of my life on that machine."[8]

He was still avidly reading the muscle magazines, of course, and the "double split" routine that Arnold was said to be using was featured throughout the Weider publications. Mike decided that if this was how the greatest bodybuilder in the world was training, there had to be something to it. Arnold became his new bodybuilding idol.[9] Creating his own version of the exercises he saw the "Austrian Oak" performing in the magazines, he started training three hours a day, six days a week.[10]

But simply getting bigger and stronger wasn't his sole objective; Mike wanted to become a champion bodybuilder, just like John Grimek, Steve Reeves, Larry Scott, Bill Pearl, and Arnold Schwarzenegger. He wanted to be that person who could produce out of the raw material of sinew and bone a form of human statuary, an aesthetic presentation of human strength, power, and beauty. "What's wrong with men wanting to look better?" he asked. "Taking pride in yourself, taking care of your body, what could be a more noble end? If people practicing the piano seven hours a day is a noble end, what's wrong with seven hours weightlifting?"[11] It was, he believed, a realization of the ancient Greek ideal of a healthy mind in a healthy body.[12]

Besides, to the mind of an 18-year-old male, what would be the alternative? To simply resign oneself, as his parents had, to the inevitable decay of life? Where was the contentment to be found in watching one's body slowly deteriorate? By contrast, bodybuilding offered a virtuous quest that culminated in the practitioner looking like a Greek sculpture, and, if the ads in the muscle magazines were to be believed, standing out among one's friends and becoming an object of desire to beautiful women. It was a no-brainer.

But just as Praxiteles required the precise tools (chisels, hand drills, abrasive powders) necessary to bring his vision of physical perfection to life in marble, the physique artist who was looking to sculpt his body required specific tools of his own to bring forth the superhero within. And this consisted of weights, proper nutrition — and anabolic steroids. Mike began using steroids at the age of 19. It's unknown who introduced the drugs to him, but once they connected with his already well-built physique, his muscles responded rapidly.[13] So much so that by late January of 1971, he entered his first bodybuilding competition: the Mr. Lancaster contest.[14] The major problem he had to contend with in the weeks leading up to the competition was an old one: his inherent shyness, which was so bad he had trouble even looking at himself in a mirror in order to check his muscular development.[15] Fortunately, he was able to push through this obstacle, and, on Saturday, January 23, 1971, before 300 spectators at Warton Elementary School in Lancaster County, he edged out his nearest rival, Jim Tierney, by 34 points (277–243) to win the Mr. Lancaster title.[16] Winning that first contest gave the young man a tremendous boost in confidence. "There were a lot of good bodybuilders in that area," Mike recalled. "It's an area populated by a lot of German people — strong stock. There was a high premium placed on physical performance, sport, strength, and bodybuilding. And they had their annual contest, and I won rather handily. I had beaten some of the guys from the city who I used to look up to. So, that provided some very important motivational fuel to keep going."[17] Mike's journey to the summit of the bodybuilding mountain had begun.

Within the year he had won Mr. Pennsylvania[18] and placed second at the Mr. Teenage America in Cleveland, Ohio (where he was also considered to have had the best arms, legs, back, and chest in the competition).[19] All these accomplishments occurred while Mike was in the Air Force and living in Maryland. Meanwhile, 135 miles north, in Ephrata, the Mentzer household had been turned upside down. Harry's relationship with Alta Jean Markley McCord was now no longer a secret. The news resulted in arguments and yelling. Marie was constantly crying and phoning relatives to vent. She called her parents in Los Angeles,[20] her sister in Hollywood, Florida, and her brothers in Lafayette Hill, Pennsylvania, and Van Nuys and Northridge, California.[21] Harry moved out of the family home and Marie initiated divorce proceedings against him, citing grounds of "indignities,"[22] which, in the State of Pennsylvania, is interpreted as occurring whenever "one party made the other's life unbearable."[23] Her depression returned.

With Mike away from home, all his younger brother, Ray, could do was look on in solitude as his parents' marriage imploded. The family home on

177 Chestnut Street went up for sale, and the proceeds were put towards the purchase of houses for Marie at 56 East Chestnut Street in Ephrata, and Harry (a little over 14 miles away) at 125 Broad Street, Lancaster.[24] Ray opted to live with his mother and busied himself by giving all his energies over to high school athletics. He was featured in the local newspapers seven times between 1970 and 1971; four times for football[25] and three times for wrestling.[26] He became the first wrestler in Ephrata High School history to ever make it to the regional championships.[27] Although concerned for his 17-year-old brother's welfare, in truth Mike was glad to be away from what had once been his family. His mother, understandably, only wanted to talk about Harry's betrayal, and how hard her life had now become. It didn't leave room to talk about much else.

Her depression was also a cause for concern. To better understand what she was going through, Mike spent what little spare time he had studying psychology. He read voraciously the works of Sigmund Freud, Carl Jung, Wilhelm Reich, Ronald David (R.D.) Laing, and Thomas Szasz.[28] He sought out part-time jobs in neurology clinics, emergency rooms,[29] and mental institutions[30] to better observe the symptoms and treatments of mental illness firsthand. It was during this time that he resolved to become a psychiatrist.[31] According to Mike:

> I remember reading in an interview with [Allen] Ginsberg a Latin expression which was translated to the English: "Nothing human is foreign to me." And I remember being struck by the profundity of that statement and it sort of became my credo. That's one of the reasons I gravitated to psychiatry and psychology; I felt that nothing that any human being experienced was something divorced from myself. I've always felt that I've had a certain capacity to empathize with what was going on inside people. I could get behind their experiences and experience what they were feeling. And that is sort of in accord regarding the human experience and feeling things such as disappointment, grief, sadness, unhappiness [read: his mother's depression]. To not feel these things is really an abdication of our humanity and is something we should allow ourselves to feel and not be overwhelmed by. It's one of the essential aspects of being alive as a human being.[32]

Try as he might, however, Mike made little headway with his mother. When he tried to speak with his father, Harry knew nothing about mental illness and deflected any conversation of personal matters so that they didn't creep into territory that might involve his infidelity to the family. Consequently, the topics discussed were largely superficial in substance. Moreover, neither parent wanted to talk about Mike's bodybuilding ventures. Given the choice between speaking with someone consumed by self-pity and someone whose discourse was superficial, Mike opted to keep his own counsel. "Like most young obsessives, I responded to the disapproval of my friends and relatives by withdrawing into the insulated world of the gym," he said. "I pursued my goal on my own and for years I continued despite their scorn because I was striving for a noble goal — perfection of the human form. It wasn't until many years later that I realized their disapproval was more historic than experiential, rooted in sociological dogma, man's age-old vacillation about the body, an attitude that has swung from the Greek ideal of a healthy mind in a healthy body to the Victorian rejection of the body and its needs."[33]

Any guidance or advice he needed could be located between the pages of the books he read, which spoke to his interests with far greater authority than his mother and father could. As for his father's new paramour, well, she held no place in his life at all and never would. If his parents had any interest in the details of his recent forays into bodybuilding competition, they could read about it in the local papers, just like everyone else. Mike developed, in his words, an "intense interest in how the mind worked,"[34] and was further interested in how the mind and body connected, and what effect each had on the other. To this end, he began to explore Zen through the writings of Shunryu Suzuki and the mind/body musings of Yukio Mishima.[35] The latter struck Mike as a man who had made the connection. In Mishima's book, *Sun and Steel*, the author waxed euphoric about bodybuilding's way of strengthening the mind and spirit:

> The groups of muscles that have become virtually unnecessary in modern life, though still a vital element of a man's body, are obviously pointless from a practical point of view, and bulging muscles are as unnecessary as a classical education is to the majority of practical men. Muscles have gradually become something akin to classical Greek. To revive the dead language, the discipline of the steel was required; to change

the silence of death into the eloquence of life, the aid of steel was essential.

The steel faithfully taught me the correspondence between the spirit and the body: thus feeble emotions, it seemed to me, corresponded to flaccid muscles, sentimentality to a sagging stomach, and over-impressionability to an oversensitive, white skin. Bulging muscles, a taut stomach, and a tough skin, I reasoned, would correspond respectively to an intrepid fighting spirit, the power of dispassionate intellectual judgement, and a robust disposition.[36]

Proceeding, Mike made room on his bookshelves for the writings of psychologist William James (whose essay "The Energies of Men" particularly intrigued him)[37] and the sports psychologist Bruce Ogilvie.[38] But it was Wilhelm Reich, R.D. Laing, and Thomas Szasz who proved to be the most impactful psychologists on the young man's psyche.[39] He considered Laing and Szasz "brilliant thinkers" who were "all but pilloried by the psychiatric establishment for their proclaiming that schizophrenia is not a disease, but a label used to control those whose behavior and use of language differ from the norm. A disease is caused by an invasion of the human body of harmful entities referred to as germs. Certainly, there is no such entity that causes so-called mental disorders, especially those which manifest primarily in the use of metaphors and language that makes others uncomfortable. In fact, every human being at times uses language and metaphors that are illogical and, not infrequently, are as hard to decipher as those used by some mental patients."[40] Their words offered hope that mental illness, per se, was not something bad or anything to be ashamed of; it was simply misunderstood by society and by many within the psychiatric establishment.

That was all well and good (if not without controversy) in the treatment of what was commonly held to be purely psychological disorders, but neither Szasz nor Laing addressed the mind-body connection. That was Wilhelm Reich's domain. And the more Mike read of Reich, the more he liked what the doctor had to say:

> Reich was one of the first psychotherapists to take a physical approach to the mind/body question. In the 1930s he broke from the "talk therapy" of his mentor Freud and pursued

the problem on a more biological level. Reich theorized he couldn't work on the psyche without working on the soma, or body, as well. His work led to the formulation of a therapy he called "orgonomy," which involved the freeing of dammed-up biological energy through the application of pressure to certain "holding points" in the muscles. He also used a series of exotic exercises to accomplish the same end. Reich discovered the existence of a continuous bioelectric field he called the "orgone," a field of energy running from the center to the periphery of the body. "Physic health," Reich said, "is characterized by the alternation between unpleasurable struggle and happiness, error and truth, deviation and rectification, rational hate and rational love; in short by being fully alive in all situations of life." He felt that such states of being as pleasure and anxiety, seemingly antithetical, actually stem from the same energy source. Pleasure, Reich felt, is the subjective sensation of expansion, the flow of the orgone energy from the center of the body to the periphery, while anxiety resulted from the stoppage of this energy flow by what he called "armoring," which is really muscular tension. Reich maintained that unless our physical and biological energies are discharged, they will eventually consume us. This discharge can be sexual, through the orgasm, Reich says, or purely physical, through exercise.[41]

What the doctor wrote about meshed nicely with what Mike perceived implicitly about the body's effect on the mind. Reich wrote about this new "orgone" energy rhapsodically and convincingly. Some likened it to the chi energy described in ancient Chinese medicine,[42] or the Hindu and Buddhist concepts of chakras and prana energy.[43] Reich even discussed his findings over a five-hour period with Albert Einstein at Princeton.[44] Nothing resulted from their meeting, however. This didn't deter Reich; he continued his investigations into this new energy form and even built and sold contraptions that were said to be "orgone energy accumulators." That's when the United States Food and Drug Administration (FDA) stepped in.

Reich was ordered to stop selling his devices, and, when he violated the injunction, he was declared a medical fraud by the FDA, and ultimately sent to jail. On August 23, 1956, six tons of Reich's papers, journals, and books, were seized by the FDA and burned in New York, including books such as *The Mass Psychology of Fascism* and *The Sexual Revolution*, which had nothing at all to do with his theories on orgone energy.[45] The 2015 edition of the *Encyclopaedia Britannica* stated, "In the 21st century some considered this wholesale destruction to be one of the most blatant examples of censorship in U.S. history."[46] But there may have been other reasons for the government to want Reich squashed under thumb. He wrote about sex rather cavalierly for the times, which in a puritanical society such as America's in the 1950s was viewed as an attack upon the very social and moral fabric of the nation. Webster Schott, writing for the *Washington Post*, suspected that the government's punishment of Reich was solely about his views on human sexuality:

> But the larger reality of the proceedings against Wilhelm Reich and his Orgone Institute at Rangeley, Maine, is that he was also convicted of sinning against society. He conspired to remake it. He believed he could free us all from a worldwide "emotional plague" through the fullness of sexual orgasm.[47]

Perhaps. But the story of the martyred psychologist, and the fact that it was the U.S. government that shut him down and declared his life's work to be quackery, appealed to Mike's sense of compassion.[48] Here was a man on to something (the mind-body connection), and the heavy hand of a paternalistic government had swatted him down. To an individualist like Mike Mentzer, it was yet another example of the herd versus the individual — those willing to be yoked versus those who sought the freedom to effect positive change. There had to be something to Reich's methods — why else would the FDA move to trample him underfoot? He immediately signed on for Reichian therapy sessions with the Philadelphia MD Mel Thrash.[49] "Several years ago," he wrote in 1980, "I underwent a period of Reichian therapy and my observations during that time validated for me Reich's notions about energy flow. After each weekly session of special manipulations and exercises, I left the doctor's office free of even the slightest trace of muscular tension and anxiety. This feeling usually lasted for several days before wearing off."[50] That he was already experiencing episodes of anxiety that were serious enough to require professional therapy is telling. But apart from the psychological benefits, however, Mike discovered that Reichian therapy also helped him with his physique presentation in bodybuilding competition. A newspaper from the time reported that Mike underwent treatment for 15 months:

> For him, he says, the therapy was mostly an intellectual pursuit. But, he says, it helped him with his stage presence. It has helped him to express himself as he moves from pose to pose in almost balletic fashion, and to convey mood.[51]

Mike drew comparisons to more current therapies that were similar to Reich's, such as Alexander Lowen's "Bioenergetics" and Ida Rolf's "Structural Integration," which similarly "recognize the need to relieve a person's dammed up energies" and included "the manipulation of muscles as an integral part of each session."[52] A new goal now entered Mike's mind; not only was he going to win the Mr. America title but he would go through medical school and become a Reichian psychiatrist.[53]

That a bodybuilder would use Reichian therapy for bodybuilding competition was unheard of. And yet Mike Mentzer did it, pressing mind and body into service for the attainment of cognitive well-being and muscular expression. With mind and body now believed to be all of a piece, Mike was literally "all systems go" as he prepared for his assault on the Mr. America title. But then another problem settled in. "Curiously enough," Mike said, "around the time of entering the Mr. America contest, I was considering giving up entirely."[54] Looking at his schedule in 1971, it isn't hard to see why. He was a medic in the Air Force,[55] which had him working 12 hours a day; he had a girlfriend and a part-time job;[56] and his bodybuilding progress — despite his steroid use — had ground to a halt:

> I started to notice that my progress was slowing down and even at one point came to a screeching halt. I was training on the typical marathon type of training routine — twenty sets or more per body part for six days a week, and I hit a plateau in my progress that I couldn't overcome using the twenty sets per body part system. At that particular juncture I thought that things that were printed [in the muscle magazines] were true, otherwise they couldn't be printed. Who was I to judge the collective wisdom of all these bodybuilders? So, I didn't judge. I just read, accepted, and swallowed whatever it was that

was handed to me.⁵⁷ . . . By that time, I was training at least eighteen hours a week and nothing discernible was happening except that I felt tired all the time. Then I began to compound my mistakes. I reasoned that if three hours a day wasn't enough time in the gym then I would spend four, five, or even more hours if necessary. Luckily for me there just weren't enough hours in the day, or enough energy in my body, to handle the full-time Air Force job and full-time workouts. And I began to think that if developing a Mr. America physique meant giving up my entire social life and a third of my waking hours, it might not be worth the effort.⁵⁸

This certainly was not a situation an aspiring bodybuilder preparing to enter the biggest competition of his life wanted to find himself in. Perhaps owing to his age (he was just 19), Mike plodded on with his training, dieted until his bodyfat was down to a single digit, and then made the trek 96 miles north to York, Pennsylvania, to compete in the 1971 AAU Mr. America contest on June 12. He was there alone, of course. His parents didn't show up, despite living only 40 minutes away.

Those who did make the effort to attend included *Muscle Training Illustrated* publisher Dan Lurie, who was always on the lookout for new talent to promote his products and compete in his contests, and the Mr. Olympia champions Arnold Schwarzenegger and Sergio Oliva,⁵⁹ who likewise wanted to check out the young lions. The pair were preparing to face each other in a rubber match to decide Mr. Olympia supremacy in three months' time.

Backstage, the competitors stripped down and began to pump up their muscles prior to the prejudging. Looking around, Mike was feeling pretty good about his chances. Assessing the condition of the competitors in the pump-up room, he saw some faces he recognized: Ken Covington, Robert McNeill, and James Handley, all from Pennsylvania. There was Ed Corney, who had appeared on the cover of the December 1970 edition of *Muscular Development* magazine, and Bill St. John, who was the cover man for the February 1969 edition of *Strength and Health*. It was also expected that Ken Waller would be competing. Waller was a six-foot, 230-pound ex-Marine, powerful and massive, who had recently won the AAU Mr. World title. However, word soon trickled throughout the backstage area that Waller had been disqualified for appearing in an ad in a magazine, which, given that the AAU was an amateur and not professional organization, was considered grounds for his disqualification.[60]

As Mike continued pumping up along with the other contestants, 19-year-old Casey Viator entered the room. It was like a bomb went off. Fresh off his AAU Junior Mr. America win only three and a half weeks previous,[61] Casey was clearly in a class of his own. "We all stripped down backstage," Mike recalled, "and I saw this 19-year-old kid looking like Mr. Olympia and I went through the roof! I couldn't believe my eyes!"[62] It was obvious that with Casey now in the competition, everybody else was competing for second place.

Indeed, when the dust had settled, Casey was crowned the new AAU Mr. America, the youngest person to ever win the title.[63] He beat the second-place finisher, Pete Grymkowski, from Rochester, New York, by 27 points (377–350).[64] As for Mike, he finished a distant tenth (with 319 points).[65] He did, however, place second to Casey in the best arms and best legs categories,[66] and *Muscular Development* magazine reported in its coverage that some thought Mike should have won the best arms contest.[67] Despite a disappointing placement, Mike Mentzer had made an impact.

As his 18 hours a week in the gym had landed him in tenth place, Mike wasn't sure if he had just entered his last bodybuilding competition. It had been a lot of toil for not even a sniff at the title. As Mike packed his bodybuilding paraphernalia into his gym bag, Casey Viator approached and introduced himself. "You've got good genetics," he said. Mike smiled and shrugged. He wasn't sure what Casey was talking about.[68] The topic then switched to training; Mike had to know what secret method this muscular marvel had used to become so big and ripped. When Casey told him that he was only training three days a week for 45 minutes a workout, Mike was thunderstruck.[69] Casey further told him that he was training with Nautilus machines, following the principles of high-intensity training under the watchful eye of a man who lived in Florida named Arthur Jones. He added that if Mike wanted to learn more about the training system, he should give Arthur a call. He scribbled down a phone number onto a slip of paper and handed it Mike.[70]

Over the next several days, Mike gave the matter some serious thought. Training three days a week for 45 minutes a session seemed to Mike an awful lot like what he had been doing when he first started training. Surely this couldn't be right. Questions began to percolate: Hadn't bodybuilding progressed since then? Weren't the physiques of champions like Bill Pearl,

Larry Scott, and Arnold Schwarzenegger proof that training more frequently resulted in building bigger muscles? Granted, the steroids helped in this respect, but no champion bodybuilder Mike knew of trained in such an abbreviated fashion. If Arthur Jones's method could do for him what it did for Casey, wasn't it worth a phone call to find out more about it? After all, if what Jones advocated didn't make sense, Mike was under no obligation to switch over to such a program. But if it did make sense, it might mean a first-place finish at next year's Mr. America contest.

Mike decided to make the call.

CHAPTER SEVEN

NAUTILUS EMERGES

Arthur Jones was an intriguing character. Possessed of a brilliant and highly analytical mind, he hailed from a family that boasted a long line of medical doctors.[1] Arthur read his father's entire medical library by the age of 12,[2] dropped out of high school in grade ten,[3] and hit the road in search of adventure.[4] He certainly found it:

> I've done 50 things in my life, any one of which another man would give anything to have done once. . . . I've been the length of the Congo, Nile and Amazon. I've captured an adult crocodile and an African elephant: I've run a jeep into a tree at 60 mph, been bitten by poisonous snakes 24 times, and hundreds of times by nonpoisonous snakes, survived a couple of plane crashes that weren't my fault, been chewed up by a lion and several other cats and been shot six times, axed once, and stabbed on occasion. It's been exciting.[5]

"Exciting" is almost too mild an encapsulation. Apart from the above, a short list of some of his further adventures would include the following:

- Being involved in armed conflicts around the world.[6]
- Creating a stabilizing mount for movie cameras.[7]
- Being accused by the Federal Bureau of Investigation and the Central Intelligence Agency of smuggling guns and perhaps bombs into Cuba.[8]

- Being taken to court for tax evasion by the Internal Revenue Service.[9]
- Being an accomplished pilot of both large and small airplanes.[10]
- Flying a Boeing 707 into Zimbabwe, where he airlifted 63 elephants marked for government slaughter to safety in America.[11]
- Constructing a private airport on his 550-acre property in Marion County, Florida, along with an animal sanctuary that included 600 crocodiles, 500 snakes, 17 African elephants, an adult gorilla, and three white rhinoceroses.[12]

Along the way he burned through six marriages,[13] fathered four children,[14] and created Nautilus exercise machines, which would prove to be his ticket to fame and fortune.

A Nautilus exercise machine was nothing more or less than a "rational barbell," Arthur claimed.[15] Human joints rotate in a semi-circular arc, but barbells provide only linear resistance. Consequently, he reasoned, working a muscle through its full range of motion was impossible with a barbell. Arthur further understood that if this problem could be solved, a completely new form of exercise could be introduced to the world that made it possible to achieve "total fitness" from a singular activity. He set about designing and manufacturing exercise machines that would simultaneously optimize flexibility (as the limbs would move from their fullest possible extension to their fullest possible contraction); build strength (as the resistance was increased on a progressive basis) and enhance cardiovascular fitness (as all metabolic pathways, including the aerobic, are engaged via the muscular system).

Not content with simply formulating a hypothesis on this matter, he spent 30 years of his life developing prototypes for what would become the first line of Nautilus machines (one machine for each major muscle group of the body), which he released into the market in 1970.[16] He then spent considerable money to fund studies that tested the machines and his exercise hypotheses at academic institutions such as Colorado State University,[17] West Point Military Academy,[18] and the University of Florida.[19] Both the machines and the exercise theories proved successful and, within a decade or so of their creation, *Forbes* magazine listed Arthur Jones as one of the 400 richest Americans, with a net worth of "at least 125 million dollars."[20]

But there was also a dark side to the Nautilus inventor. For one thing, he claimed to have killed some 73 men over the course of his life;[21] for another, he wasn't exactly a paragon of clean living, subsisting primarily on a diet of black coffee and cigarettes.[22] A workaholic by choice, Jones was certain about what he was certain about, and wasn't concerned in the least what others thought.[23] When approached by exercise scientists who claimed that they could conduct studies to prove the validity of his training theories, he dismissed them outright, believing them to be modern-day sophists; a true scientist wouldn't go into any study knowing what the outcome would be beforehand.[24] Nevertheless, to any young man who desired to be rich or learn a science-based approach to bodybuilding and to live an adventurous life, Arthur Jones had a checkmark in each box.

Mike's initial attempt to phone Arthur proved unsuccessful, as the Nautilus machine inventor was away from his office. Mike left a message with the receptionist indicating who he was and why he was calling, with the expectation that Arthur would most likely get back to him later that week. It wouldn't take that long:

> At three o'clock in the morning he rang me back, which shocked me, but Arthur took it in his stride. He told me Casey had spoken to him about me. It wasn't really a conversation; it was a lecture, during which he explained to me in the most precise, scrupulously objective language possible, the actual science of productive bodybuilding exercise; the nature of the cause and effect relationship between intense exercise and muscle growth, and, why, in light of the body's limited recovery ability, such exercise had to be brief and infrequent if it was to be productive. During that conversation I realized I was not the expert I had thought. What amounted to mindlessly thumbing through muscle magazines and memorizing training routines doesn't make one an expert. I realized that I knew little of value about exercise, while this man knew a lot about exercise.[25]

The disquisition went on for two hours.[26] After Mike hung up the phone, he had trouble getting back to sleep that morning. Arthur had shared so much information with him that it was hard to digest it all. What Arthur told him was so radically different from the pervading bodybuilding worldview he had held since reading about Bill Pearl, Larry Scott, and Arnold Schwarzenegger that, initially, Mike refused to accept it. "There was a short time during which I resisted some of what Jones told me," he recalled. "While I grasped it intellectually, and recognized its validity, I still had operating in my subconscious the premise that 'more is better.' And I had to work with that."[27]

An accident in the Air Force gym would result in Mike soon having ample time to think about the matter in greater depth. It occurred while Mike was performing one of his 20-set chest workouts. During a set of flat bench dumbbell flyes, he lost control of the dumbbell he was holding in his right hand. The velocity of the dumbbell's descent increased the forces brought to bear on his shoulder joint, hyperextending tendons and ligaments.[28] He heard a loud *pop* and felt a jolt of pain in his right shoulder. The weight crashed to the floor. He knew instantly that he had suffered a severe injury. Mike stood up and rubbed the injured joint, hoping to increase circulation into the area. However, when he tried to move his upper arm, he discovered it would not leave his side.[29] He quickly made his way to the base clinic, where the resident physician forced his upper arm back into place. A sling was provided to remove the tension on the shoulder and Mike was given instructions not to lift any weights at all for the next several months.[30]

Eight months prior to the AAU Mr. America contest, and a mere one month after winning the 1970 Mr. Olympia title, Arnold Schwarzenegger flew to Florida.[31] He wasn't traveling alone. Shortly after Paul Graham had been trundled off to the Terminal Island Federal Correction Institution, Arnold had convinced Joe Weider to bring Franco Columbu to America. Columbu was born and raised in Sardinia, Italy, but had moved to Germany, where he met and trained with Arnold during the 1960s. Weider, initially, was reticent: Franco was only five foot five,[32] and by this point hadn't registered much of an impact in the European bodybuilding world. Indeed, he hadn't won a single contest.[33] Moreover, while Franco was certainly powerful and had a large chest, his arms were nothing to write home about, and, for marketing purposes, big arms sold a lot of product in Joe Weider's world. When Joe asked why he should invest money in bringing this guy across the pond, Arnold answered that if the two were reunited as training partners, he was sure to improve even more rapidly.[34] Joe shook his head; he simply wasn't interested.[35] It was then that Arnold initiated a strategy that would always work out to his advantage in dealing with Joe; he appealed to his business interests:

Joe was never going to buy the sentimental argument, so I put it in commercial terms. "Bring Franco," I told him, "and you're going to have professional bodybuilding locked up for years! You're going to have the best tall man in the heavyweight division" — meaning me — "and the best small man in the lightweight division."[36]

The prospect of having professional bodybuilding locked up for years made sound economic sense to Joe. Moreover, if Franco's being in America meant that an improved Arnold Schwarzenegger would be entering contests and marketing Joe's products, that could only be good for business. An in-shape Arnold made the phasing-out of the problematic Sergio Oliva much easier; Arnold would be the new Mr. Olympia and promoted not only as Joe's "student" but as the poster boy nonpareil for Weider products. And if Franco could appeal to the short wannabe bodybuilders who bought Joe's products, bringing the "Sardinian Samson" to America might be a pretty good move. And so, by June of 1969, Franco Columbu was in California, sharing an apartment with Arnold and being paid $80 a week to appear in Joe's magazine articles and ads.[37]

Most likely looking to pad their purses, or perhaps to try and leverage a greater stipend out of Joe, the two friends made the trip to Florida to test the financial waters with Arthur Jones. After all, Arthur's Nautilus empire was starting to emerge as a force unto itself; Jones had articles published every month in *Iron Man* magazine, his machines were selling at a rapid pace, and there was even talk of him starting an entirely new bodybuilding contest, one that would include an independent body of doctors who would "determine accurate body-part measurements, drug usage, performance ability, and related physiological factors" and a $25,000 cash prize for first place.[38] Given that the first-place prize money for winning the Mr. Olympia contest in 1970 was $1,000,[39] Arthur believed that "with a chance at a $25,000 cash prize, you can be reasonably sure that 'everybody' will be there."[40] As $25,000 in 1970 would be the equivalent of around $200,000 in today's dollars, his reasoning wasn't out of line.[41]

While Joe wouldn't have cared about Arnold and Franco heading to Florida to try out Arthur Jones's Nautilus machines, if he thought for one minute that he might lose the pair to Arthur, *that* would be a problem. Not only had he taken substantial legal and financial risks in bringing both bodybuilders to America, but Arnold was now the face of his company and product line. If it got out that Arnold was being trained (in the public's eyes) by Arthur — not the Master Blaster — and that he was not using any protein supplements (as Arthur thought they were useless), it could potentially lose Joe millions. If it was a leverage move on Arnold's part, it was a good one.

The truth, however, was that Joe needn't have worried. While Arthur was certainly impressed with Arnold as a bodybuilder,[42] he didn't like him as a person[43] and had zero tolerance for Arnold's ego. This was made abundantly clear to the future governor of California shortly after Arthur had picked him up at the Orlando International Airport.[44] They hadn't made it halfway back to Nautilus headquarters when Arthur had had enough of the Austrian. Ellington Darden, who worked alongside Arthur Jones for 17 years as his Director of Research,[45] picks up the story:

> Schwarzenegger had just won his first Mr. Olympia title at the age of 23, and Jones just presumed him to be a serious, hardcore, no-BS kind of guy. Instead, he got a monologue for most of the 50-minute trip from the airport to Lake Helen. "For 30 minutes, all I hear is how big, strong, and great Arnold is, and it's difficult to understand him with this heavy Austrian accent," Jones said. This was an unusual situation for Jones, who was and is an aggressive monopolizer of conversation. Jones had hoped that when they got to the freeway — after a half-hour of start-stop driving on surface streets — the bodybuilder would relax and let Jones talk for a bit. "But, no, he gets worse — he's more boisterous. He's sitting bolt upright in the seat, looking around like a male giraffe in heat and still shouting his gibberish. So, without saying anything, I calmly pull over on the right shoulder. Stop. Cut off the engine. Get out of the car and walk around to Arnold's side. Open his door, grab him by his shirt collar, jerk him out of the seat, stand him up, and look him right between the eyes. And yes, he's still talking, but it's more of whisper." Jones explained, in a way only Jones could, that if the bodybuilder didn't shut up, he'd get his ass whipped by a man twice his age and half his size. Worse, it was going to happen at that moment, right there on the shoulder of Interstate 4. "Arnold stopped talking,

grinned a bit, and nodded his head. Although I had difficulty comprehending his German, I guarantee he understood my English. And he knew I meant every word."[46]

It's also possible that Arnold saw the Colt .45 tucked into Arthur's waistband (he never went anywhere without it),[47] which would have provided further reason to take his host seriously. The introduction now out of the way, Arthur drove the two bodybuilders to the training compound at Nautilus. Casey Viator had followed Arthur's training advice to the letter, as had Sergio Oliva, and both had appeared bigger, fuller, and in the best shape of their lives when competing in 1971. Their workouts (and Casey's in particular) during this period were renowned for their over-the-top intensity. Arthur held that intensity had to do with the percentage of momentary muscular effort one was capable of exerting, a factor involving three things: the amount of weight the muscle(s) was/were made to contract against; carrying each set performed to a point where another repetition was impossible despite the trainee's greatest effort; and the time it took to complete all of the prescribed exercises for a given workout. This meant that there was no rest between exercises — it was one after the other until the workout was over. Once the workout was completed, the trainee would take the next day off to recover and adapt and then train again.

Arnold, as the reigning Mr. Olympia, and particularly after his boasting about "how big, strong, and great" he was while in the car on the way to the gym, was expected to not only perform his workouts in such a fashion while at Nautilus, but to excel at them. While he would write in his *Encyclopedia of Modern Bodybuilding* about how important it is that one train to a point of muscular failure,[48] talking the talk was one thing, but walking the walk was something else entirely. Casey Viator recalled that "Arnold just couldn't get into the intensity part of it. He was used to going so far, backing off, resting, then doing another set. But our workouts were very, very, very intense, and there was no resting. He kept wanting to really get into it . . . and he seemed to be improving. But the last time Arnold tried to workout at the Quonset hut, in the middle of the session he crawled outside and spilled his guts on the grass. We didn't see him after that."[49]

Arthur, simply put, was not impressed. "I couldn't ever get him to work to failure, not even on one exercise," he lamented. "He'd strain and make terrible faces, but I can recognize the difference between faking failure and real failure. Arnold's was faked. But afterward, he'd talk like he'd had a great workout."[50] Another disappointment awaited the Nautilus mogul when he measured Arnold's arm and discovered it was not the 22½ inches that Joe Weider had claimed in his ads,[51] nor the 21½ inches that Arnold stated in his mail-order courses.[52] Instead, after pumping his arms slightly, Arnold's right arm taped out at 19⅞. Arthur believed that had he not pumped blood into them, his arms wouldn't have been more than 19½ inches.[53]

The Arnold-Arthur relationship was never going to happen.

CHAPTER EIGHT

AUTHORITIES BY PROXY

Despite being a teenager when he won the Mr. America title (or perhaps because of it), Casey Viator was never particularly motivated to fully understand the training principles that Arthur Jones advocated. "Arthur referred to Casey Viator as 'a child in a gorilla suit,'" Mike recalled. "Casey used high-intensity training, but he never understood it. He just did what Arthur told him."[1] Casey had always been content to let whoever signed his paycheck do the figuring on such matters.

While he had won contests prior to the 1971 Mr. America without having to delve too deeply into such things as physiology or the biomechanics of lifting weights,[2] these had been minor contests where the competition hadn't really been much of a threat to Casey in terms of their muscle size. The Mr. America, however, attracted competitors of a different breed altogether; their muscular mass was bigger, their conditioning was greater, and their ability to pose and otherwise display their muscular development was almost effortless. In addition, many of the Mr. America contenders were in their twenties and thirties — well out of their teens and in the prime of their lives in terms of strength and muscle size — and had already been competing for decades. Casey needed to improve rapidly if he was going to be able to compete with these bodybuilders. Fortunately, once he came under the wing of Arthur, using the latter's Nautilus machines and training principles, his physique improved dramatically.[3]

Following the contest, Casey's picture appeared on the covers of *Iron Man*, *Muscle Training Illustrated*, and *Muscular Development* magazines, along with reports of his three-day-per-week low set training routine, which stood in sharp contrast to the 20-sets-per-body-part, six-day-per-week training touted in the pages of *Muscle Builder* magazine by Joe Weider. Not that Joe's "students," Arnold Schwarzenegger and Franco Columbu, paled by comparison.[4] Arnold, after all, was the reigning Mr. Olympia, and, to ensure that he would remain that way, the Weider brothers disqualified Sergio Oliva from competing in the contest that year. Indeed, Arnold won the 1971 Mr. Olympia, held that year in Paris, France, by virtue of his being the only bodybuilder in the contest.[5] Fortunately, as in previous presentations, the Mr. Olympia was boxcarred to the Mr. Universe competition, so fans at least got to see an actual bodybuilding contest prior to Arnold being declared Mr. Olympia for 1971. But even that contest was bizarre; the judges selected Ahmet Enünlü from Turkey over the more popular Englishman Albert Beckles as the winner of the Medium Height Class of the competition. When the crowd loudly expressed its displeasure with the selection, Ben Weider called an emergency meeting of the judges and, soon thereafter, Enünlü was relegated to second place and Beckles was announced as the winner.[6]

The reason the Weiders gave for Sergio's disqualification was that he had competed in a rival organization's contest in London, England, some months previously.[7] Arnold had also intended to compete in that same contest, but once the Weider brothers found out, both men wrote letters to Arnold warning him that he would be disqualified if he did, and that the taps from which flowed all of the fame and fortune he had enjoyed thus far could be shut off just as fast as they had been turned on.[8] No such letters of forewarning were written to Sergio, however. He would only learn that he wasn't allowed to compete upon his arrival at the contest.[9] And when it was discovered that Franco Columbu also had competed in a non-IFBB contest a year previously, it was announced that Franco was suspended as well.[10] That was all right; Franco had already had a pretty good year as it was. Indeed, making the move to California in 1969 to promote Weider products proved to be just the ingredient that had been missing from Franco's competitive arsenal. While his physique hadn't been deemed exceptional enough to win Mr. Europe, Mr. World, or Mr. Universe prior to 1970, once he signed on the dotted line with Joe, he suddenly became a force to be reckoned with; winning all three of those titles within one year (1970–71). Granted, the contests he won were all run by the Weider-controlled IFBB, but that aside, it was quite an impressive turnaround for signor Columbu. It is worth noting that Arnold had not only appeared in but won the very same contest that Franco had entered that resulted in Franco's disqualification.[11]

After the 1971 debacle, the belief that the Mr. Olympia contest was a competition to determine the best-built man on the planet had taken a serious hit. There was now a hint that it was simply a pageant to honor the latest ambassador of Weider products (and the IFBB's actions left no doubt as to which bodybuilder this was). Sergio was clearly on his way out of the federation. Not only had Arnold's arrival on the scene made the Cuban expendable as far as Joe Weider's business interests were concerned, but (even more directly threatening to Joe's reputation) it was already public knowledge that Sergio was being trained by Arthur Jones, whose high-intensity training method was the exact opposite of what Arnold was employing, and what Joe Weider was promoting as being part of his Weider system of bodybuilding. In a not-so-subtle effort to defend his turf, Joe made sure to put the word out in *Muscle Builder/Power*'s report of the 1971 Mr. Olympia contest that Sergio had lost the contest because he was no longer training the Weider way:

> Sergio was in as good shape as I've ever seen him. But he makes too many concessions to bulk-madness. Apparently he refuses to train properly because a lack of muscle-density holds him back from being totally unstoppable. Arnold and Colombu [sic] are definitely in his class. With greater density to complement his awesome size, shape, and proportion, Oliva would be peerless. If Sergio would hit California this summer and pick up some more tips from Joe Weider, who originally brought him to prominence, he might easily regain *Mr. Olympia* in 1972.[12]

There was only one "trainer of champions" in the bodybuilding world, was the message.

The fact that Arthur had poached one of Joe's former Mr. Olympia champions left a sour taste in the mouth of the Master Blaster, who then decided that he could play that game too. Joe now made it his mission to get Casey Viator to jump ship from Nautilus to the Weider team. He made the young bodybuilder an offer. Casey considered it. He even flew to California to meet with the bodybuilding mogul. However, at the 11th hour, Casey changed his mind and returned to Florida to continue working for Arthur

Jones.[13] Matters were made worse for Joe when Arnold wrote a letter that was published in *Iron Man* magazine praising Arthur's methods and machines:

> ... visit Mr. Jones and try his machines yourself. Because that's the way I did it. I gained four pounds and increased my arm size in the first three days of training on the new equipment, and I am making immediate arrangements with Mr. Jones to obtain several of his machines for my use in California. If this is not my true opinion, then I will give up all of the titles I have won in the past. I really believe that the new machines are fantastic. Otherwise, I would not write this.
> — Arnold Schwarzenegger, five times Mr. Universe, Mr. World, Mr. Olympia.[14]

It had to be a blow that Arnold, the current Mr. Olympia and the very face of the Weider system, had publicly endorsed the high-intensity training method and equipment of Arthur Jones. It certainly rendered null and void the critique of Sergio that appeared in *Muscle Builder* magazine. Joe now viewed Arthur as a bona fide threat to his reputation and his business,[15] and he would use his magazine to attack both Jones and his Nautilus machines over the next several years in an effort to bring down his rival.

By mid-1972, eight months had passed since Mike's shoulder injury. He was still working 12-hour shifts every day in the Air Force as a hospital technician[16] and brought in extra money conducting EKG stress tests on cardiac patients under the care of a local DC physician.[17] While still passionate about bodybuilding, Mike entertained no notion about his passion becoming his profession. His career goal was to become a "radical psychiatrist,"[18] employing the teachings of Freud, Laing, and Reich when he became licensed.[19] In preparation to eventually attend medical school (a medical degree was required prior to becoming a psychiatrist), he was reading a lot of psychology books, in addition to obtaining experience in fields related to medicine. As for bodybuilding authorities, Arthur Jones seemed to him the only individual who took a scientific, logical approach to the subject:

> From the moment I hung up the phone I constantly reflected on what he had communicated, reflecting on my experience, connecting his thoughts to what I already knew. I became fully

convinced that this guy knew what he was talking about and that he was right! I was very impressed by how different he was from the average; he was a high-level intellectual sociologist; he understood the nature of science gained through scientific observations; he understood logic and how to apply it. He had a great influence on how I thought about training. But, even more important, the way I thought about *thinking*. While my parents and teachers had paid what amounted to in retrospect only superficial lip service to the values of thought, logic, and reason, Arthur Jones on the other hand was absolutely passionate about them — this impressed me very, very much.[20]

Arthur was also the only individual in the bodybuilding industry conducting any research into the field of bodybuilding exercise, and Mike continued to touch base with him periodically to see what muscle-building information Nautilus was turning up. As with his studies in psychology, Mike looked to external authorities at this point in his life for information. He was, of course, still reading the various bodybuilding magazines for motivation, as he had not abandoned his dream of someday winning the Mr. America, Mr. Universe, and Mr. Olympia titles.[21] And through his conversations with Arthur, in addition to reading about the political fiasco that was the 1971 Mr. Olympia, he was becoming aware of the commercial machinations that were going on behind the scenes in the world of professional bodybuilding.

Despite not training for quite some time, Mike still retained a considerable amount of muscle mass. Enough, at least, that he felt comfortable accepting a request to guest pose at the Mr. Lancaster contest on May 20, 1972.[22] When the Atlanta press arrived in DC to do a story on the curious world of bodybuilding, they approached Mike for a comment and were shocked to discover a bodybuilder who actually had a brain in his head. They devoted an entire column to him:

BRAIN PLUS PHYSIQUE:
WEIGHTLIFTER HAS STRENGTH PLUS IQ

WASHINGTON. Mike Mentzer, who can deadlift 550 pounds, wears baggy woolen shirts. Still, frustrated women grab his arms. That's okay, but no longer for him those sleeveless tight-around-the-torso tee shirts that he filled as an ultra-bulk teenager. Some days the proud Mentzer, 20, almost Mr. Teenage America last year, even ponders tossing aside bodybuilding the way he discarded the brute shirts. "There's so much politics involved," groans the young serviceman who fits no popular conception of a steel-hefting imbecile.

Mentzer is nearly finished reading *Inside the Third Reich*, the memoirs of Hitler's master architect. And he recently rediscovered Shakespeare, whose *Romeo and Juliet* fills Mentzer's 50-inch (unexpanded) chest with tenderness. "I'm a sentimentalist," he declares, dark eyes glaring with the seriousness of such revelation. Introspective, absorbed in psychology as well as body, he wavers toward being an agnostic, wants to be a medical doctor, grows melancholy over *Love Story*, and has a fine disdain for the toadying involved at physique contests. "It's sickening," he says. Now an Air Force hospital technician, Mentzer has been stationed at Andrews AFB for more than a year. "When I first came down here," he recalls, "I thought Andrews would have tons of weights, gold-plated, barbells."

But only one dusty Universal lifting machine confronted the truck driver's son, then 19, who had been struggling with weights since age 11 — often against his father's wishes. Undaunted at Andrews, Mentzer invented his own exercises. Alone, he sweated three hours a day, six days a week. Last year, he was Mr. Pennsylvania, finished second in the Mr. Teenage America contest and placed 10th in Mr. America competition. Exactly what led an apparently otherwise sane young romantic into the world of the tortured bicep and the puffed pose? Vanity, he readily admits, and an obsession to be different.[23]

The Atlanta reporter also happened to witness a clash backstage at a local amateur bodybuilding contest, where Mike stepped in to save a young bodybuilder who was almost taken advantage of by two photographers:

> Such vanity did not stop Mentzer from quickly dismissing two photographers soliciting several pictures, including nude photos, after one contest. He sent them packing with all the

authority of a young man who can bench-press approximately 400 pounds.

Despite such an incident, Mentzer insists that bodybuilding generally is free of homosexual overtones. The problem with bodybuilding's image, he says, is that a display of the physique essentially is a passive event, despite the effort accorded the making of the physique. "Our society equates passivity (of display) with female," he claims. Consequently, he thinks, American males tend to view the bodybuilding business gingerly.[24]

Mike always felt the need to use his experience to protect young bodybuilders from being exploited. Many years later, the gay and lesbian publication the *Advocate* inquired why he hadn't posed nude for photographs:

> Because right now all of my activities are limited to the regular muscle magazines you see on the newsstands. They don't publish nude pictures. Why thrust that on the average 14-year-old kid out there in America, who is already struggling with his sexual identity? Something like that would confuse him all the more. I'm not arguing for or against homosexuality, but in this case, let's face it, every young male comes to a point in his life where he's confused about his sexual identity — where he's given a choice at the crossroads — and the people who publish those magazines are aware of that. So why confuse the issue for the kids?[25]

While Mike was busy protecting the naïve and innocent in Washington, DC, back home in Ephrata, things between his parents had reached a dramatic crescendo. Three weeks before Mike's guest posing exhibition at the Mr. Lancaster contest, Harry and Marie's divorce was made official.[26] The divorce weighed heavily on Mike's younger brother, Ray. He began spending more time alone, read more, and quit all team sports in the summer prior to his final year in high school.[27] He looked on as his dad was remarried to Alta Jean Markley that June.[28]

The day after he graduated from high school, Ray packed a bag and headed east to Washington, DC.[29] The siblings had kept in touch during

Mike's absence, and Mike thought it would do his little brother good to get out from under the dark cloud that hung above the house on 56 East Chestnut Street and move in with him for a while. Through his connections in the medical field, he found Ray a summer job working in the central supply of a nearby hospital.[30]

The brothers hadn't been reunited long when their old friend Dave Mastorakis called. He was now serving in the National Guard and said he would be coming through DC. He wanted to know if Mike wanted to get together once he hit the nation's capital so that the pair could catch up. Mike thought that was a great idea and agreed to meet his old friend when the bus pulled into the Washington terminal.

When Dave stepped off the Greyhound, he was greeted by Mike with Ray in tow. Mike announced that he had been able to score three tickets to the Rolling Stones concert on the evening of Tuesday, July 4, 1972, at Robert F. Kennedy Memorial Stadium. Being reunited with old friends on the Fourth of July and seeing the "Stones Touring Party" live made for a memorable night. "I spent a day and a half with Mike and Ray . . . and it was a great time," Dave recalled. But the reunion was short-lived; Dave was only passing through, and had to continue on to Springfield, Massachusetts. The Mentzer brothers saw him off at the bus station. It would be three years before the friends would see each other again.[31]

When summer ended, Ray announced that he was heading southeast to Colorado; he wanted to experience the mountains and pursue a university education in the Centennial State.[32]

Once more, Mike Mentzer was on his own.

CHAPTER NINE

THE CUBAN MUSCLE CRISIS

The 1972 Mr. Olympia contest took place in Essen, Germany. Sergio Oliva had redoubled his focus and hadn't entered any other contests in the months leading up to it. There would be no disqualifications this year; his sights were set firmly on reclaiming the title.

The show was co-promoted by Arnold's good friend and long-time fan (and Weider ally) Albert Busek,[1] which meant that Busek had a hand in the selection of judges. Arnold evidently felt he had an in with the promoter as, having become friends with the new owner of Gold's Gym, Ken Sprague, he invited him overseas to be a judge. However, when Sprague landed in Germany, he was met with a surprise. "Arnold wanted me to travel to Essen and judge the contest," Sprague recalled. "[But] after arriving in Essen, the promoter, Arnold's long-time friend, had already set the panel."[2]

Sergio claimed that his training with Arthur Jones had resulted in his achieving a level of condition that was "miles" beyond the competition.[3] It's not clear if he was still training with Arthur at this point (nobody who worked at Nautilus at this time recalled seeing him there), or whether he simply was still employing Arthur's methods on his own. Regardless, Sergio entered the contest in what most pundits believed was the best shape of his bodybuilding career.[4] Arnold likewise came into the contest in good shape, although Frank Zane, who also competed in the Mr. Olympia that year, believed the Austrian still needed another month of dieting and training to dial in his physique to where it should've been.[5]

Nevertheless, at the end of the day Arnold defeated the vastly improved Sergio by four points[6] (one judge incredibly had Sergio in fourth place[7]). It would prove to be one of the more controversial decisions in the history of the Mr. Olympia contest,[8] as even Arnold would concede that, had he been on the judging panel, he would have voted for Sergio.[9] But this admission would come decades later. In the immediate aftermath of the contest, Arnold was positively crowing about how he had outwitted both Sergio and the judges by convincing them to hold the prejudging in the pump-up room, as it was larger — and darker: "I was far more interested in the paint," he said. "It hadn't occurred to Sergio that my white body would stand out against the dark wall behind us, while his would blend right in. To this day I believe that was how I got the edge. In a nutshell, the judges saw more than I actually had that day in Germany. Sergio suffered for his blindness."[10]

It's an interesting story, even if the photos taken during the prejudging of the contest don't support it. The wall behind the competitors during the prejudging was light, not dark, and Sergio's physique stood out just fine and did not blend into the background at all. In any event, Arnold was given the victory, and Joe Weider now had a three-time Mr. Olympia winner to promote his products. As Arnold recalled:

> Joe Weider had one goal in mind, and that is that I win every competition, that I'm on the cover of his magazine. That I sell a shitload of food supplements for him. And that everything that I did, he would use the name Weider for it. So, when I came up with splitting my biceps training with my triceps training, he called it "The Weider Split Routine." So that was the deal.[11]

With the 1972 Mr. Olympia contest now in the rearview mirror, Joe Weider felt emboldened to go on the offensive, and spent the next fifteen months attacking both Sergio and Arthur Jones in his magazines.[12] And the attacks — particularly against Sergio — were juvenile if not libelous. To wit:

- "Sergio Oliva, A 'Chicken' Without a Head."[13]
- "Unfortunately for Oliva . . . when his head eroded, so did his memory."[14]
- "[Dan] Lurie had paid Sergio — a whore even then — to endorse his products."[15]
- "Sickening narcissism and weak ego."[16]
- "The man loves himself too much to admit Arnold is better."[17]

Such ad hominem attacks were bizarre. Never had a bodybuilding magazine that was the official journal of a particular federation devoted so much ink to attacking one of its former champions, particularly a champion who consensus indicated was in better shape than the man who won the contest (and this supported by the victor's own words on the matter). Evidently, all the above was printed because Sergio was (somehow) "making a mockery of the sport that we are trying to upgrade."[18] How Sergio had accomplished this by merely competing in a contest was not explained, while the irony of Joe's own actions in printing such attacks was evidently lost on the Master Blaster.

So much for Sergio. Joe next aimed his cannon at Arthur Jones and the latter's business — the Nautilus exercise machines. Arthur was a threat that needed to be stamped out once and for all. Joe began a lengthy and relentless publishing campaign designed to undercut Jones's credibility in the bodybuilding industry. Each issue of *Muscle Builder/Power* featured "interviews" with various luminaries within the industry criticizing Arthur's machines, a sampling of which follows:

- Arnold Schwarzenegger: "I came back [from visiting Nautilus in 1970] looking terrible. You [Joe Weider] and others said I never looked so fat. And I lost three-quarters of an inch off my arms . . . and I really gave the biceps-curling machine a good, honest test. . . . I don't feel that the Nautilus machines even come close to training with the standard barbell, dumbbells and pulley equipment. It is my honest opinion there is no comparison at all."[19]
- Ken Waller (1971 IFBB Mr. America): "I lost about three-quarters of an inch from my arms!"[20]
- Vince Gironda (Hollywood gym owner): "The basic technical concept is erroneous; . . . it is far too costly for what little it can do; and . . . Its appearance alone turns many persons away — frightens and confuses them."[21]
- Frank Zane (1968 IFBB Mr. Universe): "These Nautilus machines are mainly a gimmick. . . . I actually dislocated my right shoulder."[22]
- Roger Callard (Arnold's training partner): "Everyone I know who used these machines extensively became smooth."[23]

- Serge Nubret (1970 IFBB Mr. Europe, Tall Division): "I felt nothing except a little pain . . . The gadget provided a little pump but strained my biceps in a weird way. Fortunately, I stopped before causing any real injury."[24]

And finally, Joe Weider himself appeared in print to fire the final torpedo into the hull of the equipment company:

> Bodybuilders have learned through the years that all the standard weight-training equipment is what works! Also, that the multiple-set system is best with its many variations as super-sets, tri-sets, forced-reps, split-systems, half reps, etc. — and they know that every "Mr. Muscle" winner is a product of this type of training, not anything else! Period! Arthur Jones tried to disturb all this . . . to sell his Nautilus equipment, he was willing to destroy almost every existing physiological and anatomical fact and method of training that is known to be sound by replacing it with equipment and exercise methods that are erroneous in concept and application. All factual and result-producing methods and equipment were "destroyed" by Jones' gospel — his revolutionary bodybuilding philosophy — just to push his Nautilus equipment on unsuspecting persons.[25]

Joe went on to conclude that, "I publish MUSCLE BUILDER magazine just for this reason; to teach my readers what is right and what is wrong. I publish what has been proven to be effective and expose that which hasn't been of any value . . . and I will continue to do this. My main love is bodybuilding, and the wonderful people who want to be involved in it . . . !"[26] The article ended, conveniently, next to an ad for the Weider System, which featured photos of Arnold Schwarzenegger, Frank Zane, Franco Columbu, Chuck Sipes, Mike Katz, Dave Draper, Larry Scott, and (just to drive the point home) Sergio Oliva, and promised that one could "gain 2-inches on your chest" and "1¼-inches on your arms the first week when you train like the champions." The ad further went on to claim that "the training principles developed by Joe Weider, worlds [sic] greatest trainer of champions has taken the champs into the space age of bodybuilding — where 20-inch arms, and 54-inch chests are the norm — instead of the former 15-inch arms and 44-inch chests. Why don't you enter the space age of bodybuilding, too. Start training like the champs and use the Weider system to put up to 3-inches on your arms and over 4-inches on your chest in just one month."[27]

These were (and remain) staggering (and as yet unsubstantiated) results. Moreover, according to Ellington Darden, the research director of Nautilus Sports/Medical Industries, "Jones later discovered that the primary interviews, between Joe Weider and five champions, were fictitious."[28] Amusingly, on page 53 of the issue in which Joe claimed to be the light of truth for bodybuilding, there appeared an editor's note that stated, "Arnold is presently working with the Weider Research Clinic on a new Weider principle that we believe will revolutionize forearm training." This was high comedy indeed, coming from the man who had sworn to teach his readers "what is right and what is wrong." In point of fact, there never was (and never would be) a "Weider Research Clinic." As the renowned Canadian writer and marketing executive Jack Neary, who worked for Joe Weider as a writer for *Muscle Builder/Power* during the 1970s, recalled:

> I grew up reading the magazines . . . and it was always about the "Research Clinic." And I remember when I first met Joe and we were driving in his Lincoln Continental. I said, "Oh, I'd love to go to the Research Clinic!" And he was sort of embarrassed and flustered, and kind of hemming and hawing. And he admitted to me, "Well, there is no Research Clinic, you know; it's just something we made up." And I was like, "what are you?" I thought there were guys in white coats with clipboards.[29]

Be that as it may, Joe indicated to his loyal readers that he was exposing Nautilus for the purpose of giving bodybuilders the truth. But the truth Joe was communicating had little to do with the advancement of bodybuilding methods. According to Arnold, it was all about making money:

> I had to go and work with him and say, "Joe, you're selling your products. You're making millions of dollars. I want to also sell some products of mine. All I need from you is give me advertisement space in your magazine." I wanted to make money and I wanted to turn one dollar into two.[30]

Arnold's willingness to promote the Weider System, the Weider Research Clinic, and Weider nutritional products brought in a lot of money for Joe. And so, the Master Blaster did what he could to keep his cash cow happy and content while in his stable. Indeed, when Arnold decided he wanted to purchase a six-unit apartment house in Santa Monica to broaden his real estate portfolio, Joe Weider was the one who loaned him the $10,000 down payment to acquire it.[31]

The public attack by Weider and his bodybuilding cronies left Arthur Jones unimpressed;[32] he had a low opinion of bodybuilders to begin with,[33] and an even lower opinion of bodybuilding magazine publishers.[34] Presently, his interest lay in devising a means of testing how quickly his methods and machines would cause an individual to regain previously held levels of muscle mass. To this end, in concert with the University of Colorado, both he and Casey Viator took part in what was labelled an "experiment," but that was really a demonstration.[35]

Arthur, a man of decent if not exceptional genetics for building muscle, hadn't trained in quite some time. His bodyweight had fluctuated between 145 and 160 pounds since the early 1960s,[36] but was presently down to about 144.1 pounds.[37] Casey, a muscular phenom who had competed at a bodyweight of 218 pounds when he won the Mr. America title in 1971,[38] had suffered an accident and an allergic reaction to an anti-tetanus shot.[39] He was forced to stay out of the gym for quite some time and lost considerable muscle mass. Moreover, Arthur wanted him to lose even more weight prior to starting the experiment. By the time Casey arrived in Colorado to begin the study, he weighed an emaciated 167 pounds.[40]

Using Nautilus machines exclusively and Arthur's high-intensity training methods, the two men worked out three days a week, typically performing but one set per exercise. Each exercise was taken to the point of positive failure; that is, the point where another repetition was impossible. On certain exercises they only lowered the weight, making use of certain machines that had foot pedals that raised the weight for them. Arthur was of the belief that the lowering, or "negative" portion of a repetition, was "one of the most important factors involved in exercise for the purpose of increasing strength and muscle-mass."[41] Arthur performed 14 workouts (he would later claim that he performed only 12)[42] over a 22-day period (from May 1 to May 23), with each workout lasting from as little as nine minutes and 14 seconds to as long as 35 minutes and 45 seconds. He performed between nine and 14 exercises per workout, usually for one set each. His total training time for the month was just under five hours.

Casey, likewise, performed 14 workouts, but over a 28-day period (May 1 to May 29),[43] with each workout lasting between 25 and 42 minutes. He typically performed 12 exercises per workout, but sometimes that number dropped to eight and other times it climbed to 13. Like Arthur, Casey typically performed one set for each exercise. His total training time was just a little over seven hours for the month.[44]

At the beginning and end of the study, both men's weight and body composition were tested — and the results were staggering. Arthur Jones, it was discovered, had regained 15.44 pounds of muscle, while Casey, who was both a genetic marvel in terms of muscle mass and more underweight than Arthur when the study began (and undernourished), ate everything he could get his hands on and ended up regaining 63.21 pounds of muscle.[45] Dr. Elliott Plese, the physiologist from Colorado State University who oversaw the experiment, wrote about the study, as did Arthur Jones.

Joe Weider and his champs could condemn Arthur and his machines in issue after issue of *Muscle Builder/Power*, and but all it took was one article about the study to appear in *Iron Man* featuring before-and-after photos of Casey Viator to get bodybuilders talking and launch Nautilus into the stratosphere. Arthur Jones may not have trained a Mr. Olympia winner, and despite his stating no fewer than three times in the *Iron Man* article that the results Casey achieved were extraordinary and beyond the reach of most trainees,[46] the fact remained that he had trained a bodybuilder who had regained 63 pounds of muscle in a mere 28 days as a result of using Arthur's methods and machines. And that, to most aspiring bodybuilders, athletes, and coaches, was far more impressive.

Sergio Oliva was still angry. He was convinced that the judging panel at the 1972 Mr. Olympia was rigged.[47] Looking to satisfy his competitive urge, he decided to enter the IFBB Mr. International contest and perhaps the Mr. International Azteca contest (both competitions being held on the same day) in 1973 in Tijuana, Mexico. The contests were promoted by the former (1959) Mr. Universe winner Eddie Sylvestre. Unbeknownst to Sergio, however, both Joe and Arnold believed that the Mr. International would be a good title for Arnold to add to his collection as well. And so, the Master Blaster and his "student," along with a small entourage, traveled south from California to Tijuana for the competition.[48] Neither man knew that Sergio would be one of the competitors.[49] For his part, Arnold was still a few weeks away from being in Mr. Olympia shape, but given the caliber of the competitors he suspected he would be facing in this contest, his size, status in Joe's magazine, three Mr. Olympia titles, and the fact that the Mr. International was an IFBB-sanctioned event, he was convinced that he had sufficient ammunition to win the competition. And, just to make sure the decision would fall the right way, Joe brought three judges to Mexico as well.[50] Not long after arriving in Tijuana, Joe discovered that Sergio was competing, which threw him into panic mode. In a last-ditch effort to assert some influence over the outcome of the contest, Joe invited Eddie Sylvestre to dinner the evening prior to the competition. According to bodybuilding journalist Rick Wayne:

> During postprandial deliberations Weider remarked that he'd invested too much money in Arnold's career to risk the latter's defeat by Oliva. Sylvestre said he took that to mean Weider expected him to guarantee a victory for Arnold, which was "totally out of the question!"[51]

With an Arnold victory now in doubt, and despite having traveled 137 miles from Los Angeles to Tijuana for the event, Joe decided not to enter Arnold in the contest.[52] Joe and Arnold, along with Franco Columbu (who also made the trip south to Tijuana to witness Arnold compete), resigned themselves to the prospect of simply being spectators. In truth, it wasn't much of a show, as Sergio plowed through his opposition and won the title handily. And when the massive Cuban took notice of Joe and Arnold seated in the audience, his resentment quickly rose to the surface. He issued a challenge for Arnold to come up on stage and pose off — *mano a mano* — before a judging panel that had *not* been selected in advance by Joe Weider.[53] Joe refused to let Arnold up on the stage.[54] The audience roared its disapproval.[55] Looking to protect his cash cow, but also leery that the crowd had whipped itself into an anticipatory lather to see Sergio flex his considerable muscle against someone with a name in the sport, Joe Weider looked on as Franco Columbu bounded up on stage to accept Sergio's challenge.[56] Franco went through a posing routine and Sergio did likewise.[57] And, although Sergio dwarfed Franco, Eddie Sylvestre, in an effort to calm the choppy waters, ended the impromptu competition by raising the hands of both men, indicating the pose-off to be a draw.[58]

Joe Weider knew that the optics weren't good. But they were even worse when he attempted to explain to his readers why he had allowed Franco to accept Sergio's challenge in Arnold's stead:

> Sergio trained specifically to be at his best for this show, while Arnold and Franco had four weeks left of shaping up and cutting up to be at their contest best.[59]

It was a weak excuse. If neither Franco nor Arnold was in shape to take on Sergio in Tijuana, then Joe shouldn't have allowed either of his two contracted bodybuilders up on stage. After all, Franco would be entering the forthcoming Mr. Olympia as well as Arnold, and surely what was good for the goose should have been good for the gander. However, rather than risk Arnold's appearing second-best, Joe thought it best to sacrifice the lesser-known (both from a competition and marketing perspective) Franco to the baying crowd, rather than the man whose career he had told Sylvestre he had "invested too much money in." This, despite Joe's own admission that Franco "wasn't even in shape or ready for this contest."[60]

Franco, in other words, was expendable. Arnold wasn't.

Joe Weider was agitated at having been put in such an embarrassing predicament. He immediately hatched a plan to get back at Sergio. He knew the bodybuilder intended to enter the 1973 Mr. Olympia contest and, if Tijuana was any indication, he was sure to arrive in unbelievable shape. That could be a problem. But it was a problem that had an easy fix; the IFBB simply suspended Sergio from the Mr. Olympia competition — again. This time for having entered Dan Lurie's WBBG Mr. Galaxy Contest.[61] "The problem here," as bodybuilding historian Randy Roach points out, "was that Sergio had actually entered and won Lurie's Mr. Galaxy title well over a year earlier in April of 1972. Weider had more than ample time to disqualify Oliva for such an act, and would have also known that a showdown between Sergio and

Arnold in New York that year was highly unlikely."[62] Just for good measure, the Weider-controlled IFBB stripped Sergio of his Mr. International title as well, awarding it to Franco, who hadn't even registered to compete in the contest, hadn't participated in the prejudging, and only did a brief posing routine at the end of the competition.[63] And if that wasn't enough for Sergio to get the message that he was no longer welcome as a competitor in the IFBB, Joe wrote an article in *Muscle Builder/Power* that made it clear that he would never beat Arnold:

> However, since the "so-called" Myth isn't the greatest in the world like he thinks he is (three straight loses [*sic*] to Arnold, plus one to Bill Pearl), I think it is a good idea to explode the Myth in our next issue. I will personally do an article on his muscular development in which I will present my view and analysis of why Sergio is not the unbeatable "King of Bodybuilders" that he would like everyone to think he is . . . and why, in my opinion, that he will never beat Arnold![64]

This coming from the man whose brother ran the IFBB made it clear (in case there was still any doubt) that the Mr. Olympia contest was no longer about determining who possessed the best physique in the world. When the 1973 Mr. Olympia contest took place in New York in October 1973, Arnold only had to overcome the French bodybuilder, Serge Nubret, and the diminutive Franco Columbu. It was an easy and deserved win, given the competition.[65]

Joe's business investment was well protected.

CHAPTER TEN

A NEW APPROACH

In January 1974, Mike Mentzer decided it was time to go on a diet and resume training.[1] He hadn't worked out in almost three years,[2] and his bodyweight had crept up to an alarming 245 pounds.[3] But on a positive note, his injured right shoulder had finally healed. It was also time for him to seriously consider what he was going to do after the Air Force, as he was slated to be honorably discharged that February.[4]

Mike had maintained steady if intermittent contact with Arthur Jones since 1971,[5] and by now was firmly of the opinion that the high-intensity training approach and Arthur's Nautilus machines were the way to go. He decided he would check them out firsthand and head south to Arthur's compound once his discharge from the Air Force became official. In the meantime, he looked around Maryland to see if he could find a gym that had Nautilus equipment in order to familiarize himself with the machines. Eventually he found one: the Spartan Health Club.

Nestled behind an auto parts warehouse in the Temple Hills section of Prince George's County, the Spartan Health Club was described by one scribe as having "the homey atmosphere of a neighborhood bar."[6] It consisted of three rooms: a large mirror-lined one with barbells and dumbbells; a second, smaller room that contained several Nautilus machines;[7] and a third room with three stall showers and two rows of tiny lockers.[8] The Spartan Health Club instantly became Mike's favorite gym and would remain so for the rest of his life.[9] The various signs on its walls were admonitory: "Return All Dumbbells To Proper Place On Rack" and "DO NOT Drag Weights On

A New Approach

Mat."[10] It smelled of sweat and effort. It was, as the same newspaperman indicated, "a place to work, a place to build the human body."[11]

It was while training at Spartan that Mike met another aspiring bodybuilder, Roger Schwab, a man who would one day become one of the most successful gym owners in Maryland, and later a head judge for the IFBB. "A psychiatrist introduced us, a Reichian psychiatrist," Schwab recalled. "His name was Mel Thrash. He was an MD. He lived in Philadelphia and somehow or other, he knew Mike. And when I first went down to the Spartan gym by myself, Mike was there, and we hit if off immediately. And he trained hard, you know, from that first workout. Every workout we did was hard, and every workout we did was virtually the same over the course of an entire decade: we used Nautilus machines, training the whole body three days per week."[12] Mike also spoke with Roger about his interest in the work of psychologist Wilhelm Reich:

> He mentioned to me on numerous occasions that he was fascinated by the orgone. Reich, you know, was friends with Einstein. I mean, this was *way* beyond my pay grade. Right or wrong, the orgone energy, as Mike explained it to me, was a very sexual thing. He talked about it a lot. He didn't want to be just a psychiatrist. He wanted to be a Reichian psychiatrist.[13]

The two men became fast friends.

It was at this time that Mike's dream of returning to bodybuilding competition returned.[14] With the idea of heading to Nautilus that March, he went on a zero-carbohydrate diet (which was in vogue with bodybuilders in the 1970s, to lose bodyfat) throughout the months of January and February,[15] and started on a very abbreviated workout routine in the hope of getting back into reasonable shape. In a profile piece on Mike that appeared in *Muscle Builder* magazine some years later, Rick Wayne wrote about this period of Mike's life:

> Mike had no fixed goal in mind, except maybe to trim down somewhat. He remembers doing just two exercises a body part, ten sets per workout. He trained the whole body in one

session . . . A session that comprised just five exercises. "But the truth is I started making such rapid progress I was amazed. That, of course, says a lot about my genetic structure . . . or maybe the efficacy of the form of training I was doing at the time. Maybe both. Before you knew it my mind was functioning correctly again, and I was thinking about competing."[16]

While Mike was pleased that his bodyweight was down 50 pounds, the dieting and occasional fasting required to achieve the weight loss had left him weak and gaunt.[17] Nevertheless, in early March of 1974, he left Washington, DC, and traveled 814.7 miles south to DeLand, Florida.[18] Once settled in, he put pen to paper and wrote Dave Mastorakis of his experiences at Nautilus thus far:

March 1974
Dear David,

Well, as you have surmised after reading the envelope, you know that I made it down to Arthur's. I left last Monday at 1:30 p.m. and arrived the next day, Tuesday, at approx. 4 p.m.; Arthur has been treating me like a king ever since. He has bought most of my meals & has spent a lot of time with me. Casey has been nice to me also, helping me to find a job and helping with my workouts. Casey looks fantastic by the way; his arms are huge & cut up, as is everything else.

The gym we workout in is right at the factory & has all the machines. Casey and I workout together every Mon., Wed & Frid at 5 pm before anyone else comes. Ell Darden & Arthur are at every workout, making sure we push hard & use correct form. I got down here weighing 195, and Arthur said I still was a little fat. My arms and thighs had a lot of veins showing when I got here, but now you ought to see them. It may be partly psychological, but I can see myself growing & the veins are becoming more prominent. I went on a zero-carbohydrate diet before I got here and now I am on a diet comprised of 60% carbs & only 13% protein & the rest fats. Yes, you read it correctly, 60% carbs!! Arthur & Ell believe they are by far more important when you are stimulating muscle growth. Arthur believes I can gain at least one pound a day for the next three weeks & at the same time lose ⅓ lb. fat a day.

We are doing as much negative accentuated [training] as possible. He has us doing everything slowly, controlled, & deliberate. He says you have 3 different levels of strength: positive, contracted & negative. You're strongest in the contracted, then 2nd strongest in neg. & of course weakest in positives. So, if you can curl up a weight then you should be able to hold it easily in the contracted position since, as I said, you're strongest in the contracted or static position. He makes us do the positive relatively slowly then hold it in a tight controlled position for a second & then lower it slowly. When you can no longer hold it easily in a controlled position then you should cease the set, because if you can't hold it in a contracted position that means you didn't raise it purely by muscle, otherwise you would be able to hold it in the contracted position since that is by far the strongest.

He thinks that at our peaks Casey can have a 19½+ arm & I can have 20+, since my muscles are a little longer.

Let me know when you're coming down — you gotta see his new squat machine, I believe it's their best machine. It works your thighs in a full range of movement like you could not believe.

Write back & I'll tell you more.

Your best friend
Mike
P.S.: Tell me all about your training.[19]

Trying out the new Nautilus machines made Mike feel like a kid in a candy store. He couldn't wait to tell Roger Schwab about his experience, and, on April 2, he placed a phone call to him. Roger was fascinated by Mike's report and jotted down the following notes during their conversation:

Mentzer's Workout As Described To Me 4/2/74:
8:30 p.m.
<u>Confidential</u>

1. Double Shoulder

2. Negative Chins — On Multi [Exercise Machine]
3. Double Chest (110 [lbs.] flyes; 160 [lbs.] Press)
4. Regular Chin — On Multi
5. Omni Chest — ("fantastic machine")
6. Regular Dips — On Multi
7. Pullover Torso
8. Pulldown B.N. [Behind Neck] (220 lbs!!!!!)
9. B.N. [Behind Neck]
10. Curl (On Monday — Original Curl, on Wed & Friday Omni Curl — negative)
11. Triceps — ditto
12. Wrist Curls — Multi
13. Curl — Multi Exerciser (I didn't ask how he did these)
14. Triceps — Multi with a towel
15. Wrist Curl — Multi
16. Shrugs (didn't ask how he did it)
17. Neck work on B.N. (didn't ask how he did it)
18. Compound Leg
19. New Squat machine — One leg at a time — two platforms
20. Leg Curl
21. Geared Hip & Back

REMARKS

1. Says they sometimes do legs first.
2. Trains very hard 3 days a week.
3. Concentrate on pre-extension in every exercise.
4. Contract 1-2 seconds, lower slowly.
5. Positive work on Monday — negative accentuated Wed & Friday (Laterals on Double Shoulder, Flyes on Double Chest, always done positive).
6. Casey — Arnold — Equal.
7. Rheo H. Blair — Firm believer in 18 hours per night of sleep. "Only an ass would listen to him" — quote from Mike Mentzer to which I readily agreed.
8. "Regular bread as much as possible. Some football players encouraged to eat 1–2 loaves a day" — Arthur Jones.

9. "White bread has five essential nutrients, forget about whole wheat" — Arthur Jones.
10. Mentzer needs 3,000 calories at rest, 1,000 extra calories due to workouts (4,000/day)" — Arthur Jones.
11. "I take no vitamins, no protein, high carbs, low protein. I have gained 8 lbs. in 8 days, definition much better, developing tremendous vascularity in the thighs."
12. Casey hates Darden.
13. Mike is going to train in DeLand in preparation for the Mr. USA. He will enter. If he wins, he will stay in DeLand for the Mr. A— 1975. If he does not win, he will leave DeLand and enroll in the Univ. of Maryland. The junior college in DeLand isn't worth shit.
14. Casey was in auto accident — not serious.
15. Gossip in DeLand — How great Bob Birdsong looks — I verified that gossip.[20]

Ten days later, Mike fired off another missive to Dave Mastorakis:

April 12, 7:00 pm, 1974
Dear Dave,

I have to apologize after reading your letter. I was just kidding in my last letter when I said that Arthur had new secrets; I guess I was a little vague. No, he has no secret principles.

Last week Arthur measured my arms, and they were 18" cold — up ⅜" since I got here. He seemed disappointed and said he'd expected me to gain faster. Casey's arms are slightly over 18" cold but have no fat, whereas mine, although not fat, aren't as cut as his. Actually, Dave, I'm quite pudgy, not really very cut up. You have to remember that I hadn't trained seriously until the end of this January; and then I weighed 200 fat lbs. When I found out about my early A.F. discharge I went on a zero-carbo diet so that I wouldn't be too fat when I got here in March. Well, when I arrived here, I weighed 195 but was still not real cut up. A zero-carbo diet I have since found out, causes your tissues to lose a lot of fluids and since your muscles are 75%–90% water, you lose a lot of muscle tissue, which is what happened to me. So, my first gains since I've been here have been due to the restoration of all that lost fluid from the zero-carbo diet.

As far as your diet goes, I think I have the answer. Since you want to cut-up but still need carbos, I would recommend you do what I'm doing: count calories instead of carbs, keeping your carbo percentage relatively high with your protein percentage down. Buy a calorie counter & make sure you don't go over 2,000–2,500 calories a day. Make sure that at least 50% of it is carbos. I was putting weight on too fast, so Arthur had me drop my daily calorie consumption back to 2,800 while maintaining a high carbo percentage. It's okay to run, but don't do it on your off days; run after your workouts. Your off days are for recuperation. If you don't see a difference in your cuts after about a week on the 2,500 calories a day diet, then cut to about 1,800. You don't need more than 80 grams of protein a day at your weight, so make sure the rest is carbs. It doesn't matter too much how or when you eat your meals, as long as you don't go over the limit. On the next page is the routine:

Monday (positive), Wednesday, Friday (negative accentuated)

In Sequence:

1. Leg Ext. up to 12 reps (superset these two)
2. Leg Press
3. Squats — go down until your buttocks reach your calves — all the way down, good form — 2 sets 10 reps
4. Leg Curls — 2 sets on positive [day] — 1 set negative day
5. DB side laterals (superset 1 cycle)
6. Press Behind Neck
7. Chin Behind Neck
8. Chest Machine (superset 1 cycle)
9. DB Incline Press
10. Regular Palm-facing-you chins (1 set)
11. Pullover on Scorpio (slow, strict for 2 cycles)
12. Pulldown on Scorpio
13. 1 set of Bench Press on Incline to neck (1 set)

A New Approach

14. 1 set of regular BB curls — 8–10 reps to failure — really bust ass until the bar drops from your hands
15. 1 set Triceps Pushdowns on Lat machine
16. Dips — superset with pushdowns do them up slow and down slow — very deliberate
17. Wrist curls 1 set
18. Curls again
19. Dips
20. Wrist curls
21. Shrugs — do these after number 12 one or two "strict" sets.

I know that you are better in form than most bodybuilders, Dave, but you can't emphasize it too strongly. Up slow, hold, down slow. Make sure you allow the muscle to fully extend & "stretch" at the beginning of an exercise. This "pre-stretch" is extremely important. It stimulates more muscle fibers to come into action during the contraction. Full extension — full contraction! Very important — "PRE STRETCH."

Go through the workout fairly fast, according to your cardiovascular capabilities. You should see their new Squat Machine. Wow! It is so great you wouldn't believe it. You do one leg at a time. It forces your knee up into your chest and you push down from there; talk about full extension — Wow!

Well, any more questions write back fast. Come on down here if you can.

Your best friend,
Mike

Call Arthur & tell him you heard me talk about it; tell him you have a professional gym.
New squat machine. Very rough sketch.
Shoulder pads
Hand grips
Foot pads
Weight stack
Big cam

I'm not sure how the chains are attached. It's the best machine. You ought to get it.[21]

Although Mike was enjoying training in Florida, his heart was slowly moving away from the south and back to a girl in Maryland whom we only know by the name of Debbie. He told the author a little bit about her during a conversation we shared in the months prior to Mike's passing. He evidently had been head over heels in love with her, overwhelmed totally. He had once made the statement that:

> While I am very attracted to WOMAN — capital letters — in general, I have found over the years that I have been attracted to the point of pursuit rather rarely. But when I am attracted to a woman, it's usually a very strong overwhelming attraction and I'll pursue her for all I'm worth. In looking over the women I have been attracted to over the years it's really rather difficult to put my finger on any common denominator as they all seem rather diverse in their qualities. I've been in love with blond women, dark haired women, introverted, extroverted, well-built women, not so well-built women — the whole gamut. In looking back, however, to the initial attraction — and it's always an initial attraction — again, I'm overpowered immediately by the women I've pursued, or I just didn't pursue them. It wasn't something that developed over a period of time. In the majority of cases, it was something in their eyes, a vulnerability. I think it was Shakespeare who said "the eyes are the window to the soul" and I think it's very true. I judge most people initially anyway by their eye contact and what it is I get from their eyes — and especially so with women. It's really a great ineffable to me; it's something mysterious, it's a chemistry with the eyes. It's a certain vulnerability or emotional sensitivity which can't be hidden when looking at the eyes. Many people try to hide their sensitivity or their emotional vulnerability through different character traits, but the eyes never lie.[22]

When he stayed overnight at Debbie's parents' house, the two were not allowed to sleep together. But, unable to bear being apart from her, when

A New Approach

everybody went to sleep at night, he brought his pillow and blanket to her bedroom door and lay down on the floor outside of it and slept there. Such was the emotional pull this girl had for him in 1974. He spoke about this, along with the fact that he would soon be leaving DeLand, in his next letter to Dave:

> June of '74
> Dear Dave,
>
> I have to humbly apologize for not writing sooner. Two weeks ago, I went back to Maryland for eight days and two of your letters arrived here in Florida while I was up there, so don't think I forgot about you, old buddy, OK?
> I missed Debbie so bad that I had to go see her. You can understand that, I'm sure.
> Things down here have taken on an unpleasant turn. The fellow I'm living with is moving within two weeks and I can't possibly afford staying here for $180 a month. I also was accepted to school back in Maryland as a state subsidized student, which means it would be so cheap that I'd be a fool not to go. So, rather than spend the couple of hundred dollars necessary to get re-established in another apartment here, I've decided that the most practical and logical thing to do is move back to Maryland.
> I must let you know that there are other considerations involved in making this decision than the one mentioned above.
> The big thing is lack of progress. Arthur is hardly ever around anymore, and I just can't push myself when he is not there. I really haven't made any progress for six weeks. Arthur apologized to me yesterday for not being around more, but said he was just too busy, which I said I understood. I do understand him being too busy, but that is not enough to make me want to stay.
> The most important factor in my decision to return north is Debbie. I talked to her on the phone the other night and I sensed that she is slipping away from me. I feel so empty without her that I feel I'll die unless I get back with her. Over the past several months I've come to love her so much that I

can't bear to be without her. Nothing else is important unless you have someone to love and love you. I do regret having to go back — having only been here 2½ months — but all practical considerations dictate that I must.

I'm glad to see you placed so high in the Mr. Eastern A.

Dave, that low-carb diet is very dangerous. People are actually dying from it, really. You will lose fat, yes, but you'll also lose muscle. Your best bet is an all-around balanced low-calorie diet. Have you tried it? Let me know.

I'm happy that you finally have Nautilus. Would you believe you have more machines to work with than I do? Really. We have no compound, no triceps machine, no pulldown machine, no behind neck & no infimetric. That is another reason I'm leaving; we have more machines in Maryland.

Most of the time there is no chest machine either. The gym here is really a storage area & whenever they need a machine, they take it from our supply.

Well, don't write back because I'll be going back to Maryland very soon, so I'll contact you.

Your best friend,
Mike[23]

And so ended Mike's time at Nautilus. In reflecting on the situation years later, he concluded:

> I didn't like it so much. I got to spend some time with Arthur, which further impressed me, but I didn't make much progress. I was very disappointed . . . I didn't adjust to the situation psychologically very well. I was very involved with a young lady back in Washington, DC, and . . . she wasn't urging me to go back, but I missed her. My heart wasn't into it.[24]

Although he returned to Maryland somewhat disappointed, by July Mike was back at the Spartan Health Club and putting the high-intensity program he had used in Florida into effect.[25] One of the bodybuilders at Spartan

A New Approach

who encountered Mike at this time was 20-year-old Michael Levenson. His memories remain vivid to this day:

> In the summer of '74 I walked into the Spartan Health Club in Marlow Heights, Maryland. It was late morning, and the gym was empty except for a nondescript heavy-set guy banging out a full body workout. It gradually dawned on me just how incredible the weights he was using were, and also the intensity he was employing. Mike trained three times a week, full body workouts with two to three sets per muscle group till absolute failure. His workouts were unbelievably intense and lasted approximately forty-five minutes each. He grew very quickly. I remember asking him his weight and he said, "about 250." He was huge. That was my introduction to a twenty-three-year-old Mike Mentzer. A future great. I gradually got to know Mike and he discussed with me his workout theories and philosophies about life — it made a huge impression on me. I still think of him fondly and the profound effect he had on everyone at the gym. He was a brilliant guy and far ahead of his time.[26]

Mike still wanted to win the Mr. America title, but as psychiatry was going to be his profession, he knew that his education was the top priority. In order to obtain the credits necessary to gain admission to the University of Maryland's premed program, in the fall of 1974, he enrolled in an arts and sciences program at Prince George's College.

CHAPTER ELEVEN

RELATIONSHIPS

B>ased in Largo, Maryland, Prince George's Community College provided (and continues to provide) higher-level education to those seeking to further their academic studies or better prepare for the workforce. To some, such as Mike Mentzer, it was a necessary stepping stone that allowed him to pick up some helpful science credits before entering the University of Washington to pursue a career in medicine.

The school had been in operation since 1958, with its main campus opening in Largo in 1967, seven years prior to Mike's enrollment. The school would prove to be an important part of Mike's life, as it was at Prince George's that he met Cathy Gelfo, a woman who would win his heart and, perhaps more importantly, keep him centered emotionally for the next eight years. Cathy came from an athletic family. She and her sister and two brothers were heavily involved in football, basketball, baseball, skiing, and soccer.[1] However, by the time she entered high school, Cathy had put her athletic pursuits behind her. She became a cheerleader — and popular. With popularity, however, came some bad habits. Soon she was smoking half a pack of cigarettes a day.

By the time she entered college, she was dismayed to learn that she was 20 pounds overweight and decided to do something about it. "I couldn't have run a mile on the track if you had paid me," she recalled. "I was filled with new fears concerning my capabilities and was for the first time feeling at odds with my surroundings. I felt too vulnerable! Gone was the feeling 'I can do it.' After analyzing the situation, I decided I had to get back in touch with developing my personal strength and overall fitness. I have always been attracted to strong people and I wanted to be one myself." Together with a girlfriend, she enrolled in a weightlifting class at college. To her shock, she discovered that they were the only women in a class with 50 male students. But Cathy was diligent and committed herself fully to the weight training program. She actually came to enjoy it. "The riding joke in the class was for the instructor to come into the room and tell me that Don Shula from the Miami Dolphins was in his office and wanted to talk to me about a contract," she quipped. However, it wasn't until January 1975 that she learned about bodybuilding. That was when she first laid eyes on Mike Mentzer. "It was the first day of the new semester at college," she recollected. "I entered the room where my Philosophy II class was to be held.[2] I took a seat in the front of the room and out of the corner of my eye I spied what had to have been the biggest guy I had ever seen. I later found out that this man was Mike Mentzer. Mike and I took a liking to each other immediately, much to the chagrin of my current boyfriend. I remember how fascinated I was with Mike's physical strength as well as intellectual integrity. Many times, he would take a bundle of schoolbooks from me, books that were heavy, but were a mere toy for him."

Soon thereafter, Cathy broke up with her boyfriend, and Mike stopped seeing Debbie. Going forward, Mike and Cathy were inseparable. Cathy was intrigued by Mike's bodybuilding and wanted to learn more about his approach to training — and whether it was something she could do. "Well aware of my reservations concerning women who train, Mike convinced me that women do not become masculine and develop large muscles," she recalled. "He convinced me that women who train enhance their feminine form, and that because of our hormones needn't worry about big muscles. With what seemed like unlimited support and encouragement from Mike I began serious weight training. By 'serious,' I mean that weight training became a part of my lifestyle."

Meanwhile, 1,740 miles away to the east, Colorado wasn't working out for Ray Mentzer. He'd started off college well enough; for the first time in his life, he claimed, he was getting straight A's. But it didn't last long. "I went to college, but I realized that was inhibiting my thinking," he recollected of the experience. "They tried to institutionalize my way of thought. I rebelled as a straight-A student my junior year and quit."[3] That may well have been true. And it most certainly would have been the reason he offered to his parents. However, his extracurricular activities may have played a significant role in his dropping out of college sooner than he had planned. "I wasn't training or playing any sports. I was drinking and partying, but through it all I was a loner," he said. "Before long, I couldn't face my lifestyle. I had lost my physique. My self-esteem plummeted."[4] Ray would most likely have kept the truth from Mike as well, understanding that his older brother placed a higher value on intellectual development than partying.[5]

Ray seemed lost. But then a friend from Ephrata made a surprise stop in Colorado and looked him up. "My friend talked me into going for a workout," Ray told an interviewer four years later. "We really hit the weights and I got so psyched up I haven't stopped lifting since."[6] Perhaps to get his little brother back on track, Mike once again extended an offer for Ray to come to Maryland and stay with him until he figured out what he wanted to do with his life. Ray accepted and, shortly thereafter, found employment as a pool manager and rented a place of his own in Calverton.[7] Cathy recalled watching the brothers hit the iron shortly after being reunited:

> I had been in gyms before, but never had I seen anyone train like Mike and his brother Ray. The energy that they expended and the pounds that they lifted served to thrill as well as frighten me. I wanted to know what it felt like to lift such heavy weights and would sit for hours talking to Mike about his training concepts.[8]

Looking to get his competitive feet wet again, Mike traveled to his friend Dave Mastorakis's home state of Massachusetts and entered the Mr. East Coast contest. He ended up placing second in the Medium Class to Len Archambault, the man who would go on to win the competition. Dave won the Short Class, and Mike won the subcategory awards for best arms and best back, which wasn't bad for a guy who hadn't competed in three years.[9] Feeling confident, Mike set his sights on taking another run at the 1975 Mr. America title, which was promoted that year by Franco Columbu in Los Angeles, California.

Relationships

About the time of Mike's second place finish in the Bay State, *Sports Illustrated* came out with a profile piece on the sport of bodybuilding. Arnold Schwarzenegger, the current Mr. Olympia champion, was the centerpiece of the article. While Arnold made sure to give props to the sport, he also said things that must have come as a shock to Joe Weider when he read them:

- "Joe Weider is not my coach."
- "Joe has his own goals, though I do not agree with many of them."
- "All of these magazines — Weider's, Hoffman's, Lurie's — I call them comic books, circus books!"
- "Why won't these guys get together? I will tell you why. It is because none of these silly people are really interested in bodybuilding anymore. They are interested only in the money that can be made from it."
- "I ask Joe why he prints such junk — why is everybody bombing and blasting and terrorizing, all those silly words? Joe says it sells the magazine. Period."
- "I would like to get hold of Joe's magazine . . . but he will not give up such a sales manual."
- "I will have to start my own magazine, a *real* magazine, a bodybuilding magazine, not just something to sell products to 14-year-old boys."
- "When Franco and I got permission from Ben Weider to promote the Mr. International show at the Embassy, I wanted to have it on TV, to sell it to TV. A guy I contacted said yes, they were interested, you know, but first show us what bodybuilding is all about. All I had to show was Joe's magazine, and they looked at it and then they were all laughing. They thought the show would be the same thing as the magazine. 'I will call you,' the guy says. 'Don't bother,' I said. I was embarrassed."[10]

It's doubtful that Arnold ever spoke so truthfully about Joe Weider and the bodybuilding world before or since. But even without Arnold's corroboration, it was evident that *Sports Illustrated* saw through Joe Weider's motives:

> Although Joe Weider bills himself as the "trainer of champions" and the discoverer of the "Weider Principles" of weight

training, his motives were by no means altruistic. En route to becoming millionaires, both Weider and Hoffman expanded their product lines to include hundreds of diet supplements, special exercisers, tanning oils and magic lotions.

The Hoffman-Weider war, now a three-cornered affair with the rise of Dan Lurie of Brooklyn as a publisher and contest sponsor, has helped bodybuilding in some ways, but has hurt it in others. The partisans scream at each other in their respective muscle magazines, calling builders affiliated with other entrepreneurs cowards and tricksters[11] and generally producing an abysmal level of trade journalism. Anyone leafing through these magazines is likely to find support for his worst suspicions of bodybuilding — and bodybuilders.[12]

It was apparent that some cracks had formed in the plaster of Arnold and Joe's relationship. Perhaps fortunately for Arnold, the article didn't hit the newsstands until two days after the 1974 Mr. Olympia contest had concluded.

The 1974 Mr. Olympia took place in the Felt Forum in New York City's Madison Square Garden, and Arnold was at the top of his game. He came in weighing a career-high 237 pounds — all of it muscle. Weider and the IFBB, perhaps to make Franco Columbu more marketable, changed the format of the competition.[13] They divided the competitors into two separate categories: "Over 200 Pounds" and "Under 200 Pounds." The winner of each would then face off for the "Overall" Mr. Olympia title. Such a move allowed Joe to claim in his ads and articles that his "students" Arnold and Franco were both Mr. Olympias in their respective categories (Arnold's earlier suggestion of Joe having the best small man and best tall man in order to lock up professional bodybuilding had not fallen on deaf ears). Then, Arnold would go on to win the "Overall" Mr. Olympia, defeating the best "Under 200 Pounds" winner. It was a way of establishing a pecking order in the sport, which underscored Franco's position of being the best "Under 200 Pounds" bodybuilder. It was a great imprimatur to have for marketing Joe's products, as both the Over and Under 200-Pound Mr. Olympia Class winners were endorsing his supplements and training system, and it really didn't impact Arnold's status in the least. So long as Arnold was competing, it was obvious that Franco would never win the overall Mr. Olympia title, but it still allowed Joe to squeeze every dollar he could out of his investment in the shorter Franco Columbu.[14]

Not that Franco would have an easy time of it in this new division, as Frank Zane — the man who had defeated Arnold at the 1968 Mr. Universe contest — was in top shape. The judges ultimately settled on Franco as the Under 200-Pound Mr. Olympia winner.[15] The Over-200-Pound Division was expected to provide Arnold with a challenge even greater (in terms of muscle mass) than Sergio Olivia in the form of 21-year-old Lou Ferrigno (still three years away from becoming television's *Incredible Hulk*), who would be stepping onto the Olympia stage for the first time. At six foot five and weighing by some guesstimates 260 pounds,[16] he was believed to be the only bodybuilder on the planet who could make Arnold look small in the judges' eyes. But that would have been an upset for the ages, which simply wasn't meant to be on this day. Arnold was at his biggest and sharpest, while Ferrigno had evidently dieted too severely and lost some of his muscle mass. It was an easy win for Arnold.[17]

When Joe's magazine came out with its report of the contest, some interesting information came to light; it was announced that both Arnold and Franco were contemplating retirement from the sport.[18] This was not good news for Joe Weider, particularly given his new self-anointed title: "Trainer of Schwarzenegger, Columbu, Zane, and other champions since 1936." If Arnold was thinking about retiring, Joe had to make hay while the sun was still shining; he featured Arnold in no fewer than 17 ads for his products and three articles, in the same issue of *Muscle Builder/Power* that carried the report of the 1974 Mr. Olympia contest.

Unfortunately, this particular edition of the magazine (March 1975) also provided further support to *Sports Illustrated*'s condemnation of Joe's "abysmal level of trade journalism." Joe's scribe, George Kaye, took another (by now almost obligatory) shot at Sergio.[19] He then went on to pen incredibly sexist comments about the female contestants in the Miss Americana contest,[20] in addition to mocking a homeless woman in New York City.[21] This was topped off by an insensitive anti-Semitic comment — particularly bizarre in a magazine owned by a Jewish publisher.[22]

By this point in time, Arnold didn't have much use for Joe. He had already made decent money from his bodybuilding and fledgling real estate enterprises, and had long wanted to get into acting, just as his former bodybuilding hero Reg Park had. Not only was there fame to be had in that profession, but considerably more fortune. Unlike most neophyte actors, Arnold's foray into this new field started off with a leading role. In 1970, he was the star of a quickly forgettable film (he got the part through the efforts of Joe Weider) entitled *Hercules In New York*.[23] It is doubtful the film ever received a theatrical release, but it would later enjoy a modest success as a VHS rental. The film proved so unwatchable that its copyright was put up for sale on eBay in 2005 with the minimum bid set at $250,000.[24]

Arnold's first foray into movies was not without its problems. The producers thought his accent too thick, and so had his dialogue in the film dubbed in by another actor.[25] And then there was the issue of his last name, which was too much of a tongue-twister for the average American moviegoer to attempt. It was at this point that Arnold Schwarzenegger, at the prompting of Joe Weider, briefly changed his name to "Arnold Strong," with the hope that this would be catchier and remove one of the impediments to his becoming a major movie star.[26] But neither the voice dubbing nor the new last name proved sufficient to save the film.

It was not an auspicious start.

Arnold's next acting role was a very minor one and didn't come until four years later, in 1973, when he had appeared (uncredited) as one of several thugs in the Elliott Gould movie *The Long Goodbye*.[27] In 1974 he landed a supporting role in the Lucille Ball made-for-TV movie *Happy Anniversary and Goodbye*.[28] In 1975, he filmed another co-starring role, this time in the movie *Stay Hungry*,[29] which was released a year later.

But then, seemingly out of nowhere, a writer, Charles Gaines, along with photographer George Butler, combined to produce a book on bodybuilding entitled *Pumping Iron*, which, upon its release in 1974, surprisingly became a bestseller.[30] The book featured Arnold liberally throughout its pages, as he was the reigning champion of the sport, and both men found Arnold's personality to be compelling. Arnold was forthright with both Gaines and Butler about his obsession for power, telling Butler, "My relationship to power and authority is that I'm all for it. . . . People need somebody to watch over them and tell them what to do. Ninety-five percent of the people in the world need to be told what to do and how to behave."[31] The book proved so successful that one year later Butler decided to produce a documentary on it.[32] The only problem was that Arnold had no interest in competing again.[33] This changed, however, when the filmmakers offered him $50,000 to come out of retirement for the benefit of their cameras.[34] Arnold was receptive to the paycheck, and thought starring in a documentary wouldn't be a bad way to get his name out amongst the moviegoing public.

Relationships

As was getting to be the norm for the Mr. Olympia contest, the 1975 Mr. Olympia was scandalous. For openers, the contest was sanctioned — with the blessing of the IFBB and Ben Weider — to be held in Pretoria, South Africa. Apartheid[35] was still very much in place, and most people who were directed by any sort of moral compass were not looking to do any favors for the South African tourist industry. Indeed, only a year before, the United Nations had expelled the nation of South Africa because of apartheid.[36] The IFBB, however, didn't consider this an impediment to staging their premiere bodybuilding competition on South African soil. The federation had embraced South Africa as a viable venue shortly after Arnold had visited there in 1972.[37] The South African sports minister, Piet Koornhof, told him that South Africa would love to host a sporting contest like the Mr. Olympia — and that money was no object. When Arnold returned to America, he couldn't wait to share the good news with IFBB president Ben Weider.[38]

Arnold's own comments appeared to indicate he had no problem with apartheid. He had, for instance, allegedly told journalist/bodybuilder Rick Wayne that "if you gave these blacks a country to run, they would run it down the tubes."[39] He could not have been unaware of the racial segregation that existed in the country, as he had visited South Africa many times over the years,[40] beginning in 1967, when Reg Park, his boyhood hero, brought him there to stay with him in at his home in Johannesburg for a series of bodybuilding exhibitions.[41] Arnold was starry-eyed at Reg's lifestyle, which included servants.[42]

Most of the bodybuilders were taken aback when they learned that South Africa was even in the running to host the Mr. Olympia contest.[43] But to the IFBB, institutionalized racism was one thing but business was another matter. All that was required to smooth the waters with the IFBB was a pledge that the competitors would be treated fairly and that several hundred thousand dollars would be paid to the IFBB in sanctioning fees.[44] In July 1973, Joe Weider's *Muscle Builder* magazine broke the news:

> IFBB Congress Precedes Championships — Great Organizational Progress Made On October 19, 1973, in Geneva, Switzerland. . . . Of the many issues discussed, the most vital was the voting into IFBB membership of the Union of South Africa. This controversial nation has been barred from many international sports associations because of its racist policies. However, they

sent black (Mr. Thabebe) and white (Mr. Bester) representatives to plead their case. The IFBB was assured that no discrimination of any kind would be permitted in their national federation, nor would any prejudice attend possible international meets in that country. Consequently, South Africa was warmly accepted into the IFBB brotherhood and was also awarded the 1975 World Bodybuilding Championships by a vote of 35–0, with Pakistan and Yugoslavia abstaining.[45]

The next problem reared its head when Serge Nubret, the French bodybuilder who had lost to Arnold in the 1973 Mr. Olympia, arrived in South Africa in phenomenal shape.[46] Not that he was expected to defeat Joe's poster boy, but an in-shape Serge could pose problems — if not to the judges, at least to those who viewed Butler's documentary of the competition in theaters. If moviegoers thought Nubret looked better than Arnold, for instance, it would take some of the luster off the film's intent (indeed, its thesis) of positioning Arnold as the greatest bodybuilder in the world. It was decided that the Frenchman's entering the competition wasn't worth the risk. Ben Weider took Nubret aside and promised him that he would win the next year's Olympia if he would withdraw from this one.[47] Nubret balked at the suggestion. "I had already trained for an entire year without respite," he said, "and have never felt so good, so strong, so sure of myself."[48]

With Nubret refusing to remove himself from the contest, the next step was for the IFBB to do it for him. Taking a page out of their playbook in dealing with phenomenal Black bodybuilders such as Sergio Oliva, they informed Nubret that he was disqualified.[49] The reason? He had appeared in a pornographic film, which, the IFBB decided, reflected badly on the lofty morals of the sport of bodybuilding. Nubret denied any such thing.[50] It was then brought up that he had competed in a non-IFBB-sanctioned event in Spain.

Nubret was out.

For the next two weeks, Nubret, who, apart from being a competitor, was also on the executive of the IFBB and had been instrumental in securing both the contest venue and sanctioning fee in South Africa,[51] sat around and watched his hard-earned conditioning deteriorate.[52] But then, at the 11th hour, the producers of *Pumping Iron* decided that the Frenchman would actually make for a good addition to the film. Ben Weider was not blind to the upside that a successful film based on a bestselling book could provide to both the IFBB and the Weider supplement business, and so the order came down from on high to waive Nubret's suspension. However, while he was allowed back into the contest (and documentary), Nubret had lost his competitive edge as a result of the two-week hiatus.[53]

One reason why the Weider interests may have been concerned (at least initially) about Nubret was that Arnold, while in great shape, had been unable to regain all the muscle mass he had displayed at the Mr. Olympia contest the year before. In the 1974 Olympia he weighed 237 pounds and was shredded; there wasn't a trace of fat visible on his body. However, after the competition Arnold dropped his bodyweight to 210 pounds for his supporting role in the movie *Stay Hungry*.[54] By the time production wrapped in the summer of '75,[55] he had four months to regain his former size and diet down for the Mr. Olympia contest, which took place on November 8, 1975.[56] He resumed his steroid use, which, according to Arnold, usually lasted anywhere from six to eight weeks before a contest,[57] and which, according to his friend and occasional training partner, Jerry Brainum, always saw his muscle mass blow up almost before his eyes:

> Arnold, I can tell you, was very responsive to the drugs because when he would compete, he'd get on the drugs. Then, after the contest, he'd get off it. And about maybe eight weeks after the contest he looked like a shadow of himself. Those huge slab-like pecs he had would disappear, there'd be no deltoids, the forearms would get skinny, skinny legs . . . the physique was worlds apart from his Olympia physique. And then, as a contest drew close, let's say maybe eight weeks before, he'd start the more intensive training. He'd start coming in twice a day and he'd get on the drugs, and you could see him change.[58]

Arnold typically began his contest training three to six months out from a competition,[59] and then would start cutting his calories roughly two to three months prior to the show,[60] so he was in familiar territory. However, this time around his muscles weren't responding as they had previously. Indeed, on the day of the contest he weighed (depending on the report) either 220 or 225 pounds,[61] which had him down either 17 or 12 pounds from the muscle size he had displayed the year before.

One may speculate that when Nubret showed up in Pretoria weighing a rock-solid 212 pounds, it may have been feared that Arnold lacked the mass necessary to thoroughly dominate the Over-200-Pounds category of the competition, particularly when Lou Ferrigno would be stepping on stage at 268 pounds.[62] In the event, however, Ferrigno wasn't in the condition that Arnold was, and Nubret had lost 12 pounds of muscle. Neither man posed a serious threat to Arnold, who would go on to win the Over-200-Pound Division with ease. Given the previous year's new structure of dividing the competitors into two weight classes, it meant that Arnold would once again be posing off against Franco Columbu for the overall title. At six foot one versus five foot five, Arnold had more than enough mass to vanquish the smaller challenger — although the scoring was surprisingly close (four judges voted for Arnold, three voted for Franco; Arnold ended up winning by a single point),[63] causing Franco to complain afterwards that he thought the contest had been fixed for Arnold to win.[64]

But then came a plot twist; after being awarded the title, Arnold took the microphone and announced to the crowd that he was retiring from competitive bodybuilding. The good news, however, was that he, together with his new partner, the former mayor of Worthington, Ohio, Jim Lorimer, would be the promoters of the Mr. Olympia contest going forward, starting the very next year in Columbus, Ohio.[65]

And with that, Arnold Schwarzenegger stepped away from bodybuilding competition.

PART TWO
THE LION

With a dark glance wily Odysseus shot back, "Indecent talk, my friend. You, you're a reckless fool — I see that. So, the gods don't hand out all their gifts at once, not build and brains and flowing speech to all."

— Homer, *The Odyssey*

CHAPTER TWELVE

A MAN OF SCIENCE

The 1975 IFBB Mr. America contest was fast approaching, and it was a contest Mike believed he could win. From what he could ascertain, his chief competition would be Roger Callard, a bodybuilder who was on the rise. Given that Roger had won the Medium Class at the IFBB Mr. Western America in 1974, along with the fact that he was Arnold's training partner and was already receiving publicity in Joe Weider's magazine,[1] the smart money was on Roger to add the Mr. America trophy to his collection in 1975. Mike knew he had his work cut out for him.

Apart from his training and diet needing to be on point, Mike had heard enough through the bodybuilding grapevine to know that he would need to up his steroid intake in order to have a chance. He had been taking three Dianabol tablets a day, but that wasn't going to cut it, not when the other competitors were already stacking steroids, making use of both tablets and injectables. "He said taking in an exogenous dose would signal his body to stop producing normal testosterone, so he needed to at least double a normal dose," Mike Levenson recalled. "He got his anabolics from a doctor that he worked for part time, Paul DeVore."[2] According to Levenson, Mike now added the injectable steroid Deca-Durabolin to his regimen.

But Mike knew enough about steroids to have concerns. He had blood tests taken periodically to ensure that nothing untoward was happening physically. "I looked into the steroid thing closely, and I knew that there was a certain amount of risk involved," he said. "But obviously if I wasn't willing to tolerate some of the risks, or any of the risks, I wouldn't do it. I was convinced that the risk was relatively slim if I didn't abuse it, and I don't think that I abused it. I went higher than the doctor would recommend but stayed within the far end of the recommended dosage range. I never stayed on it for more than ten, 12 weeks — at the longest — and never had any problems."[3] That might have been true for any physical side effects from the drugs, but it was their potential psychological side effects that worried him the most. Given that depression ran in his family, along with the fact that the literature on steroids indicated that they could exacerbate such a condition, he had cause to be concerned.[4] "Many people fear that taking steroids will adversely affect them physically," he said. "I'm more concerned about the way they might have affected me psychologically or my personality. Scares me to death!"[5] For the moment, he parked his fears, took the steroids, and focused on his training.

Unlike most of the competitors he would be facing, who largely copied the Weider/Arnold method by training twice a day, six days per week for two hours a workout,[6] Mike limited his training to whole-body workouts performed three days per week, with each workout lasting one hour.[7] In other words, while his competitors were training up to 24 hours a week, Mike was training only three. It was a radical (and, if successful, revolutionary) departure from the norm. His training, coupled with the strict diet he had started seven months prior to the contest, saw him tipping the scales at a rock-hard 196 pounds when he arrived at the Embassy Auditorium in Los Angeles on the day of the contest.[8]

Mike was confident and fully expected to win. And this feeling held right up until Robby Robinson, a Black bodybuilder from Tallahassee, Florida, walked into the pump-up room. Robinson was a newcomer; nothing had heralded his arrival to the contest. But even then, he was one of the greatest physiques in the history of bodybuilding. His biceps rivaled Arnold's, and his back had a V-taper that had to be seen to be believed. Not only that, but he had arrived at the competition in diamond-hard condition. Mike knew as soon as he saw him that he was looking at the winner of the contest. "Upon reaching backstage and seeing Robby, I realized that I was not going to win. I didn't take it hard, either. If I didn't win, I didn't really care about second or third. I knew Robby was going to win, and he did very handily."[9] While Robby won the contest. Mike's physique caused the muscle media to take notice:

> By far the closest competition of the contest came in [the Medium] class. The first three men — [Robby] Robinson,

Roger Callard and Mike Mentzer all looked sensational. Robinson's massive muscularity prevailed in a real donnybrook. Roger Callard made fantastic improvement during the past 12 months and received two first place votes to Robinson's six; Mike Mentzer, a sensational newcomer, had one first place vote and wound up an easy third. Both Callard and Mentzer are bona fide future Mr. America material.[10]

One of those in attendance that day who was particularly impressed with Mike was the Master Blaster himself. "I remember very clearly being backstage pumping up for the prejudging and I couldn't get over the fact that Joe Weider was back there, and he would spend all his time staring at me," Mike recalled. "I was literally shocked; I thought, 'Geez, I knew I looked good, but I didn't think I looked *that* good."[11] Joe was so impressed, in fact, that he invited Mike to take part in a photo session two days later at the Los Angeles studio of Weider photographer Russ Warner, a man who had photographed every top bodybuilder from Steve Reeves to Arnold Schwarzenegger. Mike was flattered beyond belief. He was still naïve to the extent of the political and commercial goings-on within the industry, and to be taken notice of by Joe Weider was, from his limited perspective, a huge honor.

On the Monday after the contest, Mike attended the photo shoot and went through a series of poses for Warner's camera. After the session, Joe told Mike to come up to his offices in Woodland Hills so that his staff writer, Gene Mozee, could interview him for *Muscle Builder/Power*. When Mike arrived at 2100 Erwin Street the next day, he couldn't help but be struck by the opulence of Joe's place of business. The building itself was just under 42,000 square feet, comprising two storeys of glass and concrete, with a white marble façade that covered its exterior. Indeed, white marble was everywhere; marble steps led up to its front doors, which opened to a sun-splashed atrium and white marble floors. Just beyond the reception desk, a 20-foot waterfall cascaded down a marble wall. An impressive staircase led up to the second floor, where the Master Blaster's magnificent office was situated, featuring a huge window that looked out over Erwin Street and Joe's massive Louis XIV–style desk. Impressive surroundings, to be certain, particularly to a young student from Maryland.

After being given a tour of the premises, Mike sat down with Gene Mozee. "I spoke at length about the high-intensity training program," Mike recalled.

"Gene, during the interview, was quite surprised that I was only training three to five sets per body part, only three days per week."[12] While the bodybuilding orthodoxy was certainly surprised by Mike's training approach, they couldn't argue with his results. After the interview, Mike thanked Gene and Joe, and walked down the staircase to the reception area. On the wall next to the stairs were hung huge oil paintings of Weider champions Rick Wayne, Larry Scott, and Arnold Schwarzenegger. As he exited the building and descended its marble steps into the warm California sunshine, he felt as if he were in another world, which, in some ways, he was. If Gold's Gym could be said to be the Mecca of bodybuilding,[13] the Weider building was its Nirvana. Mike had just been "discovered," and it was summertime in California. For a young bodybuilder, it was hard to imagine anything better than this.

As Venice was where Gold's Gym was located, Mike made a point of checking out the facility to see what famous faces might be working out. However, upon arriving at Gold's he was surprised to discover that George Butler and his camera crew had taken over the gym for the filming of *Pumping Iron*. But in amongst the crowd that day, Mike spotted his Maryland chum, Roger Schwab. "I was there as a guest of John Balik, who was very friendly with Arnold," Roger recalled. "We had breakfast that Saturday morning at Arnold's place. I remember it well, because Dave Draper had made this huge bed for Arnold; a big timber-like bed. And I remember seeing the syringe he [Arnold] used; I think it was loaded with a German [steroid] drug called Primobolan. I was reading *All the President's Men*, by Woodward and Bernstein, and Arnold made some wisecrack to me that, 'Schwab, what are you, an intellectual?' Then we took a car to Gold's Gym. It was me, John Balik, and Arnold. And Arnold walked into Gold's Gym with me right behind him. Ed Giuliani ran up and jumped into his arms. If you remember the movie, you remember that. And the whole thing was about Arnold."[14] Indeed, at the six-minute mark of the film, the viewer can see both Roger and Mike in the background watching Arnold's entrance. A few seconds later, Mike can be spotted seated at the end of the reception counter, sipping a beverage and looking on with a bemused expression while Arnold banters with bodybuilder Ken Waller.

Mike would compete twice more in 1975, winning the Junior Mr. America, and placing third at the AABA Mr. USA., behind Roger Callard.[15]

Come September, Mike was back in Maryland. He resumed his classes at St. George's College and returned to his job with Dr. Paul DeVore. Needing more money, he found additional part-time employment working for another Maryland physician, Dr. John Ziegler.[16] Physically, the doctor cut an imposing figure, standing six foot four and weighing 275 pounds.[17] He was a weightlifter himself, and the physician for the American Olympic weightlifting team.[18] But it was his mind that Mike found most fascinating. The doctor had played a significant role in the creation of Dianabol, the steroid that all of the top bodybuilders were using at the time. Given the abuse of the drug by the bodybuilding community, Ziegler had grown to regret the role he played in its development. But apart from this "dubious distinction," as Mike referred to it,[19] he had been particularly impressed by Ziegler's creation of the Isotron Mark VIII, a forerunner to today's electrical muscle stimulation machines. According to Mike:

> It worked on the principle that since muscles contract as a result of electrical stimulation from the brain, in order to achieve maximum results, what you have to do is bypass the motivational shortcomings (mental drives) of the individual. This is done by applying an exogenous electrical source to the muscles, so that contractions can always be maximal. "Exogenous" means from outside the body — instead of the electrical stimulation coming from the person's own brain via the nerves, it would be supplied via this machine. [Ziegler] had three different size pads for different size muscle groups, and one pad, for instance, would wrap around the biceps. The technician would hold this pad on the biceps while you'd be lying on this table covered with a towel soaked in a saline solution; a liquid containing salt such as sea water, which has a relation to conduction of electrical current. Dr. Ziegler claimed the saline was his own special solution; that it was exactly the same solution as was inside the interstitial fluid of the muscle in the body. There was a current control dial on the machine with numbers ranging from one to twelve — twelve being the highest. As you turned this dial up towards twelve, the electrical stimulus going into the muscle would increase. That stimulated the muscle to contract, and the contraction would

become harder and harder in intensity. This would happen until finally every single muscle cell within that given muscle would be activated. Through normal conscious direction, only on the order of thirty percent of a single muscle might be stimulated at one time. With this machine, again, you don't have that shortcoming. You can stimulate one hundred percent of that muscle, and surrounding muscles, even at one time.[20]

Ziegler's primary motive in creating the machine had been to stimulate and rehabilitate the muscles of injured athletes and those who were handicapped or had lost the use of certain limbs. He hired Mike to assist him in treating those most in need of such therapy.[21] Word about the new contraption quickly spread throughout Maryland and surrounding regions, and soon the local press came calling. When it was discovered that Mike was also using the machine for bodybuilding purposes, their curiosity was piqued:

But like a hero with a secret weapon, Mike Mentzer is not counting on his barbells alone. Twice a week, he drives out to Olney and the very rural office of Dr. John Ziegler, physical medicine specialist and inventor of something called the Isotron Mark VIII. "Without that machine," he says, "it might take me eight years to reach my maximum potential. With it, I'll do it in three. It's something I have that the others don't. It can push you over the top." Mike Mentzer, however, has no qualms at all about the Isotron Mark VIII. Seated on a table, he puts the small pad connected to the machine by a long cord on his calf muscle and within seconds it pops up like a slice of toasted bread, hard as rock. For $15, which gives him eight to fifteen minutes on the machine, he gets what he feels is the equivalent of three to five hours with weights. "It's not magic, it can't get you to outstrip your hereditary, genetic potential," he says, "but it gets you there faster." And getting there, getting the best possible body in the shortest possible time, is just what Mike Mentzer wants.[22]

To Mike, he was simply making use of a new advance in science. It was the same way he viewed his ingestion of anabolic steroids;[23] the hormones were an advancement in the science of biochemistry that would aid a bodybuilder in his quest to build larger and stronger muscles. Similarly, using Nautilus machines was only taking advantage of a technology that permitted one to train a muscle through its fullest possible range of motion, rather than making do with a barbell that only provided effective resistance to muscles throughout but one part of their range of motion.[24] From Mike's perspective, the Isotron Mark VIII was a scientific device that allowed a trainee to overcome the motivational shortcomings of the human psyche in outputting the physical effort and energy required to stimulate an adaptive response from one's body. Mike believed that one should make use of such scientific options in the pursuit of one's goals — or at least a rational bodybuilder should. "The guy who trains the smartest wins," he said.[25]

He had reason to feel this way. After all, belief in the wonders and power of science was on the rise. The 20th century had already witnessed the creation of insulin, television, penicillin, the airplane, the electron microscope, the jet engine, the helicopter, the first electronic digital computer, the kidney dialysis machine, synthetic cortisone, contact lenses, the microwave oven, nuclear power, space flight. Apollo lunar landings were almost commonplace, with no fewer than six having occurred between 1969 and 1972.[26] This was science. This was progress. This was the future. In Mike's opinion, those who ignored scientific breakthroughs, who instead opted to embrace tradition in their bodybuilding pursuits, were simply Luddites who badly needed to update their calendars to the 20th century.

A name that Dr. Ziegler mentioned repeatedly to Mike during their time together was that of Dr. Hans Selye, a scientist and professor at McGill University in Montreal. According to Ziegler, Selye's pioneering studies on the physiology of stress had a tremendous impact on the doctor's understanding of how the human body worked. Moreover, Ziegler confessed, it was Selye's research that was responsible for shaping his own views on training and the use of the Isotron Mark VIII.[27] Not long afterward, while browsing in a secondhand bookstore, Mike happened upon Selye's book *The Stress of Life*. He immediately purchased it, took it home, and read it cover to cover.[28] By the time he had finished reading, he saw a direct connection between the science of stress physiology and bodybuilding.[29]

Selye revealed that irrespective of what the stressor was that acted upon the body, be it pleasant or unpleasant (and everything was a stressor, according to Selye), the body responded in *exactly the same way*. Its initial reaction was a stage of alarm during the application of the stressor. This was followed by a stage of resistance, during which there was a biochemical call to arms, so to speak, as the body attempted to defend itself against the stressor. And, if the stressor persisted, it would eventually overwhelm the body's resistance, causing it to enter a stage of exhaustion, whereupon a breakdown within the body occurred. Again, this was a universal phenomenon (or syndrome) and applied to any stressor, from a virus to exercise.

Mike noted two examples where this occurrence clearly took place. The first was the body's reaction to ultraviolet sunlight; the second, the skin's reaction to friction. In the first instance, being exposed to ultraviolet sunlight, the body immediately mobilized its forces and began to produce melanin as a protective pigment against the intensity of the sun's rays. However, if one stayed out in that sunlight too long, the body quickly entered a stage of exhaustion, and rather than the formation of a tan (the protective barrier), the skin would burn, blister, and break down. In the case of friction, the alarm reaction corresponded again to the application of the stressor; say, the palm of one's hand rubbing against the wooden handle of a shovel while digging a hole. During the body's stage of resistance, the body would produce a protective barrier of tissue, a callus. However, if the friction continued beyond this point, the callus would become a blister and there would be a tissue breakdown (a stage of exhaustion).

Mike saw that a similar situation existed when one exercised a particular muscle. Initially, the stressor of exercise caused the body to go into an alarm reaction; more fibers were recruited and fatigued. During the stage of resistance, the body would defend itself by building up or enlarging upon its existing level of muscle tissue, much like the skin would build up a callus to protect itself from the stressor of friction. If, however, the exercise was carried on for too long, if too many sets of exercise were performed for too many days in a row, there would be a breakdown. Rather than building muscle, the body would continually be losing energy and breaking down muscle fibers, which would result in the muscle becoming weaker and smaller.

Even more interestingly, if the intensity of the stressor that was brought to bear on the body was too low, such as if one went out into the ultraviolet sunlight in November, one could tolerate such exposure for hours, even days.

The body would not even need to enter an alarm stage, and the adaptation process would not be triggered. To one seeking to develop a suntan, this would be the wrong stimulus, as it was insufficiently intense to trigger the desired adaptive response. By contrast, stepping out into the ultraviolet sunlight in summer brings about an immediate alarm reaction, and one has to be extremely cautious not to overexpose oneself to the ultraviolet rays for fear of entering the stage of exhaustion. To the same suntan seeker, this would be the proper stimulus, but it could not be tolerated for very long. Considering this, it was obvious that the intensity of the stressor was key in whether or not the General Adaptation Syndrome was triggered into motion — whether for developing a suntan or larger and stronger muscles.[30]

Seeking additional support for this phenomenon as it pertained to bodybuilding, Mike started reading physiology textbooks, particularly textbooks that examined the role of intensity in the muscle growth process. Foremost among the researchers was Arthur Steinhaus, an exercise science professor from Chicago.[31] Steinhaus had traced the history and studies conducted on the principle of intensity in stimulating strength adaptations. Mike's eyes were opened even wider by what he read:

- "Muscles hypertrophy in proportion not to total work done but to the intensity factor, i.e., work done in a unit of time."[32]
- "Muscles grow larger and stronger when they are 'overloaded,' i.e., made to carry loads greater than ordinary. Thus hypertrophy is related primarily to the intensity of exercise, not to its duration."[33]
- "As early as 1905, Roux observed that the muscles of various athletes differed and that not all muscles in one athlete were equally large. He postulated that the size and strength of muscles were related not to the total amount of work done but rather to the amount of work done in a unit of time, i.e., to the intensity factor. This is well illustrated in the muscles of the miler and sprinter. The miler does more work than the sprinter but, in comparing intensities, the 10-second man runs 30 ft. per second and the four-minute miler only 22 ft. per second. Therefore, the sprinter has larger muscles."[34]

What Mike was seeing in the scientific literature were scientific principles; specifically, the principles of intensity and adaptation. What he wasn't seeing in the scientific literature were any references whatsoever to Joe Weider, Dan Lurie, or Bob Hoffman. When he looked into nutritional science textbooks, once again not one bodybuilding publisher was referenced. There was no mention of "Crash Weight Gain Formula #7" or "Protein from the Sea." In fact, there wasn't a particular emphasis on the need for any supplemental protein at all.[35] "At this point the muscle magazines ceased to be any authority at all in my mind," Mike recalled.[36] "The works of Hans Selye, Wilhelm Reich, Arthur Steinhaus, and Per-Olof Åstrand became my constant companions, slowly pushing the piles of muscle magazines into the corner. At this point, too, I began to realize that proper nutrition was a lot more than just stuffing myself with protein. Now the nutrition books moved in, and the muscle magazines were stored away. [Medical researcher] Ronald Deutsch and [nutritional scientist] Jean Mayer vied with the exercise physiologists for my time, and my training bag had more books than clothes in it."[37]

Mike's research into the science of exercise impressed Dr. DeVore, who asked Mike if there was any evidence of resistance training producing a cardiovascular effect. DeVore's patients suffered from a variety of health issues, ranging from obesity to high blood pressure, and high-impact activities such as jogging simply weren't options. It just so happened that Mike was reading the work of Swedish physiologist, Dr. Per-Olof Åstrand, who had written: "The cardiac output at a given submaximal oxygen uptake is in many types of exercise similar . . ."[38]

If the above was true, would the muscular demands of weight training suffice to produce a cardiovascular effect? Mike found the answer in another bit of research that had been conducted by Dr. James Peterson at West Point Military Academy in 1974.

The study was a game changer. Dr. Peterson selected 21 athletes from the academy's varsity football team. Using ten Nautilus machines (and only Nautilus machines), the subjects were instructed to train intensely enough to elevate their pulse rates and to move with minimal rest from machine to machine so that their pulse rates remained elevated throughout the training session. The sessions were repeated three days per week on alternate days. After six weeks, Dr. Peterson tabled the data. The results were shocking:

> It was demonstrated that a strength-training program, when properly conducted can have a positive effect on the central components of physical fitness. Contrary to widespread opinion,

not only will . . . strength training produce increases in muscular strength but will also significantly improve an individual's level of cardiovascular conditioning. The data suggests that some of these cardiovascular benefits apparently cannot be achieved by any other type of training.[39]

Armed with the data from doctors Steinhaus, Åstrand, and Peterson, Mike went to Dr. DeVore and presented his evidence in support of starting a resistance training program for his patients. The doctor recognized that Mike was onto something. They initiated a training program for DeVore's patients that was designed and carried out under Mike's supervision. The program proved a tremendous success. "Without exception," Mike said, "there was a marked increase in the cardiovascular fitness level of the people in the program. One 60-year-old man actually doubled his fitness level in only two months."[40]

Mike was now even more convinced that science — not tradition — was the future, and, as the 1976 Mr. America contest was fast approaching, he brought the science he had learned into the gym with him. Dr. DeVore recalled that "because of the fact that his responsibilities as a pre-med student (and hopefully as a medical student in the near future), as well as his duties as a cardiopulmonary lab technician would predictably demand more and more of his time, he felt that 1976 would be a 'now-or-never' year in his quest for the Bodybuilding Championship of America."[41]

The doctor was right. Mike was at a crossroads; his academic workload was only going to increase — and bodybuilding wasn't paying the bills.

CHAPTER THIRTEEN

MUSCLES, MASCULINITY, AND MR. AMERICA

All of Mike's energy and what little spare time he had were devoted to his preparation for the Mr. America contest — and facing Roger Callard again. But his devotion to his studies, to his jobs, and to his girlfriend had paced him out of step with the rest of the bodybuilders who worked out at Spartan Health Club:

> One day I overheard a chance remark by one of the bodybuilders at the gym where I trained: "That Mentzer sure ain't one of the boys." One of the boys? Although I had always felt that I was different from my friends, I had never actually pinpointed the difference. Now, however, faced with the offhand verdict, I began to wonder what it meant. As time went on, I began to see evidence in everything I did that I was not, in fact, one of the boys, had never been one of the boys, and had absolutely no desire to ever be one of the boys. I had always been a loner, preferring my own company to group activities of any kind. Whenever the guys at the gym tried to get me to go carousing and skirt-chasing, it seemed I always declined. I either stayed home with a book or went out with a girl, just the two of us. Then when Monday evenings rolled around and the boys congregated at the gym, they would turn the air of the locker room blue with their lurid accounts of bottles emptied and nubile girls debauched. For all I know some of it might even have been true. But true or not, that kind of talk had always

struck me as the lowest of low rent. I kept my trap shut, and my taciturn manner set me off further from the boys.[1]

Mike had studied enough psychology by now to recognize the Type A personalities who hung out in the gym, and who associated their vision of masculinity with the number of women they had slept with, how big their arms were, and how many strokes to their egos they had received, and who always seemed to be after more power (particularly over others), possessions, and money. To settle for obtaining merely a modest measure of such things was never enough; whenever a summit was reached in any of these areas, dissatisfaction set in. Their identity and sense of masculinity was bound up in the process of acquiring more.[2]

Such a limited concept of masculinity was foreign to Mike's psyche. "This kind of imbalance in the male personality serves neither the individual nor society," he said. "Quite often individuals indulging in exclusively masculine behavior are seeking to prove their self-worth with little or no regard for authentic self-expression. While this person may be thought of as traditionally masculine, he may not necessarily be characterized as psychologically strong. This type of personality is most often emotionally impoverished, incapable of expressing love or affection and missing out on the subjective side of human nature."[3] Some years later, Mike wrote an article on this topic that warned young bodybuilders that looking to him (or others) for their sense of masculinity was a mistake:

> A man can spend his entire life compulsively engaging in activities that prove his masculinity. When a bodybuilder must reassure himself again and again with his muscles and his victories, his body becomes a crutch. So long as he continues to look outside himself, he will never satisfy his need to prove himself a man. His only salvation lies in being able to reject these "false gods" and have the courage to look inward. A great deal of strength is required for a male to end his search for identity, listen to his inner voices and decide what makes him happy. Rather than try to become masculine, which is to try to become something outside himself, a truly strong man will look at the richness and texture of his own experience and from that create the kind of person he wants to be, to become

more of the person he already is. While the ability to please women, make pots of money and have muscles up to the eyeballs may be proof of a certain degree of external mastery and hence masculinity, the individual must ask himself what he has done to cultivate inner mastery. Does he, for instance, have a solid sense of who he is? Does he acknowledge his need for interrelatedness, for touching, for helping others and the need to be helped by others? How well does he stand up under stress?

A man that spends all his time tending his muscles while allowing "inner landscape" to lie fallow will inevitably end up spiritually bereft, unable to enjoy the fruits of his labor. He must be free to choose his lifestyle and individual mode of expressing his masculinity. Lasting health and happiness will only be his when the individual successfully integrates external mastery with inner skills. If this article did not create a new concept of masculinity, it's because every man must find his own.[4]

It was evident to all who crossed his path that Mike Mentzer was a different breed of bodybuilder. He was cerebral and self-confident. At this point in his life, his mother's affliction was keeping its distance. He believed in himself and in his ability to think clearly and logically. It was a mindset that he brought with him to the gym. During the winter of 1976, with brother Ray as his training partner, Mike hit the iron ferociously. Soon he was performing 1,200-pound leg presses, squats with 565 pounds, 300-pound presses behind neck, 460-pound bench presses, 385-pound incline presses, and 600-pound deadlifts.[5] He trained quickly, with minimal rest between exercises, recognizing that time (per Arthur Steinhaus's teachings) was an important factor in the intensity of his workouts. Recalling Steinhaus's sprinter analogy, he decided to move as quickly as possible between exercises for the greatest metabolic effect:

> I liken my training to that of a sprinter. I train fast, of course, and as heavy as possible, in as short a period as I can manage. Sprinters carry their bodyweight over a distance of, say, a hundred yards in a short time . . . as short a time as they

can. While I am not running, I nevertheless move heavy weights distances, as fast as possible. The intensity is actually greater than the sprinter's, on account of the fact that I can adjust the amount of weight used; the sprinter moves only his bodyweight. I can increase my training poundage — the training intensity — at will. Intensity is a function of power input. You move weight distances in a certain amount of time. So, if you can increase the weight, increase the distance, and decrease the speed, well, then you'll be increasing your power input geometrically.[6]

He shared his workout records (weights, repetitions, sets, and workout duration) with Dr. DeVore. The doctor plugged the data into a spreadsheet to obtain a pounds-per-hour calculus to objectively measure Mike's progress:

Mike Mentzer's usual exercise training schedule (i.e., prior to the eight-month period before the October 1, 1976, contest) consisted of three or four sessions per week, each lasting about two hours. He would lift a total of about 20 tons of weight during each two-hour session. His goal during the eight months prior to the 1976 contest was to double the intensity of each of his exercise sessions! With this stated goal in mind, he was eventually able to increase the intensity of his workouts to the point that he was lifting 40 tons per hour![7]

Mike's motivation for training received a considerable boost when the April 1976 edition of *Muscle Builder/Power* hit the stands. A friend told him that he'd seen the issue — and that Mike was on the cover! Mike was stunned. He rushed to the nearest newsstand and purchased several copies[8] and then ran back to his apartment in College Park to telephone Joe Weider:

As it turned out, one of those photos from Russ's photo session ended up on the cover of *Muscle Builder*. I was ecstatic. I didn't know it was going to be on the cover; I don't think Joe told me it would be. But it did, and I remember being at the newsstand in Washington, DC, and running home and calling Joe and thanking him for it.[9]

Joe attempted to capitalize on the young man's enthusiasm: he extended an invitation for Mike to move to California, to join the Weider team, just as Arnold and Franco had. To the Master Blaster's surprise, however, Mike turned him down. His priority was to get into medical school.[10] Even Joe Weider had to respect the young man's decision. Besides, there was no shortage of bodybuilders in Southern California who were hungry for publicity and who would endorse any of Joe's products sight unseen in exchange for exposure in his magazine. Upon hanging up the phone, Mike once again leafed through the magazine. To his delight, he discovered that not only did he appear on its cover, but also in a four-page spread containing the interview he did the previous September with Gene Mozee. This was heady stuff for a 24-year-old college student in Maryland. "It was the greatest inspiration I could receive," he recalled. "It really fired me up!"[11]

Approximately 2,296 miles away to the northwest, a 21-year-old sports reporter for the *Albertan* (now the *Calgary Sun*), Jack Neary, was reading the same issue. He didn't share Mike's enthusiasm:

> I remember the first impression Mentzer made upon me. Of course, I did not know him when I first heard of him — he was on the east coast in Maryland, and I was a mere bodybuilding fan in Canada. Mentzer appeared on the cover of *Muscle Builder* magazine in the late spring of 1976. His countenance and massive torso graced the inaugural issue of the "new look" *Muscle Builder*.
>
> The photograph showed Mentzer in light blue posing trunks. He was in a rather relaxed posture with his fists turned knuckles-in at his sides. A striking portrait, appearing at a time when Mentzer had hardly cracked the social register of the sport. "Who is this guy?" I remember asking myself. There was a cocky tilt to his head and a look of confidence on his face. It made me uncomfortable, as I recall, to see a cover man of whom I knew nothing. The story inside proved even more disturbing, for it quoted Mentzer saying in one year he would beat Arnold.[12] My hero. The article was about Mentzer's rather iconoclastic training system. So outrageous did his three-sets-per-bodypart routine seem to me that I actually laughed aloud and took it all as a bad joke: I mean, one just couldn't build muscle

doing 20-minute workouts only three times per week. How were we to take this bit of news when Arnold and Franco and half a dozen other Weider boys had been extolling the virtues of the double split 20-set-per-bodypart system on the pages of the very same journal for years? Not very seriously, I should think. My introduction to Mike Mentzer, via the columns of *Muscle Builder*, did not rest easy in the brain pan. Not only did he challenge everything I had thought to be correct about training, but he suggested the reigning king of the sport, Arnold Schwarzenegger, was no further away from him than a year's worth of this foolish training.

"Another cocky east coast guy," was my first impression.[13]

Who would have known that a year later Jack would be sleeping on a couch in Mike's apartment and be the top writer for Joe Weider's magazine?

Ray Mentzer's interest in competitive bodybuilding had returned. Despite Ray having only competed twice in his life, Mike's placing at the 1975 Mr. America had inspired him. Ray's first contest, six years previously, was the AAU Teen Mr. America contest, where he had finished a distant tenth behind Mike (who placed second) and (then) newcomer Lou Ferrigno (who finished fourth).[14] He entered the Mr. USA contest in 1975, along with Mike, but failed to crack the top five in the Tall Division. However, seeing the progress his brother had made over the past year, and how Mike's picture now adorned the cover of *Muscle Builder/Power* magazine, Ray thought bodybuilding competition was worth another shot. He told Mike that he wanted to enter the forthcoming 1976 Mr. America contest alongside him. Mike offered encouragement; he explained the whys and wherefores underlying the high-intensity training approach he was using, in addition to sharing his diet methods and steroid regimen. "My enthusiasm for bodybuilding rekindled, I resumed serious training, intent on becoming a top bodybuilder," Ray recalled.[15]

The hardest part of Mike's workouts was summoning the motivation required to push each set of every exercise to the maximum. To surmount this mental obstacle, he did what he could to cultivate a high-intensity mindset. He listened to music that psyched him up — rock music, such as that of

Led Zepplin, or classical music, such as Wagner or Tchaikovsky, seemed to do the trick. He read authors such as Jack London, who wrote stories of human beings grappling with nature and the great efforts of will they put forth in their struggles.[16] And then there was Nietzsche. The latter's "superman theory" leapt from the pages of his books and struck a resonant chord within the young man's soul.[17] Nietzsche's admonitions to surmount the group, the mass of mediocrity, to become what you are fully capable of, his praise of individualism and the will to power, Mike found to be particularly helpful and, above all, inspiring.[18] Augmenting the writings of the Good European were the writings of Dr. Maxwell Maltz in his book *Psycho-Cybernetics*, which indicated that one could actually program one's mind through techniques such as visualization to become successful in any chosen field of endeavor. Mike was particularly struck by this passage:

> Experimental and clinical psychologists have proved beyond a shadow of a doubt that the human nervous system cannot tell the difference between an "actual" experience and an experience imagined vividly and in detail.[19]

What further appealed about Maltz's theories was the fact that the doctor based certain of them on the research of Hans Selye. Mike employed Maltz's visualization technique while lying in bed every night before he went to sleep. He visualized his ceiling as a movie screen and saw projected upon it images of himself growing stronger, lifting heavier weights in his workouts, and, ultimately, winning the Mr. America contest. He continued to do this until the images became so real that he believed that he had willed the wish into reality.[20] Such ultra-intense mental focus resulted in ultra-intense workouts, which, in turn, resulted in a startling transformation in Mike's physique. According to one newspaper report: "His thighs increased from 25 to 27 inches: calves from 17.5 to 19 inches: biceps from 19 to 20.5 inches."[21]

This was all well and good, but it meant nothing to Roger Callard. During a conversation with Jack Neary three weeks prior to the contest, he claimed that he didn't consider Mike Mentzer to be a threat at all. "I'm not even worried about him," he'd said. "I've already beaten Mentzer twice before. He shouldn't be hard to beat again."[22] Danny Padilla, however, had a different take. "Padilla held Mentzer in higher esteem," Jack reported, "and had mentioned, in his own quiet way, that Mentzer would be the biggest challenge."[23] By the time the Mentzer brothers arrived in New York for the contest, it didn't matter what the individual competitors' opinions were; it was now up to the judging panel.

The competition was held on October 2 at the Felt Forum in Madison Square Garden, perhaps the most impressive sporting and entertainment venue in the western world.[24] It was home to the New York Rangers of the NHL and the New York Knicks of the NBA, it was where Muhammad Ali and Joe Frazier had slugged it out in what had been dubbed "The Fight of the Century," and both Elvis and John Lennon had performed on its stage.[25] For Mike, the venue was light years removed from competing in the Wharton Elementary School auditorium in Lancaster County, where he had won his first bodybuilding contest only six years previously.

Arnold Schwarzenegger also made his way to the Big Apple to serve as one of the judges at the competition. He was fresh from his first promotion of the Mr. Olympia contest with partner Jim Lorimer in Columbus, Ohio, which had taken place only two weeks previously.[26] The 1976 Olympia was a success, despite the sport's biggest stars being absent. Arnold, of course, had retired, Lou Ferrigno had quit bodybuilding to play football,[27] and Serge Nubret had received a four-year suspension immediately after *Pumping Iron* had wrapped.[28] The Frenchman was also stripped of his executive position as vice president of the IFBB.[29] The removal of these three bodybuilders from the competitive ranks left a gaping hole in the talent roster. The Heavyweight Division of the Mr. Olympia featured journeymen Mike Katz and Ken Waller, but they didn't possess the kind of physique that would captivate a hard-core bodybuilding public. Still, the show went on. To nobody's surprise, the contest boiled down to Frank Zane versus Franco Columbu. Both were impressive bodybuilders, to be certain, but not ones who moved the electricity meter all that much. As Franco had finished second to his best friend Arnold in 1975, and as Arnold was co-promoter of the contest (and thus the one who selected its judging panel), not to mention that Franco was being heavily publicized in Joe's magazines, his being declared the winner of the 1976 Mr. Olympia was pretty much a foregone conclusion.

However, at least one of the judges was surprised at the result:

> Jacques Blommaert of Belgium, a contest judge with 25 years' experience disclosed that though he and his brother Julian, also a top judge, had had a falling-out with Zane a few years

ago, a niggling rift at best, he still scored Zane high: 18 to 17 for Zane over Columbu in the first scoring round, and 19 to 19 for both in the final round — an edge of one point in favor of Zane. "Personal relationships do not interfere with my judging," says the popular Belgian gym operator. "I feel secure in my choice. I know that two other judges also voted for Zane. Personally, I feel the title belonged to Zane."[30]

Shortly after Jack Neary had made the move from Canada to California to work as a writer for *Muscle Builder/Power*, he was dispatched to the east coast to cover the Mr. America contest. There were worse places to go for a weekend. After checking into his Manhattan hotel, Jack made his way over to Madison Square Garden to check out the goings-on amongst the competitors who had already gathered within a large room in the bowels of the building to change and prepare for the competition. He spotted Roger Callard, along with Danny Padilla. Both were seated talking with two other bodybuilders, only one of whom Jack recognized. That was Ken Covington, a bodybuilder who placed second to Robby Robinson in the Medium Class at the 1975 IFBB Mr. World contest.[31] The mystery man was a competitor whom Jack described simply as a "massive guy in a blue sweatsuit."[32]

"Hey man," Covington said to Callard, "just wait till you see me this year. I've got something special for you. When you see me, you better be worried!"

Callard smirked. "Yeah, you looked good last year, but you've got to work on those calves. Get yourself some calves." With that Callard pulled his pant leg up and revealed what Jack described as "a giant, flexed parasite hanging from his shin."

"Somehow my calves just don't want to grow," Callard said sarcastically.

"That isn't a *calf*, that's a *cow*," said the massive guy in the blue sweatsuit.[33]

This caused Jack to chuckle. It was an apt metaphor. At this point, a contest official asked the man in the blue sweatsuit what his measurements were.

"My arm taped is 20½ inches — cold. Calves are 19 inches."

The official scribbled the information dutifully onto a sheet of paper on his clipboard.

"Thanks Mike," he said.

Jack raised an eyebrow. "So, this is Mike Mentzer," he thought to himself.

Soon it was time for the prejudging. Forty competitors in three different weight classes were vying for the title.[34] One of them was Mike's good friend Dave Mastorakis, who had switched over to Mike's high-intensity training program as a result of their correspondence two years previously.[35] Jack believed Danny Padilla was a shoo-in for the title — at least prior to the prejudging. He changed his mind when Mike walked out on stage. "Audible gasps came from people's mouths as they first saw Mentzer," he wrote. "He was in tremendous condition. He had excelled far beyond the condition we saw him in on the cover of the magazine."[36] A man seated next to Jack at the contest pointed at Mike's calves and yelled, "Look at those calves! The best calves in the world!" While Mike's calf muscles struck Jack as being big, he didn't believe that they were the best on the planet — and told the man so. Unfortunately, he said this within earshot of Cathy Gelfo, who proceeded to burn a hole through the back of the young reporter's head with her eyes. "My suggestion that Mentzer's calves were not the greatest this end of the universe left me open to a good deal of psychic malcontent and bombardment from Cathy," Jack recalled.[37] She would tell him two years later that she hated him for an entire year for what he said about Mike's calves. Jack took it in stride as part of the job. "I have learned to limit my criticism of Mentzer to moments when she is beyond hearing range," he said. "One can only withstand so much psychic weaponry, and Cathy wields her fair share."

Seated next to Jack was Arnold Schwarzenegger, who felt compelled to tug on the reporter's arm as Mike was posing and whisper, "Look at that! Look at the way he hits his side chest pose — so basic, so pure!"[38] High praise, indeed coming from the bodybuilder who was said to "own" this very pose. By the time the evening finals rolled around, the crowd, which Jack reckoned totaled approximately 2,500,[39] was electric. The Short Class was won by Danny Padilla, with Arizona's Carlos Rodriguez placing second and Dave Mastorakis placing third.[40] Next came the prejudging for the Medium Class. The energy from the crowd when Mike Mentzer and Roger Callard walked out on stage was palpable. It was clear that Mike's previous losses to Callard didn't mean a thing. As Jack reported:

> Mike Mentzer created a small sensation amongst the sparse gathering at the prejudging. The evening show performance had a crowd of about 2,500 literally sucking in gulps of air in amazement. He was every bit as thick as he was reputed to be and more. I had been spending much time before this contest

with Roger Callard, quietly marveling at his condition and wondering how anyone could possibly beat him for Medium Class honors. But next to Mentzer, Callard looked thin. Please allow for hyperbole . . . in terms of muscle size and thickness Mentzer breezed the class. Callard, who had been dieting strictly the past week, appeared to have smoothed out thanks to an improperly gauged zero carbohydrate diet. Two days before in his Santa Monica apartment, Callard whipped off his jersey and displayed an intricate network of cuts, striations and veins zigzagging freelance across his golden set of lumps. But in a last-second quest for an extra cut or two, the poor guy went flat. And it showed oh so sorely at the prejudging . . . after losing to Roger two times before, Mike Mentzer looked every inch a winner.[41]

After the prejudging, Danny Padilla overheard Arnold berating Callard, stating "Mentzer blew your shit away!"[42] The former Mr. Olympia winner was not happy about this, but in the end, Arnold was the only judge to give Callard a first-place vote; the other eight judges awarded their first-place votes to Mike Mentzer, making him the winner of the Medium Division.[43]

That didn't stop Arnold from asserting his influence over the judges when the Tall Class — with Ray Mentzer — took to the stage.[44] Mike looked on from the wings as his little brother more than held his own against the best bodybuilders in his class.[45] Bodybuilding scribe Rick Wayne felt obliged to state:

> No doubt about it, the 1976 IFBB American Championships were dominated by the Mentzers. The whole thing turned out to be little more than a showcase for Mike and Ray Mentzer, an opportunity to show off the results of their scientific bodybuilding endeavours.[46]

But it was not to be. Jack reported that:

> At only 21 years of age, Florida's [Jorge] Navarette. . . . had already won the support of muscle main man Schwarzenegger, whose telling influence over the judges' panel earned Navarette the enviable tour de force of winning the Most Muscular award.

"I told the judges to watch this kid's most muscular pose, it looked that good," explains Schwarzenegger. "After they saw that pose, we all decided unanimously." ... Navarette, whose intelligence gives the sport an enlightening prospect, battled to a close victory over Mentzer's "little" brother Ray.[47]

Navarette might well have won the division without Arnold's help, but "a close victory" may have just been close enough to go the other way had Arnold not opted to direct the judges' attention his way. Nevertheless, in only his second bodybuilding competition in six years, Ray could take some pride in finishing second in his height class. The final placings for the overall title of Mr. America were then announced. As reported by Jack Neary:

> Mike Mentzer, if Thornton Wilder will pardon me, nipped Padilla for the overall title by the skin of his teeth! Only a ½ point separated them. While it was not announced in what order the runners-up finished, it was assumed that Roger Callard placed third and [Jorge] Navarette fourth.[48]

Mike Mentzer was Mr. America.

So many memories now flashed through his mind: he saw his 15-year-old self, scribbling down the bodybuilding titles he intended to win in the margin of *Muscle Builder/Power*, and his 20-year-old self in the gym, injuring his shoulder. He reflected on his research into muscle physiology, psychology, and philosophy — all in the quest to bring science out of the classroom and into the gym. He recalled his two failed attempts — four years apart — at winning this contest, and his persistence to keep trying. And then he looked at the trophy that had been placed at his feet and found himself fighting back tears:

> I can remember, even before they called my name out, knowing I was going to win. And I felt the emotion welling up in my chest and I had to really keep myself from crying. It was such an exciting moment. And I remember standing on stage and being very, very aware of everything that was going on; the audience, the people behind me. And making a definite attempt to never forget this moment — every impression: sights,

sounds, smell, everything — and I still have that impressed on my mind. That exact moment, everything, the feeling... it was great.[49]

Winning the Mr. America title meant that Mike was eligible to compete in the IFBB World Championships (previously known as the Mr. Universe). In fact, not only was he eligible to compete at the contest, but he was also expected to. The MC told the crowd that Mike, along with Danny Padilla and Robby Robinson, would form Team USA for the World Championships, which were to be held in Montreal in four weeks' time.

But that was still a month away. Right now, after four months of dieting, all Mike Mentzer wanted was something to eat.

CHAPTER FOURTEEN

DESTINY BECKONS

As soon as the Mr. America contest concluded, Jack Neary was backstage looking to get some statements from the competitors for his report. He spotted Mike Mentzer and approached the new champion, notebook in hand. Jack had no intention of leading with a softball question, such as "How does it feel to win Mr. America?" He had a more direct query in mind.

"Do you still think you can beat Arnold in a year?"

Mike suddenly straightened up.

"Ah . . . well, I might have been a little hasty in saying that."[1]

Both men laughed. It was, to borrow from Bogey in *Casablanca*, the beginning of a beautiful friendship. "I really liked Mike," Jack recalled. "I was really impressed by his intelligence, his sound thinking. He's an incredibly good speaker, he expresses himself so well, so logically, so clearly — which is unusual for a lot of athletes. I remember warming to Mike right from the beginning."[2] Danny Padilla appeared and shook Mike's hand.

"Look, didn't I tell you Mentzer would be the man to watch?"[3]

The trio continued to converse for several minutes until Jack was satisfied that he had sufficient material from them to flesh out his article. He then moved on to interview some of the other competitors.

Mike made his way to the competitors' room, changed into his street clothes, and then made his way to the lobby of Madison Square Garden to hook up with Cathy. As the pair were heading for the exit, they were approached by Arnold Schwarzenegger. Arnold offered his congratulations; the two men shook hands and then went their separate ways.[4] The first meeting between the two was over almost as soon as it began. Once outside, Mike and Cathy made their way to the nearest restaurant. Mike was ravenous.

Eight months out from the contest, Mike weighed 232 pounds. At that point he was ingesting 4,500 calories a day and his bodyfat was hovering around 22 percent. Four months later, he began his competition diet, using a special nomogram that factored in his age, height, and weight, and reduced his calorie intake to 2,575 a day — exactly 1,000 calories below what he had calculated his maintenance level of calories to be.[5] In a severe calorie deficit, the body will lose a combination of fat and muscle; however, the steroids Mike consumed served to preserve and even build his muscle mass while dieting, so that most of the weight Mike lost was bodyfat. He once told the author:

> I've tried dieting without steroids and have lost as much as nine pounds in one week, a certain amount of which was muscle. On steroids, I'd gain two pounds the first week — even though I was on low calories and losing fat. I'd end up losing the same amount of fat ultimately, without losing the pounds, which meant I was gaining some muscle mass at the same time. That phenomenon first manifested itself back in 1976, when I was training for the Mr. America. The previous year I'd entered at 196 pounds — ripped — and got third place behind Robby [Robinson] and Roger Callard, and I was considered a favorite for the next year. I assumed that in order to be improved and still be cut the next year, I'd probably have to weigh around 202 pounds, so I started my dieting six weeks in advance [at a bodyweight of] 216. Three weeks later, after three weeks of starving — at that time I was on zero carbs — I still weighed 216. I thought, "What am I going to do? I'm starving, I'm training, and I'm not losing any fat!" In fact, I was gaining muscular mass at the same time.[6]

Three months later, Mike's bodyfat was down to 12 percent. With one month to go until the contest, he reduced his calories again — markedly. Living on approximately 600 calories a day, on a diet which consisted of two or three ten-ounce cans of "Nature's Inn Protein Density Drink," three to six ounces of broiled fish or chicken, Theragen-M (a prescription multi-vitamin used to prevent vitamin deficiency), vitamin-mineral supplements, two tablets of dolomite, and 40 mEq of potassium chloride,[7] it was a bland existence — but it worked. By the end of the month, Mike was down to 209 pounds and his bodyfat, according to Dr. DeVore, "reached a level that made conversion from existing tables impossible, but we estimated that his total body fat couldn't be more than two percent on the basis of these skin fold measurements."[8]

Now that the contest was over, however, so was the dieting — and every cell in Mike's body was now crying out for the macronutrients they had been denied for the past month. Finding a restaurant, Mike and Cathy sidled into a booth together. Within minutes, Mike had polished off two slices of cheesecake and six heaping scoops of ice cream.[9] He knew he couldn't indulge this recklessly for long, however — not if he wanted to have any chance of defeating Robby Robinson at the World Championships in four weeks' time.

News of Mike's Mr. America win spread quickly; articles appeared in the nation's newspapers from New York to Texas over the next eight months.[10] Even his father called to offer congratulations. But the chasm between Harry and his son hadn't been bridged. "It's a point of everlasting grudge," Mike said. "It's very easy to support a winner. But when I needed the support, it was withdrawn."[11] But this didn't prevent a Lancaster County contingent consisting of Harry, his brother Charles, and Charles's son, Sid, from attending the World Championships on November 5 in Montreal to lend emotional support. Ray Mentzer also made the trip.[12]

The venue was Montreal's Claude Robillard Centre, which had been constructed especially for the 1976 Summer Olympics.[13] Three thousand fans purchased tickets to witness the competition and a reported 5,000 more were turned away at the door.[14] ABC's *Wide World of Sports* (with Arnold as its in-studio guest) was on hand to televise the event for broadcast throughout North America.[15]

The prejudging proved to be a war of attrition, lasting some seven hours. The evening finals took up four hours.[16] But then, there were athletes from 51 nations competing in the contest.[17] The IFBB instituted new changes to their rules for this contest; there would no longer be an overall winner of the competition. Instead, the winner of each division would be declared "World Champion."[18] But the divisions themselves had changed; whereas in the past the divisions had been arranged according to height (Short, Medium, and Tall), the classes were now demarcated by weight:

- Lightweight — up to and including 75 kilograms.
- Middleweight — over 75 kilograms, up to and including 90 kilograms.
- Heavyweight — over 90 kilograms.[19]

There were 19 competitors in the Middleweight Division alone[20] — the weight class featuring the highly anticipated showdown between Robby Robinson and Mike Mentzer. "I didn't really think that I beat Robby — until that night," Mike recalled. "I thought I'd gotten a greater audience reception and people were coming up — Lou Ferrigno and Boyer Coe — saying, 'Hey you could really win this thing!'"[21] Mike certainly was in great shape; his muscle mass was at a peak, as was his conditioning. But Robby's star within the bodybuilding firmament was on the rise; he had already appeared on the cover of *Muscle Builder* magazine twice and was billed as being a "Weider pupil."[22] Moreover, Robby was always lethal in any competition he entered — and the 1976 World Championships would prove to be no exception. An in-shape Robby was always kryptonite to Mike. "In the back of my mind, and in my heart, I knew there was no way I was going to beat this guy," he said. "Not only did I think he looked better, but he was getting all the publicity. And I noticed that Ben Weider was introducing him to all the Montreal dignitaries in the audience, while he didn't even shake my hand; didn't even recognize my existence."[23]

While it proved to be a close battle, Robby won the Middleweight Class with 188 points. Mike came in second with 185 points. The third member of the American team, Danny Padilla, finished in second place in the Lightweight Class, losing out to Egypt's Mohamed Makkawy.[24] Nevertheless, the U.S. team placed first overall, with second place awarded to Austria, third to Barbados, fourth to Egypt and Australia (a tie), with sixth place awarded to Turkey.[25]

After commiserating briefly with his relatives, Mike was on a plane headed back to Washington, D.C. Robby, the new Middleweight Mr. Universe champion, headed back to California — and a surprisingly uncertain future.

While Robby had been receiving publicity in Joe's magazines, he wouldn't receive anything else. Robby had competed steadily and successfully since 1974. During that time, he won the Mr. Southeastern USA and Mr. USA titles and placed second in his division at the Mr. America contest. Each competition was run under the auspices of the AAU, a rival federation to the Weider's IFBB. However, in 1975 Robby switched allegiances, jumping ship to the IFBB, and promptly won its Mr. America title. He then went on to add the IFBB Mr. Universe trophy to his collection.[26] It was in 1975 that he received a letter from Joe Weider, inviting him to move to California, where he could train among the champions at Gold's Gym.[27] Gold's was where Joe sent the photographers and writers from his magazine to take pictures and interview the bodybuilding champions about their training methods. Robby believed Joe's invitation to be the start of something big; he suspected that he would be offered a contract along the lines of what had been offered to Arnold and Franco. And why wouldn't he? After all, both Arnold and Franco were retired from the sport (Franco immediately after winning the 1976 Mr. Olympia title), which meant that Joe needed to lock up the next bodybuilding sensation. And, with the IFBB Mr. Universe title now in his back pocket, Robby was the logical candidate. "I set up an appointment, I went up to see Joe Weider," he recalled. "And [in] my first indoctrination to bodybuilding, [Joe said] 'I don't give Blacks contracts.[28] Blacks on the covers don't sell magazines.'"[29] Robby was understandably furious. Arnold had a contract, Franco had a contract, and when Robby saw the April 1976 addition of *Muscle Builder* with Mike on its cover, he assumed that Mike had a contract as well. To his mind, Joe had sent Mike to La Belle Province as his Great White Hope:

> Weider needed a new White Hope to compete against me. It would be the big, thick Mike Mentzer. . . . Mike was handsome with his parted-down-the-middle black hair and thick mustache. . . . In 1976, he won the Mr. America contest, competing in the medium weight group. The Chief rolled him out on the cover of *Muscle Builder* and gave Mike and Ray a contract. The Weiders sent Mike to the Universe contest, to go muscle-for-muscle with the Black Prince.[30]

The truth, however, was that Mike didn't have a contract with Joe. All his expenses were paid out of his own pocket with money he earned from the two jobs he was working. While Joe had offered Mike a writing job at his magazine, Mike had turned him down, opting instead to complete his college education. He was on his own. Ray didn't have a job or a contract with Joe Weider either. In fact, he would never be offered one. By 1976, Mike had only appeared on the cover of *Muscle Builder/Power* once and had a single profile piece devoted to him. By contrast, during that same year, Robby was featured on two covers of the magazine, was the subject of four separate profile articles, featured in eight training articles, given considerable photographic and written coverage in six contest reports, had appeared three times in ads for Joe Weider's supplements, and random shots of him were liberally sprinkled throughout the magazine. It certainly appeared that, contract or not, Robby Robinson was being heralded as the new superstar in bodybuilding. Such exposure certainly put his name out there, not only for the fans but for the judges. It was evident that Joe was promoting him heavily. And he was doing so without having to pay the bodybuilder a nickel. Robby knew he was being exploited, but the exposure he was receiving, along with the titles he was winning, kept his anger in check. At least for the time being.

In January of 1977 Mike entered the University of Maryland for his junior year, where he began studying premed with a major in psychiatry.[31] His grade point average was an impressive 3.7 (approximately 92 percent).[32] "I had excellent teachers there," Mike recalled, "especially in genetics, physical chemistry and organic chemistry."[33] He continued to train, but found that whole-body workouts performed three days a week were taking too much time out of his day (two hours per workout) and the energy debt created by such high-intensity workouts left him exhausted to the point that he couldn't get out of a chair immediately after a workout. This was a problem, given that he had work and school and responsibilities. Recalling Hans Selye's tri-phasic model of the General Adaptation Syndrome, Mike recognized that he had entered the "stage of exhaustion"; his whole-body workouts were simply taking too long. He cut his workout in half, training legs, chest, and triceps on Mondays and Thursdays, and back, shoulders and biceps on Tuesdays and Fridays. The change made an immediate difference:

> I knew that high-intensity training was the best, there was no question about that. But I couldn't put up with that kind of exhaustive effect immediately after the workout. I had to either go to a job or back to school, and all I could do was to collapse in a heap and sleep. Really, the build-up of lactic acid was so quick, so dramatic, and so severe that until my

body metabolized it — usually about two hours later — I was almost incapacitated. I found that by splitting the routine, doing half the body one day, and the other half the next, the fatigue was much less than half. You would think it would only be half, but apparently after a certain point, in terms of volume in training, the exhaustive effects grow geometrically as opposed to arithmetically. I found that I could get the same benefits from high-intensity training while avoiding the overwhelming exhaustive effects of the full-body three-day-a-week routine.[34]

On January 18, Mike found himself back on stage with Robby Robinson. However, this time around it wasn't to compete in a contest but rather to promote the release of the *Pumping Iron* documentary in New York. Mike and Robby, along with bodybuilders Franco Columbu, Mike Katz, and Ed Corney, were brought up on the stage of the Plaza Theater to engage in a mock competition in front of a full audience prior to the screening of the film. Cathy made the 205-mile trip northeast from Maryland as well, but, upon her arrival, Mike was quickly separated from her by one of the organizers to be photographed with Franco alongside former movie star and socialite Paulette Goddard.

Despite the status the film enjoys today among bodybuilding fans, *Pumping Iron* almost wasn't completed, as its producers ran out of money after shooting some 100 hours of footage. To obtain additional financing, on February 25, 1976, producer George Butler put on an exhibit at Manhattan's Whitney Museum of American Art, featuring Arnold Schwarzenegger, Frank Zane, and Ed Corney posing on a rotating dais. Over 5,000 people attended, paying five dollars each, which raised the $25,000 Butler required to complete the documentary.[35]

But Joe Weider wasn't pleased with the Whitney event. None of the three bodybuilders were in contest shape; they were off steroids, untanned, and smooth in appearance. To the patrons of the museum, the trio's muscle development was well above average, and for an event billed as "Articulate Muscle: The Body as Art," the physical development of Schwarzenegger, Zane, and Corney was certainly sufficient. But to a marketing man like Joe, having his star pitchman appear in public in anything less than top shape, and at an event in one of the media capitals of the world, wasn't good for business. The Master Blaster vented his spleen in an article in *Muscle Builder/Power* entitled "Speaking Out." The piece lamented that "Schwarzenegger and Zane appeared at the Whitney Museum of American Art's presentation of 'Articulate Muscle' considerably short of top shape. It made history, but they weren't their best. They owed it to themselves and posterity, but they missed the chance."[36]

Joe wasn't alone in his disappointment; *Sports Illustrated* was also unimpressed, but for different reasons:

> Not long ago, New York's Whitney Museum did some inept but well-intentioned pioneering with a symposium called "Articulate Muscle: The Male Body in Art" — a presentation of three Mr. Universe types as living objects of art. It was rather ironic that bodybuilding, a sport with a low repute in this country, was the one to bridge the gap between art and athletics and that its classical implications were substantial enough to be celebrated in a world-famous and highly respected museum. Yet the more than 2,500 people attending this supposedly exciting and ground-breaking esthetic happening left feeling as if they'd just been to a compulsory night-school class.[37]

Even Arnold, the magazine reported, was embarrassed by the event. He was quoted as saying, "In a personal sense it was terrific. But in every other way, it was a total disaster."[38] But that was in 1976. One year later, the edge of Arnold's embarrassment was beveled somewhat by the fact that *Pumping Iron* was completed, and its New York début was a star-studded affair. Apart from Goddard, the singers James Taylor and Carly Simon attended, as did actors and actresses such as Carroll Baker, Jennifer O'Neill, and Anthony Perkins. New York's *Daily News* devoted a full page to the gala event.[39]

All the glitz and glitter that now enveloped the sport of bodybuilding made it hard for Mike to focus on his seven hours per day of organic chemistry study when he resumed his classes at the University of Washington. At this point in his life, Mike was impressed with Arnold. To be the center of that kind of attention; to have a major documentary made on bodybuilding in which you are the star attraction — and a film crew standing by recording your greatest competitive triumph — what an incredible feeling of satisfaction that must be! Mike had been present only when the first scenes of the film were shot at Gold's Gym during August 1975. Who would have known that *that* would turn into *this*? The film's success deepened Mike's pride in being a competitive bodybuilder. But Mike felt that he was being pulled in two directions. He was torn between following his head — completing his education and becoming a psychiatrist — and following his heart by devoting himself solely to bodybuilding. By February 1976, his internal conflict reached a tipping point.

"I was walking the half-mile between classes at the University of Maryland campus, and it was freezing," he recalled. "I didn't have any money. I was moonlighting; I didn't have a lot to spend on my girlfriend and wasn't seeing her as much as I wanted to see someone whom I was crazy about. I was studying up to seven hours a day on chemistry alone and I was working out also. Plus, I was becoming disillusioned about becoming a psychiatrist and tired of being broke."[40] Seeking merely to warm up a bit, he entered the library at the University of Washington and ventured over to where the magazines were kept. Scanning through some back issues of *Sports Illustrated*, he was surprised to find an edition that contained an article about Joe Weider. He sat down and read the article. A passage caught his attention:

> Weider doesn't let detractors get him down. "I have great excitement and enjoyment in life," he says. "When I was 12 I read Nietzsche. I admired him for his truthfulness and because he stressed the total importance of the individual and the intellect. The trouble with men is that when they shed a little light on mankind they want to turn it into a religion, a philosophy, an *ism*."[41]

That Joe was a fan of Nietzsche impressed Mike,[42] who by this point in time was reading quite a bit of the philosopher himself. A thought came to him: "I wrote him a letter letting him know about my particular interest in philosophy," Mike recalled. "And that, believe it or not, got him kind of excited. He liked the fact that perhaps there was a bodybuilder out there who was not only soon to win top titles but was something of an intellectual perhaps. I received a letter back from him re-inviting me to California. I was in college at that point and decided to finish out that semester. What I decided to do was, in June of that year, fly out to Vancouver, British Columbia, and compete in the Mr. North America contest, which was going to be attended by Joe, and then fly down to California with Joe from British Columbia and discuss further the possibility of my relocating."[43]

About the time Mike wrote his letter to Joe, Jack Neary was packing his bags. He'd had enough of California and was homesick for Canada.[44] He'd grown bored writing about bodybuilders' training routines. Jack had a creative mind, but his creativity had reached its limit in trying to find different ways to describe the exercises that bodybuilders employed in their workouts. "After a few years I just found it to be an incredibly narrow world," he recalled. "I had previously been a news reporter, covered general news . . . and I just found that there are only so many ways you can describe how to do a donkey calf raise, you know?"[45] Becoming Los Angelized never took with the transplanted Canadian. He headed home to Alberta. Not that Jack had forsaken bodybuilding by any means; he quickly found a job as the international editor of a new bodybuilding publication, *Looking Good*, which was published and edited by the Canadian entrepreneur Cal Smith. As Smith wanted substantial coverage of the Mr. North America contest to appear within his magazine, and as the contest would be taking place in Jack's neighboring province of British Columbia, Jack was given the assignment of covering it for the fledgling publication.

Ray Mentzer, meanwhile, was encouraged by his placing at the 1976 Mr. America contest. Later that year he placed third in the Tall Class at the Mr. Eastern America, and then won his first contest: the Mr. Eastern USA. He entered one contest in 1977, placing second in the Heavyweight Class of the IFBB Mr. America.[46] Mike encouraged him to enter the Mr. North America competition along with him; having two Mentzers gunning for the title would be good motivation for the brothers leading up to the contest.

While the bodybuilding press had been largely silent about Mike since his Mr. America win, America's newspapers found him fascinating. The *New York Times* had called,[47] the *Washington Post* devoted three pages to him, and the *Baltimore Sun* featured Mike in a six-page spread in its *Sun Magazine* supplement.[48] The young bodybuilder certainly displayed no hesitation in speaking his mind:

- *On the muscle magazines*: "Since their reason for existence is to sell products, they have to talk everyone into believing they could become top bodybuilders if they take the magazines' products and train the way the magazines tell them to train. But most top bodybuilders are top bodybuilders not because they possess any great talent or scientific genius but because they had the genetic potential, just as O.J. Simpson had the genetic potential to be a great football player. So, a falsehood is perpetuated by the magazines for the sake of selling products."

- *On Joe Weider*: "He was confused as to how to deal with me for a while. I don't try to alienate him; I just haven't done anything servile."
- *On* Pumping Iron: "I liked it a lot, but it did tend to neglect or avoid areas of bodybuilding I thought should have been presented to the public. Just like now they're delving into all the aspects of pro football — the drugs, the homosexuality, the pay-offs — they're going to have to delve into all these aspects of bodybuilding."
- *On Arnold Schwarzenegger*: "He could have been better if he'd have trained properly. He trained four hours a day, six days a week. I train four days a week, for an hour or an hour and a half. Most bodybuilders laugh at an hour workout, but most bodybuilders overtrain. The time I spend in the gym is much more productive."[49]

Such off-the-cuff comments, spoken candidly and without filter, caused Ray to express concern to the reporter that Mike's outspokenness could hurt his placings in future contests.[50] The journalist wrote that while Mike agreed with his brother's sentiment, facts were facts; he held to his sincere belief that "if he develops his physique to its potential, no one will be able to deny him his honors or publicity, no matter what he says."[51]

As the reader will surely know by now, such a belief was the epitome of naïveté. Such would only hold true if the IFBB contests Mike chose to enter were concerned solely with rewarding the best physique and did not factor the Weider/Arnold/commercial component into the calculus. Ray had reason to be concerned, particularly given his older brother's comments about Arnold. After all, the *Pumping Iron* star had recently revealed to *Rolling Stone* magazine that he had no compunction about taking steps to "fuck up" anybody who had the audacity to believe he was better than him.⁵² Mike was being reckless; he was waving a red flag in front of the biggest bull in the arena.

The 1977 Mr. North America competition took place on June 4, 1977, at the Queen Elizabeth Theatre in downtown Vancouver. Every one of its 2,575 seats⁵³ was occupied by an eager bodybuilding fan. Even the politicians got caught up in the enthusiasm. Vancouver's mayor, Jack Volrich, declared it "Bodybuilding Week." Canadian Pacific Air Lines donated the first prize award (two round-trip tickets to Australia, with stopovers in Fiji and Hawaii), valued at $3,800.51.⁵⁴ The CBC, the nation's television network, showed up to cover the event, and several top bodybuilders, including Barbados's Darcy Beckles and California's Dave Dupre (who had appeared in the *Pumping Iron* documentary) came to British Columbia to compete.

When Mike and Ray arrived, Mentzer the elder was promptly whisked off to a local television station (CKVU), which devoted the better part of its two-hour *Vancouver Show* to promoting the forthcoming contest. The hosts of the program were intrigued by Mike's radically different approach to training and asked him to elaborate on it. "There are two kinds of training," he explained. "There is hard training and long training. I train hard and fast. I only do four sets per body part. I will superset exercises and each set is done to failure. By the last rep the weight cannot move no matter how much force is exerted. When you train like this, all you need is four sets, twice a week. If more guys followed this type of training, bodybuilding would be revolutionized."⁵⁵

In Jack Neary's report of the contest he made it clear that "even to hint that Mike Mentzer might not win the overall title would have been blasphemy." Mike was certainly in the best shape of his career. "He devastated the audience with his thickness," Jack wrote. "His leg development is as massive as anyone's ever was. Indeed, the immensity of his thighs forced him to stand with the feet considerably far apart as if to assume the position of an inverted Y. He was at least thirty percent better than at last year's World championships if a numerical value can duly record a man's improvement."⁵⁶

Mike easily won the Medium Class and the Overall championship, in addition to picking up subcategory awards for best arms and best legs. Younger brother Ray, however, had yet to find his stride and came in third in the Tall Class behind Beckles and Dupre.

Joe Weider was delighted by what he saw. After the contest, Joe and Mike boarded a plane bound for California. During the flight, Joe put a sharper point on his offer; he would pay Mike $200 a week for the remainder of the summer and help him find a place to live. In return, Mike would appear in some ads for Joe's products and write articles for *Muscle Builder/Power*. Joe liked that Mike had a talent for writing; having recently lost the talents of Jack Neary, he could now replace the Canadian scribe with a writer who could also win contests and market products — and for considerably less money than he paid Jack. At the end of the summer, if Mike didn't find the arrangement satisfactory, he could always return to the University of Washington when the fall semester started and not have missed a step. But if it turned out that Mike liked the experience of working in California — which Joe would do everything in his power to ensure — their arrangement could be renegotiated.[57]

For all the disparaging comments leveled at Joe Weider over the decades, not one of them indicated that he wasn't an exceptional judge of bodybuilding horse flesh. He believed that Mike's combination of chiseled good looks and a muscle mass level that reminded him of the Farnese Hercules,[58] was something he could use to his considerable financial advantage. Moreover, Joe would have no trouble putting forth the young man as a spokesperson for bodybuilding: Mike was not like the other iron-pumpers that the Master Blaster typically dealt with. Here was a young man who truly was an intellectual, who was just as at home discussing philosophy and science as he was sets and reps. Yes, getting Mike to stay in California was Joe's top priority moving forward.

Although he didn't know it at the time, when Mike Mentzer stepped on that plane in British Columbia, he was saying a permanent goodbye to the east coast and the University of Washington. He was about to say hello to a future that nobody could have predicted.

CHAPTER FIFTEEN

A PEEK BEHIND THE CURTAIN

As the commercial airliner arched its way through the sky, soaring 35,000 feet above the mountains and rugged terrain that separates Vancouver from Los Angeles, Joe spoke with Mike at considerable length. He painted a picture of fortunes to be made, mild temperatures, celebrities, and a career that would eventually see Mike's face chiseled onto the Mount Rushmore of bodybuilding legends. By the time the plane touched down on the tarmac at Los Angeles International Airport, Mike was sold.

"I clearly remember the exact date that I arrived in California," he recalled. "It was June 6, 1977."[1] Mike and Joe were greeted at the airport by Ken Sprague, the owner of Gold's Gym, who offered to put the new arrival up for a few weeks.[2] Ken put the word out at the gym that Mike was looking for a place to stay until an apartment could be found for him. According to Ken, it was decided amongst the members that bodybuilder Bill Grant's apartment would be a good fit.[3] However, the two bodybuilders couldn't have been less compatible. "I remember the roommates," Ken recalled. "Two distinct personalities: Bill was outgoing, messy, and always had a girl over. Mike was quiet and neat."[4] Mike had a different memory, describing Grant as "an absolute maniac."[5]

Eventually, a suitable apartment was found, conveniently located in a fourplex owned by the aunt of Joe's wife, Betty.[6] It was not the first time that one of Joe's employees had lived in the building. Indeed, a previous tenant was none other than Jack Neary, who remembered it as "a little four-unit building on South Beverly Glen [Boulevard] in West Los Angeles. And [Betty's aunt] Ann Brosmer lived in the front apartment, and the back apartment was for rent. It was a really nice little place. One bedroom had a little lemon tree outside on the patio — that stuff you just would never get on the Canadian Prairies."[7]

Cathy Gelfo, meanwhile, was tarrying in the couple's apartment back in Maryland. While she loved Mike and wanted what was best for his career, she also had a huge decision to make. Should she head west while Mike pursued his dream, or should she stay and focus on her own career? She was, after all, very much a part of the relatively recent women's movement,[8] and believed her future career to be every bit the equal of Mike's. In this, Mike supported her; if she wanted to remain in Maryland, he would respect that. One month later, however, Cathy had made her decision and was living with Mike in the apartment on Beverly Glen.[9] "Mentzer hasn't a stauncher supporter than Cathy," Jack would write in *Muscle Builder/Power*, "who, in spite of her unlimited admiration, may be his own worst enemy. When it comes to *her* Michael, she is the least objective person I know. He is unbeatable in her eyes. Cathy is barometer to Mentzer's moods. If he is down, she may sink even lower. She becomes angry when someone doesn't applaud Mentzer's performance at an exhibition or contest. I have never heard Cathy criticize the man about bodybuilding, which is testimony to an unwavering loyalty."[10] Her loyalty to Mike was certainly reciprocated. "She's the best thing that's ever happened to me," he told Jack. "I've never heard a word of discouragement from her. If I broke up with her today, I'd never find someone to replace her. Never."[11]

Knowing that Cathy's comfort level was the key to keeping Mike in California, Joe went out of his way to make the newcomers feel welcome. Twice a week he would take them out for dinner; on weekends they were invited to his home. There, Joe would show off his art collection and discuss philosophy with Mike into the wee hours of the morning.[12] They also talked bodybuilding training, and Joe seemed fascinated by Mike having constructed a training method based on valid scientific principles.[13] Some, such as Ken Sprague, believed that Joe saw an idealized reflection of himself in the young bodybuilder. "I knew Joe quite well. I suspected Joe vicariously identified with Mike. Both were facially similar; Mike/Ray resonated as Joe/Ben; Mike had the muscle mass that Joe dreamed of for himself."[14]

Joe couldn't wait to get Mike on the cover of his magazine again. Mike appeared on two covers in 1977, and Joe began touting him both as a "Weider pupil" and as the heir apparent to the Mr. Olympia title.[15] Mike's job title was "associate editor" for *Muscle Builder/Power*. Unlike all the other bodybuilders who came before (apart from Rick Wayne), Mike could write. "When he came to explaining his training methodologies, he could communicate them so well," Jack Neary said. "His articles were so beautifully written. And he was the only guy I knew of the bodybuilders who could write. Rick Wayne, of course, wrote his own stuff, but all the other guys had ghostwriters, which were usually me, Armand Tanny, Bill Reynolds, or any of the other guys that worked for Joe. The articles always appeared under the byline of 'Arnold' or 'Frank Zane,' or whoever, but, but it was really someone else writing the stuff based on an interview."[16]

Mike turned out to be not only a good writer, but also a prolific one. He wrote detailed articles on how he trained each muscle group — from his arms to his calves. He not only gave descriptions of how he performed each exercise, but in a radical departure from most training articles that appeared in the magazine, he explained the anatomical function of the muscle groups being trained, and which exercises best aligned with these functions. The readers of *Muscle Builder/Power*, who were used to reading the by-now standard six-days-a-week, 20-sets-per-body-part training methods, were fascinated at the contrast. Mike's abbreviated high-intensity training offered hope to those who didn't wish to live their lives in the gym in the pursuit of their bodybuilding goals. Letters flooded into the Weider offices wanting to learn more about Mike's methods.[17]

Mike's scientific approach caught on, as did his erudition. Readers sensed that this was a person who knew a lot about a lot of things. And so, the subjects they wrote to him about extended beyond the mere confines of the gym. Soon he had his own question-and-answer column, "Ask Mike," which was devoted to answering queries on topics that ranged from genetics, stretch marks, vitamin B-15, and anabolic steroids, to masturbation, motivation, dealing with parental pressure, and individualism. Given Mike's soaring popularity, Joe encouraged him to write and self-publish his own bodybuilding courses. Other bodybuilders had done so and reported that it was a solid means of supplementing their income. Joe wasn't interested in paying his bodybuilders or writers any more money than he had to, but he was willing to provide them with free ad space in his magazine. It didn't cost him anything to do this, and it ensured (in the bodybuilders' case) their presence in *Muscle Builder/Power* each month. He offered Mike a full page in each issue to market his courses. If the training courses sold, great. If they didn't, that was on Mike.

But mail-order was risky. It cost a considerable sum to have the training booklets printed, and there was no guarantee that the product would sell. Moreover, not everyone could build an empire from the enterprise. That was reserved for the titans in that field, such as Charles Atlas, who, by the 1950s, had successfully sold the better part of a million of his "Dynamic Tension" mail-order courses to the public and was averaging up to 40,000 new sales every year.[18] The market size was considerably smaller for a subculture like hard-core bodybuilding. Even Arnold, with all the publicity he had received over the years in Joe's magazines, had had a tough go of it — at least initially. Despite reports that he made his first million dollars in mail order,[19] the reality was that four years into his mail-order business, Arnold's annual income was hovering somewhere between $40,000 and $60,000 — and this was an aggregate of the money he was paid from Joe, what he made from competing, conducting bodybuilding seminars, posing exhibitions, and his mail-order sales.[20] For the better part of a year, it didn't look like his mail-order business was going to get off the ground, largely because Joe was dragging his heels. First, he had promised to have one of his staff members write the training courses for Arnold. This took several months. Then Joe neglected to pay the printer to publish them.[21] This put Arnold in a precarious position; he had ads running in the magazine each month and money was coming in, but he had no product to ship. According to his girlfriend at the time, Barbara Outland Baker, it made for a tense situation:

> Waiting as long as six months to a year after the expected delivery date, his mail order customers were fuming. Dramatic appeals from young boys, terse letters from their fathers, illiterate threats, and lawyers' missives put Arnold in a quandary. Legally he was solid as long as the collected monies remained in the bank. . . . Joe would just tell him, "Relax. It will all get done." But P.O. Box 1234 posed a wicked polarity each day. Would new checks and ready cash await him or poignant letters of desperation? Arnold was unusually irritable. What he wanted was a load of money, not two loads of complaints . . .[22]

George Butler recalled seeing Arnold examine each piece of mail that came in, holding the envelopes up to the light to see if they contained a check or cash. If they did, they went onto the kitchen table for processing;

if they didn't, he simply threw them into the trash.[23] At one point in 1970, after having grown frustrated from waiting for Joe to uphold his end of their arrangement, he wrote the Master Blaster a letter, stating "Please let me remind you about the training courses to make them ready as soon as possible; otherwise I get too many complaints. Please print enough so I can sell 7,000 to England and 7,000 to South America. I have to get $15,000 as soon as possible so we can pay 30,000 dollars for an apartment building. I save every penny I can save."[24] Significantly, it was Joe loaning Arnold $10,000 as part of the down payment on that apartment building — rather than mail order — that would put Arnold on the path to his first million dollars.[25]

In Mike's case, however, the Master Blaster had nothing to do with the writing and the printing of the courses. He also had nothing to do with paying for Mike's apartment; that was Mike's responsibility — and Mike was fine with that.[26] He quickly set about writing a training course outlining the whys and wherefores of his method, in addition to writing booklets for training individual muscle groups (legs, chest and back, arms, and shoulders). He changed the name of his training system from the pedestrian "Contraction Control Method," which Joe's writer Gene Mozee had initially christened it, to the catchier "Heavy Duty" system. Now he needed to save up the money to cover the printing bill, and that would take a while.

Meanwhile, Cathy was having a hard time of it. Being on the west coast and away from her family left her homesick. Mike did what he could to keep her spirits up, but there was no denying that a seismic event had disrupted their lives with the move to California. Joe and Betty Weider were no substitute for Cathy's family and friends back in Maryland. Both Mike and Cathy would have to make the adjustment together.[27] Not helping Cathy in her adjustment were the letters that were arriving from female fans of her boyfriend. Even Mike was shocked by their content:

> They are very, very explicit; going into great detail about what they'd like to do to my body. I've even gotten phone calls at Gold's Gym from women I've never talked to in person who immediately launch into great detail about what it is they think I want, and what they want to do to please me sexually. These women are really kind of crazy when you think about it. For all they know, I could be a masher myself, a Jack-the-Ripper type. Really, a woman has to be sick or distorted to get that explicit

with someone they don't even know. Of course, what they're responding to is an image of me portrayed in the magazines. And, of course, many times the image that the public has of a personality, or a celebrity figure, is not totally accurate.[28]

Between being there for Cathy and preparing his training courses, Mike also had to be in the Weider offices every day to write his articles for the magazine.[29] In addition to this, he had to summon the mental motivation and physical energy required to train and diet for the 1977 World Championships in Nîmes, France, which was now only a couple of months away. While he had no trouble showing up at Gold's Gym for this purpose, Mike found that his focus was lagging:

> I shouldn't say I *couldn't*, but I just *didn't* invest the same energy, the intensity, into my training as I had the year before. Winning that Mr. America was crucial to me. I wanted it very, very badly. For that one year preceding the Mr. America I trained with as much intensity, if not more, perhaps, than I had for any other contest. After winning the America, there was a bit of a letdown; everything else after that seemed anticlimactic. The summer of '77 I did not train with that deep, deep drive that I had felt before when I trained for the America. That was not due to a deviation from the [training] theory, it was psychological.[30]

"Mike did not interact in a friendly, bantering manner that was typical of the Gold's crowd," Ken Sprague recalled. "He rarely if ever smiled in the gym; he kept to himself. Self-absorbed is an accurate description of his affect. He was neither liked nor disliked. Little if any interactions with the guys outside the gym. In short, he was not 'one of the guys.'"[31] And while the bodybuilders training in Gold's may have been indifferent to the new arrival, other opinions were anything but apathetic. Rick Wayne, for example, was not a fan, writing: "Just over a year ago, the bodybuilding grapevine buzzed with the rumor that Mike Mentzer had discovered a system of training that was completely revolutionary, that spat in the collective face of all established systems of modern bodybuilding. At first, most serious bodybuilders dismissed the whole thing as so much cock-and-bull, while the various authorities scoffed at the idea."[32] But Rick was old-school, having competed throughout the 1960s into the 1970s. The methods that he, Arnold, and the other champions of that era used were the high-water mark as far he could see. That a newcomer like Mike should claim that he used science to create a better way to train was, to Rick, little more than hubris. "I remember when Mike first came to Weider," he said, "and it was obvious he had read a lot of my stuff, and it was obvious, too, that he didn't like that I was obviously a super-fan of Arnold — that we had background, all that kind of stuff. So, it was very quiet [between us]. And he was always a very cerebral guy as well. . . . And dare I say it, I always thought there was something odd about Mike. I did not go for his training system, for obvious reasons."[33]

It came as no surprise, then, that when Rick was assigned to write an article on Mike's training method, he sought out comments from his old-school comrade Arnold Schwarzenegger. The pair had hooked up to attend gym-owner-cum-contest-promoter George Snyder's Mr. Eastern United States contest in Warrington, Pennsylvania. They looked on as Mike walked on stage to guest pose at the start of the contest. As he was guest posing rather than competing, he hadn't dieted down to single-digit-percentage bodyfat, but his muscle mass was certainly on full display. As Mike went through his posing routine under the lights, Rick nudged Arnold to get his comments. "Okay, so he's pretty big," Arnold began. "Maybe he's even *too* heavy." Then came the hammer: "The guy needs more quality muscle. He needs cuts . . . striations, if he's planning to go anywhere. He's got to chisel his triceps from the biceps, his pecs from the deltoids."

"Surely, that will come in the next few weeks," Wayne replied, playing (in his words) "devil's advocate."

"It'll come my ass!" Arnold exclaimed. "You can't get that finished professional look merely from a low carbohydrate diet. He thinks he's so clever with that three sets twice a week crap training of his. He'd better smarten up and start bombing six days a week. Some body parts need at least 20 sets."[34]

After recording Arnold's verdict for posterity, Rick couldn't wait to share it with Mike.[35] Perhaps a dressing-down from the six-time Mr. Olympia winner would present the young maverick with a reality check. But if the journalist was looking for contrition, he soon found out that he was speaking to the wrong person. "Mike listened and then he gave me his forgive-them-they-know-not-what-the-hell-they're-talking-about look," Rick reported.[36] Having withstood Arnold's salvo, Mike returned fire. "That's the trouble," he began, "just because Arnold beat those other guys for the Mr. Olympia doesn't mean he has any idea what he is talking about or that he knows anything about scientific bodybuilding. But people will look at his titles and his twenty-two-inch arms, and they will assume he has been training correctly all these years. Arnold is great *in spite* of his erroneous training concepts."[37]

A pushback was *not* the response Rick had anticipated. The former bodybuilding champion attempted to put Mike in his place by laying down a trump card of his own: "I reminded Mentzer that Robby Robinson, Lou Ferrigno, Danny Padilla and a host of other champions had achieved superstar status via the pump twenty-sets system."[38] But Mike was having none of it. "It all goes to prove how much more they might have achieved with scientific training procedures. You, me, Arnold, Sergio, Robby, the champs, we are all the thoroughbreds of the human race. We started off with definite genetic advantages that a lot of other people don't have. That is why the top bodybuilders made the grade."[39]

Mike let pass Arnold's comments about thinking he was clever and his attempt to categorize his training system as "three sets twice a week crap." These were simply logical fallacies; the first an ad hominem attack; the second — since Mike was training four times a week using up to five sets per body part — simply a straw man fallacy. As for Arnold's opinions on how he *should* be training, Mike proceeded to decimate each one in turn:

- *"The guy needs more quality muscle"*: "The key to building big muscles is simply training *intensity*. This is backed up by scientific facts. The harder a man trains the less amount of training he will be able to do. It's like the long-distance runner and the sprinter. The sprinter always has larger calves and yet he actually engages in only a small fraction of the amount of work done by the distance runner. The distance runner has great lean muscles, while the other tends to have more muscular mass. It's his type of running that prevents the sprinter from doing a lot of long-distance work. But he builds massive calves. Hard bursts of training is exactly what it takes to build big muscles."
- *"He needs cuts . . . striations, if he's planning to go anywhere. He's got to chisel his triceps from the biceps, his pecs from the deltoids"*: "Well, as I have already pointed out, the correct way is to build muscles to their full potential and then diet to bring out

the cuts and striations. You take a guy who has never trained, put him on the appropriate diet and you will see his small, untrained muscles quite clearly."

- "*He'd better smarten up and start bombing six days a week. Some body parts need at least 20 sets*": "Arnold's idea that the more sets a guy does the better is most erroneous. It is more than wrong, it is *simplistic*. Some people figure that if two sets can do that amount of good, twenty will do *even more good*. Nonsense, of course. Generally, muscles respond essentially to the same stimulus. I was going to say earlier that there is no man alive, no matter how fit, who can sprint at top speed for a mile; he's running too hard, too intensely, to last a mile. The same principle applies to other physical activities. The harder you engage in it, the more intensely you push yourself, the less of it you will be able to withstand. I doubt anyone will question my judgement when I say that those bodybuilders who claim to do twenty sets a body part, who say they train three hours a day, six days a week, are not training hard. True, they are training diligently and long. But they are not training *hard*. There's a difference between hard training and training for long periods. Just as you cannot run hard and long, so you cannot train hard for three hours at a time. You can't train hard and long. They are two mutually exclusive factors. Impossible to do at once."[40]

"But what about the calves?" Rick asked.[41] After all, gym lore had it that the calf muscles required far more training volume than other muscle groups did. Arnold had stated this in his books.[42] The question caused Mike to chuckle[43] in reply: "The calf is precisely the best body part to prove exactly how stupid the twenty sets rationale really is. You hear it said that because a man walks all day long and his calves have grown tough and dense from the activity, you must give them extra work if you want them to grow . . . Extra work meaning more sets. The truth is that they need more *intense* training. Twenty sets of this and that will only overwork them."[44]

Mike had thrown down the gauntlet at Arnold's feet — and his comments appeared in Joe's magazine for the bodybuilding public to read. Once again, he had poked the bear. But Mike didn't care; facts were facts. And if Arnold didn't like them, that was his problem. From Mike's perspective, bodybuilding was suffering from a self-imposed Dark Ages, from a lack of science in the discipline in favor of the cult of personality. It was clear to him that Arnold had built his body with a hit-or-miss approach. If it were solely his training methods that produced his level of muscular development, then all the bodybuilders that followed his methods over the past seven years would be as big as he was. This clearly wasn't the case, as there wasn't another Arnold anywhere in sight.[45] Mike did not want to contribute to this situation:

> I'm not trying to push my personality. I'm trying to push the facts! Guys like Arnold expect people to accept what they say because they've won a few titles. Sure, they've won some titles, but doesn't mean they necessarily know the right way or the quickest way of doing things. I don't want people to accept what I say because I've won a few titles and [they] look up to me; that doesn't mean a thing. This stuff is based on very sound, well-authenticated scientific facts. The stuff that isn't scientific fact is so common sense that no one could deny it. I don't try to give anything in these books or my seminars that isn't already known. All I did was put it in book form and adapt it to fit bodybuilding. Anyone can go into any book on physiology or nutrition and learn the same thing.[46]

When Joe Weider was asked whose approach — Arnold's or Mike's — was correct, he sat on the fence. "Arnold and Mike are both correct," he said, "for the fact is that each has found, through the Weider Instinctive Training Principle, what system works best for them."[47] In other words, given that both horses were in his corral at the moment, he wasn't going to risk upsetting either one so long as he could claim that both endorsed his "Weider Principles."

But Joe's eyes had strayed of late. His financial bread and butter had always been teenage males who wanted to build big chests and mighty biceps. Arnold had been the perfect pitchman for this crowd, as these were his two best body parts. But Arnold wasn't competing anymore, and the current Mr. Olympia champion, Frank Zane, was a poor replacement. Despite defeating Robby Robinson for the title in October of that year, Zane stood five foot nine and weighed no more than 190 pounds soaking wet.[48] He was known for his symmetry — not his chest and arm size. And while Mike certainly had muscle mass, with big arms and a broad and square chest that drew comparisons to former champion Steve Reeves,[49] his arm size was largely due to the girth of his triceps, not biceps, and his chest was not over-the-top bulbous and fibrous like Arnold's. Joe needed a high-level bodybuilder who had a massive chest and huge, egg-shaped biceps to recapture the profitable teenage male market he enjoyed when Arnold was at his peak. And that's when the Master Blaster saw Kal Szkalak.

At five foot ten and 210 pounds, Kal Szkalak had hit the bodybuilding world like a nuclear bomb in 1976, winning the AAU Mr. California and Mr. America titles in quick succession.[50] In June of 1977, he won the IFBB Mr. USA, edging out Ray Mentzer, which qualified Kal to compete in the World Championships.[51]

Born in Budapest, Hungary, Kal had immigrated with his family to America 11 years previously.[52] He was raised in Delaware, where, according to his account, he became an exceptional athlete.[53] Unlike Mike, who grew up idolizing Steve Reeves and Bill Pearl, or Arnold, whose bodybuilding inspiration was Reg Park, Kal's bodybuilding hero lived much closer to home. "When I was first into bodybuilding, I never really followed the star scene too much," he said. "My idol was myself."[54]

Kal was handsome, and (obviously) confident. And he had reason to be — even in the earliest articles written about him, he was being compared to Arnold.[55] His chest was massive, and his arms were reportedly 20 inches in circumference.[56] Even his shoulders and back development placed him at the uppermost level of the sport.[57] Unfortunately, his leg development was also compared to Arnold's — which wasn't a good thing.[58] Kal's legs simply lacked the size and fiber density that the muscles in his upper body possessed. This left him with a proportion issue that could never be resolved. However, in competitive bodybuilding, paying lip service to the importance of physique assessment standards such as proportion was one thing, while insisting on implementing these factors as part of the judging criteria was something else entirely. In Randy Roach's book *Muscle, Smoke & Mirrors, Volume II*, for example, he reports that in Kal's Mr. California victory, the promoter of the contest, Ken Sprague, picked the judges and let it be known that Kal, who trained at Ken's gym, should win the contest. The judges, ignoring the imbalance in the young man's physique, did what they were told, and Kal won the competition. He then rode the wave of this momentum into the

AAU Mr. America competition, which was held several weeks later, winning it on his first attempt.[59]

Whether or not there would be a similar attempt to influence the judges on Kal's behalf at the forthcoming World Championships in order to fast-track his entry into the 1978 Mr. Olympia remained to be seen. But for those who had eyes for such things, the warning signs were already present. Within the first issue of *Muscle Builder/Power* that featured Kal's image on its cover was the statement: "Joe Weider has expressed keen interest in Kal's future. No doubt, with Kal's determination to succeed plus Joe's penchant for turning regular champions into superstars, we'll be hearing a lot more of Mr. Szkalak."[60]

The city of Nîmes dates to 6000 BC, when it was settled by the Volcae Arecomici, a Celtic tribe, who built a sanctuary around a natural spring. In 120 BC, the Romans took it over, and remnants from their occupation still dot its landscape.[61] Nîmes was always a desirable piece of real estate, it seemed, for it was subsequently taken over by the Germans and Arabs before becoming attached to the French crown in 1229.[62] However, on November 6, 1977, a takeover of a different sort would occur.

When Mike and Cathy arrived in France and checked into the hotel where the competitors were staying, whom should they spy strolling about the lobby but Jack Neary. The journalist had decided to give Joe Weider another chance and was sent to Nîmes to cover the contest for *Muscle Builder/Power*. Their reunion was respectfully brief, as Mike and Cathy wanted to get to their hotel room to decompress after their 16-hour flight, while Jack wanted to get a feel for the venue as well as interview some of the other competitors.

The World Championships (or Mr. Universe) was the biggest amateur contest in competitive bodybuilding, the gate through which an amateur bodybuilder had to pass to earn his pro card and turn professional. The winner from each of the three categories — Heavyweight, Middleweight, and Lightweight — would be eligible to compete in the 1978 Mr. Olympia contest.

As soon as the heavyweights strode onto the dais, it was obvious that the contest was between Szkalak and Mentzer. However, now that they were standing together on stage, the shortcomings of the former were glaring.

"Kal was impressive, there's no question" Jack recalled. "I mean, he had the 'prison workout muscles,' the big pecs and the big biceps, and those are the ones that really capture the audience's attention a lot of the time. And they could help mask weaknesses. Mike was by far more balanced — way, way better symmetry, way better lower body development. It was flawless, you know, like he had no real weaknesses."[63] The judges evidently thought so, too. When the prejudging ended, one of the judges approached Mike and told him he had already won.[64] As bodybuilding contests were won or lost in the prejudging and the evening show was primarily for the benefit of the fans, the show had already been adjudicated. Jack's report of the contest established this beyond question:

> The judges' score sheets show that Mentzer scored 279 points from the prejudging; Szkalak with 269. A considerable margin. After an hour and a half of deliberate comparison over three rounds of judging — relaxed, mandatory, and optional posing — seven men (who pride themselves in their objectivity) established in all rounds, that Mentzer had the superior physique. Yes, a ten-point difference would seem to indicate that.[65]

Unbeknownst to Jack, however, the contest wasn't over yet. It was decided (for reasons the reader is free to speculate on) that all of the prejudging scores should be thrown out, and that the contest would be decided by the level of audience applause for the competitors during the posedown.[66] This was the first and only time that a contest of this magnitude — the premier jewel in the crown of international amateur bodybuilding — would be have its winner determined solely by an activity that up until this event was used to entertain the crowd[67] and buy the judges the time they required to tabulate their scoring. Mike certainly was not aware that the evening posedown was now what the entire competition was going to be judged upon.[68]

When the posedown concluded that evening, Kal Szkalak was declared the winner. For the second year in a row, Mike had placed second at the World Championships. However, losing to a phenom like Robby Robinson was one thing, but, truly, nobody had seen this one coming.[69] Even Kal seemed surprised. "I pulled an upset," he said. "I was as shocked as Mike when my name was called. I really didn't know if I had won."[70] Canada's Roy

Callender, who had just won the Middleweight Division of the contest, was approached by a reporter who offered his congratulations. "Thank you, but I cannot feel happy right now," he replied. "Not after what has happened to Mike. I cannot believe it. Just don't talk to me."[71] Ben Weider, along with several members of the IFBB's top brass quickly surrounded Mike. Ben promised that he would investigate the matter personally,[72] but he never did.

Kal Szkalak was the new IFBB Mr. Universe — and his next stop was the 1978 Mr. Olympia. Cathy Gelfo was in tears; she threw herself at Jack Neary, sobbing.[73] Jack was stunned at what had just unfolded.[74] Mike looked lost.[75]

CHAPTER SIXTEEN

THE CHALLENGE TO THE THRONE

"I guess even gods are mortal some time."[1]

Jack was sitting on the edge of the bed in Mike and Cathy's passenger cabin when he made the comment. The ice cubes in his glass of Coca-Cola clinked with every slight shift of the train as it made its way along the tracks from Nîmes towards Nice. It was one o'clock in the morning, several hours after the contest ended, and Jack's initial disbelief at the result had long since given way to attempting to view that particular drop of water within the bigger stream of life. He had morphed from Bob Woodward into Albert Camus.

Mike reclined on the bed in his cabin, and, with Cathy lying by his side, picked up on Jack's sentiment. "For some reason I just can't get too excited about this whole thing," he said. "Maybe it just hasn't hit me. But how can I take the opinions of men with pencils in their hands seriously?"

Jack perked up. "When you really think of it . . . what is bodybuilding?" he asked rhetorically. "You have this long lineup of huge guys, guys who have spent much of their lives in a gym with iron barbells and equipment and they've tortured themselves to build all this mass. And now they stand on a stage somewhere far from home and parade around, and some man half his size has a pencil and makes a few marks on paper and decides which body is the best. Yes, a lineup of men as close to physical perfection as man can come. People looked at as Greek gods from the pantheon. Men with huge followings, revered as idols. In the eyes of the masses, they are Heaven personified, and then a group of other men, called judges, more or less mortals when you think of it, come along and topple the celestial pedestals these gods rest upon. One physique contest and it can all come crashing down to reality. And the crazy thing is that a decision from a complete stranger affects the bodybuilder's whole life. Dreams are made or broken by the pencil marks of a guy's observations. You have to ask yourself, who sets the standard for which these bodies are judged? I mean, who says that big calves and a small waist is *the* look? How do we know that someday, maybe, it won't change?" He paused before adding, "It becomes so damn impersonal, doesn't it?"

"That's why I can't get too worked up over this," Mike replied. "I mean I have thought of this sport that way many times." A realization now washed over the vanquished competitor, and he laughed. "God, *that's* getting existential!"

By the end of the week, Jack was back in the Weider building, tapping out the contest report on his Smith Corona electric typewriter and trying his best to stave off the jet lag that attends crossing the Atlantic twice over a nine-day period. Someone appeared at his desk and picked up the small stack of completed pages and began reading them. Looking up from his desk to see who the interloper was, Jack was surprised to see Kal Szkalak. "You aren't going to make a controversy out of the prejudging, are you?" the new Mr. Universe inquired. "No," Jack replied coolly. "I won't make a controversy out of it. There already is a controversy, I'll just explain what happened."[2] Kal stared at him for a moment before returning the pages to the top of the desk and walking away.

Jack was staying at Mike and Cathy's place until an apartment closer to work could be located.[3] As Cathy had recently returned to Maryland to visit with family, her absence gave Mike and Jack free rein of the place to do as they wished. The dwelling had gone to shambles during her absence; forgotten editions of the *Los Angeles Times* and the *New York Times Book Review* competed for floor space, and books were omnipresent. A pile of them was stacked up on a large table — philosophy tomes by Nietzsche and Sartre, poetry books by Walt Whitman, and several Henry Miller novels. Jack considered the table to be "nerve center of the room."[4] But all work and no play made for dull boys, and the pair soon got it into their heads that an evening of drinking was in order. Jack would later describe the experience:

> It was important, Mike Mentzer told me, that we find the green Chartreuse and not the yellow. The urgency in his voice

indicated the green kind commanded the more fearsome wallop of the two liqueurs.

"It's like sparklers going off in your head," he said, turning the bottle around to check the label. Seconds later, the great arm reached up to the highest shelf. The hand groped blindly past the first row of bottles and closed around one further back, as if it were a special treasure tucked away from view — much as a child will stash the last of his favorite chocolate bars underneath bags of potato chips until he can return to his neighborhood confectionary with more money.

Mentzer brought the bottle down, scowled at it for a moment, then hefted it in his palm, checking its weight as a grocery shopper might with a grapefruit. "*This* is the stuff," he said. "The *green*."

He pursed his lips and squinted violently; it was a gesture that suggested the considerable potency of the drink. Our fate had been secured. With sanguine disposition we resigned ourselves to the prospect of some serious drinking.

The bottle was opened en route to Mentzer's West Los Angeles apartment. The obligatory first sips were in order. Mine was a rather conservative one: Mentzer's warning of sparklers in the head had not gone unnoticed. I rolled the liquid around on my tongue for a few seconds before letting it slide lazily into the gut. A fiery sensation had worked itself up within my mouth and, truly, small explosions or pops of alcoholic fireworks created a flurry of activity in there. One felt compelled to borrow from Jackie Gleason:

"Mmmmmmmm, that's good booze!"

Mentzer was receiving a vicarious thrill from all this. He reached for the bottle and took a healthy swig of the stuff. I could see him working the liqueur around furiously in his cheeks; a great deal of sloshing could be heard. Indeed, each drinking man has his own private ritual of enjoying his first taste of the evening.

"Damn," he said.

"What?" Was he throwing a damper on the festivities so soon?

"I don't think we got the green kind . . . this is the yellow."

He peered intently at the bottle, maneuvering its form so that a slice of passing streetlight illuminated the contents.

"What color is this?" Mentzer thrust the bottle under my nose.

"Looks yellow to me but the hues are similar. It's an honest mistake."

"I never seem to get this right. I'm color blind, you know. Have a difficult time picking one color from the next."[5]

This last revelation Jack found to be typical of Mike's candor; the man was devoid of pretentiousness. "I was struck by this admission of vulnerability," he recalled. "I remember Mike as the definition of confidence. Not smug or cocky, but self-assured. Mike had a belief in himself I rarely saw in other bodybuilders from that golden age."[6] Upon their return to the apartment, the tumblers were brought out, filled with ice, and the Chartreuse poured. The drinking continued. Soon Mike brought out a stack of muscle magazines and dropped them on the table in front of the couch. Jack had to quickly pick up his drink to avoid it being knocked off the table. Mike leafed through one of the magazines until he came to a picture of Arnold Schwarzenegger flexing his biceps.

"Shhhhhooooo!" he said, almost under his breath. "This is *unbelievable*."[7] While strongly disagreeing with Arnold's training approach, Mike still held the Austrian's physique in high regard. He turned the page so that Jack could see the image. Jack nodded his approval. After another sip of Chartreuse, Mike rolled up his sleeve and flexed his arm. "The nexus between the printed image of Arnold's mightily peaked upper arm and Mentzer's own offering presented the evidence that there before me, smitten with a somewhat spirit-induced mood of euphoria, was a prospective successor to the Austrian Oak's heralded title as the greatest bodybuilder in history," Jack recounted. "Never before had a top bodybuilder displayed such physical potential as Mentzer. The muscle lengths and bellies, the insertions, tie-ins, and fullness of each muscle group conjured up thoughts of all the natural resources one needs to create a Superman."

By now the alcohol was doing its job.

"Someday I am going to surpass . . ." Mike intoned, pointing at Arnold's picture.

"That remains to be seen," Jack replied, the Canadian love of argument coming to the fore.

"Hey, I have no doubt in my mind that I will beat this. I have the greatest potential of any bodybuilder. I can see myself going past what Arnold ever developed."

"Mike, I know you're good, and you're sure to get better — but Arnold? I can't see anyone surpassing him for quite a while. Sure, Arnold had weaknesses, but when you put it all together, forget it."

"Well, I'm not going to argue about it. But know what I'm capable of and I know what I'm going to do."

Jack shrugged. "Yes, there was no sense arguing about the future," he thought to himself. "Mentzer is, after all, an existentialist, having been heavily influenced by the writings of Nietzsche and Sartre. His fate was in his own hands. He could control his own existence. We would wait and see."

Mike put down the magazine and picked up another. It was the April 1976 edition of *Muscle Builder/Power* — the one with his image on the cover.

"Now *that's* the best cover I've ever seen," he said with mock seriousness.

"I thought differently," Jack opined. "When I first saw that I thought you were a cocky east coast guy who thought he could beat everybody."

"Oh, I still do," Mike replied facetiously.

"After your victory at the 1976 America, you told me that cover helped you improve 95 percent. I don't know where you got that exact number, but I'll take your word for it."

"Yeah. When Joe Weider put me on the cover, I was so surprised. It was the greatest inspiration I could receive; it really fired me up."

"What about the second cover, after your America victory?"

"Well, that was great too, yeah, but nothing tops the first cover. What a thrill! I remember rushing into the drug store after I heard I was on it, bought up a pile of copies. I had a very favorable reaction back home. Of course, it's better than ever now. All the things that Joe has done to help me — all the constant publicity — is good. It keeps your name up there where people can see it. I like to think I've helped Joe, but, you know, he didn't have to do all he did for me."

The drinking and the banter continued into the wee hours of the morning. It was, indeed, the best of times. Jack was 22. Mike had just turned 26. They both were living in sunny California and writing for an increasingly popular magazine. Jack recalled those days with fondness:

> Our friendship flourished from there. We became very close. There was a sense in those days that the whole world lay before

us daring us to devour it. I well remember pulling the occasional all-nighter with Mike racing against deadline, as we desperately pounded out stories for our boss, Joe Weider. We consumed Balzacian amounts of coffee and other substances to see us through to dawn. After these writing marathons, we often rewarded ourselves with grand feasts at Mike's favorite restaurant, The Palm, in West Hollywood. His appetite for Nova Scotia lobster deserved an entry in the *Guinness Book of World Records*. I saw him eat a lobster the size of a Labrador retriever.[8]

In time, Jack found an apartment to his liking and moved out on his own, but the two friends remained in close contact. Mike even talked Jack into being his training partner — and Jack gained 20 pounds in one month utilizing Mike's "Heavy Duty" system.[9] Even after Cathy returned from the east coast, the friendship continued; the trio would go out for dinners, watch movies, frequent bookstores, discuss literature (both men were fans of Henry Miller), and listen to music by artists such as Elton John, the Beatles, the Rolling Stones, Fleetwood Mac, and the Eagles, and particularly the classical music of Beethoven and Wagner.[10]

Mike's popularity was rising amongst the magazine's readership, and when the first ad for his bodybuilding courses appeared in the April 1977 edition of *Muscle Builder/Power*, the mail-order sales were beyond anybody's expectations. Indeed, within two years of releasing his training booklets, and in combination with his seminar and exhibition fees, Mike was bringing in $200,000 a year[11] — about $140,000 a year more than Arnold did from bodybuilding during his peak years.

Back in Maryland, seeking to capitalize on Mike's recent popularity, Dr. Paul DeVore wasted no time cobbling together a nutrition book based upon how Mike had dieted for the 1976 Mr. America contest.[12] The doctor envisioned a two-book publishing venture. Having witnessed the massive success of fellow physician Kenneth Cooper's book *Aerobics*, DeVore thought the time was right for a book on the cardiovascular weight training program Mike had created for his patients, which DeVore christened "Cardionics." Mike was fine with DeVore's plans for the diet book but thought having his name on an exercise book could lead to problems. The circuit-training program he created to improve the cardiorespiratory fitness of the doctor's patients back in Maryland was far different than what he was advocating in his courses for bodybuilders. He didn't want his name appearing on two different exercise programs, which would only serve to confuse both would-be patients and aspiring bodybuilders. DeVore ended up self-publishing the diet book; the training book stayed on the shelf.

Mike's popularity amongst the readers of *Muscle Builder/Power* was such that he was allowed to get away with exposing the supplement business — including Joe's stock pitch that bodybuilders needed more protein to build bigger muscles:

> Most of us think muscle equals protein. When you think of protein, you think of muscle and when you think of muscle, you think of protein. It just so happens that muscle is comprised of 70 percent water, 22 percent protein, and 6 to 8 percent lipids and inorganic materials. So the primary constituent of muscle tissue is not protein but water. I know bodybuilders have been told for years that because they are indeed bodybuilders, and very different from the average person, they need more protein. This is not necessarily true. Keep in mind that muscle growth on a daily basis is very slow. Ten pounds gained in one year comes out to less than 12 grams gained per day — that's less than half an ounce of muscle gained per day, and most of that is water. How much extra protein do you think you need to gain 12 grams of muscle a day, most of which is water anyway? Obviously very little. Again, I can't emphasize it enough, don't overemphasize protein in your diet. Remember that muscle tissue is comprised mostly of water. That doesn't mean, however, you should drink gallons of water every day, either, to hasten the muscle growth process. Your body has specific needs each and every day for all the basic food nutrients. When you eat an excess of any one of those nutrients you don't utilize more of that nutrient for growth or for anything else. So don't eat much more than you need to maintain yourself and concern yourself more with training hard and eating just a well-balanced diet. The reason protein has been so overemphasized is because the protein hucksters can't sell you water through the mail. Again, this is where the commercial interests have distorted the true picture of bodybuilding reality.[13]

For a bodybuilder who was employed by Joe Weider, to say such things could be viewed as being just this side of heresy. And yet Mike was doing just that in his training courses and in his seminars. Apart from the science Mike imparted, even more impressive to the younger readers of the magazine was the confidence he exuded, both in his writings and when he spoke in seminars. He challenged with certainty all the sacred traditions in bodybuilding — and wouldn't bend his knee to anybody, including Arnold Schwarzenegger, as the following question-and-answer from his "Ask Mike" column illustrated:

Q. "Mike, you say that very few people can gain even ten pounds of muscle a year. If so, how do you explain the fact that Arnold went from 210 pounds after filming *Stay Hungry*, up to 235 pounds in a few short months to win the 1975 Mr. Olympia?"

A. "First of all, Jim, Arnold didn't go from 210 pounds to 235 to win the Olympia in a few months. He went from 210 pounds to only 225 pounds in four months to win the Olympia, a gain of fifteen pounds. You must keep in mind however that Arnold was gaining back size he had already built and lost. The regaining of previous mass is quite easy, certainly much easier than the acquisition of new muscle weight. There exists a 'tissue memory' that makes growth easier the second time around. The most dramatic example of this tissue memory was in the case of Casey Viator, 1971 Mr. America. On May 1 of 1973 Casey weighed a meager 166 pounds following an industrial accident. Only twenty-eight days later Casey had gained back to his best weight of 212 pounds, a demonstrable gain of some forty-six pounds. His actual gain of muscle in that one-month period was an incredible sixty-two pounds as isotope studies revealed that Casey had lost over seventeen pounds of fat during the month. How did he do it? Casey trained for thirty minutes three times a week for four weeks! That comes out to a total of six hours of training to gain back sixty-two pounds of muscle. This study was conducted by the exercise physiology department of Fort Collins University, so the figures are scientifically accurate.

"How did Arnold gain back his fifteen pounds in four months? He trained every day for four hours, as he has often stated in *Muscle Builder*. Training six days a week, four hours a day for four months equals 288 hours to gain back fifteen pounds. So, it took Arnold 288 hours of training to gain back fifteen pounds while it took Casey six hours of training to gain back sixty-two pounds of muscle. In both cases Arnold and Casey were regaining muscle which again is easier. . . . How can Casey's superior achievement be explained? Well, I know Casey was following an ultra-high intensity workout very similar to Heavy Duty methods. While this may not explain it fully, it certainly must be taken into account."[14]

Mike's approach to training was rapidly gaining support and popularity among the bodybuilding fans. In fact, the demand for him to appear for exhibitions and seminars had risen so high that Mike felt obliged to ask Joe if he could forgo having to appear in the office on a daily basis. Joe was fine with this and switched Mike's title from associate editor to writer. So long as Mike submitted his articles on time, there was no problem.[15]

Arnold Schwarzenegger, meanwhile, had developed a problem with Ben Weider over the sanctioning fees Ben wanted paid in order for Arnold and his partner, Jim Lorimer, to promote the 1978 Mr. Olympia contest.[16] Given that Arnold had brought a lot of money into the Weider coffers over the years, as a token of their gratitude Ben hadn't charged Arnold and his partner a sanctioning fee to host the Mr. Olympia contest in either 1976 or 1977. However, Ben made it clear that the duo would be paying for the privilege thereafter. This rubbed the Austrian Oak the wrong way. After all, in 1976, he and Jim had only walked away with $5,000 each after the contest.[17] Now Ben was telling them that a $5,000 sanction fee had to be paid to the IFBB or he would find someone else to promote the competition.[18]

About this time, another aspiring contest promoter, New York's Wayne DeMilia, appeared on the scene with the idea of creating a new professional contest — "The Night of Champions." It seemed a solid idea; bodybuilding was growing, the public was hungry to attend more high-level competitions, and it gave professional bodybuilders an opportunity to make more money.[19] It was a nice sentiment, to be certain, but when Ben Weider caught wind of Wayne's intention to run a professional bodybuilding contest under the imprimatur of the IFBB, he phoned the fledgling promoter and demanded his pound of flesh. Ben announced that he wanted to be paid a dollar per seat, which, given that Wayne's venue was purported to be the Town Hall Theater in Manhattan, he calculated to be $1,500.[20] Wayne was confused by the demand because when he had run the idea of creating a new pro show past Arnold, who, after all, was the Chairman of the IFBB Professional Committee (and had been since 1975),[21] the former Mr. Olympia winner made no mention of any sanctioning fees at all.[22] But Ben Weider's edict was final: all professional shows would have to pay a fee, and neither the Mr. Olympia nor Wayne's proposed Night of Champions contest was exempt.

Upon discovering that Ben had contacted Wayne directly, Arnold did likewise. He phoned the would-be promoter that informed him that under no circumstances was he to pay Ben Weider anything. Such a directive from a member of the IFBB clearly undermined the authority of its president. Clearly, Arnold believed that there was strength in numbers; if the two promoters stood together, perhaps neither of them would have to pay a fee. Wayne confessed to Arnold that, alone, he just didn't have the power to say no to Ben Weider. Indeed, from where he was sitting it looked like it was Ben's way or the highway. Arnold wasn't interested; he'd already communicated what he had to say about the matter and hung up the phone.[23]

Not hearing anything from Arnold in the weeks that followed, Wayne went ahead with his Night of Champions contest on May 6, 1978.[24] The contest, won by Robby Robinson, proved to be a great success with the bodybuilding public, and Ben Weider left the auditorium with a spring in his step and a check for $1,500 in his pocket.[25] The night after the competition, Wayne received another phone call from Arnold, this time inquiring if he had paid Ben the sanction fee. When Wayne replied that he had, Arnold hung up on him — again.[26]

More alarming to Arnold was the news that Gold's Gym owner Ken Sprague had started promoting bodybuilding contests — both amateur and professional — and Ben hadn't charged Ken any sanctioning fees at all.[27] But then Ken and the Weider brothers had a mutually beneficial arrangement in place. Ken had used his business acumen to bring the AAU (long controlled by Weider rival Bob Hoffman) into affiliation with the IFBB.[28] This resulted in Ben now controlling all amateur bodybuilding in North America. This had been a huge victory for the Weiders — and they had Ken to thank for it. Ken further allowed bodybuilders to be photographed in Gold's Gym for the numerous training articles that appeared in Joe's magazine. In return, the bodybuilders all wore Gold's Gym T-shirts and tank tops, and the gym received further acknowledgement in the magazine's photo credits. This underscored the impression that Gold's Gym was indeed the Mecca of bodybuilding; it was where the champions — both amateur and pro — trained.[29] In six short years (1972–78) under Ken's stewardship, Gold's had become an industry unto itself. Seeking to expand his brand, Ken's foray into promoting contests seemed a natural progression.

Rubbing salt in Arnold's wounds, Ken's contests were phenomenally successful. In July 1978, for example, Ken sold over 6,000 tickets to his "Gold's Classic" competition at the Los Angeles Shrine Auditorium, with those in the first five (main floor center) and the first three rows in loge paying $50 a seat.[30] He even had the juice to bring in Sylvester Stallone, late of *Rocky* fame, to hand out trophies to the winners.[31] Unlike Frank Zane (the winner of the Schwarzenegger/Lorimer-promoted 1977 Mr. Olympia contest), who received the paltry sum of $5,000 for his efforts,[32] the winner of Ken's Professional World Cup — Robby Robinson — was allowed to choose between a Cadillac Seville or its cash equivalent ($20,000), whichever he preferred.[33] In terms of cash prizes and how much money the promoter took home, Ken Sprague was operating on a different (and far superior) level. "I would think he [Arnold] was jealous of Ken Sprague's success," Joe Weider said. "He looked upon Ken as a competitor to him in promoting his shows and stealing some of Arnold's, you know, thunder."[34] It certainly appeared that way.

But as someone who, in George Butler's words, had designs on becoming "the king of the earth,"[35] Arnold had no intentions of relinquishing his power in the bodybuilding world. Indeed, he had already set in motion a plan to expand it. Arnold was putting the pieces in place to stick it to Ken Sprague and the Weiders. His contract with Joe Weider had expired in July 1977,[36] and while the pair had spoken about renewing it, Joe had been slow in finalizing it.[37] Moreover, Joe had signed a contract with Kal Szkalak in 1976, which ended in September 1977.[38] He evidently wanted to see how a renewal with Kal played out before committing to a contract that Arnold would no doubt want sweetened quite a bit. Arnold was still receiving free ads in Joe's magazine, of course,[39] and was still handling the Mr. Olympia promotion, but as far as Arnold was concerned, he was a free agent. He had already appeared on the cover of *Inside Kung Fu* (March 1976), which went on to feature two articles written on his training methods by Gene Mozee (an ad for his mail-order courses also appeared on the back cover of the magazine). In addition to this, Arnold had recently signed a one-year deal with a new bodybuilding magazine, *Muscle Digest*, which featured him in articles and published an interview.[40] Joe believed that Arnold was attempting to take a page out of his playbook: if Arnold could control the new magazine, he would be bodybuilding's new kingmaker.[41] Now all Arnold needed was a new gym; he could then convince all of the top bodybuilders to train there. When this happened, he would unplug the source of Ken's power with Joe Weider.

Arnold had ceased going to Gold's Gym[42] when he learned that Joe Gold, its original owner, was considering opening a new one in Santa Monica. With *Muscle Digest* on board and Joe Gold opening a new facility, Arnold's plan was proceeding without a hitch — until Ken Sprague learned of it. A former law student with a litigious hair-trigger, Ken sent a reminder to Joe Gold through the appropriate legal channel that when Ken had purchased Gold's Gym, Mr. Gold had signed a non-compete clause;[43] if he proceeded in opening the new gym, he would be doing so at his financial peril. This backed Joe Gold off. But then, perhaps out of sympathy, Ken relented; he would allow Joe to open a new gym, but only with the following stipulations: he could not use the Gold name, could not have photos taken in the gym (that would appear in a magazine) for three years, and he had to pay Ken an undisclosed amount of money.[44] Joe Gold was happy with the arrangement, and his plan to open the new gym proceeded.

Ken suspected that Arnold was financially involved with the new gym, perhaps as the owner of the building it would be operating out of. He wasn't certain about this, but the possibility was why his agreement with Joe Gold stipulated that no photographs were to be taken within the new facility. That clause protected the business relationship Ken had with Joe Weider.[45] In any event, Joe Gold's new facility opened in 1977. It was called World Gym.

Arnold did what he could to get the top bodybuilders who were presently members of Gold's to switch their allegiance to World Gym.[46] And one of the first he convinced to jump ship was Kal Szkalak.[47] Arnold had taken an interest in Kal. Not that he cared anything for him personally, but he knew what Kal meant to Joe Weider's future business plans. It was evident that Kal had all the physical attributes that Arnold possessed, plus there was no accent issue to contend with. The guy had star potential written all over him. He had already appeared on the cover of the July/August 1978 edition of *Muscle Digest*, and the accompanying article included the subheading

"Arnold's Successor?" The Austrian Oak knew which way the commercial winds were blowing. "Arnold was no dummy," observed Ken Sprague. "He understood the challenge to his eminence in the magazines, not wanting to lose the 'bird in hand' of the magazines as he pursued an acting career."[48] Sensing that he was potentially being phased out by the new arrival, Arnold employed the maxim of *keep your friends close and your enemies closer*.

Having gained Kal's trust, it was easy to lead him where Arnold wanted him to go. It was reminiscent of the scene in the documentary *Pumping Iron* where Arnold indicated that his best friend, Franco Columbu, was like a little child, who, when he came to Arnold for advice, could easily be directed onto the wrong path. "It's not that hard for me to give him the wrong advices [*sic*]," Arnold had said. Upon seeing the film, Franco was incensed by the statement.[49] But that was all water under the bridge now.

While giving Kal the wrong training advice might hurt the young bodybuilder competitively, Arnold had his mind set on using the current Mr. Universe champ for another, grander, purpose. He wanted to send a crippling torpedo directly into the hull of the Weiders' business enterprises. He convinced Kal that they should start a union. This would allow bodybuilders to compete in any contests they wanted — in any bodybuilding federation — without having to kowtow to Ben Weider and the IFBB.[50] Kal agreed: Who was Ben Weider to dictate what the bodybuilders could do, where they could compete, and how much money they could earn from the sport?[51] Arnold found it relatively easy to get Kal on board with his plan.

With talk of a union (and Arnold's support of it) spreading among professional bodybuilders,[52] Arnold now went on the offensive. He attacked Gold's Gym and praised World Gym in public forums. By this point, Ken Sprague had had enough.

What happened next was published in the newspapers:

SCHWARZENEGGER SUED

LOS ANGELES (AP) Muscleman Arnold Schwarzenegger has been sued for $3 million by Joe Gold's Gym in suburban Santa Monica for alleged libel. The suit filed in Los Angeles Superior Court Thursday alleged as libelous an article by Schwarzenegger in the February issue of Musclemag International, which said that going from Joe Gold's Gym into another Santa Monica facility, World Gym, was "like stepping from an outhouse to a palace." The suit also said a statement in Schwarzenegger's biography, "Arnold: The Education of a Bodybuilder" that "Gold's Gym is now World's Gym" was damaging, because it implied Gold's Gym had gone out of business.[53]

The lawsuit got underway in Los Angeles in July 1978. And in what must have been a shock to Arnold, a sworn statement in support of the prosecution came from none other than the Master Blaster himself.

CHAPTER SEVENTEEN

BETRAYALS

Joe Weider ascended the concrete steps and entered the 26-floor building at 10100 Santa Monica Boulevard. The elevator — one of 12 servicing the structure — carried him up to the seventh floor and the law offices of Chung and Tinberg.[1]

Awaiting his arrival in suite 750 were Ken Sprague and his lawyer, Sidney Tinberg. Joe had made the drive from his mansion in posh Hancock Park[2] that day to give sworn testimony in the *Joe Gold's Gym, Inc. v. Arnold Schwarzenegger* lawsuit.[3] The date was July 20, 1978, and the information he was about to provide about Arnold Schwarzenegger could prove both shocking and disturbing to fans of the bodybuilder, who up until recently had been the poster boy of Joe's empire:

- *On Arnold having become a success on his own*: "We photographed him. We prepared articles on him, gave him nutrition, and financed him and paid him a weekly check. . . . I gave him, I believe, $200 a week and ads in the magazine. I presume what I paid at the time, he must have taken in half a million dollars or so. . . . when I brought him over from Europe, he had no way of making a livelihood. He couldn't speak English properly and he had no profession. So, I actually helped him to get on his feet, to get him some money so he can train, he can go to drama school, and take business lessons. We helped him with his schooling, too. When he made some money I advised him to buy property and when he made money from his courses and money I gave him, I advised him to buy property and where to buy it and how to accumulate some security. . . . We helped him when he was in his movies with dialogue and copy, and we did everything that we could for him."

- *On Arnold's claim to have been a manager of a gym in Germany prior to coming to America*: "[Arnold] says in his book, that he ran a gym in Munich. But he didn't. He worked in a gym. He worked and slept at a gym with Franco, and he didn't have any money at all. . . . From what I know Franco told me that the police were after him for various violations of traffic and fights and so forth. He got out of Germany just in time."

- *On the reason for Arnold wanting to start a bodybuilder's union*: "I figure if he makes his union it will be like the I.F.B.B. He figures most likely he wants to be like me so that he can have work with World Gym like I work with Gold's Gym. He figures we have *Muscle Builder*, that he would work with [*Muscle Digest*] magazine. In other words, he is trying to run bodybuilding."

Things took a weird twist when Tinberg followed up on this point:

> **Tinberg:** "Has Arnold ever made statements to you that were derogatory about Ken Sprague or Gold's Gym?"
> **Weider:** "Yes."
> **Tinberg:** "What were the substance of those statements?"
> **Weider:** "Oh, he would say that he doesn't like Ken because he was gay. He didn't like any gay people in the business. He says that he can't trust Ken Sprague and he said that the place had loads of queers who would come there and pick up guys. He said that Ken was getting too much power in the gym, things to that effect."
> **Tinberg:** "Did he say these on more than one occasion?"
> **Weider:** "Yes. He said them on more than one occasion. I told him, 'If that's the case, why did you train at Gold's for all these years? You were training there, you took pictures with Ken Sprague, you wrote articles about how great the gym was, and everything, and if you are against it, why were you working with *Muscle Digest*, because [from] what I know, the editors there are gay as could

be.' You know, so I knew that wasn't the answer at Gold's Gym. I know that a lot of guys there hustle, too."

Tinberg: "You mean at World Gym?"

Weider: "At World Gym. So, I told him it is illogical and I don't think that is the real situation."

Tinberg: "What did he say to that?"

Weider: "He just smiled like I knew what I was talking about and let it go. He was basically, in my opinion, jealous of Ken Sprague. You see, Ken has Gold's Gym, Ken is running the show. He is in with the AAU and he has got a lot of strength. He is making some money and he is making a name for himself, and Arnold just didn't like to see that happen. He wanted to be the kingpin all the way down the line."

[. . .]

Tinberg: "He is trying to be a junior Joe Weider?"

Weider: "But he will never be a junior Joe Weider because he is prejudiced and he doesn't love the sport and he uses the sport."

Tinberg: "How is he prejudiced?"

Weider: "Well, because he singles out certain people he likes and he singles out certain people he doesn't like. He singles out certain bodybuilders he likes and he makes no bones about it, and certain ones he doesn't like. As long as they toe the line with him and obey him, then, you know, and he can use them, those are the people he would work with."

Tinberg: "Which are some of the bodybuilders that he likes?"

Weider: "Well, he likes Kal Szkalak, he likes Ed Corney, and he got along well with Frank Zane, I guess, up until recently. He found out he couldn't use Frank Zane. And there are some others."

Tinberg: "What about the ones he doesn't like?"

Weider: "Everybody that [still] trains at Gold's Gym, he hates. You know, he will say hello and be civil, but he hates them all. He doesn't like Robby [Robinson], he doesn't like Mike [Mentzer], he doesn't like [Danny] Padilla, and so forth."

Tinberg: "Is Arnold prejudiced against blacks?"

Weider: "Well, I would say so."

Tinberg: "Has he made any statement or actions to you that would indicate that he is prejudiced against blacks?"
Weider: "He is a prejudiced person. He just doesn't like minorities."
Tinberg: "Has he said anything to you about Jews?"
Weider: "Well, he doesn't come right out and say, 'I hate Jews.' He has ways of saying things."
Tinberg: "For instance, do you know of an example?"
Weider: "Well, he said that the movies are controlled by Jews, or he would say that he went to Israel and the Jewish people there are animals. Or he will use things along those lines."
Tinberg: "Do you know if he is a member of any Nazi organization?"
Weider: "I wouldn't know, but he admires Hitler and all that stuff."

If what Joe Weider testified to above was true (and the author is in no position to ascertain whether it was or was not), it may have spoken more strongly to Joe's character than it did to Arnold's. Evidently, so long as Arnold sold products for him, Joe was willing to keep his mouth shut about Arnold's alleged character flaws. It was only when Joe perceived that Arnold was trying to cut into his business territory that the Master Blaster brought out the knives, spilling the beans on his former "student" in order to protect his fiefdom. And make no mistake, what Joe Weider was putting out there under oath were allegations that carried the potential to end Arnold's career. Indeed, had it been made public in 1978, it would have terminated the Terminator's career in Hollywood well before it began, and most certainly would've derailed any political ambition he might have held. It further indicates the extent of the divide that had formed between Joe and Arnold, underscoring why Joe was actively searching for a bodybuilder who could replace the former Mr. Olympia winner as the new face of his product line. And when that face ultimately became Mike Mentzer's, it explains why Arnold and his allies in the bodybuilding world (as we shall see) went out of their way to castigate Mike and his physique in the bodybuilding press. But the author is getting ahead of himself.

Fortunately for Arnold, the lawsuit would be settled, and the depositions, along with Joe Weider's sworn statement, were put into boxes and filed away. There they would remain under wraps until Ken Sprague reopened them and shared its contents with author Randy Roach, who excerpted it in Volume II of his trilogy, *Muscle, Smoke & Mirrors*. But this came 33 years later (2011), well after Arnold had made his millions as a cinematic superstar and just after he completed his final term as the governor of California. In 1978, however, all of this still lay before him, and he had a Mr. Olympia contest to promote — and a bodybuilding union to get off the ground.

In the meantime, it was all systems go for Ken Sprague and Gold's Gym. Ken's next promotion was the 1978 Gold's Classic bodybuilding contest (held a mere nine days after Joe Weider's sworn statement had been entered into evidence), which featured no fewer than four bodybuilding competitions taking place on the same day — and at the same time.[4] The Gold's Classic featured the 1978 AAU Teenage Mr. America, the 1976 AAU Past 40 Mr. America, the USA vs. World Challenge Match, and the IFBB Professional World Cup. The poster Ken created for the event referred to it as "The Greatest Bodybuilding Contest in History."[5]

The hype enticed both Mentzer brothers to enter the USA vs. World competition. Ray was looking for some exposure to get his bodybuilding career off the ground, having lost his division to Pete Grymkowski at the 1977 IFBB Mr. America and losing to Kal Szkalak at the IFBB Mr. USA the previous summer. He wanted to be like Mike, to live in California and become a full-time bodybuilder. Living on the east coast and working at a pool company only served to fan the flames of Ray's ambition in this regard.[6] The USA vs. World competition would mark the third time (the previous two being the 1971 AAU Teen Mr. America and the 1977 IFBB Mr. North America) that the Mentzer brothers would be competing against each other.

According to Rick Wayne's report of the contest in *Muscle Builder/Power*:

> The American team was devastating. There was Mike Mentzer and his brother Ray, Ron Teufel too. The three could also have taken on Mars and Saturn, never mind the world. Mike's posing has improved beyond the horizons of my vocabulary (what a copout for a writer that line seems to be). He was big and he was confident. His definition was never better. And the improvement in his back had the crowd hollering for more. Ray Mentzer, though slightly behind big brother, was at his best. He has taken to duplicating some of Mike's incredible leg poses, which provided ample excuse for pandemonium at the Shrine auditorium.[7]

While Mike won his division of the contest easily (Ray would place second in the same division), the USA vs. World was a contest Mike entered simply to keep sharp in preparation for another run at the World Championships, which were set to take place in Acapulco, Mexico, in four months' time. "After losing the '77 Universe I realized that my back was literally against the wall," he said. "If you lose it after three times, you may as well forget it because your image in the minds of the judges goes down. I knew that I had to win the '78 Universe or kiss it goodbye."[8] With his bodybuilding future hinging on winning this contest, the talk of Arnold Schwarzenegger and Kal Szkalak starting up a bodybuilders' union was something he simply wasn't interested in investing much time in — at least initially. But the politics of the matter soon got the better of him. After all, Harry Mentzer was a member of a trucker's union, so Mike knew something about such things, if only in a peripheral way. The fact that bodybuilders such as Kal and Robby Robinson — straight shooters both — were in favor of the union caused him to take the matter seriously. The only potential problem that he foresaw was Arnold's involvement, as he had never known Arnold to do anything for anybody's benefit but his own.

Mike had crossed paths with the Austrian Oak on several occasions since moving to the west coast. Bodybuilding was a small world; if Joe or someone hosted a get-together, most of the bodybuilders were invited, and Mike and Arnold sometimes found themselves together in the same room. "For a short time, we became, not good friends, but acquaintances," Mike recalled. "We had some interesting conversations together alone. I was a young guy, new to California, a little bit in awe of Arnold. I wasn't as developed philosophically and intellectually as I was to become later. I didn't know how to perceive moral qualities. I just responded to what you sensed about people. I was never crazy about the guy because I didn't like his unwarranted arrogance. I was clearly aware that he was not a person of the stature he thought he was."[9]

But Kal, Robby, and a cadre of disgruntled bodybuilders held a different view. To them, Arnold was just the person who could pull off bringing a bodybuilders' union into existence. And they had good reason to believe it. Thanks to *Pumping Iron*, Joe's magazine, and numerous television appearances, Arnold was the face of bodybuilding. He had played a major role in building the Weiders' empire, he was the head of the IFBB Professional Committee, and, most importantly, Arnold had told the bodybuilders that he would back their play. And so, when Arnold and Kal called for a bodybuilders' summit at World Gym, Mike felt obliged to attend.

The meeting began with Kal announcing that he was the chairman of the union and Arnold its treasurer.[10] A fellow named Mike Besikoff was introduced as the lawyer for the new union. Kal explained that the aim of the union was to ensure that professional bodybuilders obtained a fair deal from promoters, and that it would seek to implement a guaranteed minimum wage for bodybuilders who gave posing exhibitions and seminars. This would hold contest promoters' collective feet to the fire; there would no more missed paydays because the organizers of events didn't get the audience turnout they had anticipated.

Next, it was Arnold's turn to speak. He stated that he would be the man responsible for "generating union funds" and that membership in the union was restricted to *only* pro bodybuilders. Mike, who had yet to turn professional, thus was not eligible to join.

When news of the World Gym summit reached the ears of Ben Weider, he hastily dispatched letters to all parties concerned. He quickly called for a meeting to take place the day after the Gold's Classic competition. The venue: the Santa Monica Holiday Inn.[11] Ben intended to nip the potential uprising in the bud before it blossomed. With Arnold firmly in their corner, on the night of the meeting Kal, Robby, and the rest of the bodybuilders made their way to the Holiday Inn with a large measure of confidence. They believed big changes were coming. Once again, Mike decided to attend.

Upon his arrival, he observed Ben Weider, along with Oscar State (who was now the general secretary of the IFBB) seated at a head table that was set up at the front of the room. Conference chairs were placed in front of the table and were already filled by movers and shakers within the industry: people such as bodybuilding promoters Ken Sprague, Wayne DeMilia, and Charlie Blake; gym owners George Turner (St. Louis), Leo Stern (San Diego) and Bill Pearl (Pasadena); executives Jim Manion (then current head of the AAU), Jacques Blommaert (IFBB Belgium), and Albert Busek (IFBB Germany). Joe Weider, of course, was present, flitting from person to person, hoping to give the impression of impartiality. Mike recognized the bodybuilders who were present: Kal Szkalak, Robby Robinson, Manny Perry, Danny Padilla, Ed Corney, Roy Callender, Bill Grant, and Kent Kuehn, as well as Steve Davis and Dave Johns (the last two currently under suspension from the IFBB). *Muscle Builder/Power* writers Rick Wayne and Jack Neary were also there, in addition to photographer Craig Dietz. All told, some 40 people had packed themselves into the conference room.[12] The only person absent was Arnold Schwarzenegger.

Thirty minutes after the meeting started, Arnold entered the room,[13] just in time to hear Kal Szkalak tell Ben Weider that he hoped the IFBB would work with the union.[14] With over 100 member countries now in the IFBB, Kal suggested that the union would actually serve to lighten Ben's workload, as he would no longer have to deal with promoter/bodybuilder issues.[15]

Ben was having none of it, however.

"How can I trust the remarks you just made, how can I accept you as a friend of the IFBB, when you persist in writing disparaging things about us and our federation?" Ben shot back,[16] presumably referencing some of Kal's recent comments in *Muscle Digest* magazine. As far as protecting the bodybuilders from unscrupulous promoters, Ben continued, he had heard from several promoters who had paid bodybuilders to guest pose only to have the bodybuilders show up out of shape, which hurt the promoter's credibility with ticket buyers. In another instance, a bodybuilder agreed to guest pose for a certain fee but then demanded more money than had been agreed upon or else he wouldn't pose, leaving the promoter the option to either capitulate or refund monies to the customers. Perhaps it was the promoters who needed a union rather than the bodybuilders, Ben quipped.[17]

The bodybuilders were on their heels. They now turned to Arnold. It was time to bring the heavy artillery into battle. Mike leaned forward in his seat. Arnold stood up and began by stating that he had once had a bad experience with a promoter in Mexico several years back.[18] He said nothing further.

That was *it*? This was the ammo Arnold had brought to the battle?

"[Arnold] could not say that bodybuilding promoters were a bunch of crooks," the editors at *Muscle Builder/Power* reported. "Indeed, apart from the named transgressor no one could recall a single instance where a promoter had been dishonest with a bodybuilder."[19] Arnold now read the room, and sensing that the union idea wasn't going to fly, he did something that shocked his comrades in arms. According to Robby Robinson:

> Arnold stood up, walked to the front, kissed Joe and Ben on their cheeks and walked out of the room. All our jaws dropped because we thought we had Arnold's support behind the union. We had all talked about it and agreed that if we came at them

as a group, they would have no choice. Now it was clear whose side Arnold was on.[20]

According to the article that appeared in *Muscle Builder/Power*: "At the end of the day the consensus was that whatever bodybuilding needed at this point in time it was not a union run by Kal Szkalak and Arnold Schwarzenegger."[21] Some years later, Wayne DeMilia would tell author/historian Randy Roach that after the meeting had broken up that night, he approached Ben Weider and asked him what Arnold had whispered into his ear prior to his departure (at the time Arnold kissed his cheek). Ben replied that Arnold said he "had to go to a meeting but that he fully supported the IFBB," which left poor Kal Szkalak floundering on his own. Ben added that he "didn't trust Arnold at all."[22] It was certainly clear to the bodybuilders that Arnold had been playing both sides against the middle in the affair. But then, why wouldn't he? He couldn't lose; if the union was established, he would have been in control of it — the Jimmy Hoffa of professional bodybuilding. If the union didn't get off the ground, then Kal Szkalak would be the fall guy.

The passage of several weeks proved insufficient time to heal the wound to Kal's pride from the union calamity. A kaleidoscope of emotions flitted through his mind, and none of them were pleasant. Matters weren't helped when he pondered what the failed union attempt might mean to his professional bodybuilding career. After all, it wasn't just bodybuilders who were present at that meeting, there were also promoters; people who paid bodybuilders money for guest posings and seminars, and who provided platforms for them to sell their products. This was a serious source of income. If Kal was now viewed as the bad guy, then most of the promoters who worked hand in glove with the Weider brothers would have nothing to do with him. Kal's dream of earning a living from professional bodybuilding might have ended just as it was starting.

And then Kal spied the February 1978 issue of *Muscle Builder/Power* — the one that featured two large pictures of him on its cover. Flipping the magazine open to the table of contents, his anger rose. There was a photo of Kal hitting a double biceps pose while standing in front of Joe Weider. In the image, Joe's right hand was tucked under Kal's arm as if he were helping him with the pose — as if they were a *team*. It was the only photo on the page, and right next to it was the caption: "Joe Weider, Trainer of Champions since 1936, did it again! Joe poses proudly with Kal Szkalak, another Weider Superstar, 1977 World's Champion Body Builder." Now Kal was livid. Joe had nothing to do with what he had gone through to win that title (at least, as far as he knew). When Kal's contract with Joe had ended, Joe promised that he would continue to pay him for any use of his photos and any ghost-written articles that had appeared "by Kal Szkalak" in his magazine. But the contract had expired the better part of a year ago, well before this edition of the magazine went to press, and, to date, no money had arrived in Kal's bank account. According to Jack Neary, this was common practice for Joe; he would promise astronomical sums, but then never follow through with his pledge. He'd even promised Jack that if he kept training hard, he would put him on the cover of the magazine and pay him $50,000.[23] Most of those who worked closely with Joe, such as Jack, typically laughed off his grandiose promises. Kal, however, was of a different mindset.

Filled with rage, Kal hopped into his car and made a beeline to Joe's offices in Woodland Hills. Upon arriving, he entered through a side door, ascended the stairs, and marched directly to the photo library, where all of Joe's photographs of the various bodybuilders were kept in alphabetized files. Jack Neary, who was in the office with Joe at the time, vividly recalled what happened next:

> It was kind of a rainy fall day and Kal suddenly came barreling into the studio area leading towards the photo library. He went straight for the drawer, and he scooped up armfuls — like he's got all of the photos from the "S" files, including those of Schwarzenegger. And as he was running back out Joe said, "What are you doing?" And I give Joe credit; he stood in front of Kal. Now Kal was a big guy, and Joe was a 57-year-old man, and he stood his ground. And Kal ran into him like an angry rhino, knocked Joe on his ass and dropped half the pile of photos in his arms. And they both hit the floor and Joe was kind of grappling with him and I said, "Joe! Joe!" I was trying to pull Joe off. I'm like, "No, Joe! You don't want this to escalate! This could end badly!" So Joe kind of backs off, and Kal managed to scoop up enough; he got away with

about 300 shots and runs down the stairs and away. Joe is in a rage. "Call the cops! Call the cops!" I said, "What are the cops going to do?" And then Joe got his lawyer on the line and the next thing is that lawsuits are being threatened.[24]

After work that day, Jack couldn't wait to share what had just gone down with Mike. "I shared the rhino charge of Kal with Mike," Jack recollected. "As I recall, he laughed and found the whole thing amusing."[25] Several days later the phone on Jack's desk rang. It was Kal Szkalak on the line. "I've been told that there's a lawsuit pending or something," he said. "And I have to return the stolen goods." After a pause he added, "So, I want to organize to do that *with you*."[26]

The handoff was set to take place that night in the parking lot of the Santa Monica Airport. "It was like a clandestine drug deal," Jack recalled. "I pulled my Volvo up and he had his Camaro. All the pictures were bent and tattered from the collision with Joe. They weren't in the greatest shape, but he did return them. There was a big stack, and I just put them on the car seat beside me and drove them home and delivered them to Joe the next day. But there was a lawsuit."[27]

Suddenly, the man who had been touted as the second coming of Arnold Schwarzenegger was on the outside looking in. Joe would have to look for another bodybuilder to replace Arnold as his poster boy. Kal concluded that his recent actions would scuttle any chance he might have of winning the 1978 Mr. Olympia contest. But then, word had it, along came Arnold Schwarzenegger, Kal's mentor,[28] coaxing him to enter the competition.[29] After all, Arnold was the promoter of the contest — not Joe Weider. This meant that Arnold would be the one to select the judges. Kal's beef with Joe wouldn't be a factor. Soon Kal was convinced that if he entered the competition, he would get a fair shake and a level playing field. And so, he entered — and was rewarded with a fifth-place finish.

Frank Zane, the sub-200-pound defending champion, was declared the winner of the 1978 Mr. Olympia contest. *Muscle Builder/Power* reported that Zane's victory that day wasn't because he had any outstanding muscle groups, but rather it was his *lack* of exceptional development that resulted in a more balanced, symmetrical look, which the judges evidently considered to be more important than muscle mass.[30] In the very Mr. Olympia contest that had placed crowns on the heads of mass monsters such as Sergio Oliva and Arnold Schwarzenegger, muscle mass — or at least having over 200 pounds of it — was no longer a good thing. And it wasn't that Kal lacked definition; the consensus, including the one published in *Muscle Builder/Power*, indicated that Kal "was certainly as muscularly defined as any of the contenders,"[31] which obviously included Frank Zane. Mike Mentzer, who had made the trip to Columbus, Ohio to watch the competition, concurred. "There wasn't an ounce of fat on his entire body," he said.[32]

When Kal's name was called out for fifth place, a chorus of boos greeted the judging panel's decision. Kal smiled to himself. *Fell for it again.* He stepped forward and placed his left foot atop his right, stretched his arms out to the side and dropped his head onto his right shoulder.[33] The crowd didn't have to be Christian to understand the message he was communicating. "Mike was there and told me about it," Jack recalled. "Mike was stunned. I remember him saying, 'You would *not believe* what I saw. It was crazy!'"[34] Joe Weider opined that "Kal has crucified himself thinking he will win the Mr. Olympia when his legs are way out of proportion to the rest of his Herculean upper body."[35] The smaller, less developed legs that were good enough in the judges' eyes to win the World Championships and allow Kal to turn professional, were now deemed an impediment to his winning a professional bodybuilding contest. But consistency had never been a hallmark of an IFBB judging panel.

Kal walked off the stage and out the Weider bodybuilding world. He would never compete in another IFBB contest. Albert Busek, Arnold's friend who attended the failed union meeting, would say — 21 years later — that "I was a judge at the 1978 Mr. Olympia and Kal had absolutely no chance to be a contender for the title, period."[36] Indeed.

With Kal out of the picture, Joe still needed a bodybuilder with similar muscle mass to sell products for him. Not that Frank Zane wasn't marketable. He was. In fact, he had been appearing in Joe's magazine ads since the late 1960s, marketing everything from "Muscle Food Candy" to "Muscle Rub" liniment. His physique was incredible, like something a Renaissance artist would have created; great definition and a muscular symmetry that was pleasing to the eye. But Joe's market wasn't the arts community. It was young males who coveted huge, superhero-type muscles — and Frank just didn't have them. Looking around his environment Joe saw no shortage of big, muscular physiques.

Robby Robinson, of course, was a standout. But in Joe's mind, Blacks didn't sell magazines, and minimal magazine sales meant minimal eyes reading his ads. Consequently, great Black bodybuilders like Robby, Darcy Beckles, Bill Grant, and Dave Johns weren't viable options for the Trainer of Champions. Joe's eyes then came to rest upon Mike Mentzer. Mike was not only popular, but he was also strikingly handsome, with hazel eyes and a mustache that rivaled Tom Selleck's — and he was built like the proverbial brick shithouse. Plus, he was intelligent, well versed in science, psychology, and philosophy, and had a premed background. Moreover, he was preternaturally articulate; no one who spoke with him came away unimpressed. This was a guy who could successfully sell Joe Weider's products in many markets.

Joe Weider had found his replacement for Arnold Schwarzenegger.

CHAPTER EIGHTEEN

PERFECTION IN ACAPULCO

There was nothing Arnold could do to stop Mike from becoming Joe's new poster boy — at least not at the moment. He couldn't befriend him to ultimately mislead him because, unlike Kal Szkalak, Mike didn't trust Arnold. Mike had witnessed firsthand how Arnold had betrayed the Hungarian, both in the union fiasco and at the 1978 Olympia. Besides, Mike was never one to curry anybody's favor in the hope that a few crumbs might be thrown his way. He had made it this far on his own, and that was the way he intended to play it going forward.

With the World Championships less than six weeks away, Mike was focused on getting into his best shape and claiming a title that had eluded him on two prior occasions. He had started keeping a journal prior to competing in the Gold's Classic show,[1] in which he made entries on his workouts and any variations he employed — from weights and sets to protocols and training frequency — to see what effect each had on his physique. He further noted his calorie intake, steroid use, and aerobic activities in his quest to build muscle and lose fat. Knowing the mind and body to be integrated, his daily entries also included notes on his emotions and thoughts. Each entry taught him something about himself.

Mike trained alone, four days a week, with each workout now lasting only 30 to 45 minutes.[2] He averaged two to four sets for smaller muscle groups, like arms,[3] and up to six sets for larger muscle groups like back, employing high-intensity techniques such as forced repetitions and negatives on each and every set.[4] He trained almost exclusively on Nautilus machines and became so strong on several of them that he was using the entire weight stack plus additional weights.[5] He also engaged in daily aerobic activity, typically bike riding for 30 to 40 minutes per session.[6]

While most high-profile bodybuilders of Mike's era, such as Arnold Schwarzenegger and Franco Columbu, publicly denied that they used steroids for competition,[7] Mike was always up-front about his use of the drugs.[8] He was, after all, intellectually invested in seeing the sciences brought to bear on bodybuilding — and chemistry, last he checked, was one of the sciences. More significantly, he believed that lying was more immoral than taking steroids. As he once told the author: "The kind of bodybuilders that annoy me the most are the ones who lie about their steroid use — especially top champions. I think the bodybuilding world has forgotten about this: that lying is immoral. Taking steroids is not immoral; it's a personal decision that affects no one but the individual."[9] It must be remembered that this was 1978; steroids would not become an illegal substance in the United States until 12 years later, with the passing of the Anabolic Steroids Control Act of 1990.[10] Mike wrote several articles for *Muscle Builder/Power* in response to the voluminous inquiries he received about steroids, and he believed the best response was to be completely candid. Yes, there were risks involved. No question:

> Since writing about steroids openly in *Muscle Builder*, I have been swamped by letters requesting advice on how to best take them. While your interest is highly appreciated, I must point out that I am not a physician. And even if I were, it would not be ethical to prescribe through the mail. Besides, I don't know the safest and most effective way to take steroids. My experience with them has taught me certain things, but I would never suggest that my observations are absolutely correct or valid. Taking steroids is a very chancy thing. These substances are not vitamins; abusing them could be fatal. My position remains as stated in my articles. I would never advise anyone to take them because this is a highly personal decision. If, however, you are resolute in your intent to take them, please don't be indiscriminate. Do so only under your doctor's supervision.[11]

But if steroids were chancy, they were also necessary if a bodybuilder wanted to compete at the highest level of the sport. And as the highest level of the sport was where Mike wanted to compete, he opted to take the drugs — and was candid about doing so:

> I have never hidden the fact that I've used steroids, I realize that any further attempts at self-disclosure could justifiably be interpreted as a rationalization, or even atonement for my own reluctant use of drugs. Without being prompted, I will admit to a nagging concern and worry about the associated health risks. What sane and rational individual wouldn't? Any drug, including caffeine and aspirin, has the potential to induce physical harm. The point is, being fully cognizant of the risks, I persist in using them. At this point in my life, I have decided that winning physique titles and living the life of a top bodybuilder give direction and meaning to my life. These drugs have been around long enough to establish whether or not long-term intermittent use causes serious, irreversible side effects. Having used steroids for many years without any visible impairment, I will probably continue to use them prior to future competitions.[12]

Concerned that young bodybuilders were proceeding with steroid use blindly, taking many times the dosages that upper-echelon bodybuilders used, Mike did something that was unprecedented: he wrote an article detailing exactly what brands and dosages he employed when preparing for a contest:

> The dosage which I employed the last six weeks leading up to the 1976 Mr. America was moderate and well within the recommended dosage range. My intake then was 100 mgs. of deca-durabolin every three weeks and 15 mgs. of dianabol a day. I was more than happy with the results I was getting at that time and never gave serious consideration to upping the dosage. Once I arrived in Southern California and heard stories of the massive doses others were reportedly taking and getting great results, I began to wonder if I too shouldn't do the same. I began to fall prey to the insidious and coercive charm of the "more is better" logic. The logical reasoning and keen judgment for which I usually pride myself suffered further

breakdown under the intense pressure I felt to win the '77 Universe in Nîmes. At the time, I saw that contest as pivotal in my career with a loss meaning possibly the end. . . . My compulsion to win led me to increase my anabolic intake for the Nîmes Universe to 200 mgs. of deca-durabolin every three weeks along with a weekly shot of 100 mgs of Primobolin and up to five dianabols a day. For the first time in my fledgling career, I encountered water retention problems. I went to Nîmes puffy, lacking the hard razor ripped look I had when I won the America, and lost to Kal Szkalak. Apparently, I took too many steroids and retained water under the skin as well as in the muscle. The saga didn't end in Nîmes of course, I am still competing and still using steroids, but I am also learning from my experiences. I know now that the benefits I derive from steroid usage come from small to moderate doses, taken for brief periods, intermittently through the year, usually before a contest.[13]

A month before the competition, Mike dropped his calorie intake to only 500 per day.[14] This put his body into a perpetual state of ketosis (fat burning). He used Ketostix to test his urine for the presence and concentration of acetoacetic acid; an indicator that he was burning bodyfat (rather than glucose) for fuel. Mike's biology and organic chemistry background taught him to augment his diet with potassium tablets when in periods of heavy ketosis, so that his energy didn't bottom out. "Before I discovered the importance of supplemental potassium on a low-carb diet, I found myself at times so overwhelmingly fatigued that I literally couldn't get out of a chair," he said. "When you're mobilizing that much bodyfat, you excrete a chemical known as ketones, and your body's potassium has a very strong chemical affinity for ketones. And when you urinate, you urinate the body's potassium out with the ketones. But as long as you keep your potassium high enough, you'll have an abundance of energy. I required less sleep, and I got through my workouts okay."[15]

To keep his motivation primed during this period of privation, Mike once again found the writings of Nietzsche to be helpful. "I don't know how readers will relate to this," he told bodybuilding journalist Bill Reynolds, "but my training partner during my Universe workouts — and this is meant somewhat facetiously — was Nietzsche. I was reading his works four to five hours a day before Acapulco. Reading him puts me in a certain state of mind and being. He intensifies my state of being. He's a very intense writer of a very intense philosophy. I was particularly reading his *The Will to Power*, and just reading it made me feel more powerful. He talks a lot in there about building a strong will, and about accomplishment through determination and will power. Reading him was great for psyching me up."[16] Mike was also reading the American physician / psychologist / pragmatist philosopher William James, and particularly his book *The Energies of Men*, which contained two passages that caught his attention:

- "Compared with what we ought to be, we are only half awake. Our fires are damped, our drafts are checked. We are making use of only a small part of our possible mental and physical resources."[17]
- "Either some unusual stimulus fills them with emotional excitement, or some idea of necessity induces them to make the extra effort of will. Excitements, ideas, and efforts, in a word, are what carry us over the dam."[18]

Mike related James's observations to his contest preparation. He weighed up what winning or losing would mean to his career; if he won, he could turn pro and enter contests that awarded victors prize money rather than trophies. If he lost, his bodybuilding dream would be over. Winning, then, became his "idea of necessity," which served to prompt him to apply the required "extra effort of will" during his workouts. By the week of the contest, Mike felt his energy peaking. The novelty of this experience caused him to write in his journal:

> The notion that all of this tortuous preparation, privation, and relentless pursuit has lifted me on to a new and higher level of existence has become increasingly apparent to me. Life has assumed a greater meaning in the process. While there is an element of tension and discomfort associated with this "elevated" existence, I can only say I thrive while caught up in it, and am generally most stimulated in every area — intellectually, emotionally, and spiritually . . . Nietzsche's will

and sense of life waxed their strongest during those periods of greatest physical hardship . . . There must be some trigger mechanism which liberates a tremendous reservoir of strength and energy that results in this experience of vastly increased vigor and vitality.[19]

Mike and Cathy arrived in Acapulco the week of the contest, content in the knowledge that Mike had done all that he could in terms of preparation. He was *ready*. The competition was well publicized, and not just in the local media; the Associated Press and CBS Sports were on hand to cover the event. Convinced that he had lost the title to Kal Szkalak the previous year owing to the Hungarian's greater definition, Mike had made it a point to improve that aspect of his physique. Evidently he succeeded, as not only did current Mr. Olympia Frank Zane (who was on hand as the color commentator for the CBS telecast) offer his approval,[20] but, upon laying their eyes on him, the producers for CBS decided they wanted to make Mike the subject of a 30-minute episode of their TV series *CBS Sports Spectacular*.[21] As part of their "B-roll" footage for the program, they had Mike go through his posing routine against a backdrop of bleached-white rocks and the azure water of Acapulco Bay. A cadre of photographers, some professional, some amateur, looked on during the filming and snapped away furiously with their cameras.[22]

Mike knew that his competition for the title would not be quite as stern as he had faced in previous World Championships. Robby Robinson and Kal Szkalak were obviously absent, the former having moved on to the Professional Division and the latter suspended from IFBB competition. But a German entrant, Jusup Wilkosz, was huge and ripped, and looked ready to give Mike a serious battle.[23]

When the doors to the Centro de Convenciones Acapulco opened for the contest, it quickly filled with 2,700 fans.[24] Each class competed separately before seven different judges (21 in all).[25] A total of 95 competitors from 43 nations would be battling it out to win the Mr. Universe title in the Lightweight, Middleweight, and Heavyweight Classes.[26] Mike's teenage hero, Bill Pearl, recently appointed head of the Professional Judges' Committee, was on hand to help run things from backstage and to hand out the trophies to the winners of each division.[27]

The contest began with the Lightweight Division and culminated with the Heavyweights. Carlos Rodriguez from Tucson, Arizona, won the Lightweight

Class with 298 points,[28] just two points shy of a perfect score. California's Tom Platz claimed the Middleweight title with a score of 294.[29] And then came the division that most of those in attendance (and millions more throughout North America who were watching the broadcast on television) wanted to see: the Heavyweight. After each competitor had gone through his final posing routine, master of ceremonies Oscar State walked to the podium and leaned into the microphone: "Ladies and gentlemen. The winner, with a perfect score of 300 points — the first perfect score ever awarded in the history of international bodybuilding competition — the new Mr. Universe: Mike Mentzer of the United States!"[30]

Pandemonium broke out; chants of "Ment-zer! Ment-zer!" filled the auditorium.[31] The CBS camera crew rushed onstage to record Mike's reaction, while the Associated Press quickly filed its report so that newspapers around the country could pick up the story. And it was newsworthy. As Oscar State had announced, Mike Mentzer was the only Mr. Universe winner in the history of the competition to be awarded a perfect score — even the highly celebrated Arnold Schwarzenegger never earned such an honor in international competition.[32] In its "flash report" of the contest, *Muscle Builder/Power* proclaimed that "Mentzer returned with a vengeance in a performance that was nothing if not perfect. At a bodyweight of 216, entirely ripped, flexing flawlessly, he accomplished the impossible — a 300 score in international competition."[33]

Mike Mentzer had just made bodybuilding history.

CHAPTER NINETEEN

TURNING PRO

One would be forgiven for assuming that winning the Mr. Universe title with the first perfect score in bodybuilding history would have made Mike Mentzer deliriously happy. But such was not the case. Instead, he was perplexed.

The day before the contest, he had been as ripped as he had ever been. But perhaps from the steroids or the combination of sodium-rich seafood and water he consumed the night before,[1] the space between his muscles and his skin had stored fluid, which compromised his definition on the day of the show. He didn't think he was as sharp as he could have been.[2]

"Getting the 300 points and winning by 30 over Wilkosz of Germany leaves me with mixed emotions," he said, immediately after the competition. "It's almost embarrassing to me on one hand, and an honor on the other. I personally didn't think I was that much ahead of Wilkosz, who was very ripped. If I had been as cut as the day before the show, I'd have been more comfortable in accepting that 300." He paused and then added, "Actually, nobody deserves 300, since everyone has a flaw here and there."[3]

Alarmingly, rather than experiencing elation from his victory, Mike lapsed into a deep depression. "There was a tremendous post-contest depression that set in almost immediately after my name was announced. I've always felt somewhat of a depression after a contest, because the most exciting thing for me is the preparation, and winning is always somewhat of an anticlimax. This time it was such a severe depression that I almost started crying after the contest, not from joy, but from the depression."[4] It was a peculiar emotion to be feeling after achieving one of the greatest feats in bodybuilding history and may have been his first inkling that the mental health issue his mother suffered from had now knocked upon his door.[5]

Mike tried to understand the cause of his depression and concluded (perhaps too hastily) that it was "probably due in a large degree to a slowing of the high state of existence I was in while preparing for the Universe. After the super intensity of training, dieting and mental preparation, it was a letdown to be back to normal."[6] He may have been right. However, when recalling the incident some 15 years later during an interview with bodybuilding journalist Peter McGough, he still couldn't explain it:

> There was a point where I was thinking, 'What did I go through all of that for?' But it was an emotional thing, I hadn't thought about it, and it wasn't based on anything rational. I'm not sure what caused it.[7]

If, as Mike assured himself, it was simply his coming down from the elevated plane of existence he had enjoyed during contest preparation that triggered his depression, a cure was on its way. His Mr. Universe victory enabled him to now enter professional contests, and 1979 had a slew of them to choose from. Wayne DeMilia, Charles Blake, and Karen Clarke (the promoters of the first Night of Champions professional contest in New York the previous year), were looking to sign up bodybuilders to compete in three pro shows they would be promoting prior to the 1979 Mr. Olympia. According to *Muscle Builder/Power*, apart from the above trio, the IFBB also sanctioned three additional pro contests that year: George Snyder was promoting one in Pennsylvania; Warren Langman would be promoting one in Canada; and, surprisingly, Paul Graham was promoting a pro show in Australia.[8] The "crocodile wrestler" had apparently exited prison into the open arms of Ben Weider. The IFBB, along with Arnold (who was head of its Professional Division) not only awarded Graham the right to promote a professional bodybuilding contest but also named him the new president of the IFBB Australian Bodybuilding Federation.

Given Mike's historical triumph in Acapulco, the trio of DeMilia, Blake, and Clarke was keen to sign him up to compete in three pro shows they were promoting on February 3 (in Florida), April 7 (in Pittsburgh), and May 12 (in New York).[9] But entering three contests in four months was a big ask and, for the moment, Mike wasn't sure he was up to it. He thought it best to compete in only one their shows. "My first professional show will be at the April 7 Night of the Champions in Pittsburgh," he'd said. "The February 3rd show is too soon after the Universe for me. I want to be off the drugs for several months, and I just need a little break in the training intensity and severity of the diet. I can't maintain a high degree of muscularity too long without just becoming a nervous wreck."[10]

While pleased with the improvements he'd made to his body in winning the Mr. Universe competition, Mike knew that he had been far from the "perfect" his 300 score had indicated. His goal remained to build "the ultimate physique,"[11] which meant he needed to build more size and create sharper definition. In November 1978, Mike conducted a bodybuilding seminar at the Chicago gym of former Mr. America Bob Gajda. Among those in attendance was Tony Garcy, one of America's more celebrated weightlifters.[12] Tony was on the American team that competed in the 1964 Tokyo Olympics, where he finished fourth in the Lightweight Division.[13] After the seminar, the two men struck up a conversation. During the discussion, Mike learned that Tony had a PhD in exercise physiology. This led to a discussion about the science underlying Mike's approach to bodybuilding exercise:

> Tony and I discovered that our thoughts regarding intensity, the adaptive response and recovery ability were along the same lines. Tony agreed that intensity was the single most important factor influencing the growth of skeletal muscle. I explained to Tony how I had been using pre-exhaustion and relatively heavy weights to up my training intensity, but that recently my progress had slowed almost to a complete halt despite my most intensive efforts. Drawing upon his extensive knowledge of the physiology of stress, Tony pointed out that I had adapted fully to the pre-exhaustion method,[14] which was no longer sufficient in intensity to induce growth stimulation. What I required was a new training method that provided for the possibility of even more intense contractions, while avoiding the ischemia and build-up of metabolites such as lactic acid that might prevent such ultra-intense effort.[15]

Upon his return to California, Mike cracked open one of his physiology textbooks to see if he could find a solution to his dilemma. The book was *The*

Biology of Physical Activity by D.W. Edington and V.R. Edgerton, and there, in the chapter entitled "Circulatory Factors in Exercise," he read the following:

> Muscle contractions can become so intense that blood flow to that muscle is decreased. . . . In effect, not enough time between contractions was permitted for the vasculature to fill before the onset of the subsequent contraction. Blood flow to working muscles does not decrease at high work intensities when the duration of contractions is short enough and the duration of relaxation is long enough.[16]

Armed with the knowledge of the need for intense muscular contractions to stimulate growth, and now with a better understanding of how to assist his circulatory system in achieving this, Mike set off for the gym to experiment with a new protocol:

> I would do one set of four reps for each exercise. Never did I do more than three total sets per body part. I experimented at first by resting fifteen seconds between reps. Other times I rested for seven seconds. Fifteen turned out to be too long and seven seconds too short. I also tried six reps per set, but I found it too taxing, and it immediately led to overtraining. Doing four reps, with the ten-second rest-pause, I increased every single exercise at least twenty pounds per workout until I finally had improved sixty-six percent on each one. My size, of course, increased also.[17]

By January 1, 1979, Mike's improvement was such that he decided he would compete in the 1979 Southern Professional Cup in Miami. It would be his first professional contest.[18] Things took a serendipitous turn the week prior to the competition when CBS Sports broadcast its 30-minute profile on him, which highlighted his perfect 300 score at the World Championships.[19] "Within days after the subsequent airing of the CBS piece," Mike recollected, "I was contacted by a major public relations firm that secured me a book contract, a poster contract, and appearances on several national TV shows, all in short order."[20] Mike's star was on the rise, and, to top it off, by the time he arrived in Miami he was in the best shape of his life.

But Mike was a rookie. This was his first pro contest. By contrast, Robby Robinson, the "Black Prince," was not only a veteran of professional bodybuilding competition, but the king of the hill. He'd already won the first ever Night of Champions and World Pro Cup contests and had placed a close second to champion Frank Zane in both the 1977 and 1978 Mr. Olympias. Moreover, the prize money he'd earned through his contest placings, in addition to the lucre that flowed into his pockets from seminars, exhibitions, and product sales, made him the highest-earning professional bodybuilder in the sport, generating in excess of $100,000 in 1978 alone.[21] It's true that he didn't have a contract with Joe Weider, but his burgeoning bank account proved he didn't need it. Given that Robby had previously defeated each competitor (either on the amateur or professional circuit) who would be appearing in the Florida show, he arrived for the Southern Pro Cup brimming with confidence. He considered it a homecoming of sorts. After all, he was raised in Tallahassee, Florida,[22] and was so certain of victory in this contest that he paid for his mother and sisters to come to Miami and watch him in action. Surprisingly, they had never attended any of his bodybuilding competitions before,[23] and Robby wanted them in the front row to witness him awarded first place — and the $4,000 winner's check.[24] The last time Mike and Robby had competed against each other was three years previously, at the World Championships in Montreal. Then, they were both amateurs and in their twenties. Robby was now 33 and entering his fifth pro contest. Mike was 27 and had zero experience at this level of competition. Robby expected to blow Mike off the stage.

Bill Reynolds was a physical education teacher with a PhD in psychology from the University of California, Berkeley, when he began writing articles for Bob Hoffman's *Muscular Development* magazine in the late 1960s. He had an amazing capacity for churning out articles in a matter of hours that took most writers in the bodybuilding world weeks. It wasn't long before Joe Weider saw him as an asset and had him writing articles for *Muscle Builder/Power*. By 1978 Bill had worked his way up the corporate ladder to become the magazine's editor-in-chief. One of the things he enjoyed most about his job was the travel. And so, he took it upon himself to cover the Florida Pro Cup for the publication.

Upon his arrival in Miami, he checked into his hotel and placed calls to most of the competitors to set up interviews. When he finally connected with Mike Mentzer, Mike suggested that the two meet at a nearby Howard Johnson's; the interview could take place over a bowl of ice cream.[25] Bill wasn't sure he had heard Mike correctly — ice cream? What bodybuilder ate ice cream prior to a contest? Bill's hearing proved to be fine, however, when the pair sat down in the restaurant and Mike ordered a large bowl of the confection. If Mike's consumption of ice cream prior to the biggest contest of his life came as a surprise, Bill's jaw hit the table when Mike next ordered a double vodka gimlet. Seeing the surprised look on the editor-in-chief's face, Mike felt an explanation was in order. "My diet is now more in tune with the human body's biochemistry than with any program I've ever followed," he said. "By reducing total calories in any diet, a person will lose fat weight. The primary way I reduced calories for this competition was to cut back drastically on my consumption of fats — no beef, then — and reduce my protein intake to 60 grams per day. Undoubtedly, this sounds incredible to you, but your body does not need more than that amount to build huge muscles, since it is perfectly capable of manufacturing its own protein from other foods."

Bill understood the reasoning behind reducing calories to lose fat, but why was Mike consuming products laden with sugar?

"The body's preferred source of fuel for energy production is carbohydrate, so my carbohydrate level is high to keep my training energy and daily energy levels up," Mike explained. "That's why I'm eating ice cream before the contest. In fact, I've had at least three scoops every day this week and am still cutting up. As long as I keep my daily caloric intake under a certain level, I get progressively more defined."

Mike also shared with Bill his use of the Rest-Pause training protocol. Bill was intrigued and wanted Mike to write an article on the method for *Muscle Builder/Power*. "I've never been as big or cut as I am today," Mike stated. "And my chest has improved so much it will shock some of the competitors. And yet it's never been so easy to get into shape. I'll be at all the pro shows this year, except the one in Australia. Unfortunately, I had already scheduled a seminar and posing exhibition that day. This new type of training has given me incredible results, and my new low-protein/high-carbohydrate diet is easy to live with, yet it strips off fat like hot water on snow. I'm taking an extremely low level of drugs, and for the next show I'll probably be totally natural." That would be incredible — if it was possible. Bill hadn't seen Mike stripped down yet, so for all he knew, Mike was just talking. The proof would be in how he looked onstage.

The morning of February 3, Mike entered the Gusman Cultural Center, the venue for the competition. He kept his eye peeled for Robby Robinson, the one man he knew from experience was always a massive threat — if he was in condition. And the word amongst Mike's fellow competitors was that the Black Prince had never looked better. But Mike took their reports of Robby in stride. "I knew that I was in my best shape, and it would take a *monster* to beat me," he recalled. "Prior to the prejudging, backstage, when we were all stripping down, the one guy I knew that I had to worry about was Robby. And when I saw him stripped down, I thought, 'There's *no way* this guy's going to beat me.'"[26]

From his seat in the front row of the auditorium, Bill Reynolds could see that not all of the contestants were in their best condition.[27] Boyer Coe, for example, a four-time winner of the Mr. Universe title, had decided to reduce his competition weight closer to what Mr. Olympia Frank Zane's was (as being more defined was what winning competitions was all about as of late). But while Boyer looked good, he didn't look good enough to threaten either Mike or Robby for the win. Danny Padilla also was not as sharp as he had been in prior contests.[28] But when Robby walked out on stage, his body confirmed the rumor that was circulating: he was in his all-time best condition. "To say Robby had peaked perfect would be an understatement," Bill wrote in his report. "He's probably never been in better shape — huge, proportionate, muscular with white highlights dancing from his writhing muscles and an occasional glint bouncing from his gold front tooth."[29]

But then came Mentzer.

Bill immediately recognized that Mike's self-assessment earlier was not only accurate, but understated:

> The improvement he has made since the Universe only three months ago is almost unbelievable. He's added so much size across his chest and shoulders that one could be fooled into thinking he had undergone some sort of anatomic transplant. Still, his most startling improvement is overall muscularity. Mike was as cut up as anybody in the show, and added to his usual size and flawless proportions, this finishing touch ultimately made him unbeatable.[30]

After the prejudging, the judges had Mike ahead of Robby by three points (200 to 197).[31] Mike was pleased; his science-based approach to training had paid off. "I had cut my workouts back to only seven sets [total] and achieved one of my most heavily muscled conditions," he recalled. "I remember my muscles even feeling *heavier*. I was more heavily muscled at that contest than at any other contest."[32] When the finals got underway a few hours later, he looked even better. According to Bill Reynolds's report:

> Whatever he had done in his diet and training, the end result was incredible — especially with the effectiveness of Mike's posing to stirring strains of Wagner's classic *Funeral March for Siegfried*. With every new pose, the crowd roared more loudly, and with each roar the residential sound level built higher, until there was danger of plaster rattling loose from the ceiling and falling on the crowd. When Mike jumped down from the posing dais, he knew in his heart that he had won![33]

Mike not only won the contest, but he had also made history again, receiving the first perfect score awarded in a professional bodybuilding competition.[34] Robby was furious; the judges had spoiled his homecoming party. "Robby, it was a pleasure beating you," Mike said as he shook hands with the Black Prince after the contest. Robby, mistaking Mike's comment for trash-talking, fired back: "You didn't beat me, they *gave* it to you."[35] But the truth was that Mike respected Robby as being the best professional bodybuilder in the world; his comment was simply underscoring what an honor it was to have *finally* defeated him in competition. When interviewed by Bill Reynolds afterwards, Mike put a sharper point on the matter. "I'm very proud to have defeated such a great champion as Robby Robinson," he said. "Now I am preparing for the next Night of the Champions production in Pittsburgh on April 7th. I've got to keep progressing."[36]

While awaiting the flight back to California the next day, Mike, Bill Reynolds, and one of the other bodybuilders from the competition sat down in an airport cafeteria. Mike ordered coffee. When the server delivered the beverage to their table, she also deposited several small plastic containers of coffee creamer. The bodybuilder who was sitting with Mike and Bill picked one of the containers up and scanned its label. Scowling, he muttered, "God, I can't use this shit! It's full of chemicals!"

"What about all the steroids you put into your body?" Mike asked.

"Well," the bodybuilder replied, "you have to draw the line somewhere!"[37]

Mike and Bill found the irony hilarious. The other bodybuilder shrugged in resignation.

Winning his first pro show, particularly with another perfect score, left Mike feeling content and confident. He looked ahead to what promised to be a very bright future. For the moment, the hounds of depression were keeping their distance.

CHAPTER TWENTY

THE BLOWS OF FATE

The party had been going on for quite some time in Mike and Cathy's apartment. Joe and Betty Weider were there, along with Lou Ferrigno and photographers Artie Zeller and John Balik. Bill Reynolds was in attendance, as were Casey Viator (who had recently made the trek from Louisiana to California to pursue professional bodybuilding), Albert Busek, and Jack Neary. Everybody was crammed into the living room and kitchen area of the apartment to celebrate Mike's first professional win.

Ray Mentzer was present as well. In fact, he'd been sleeping on the sofa at Mike and Cathy's place for the past eight weeks, ever since he packed in his job with the pool company back east. Feeling confident after his close finish behind Mike at the USA vs. World competition seven months previously, Ray decided that he would devote his full time to bodybuilding, and that his future lay in California.[1] Jack knew both Mentzer brothers, Mike better than Ray. In truth, nobody really knew much about Ray, other than he looked like Mike's twin. But that was where the similarity ended. Whereas Mike was cerebral, soft spoken, and a caustic wit, Ray was none of these things. He was like a version of Mike that might exist in a parallel universe. Certain of Mike's friends, like Roger Schwab, thought he was dangerous.[2] Ray was known to have a flash temper and didn't think twice about fighting — anybody. And given his tremendous strength, he was a formidable and highly intimidating person to disagree with.

Jack thought (perhaps with Mike's prompting) that Ray might be a good subject for an article. And after a few drinks, he made his way over to where Ray was standing to speak with him. Ray was with his girlfriend, Pam

LaMarca. Jack said hello to Pam and was informed that she was presently working on her thesis for a master's degree from the University of Colorado, which is where she and Ray had met five years previously. They had been seeing each other on and off since then, but things between them had become a little more serious of late; Ray had just found an apartment of his own and the two would soon be living together.

When the conversation switched to what Ray was doing, the younger Mentzer brother volunteered that he was currently working at a posh fitness center, where he trained wannabe bodybuilders. He didn't care for the vocation but conceded that "it's better than nothing." He told Jack that he didn't understand how any bodybuilder could expect to lift weights all day and not work full time. "I know I'd go crazy if I just sat around all day," he said. "My workouts only last 30 minutes, three days a week. I've got lots of energy and I have to put it to use."

Jack wanted to know why he left the swimming pool maintenance business. "It seems like my life is always going in cycles," Ray replied. "Every three years or so my life changes. I look for a new experience and move to a new part of the country. I was having problems with my partner in the swimming pool business back east, so I shut the whole thing down, then found the fortitude to uproot myself from a comfortable situation and come here. It's a frontier thing, a new challenge. I can adapt to any social situation. I don't harbor any great expectations this early, but I feel I'm always getting better. I can't think of an amateur heavyweight in America who I can't beat. Actually, the only person I have to compete with this year is myself. If I don't make the mistakes I made last year, I can be heavyweight Mr. Universe." Certainly, the young man's confidence — or rather his bravado — appeared quite high.

Ray proceeded to tell Jack how he had lost his edge for the 1978 AAU Mr. America contest, held five weeks after the USA vs. the World competition. "I got insecure after the L.A. contest, and I tried some thyroid drug — it made me puffy. It also seemed to eat my muscles. That was depressing to see. I'll never mess with thyroid again. I was also burning too many calories. I was working long days in the sun and training very hard, and I became depleted." But he had his shit together now, he said. He was going to take another run at the AAU Mr. America that coming September. And, after that, who knew? Maybe he would enter the World Championships, which were being promoted by Arnold Schwarzenegger and Jim Lorimer that year and held on the same weekend (and in the same venue) as the 1979 Mr. Olympia contest. If he won the World Championships, he would qualify to enter the Olympia. It was (remotely) possible that he and Mike might be battling it out for the biggest title in bodybuilding in only four months' time.

It was obvious to Jack that Mike was Ray's hero. He got the feeling that Ray didn't want to just be *like* his older brother, but actually wanted to *be* him. When Mike went into football, so did Ray; when Mike started lifting weights in the basement of his parents' home, his little brother did too. When Mike grew a mustache, so did Ray. Both wore glasses. When Mike went into bodybuilding, Ray followed suit. He adopted Mike's training protocol, took the same steroids, and attempted to parrot his older brother's extensive vocabulary, albeit not always correctly. He even read the same philosophy books that Mike did (although he may not have understood their contents quite as thoroughly), and he listened to the same classical music. Mike wrote magazine articles and training courses, and just been signed to do a three-book deal with a major New York publisher. By contrast, Ray's attempt at article writing was an unmitigated disaster. Mike was making more than six figures a year running a successful mail-order and seminar/exhibition business, and that was the kind of success that Ray coveted most of all.[3]

But what Ray lacked in refinement, he made up for in street smarts; he could read people accurately and immediately in a manner that Mike never quite acquired. Indeed, for all his intellect, there was a simple, almost child-like naïveté about Mike — a character trait that he was aware of but that was too deeply ingrained to change.[4] He believed that people were people, and he made no differentiation as to race, creed, color, or background. From his vantage point, everybody was the same (his forays into physiology had convinced him of this). Mike saw no reason to suspect that complete strangers weren't fundamentally like him, i.e., benevolent and seeking to learn. Such a perspective was completely foreign to Ray. Having spent more time with his Marine Corps father than Mike had (particularly after Mike enlisted in the Air Force), Ray believed it was a tough world out there, and everyone you met was looking to play you for a sucker. He had his guard up constantly. It's safe to say that only a few people ever made it into Ray's inner circle, and fewer still would remain there.

"He paled in comparison to Mike in terms of intelligence, charm, and confidence," Jack noted. "Ray was a nice guy, but he always struck me as fundamentally insecure. He worshipped Mike, but he envied him also."[5] Ray, of course, bristled at any comparison with his older brother. "I don't know why people think I'm trying to be like Mike," he said. "Obviously, we look alike because we're brothers and we both believe in the same basic training principles. But it only goes as far as that. I'm an individual and I'm motivated. We're always competitive, and I'd like to beat him. If there's any talk of sibling rivalry, I just keep neutral. I'll let it outgrow itself. I'm going to set my own precedents and show my wares in my own way."[6] That remained to be seen. Certainly, it was the right sentiment, even if one could find no support from Ray's personal history for believing it.

Before Jack left the party that night, Joe Weider pulled him aside and told him he wanted him to write a profile piece on Arnold, who evidently was back in Joe's good graces again. Moreover, Arnold's popularity was on the rise, and Arnold's success — at least as Joe wanted it communicated to the magazine's readership — was an example of what could happen when one lived the Weider lifestyle. Jack said he would write the article and called Arnold the next morning to arrange a time for the interview.

Upon Jack's arrival at Arnold's place later that afternoon, the Austrian Oak was only too happy to talk about himself. He made sure to tell Jack that he had recently discussed politics with Henry Kissinger (in German, of course), that he had been invited to play tennis in the Robert Kennedy Celebrity Tournament, that he had appeared on the cover of the 75th-anniversary edition of the *Hollywood Reporter*, had dined at the White House and driven a tank across the Israeli desert. And there was more. He had been photographed with Muhammad Ali, Candice Bergen, and Christopher Reeve and been invited to join the President's Council on Fitness, an invitation which he declined. "I don't want to be just a *part* of it because you can't get anything done. I want to be the head of it. No monkey business." And the final tidbit Arnold dropped on Jack's plate was that he was now dating Maria Shriver, the daughter of Eunice (née Kennedy) and Sargent Shriver.[7] These were impressive things to have on one's résumé, to be certain. When Jack inquired whether he missed bodybuilding competition — the activity that had first brought him to the world's attention — Arnold shook his head. "I never think if I could beat the current top guys. I'm at ease with myself. I still consider myself to be the best there ever was. No one has come along yet who is better than I was, or Sergio was."[8] But then, in a relaxed moment, a closely guarded thought passed his lips: "I think muscle-for-muscle, Mike Mentzer could get there."[9]

A few days later, Mike arrived at the Weider building and dropped off the article that Bill Reynolds had requested on Rest-Pause training. Bill passed it along to Joe, who, true to form, tacked on a sidebar to the piece indicating that Rest-Pause was a Weider Principle.[10] But things were going so well for Mike at the moment that he only rolled his eyes at Joe's misappropriation. With his mail order bringing in $200,000 a year, and the press dubbing him the "heir apparent to Arnold Schwarzenegger" and a "budding legend," there appeared to be nothing but blue skies ahead.[11] And now that he had successfully turned professional and had a stable income, Mike and Cathy decided to get married.[12]

The two were cut from the same cloth; both were intellectually oriented, and both loved exercising, albeit for different purposes. Cathy worked out to stay strong and keep her weight in check, while Mike used it as a tool to earn his living. It was a perfect pairing. Frank Zane and his wife, Christine, were both actively involved in bodybuilding and had been for some time, but Mike and Cathy were bodybuilding's new power couple. Even Joe Weider admired Cathy's independent spirit, and wanted an article written about her for his magazine. He assigned a female reporter, Laura Mishima, the task of discovering what Cathy Gelfo was all about.

The reporter spent a day with Cathy, accompanying her to the gym to watch her work out, then out for lunch, where some probing background questions were asked about her beliefs, continuing education, and how she first met Mike. Over lunch, Cathy spoke clearly, articulately, and progressively. "In this society," she said, "women have been taught to be the underdogs, constantly in need of protection. We are labeled the 'weaker sex,' while men are encouraged to be more aggressive. Madison Avenue has sold us a bill of goods — who to hook, how to look, what eye shadow to buy — and I refuse to accept it."[13] In terms of education, Cathy was a sociology major while at the University of Maryland and had transferred to UCLA to complete her degree. "I want to get straight A's," she said. "I want to go to law school. This may sound corny or trite, but I want to be my own person. I want to be self-sufficient. I have a good idea of my capabilities and potentials. I am confident in me."[14]

Regarding her relationship with Mike, Cathy shared with the writer that they first met in a philosophy class at college. They sat together in class, but at the time she was dating someone else. Sometimes, however, they would skip class together and sit under a tree on campus and talk philosophy. Mike would read Walt Whitman's poetry to her. He was particularly taken by Whitman's "One Hour to Madness and Joy," and its passages:

> O the puzzle, the thrice tied knot, the deep and dark pool, all untied and illumin'd!
> O to speed where there is space enough and air enough at last!
> To have the gag removed from one's mouth!
> To have the feeling to-day or any day I am sufficient as I am.
> To ascend, to leap to the heavens of the love indicated to me!
> To rise thither with my inebriate soul![15]

Their relationship then was purely platonic. It would be eight months before the subject of bodybuilding even came up.[16] "He was shy," Cathy said. "And he always wore baggy clothes to hide his physique. This was before [the documentary] *Pumping Iron*, and I guess he didn't want to be a 'freak' on campus. . . . I remember he was always dieting, and one day in the cafeteria he was so hungry he devoured my apple. He fasted once a week. After he lost forty pounds I noticed and said, 'Hey, have you lost weight?'" Mike explained that he was a bodybuilder, but Cathy didn't really understand the term. Later that summer, Cathy went to Europe, where she ended her relationship with her boyfriend, while Mike stayed behind and entered the 1975 IFBB Mr. America contest in Los Angeles. When they returned to school that fall and inquired what each had done over the summer, Mike told her about his third-place finish in his height class at the Mr. America contest. Cathy was bemused.

Soon they had their first date. "We went out for Chinese food and that night while we were watching TV, Mike said, do you want to see my calves? I couldn't believe what he asked me. And when I saw his calves, I couldn't believe them either! They're the greatest in the world," she told the reporter, with a fair degree of partiality. "Later, when he met my family, I would say, 'Show them your arms!'" The interview concluded with Cathy speaking about her passion for weight training. "I'm no glamour girl," she said. "I don't like the image. I'm not in the gym to impress anyone or to get a man. I don't smile and smell sweet while I'm training. I'm there to improve, to get stronger."[17]

Cathy was certainly no stranger to the press since dating Mike. In 1977, she told a Baltimore news reporter that she was "first drawn to Mike by his mustache, not his body,"[18] while in 1976 a member of the news media wrote that Mike "lives with a woman who is active in the National Organization for Women and supports the feminist movement."[19] It was certainly true that Cathy wasn't the type to take a backseat to anybody, which was one of the features that attracted Mike to her in the first place.

From Mike's perspective, while the news reporter's description of Cathy was certainly apt, it was also superficial; Cathy was far more than simply a person seeking to redress the imbalance that patriarchal sexism had created in American society — she was her own person. And that was how it should be, he thought. Mike and Cathy were not two people sharing a brain, but two individuals who took responsibility for their own lives. It just so happened that their values were such that they were strongly attracted to one another. In other words, as he once told the author, the primary consideration in any meaningful relationship was that the two individuals shared a mutuality of values:

> There's only one proper basis for choosing friends, and that is mutuality of values. Most people exercise no discrimination in terms of thought or values in defining any relationship that they might be involved in or about to be involved in, whether it be the choice of a boss, a friend, a lover, associates at work, whatever. The only rational way, in the realm of friends, to make a choice is through mutuality of values. How could I possibly share something if we didn't share the same values?[20]

Cathy was yin to Mike's yang; it wasn't so much that they were two distinct entities, but, as Aristotle was reputed to have said, "one soul dwelling in two bodies."[21] They hadn't yet set a date for their marriage,[22] as neither was big on tradition, but that didn't stop them from purchasing a house together in Palm Springs.[23] "The reason for it was that I was looking for a real estate investment and didn't want to invest in the Los Angeles market because it was so overpriced," Mike said. "But then also at the time that I started looking around for a place I began growing very alarmed about the increasing rate of violent crime in Los Angeles. During that period when I was looking for a real estate investment, my own neighborhood in West L.A., which is considered a 'good' neighborhood, formed a neighborhood 'watch' group to protect themselves — and that really freaked me out. I thought rather than live in an armed fortress I was just going to leave the area entirely. So those two motivating factors led us to Palm Springs."[24]

With his personal life proceeding smoothly, Mike directed his focus to his next pro contest, the 1979 IFBB Pittsburgh Professional Invitational, which took place on Saturday, April 7, 1979, within the 3,700-seat Syria Mosque, which, despite its name, had never been a building for Islamic worship.[25] Once again, Robby Robinson was there to compete and, once again, had arrived in great shape. Ditto for competitors Pete Grymkowski and Roy Callender. Unfortunately for all of them, Mike was in even better shape than he had been in Florida. "My muscles were filled to the brim with glycogen and my skin was extremely tight, adhering to the muscles almost like a cellophane," Mike recalled. "I remember being impressed for the first time with my pecs, looking down at them under the light backstage and seeing deep striations and I thought, 'My goodness; I'm even better now than I was at the last show. And I was better at the last show than I was at the Universe, so everything's going well."[26] And so it seemed. Indeed, by the time the prejudging wrapped up, Mike had chalked up another perfect score.[27] His second pro victory seemed a foregone conclusion. But his youthful hubris led him a little too close to the sun:

> During the prejudging I was in the best condition of my life. But after the prejudging, I made the mistake of going out and eating indiscriminately. At that point I didn't understand diet and fluid intake as well as I was to later. I learned about it, in part, from the mistakes that I had made after the prejudging of that contest. I remember going out right after the prejudging and eating four or five pancakes with butter and syrup and drinking several glasses of orange juice. And then going to the final show that night and being clearly aware myself that something was not as it had been that morning.[28]

The high-carbohydrate consumption caused him to retain water, which blurred his muscular definition. It was a situation not unlike what had beset him in Acapulco in 1978. He had been able to get away with it then, given the caliber of competition, but this time around he would be facing Robby Robinson, and Mike knew if he wasn't at his absolute best, Robby had what it took to knock him off his pedestal. And that's exactly what happened. The Black Prince avenged his loss to Mike at the Miami contest and rallied to win the Pittsburgh show. Mike had to settle for second place. *Muscle*

Builder/Power's Bill Reynolds was present backstage to get the reactions of certain of the competitors. Robby was over the moon. "It feels great — well worth all the training and dieting," he said. "To turn the tables on Mike makes victory seem even more sweet."[29] To Bill's surprise, Mike accepted his defeat with grace:

> Mentzer, less dejected than one would expect, had a few words for this reporter. "Nobody's going to win them all this year and it's no disgrace to lose to Robby. I have nothing against the judges, or anyone connected with this contest. You win some and you lose some. Actually, I knew I would be second and started walking on stage even before my name was called. In Florida, I had a gut feeling that I was winning all the way, but this time my instincts told me I was losing. What else can I say?" I can say it's a genuine pleasure to see a gentleman and a sportsman take defeats in the same manner as victories — with dignity and grace. Mike is seven years younger than Robby and has many victories ahead of him.[30]

The contest placing was a disappointment, but, on a personal note, there were positive signs coming from back home in Ephrata. While Mike and Ray had always kept in contact with their mother throughout the years, Mike had never felt particularly close to her. They were miles apart philosophically;[31] she was a devout Catholic and Mike an avowed atheist. But over the past several months, mother and son had been communicating more frequently and affectionately. Mike wanted Marie to come to California for a visit. Better yet, after his next pro show — the New York Night of Champions II on May 12 — she could travel with him to Europe. There was a big world outside of Ephrata, PA, and Mike wanted her to see it.[32] Marie had never once left American soil; Mike could easily book a seminar in Italy, which would allow his mother to visit the homeland of her ancestors. Both were excited at the prospect.

But then just as things were looking so promising, Mike hit a wall. His body wasn't responding to his workouts as it had previously. He attributed this to simply having exhausted his energy reserves. He had already entered two contests, traveled extensively to conduct seminars and exhibitions, written several columns and articles for *Muscle Builder/Power*, started writing a book on training for a New York publisher, and appeared as a guest on the nationally syndicated *Merv Griffin Show*[33] — all within a span of two months. This, coupled with months of draining his muscles in the gym while on a significantly reduced calorie diet, had left his gas tank running on nothing but vapors. "I'll never again compete in so many contests, give seminars and exhibitions so close together," he said. "I was just tired, and my body reached a point where it wouldn't respond to training."[34]

Mike and Cathy arrived in New York City on Friday, May 11, the day before the contest, and checked into the Hotel Beacon, a 24-story building located at the corner of 75th Street and Broadway. The venue for the competition was the (then) 50-year-old Beacon Theatre, which was conveniently located next to the hotel. Also arriving in New York was their friend Jack Neary, who was in the Big Apple to write the report for *Muscle Builder/Power*. The trio hooked up shortly after Jack had hit town and, over a light lunch in the hotel restaurant, they decided to indulge in a bit of sophistication by visiting the Museum of Modern Art. And it was there, in the very cultural hub of Manhattan, that Jack had a wicked idea:

> We were walking through this very quiet gallery, it was like a cathedral. And there were all these beautiful sculptures, like Henry Moore sculptures. And I dared Mike; I said, "Mike, you ought to whinny like a Lipizzaner stallion through the gallery, it will be hilarious!" And he did it! He started whinnying with his hands up like a horse's hooves and kicking up his legs. And of course, he's a big guy, like 235 pounds — and people are looking at him, and heads are turning, and security guards are moving over and, you know, it's like, "What the hell is going on here?" And he did it for quite a long time, like a good minute, and nobody did anything! He wasn't touching or knocking anything over, but it was just hilarious! It must have traumatized the hell out of some of those snooty New York art patrons, you know? But Mike was always up for a bit of a lark like that.[35]

Mike and Cathy were still in good spirits later that evening when the phone rang in their hotel room. Mike answered, whereupon a stern voice on the other end of the line informed him that he was speaking with Marie Mentzer's doctor. Cathy could tell by reading Mike's face that the news wasn't good.[36] Mike was ashen when he hung up the phone. His mother had apparently been ill for some time;[37] her condition was terminal.[38] He turned to Cathy in muted despair. She did what she could to help him keep it together emotionally,[39] but Mike's mind was swimming. Had he not been under a contractual obligation to compete the next day, he would have caught the next flight out of LaGuardia to Pennsylvania.[40]

The morning of the contest, Mike was a somnambulist. He went through his posing routine but just couldn't get into it.[41] "In spite of the fatigue," Jack wrote, "Mentzer was, as usual, impressive. The muscle size and shape was all there, only a touch more definition would have made him spectacular. . . . Mentzer was stunning at his victory in Miami, a notch below that for Pittsburgh, and even further below that for New York. He had faded, while Robinson hadn't."[42] Indeed, Robby was in excellent shape, and Danny Padilla had improved markedly. Mike didn't care. Winning a bodybuilding contest was the last thing on his mind at the moment.[43] At the conclusion of the competition, Mike ended up in third place, behind Danny Padilla and the winner, Robby Robinson. It was the best he could do under the circumstances.

Early the next morning, Mike checked in with Marie's doctor, said goodbye to Cathy, and boarded a plane bound for Europe for a series of seminars that had been arranged in advance by Albert Busek. During the flight, he had plenty of time to reflect on what he was leaving behind in America. He tried to think about things other than his mother's illness. Upon arriving in Europe, Busek did what did what he could to make Mike's stay comfortable, including taking him to places where he could indulge in his passion for ice cream.[44] While the two-week seminar tour of Europe was a success, Mike's mind was on his mother, who was hooked up to a variety of tubes some 3,987 miles away across the North Atlantic Ocean.

When the tour concluded, Mike caught an eight-and-a-half-hour flight from Germany to Philadelphia, rented a car, and pushed its gas pedal to the floor as he tore along I-76 west towards Ephrata. He wheeled into the parking lot of the Ephrata Community Hospital and sprinted towards its front doors. "I had just enough time to see my mother alive for the last time before she died," he recalled. "In fact, her doctor had kept her artificially alive with her heart beating for my sake with injections of very powerful steroid drugs. After I had seen her, the doctor mercifully ceased the injections, and my mother died a few hours later."[45]

Mike returned to his car and drove — for hours. He couldn't stop the tears.[46]

CHAPTER TWENTY-ONE

PLAYING WITH FIRE

It seems a strange thing to say, but Marie's passing hit Mike much harder than it should have. Of course, she was his mother, a human being for which there is no replacement in one's life. It is normal and understandable that he would grieve. But the depression Mike suffered after her loss was so powerful and overwhelming that for six weeks afterwards he found it difficult (and at times impossible) to get out of bed.[1] He knew from his psychology studies that this was a dangerous sign.[2] Even more concerning, he understood that the magnitude of his depression was a dark reminder that while his mother had passed away, her mental illness had not; it had now been visited upon her son. And for the moment, Mike was powerless to escape its grasp.

He continued to read, hoping to find some insight into the mind that would alleviate his condition, but after a while it was all just words on a page rather than the reality he was experiencing. "Only a few months before I had read in *The Psychology of Sport*, Dorcas Susan Butt's informative book, that athletes are motivated by three distinct energies: aggression, neuroticism and competence," he recalled. "All three energies contribute to an athlete's motivation but one usually predominates. Suffice it to say that most of my energy was taken up in neurotic conflict at this time. Strangely enough, the undermining of confidence was not restricted to the area of physical performance but spread to other areas of my life. For a time, life in general became very problematic."[3] Unfortunately, the recognition that he was in the throes of what was (hopefully) a brief interlude of neurosis didn't alleviate it.

Ray had also taken his mother's death hard, but he hadn't inherited her affliction. Perhaps because he had a contest coming up sooner than Mike,

Ray was able to keep his grief in check by working out. He had no trouble throwing himself full throttle into his training and dieting for the forthcoming AAU Mr. America contest, which was set to take place on September 8 in Atlanta, Georgia. While never one to suffer the pangs of clinical depression, Ray nevertheless had his own psychological issues to contend with. It might be said that he was suffering from a crisis of his own choosing, as he was still opting to be a carbon copy of his older brother. This meant that with each passing year he was in this mindset he was moving further and further away from himself. Apart from choosing to look like Mike in appearance, he took to copying his mannerisms. Like Mike, Ray kept a journal; like Mike, he used high-intensity training protocols — and it went on from there. He followed a reduced-calorie diet that included ice cream, he listened to Wagner and read Nietzsche.[4] If, as he told Jack Neary, he was trying to create a distinction between himself and his brother, he was heading in the wrong direction. This being said, Ray's copying Mike's training method was paying dividends. "[I was] getting gradually stronger and more massive every week," he said.[5] Indeed, everything was starting to come together for Ray in a manner that had never happened before. Everybody who saw him engage in his posing practice came away convinced that he had an excellent shot at winning the Mr. America.[6]

By contrast, Mike was miles from where he needed to be — and the Mr. Olympia contest was only three months away. He understood that something of a biochemical nature had occurred in his brain and that it simply wasn't producing the necessary chemicals to right his emotional imbalance. He decided to self-medicate, to do what he could to chase away his depression if he was to have any chance of winning the highest title in professional bodybuilding. Once again, he looked to the science of chemistry. He spoke with a doctor and received a prescription for amphetamines in the hope that they would serve to restore his mental equilibrium. "In 1979 I started getting amphetamines from a doctor," he recalled. "Not for the purpose of getting high — that was the furthest thing from my mind. I didn't like getting high, as a matter of fact. I had stopped smoking marijuana many years before. I had read some of the literature on amphetamines. Of course, it was something that was not encouraged, just as steroids weren't."[7]

Amphetamines were certainly nothing new to American (or European or Asian) culture. They were first synthesized in the late 1800s, and a variant (methamphetamine) was developed by a pharmacologist in Japan in 1919 to produce feelings of "alertness and well-being." By the 1930s they were utilized in the United States to treat asthma and narcolepsy, available as an over-the-counter treatment for such maladies in addition to being a go-to treatment for nasal and bronchial congestion (as a bronchial dilator) resulting from the common cold.[8] During World War II, the Axis Powers and the Allied Forces had supplied their troops with amphetamines (Allied) and methamphetamines (Axis) as the drugs "increased their confidence and aggression, and elevated morale."[9] The 1950s saw the use of the medicine expanded to treat conditions of obesity and sinus inflammation, and "pep pills" or "bennies" were sold to truck drivers, homemakers, athletes, and college students to help them stay awake and keep active.[10] Right from their inception, then, amphetamines had been proven to induce "a sense of well-being and a feeling of exhilaration" in addition to "lessened fatigue in reaction to work"[11] — and these were properties Mike was desperately in need of to counteract his depression and prepare for the Olympia. Like many college students in the 1970s, he had used them before. Jack Neary recalled an occasion when he and Mike used Black Beauties (amphetamine/dextroamphetamine capsules)[12] to help them meet a writing deadline:

> I smoked a bit of weed and taken some peyote and stuff along the way, a bit of acid during college, but I was not a big drug freak or anything. Nor was Mike. But Mike was very knowledgeable about pharmaceuticals, you know. His medical orientation, he just had a good head for science, and he would do the reading and the research. And there were these drugs, these amphetamines called Black Beauties, that he always had. I don't know where he got them, I presume they were a prescription. And I remember one night we both had deadlines and we had to get these damn pieces written for Joe. And I'm a horrible procrastinator; I'll put off stuff for years, but the stuff was due on the Monday morning and Mike said, "Well, here, you're going to need some help." And he gave me a couple of Black Beauties — and I was just wired! It was as if I drank ten Red Bulls or something, and I was just flying. And of course, the thoughts were flying, and the words were coming, and he and I were just churning out copy on our little typewriters because everything was this way before computers or smartphones or

anything like that. Just old-fashioned manual typewriters. And we were clacking away in the night. I don't know how he slept. And we cranked out our respective pieces and submitted them and it was good. It helped. Of course, I was *destroyed* the next day. I could barely stay awake. But Mike was an advocate of amphetamines. I mean, I don't know how often he did it, but he and I did it a couple of times.[13]

This time around, the amphetamines once again did their job. Mike was soon out of bed and back in the gym. The importance of the forthcoming competition served to heighten his motivation and keep his mind occupied, things which, in themselves, helped to keep the depression at bay:

> I noted that during the off-season, when I'm relatively inactive, my anxiety level increases and life in general seems more problematic. As soon as I'm faced with the impending challenge of a major physique competition, however, my entire psyche undergoes a profound change. My anxiety level drops to zero, and the sense of laziness and vague discontent evaporates. Everything around me — people, things, ideas — assumes a heightened sense of meaning and purpose. Like the French philosopher Jean Paul Sartre, who said he never felt more alive than when he was fighting the Germans in World War II, I find life easiest when it's hardest, i.e., when the greatest demands and privations are required. The psychologist William James noted: "It is sweat and effort, human nature strained to its utmost and on the rack, yet getting through alive, which inspire us." Preparing for a contest is my moral equivalent to war.[14]

Mike's workouts now commanded his full conscious attention, and he approached them with a powerful sense of purpose, which is reflected in the following excerpts from his journal:

July 10, 1979:

> Today is the real beginning of Olympia preparation. No more screwing around. Must stay on strict diet from here on out.

Only 89 days left! Today's was a good high-intensity workout which helped psych me up again. Weighed 218½ pounds.

Workout:

- Pulldowns: the weight stack & 45 additional lbs.
- Pulldowns: the stack, six reps to positive failure.
- Pulley Rows: 220 lbs. × 6 reps, two sets; 160 lbs. × 12 reps (all three sets in normal fashion to positive failure).
- One-arm dumbbell rows: 150 × 6 reps each arm (felt heavy).
- Nautilus lateral raises: Stack and 15 lbs., Rest-Pause.
- Presses on Universal machine: stack for 5 reps (up 2 reps).
- Rear-delt machine: stack, two reps, Rest-Pause style (too heavy). No record of diet.[15]

July 16, 1979:

Up at 5:30 AM — a little tired.

Breakfast:

½ cantaloupe:	50
1 nectarine:	75
	125

Great workout! Best this summer.
Nautilus Duo-Pullover 10 plates, 4 reps.
Nautilus behind-neck torso; stack & 10 lbs. 5 reps Rest-Pause style
Pulldowns stack & 25 lbs. × 4 reps, Rest-Pause
One-arm db [dumbbell] rows 150 lbs. 6 reps
Cable rows 2 sets to failure with the stack
Power cleans 215 lbs. × 4 reps, 250 lbs. × 1 rep, 215 lbs. × 4 reps
Stiff-Legged deadlifts 335 lbs. × 4 reps, 285 lbs. × 6 reps, 235 lbs. × 10 (break-in)

Shoulder shrugs weight stack × 4 reps, stack minus
30 lbs. × 6 reps, stack minus 60 lbs. × 8 reps
ran one time up parking structure across the street from Gold's.

Post-workout:

½ cantaloupe:	50
1 nectarine:	75
	125

Lunch at noon:

turkey	150
baked pot[ato]	125
	275

Dinner 4:00 p.m.

turkey	350
watermelon	
yogurt	450
candy	
	800

Late evening

plums	70
bread	150
	220

Total calories for day: 1,545

Today started my steroid regimen for the Olympia by taking a 100 mg shot of Deca-Durabolin, 50 mgs. of Durabolin and 2 Dianabol pills.[16]

August 21, 1979:

Up at 5:40 in ketosis.

Breakfast: cake and protein drink: 400 calories.

Workout: Worked chest and back, ran 1.2 miles before workout. Weighed 223 prior to workout.

Post-workout: muffin and melon: 250 calories.

11:15 AM: rode bike 40 miles! Wasn't too bad!

3:30 PM: chicken: 250 calories; fruit: 100 calories; baked potato: 150 calories. Total calories: 500. I was in heavy ketosis by mid-afternoon.

6:30 PM: ran 5 ½ miles!!! Most active day ever! Weighed 216 after the run vs. 223 lbs. this morning![17]

Clearly, Mike had turned a corner; both his psyche and soma were now in high gear:

> I'd found that the value I placed on the Mr. Olympia contest and my winning it had imbued not only my contest preparation with an almost transcendent sense of meaning, it had elevated everything I did — even the most trivial of tasks to a higher level of existence. My purpose followed me like a shadow; even taking out the garbage was a joy. Once, when I ran into a female bodybuilding friend of mine on the street, she said she could feel my energy a block away. I felt (to put it somewhat poetically) that I was plugged into the deep-centered rhythm of the cosmos. In fact, I felt all of a piece. Never was I at cross-purposes.[18]

And while Mike was attaining peak condition in preparation for his first Mr. Olympia contest, Ray was doing likewise for the Mr. America. The brothers trained together throughout the summer and into the fall. Ray's activity levels during this time were exceptional:

> I'd go to the gym and blast through about an hour of hard training. Then I'd ride a bicycle for one or two hours, take a break, run 5-6 miles, go see Joe [Weider], come home and practice the poses and contraction exercises he gave me, and then ride my stationary bike for another hour or two. At nights I was so keyed up that I couldn't sleep much, so I'd go for *l-o-o-ong* walks. This type of workout day would burn up 7,000–8,000 calories, while I was only taking in a maximum of 2,000 per day. Every 7–10 days I'd go crazy, however, and have to eat a lot more calories. I'd get a craving for fats and just have to eat some ice cream, but I was still losing a lot of body fat every day.[19]

The 1979 AAU Mr. America competition took place on September 8 at the Fox Theatre in Atlanta, Georgia,[20] and it was evident to everyone who saw him that day that Ray had achieved an all-time peak of condition. He bulldozed over the competition, winning not only his class, but the overall title, picking up subcategory awards for best back and best legs as well.[21] It was a total rout, and Ray's finest moment in bodybuilding competition.

Mike was so proud of Ray's accomplishment that he took time away from his own contest preparation to become his little brother's press agent. He made sure that Joe Weider put Ray on the cover of *Muscle Builder* and wrote two articles for the magazine "by Ray Mentzer." He even called the *Los Angeles Times* to inform them of Ray's victory, however the sports reporter stated coolly that bodybuilding wasn't a sport. "But the next day," Mike said sarcastically, "they ran a story on pig calling! *That's* a sport, right?"[22]

Mike's depression was long gone by this point, but his emotional pendulum had yet to find the middle. In fact, it had swung over to the other side of the spectrum. Such bipolar extremes were easily camouflaged away, however, by recent occurrences in his life. His mother's death was an occasion that understandably would have left anyone depressed. And the physical improvement he was making in preparation for the Mr. Olympia contest could account for his feelings of accomplishment and euphoria. But behind these life episodes, clearly, there was a pathology at play for anyone who had the eyes to see it. Mike's use of anabolic steroids, coupled with amphetamines, no doubt played into his feelings of euphoria (the literature on these drugs certainly bears this out). And most of his post-contest depression in the past had occurred when he went off these mood-altering chemicals. This alone would account for temporary interludes of depression, until the serotonin (and other chemicals) levels in his brain returned to normal. The nature of homeostasis is such that whenever exogenous chemicals are ingested, the body's (or brain's) natural ability to produce these chemicals endogenously is suppressed. And there is a lag time after the ingestion of such outside agents terminates and before the body starts producing them again, which leaves that chemistry considerably diminished or nonexistent. It's not unreasonable to assume that Mike's bouncing back and forth between these two mental polarities might weaken his brain's ability over time to maintain an even keel emotionally. And this, combined with what evidently was a genetically inherited strain of mental illness, meant that Mike was playing a dangerous game of tennis with his mental state.

To digress a moment, there might be said to be similarities between Mike's feelings of euphoria and those of Friedrich Nietzsche while the philosopher was in Turin just prior to his descent into madness. Nietzsche, already in the grip of a profound mental deterioration,[23] wrote letters to his friends, Peter Gast and Carl Fuchs, boasting of his preternatural health:

> Meanwhile everything is going wonderfully well. Never before have I known anything remotely like these months from the beginning of September until now. The most amazing tasks as easy as a game; my health, like the weather, coming up every day with boundless brilliance and certainty.[24]

And of his inexplicable and sudden manifestations of euphoria and joy:

> I enjoy so many silly jokes with myself and have so many clownish private insights that now and again I'm grinning for half an hour in the street, I know no other word for it . . .[25]

And:

> Just returned from a big concert, which really made on me the strongest impression of any concert I have been to — my

face kept making grimaces, in order to get over a feeling of extreme pleasure, including, for ten minutes, the grimace of tears. Ah, if you could have been there![26]

Contrast Nietzsche's statements above with the following from Mike Mentzer:

> At one point, about a week from countdown, I was taking a five-mile run down the grassy middle of San Vicente Boulevard in Santa Monica when I became acutely aware of the streams of energy careening through my entire being. I had to stifle a belly laugh for fear of appearing maniacal to the other joggers. When I woke up on the morning of the contest, I found myself in the grip of a peaking experience. Looking in the mirror at the final result of ten weeks of Herculean effort, I gave in to that belly laugh, realizing that I was in the best condition of my life.[27]

That Mike was in the best physical condition of his life certainly could not be disputed. But mentally, symptoms of a bipolar disorder had begun to manifest.[28] He knew that his use of steroids and/or amphetamines would only exacerbate inherited mental illness — he had even written a column warning other bodybuilders who suffered a similar condition against using them:

> The ingestion of artificial hormones can, indeed, induce mental changes. Various steroid drugs — not just anabolics — can cause such changes. The drug literature describes a "heightened sense of well-being," and excitement and insomnia have also been noted with steroid usage. This euphoria can be followed by depression, which can become severe enough to create suicidal tendencies. Where there is a hereditary predisposition, profound mental dysfunction may ensue.[29]

Little did he know as he typed these words that he was portending his own future.

Mike's use of these drugs was poking a sleeping dragon whose slumbers were best left undisturbed. But his plan was to be out of bodybuilding soon. He gave himself a timeline. Competitor Danny Padilla recalled that Mike "said to me, 'You know, Dan, I'm going to give this Olympia crap two years, and if I don't win, then I'm out.'[30] I'm moving forward.' He was a guy who would not sit around. He was a guy who was very big into philosophy, a very smart kid. And he had his life planned. And for him it was like, 'I will only spend two years, or this much time, in this sport, and wherever I am at that point, then I'm out and looking for something else to do.' And that was Mike's concept."[31] It is clear, then, that Mike believed if he could just walk the mental tightrope until he won the Mr. Olympia, he could then discard the drugs and their dangers and retire from the competitive side of the sport, having achieved all his bodybuilding goals, and focus on something else. At least, that was the plan.

As a result of his recent Mr. America victory, Ray Mentzer now qualified to enter the 1979 World Championships (Mr. Universe), which were to be held in conjunction with both the Mr. International and the Mr. Olympia contests that October. All three competitions were promoted by Arnold Schwarzenegger and Jim Lorimer and staged in Veterans Memorial Auditorium in Columbus, Ohio. The World Championships took place first, on Saturday, October 6. The Mentzer brothers, along with Cathy Gelfo, arrived in Columbus the day before.[32] The defending Mr. Olympia, Frank Zane, had arrived earlier that week, along with his wife, Christine, and Frank's business manager, Lee Kramer. Evidently Frank was considering getting into movies, and Kramer was doing what he could to ensure that Frank was treated like a celebrity. He rented a huge billboard by the airport which read: "Columbus welcomes Christine and Frank Zane, Mr. Olympia."[33] This let everyone know — fans, competitors, and judges, alike — who the real star of the show was.

The two-time Mr. Olympia winner was a cool customer. He was 35 years old and a seasoned veteran, having entered 22 bodybuilding competitions since 1966, eight of which were Mr. Olympia contests.[34] He appeared on no fewer than 39 muscle magazine covers over the decades leading up to the 1979 Mr. Olympia.[35] In short, Frank Zane was a man who knew his way around professional bodybuilding. At five foot nine and typically competing at a bodyweight of 185 to 190 pounds,[36] he had never bowled anyone over with his muscle mass, but the consensus was that the Zane physique had been blessed with great symmetry, proportion, and a tremendous degree of definition.

His was a look that was perfect for the era; bodybuilding was just starting to be embraced by the public, and Frank was viewed as the bridge between the superhero-like physique of Arnold Schwarzenegger and that of the common man. He was relatable. Befitting his prestige, Frank was driven to and from the venue in a limousine that his manager had procured, and even had his own private trailer parked behind Veterans Memorial Auditorium.[37] For a fellow who was said to have relatability to the common man, the champ had no interest in pumping up or interacting with the rank-and-file bodybuilders he would soon be competing against.

Upon arriving at the competitors' hotel, the Sheraton in downtown Columbus, the Mentzer brothers and Cathy proceeded to a large orientation table set up in the lobby by the promoters. Mike and Ray were given a package that contained meal tickets, badges for posing trunks, room assignments, and general information about the area. Mike glanced over the weekend itinerary sheet:

- IFBB International Congress — Friday, October 5, at 9:30 a.m.
- World Championships weigh-in — Saturday, October 6, beginning at 9 a.m. Finals — 7 p.m.
- Mr. International weigh-in — Sunday, October 7, beginning at 9 a.m. Finals — 6 p.m.
- Mr. Olympia weigh-in — Sunday, October 7, beginning at 12 noon. Finals — 8 p.m.

Seeing that nothing demanded his immediate attention, Mike and Cathy went to their room and settled in. They had arrived too late to attend the IFBB International Congress, which was unfortunate, as there were some interesting announcements. President Ben Weider revealed that Kal Szkalak was now banned for life from competing in any future IFBB competitions. Arnold Schwarzenegger (now back in Ben Weider's good books) was awarded the "President's Gold Medal," which was awarded "only to individuals who have contributed on a grand scale to the popularity of bodybuilding and the development of the IFBB." The juxtaposition of Kal's banishment with Arnold being celebrated by the same federation both men had tried to upset with the creation of a bodybuilders' union was certainly intriguing. Finally, Ben Weider announced that the 1980 Mr. Olympia contest would be promoted by none other than Paul Graham, who, Ben further announced, had just been elected to the position of vice president for the IFBB South Pacific (Oceania). Roger Walker, a former Royal Marine who was living in Australia[38] and who would be competing in the 1979 Olympia, posed the question that was on everybody's lips: "Why would Ben Weider give his baby, the Mr. Olympia contest, to a convicted felon?"[39] It's a question that has never been answered. Finally, Ben Weider informed the congress that the CBS television network would be broadcasting the 1979 Mr. Olympia and World Championships competitions — not ABC, as in the past. The latter network had not come up with enough money when it bid for the rights. Ben said he expected global viewership of the 1979 Mr. Olympia competition to reach 750 million — great exposure for bodybuilding and the IFBB. All of these decisions by Ben Weider would play a significant role in Mike's future. But for now, Mike was only interested in the impending contest.

When the World Championships got under way on Saturday, Ray was poised to take advantage of the momentum his Mr. America victory had created. He had weighed 222 pounds when he stepped on the scales prior to the prejudging and looked like he was a lock to add the Mr. Universe title to his résumé. But his chief opposition that day was Jusup Wilkosz, the bodybuilder who had placed second to Mike in Acapulco but whose muscular definition had improved dramatically since his appearance in Mexico. "Wilkosz is looking pretty good," Ray conceded, upon seeing the German backstage. He looked even better under the stage lights. Ray, it was reported, didn't fare as well. Granted, Ray's size and shape were exceptional, but he appeared to be lacking the definition that Wilkosz possessed. He also was not a close friend and training partner of the promoter Arnold Schwarzenegger (as Wilkosz was). When the contest was over, Wilkosz edged out Ray to win the Heavyweight Division and thus the Mr. Universe title. Ray's chance to compete against his brother in the next day's Mr. Olympia contest had just evaporated.

While Ray was competing, his brother was taking what last-minute steps he could to ensure that no stone was left unturned in his quest to win the Mr. Olympia title on his first attempt. Mike's journal entry from October 6 reveals his final day of preparations:

October 6, 1979:

One day to go, I can't believe it! Must watch my water intake very carefully today. Run a little, sweat a little. Was up at 7:45 AM.

Breakfast: two eggs: 150 calories; toast: 80 calories; prunes: 100 calories. Total calories: 330. Only fluids today were ½ cup coffee until 4:30, when I had a glass of Perrier. I noticed my skin thinning progressively as the day went by. I was very aware that I was excreting more than I was taking in, and my skin seemed thinner with each trip to the bathroom. At 1:30 PM I did a few light sets for all body parts and ran around the gym with a sweatsuit on to get a good sweat going. At 7:00 PM I ran for 30 minutes in the streets of Columbus. When I returned, I practiced my posing routine and got a really good sweat going.

8:00 PM: two scoops of ice cream: 350 calories; coffee.

11:30 PM: one glass of wine: 75 calories; one vodka gimlet: 125 calories. Total calories: 195. (I drank alcohol for its mild diuretic effect). I really feel READY!!! I look READY!!! I AM THERE!!! Weighed 216 this morning in sweats! Tomorrow — VICTORY!!![40]

When the Mr. Olympia contest began the next day, it quickly became clear that the contest was between Frank Zane and Mike Mentzer. Frank was said to have brought his muscle mass up from what he had displayed at the Olympia the year before. However, when he stepped on the scale that morning, he weighed only 190.2 pounds. Mike weighed in at 210 pounds,[41] almost a full 20 pounds heavier than Frank at an inch shorter in height. One might be tempted to conclude that Frank's definition was greater, but such was not the case. Mike was ripped beyond any condition he had previously displayed, causing the reporter from *Muscle Builder/Power* magazine to comment:

> There is little doubt among those I talk to that Mike Mentzer will take his class easily. When he comes out for the third

round, his posing only confirms this. He is strong, massive, in shape and confident. The only question is: can he beat Zane? The words go around, first as a whisper, then with growing enthusiasm. Yes, it is decided, he has a chance — a good chance. Serge Nubret [who was in attendance to watch the contest] agrees. "Mike is better, but Zane is the champion. We shall see." Jim Manion is of the same opinion. "If Mentzer doesn't win, it's a crime," he says. But it remains up to the judges, and nobody knows for sure.

Chris Lund, writing the contest report for *MuscleMag International*, was similarly impressed:

> After Mentzer's routine, Bob [Kennedy, the publisher of *MuscleMag International*] called over to me, "I've never seen Mike looking as good as that. He must have really trained for this one." As they stood in line under the lights and looking to the front, I couldn't believe anyone could look as perfect as Mike Mentzer. As he stood there relaxed, he looked to me to be the most complete physique the world has ever seen.[42]

The judging panel evidently thought so, too, as, once again, Mike was awarded a perfect score during the prejudging. Frank came close, being only one point shy. The two weight classes were adjudicated independently; that is, the judges never got to see the best competitors from the Under-200-Pound Class standing next to the best competitors from the Over-200-Pound Class for comparative purposes during the prejudging process. The six finalists based on the judges' scores were decided in short order: Mike Mentzer, Frank Zane, Boyer Coe, Chris Dickerson, Robby Robinson, and Dennis Tinerino.

Knowing that he was ahead of the defending champion by a single point, and wiser from his experiences in Acapulco and Pittsburgh, Mike refrained from drinking much if any fluids.[43] He did not want to risk losing any definition between the end of the prejudging and the evening finals. After the prejudging, all of the competitors returned to their hotel rooms while the bodybuilding media actively sought out restaurants to keep their energy levels primed for the finals that were set to take place later that evening. "A break between 4 p.m. and the start of the evening show at 7 p.m. in order to eat was most welcome," Chris Lund recalled. "As we waited impatiently for our food, Bob [Kennedy] asked each of us to write down our forecast for the three top places 'overall' for the 1979 Mr. Olympia contest. Strangely enough all four of us wrote the same: first — Mentzer, second — Coe, third — Zane!"[44]

With a perfect score, and carrying almost 20 pounds more muscle than Frank Zane, Mike returned for the evening finals fully confident. "I thought that I could beat Frank Zane," he recalled. "I thought that my shape and proportions were the equal of his, and that I would be considerably bigger. There's no reason why I shouldn't beat him."[45]

The finals consisted of the competitors coming out individually and going through their posing routines to music that each had selected. Then, the final six were brought back onstage together for a final posedown, where the bodybuilders struck whatever poses they wished over a brief (perhaps two-minute) period while the judges made their final analysis. The posedown was the final portion of the competition to be adjudicated. The judges received instructions to award one point for whomever they selected as the best bodybuilder during the posedown, and, given that a mere one point was all that separated Mike and Frank heading into this portion of the contest, the winner of the posedown would be the winner of the contest.

Just prior to heading onstage for the posedown, Arnold Schwarzenegger approached Mike and took him aside. They shook hands and posed for a picture, which, given their history, was completely out of character for both men. Arnold then offered Mike some advice: he should hit more poses during the posedown than the other competitors.[46] No reason we know of was given for this counsel. But Mike did what Arnold suggested. It must be remembered that this was Mike's first Mr. Olympia — winning it would be the culmination of his childhood dream. And despite his differences with Arnold regarding training methodologies, the newcomer had to respect the fact that this was a six-time Mr. Olympia winner that was advising him. Arnold knew what was required to win this title.

When the posedown began, Mike did exactly what Arnold told him. He hit his poses quickly in staccato fashion; so quickly, in fact, that the judges, who had been unable to compare the Under-200-Pound competitors with the Over-200-Pound competitors until this point, couldn't draw any meaningful comparisons as no two bodybuilders hit the same pose at the same time for comparative purposes. At the conclusion of the posedown, Frank received four first-place votes, bringing his total (prejudging plus posedown) to 304; Mike received one first-place vote, bringing his total to 301.

Frank Zane had won his third consecutive Mr. Olympia title.

"When Mike Mentzer was announced as runner-up, I definitely heard him say 'Oh no! I don't believe it,' and his face was filled with pain," Chris Lund reported.[47] But if the young upstart had been humbled, the old veteran, Frank Zane, was positively swaggering. He was informed by a crew member that Arnold, who was doing the color commentary for the CBS broadcast of the event, was waiting with a camera crew backstage to interview him. As Frank stood alongside Arnold and the television cameras whirred, Arnold asked him how it felt to win his third Mr. Olympia title. "Arnold, it feels even better than when I beat you for Mr. Universe," Frank replied.[48] Arnold's jaw went slack. He had not expected that subject to come up on national television. Frank smirked, and then continued on his way, clutching his Mr. Olympia trophy. Elsewhere backstage, Mike, Cathy, and Ray had gathered to try and make sense out of what just happened. "It is Ray who is furious," reported Bill Dobbins in his coverage of the contest for *Muscle Builder/Power*. "He took his own defeat calmly, but he cannot seem to accept that Mike hasn't won. I hope nobody bothers him; he looks in a mood to throw a punch. Wisely, the Mentzers decide to leave immediately."

The judges' scorecards were released shortly after the conclusion of the contest. In the posedown round it was discovered that both Albert Busek and Reg Park had marked Mike down to third place. Afterwards, at the victory banquet, Mike approached Reg to ask what he had done wrong to lose a contest that he had been winning up until the final round. "You have too much mass," Reg replied dismissively. This was a bizarre statement. If Mike had too much mass, it would've been evident the moment he first stepped on stage during the prejudging and he should have been marked down in points then. However, in every round of the prejudging, Reg and the rest of the judging panel had awarded him a perfect score. Reg's answer didn't make any sense — particularly in a contest that was created to select the most muscular man in the world. "What is this?" Mike asked, "Body*building* or Body *reducing*?"[49] Reg had no answer.

But Mike wasn't seeing the bigger picture. Again, he thought the problem was with himself — perhaps he hadn't followed Arnold's instruction properly. "I don't think I followed his advice well," he said. "I didn't hold each pose long enough to give the judges a good look." But if performing too many poses too quickly resulted in the judges not being able to make the necessary analysis of his physique (despite the many hours they spent analyzing his physique during the prejudging), why would Arnold have told him to do this? The answer lay within the latest issue of *Muscle Builder/Power*, which had come out several weeks prior to the contest. Inside the magazine was an article authored by Jack Neary entitled "Mike Mentzer: The Thinking Man's Bodybuilder," in which Jack had related an interesting incident:

> Not long ago Arnold called me at my office in Weiderland.
>
> He was angered by some recent comments Mentzer made about Arnold's methods of training.
>
> "Tell Mike Mentzer," Arnold's resonant Bavarian voice announced in hortatory tone, "for me that he is an asshole. I read once again where he says that my training system is wrong. I'm pissed off. The whole idea is not to knock each other, but to help. If Mentzer doesn't have anything good to say about someone else, he should keep his mouth shut. If I ever read or hear that he is knocking me again, I will see to it that nobody ever takes his training seriously. Tell him that!"[50]

While it was no secret that Mike and Arnold weren't on each other's Christmas card list, this was the first time that a bodybuilder had indicated a willingness to sabotage another bodybuilder's career and livelihood. Knowing that Arnold held considerable sway over Joe and within the industry, Jack made sure to catch up with Mike and warn him of the Austrian's threat:

> It's funny because when I shared it with Mike, he just said, "that's to be expected; it's the cat amongst the pigeons. We're ruffling feathers and that's what's going to happen. People naturally don't like it when the order of things is upended." Mike had a supreme confidence about what he did and how he did it and he never seemed to get rattled by that kind of stuff. So he just took it in stride. But bodybuilding was kind of a 'good ol' boys' club; it was a happy boat in those days

before Mike came along and kind of rocked the boat a bit. Everybody kind of just went along and, well, whatever Arnold said was gospel. And Arnold didn't like being challenged. He didn't like it, and he knew that Mike and I were getting close, and I was spending time interviewing Mike, and I guess in a roundabout way he was threatening me to threaten Mike.[51]

As Arnold was not only the promoter of the Mr. Olympia contest but also the one who selected the judging panel, he had at his disposal the means to make good on his threat. Indeed, the two judges who marked Mike down to third place in the evening show were Arnold's longtime friends, Albert Busek and Reg Park. The reader is free to make of this what they will.

And then there was Joe Weider, who had recently come to view Mike as a potential liability to his legacy as the "trainer of champions." When Jack wrote his article for the October 1979 issue, he incorporated Mike's favorable references to Arthur Jones and his Nautilus machines. The article came at a time when Joe was heavily promoting his barbell sets through his magazine and had in the pipeline several articles critiquing machines, and Nautilus machines in particular.[52] And now an article appeared on his desk wherein Mike not only didn't give sole credit to Joe for his bodybuilding success, but was singing the praises of the Arthur Jones and the machines that Joe was in direct competition with. The reader will recall that during the early 1970s Joe devoted no fewer than six issues of his magazine to attacking Nautilus machines and their creator. To have someone from within his own camp now touting the merits of the enemy's product was viewed as nothing short of a betrayal. And so, at the end of the article, Joe tacked on the following sidebar:

> Arthur Jones, who created Nautilus equipment, took full advantage of the Weider Principles of Slow-Continuous Tension, Isolation, Peak Contraction, Forced Reps and Retrogravity Training in designing his machines. While these machines make full use of such Weider Principles, we doubt that any bodybuilder can reach his full potential without using free weights. Mike Mentzer was already massive and powerful — far above the average — before incorporating Nautilus equipment into his workouts. We predict that if Mike doesn't use more free

weights — and drop at least 10 pounds of bodyweight — his chances of winning Mr. Olympia are slim.[53]

Frank Zane could have advised the inexperienced young Mentzer further on just what Joe required in a relationship and definitely on what would have increased his odds of victory significantly. Referring back to his win over Arnold in 1968, Frank recalled:

> Standing on the victor's dais with Ben and Joe Weider holding my hands overhead in victory, Joe says in my ear, "Oh Frank, always remember to praise me." "What if I can't find a reason?" I thought, "I can't believe someone is actually saying this to me." But I later came to realize that Joe was telling me exactly how to treat him if I wanted to get the most from the relationship. I should have listened, Arnold sure did. Later, Joe goes on and tells me how Arnold is going to be the greatest bodybuilder of all time and is bringing him to California to do nothing but train and pose for photographs for his magazine. "But Joe, I just beat him," I retorted. "I'd like a job like that too!" No deal. So, Arnold and Joe flew to California, and I went back to teaching math. "What do I have to do to get treated right? I just won Mr. Universe?" It didn't make any sense. Apparently, I had to do more than just win contests."[54]

Joe's sidebar proved to be a harbinger of things to come and goes some way in explaining how the 1979 Mr. Olympia contest turned out. No other bodybuilder (with the exception of Sergio Oliva — and look what had happened to him) had been so threatened or called out in Joe's magazine. Ken Sprague would bring forth another reason that Mike was not going to win the competition: there was still the animosity that existed between Arnold and Gold's Gym. "We were enemies," Ken said.[55] Frank Zane, of course, was aligned with World Gym; he even appeared along with Arnold, Franco, and Joe Gold in advertisements for the facility, which now (with Frank, Franco, and Arnold) could boast three Mr. Olympia champions. Mike trained at Gold's — he was on the wrong side of the turf war.

One former Mr. Olympia winner who flat-out believed Mike was robbed was Sergio Oliva. "Mentzer all the way," he said. "There is no doubt about it. But don't forget, Mike came from the outside; Zane was with Weider. . . . Now, if they put Zane and Mentzer together in a contest that was not Weider dominated, then Mike would have won. Zane knows that, and Zane is my personal friend."[56]

With both Arnold Schwarzenegger and Joe Weider, the two most powerful individuals in bodybuilding, looking to bring him down a peg or two, Mike Mentzer had no chance of winning the 1979 Mr. Olympia.

CHAPTER TWENTY-TWO

LEVERAGE

Mike Mentzer had been on the losing end of judging decisions before, but this one hurt. It made no sense to him. If Reg Park was to be believed, Mike lost not because he lacked definition or his posing routine was poor but because he had too much muscle mass. This, in the Mr. Olympia contest! And after he had received a perfect score in the prejudging!

One month after the Olympia, another professional competition, the Canada Cup, was held in Hamilton, Ontario. Many of the Mr. Olympia competitors entered, including Mike, Robby, Boyer Coe, Chris Dickerson and, in his first IFBB professional contest, Casey Viator.

With the exception of Dickerson, few if any of the pros were able to maintain the muscular definition they had displayed onstage in Columbus. This fact, combined with veteran bodybuilder and physique judge Bill Pearl overseeing the judging panel, resulted in no grumbling from any corner when Dickerson was declared the winner. Mike placed second. "The top two men were very close," Pearl said afterwards. "Our choice finally came down to the man we felt was in the best condition."[1]

Dickerson, who hadn't won a contest since he captured the NABBA Pro Mr. Universe title in 1974, was ecstatic about his triumph. "I didn't think I could beat the big guys unless I was in absolutely top shape," he said. "I expected a battle from Mike Mentzer and got it. He has the size, symmetry, everything. What a way for me to end 1979!"[2] For his part, Mike confessed that he hadn't considered Dickerson to be a contender prior to the competition. "The guys I was concerned about were Robby and Casey Viator. But in the lineup, I looked over at Dickerson and could see he was ripped." He then added, "Geez, I'm getting sick of seconds."³ Mike took home $3,500 for his efforts. He finished off 1979 with three second-place finishes, one third-place finish and one win. His competition prize money for the year was slightly more than $20,000.

Mike bumped into Jack Neary on the streets of Hamilton prior to the prejudging. The pair hadn't seen each other since the previous summer, when Jack wrote his controversial profile piece on him. Shortly thereafter, Jack had left the Master Blaster's employ and moved back to Alberta. He'd had enough of Joe Weider's ego and the Master Blaster's constant after-the-fact tampering with his articles:

> Joe used to have an annoying habit of meddling; he would go in and rewrite little lines or paragraphs in my articles. He did it to a lot of other guys, too. Not changing the facts or anything, but he would embellish shit about himself. He always was trying to cultivate his image. So, where I would just say "so and so would do descending dumbbell curls for his biceps," Joe would insert "the Weider Principle of descending dumbbell curls," you know? He was the publisher, I guess he could do that if he wanted to, but it never sat well with me, those kinds of intrusions.⁴

And so the writer from the prairies had gone home.

The two friends spent some time catching up. Given that Jack was now living in Canada, Joe Weider had reached out to ask if he wouldn't mind covering the Canada Cup contest for *Muscle Builder/Power*. As it wasn't an assignment that required Jack to tax his mind looking for similes to spice up a bodybuilding training article, he accepted. Mike told his friend that he was looking for a liquor store. "Mentzer wanted a glass or two of wine before the contest," Jack recalled.⁵ "It helps the muscle pump," Mike said, "and it brings out the veins."⁶ Alcohol also helped to suppress anxiety, which was evidently becoming an issue for the bodybuilder. Mike shared with Jack that Casey had called him from Florida only four days previously to inquire if the IFBB judges were on the up and up. While he hadn't made up his mind about the judges at the Mr. Olympia, Mike was confident that in a smaller contest such as the Canada Cup, Casey had nothing to worry about.⁷ Casey, it turned out, needn't have worried; he wasn't in shape and ended up in fifth place. While Jack wrote that Mike looked "not far off his best form," that simply wasn't good enough to edge out a highly defined, five-foot-six, 190-pound Chris Dickerson.⁸

On the plane ride back to California, Mike had time to mull a few things over in his mind. He was trying to figure out exactly what it was the judges were looking for as of late. He had long been of the impression that building the maximum degree of proportioned muscle mass was the goal of bodybuilding,⁹ but now the decisions were trending in the direction of more definition and ballet-like posing routines set to soft music. It seemed to him a disproportionate emphasis.¹⁰ But if *that* was the new criteria, he would have to comply. If it was more definition the judges wanted, he would see to it that his physique had it to the utmost when the 1980 Mr. Olympia rolled around¹¹ — and without sacrificing muscle mass to achieve it.

The other issue that required his attention was the fact that his contract with Joe Weider expired a few months prior to the 1979 Mr. Olympia, and the two men had been unable to come to terms on a new one. Joe put Mike on the cover of *Muscle Builder/Power* for the October 1979 issue, which was put together at the Weider offices around the time they were in negotiations. Perhaps Joe thought that seeing himself on the cover, along with Jack Neary's glowing profile piece on him, would sway Mike to renew their agreement. But when the negotiations broke down, that's when Joe added the sidebar to the article that indicated that Mike needed more barbell work in his training or else the Mr. Olympia title would elude him. This clearly was a warning to accept Joe's terms or else the positive press Mike had been receiving could turn negative. Mike didn't heed the warning and paid the price.¹² And now it was November, and he still hadn't signed Joe's contract. The Master Blaster was about to show him what happened to bodybuilders who didn't play ball.

In two articles Joe published some three months apart, mention was made of the fact that Mike had relaxed his abdominal muscles the moment it was announced that Frank Zane won the contest.¹³ This, rather than the fact that Mike received the first ever perfect score in the prejudging of a Mr. Olympia competition, was considered print-worthy. It underscored Joe's critique that Mike needed to lose "at least ten pounds of bodyweight" and start using more free weights (read: using Joe's products and the Weider training system) if he wanted the accolades to keep coming and to succeed in professional bodybuilding henceforth. It was business leverage applied to get Mike to re-sign his contract with Joe, to be certain, but coming as it did from the leading magazine in the industry, it was a criticism that soon spread throughout the bodybuilding world. It was also a negative message that carried the potential to damage Mike's mail-order business and serve to influence judges who would officiate any contests he might enter in the future. It's true that Mike had thick, fully developed abdominal muscles, but this was by choice. "I train my abs in high-intensity fashion just like my other body parts," he'd said, "because, yes, high-intensity training will make my abs thicker, which is my goal. I fully realize that the prevailing 'wisdom' has most bodybuilders performing countless low intensity sets and reps so as not to 'over develop' the abdominals. It seems silly to me that bodybuilders should want to develop large arms, chests, legs, backs, etc., and leave the abs puny. What could be more ridiculous and incongruous than a thickly developed bodybuilder of 200 pounds who has the abdominal development of a 160-pound man? Thick, proportioned developed rectus abdominus (frontal abs) set off a well-developed physique and will not thicken or broaden one's waist. The breadth of your abdominal region is dictated primarily by your pelvic bone width, which is inherited and, therefore, not subject to alteration."[14]

Mike's abdominal muscles had always been thick and fully developed in every contest he entered, and never had they been considered a malefactor. Indeed, in four of those contests since 1976, his physique was awarded a perfect score — including at the 1979 Mr. Olympia. That he should be criticized in print now — only after he hadn't signed on the dotted line with Joe — seemed more than suspicious. Moreover, that his abdominals should relax when not flexed (and when the contest was over) seemed a strange attack to make, particularly when similar critiques could be made of virtually any other bodybuilder under similar circumstances. That Mike was centered out for censure made the matter personal. In his report on the 1979 Mr. Olympia competition, for example, Weider writer Bill Dobbins dismissed many of the competitors — Padilla ("not in shape"); Robinson ("simply not in peak condition. A major disappointment!"); Steve Davis ("Lacks mass. Appears out of place here.")[15] — but made no further criticism about them. Mike, on the other hand, of whom Dobbins wrote was "almost shockingly good" — and who had just received the first perfect score in Mr. Olympia history — was criticized repeatedly in the same report. Dobbins wrote that Mike's "stomach appears to bulge somewhat."[16] That apparently wasn't sufficient to drive the point home, as the writer felt obliged to approach AAU president Jim

Manion so he could quote him as saying Mike's "belly was hanging out."[17] In a follow-up article published three months later in *Muscle Builder/Power*, the criticism was revived by bodybuilding journalist Garry Bartlett, who wrote that "Mike committed the cardinal error of relaxing his stomach, which sagged in an unaesthetic symmetry-destroying curve away from his body."[18] Garry's article actually began with a middle-finger salute to anyone who believed Mike should have won the 1979 Mr. Olympia:

> I'm fed up with listening to and reading things by Mike Mentzer's Mr. Olympia supporters! Everything I've heard or read has been opposed to Zane winning the Olympia. But Zane clearly deserved to win![19]

That such journalistic hand grenades should be lobbed in the direction of Mike and his supporters was clear indication that the political tide had turned against him. Interestingly, shortly after Garry's article was published, he was covering another contest where Mike had been brought in to guest pose. Garry was nervous after what he had written as to what Mike might say or do when they crossed paths:

> In spite of my fears, I approached Mike only to be surprised at how friendly and amicable he was towards me. In fact, his demeanor and attitude were totally opposite from the brash confrontation that I fully expected. We discussed my views and reasons regarding his Olympia defeat, and he seemed satisfied with my opinions. From then on whenever I ran into him at a contest, he always sought out my opinion and would ask, "Garry, how did my *gut* look?" He usually followed this with a knowing smile! Looking back, I think he respected my honesty and point of view in spite of not always agreeing with me. If you were going to be questioned by Mike, then you damn well better have done your homework. He was a master at debate and smelled bullshit a mile away and had very little tolerance for it.[20]

Despite Garry's criticism, the two men would become good friends.

But if Joe Weider had turned against Mike, the lay public had opened its arms to him. His newly released poster was enjoying brisk sales,[21] as was his new book, *The Mentzer Method to Fitness*.[22] He was invited onto the national television program *The Mike Douglas Show*,[23] where he explained his workout philosophy and promoted his book. CBS reached out to him to participate in their *Superstars* competition, in which champions from various sports competed against other athletes in various events that were different from their field of expertise. Mike had long argued that bodybuilders were athletes, and this program would be an opportunity to prove it against the best athletes in the world.[24]

However, Mike couldn't walk away from competitive bodybuilding just yet — there was still that Mr. Olympia title that he needed to win, a result of that promise he made to his younger self some 14 years ago.[25] Moreover, he still had a strong desire to bring science into bodybuilding. But his monthly question-and-answer column was always outnumbered by multiple other articles that Joe put into the publication that were nothing more than ads for his products. In an interview with a Pennsylvania newspaper, Mike explained the dilemma:

> The influences most responsible for shaping our current outlook on bodybuilding have been the muscle magazines. But what most people fail to keep in mind is that these are primarily commercial publications. Their primary reason for existence is to sell products, not dispense scientific facts about bodybuilding. That is not to say there doesn't exist a coherent body of scientific data, but the problem is that most of the scientific knowledge regarding bodybuilding has been published piecemeal by diverse authors in a wide variety of texts, many of which are highly technical physiological studies. What I have done is to distill the facts to the general public. These are not new facts, but they have been obscured by commercial interests.[26]

Mike recognized that he was making only minimal progress against such a strong commercial headwind.[27] He had once believed that most bodybuilders saw through Joe's hyperbole but now recognized that he was mistaken. He was disillusioned by how many believed the Weider/Schwarzenegger propaganda — that the "Weider Instinctive Training Principle" would somehow manifest in each trainee's respective brain to unerringly guide him in his training efforts.[28] A truly scientific approach to bodybuilding required that *actual* science to be applied to the discipline. Simply indulging in random workout impulses — and calling it science — was nonsense. "It is my contention," he once told writer Rick Wayne, "that bodybuilding, as it is currently practiced, is the most counter-productive, least scientific endeavor that anyone could possibly engage in. All the muscle magazines purport to be scientific bodybuilding journals. Yet, you might ask yourself, who are the scientists on their editorial boards? Who conducts the scientific investigations? Casual observation of bodybuilders in a gym can hardly be regarded as *scientific* investigation."[29] This last comment was a direct shot at Joe Weider's claim as to how he had created the "Weider System."[30] Rick, a proponent of the house system, countered Mike's contention by stating that "perhaps bodybuilders might be their own investigating agents. Their own scientists, studying new concepts, rejecting this, proving that theory."[31] Mike disagreed: "How many bodybuilders have the capacity for serious scientific investigation? How many know the least thing about scientific bodybuilding?"[32]

But how could they? The bodybuilders' only source of training information came from the muscle magazines, primarily Joe's, which were registered with the government as catalogs — not science journals.[33] And while Joe was a businessman first and foremost, he was also the man who set the trends within the industry and created its premiere contest, and whose tongue had minted the very verbiage that was spoken throughout bodybuilding gyms around the world. It was Joe Weider — through the pages of a magazine that was rapidly growing in circulation[34] — who informed the discourse bodybuilders engaged in about training, nutrition, and the sport itself. The bodybuilders chose to follow him on their own, despite the fact that the champions he claimed were "Weider pupils," such as Arnold Schwarzenegger, Frank Zane, and Robby Robinson had never been trained by him,[35] that his "Weider Research Clinic" was non-existent,[36] and that he was said to have told bodybuilder and strength coach Dr. Ken Leistner that his Weider supplements were "bullshit."[37] Joe was about the dollars, not science, and he had products to sell and money to be made. There was no return in transforming *Muscle Builder/Power* into the *New England Journal of Medicine*.

Despite a deceit that wasn't hard to decipher, Joe's marketing material had come to underpin the industry, and the uninformed culture it created was causing Mike to lose interest. When he first moved to the west coast in 1977 to work for *Muscle Builder/Power*, he recognized that extolling Joe

Weider and his products went with the job. Joe made that clear right from the beginning; it was simply the price Mike had to pay if he wanted to get away from a heavy academic workload, no money, and the sub-zero temperatures of Maryland and into a publicity machine that promised a steady but rising income in sunny Southern California.

Given how dramatically Mike's lifestyle had changed for the better, he felt genuinely beholden to the Master Blaster for the opportunity he had provided him, and had no problem at all making his gratitude known publicly through his articles and columns for Joe's magazine. But that was in 1977. The more Mike traveled, and the more seminars he gave, the more he saw that young aspiring bodybuilders — who weren't equipped to know how to separate fact from sales pitch — were being seriously misled. Every reference to a Weider Principle, every tip of the hat to Joe for being the one and only trainer of champions, and every instance where Joe salted Mike's articles with unsolicited references to Weider nutritional supplements was, from Mike's perspective, leading young bodybuilders astray. By 1980 he simply couldn't find it within himself to toe the corporate line anymore. He began speaking freely in his seminars and interviews about how the bodybuilding industry was dominated by commercial interests, and openly shared with attendees the fact that most of them lacked the genetics to become physique champions — irrespective of what Joe Weider said in his advertisements. For the first time in his life, Mike envisioned a time when he might step away from the industry altogether. He told members of the press that he saw himself out of competition and, ideally, relaxing on a beach in the Bahamas by 1981.[38] A desire to be "normal" began to grow inside him:

> "I'm looking forward to retiring as a bodybuilder," he said, "of losing a lot of this muscle and seeing what it's like to be a normal person. A bodybuilder is not a normal person." At least, concedes Mentzer, not a bodybuilder whose 5-foot-9, 220-pound structure has been acclaimed a '10.' Once Mentzer adds the professional Mr. Olympia crown to his collection, and the additional fame and money that go with it, he can settle down to being a student again. Mentzer interrupted his pre-med studies at the University of Maryland a few years ago to edit a muscle-building magazine. He says he will go back to studying to be a psychiatrist now that he is financially

secure and has accomplished his bodybuilding goals. "One of the things I'm interested in," he said, "is the effect on my own psyche and self-esteem that a smaller body will bring. I want to see my own reaction." Mentzer, for much of his life, has seen the awed reaction of lesser-developed mortals. Some abhor his custom-made body, others worship it. "I enjoy the attention on occasion," he said. "At times, though, it is tedious. I've worked at bodybuilding since I was 12, and some of the novelty and romance has worn thin. I don't see myself getting the same satisfaction forever. I don't want to be a 35-year-old competitive bodybuilder."[39]

It's true that under Joe Weider's command, bodybuilding grew as an industry, but that was largely due to the promotional arm of the Professional Division of the IFBB, which created more pro contests for bodybuilders to compete in. And credit for the increased number of professional contests was due to men like Arnold Schwarzenegger, Jim Lorimer, Ken Sprague, and Wayne DeMilia, who created more contests with more prize money, which attracted more top-level competitors and gave the photographers, writers, and magazines in the industry more content for their publications. The increased proliferation of the muscle magazines, in turn, generated more attention from the general public. The shows offered more prize money to entice the best bodybuilders to compete in their contests. The rival federations soon did what they could to follow suit, which caused the profile of the sport to grow almost organically. And, as the IFBB had the largest profile owing to the promotion its contests received through Joe's magazine, it was the federation that grew the quickest.

Since the entire bodybuilding industry benefitted from the rising tide of public awareness, Joe Weider was viewed as its benefactor, and what was good for Joe was good for the industry. As a result, Joe began to insulate himself with people who constantly praised him and his genius, and it wasn't long before he began to believe what they were telling him. His already large ego began to swell out of control.[40] Perhaps the most striking example of this was when Joe approached Robby Robinson in late 1977 and asked him to pose for a bronze bust. Robby was flattered, believing he had finally arrived; that his physique would now be immortalized alongside the huge paintings Joe had commissioned of champions Arnold Schwarzenegger,

Rick Wayne, and Larry Scott that were displayed on the walls of his office building in Woodland Hills.[41] However, after a month or so of modeling for the sculpture, when the day of the great unveiling arrived, Robby was gob-smacked to discover that a bronze sculpture of Joe's head was affixed to the sculpture of Robby's torso in the final product.[42] Joe would in fact use an image of this bronze bust of himself as his company logo to market all of his products. It even appeared at the top of the table-of-contents page in each issue of his magazine. And right next to the image Joe placed a quote from himself, "words of wisdom," as it were, in which he stated:

> Strive for excellence, exceed yourself, love your friend, speak the truth, practice fidelity and honor your father and mother. These principles will help you master yourself, make you strong, give you hope and put you on a path to greatness.
> — Joe Weider Trainer of Champions[43]

Those in the industry who benefitted from Joe's marketing and promotional efforts dismissed this insult to Robby with a smile; to them it was just one of Joe's endearing idiosyncratic quirks. But those who didn't owe their careers to the man viewed it as symptomatic of a serious psychological pathology. Joe had transformed himself from merely a bodybuilders' trainer/advisor to nothing less than Zeus himself — a god — and the bodybuilding champions were his pantheon of demigods, who stood well above the *demos*, or common person. But godlike though he had become, Joe had yet to achieve omniscience. He still hadn't found a replacement for Arnold Schwarzenegger to market his products. His attempt to use Kal Szkalak had failed miserably and it was clear that Mike Mentzer had no intention of denying scientific truths to placate Joe's ego.

Arnold, it will be remembered, had stepped away from bodybuilding competition in 1975 in order to purse a film career in Hollywood. And there was a brief moment, in January 1977, when it looked like he had successfully completed the transition. That was when he was awarded a Golden Globe as Best Acting Debut in a Motion Picture (Male) for his supporting role (after Jeff Bridges and Sally Field) in the movie *Stay Hungry*.[44] The award arrived along with the belief that Arnold would finally be able to kick aside the small boat of bodybuilding and step aboard the big ship of feature film success. However, the best he had managed since winning the prize was to appear in one episode of the television police drama *The Streets of San Francisco* (1977),[45] and a now forgotten episode of an ill-fated television series that went by the name *The San Pedro Beach Bums* (1977).[46] His character in both of these television appearances (like his role in *Stay Hungry*) was that of a bodybuilder.

If Hollywood was interested, it hadn't let him know.

But then a most bizarre thing happened: Arnold decided to enter the 1980 Mr. Olympia contest. Why he made this decision is uncertain; even he seemed confused about it in later interviews.

> It wasn't much of a decision to be honest with you. It was just one of those things on the spur of the moment; you just decide to do it and then do it, without really asking yourself much of what it really is good for what it is bad for, you know? It's just, there was no reason behind it. It was just one of those gut reaction things.[47]

And:

> One day, just a few weeks before the contest, I woke up and the idea of competing was fixed firmly in my mind. "Yes," my mind seemed to be saying to me, almost beyond my control, "you must compete."[48]

Given that Arnold was a man who prided himself on having a master plan, setting goals for each step of his life, and then achieving them, such an impulse move was completely out of left field. And 1980 Mr. Olympia competitor Roger Walker, for one, didn't buy it. "Who in their right mind could possibly believe that Arnold woke up one morning in sunny California and decided eight weeks out — after five years in retirement — that he was going to compete in an Olympia at that scale that he had never competed in before?" he asked. "This wasn't two people, three people [he'd be competing against, as in previous Olympias], this was [16 competitors], compulsory poses, etc. He'd never gone through that. Why would he put his reputation on the line eight weeks out? Doesn't make sense."[49]

In attempting to analyze the possible reasons for Arnold's return to bodybuilding competition, only two scenarios seem plausible. The first is that his ego simply overwhelmed him: he was so angry at Frank Zane for reminding the world that he had defeated the Austrian in bodybuilding competition that he had to slap him down. And then there was Mike Mentzer, whose star was rising in the bodybuilding firmament a little too quickly for Arnold's liking and who had been saying publicly that Arnold didn't know the first thing about scientific training principles. Perhaps Arnold felt that he needed to return to the dais to put Zane and Mentzer in their place. This is certainly possible. But it also seems very unlikely, as Arnold had put bodybuilding in his rear-view mirror five years previously and was now focused on his acting career. The statements of other bodybuilders were (or should have been) no longer a concern. Besides, all he needed to do was point out his six Mr. Olympia titles won in succession — more than any other bodybuilder in history — to squelch anything that Zane or Mentzer had to say. That leaves us with the other scenario: Arnold *needed* to win the 1980 Mr. Olympia in order for his master plan to proceed. This scenario makes sense, particularly given what transpired in the years leading up to his decision to enter the contest.

In late 1977 or early 1978, seemingly out of nowhere, an opportunity to play the lead in a major motion picture presented itself. Arnold was signed by Hollywood producer Edward Pressman to star in the movie *Conan the Barbarian*, which Arnold believed would start filming in the summer of 1978.[50] But problems quickly developed. First and foremost, Pressman sold his interest in the project to Dino De Laurentiis,[51] and the Italian producer didn't want Arnold in the film. He believed his accent was way too thick to be comprehensible to a North American audience.[52] Indeed, during a meeting with the producer, Arnold was actually escorted out of his office.[53]

Conan the Barbarian was Arnold's brass ring; it was a role that didn't require tremendous acting ability but rather a suit of overdeveloped muscles, which he had in abundance. However, from De Laurentiis' perspective, initially at any rate, there was no shortage of muscular actors in Tinseltown whose ability to speak English was not in any way compromised, and he had no intention of risking a multimillion-dollar investment on an aspiring actor with a thick accent who had yet to prove he could draw people into theaters to watch him as a leading man in movies. But to Arnold, the film represented much more than a chance to pad his acting résumé; it was an opportunity to make millions of dollars and acquire power. If the film was a success per his agreement, he would be guaranteed one million dollars for a sequel.[54] Pressman, in an effort to help Arnold out, and perhaps get him back into De Laurentiis's good graces, secured him two co-starring roles in the films *The Villain* (where Arnold played third banana to Kirk Douglas and Ann-Margret) and *The Jayne Mansfield Story*, where he played Mansfield's bodybuilder husband Mickey Hargitay. However, the first film flopped at the box office, while the latter presently enjoys a one-star rating on Rotten Tomatoes.[55] More significantly, his work on the two films didn't diminish the problem with his accent. Loni Anderson, the star of *The Jayne Mansfield Story*, recollected, "My heart went out to him at first because his accent was so thick that you really couldn't understand [him] and they did to have him repeat a lot of his lines."[56] De Laurentiis's opinion of the muscleman had not been without foundation.

Arnold had to find a way to convince the producer that not only was he perfect for the role of Conan, but that he — above all other muscular actors — could bring people into movie theaters in numbers large enough to ensure that the film would make back its production budget (and then some). Perhaps this is when the thought of winning one more Mr. Olympia title came to him. If Ben Weider's statement from the 1979 IFBB Congress was to be believed, the CBS telecast of the contest would be beamed into the homes of 750 million viewers, which would be incredible promotion for both Arnold and the *Conan* movie. Moreover, the promotion that would result from his coming out of retirement to claim his seventh Mr. Olympia title would put him on the cover of every bodybuilding magazine in the world over the next 12 months; again, massive publicity for Arnold — and for the movie.[57] Accent or no accent, there was no well-built actor in Hollywood and certainly no other bodybuilder in the world who could offer Dino De Laurentiis as much. Arnold winning the 1980 Mr. Olympia would go a long way in putting bodybuilding fans worldwide into theaters to see the greatest bodybuilder in the world (and the new Mr. Olympia champ) on the big screen.[58]

But this wasn't the message Arnold put out to the public to explain the reason for his comeback. He would later state to *Muscle & Fitness*, "This game is too small to knock each other. I wanted to show Mentzer and Coe that you could go into the Olympia on a very positive note without criticizing others, and win."[59] While Boyer had no idea why he was now in

Arnold's crosshairs,[60] there's no doubt that Mike had gotten under Arnold's skin. The latter's phone call to Jack Neary had made that clear. But to get the promotional support he needed to win back De Laurentiis, and to put Mike in his place, Arnold needed to win the 1980 Mr. Olympia. And to do this, he would need Joe Weider's help.

But Joe was an astute businessman; he didn't need Arnold to connect the dots for him with regard to what an Arnold win would do for Weider supplement sales. An Olympia win for Arnold could mean the return to the fold of Joe's greatest pitchman, and a new round of Weider advertising could begin. Moreover, an Arnold win would be not only a triumph for Weider products but also a victory for the Weider System over the barbarians at the gate: Arthur Jones, Nautilus exercise machines, and their champion, Mike Mentzer. It seemed every time Joe read a newspaper article on Mike, he was praising Arthur.[61] How was that good for Joe's business? If *Conan the Barbarian* had Arnold as its star, that was a multimillion-dollar PR campaign for Weider products, particularly if Arnold agreed to appear as Conan in Joe's ads. This author is not suggesting that this is precisely how things went down, but all of the above pieces were certainly in play. Again, Joe Weider was a businessman first and foremost, and consequently, no backroom deals in smoky boardrooms would have been required to draw up plans for an Arnold victory. As comedian George Carlin once astutely said, "You don't need a formal conspiracy when interests converge."

We know that Arnold spoke to Joe about his plan to return to competition, as Arnold wrote about it.[62] And we also know that Joe supported it. According to Arnold, Joe told him, "Why don't you get in there, you will make a great Mr. Olympia for a change."[63] "For a change?" What a slap in the face to Frank Zane! But then Arnold had always been Joe's cash cow, and if he won the 1980 Mr. Olympia, and went on to star in *Conan the Barbarian*, Joe Weider stood to make a lot of money.

Certainly, Joe couldn't help but be beholden to Arnold for carrying the flag of the Weider training system once more into battle and putting Mike Mentzer — and all his talk of "scientific" training — in his place.

PART THREE
THE CHILD

"Alcinous!" wary Odysseus countered, "cross that thought from your mind. I'm nothing like the immortal gods who rule the skies, either in build or breeding. I'm just a mortal man. Whom do you know most saddled down with sorrow? They are the ones I'd equal, grief for grief."

— Homer, *The Odyssey*

CHAPTER TWENTY-THREE

PREPARING FOR WAR

While Mike Mentzer and Boyer Coe were on Arnold's hit list, the Austrian also reserved a special place of contempt for Frank Zane. Arnold had phoned Frank shortly after the 1979 Mr. Olympia contest went to air, incensed over Frank's remarks during his post-contest interview. "He was so pissed off he called me on the phone," Frank recalled, "and he was screaming at me: 'How could you talk against me?!' I said, 'Arnold, you know, you have a great sense of humor when the joke's not on you, just lighten up.'"[1]

From Arnold's perspective, Frank's on-air comment had relegated his status to that of a former bodybuilder who had been defeated by the current Mr. Olympia champion. This was the message that was televised in homes around the world, with a viewing audience estimated to be more than 100 million people.[2] And with a major Hollywood production on the line, this was not the message he wanted people such as Dino De Laurentiis to hear. Arnold had no desire to "lighten up" in the face of such an impertinence. Instead, Frank's words had only served to underscore the need for Arnold to win the 1980 Mr. Olympia. He had to prove to the viewing public that Frank's 1968 victory had been a fluke and that Arnold was still the greatest bodybuilder of all time, that he was still relevant. Payback would be sweet when CBS broadcast *that* contest, as hundreds of millions of viewers would be tuning in to see a monumental ass-kicking. Zane, Mentzer, and Coe would be put in their proper place for all the world to see, and Dino De Laurentiis would be reassured that Arnold, the king of bodybuilding, was back upon the throne.

Behind the scenes, Arnold quietly stepped down as the head of the IFBB Professional Division. The vacancy caused by Arnold's departure was filled by promoter Wayne DeMilia,[3] who now headed up all the professional bodybuilding contests — save for the Mr. Olympia contest, which would be exclusively under the control of Ben Weider.[4] Arnold stepping away from the position removed him from any potential conflict of interest charge that should arise from his competing in the 1980 Mr. Olympia contest. There could not be even a hint of impropriety; it had to appear that when he defeated Frank Zane et al., Arnold's victory was on the level.[5]

In late April of 1980, Mike Mentzer, Arnold Schwarzenegger, and Franco Columbu flew to Toronto, Ontario, where they were greeted by Ben Weider. The bodybuilders were to accompany the IFBB president to the Simpsons department store in downtown Toronto to conduct a breakfast seminar that had been arranged so that the store would receive a weighty promotional push for the Weider exercise equipment it was selling. Canadian bodybuilding fans quickly snatched up tickets to the event, and every one of the 470 seats in the small conference room was occupied. Even professional boxer George Chuvalo was spotted in attendance. Many more who were unable to purchase tickets lined up outside the store on Bay Street, just to catch a glimpse of their bodybuilding heroes. Michael Moore, a writer for the *Globe and Mail* newspaper, was on hand and reported on the proceedings:

> [Ben Weider] introduced Mr. Mentzer, winner of Mr. Universe and Mr. Olympia in his division as "the greatest bodybuilder of 1980." Mr. Mentzer made a disparaging remark about the meal, quoted Will Durant with a nod to Friedrich Nietzsche about eating properly, told the audience the best diet is a balanced diet. Mr. Columbu was the first speaker to get the audience cheering when he held the microphone stand in his teeth and bent it in a right angle, then bent it again with his hands. . . . Someone else asked him about using steroid drugs to stimulate muscle growth. Mr. Columbu said he tried them in 1972 but hasn't used them since. Later, at a press conference, Mr. Schwarzenegger said he'd tried the drugs several times, though not for competitions, but he wouldn't recommend anyone using them. . . . After Mr. Schwarzenegger had disparaged people who build up their bodies but don't

have his theatrical flair to make money from their physique ("that's stupid"), one of the few women in the audience asked for some poses. The press release for the breakfast had said the three would strike poses and sign autographs for half an hour, and a number of people had brought cameras. Cheers and whistles mounted and people with their telephoto lenses and Instamatics crowded to the front. The crowd ooo-ed and aww-ed as Mr. Columbu took off his shirt and whirled through a series of quick poses. They wanted more. They wanted Mr. Schwarzenegger. Mr. Mentzer said he'd pose if Mr. Schwarzenegger would, but Mr. Schwarzenegger showed no interest. A few minutes of palaver on the stage was drowned out by encouragement from the crowd, then Mr. Weider stepped up and said it was all over. He said the hero of the film Pumping Iron (Mr. Schwarzenegger) would be in the store's sports department in the afternoon to pump people's hands, his own books and films, and Mr. Weider's equipment.[6]

Both Arnold's and Franco's statements about their use of steroids were untrue. Franco, of course, had used the drugs right up to and including his 1976 Mr. Olympia win, while Arnold used them for competition as well.[7] As one of those in attendance that day, I can recall detecting an underlying animosity towards Mike from Arnold. During his talk, Arnold looked behind him to make sure Mike wasn't in the room before stating that bodybuilders shouldn't be "so intense" with their training. He then took a shot at his fellow breakfast seminar speaker: "What works for Mike Mentzer won't work for you." Just as the words were leaving Arnold's mouth, Mike re-entered the conference room. The audience noticed this, as did Arnold, who immediately changed tack: "Uh, but then what works for me might not work you. What works for Franco might not work for you. You have to buy all of the books and all the courses of all the bodybuilders and see which one works for you." I recall this distinctly, because even then it struck me as bizarre counsel. It was like saying that aviation wouldn't work for you in getting from Toronto to Los Angeles; but then taking a ship or walking might not get you there either. That, in effect, you would have to try all forms of transportation and conveyance and see which one worked best for you. Immediately after the seminar concluded, Arnold, Franco, and Ben Weider quickly exited the building together. Mike stayed behind to converse with the fans. This impressed me, as many of us had traveled a great distance to attend the event. Mike seemed to understand this and was more than willing to spend time answering questions and signing autographs. Looking to say hello to Mike, I approached Cathy Gelfo, whom I spotted standing off to the side as Mike conversed with Chris Lund, the writer/photographer for *MuscleMag International*. I had read an article several months previously that indicated Mike and Cathy were engaged, and so I approached and started with what, in retrospect, was an inappropriate question.

"Are you Mrs. Mentzer?"

Cathy smiled and said somewhat wistfully, "Not *yet*."

Fortunately, Cathy was very friendly, and we continued to make small talk. Within a few minutes, Mike walked over to join us. We shook hands and he said, somewhat facetiously, "I thought you were trying to pick up my fiancée!" After laughing at this, I produced a bodybuilding magazine that featured Mike's photo and asked if he would sign it for me. He gladly obliged and we talked some more. Not wanting to impose any further, I excused myself, thanked him, and wished him and Cathy a safe trip back to California. Neither of us suspected that this encounter would be the start of a friendship that would last the remainder of his life.[8]

Upon returning to California, Mike began his training for the 1980 Mr. Olympia, employing every scientific principle he had learned in his quest to build more muscle. With his brother Ray as his training partner, the pair worked each muscle group to a point where another repetition was impossible despite their greatest efforts — and then pushed beyond that point with the addition of forced and negative repetitions. Mike had even developed a nuanced variation on Rest-Pause, which he called Infitonic Training,[9] which saw him perform a maximum positive repetition and then have Ray apply downward pressure on the weight stack while Mike resisted it throughout the negative or lowering portion of the repetition.

The brothers had been training on a split routine, which saw them training their legs, back, and abdominal muscles on Mondays and Thursdays, and their chest, shoulders and arms on Tuesdays and Fridays.[10] Such training required a great deal of energy output, the replenishment of which did not fall conveniently into a schedule that permitted them only three days off per week. Recognizing that they needed more recovery time between workouts, Mike suggested that they only work out again after their bodies had fully recovered and adapted, however long that proved to be. Although this sounds simple and commonsensical, it was unheard of in professional bodybuilding. Bodybuilders typically set out a routine of so many exercises, so many sets, so many days a week and then slavishly adhered to it. They relied on steroids to assist with their recovery and to produce the gains. However, Mike recognized that, steroids or not, they were still dealing with human physiology, which required adequate recovery time (lest the body slip into Hans Selye's stage of exhaustion). "There were times," Mike recalled, "when we skipped two days in between workouts — 72 hours. We would train on a Monday, skip Tuesday, skip Wednesday, and then train Thursday. So, we started training only four days out of every nine or ten days — not allowing tradition and convenience and compulsion, at some points, to supersede logic and reason."[11]

To more accurately monitor his progress, Mike subjected himself to underwater (hydrostatic) weighing.[12] This method involved weighing oneself first on a physician's scale, and then being weighed again while placed in a harness that was submerged underwater. Muscle, being denser than fat, sinks and thus registers on the underwater scale, whereas fat, being less dense, floats. The difference in weight indicated on the two scales precisely determines one's percentage of bodyfat. And after he implemented the additional rest days into his Olympia preparations, Mike's body composition analysis told an encouraging tale; in one month he gained ten pounds of muscle and lost four pounds of fat.[13] Mike's confidence in the effectiveness of his training method now had tangible, independently verified data to support it.

Arnold, likewise, was also doing what he could to win the 1980 Mr. Olympia contest, but it didn't require employing new training protocols or scientific body composition measurements. His understanding of how bodybuilding competitions were decided ran much deeper than this. He had been in contact with the man who would be promoting the contest, Paul Graham, ever since the latter was paroled from Terminal Island Federal Correctional Institution in 1972. Arnold traveled to Australia in 1974 to guest pose at one of Paul's shows, and the duo had even paired up to judge the 1975 Mr. Australia contest, a show that was not without controversy. Vince Basile, one of the competitors, claimed that he had been deliberately marked down to last place by Paul and Arnold because he had once made the mistake of loudly booing a decision at another contest Paul promoted, the Mr. New South Wales, some months earlier.[14] Moreover, five years later at that same Mr. Australia contest, which was held two months prior to the 1980 Mr. Olympia, both Paul and another judge, Paul and Arnold's friend Brendan Ryan, had been "stood down" (had their national judging credentials revoked) as a result of what the Chairman of Judges for IFBB Australia, Frank Burwash, described as "bad judging."[15] Ben Weider was notified but allowed Paul (who was a Weider distributor) to overturn Ryan's suspension.[16] This was a significant move that will factor into the story later.

But as these goings on had taken place over 9,000 miles away, in the pre-internet era, none of the American bodybuilders knew anything about it. Nevertheless, these alleged actions of Arnold and Paul suggested that objectivity in judging a contest came a distant second to putting people in their place against whom they held personal grudges. Certainly, Arnold's own judging record included some debatable decisions, sometimes to the benefit of his friends and allies. He had, after all, been the only judge to award a first-place vote to Roger Callard (his training partner) at the 1976 Mr. America contest. Arnold and Franco had once even convinced Gold's Gym owner Ken Sprague to enter the 1972 IFBB Mr. America, a contest both men were adjudicating. Ken entered to have a good time; he knew his physique wasn't at the level necessary to win such a prestigious competition. But that didn't prevent Arnold and Franco from voting him in first place (the other judges at the contest didn't see it that way, and Ken ended up fourth in his division).[17] Given the nepotistic attitude they had displayed in judging contests in the past, Arnold may have had reason to believe that Paul would do what he could to make sure the votes fell Arnold's way in the 1980 Mr. Olympia contest — particularly if there was something in it for him. And evidently there was.

Paul believed that the *Pumping Iron* documentary had been a tremendous financial success.[18] He was also aware that his friend Arnold's star appeared to be on the rise. With these two points in mind, it struck the Australian that a documentary on Arnold coming out of retirement to win the 1980 Mr. Olympia contest would be lucrative venture — particularly if Paul was the producer. Arnold, evidently, was fine with the proposed project. It must be noted that at this point in his career, Arnold had professional representation whose job it was to procure film work for their client and to negotiate his fee and backend percentages on any and all projects he might be inclined to appear in. For Arnold to appear in Paul's film and not be a profit participant is, frankly, odd, and raises the possibility that Arnold was doing so as a courtesy or favor; perhaps as long overdue payment on a debt owed Paul for keeping Arnold's name out of his mouth when he went to prison in 1969.[19] We'll never know. What we do know is that Paul would in fact produce a documentary entitled *The Comeback*, which was filmed during the 1980 Mr. Olympia contest, and it would be challenging indeed to shoot a film called *The Comeback* unless it was known in advance that Arnold would *come back*, i.e., win the contest.

More importantly, as Paul was the promoter of the 1980 Mr. Olympia, and the man who picked the judging panel for the competition,[20] his decision to devote time and money to producing such a film indicated a complete lack of impartiality. After all, as both the promoter of the contest and producer of the documentary, he now had skin in the game and thus reason to do what he could to help ensure an Arnold victory. If Arnold came up short in his quest, nobody would pay money to see a film about a guy who came out of retirement to lose the Mr. Olympia contest. And ensuring an Arnold victory was a relatively easy task; all it required was to select four (out of seven) judges who were predisposed to vote Arnold's way. And bodybuilding, being the commercially incestuous, tight-knit world that it was, Paul knew exactly who those four judges were.

But perhaps it wouldn't even have to come to that. Given Arnold's pedigree within the sport (no bodybuilder had won as many Olympias), who was to say that if he trained hard and himself got into great shape — as he had in the past — that he didn't have a legitimate shot at winning the contest all on his own? It was therefore with a justifiable air of confidence that Arnold began training for the 1980 Mr. Olympia contest. Of course, the only gym he trained in was World Gym, where his training efforts roused the suspicions of bodybuilder Danny Padilla (who would also be competing in the 1980 Mr. Olympia contest). "I was in World Gym and had seen Arnold training twice a day," Danny recalled. "And I told Mike, 'I believe this guy is going to compete. I know Arnold well enough to know that if he's training twice a day, it isn't just to go pose on the beach.'"[21]

Arnold would claim that nobody, including Paul Graham, knew about his decision to enter the competition until the night prior to the contest. That was when he said he contacted Ben Weider and Bill Pearl to notify them of his decision.[22] But this doesn't square with the recollections of Vince Basile, whose gym sold tickets to the 1980 Mr. Olympia contest on behalf of Paul Graham. Vince recalled that approximately one month before the contest, Graham told him that Arnold would be competing. In addition, the man whom Graham had hired to direct his documentary, *The Comeback*,

Kit Laughlin, claimed he knew about Arnold's entry a full two weeks prior to the contest.[23] Evidently others were aware of his decision to compete many months prior to this, as the May 1980 edition of *MuscleMag International* let the cat out of the bag:

LUCKY 7 FOR ARNOLD?

> How's this for news? Arnold Schwarzenegger confided to a close friend that . . . he may whip himself into contest shape and enter this year's Mr. Olympia in Australia.[24]

Perhaps because the announcement hadn't appeared in Joe Weider's magazine, it wasn't taken seriously. Frank Zane obviously didn't place much stock in it, as he was hard at work attempting to up his game for the 1980 Mr. Olympia. His victory over Mike in 1979 had been razor thin. He decided that he needed more muscle mass on his frame to successfully fend Mike off a second time. By early August, he claimed to be tipping the scales at "208 pounds, rock hard."[25] He wasn't in contest shape yet, but it was a good bet that he would be entering the Mr. Olympia contest weighing just north of 200 pounds — ten pounds heavier than he had been the year before.

But then disaster struck.

While he was tanning poolside at his home in Palm Springs, Frank's deck chair — with him still in it — slipped into the pool. "I felt a hard bump in the groin and sunk to the bottom, dazed," he recalled. "Crawling out there was blood gushing from my penis. The bulbous urethra was smashed. . . . I thought I was dying."[26] Frank was immediately rushed to the hospital, where he remained for eight days with internal bleeding.[27]

His stay in the hospital saw him losing muscle mass by the day. When he was finally discharged and returned home, he discovered that he had lost 15 pounds.[28] He now wondered if it was worth his entering a contest of this magnitude when he wasn't at his best. He decided to call the one man in the sport he believed he could trust: Arnold Schwarzenegger. "He'd given me contest advice for the last several years," Frank recalled, "and I really needed it now."[29]

"The word is at Gold's Gym that you took so many steroids your dick exploded!" Arnold said with a laugh.[30] To Frank, however, his bodybuilding career was at stake. He needed honest answers. Perhaps referencing the *MuscleMag*

International article, Frank wanted to know if the rumor that Arnold was going to compete in the 1980 Mr. Olympia was true. "I talked to Arnold," Frank recalled. "I said, 'I understand that you're going in [the Mr. Olympia contest].' [Arnold said] "Nah, I'm just going to go over there and do commentary [for CBS].' I said, 'What do you think I should do?' He says, 'Well, you should go to Australia and defend your title.' And so, I did, you know, because I used to go to him for advice all the time when he wasn't competing. And he'd tell me every little thing that needed to be improved. So, I sort of, you know, relied on him. But he basically backstabbed me. He set me up."[31]

In mid-August 1980, Mike Mentzer was in his home state of Pennsylvania, where he spent two weeks visiting with his old friend Roger Schwab. Roger had started Main Line Health & Fitness, already considered one of the best gyms on the east coast, which boasted a full line of Nautilus machines. He was also now a judge for the IFBB, and knew the lifestyle of professional bodybuilders. Before Mike's visit, Roger had asked his friend not to bring any injectable steroids into the Schwab household. He was married now with children and didn't want one of his kids stumbling upon a syringe. Mike, of course, complied with the request.[32] During Mike's stay, Roger learned that his houseguest had given up consuming red meat. "I remember he told me he did not eat red meat, that it always gave him trouble with acid reflux," Roger recalled. "He didn't digest it. I remember that and I do know at my house we never ate red meat, only because he was there for a couple of weeks."[33] Mike had actually given up eating beef almost two years previously, telling the Pennsylvania press: "I used to eat red meat every day. For experimental reasons, about a year ago I cut back to eating beef once every two weeks. My joint problems stopped almost immediately."[34] Roger enjoyed his time together with Mike and would look back upon the two weeks Mike spent at his house with fondness:

> Mike stayed at my house and trained at my club, Main Line Health & Fitness. He was trying to get into his all-time-best shape and wanted to become leaner for the contest, which meant he did a little bit more aerobic activity. He was riding his bicycle a lot and had his bike at my house. He was on a very, very strict diet. And like all bodybuilders at the time he ate, slept, and trained but he was training very briefly and infrequently compared to most bodybuilders. I can tell you

exactly what his workouts were because I took him through them, and during this two-week period they were exclusively Nautilus. Each one was a whole-body workout, one set to failure — just like in the old days. If you knew him well, and knew his physique, you knew that there was one area that was a constant problem for him — he'd always hold a little bit of fat just below the navel. But in 1980, in the mirror at our gym before that contest, he had veins there! He was ripped to the bone and still phenomenally massive. And he wasn't injecting anything, and he wasn't doing anything crazy like these guys do today. And he was lean. If you look at the pictures from 1980, he was definitely the most muscular man in that contest — by far. He also was great with our gym members, taking time to talk to them, sign autographs, and help them with their training.[35]

By the end of August, Mike said his goodbyes to the Schwab family and headed south to Philadelphia, where he had accepted a booking to guest pose at the inaugural Miss Olympia contest. Surprisingly, given his recent health issues, Frank Zane was there to guest pose as well.

Mike had long been an advocate for women's bodybuilding, believing that women should be free to develop to their full muscular potential the same as men were. When he saw 21 female competitors[36] who had trained hard and dieted strictly to display their muscular development, he made sure to be in the front row of the audience to applaud their efforts. He did not believe in the stereotype that it was "masculine" for males to fulfill their muscular potential and "feminine" for females to allow their muscles to atrophy in order to live up to the sobriquet of being the "weaker sex." This was 19th-century thinking as far as Mike was concerned. He wrote in one of his columns his views on the matter, which were well ahead of the curve on the subject of gender issues:

> A woman with a muscular body does not necessarily appear less feminine, just as a man with a normal or average musculature does not necessarily appear less masculine. Masculinity and femininity are traits that emanate from within the individual, expressed through behavior and personality. My advice to aspiring women bodybuilders is to stick to the superior

standard, the heroic ideal. Don't buckle under to the sticky syrup of the undemanding, the mediocre. Just as a rose is a rose, a muscular woman is a muscular woman. More power to you and I hope you continue to soar![37]

The Miss Olympia competition was promoted by George Snyder, a Pennsylvania gym owner and entrepreneur who had recently partnered with Arnold Schwarzenegger, Franco Columbu, and Bill Drake, to create a company called The Association. The purpose of the company was to use the profile of heavily promoted champions such as Arnold and Franco to attract entrepreneurs to the gym business. The Association would then sell them gym franchises, supplements, and exercise equipment such as Body Masters, which was looking to grab a piece of the market that companies such as Universal and Nautilus presently dominated.[38]

Mike Mentzer, Arnold Schwarzenegger, Franco Columbu, Frank Zane, Danny Padilla, and Boyer Coe all conducted bodybuilding seminars that weekend.[39] Boyer recalled that after his seminar concluded, he saw Arnold followed by a film crew as he made his way over to where the exercise equipment was set up. He decided to tag along to see what they'd be filming. To his surprise, Arnold began having a serious workout. Soon George Snyder approached.

"I know who's going to win the Mr. Olympia," he said.

Boyer waited for the punchline. But it never came. Instead, Snyder smiled knowingly.

"I've got it written down on a piece of paper and locked it in my safe."[40]

With that, Snyder turned and walked away.

Boyer hadn't put two and two together yet. "I should have realized Arnold was preparing for the Mr. Olympia," he said. "But it just went right over my head. [George Snyder] already knew. . . . Arnold must have conveyed to George that he was going to compete in the contest."[41] But Snyder and his partners in The Association weren't the only ones who seemed to be aware that Arnold planned to compete in the 1980 Mr. Olympia. Crossing paths with Robby Robinson backstage, Frank Zane asked him how his training for the Olympia was coming along.

"I'm not competing this year," Robby replied.

"Why not?"

"I heard the contest is fixed for Arnold to win."[42]

This was news to Frank. "I began to wonder if I'd made the right choice," he recalled.⁴³

Another person in the loop about Arnold's return to competition was Wayne DeMilia, who, as the new head of the IFBB Professional Committee, was on hand in Philadelphia to witness the Miss Olympia contest. "Ben Weider told me about Arnold's application to compete in August 1980," Wayne recalled. "He handled that then, since I was just starting in the position."⁴⁴ But apart from this handful of people, Arnold's entry was (and would remain) a closely guarded secret.⁴⁵

When his old friend Rick Wayne, who had flown in from the Caribbean to cover the Miss Olympia contest, asked Arnold if the rumor that he was going to compete in Australia had any merit, Arnold denied it.⁴⁶ It seemed that only those in Arnold's inner circle knew the truth.

It would later be claimed by Arnold that he only trained eight weeks for the 1980 Mr. Olympia contest, while the other competitors trained for a minimum of one year.⁴⁷ However, we know that he had officially signed up to compete by August 1980, and had been training hard in the gym since December 1979.⁴⁸

Since most of the competitors were under the impression that Arnold would be one of the judges at the Mr. Olympia competition, Mike Mentzer was left dumbfounded when he read a statement made by Arnold that was published in *MuscleMag International*:

> What Mike's doing is just using one or two exercises that cover the basic size and bulk of the muscle, but not really all the details, so therefore he will never have the quality of a Frank Zane, Franco Columbu, Bill Pearl or somebody like that. What he will do is get bigger, and those areas which are already fantastic will get even more fantastic, but he will never look complete or Mr. Olympia shape. People will always say, "Terrific but doesn't possess the quality physique of a world champion."⁴⁹

"How can Arnold possibly judge me objectively after making comments such as these?" Mike inquired after he read the piece.⁵⁰ But Arnold's statement wasn't

Mike hits one of the rarest poses in bodybuilding — the vacuum — while competing in the 1979 Mr. Olympia contest in Columbus, Ohio.

© Garry Bartlett

A five-year-old Mike Mentzer in kindergarten, June 1957.

Property of the author

Mike inside the York Barbell Club (Pennsylvania) during the summer of 1965.

© Dave Mastorakis

Mike at 15 years of age shows the results of three years of resistance training.

Property of the author

Mike hits some poses for Dave Mastorakis's camera while in California in 1975.

© Dave Mastorakis

Michael Levenson spots Mike Mentzer on a set of pullovers at the Spartan Health Club in Maryland in 1976.

© John Balik

Mike pumps up backstage in Madison Square Garden prior to winning the IFBB Mr. America title in 1976.

© John Balik

His triceps muscles were considered the best in bodybuilding when he was competing. This photo reveals why.

© John Balik

Mike Mentzer shortly after winning the 1976 IFBB Mr. America title. His physique was renowned for its rugged, powerful look.

© John Balik

Heavy Duty training in action. Mike gives his all during a set of barbell Preacher Curls in Gold's Gym, circa 1977.

© John Balik

Mike Mentzer researches the sciences for an article in 1977. Books by Hans Selye, D.W. Edington, and V.R. Edgerton are on the desk.

© John Balik

Mike Mentzer and his espresso machine. Jack Neary would claim that Mike made coffee "strong enough to stand an elephant on its ear."

© John Balik

Mike Mentzer's first ad for his "Heavy Duty" training system appeared in the April 1977 edition of *Muscle Builder/Power* magazine.

From the author's collection

A Mike Mentzer seminar was like attending a university class, consisting of a lecture and multiple illustrations and concepts written on a chalkboard.

Property of the author

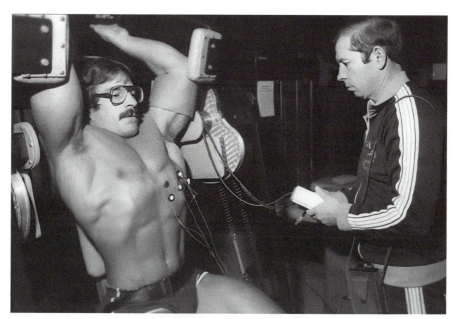

Mike Mentzer works with physiologist Tony Garcy during the development of Rest-Pause training in November 1978.

© John Balik

Mike Mentzer and fiancée Cathy Gelfo discuss Mike's mail-order business in their West Hollywood apartment, circa 1978.

© John Balik

Mike and Ray Mentzer stand with their second cousin, Joel Sweigart, during a family reunion they attended in Schoeneck, Pennsylvania, on June 17, 1979.

Courtesy of Sid Mentzer

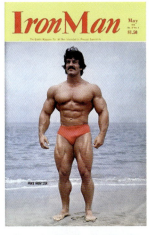 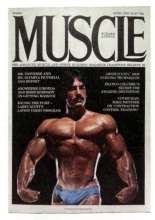 
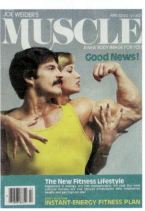  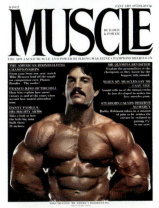
 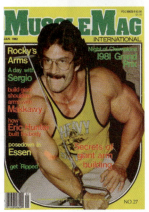 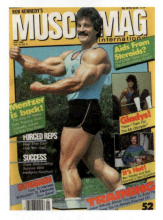

Some of the magazine covers Mike Mentzer appeared on during his bodybuilding heyday. Top row (left to right): *Iron Man*, May 1978; *Muscle Builder/Power*, April 1976; and *Iron Man*, November 1981 — interestingly, although Arnold Schwarzenegger won Mr. Olympia 1980, *Iron Man* chose this photo of Mike from the same contest for its cover. Middle row (left to right): *Muscle Builder/Power*, April 1980, March 1979, and January 1977. Bottom row (left to right): *MuscleMag International*, September 1980, January 1982, and May 1985.

From the author's collection

The famous confrontation between Mike Mentzer (left) and Arnold (right) during the competitors' meeting in the Sydney Opera House prior to the 1980 Mr. Olympia contest.

Weider Health & Fitness, Inc.

Muscularity comparisons between Arnold Schwarzenegger, Roger Walker and Mike Mentzer from the back and Arnold and Mike from the front during the 1980 Mr. Olympia contest.

Courtesy of Michael Petrella

Mike displays phenomenal back development in 1980.

© John Balik

Mike Mentzer displaying an incredible combination of muscular mass and definition while guest posing at the Eastern Canadian Championships, held in Quebec during the spring of 1980.

© Garry Bartlett

Mike was a strong proponent of Arthur Jones's Nautilus machines in his training.

© John Balik

Mike with Julie McNew, a girlfriend who provided him with both financial and moral support during his dark period. The photo was taken during a break in Julie's workout at Gold's Gym in 1986.

Property of the author

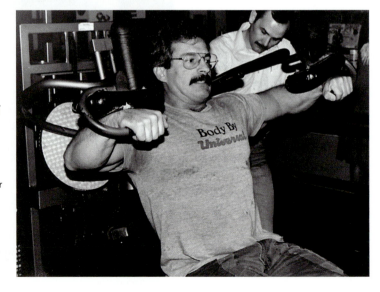

Mike Mentzer performs a set of Nautilus lateral raises in Gold's Gym in 1986.

Property of the author

The author (left) together with Mike Mentzer (right) during a break in Mike's seminar in Rexdale, Ontario, on November 15, 1981.

© Chris Lund

Mike Mentzer (second from right) and Ray Mentzer (third from right) stand in front of Gold's Gym with a group of Mike's personal training clients, circa 1992.

Property of the author

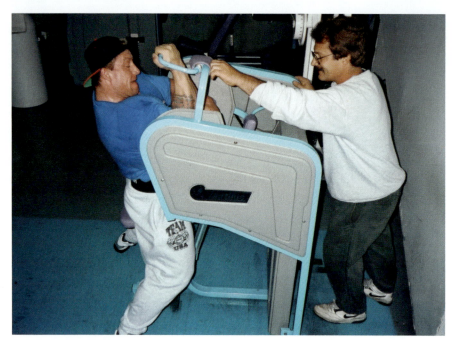

Mike Mentzer trains Dorian Yates in Gold's Gym in 1993. "He was coaching, I was the student," Yates recalled of his sessions with Mike.

Property of the author

Dorian Yates shows the immediate effects of his chest and biceps workout under Mike's supervision in the posing room at Gold's Gym in 1993.

Property of the author

Christmas with the Littles. Mike holds the author's oldest child, Riley, in his arms (the author holds his son, Brandon, while his daughter, Taylor, looks on). California, 1995.

Property of the author

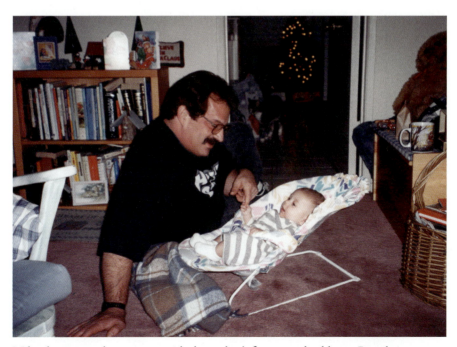

Mike shares a tender moment with the author's four-month-old son, Brandon, on Christmas Day, 1995.

Property of the author

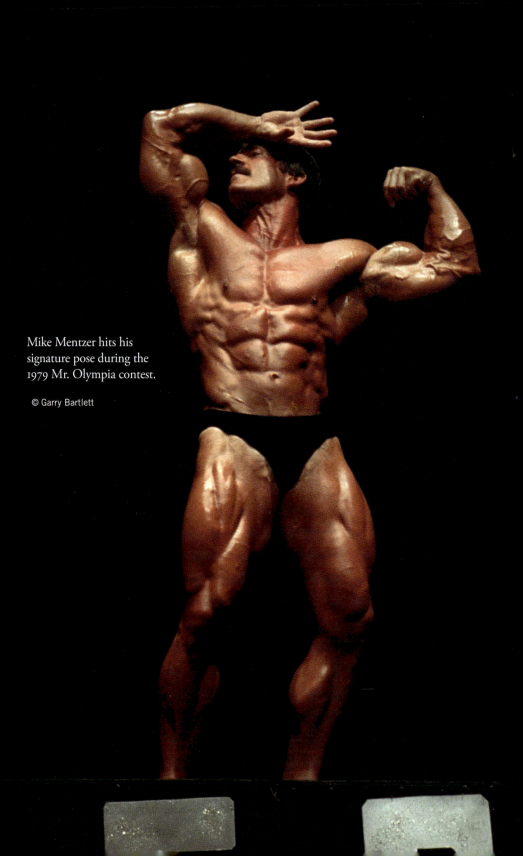

Mike Mentzer hits his signature pose during the 1979 Mr. Olympia contest.

© Garry Bartlett

just an opinion (and an incorrect one at that, as Mentzer had already won the World Championships and the Heavyweight Division of the Mr. Olympia — with a perfect score no less), but also a signal to those who would be judging the forthcoming contest. It let them know that a six-time Mr. Olympia winner, professional contest promoter, and experienced bodybuilding judge believed that the head of Mike Mentzer wasn't worthy to wear the crown.

Despite his posturing to the bodybuilding press, however, the reality was that Arnold viewed Mike as his biggest challenge — even more so than defending Mr. Olympia champion Frank Zane. Arnold had always been renowned for his muscle mass, but Mike, having gained another ten pounds of muscle, now tipped the scales at 225 pounds — the same weight that Arnold weighed when he last won the Mr. Olympia in 1975 — and Mike was five to six inches shorter than the Olympian. Arnold would need to come in closer to the 237 pounds he weighed in 1974, if he was going to outmuscle Mentzer. Moreover, Arnold had never faced a bodybuilder who had achieved a perfect score in professional competition. And despite the influence and prestige Arnold enjoyed amongst the judges he had selected for the 1979 Olympia in Columbus, Mike still almost won the contest. It was clear that Mike had gotten into Arnold's head. In the gym where Arnold trained prior to the contest, the words "MENTZER IS COMING" were written on a large piece of tape and placed across the top of the mirror that Arnold used to check how his muscular development was proceeding.[51] He even fabricated stories that he shared with his photographer friend, George Butler (of *Pumping Iron* fame), about Mike:

- "I am working on Mike Mentzer. He is the only person competing this year I have not beaten in a previous contest. Already he is too nervous to train."[52]
- "Already Mike Mentzer has left the gym this morning. I said, 'Mike, what is wrong?' He said, 'Arnold stop smiling!' I said, 'Why?' He said, 'You're driving me crazy with that smile.' . . . So, this afternoon he misses training to see a shrink. . . . And he pays him to analyze me. He should remember that another Austrian was King of the Shrinks. I could advise him for free."[53]

The problem with such tales, however, is that they can be easily fact-checked, which, for some reason, George Butler never did. For what Arnold said to be true would require that both he and Mike worked out at the same gym — which they didn't. Arnold trained at World Gym, Mike at Gold's (which Arnold hadn't set foot in since its owner, Ken Sprague, had taken him to court in 1978). Moreover, not only had Mike not missed a training session at Gold's leading up to the contest, but he had also already gained ten pounds of muscle from his efforts there. Since Arnold never entered Gold's and Mike never entered World Gym, we are left with a scenario (if we are to believe Arnold's story) that Mike popped into World Gym simply to tell Arnold not to smile. Additionally, author Randy Roach tracked down bodybuilder Mark Martinez, who was training exclusively in World Gym throughout the summer and fall of 1980. According to Roach, "Mark stated that he had never seen Mike or Ray Mentzer set foot in World Gym while Arnold was training for the Mr. Olympia or at any time."[54] In truth, Arnold hadn't laid eyes on Mike Mentzer since the latter had guest posed at the Miss Olympia contest in August. And even then, Mike's appearance was cause for concern. Rick Wayne, who was seated next to Arnold as Mike went through his repertoire commented, "There were few at the Sheraton who didn't expect Mentzer to go all the way in Sydney. His abdominals stood out under his California tan like etchings in the breastplate of a Roman centurion. And thanks to arduous practice with a noted Los Angeles choreographer, his posing had improved considerably."[55]

So, why was Arnold so concerned about Mike that he felt obliged to fabricate stories about him? Two individuals provide insight: Arnold's biographer Laurence Leamer, and Jack Neary, a man who knew both parties in the drama.

Leamer wrote:

> Another top bodybuilder, Mike Mentzer, represented far more of a threat to Arnold than Zane.... Arnold fancied himself not only the greatest champion of all time but the great philosopher of bodybuilding. He was the proudest product of the Weider system, who supposedly represented what could happen if you used Weider equipment, took Weider vitamins and supplements, and followed the rigorous Weider workout routines.
>
> Mentzer was a direct confrontation of everything Arnold represented. He was the most intellectual of any of the bodybuilders, a onetime premed student who would as likely as

not quote Jung, Freud, or Ayn Rand when he talked about training. His Heavy Duty training system was an extrapolation and elaboration of the ideas of Arthur Jones, the developer of the Nautilus fitness equipment. Mentzer said that the way to build one's body was to work out intensely and properly, but not to overexercise. Bodybuilders who worked out five or six hours a day were not giving their muscles time to recover and were hurting themselves.

Weider had condemned the Nautilus machines in the pages of his magazines, but the equipment had taken over much of the space in health clubs across America. If Mentzer won Mr. Olympia, his victory would be equally for a system that risked rendering suspect almost everything Weider did — from a workout philosophy so brilliantly exemplified in Arnold's efforts and the equipment he sold to the magazines. Weider was too powerful a figure to be seriously diminished by the mere victory of one man, but Mentzer did represent a new kind of threat to Arnold. Arnold did not read books and rarely peppered his remarks with historical or philosophical allusions. He was part of an aural tradition of learning. If he was insightful and wise about bodybuilding, there was a limit to his knowledge. Mentzer sounded far more erudite and scientific than Arnold. With victory, Mentzer would have the public platform that he sought.[56]

Jack Neary, who would end up covering the 1980 Mr. Olympia contest for Joe's magazine, published his own view on the matter:

> Indeed, there was no denying the fact that Arnold saw Mentzer as an upstart, a parvenu, a person who had suddenly gained status and wealth in the sport by way of a formidable physique and a superior intellect. Arnold saw Mentzer as a threat to his lofty position as the sport's king. The threat may have been very real. For it was Mentzer, who in his training seminars explaining his revolutionary Heavy Duty system, often pointed to the fallacies of 20-plus sets per body part, the very methods that catapulted Arnold to the top. "If you can all achieve the physique

of Arnold by using his training system, why aren't there more Arnolds running around?" Mentzer often asked his students. Surprisingly, such criticism of Arnold's training was taken personally by Arnold. He would carry a grudge a long time.[57]

In September 1980, George Butler was in World Gym taking photos of Arnold training. He expressed concern about Arnold making a comeback against the toughest field of competitors to ever enter a Mr. Olympia competition. Eddie Giuliani, the manager of World Gym, laughed at George's naïveté and told him flat out, "Well, Arnold is also very close to a majority of the judges."[58] Eddie then feigned a cough and looked over at Arnold, whom, Butler recalled was standing there smiling.[59]

While Giuliani was laughing, he wasn't joking. Paul Graham had already picked the core of his judging panel:

- Reg Park: Arnold's hero, and longtime friend.[60]
- Albert Busek: The man who discovered Arnold in Germany and first brought him to the attention of Joe Weider, and a man who passionately believed Arnold was the greatest bodybuilder who ever lived.[61]
- Mits Kawashima: A good friend of Arnold's since 1968, and a man who in 1979 went into partnership with Arnold for the Mr. Hawaiian Islands competition and who would remain his partner for the next 30 years.[62]

Four more judges remained to be chosen, which would bring the total number of adjudicators to seven. But as the competition was still some months away, there was no immediate rush. Paul extended a judging invitation to Dan Howard, another good friend of Arnold's from California (the pair had actually lived together for a while).[63] If Dan accepted, he would be added to the above three friends and business partners of Arnold, and Paul would have four out of seven judges who, at the very least, might be sympathetic to the cause, and thus ensure Arnold's victory. At which point, the three judges yet to be selected would be simply superfluous; they could vote for whomever they wished, but it wouldn't affect the outcome.

And if any of them should vote for Arnold, well, that would only be the icing on a cake that had already been baked.

CHAPTER TWENTY-FOUR

FLASH POINT DOWN UNDER

Neither Mike Mentzer nor any of the other competitors knew anything about the judging selection or what that presaged for the outcome of the 1980 Mr. Olympia.

With the contest now only weeks away, Mike entered the final and most difficult phase of his preparation: severe calorie restriction. Believing his chief competition to be the reigning Mr. Olympia Frank Zane, Mike resolved to drop his bodyfat level as low as possible. It registered 3.8 percent approximately four weeks out from the show, but he was determined to bring it down even lower.[1] To his mind, the judges at the 1979 Mr. Olympia had made it clear that Frank Zane's level of muscular definition was the ideal, and Mike was determined to create a physique that was even more ripped than Frank's but 30 pounds of muscle heavier. He had started dieting in February that year, something he normally wouldn't do until ten to 12 weeks before the competition. However, he thought it best to keep his bodyfat level as low as possible throughout that year, and then reduce it substantially in the final four weeks leading up to the show.[2] The process hadn't been that difficult initially; he'd determined his maintenance need of calories to be 2,500, and only consumed 1,800, which caused his body to dip into its fat stores to make up the difference.[3] "I carried my purpose, my goal, around with me 24 hours a day through 1980," he said. "I can remember — no matter what it was I was doing — taking the garbage out, going to the post office, everything I did had a heightened sense of meaning because I was constantly thinking about that '80 Olympia. What was it that I could do today in terms of diet, training, aerobics, and motivation to improve myself? Everything that I did was marshaled onto the side of improvement. And I probably even at a couple of points pushed myself too hard."[4]

This was an understatement.

As the contest verged nearer, Mike dramatically increased his aerobic activity to burn more fat while simultaneously reducing his calorie intake to a mere 500 calories a day. He used steroids to shunt his weight loss exclusively onto the side of fat loss, and amphetamines to deaden the hunger pangs and keep him focused on his workouts. Bodybuilding writer Jerry Brainum, who knew and trained with most of the top competitors of that era, didn't consider amphetamine use to be out of the ordinary for professional bodybuilders. "A lot of the guys took speed because it did two things: it destroyed your appetite, which made it easy to stay on a diet, and also it made them train harder."[5] According to Mike:

> I was taking amphetamines as ergogenic aids. I loved being productive. I would wake up every morning at four o'clock and read literature and philosophy for two to three hours, go to the gym, after that come home and write an article, go back down to the beach and ride a bike for 40 miles, come home, take a nap, go back down to the beach and run three-to-six miles, and then come home and pose and do some more studying, answer phone calls, do some business with the mail order. I was a productive genius. But I had lost sight of the fact that the body and the mind have limitations. I was in love with being conscious. Amphetamines had that effect on a lot of people.[6]

But the amphetamines, in concert with his high activity levels and a low-calorie diet, were drastically dropping the glucose levels that Mike's body and nervous system required to function.[7] He was running on fumes — yet still he kept pushing himself. At three different times leading up to the contest, his body gave out. "I remember one night, it was late in the evening," he recalled, "after having trained, ridden bike, running six or seven miles, and then posing, during dinner — I'm being literal here — I was so fatigued I literally fell asleep, and my head went into my plate. And I didn't know it. Cathy had to wake me up. And then later that same night when we went to bed, in the middle of the night, I messed the bed. I lost control. She had to walk me like a child into the bathroom and put me on the toilet. I remember while I was sitting there, I was confabulating, just speaking nonsensically about things in my past. My brain didn't have enough energy to function properly."[8] While Mike understood what had happened, he was still panicked by it. He stayed in bed all the next day and upped his carbohydrate intake a bit to provide fuel for his brain and nervous system. He further vowed to reduce his activity levels.[9] By the end of that day he started to feel better, but knew he was skating on thin ice.

But over the next several weeks his focus shifted from proceeding with caution to winning the contest, and he began to increase his activity levels again (while still only consuming 500 calories a day). Soon the same situation beset him. "As the contest got closer, I perhaps began becoming too intense again," he said. "I wasn't regulating my activity intelligently enough and I went through it again. It scared me the same way that it did the first time. I thought, 'What if this doesn't go away?' Or, 'What if I did some kind of irreparable damage to my energy system?'"[10]

But he so badly wanted to win the Olympia, to fulfill that promise he made to his younger self all those years ago in Ephrata.[11] He recognized that he was in the grip of an obsession — and it wasn't a healthy one.[12]

Jack Neary's on-again, off-again employment with Joe Weider was on again — but from a distance. He was no longer living in California, but from time to time Joe still paid him rather well to cover the odd contest. And in 1980, Joe reached out to have Jack cover the Mr. Olympia, which required the writer to fly from Calgary to Los Angeles to meet a connecting flight to Honolulu. After a brief stopover in Hawaii, he was to catch a plane that was destined for Sydney, Australia. It was a lot of time spent in the air; "an endless flight," as he called it.

When Jack arrived at Los Angeles International Airport, he spoke briefly with Joe Weider, who, together with his wife, Betty, was seated in the first-class compartment of the flight to the Aloha State, along with Arnold Schwarzenegger and his girlfriend, Maria Shriver. The rest of the bodybuilders leaving from California were crammed into economy. Joe offered to upgrade Jack's ticket to first class so that he could sip champagne with the well-heeled crowd, but the Canadian declined, preferring to interact with the bodybuilders.[13] Their dialogue would serve to add some color to his contest report.

During the first leg of the flight there was plenty of opportunity to catch up with industry people who Jack hadn't seen for some time. John Balik, for instance, was an old friend who was among the photographers Joe brought along to capture images from the contest. Ken Waller, now managing Gold's Gym for Ken Sprague, came out of retirement to take another kick at the Mr. Olympia can. And, of course, Jack spent some time conversing with Mike and Cathy. To the writer's surprise, a recurring topic of conversation amongst the competitors was the rumor that Arnold would be entering the contest. Jack had heard this before, of course, but didn't put much stock in it. Others, however, didn't share his skepticism. "He was at eighty-five percent a week ago," Balik said. "He hasn't looked this good since he retired. He's 225 and cut."[14] Ken Waller, however, dismissed the rumor outright. "Just think about this," he opined, "first place this year is $20,000. Arnold has got to be getting at least that for doing the color commentary for CBS. What's he going to do? Come back, risk losing and destroying the legend, or just sit back and announce on TV for the same money? He's in good shape, but not like he used to be. People don't remember how he really was."[15]

Bodybuilder Samir Bannout, who had been dubbed the Lebanese Lion, told Jack in the third person that "the 'Lebanese Lion' is going to be the Atomic Bomb in Australia! I'm holding a little water now, but as soon as I lose it, look out!"[16] Eventually, the plane arrived at Honolulu International Airport, where there was a brief stopover prior to the final leg of the journey to Sydney. Many of the bodybuilders took the opportunity to lie down on the floor of the departure lounge. It would be their last opportunity to stretch out prior to being confined to their seats for a very long flight. Some attempted to catch some sleep.

It was at this point, to shed some of the water he had indicated he was holding, that Samir Bannout headed off to the nearest restroom and posed before a bathroom mirror for 30 minutes. "He's in the washroom trying to squeeze out a little more water," John Balik cracked, which caused the group to break up laughing.

"I've been hearing about this water for eight months," Mike said. "I'm waiting to see him lose it."

"Well, he's *oceans* away," Jack quipped.[17]

An hour later, the group was thousands of feet up in the sky and heading for Australia. When the plane touched down on the tarmac at Sydney Kingsford Smith International Airport it was Monday, September 29 — a full six days before the contest.[18] Arnold and Maria were met by the contest promoter cum documentarian Paul Graham, who had a limousine ready to whisk the pair off to the upscale Hilton Hotel, which sat within the business district of Sydney. For the rest of the bodybuilders, several members of Graham's gym were on hand to shuttle them to the Cosmopolitan Inn in Bondi.

The next two days passed by uneventfully. Everyone kept to themselves. Paul Graham's Mr. Universe Gym was made available to any of the competitors who wished to train during the week and was conveniently located within walking distance from their hotel. Three days out from the contest, Mike was still doing what he could to ensure that he would be ripped by contest day, which included once again dropping his calories to dangerously low levels. He was determined to enter the Olympia in the greatest condition of his career. But once again, his body was rebelling. Competitor Boyer Coe witnessed Mike's struggles:

> The gym that we were training in in Australia was about a mile from the hotel that we were staying at on Bondi Beach. And we walked to the gym, but it was a steady walk all the way up a hill. And I remember standing at the top of the hill looking down one morning and I watched Mike come up that hill and it must have taken him a good forty-five minutes because he'd walk a while, and he'd rest a while, he'd walk a while, he'd rest a while. And finally, when he got to the gym, I said, "Are you okay?" He said, "Yeah, but I'm only eating 500 calories a day." Well, if you're only eating 500 calories a day, you're not going to have very much energy to train.[19]

Photos taken of Mike in Graham's gym that day reveal that he somehow summoned the energy to work out, but after dragging himself back to the hotel, his body began to shut down. He collapsed on his bed in utter exhaustion, unable to move a limb without being left breathless. "I was terrified," he recalled. "I had drained not just my glycogen levels but also my ATP [Adenosine triphosphate, the baseline energy source of all cellular activity within the body]. I thought, 'What if I wake up on the morning of the show and I literally don't have the energy to pose?' When I say I couldn't raise my arm without being breathless, I mean literally *breathless* — like I had just run a hundred-yard dash! I didn't know that that sort of thing was even possible."[20] In an effort to alleviate the situation, he stayed in bed most of the next day. But this time around he couldn't risk ingesting the carbohydrates that were required to remedy the problem. Doing so would result in water retention, which would blur his definition. The two prior occasions when this dilemma had beset him occurred while the contest was still weeks away. Then, he had the luxury of time; he could up his carbohydrate intake to whatever his nervous system required and deal with the water retention later. But now the contest was too close. He ingested a small amount of carbohydrates and sipped distilled water. His only hope was that his energy levels would improve throughout the night. If not, then an entire year of dieting and training was down the drain. He would confide to Jack Neary: "I like bodybuilding, but I like living better. I'm never putting my mind and body through this hell again."[21]

Two days before the contest, Arnold's physique wasn't where it needed to be either. He knew that this competition would be the most heavily contested one he had ever entered and he needed his muscle mass to be at his all-time best. However, his heavily promoted high-volume training method not only hadn't gained him more muscle mass than ever before, he hadn't even regained the muscle mass he had previously held. When he won the Mr. Olympia in 1974, he weighed 237 pounds; in 1975, he defended the title weighing 225. Then, he had blamed his inability to regain all of his lost muscle mass on the fact that he only had four months to prepare.[22] Presently, despite training for the better part of a year, it was rumored that his bodyweight was only hovering somewhere between 217 and 220 pounds.[23] His chest, shoulders, and biceps looked good, but the rest of his muscle groups — his legs in particular — simply hadn't come back. His calves still had their old size, which if a well-circulated rumor is to be believed, was the result of Arnold having had calf implants during the early 1970s.[24] But implants or not, his calves created a problem as they were clearly out of proportion with his smaller upper legs. To make matters worse, Arnold had tweaked his shoulder doing bench presses at World Gym earlier in the week and had received a cortisone injection to relieve the pain. But the drug also caused him to retain water (the overseas flight hadn't helped), which left him smooth with minimal muscle definition.[25] As a full house was expected at the venue and CBS Sports would be broadcasting the competition to millions of viewers around the world, a smooth and smaller Arnold would do little to generate much buzz for him or galvanize a fanbase for *Conan*. Appearing in the contest in such diminished condition would also seriously damage his reputation of being the greatest bodybuilder of all time. There was nothing Arnold could do at this point to increase his muscle mass; that train had already left the station. And so he was left to do what he could to increase his muscular definition. The day before the contest he went through his posing routine no fewer than 50 times, hoping to sweat out the subcutaneous water that had been retained from the cortisone injection.[26]

Across town in Bondi, Mike Mentzer had his own water issues to deal with. Evidently the small amount of carbohydrates he had taken in had caused his cells to hold more water than he wished. His energy levels had returned somewhat but at the cost of his muscular definition. His ability to function required the restoration of his ATP levels, and, to a lesser extent, his glycogen levels, but his body was in survival mode, and maintaining the water levels of all of his cells was its priority. "It's your stored glycogen that is responsible for the water — remember 70% of a muscle's composition is water — staying in the muscles," he had stated in his seminars. "And every gram of stored glycogen in a muscle contains three grams of stored water."[27] He needed the glycogen for his nervous system to function, and his muscles needed the water that bonded to those glucose molecules to retain their size — but he didn't want any more water in his system than this. To deal with the slight fluid surplus that had robbed him of some of his definition, Mike borrowed a rubber sweatsuit from Samir Bannout. Wearing it beneath a regular cotton tracksuit, he entered the kitchenette in his hotel room and closed the door. He then turned the oven up full blast and opened its door, which created what Jack Neary described as "a sauna effect of awesome intensity." Mike endured this for 45 minutes, all the while swallowing potassium tablets to keep his electrolytes intact, while a huge puddle of sweat formed beneath him on the linoleum floor.[28]

It was now a mere twenty-four hours before the contest and Paul Graham still hadn't finalized his judging panel. He had reached out to Paul Chua, then the IFBB rep for Singapore (and also the Weider distributor for that country), but visa problems had prevented Chua from leaving the country.[29] Paul was able to replace the Singaporean with Peter McCarthy, a former bodybuilder who had served as the President of IFBB Australia from 1977 to 1979 (before resigning and being replaced by Paul Graham),[30] and also received confirmation that the IFBB Belgium representative Jacques Blommaert would adjudicate.[31] These two were fine for filling out the panel, but Paul still needed at least one more judge who would be disposed to vote for Arnold in order to have the four judges required for the Austrian to win and Paul to have a successful documentary to sell. When Dan Howard arrived in Australia and saw the woeful state of the judging panel,[32] he agreed (with Head Judge Bill Pearl's prompting) to accept Paul's original invitation to be a judge for the contest.[33] Finally, Dr. Michael Walzcak was selected to fill the final judging vacancy on the panel; a move that was agreeable to both Graham and Pearl. Walzcak was a good choice, at least from Graham's perspective, as he was not only a long-standing friend of Arnold's but was also Arnold's doctor in California. However, Walzcak was also a man who, according to Gold's Gym owner, Ken Sprague, had been removed by the NPC from judging any AAU/NPC contests in the mid-late seventies shows "because of his reputation of placing his patients higher than obviously deserved."[34] Nevertheless, it now appeared that five of the seven judges selected to adjudicate the 1980 Mr. Olympia might be inclined to vote in Arnold's favor.

But appearances proved to be deceiving.

That afternoon, in a final effort to sweat additional water out of his body, Arnold made his way to the gym in Bondi for one final workout. Paul Graham's camera crew was in tow, capturing his every move. When Arnold entered the gym, he took note of those in attendance: George Butler was there to take photos for the revised *Pumping Iron* book; Albert Busek, one of the judges, was present, camera in hand, and clearly delighted at the prospect of Arnold entering the competition. Brendan Ryan was also present. Ryan was an Australian friend of Arnold's from the early 1970s, now employed by Paul Graham as the manager of his gym.[35] Arnold was among friends. Also present in the gym that day were the contest judges Jacques Blommaert and Dan Howard, who looked on as Arnold went through his workout and then followed him outside to witness the Austrian go through his posing routine.

Neither were impressed. Howard told his old friend point blank, "You're not ready."[36] Blommaert informed Arnold that he would destroy his legend competing the way he looked and tried to talk him out of it.[37] Such responses were definitely *not* what Arnold was expecting. "I saw him — *nothing*," Blommaert told Jack Neary later that evening. "People who don't know how he used to look are impressed. But he just doesn't have it. He shouldn't enter this contest. It will be a mistake."[38] Blommaert later bumped into Mike Mentzer at the Bondi gym and shared the news that Arnold would be competing in the contest. "I thought, 'Gee, that *is* interesting,'" Mike recalled. "It didn't bother me to hear that he was going to go in the show, especially in lesser condition. But even if he had been in good condition, it wouldn't have bothered me."[39]

Being told that he wasn't in good enough shape to enter the contest threw Arnold off completely. Suddenly, victory was far less certain. His plan was in danger of heading off the rails. While possible, it's hard to imagine a scenario wherein judges Park, Busek, and Kawashima would vote for anybody other than Arnold. But this still left four judges — two of whom Arnold had just discovered would be voting against him — and could tip the balance in the wrong direction.

Later that evening, the phone rang in Head Judge Bill Pearl's hotel room. Being a head judge was a task that didn't involve voting, but rather coordinating the competitors on stage for the comparisons the judging panel wished to see in order to make their analyses and render decisions.[40] When Pearl picked up the phone, he was surprised to discover that it was Arnold Schwarzenegger on the other end of the line.

Arnold was calling to inform him that he would be competing in the contest the next day. This was news to Pearl. Like most everyone else, he had been led to believe that Arnold had come to Sydney to do the color commentary for the CBS broadcast of the event. He knew nothing of Arnold having submitted his application to compete directly to Ben Weider over two months previously. Moreover, Arnold informed him, he had heard that the competitors wanted the contest to be judged as one open class; they wanted to do away with the over-and-under 200-pound weight divisions that were part of the controversy at the previous year's Mr. Olympia. He further made it clear to Pearl that he was not in favor of such a change being made.

Bill Pearl immediately smelled something fishy. How could Arnold be allowed to enter at the last minute? Why was he so insistent that there be two weight classes in the competition? Moreover, Pearl knew that at least four of the judges on the panel were very close friends of Arnold's.[41] This wouldn't have been a major issue if Arnold wasn't competing in the contest. But now that he was, Pearl sensed trouble.

Shortly after hanging up with Arnold, Pearl called competitor Boyer Coe (who was the one who had spearheaded the movement to have one class open to all competitors) and told him that there was a shitstorm heading his way. He further shared with Boyer that Arnold would be competing in the contest.[42]

Morning broke quickly on Saturday, October 4. Some of the competitors arose early, in anxious anticipation of the battle to come. Jack Neary was also awake, his mind and body still operating on Calgary's Mountain Time, which was 16 hours behind Australian Eastern Standard. Assuming his friends would be awake as well, Jack decided to head down the hall to Mike and Cathy's room. "I was in Mike's room, we were just sitting around shooting the shit, and suddenly there was a frantic knocking at the door," he recalled. "Samir was in some kind of distress."[43] The Lebanese Lion, it seemed, in a last-ditch attempt to flush subcutaneous water from his body, had ingested Lasix, a powerful diuretic that put his heart into severe arrhythmia.[44] Knowing Mike's medical background, Samir raced to his room for help. Mike understood that such a profound water loss — which the drug promoted — had robbed Samir's body of vital minerals with each trip he took to the bathroom. Mike gave Jack several potassium tablets and told him to follow Samir back to his room and make sure that he took them. He did, and within minutes, Samir's pulse returned to normal, a potentially life-threatening crisis averted.[45] According to Jack:

> Mike had a great empathy for others and, and, you know, he was a very kind soul. Mike, for all the confidence and the great Germanic logic and everything, he had a real heart about him. And this was an example of that. Where Arnold might have played a little prank to knock his opponent down a couple of notches, Mike genuinely was concerned. Mike gave him supplemental potassium tablets to regulate the electrolytes, bring his heart under control. That makes sense. I mean, potassium is super important to heart function. Too much can kill you and too little can kill you. I know this from my

kidney dialysis; that something they really monitor closely is potassium. And that was a perfect example of the kind of empathy that Mike brought to a situation. I think it was like a moment of real concern there, and Mike stepped in. He had natural leadership qualities and that's an example of that. And it's interesting that Samir would think to turn to Mike, you know, as opposed to anyone else down the hall. I think that says a lot about Mike.[46]

As the bodybuilders were sorting out their issues, the promoter and judges were dealing with some of their own. Judge Peter McCarthy, for instance, believed he had been told by Paul Graham that a mandatory meeting of the judges was to take place at one o'clock that afternoon in one of the conference rooms at the Sydney Opera House. He made his way to the venue at approximately 12:30 p.m. and struck up a conversation with Frank Burwash, the IFBB chairman of judges for Australia, and bodybuilder/gym owner Vince Basile. They hadn't been long into their discussion when a person approached and informed Peter that the judges' meeting was already underway. Flummoxed, he ran to the boardroom to discover that the meeting had in fact started 30 minutes previously.[47] Upon his entry, Paul Graham looked up from his seat at the head of the table and announced that, because of his tardiness, Peter McCarthy was no longer a judge at the contest. He was now a reserve judge,[48] meaning that he would be allowed to judge the competition, but that his score wouldn't count in the overall tally. McCarthy's place on the judging panel was to be filled (or so McCarthy believed) by Brendan Ryan.[49]

McCarthy was livid, believing he had been deliberately lied to about the time of the meeting. "I was upset and disgusted with Paul and let him know how I felt and how he had deceived me," he recalled.[50] After the meeting, McCarthy encountered Frank Burwash in the hallway and told him what had just transpired. Burwash was stunned by the news. He would write later in *Muscle Digest*:

> At no time before the contest was I, as Chairman of Judges for Australia, consulted or requested to supply names of any IFBB Internationally qualified judges to be included in the "ballot" or "judges' selection." We were just as shocked as you [the reader] to be told that the only judge to represent Australia on the Olympia

panel was Brendan Ryan, who had, together with Paul Graham, been officially stood down as national judges because of their bad judging at the "Mr. Australia" contest two months earlier. The IFBB and Mr. Ben Weider had been officially notified of this suspension at the time, and yet they "selected" this judge for the world's greatest contest, with full knowledge that he had been "stood down" as a judge on the national level.[51]

Burwash had been the one who had suspended both Paul Graham and Brendan Ryan as a result of their controversial judging at the Mr. Australia contest, but Graham, acting in his capacity as vice president for the IFBB South Pacific (Oceania), had taken it upon himself to overturn Ryan's suspension, which thus freed him to adjudicate an international competition.[52] Mike Mentzer would later state that Brendan Ryan was an investor in Paul Graham's *The Comeback* documentary,[53] an allegation the author has been unable to corroborate. What can be corroborated is that Ryan was an employee of Graham's, and, according to Arnold's former girlfriend Barbara Outland Baker, he was a friend of Arnold's going back to when she and Arnold were living together in the 1970s.[54] If Ryan was inclined to vote for Arnold, along with Park, Busek, Kawashima (and perhaps Walczak), this latest addition to the judging panel left Arnold in pretty good shape heading into the competition.

Arnold would later claim that he did not want to make public the fact that he was going to compete in case other competitors found out and dropped out of the competition rather than face him, which would have left promoter, Paul Graham, in a bad way.[55] Bill Pearl believed that Arnold was simply waiting until he had enough judges on his side. Once he received that assurance, that's when he made his announcement.[56]

In any event, Bill Pearl had seen enough. After the judges' meeting had concluded, Pearl approached Ben Weider and told him that he was out, giving as his reason that he had coached one of the competitors, Chris Dickerson, earlier in the year and that this could potentially skew his impartiality.[57] Few believed it. After all, Pearl had known that he trained Dickerson when he was first named as head judge some months previously, and he didn't consider the matter to be an issue then. Moreover, he was a judge at several of Dickerson's contest wins throughout the past year on the IFBB's Grand Prix circuit and never felt the need to recuse himself[58] — so why now?

The answer would come later, during the prejudging.

Shortly after the judges' meeting, another get-together commenced. No fewer than 50 people,[59] consisting of IFBB officials, the competitors and their significant others, the judges, and select members from the bodybuilding press corps, assembled in a dimly lit, low-ceilinged room within the basement of the Sydney Opera House. Just as the meeting was about to start, Arnold Schwarzenegger entered the room. It was a calculated move that he anticipated would shock and intimidate his fellow competitors. But by this point in time, word of his entry was common knowledge. It was expected and thus far from shocking. What was shocking, from the competitors' perspective, was Arnold's appearance. From what they could see of his physique, which was concealed only slightly beneath a tight-knit green sweater and khaki pants, it appeared that Arnold had left his muscles back in Los Angeles. As Randy Roach would note, "The bottom line was that very few, if any, of the competitors feared the physique Arnold Schwarzenegger brought to the Sydney Opera House in 1980."[60] Arnold had to have been taken somewhat aback by the fact that his big "Aha!" moment hadn't caused a ripple on the pond. He had told George Butler some months earlier that he expected "to go there, see them all be surprised, see them all freak out and have diarrhea, you know? And be confused and be upset about it and have a career that they had planned for themselves go down the tube in two seconds."[61] Instead, his fellow competitors simply looked at their watches, hoping that the meeting wouldn't last too long. They had a prejudging to prepare for.

The topic of the two weight classes was introduced to the room by Bill Pearl. He announced that he and Ben Weider had a received a petition, an ultimatum of sorts, that read: "The following Mr. Olympia competitors are in favor of abolishing the two weight classes (Under and Over 200 Pounds) and replacing them with one open class." It was signed by every competitor who would be competing — except Arnold.[62] It was a matter that needed to be resolved — quickly — before the competition could proceed.

Pearl now addressed the room.

"I'm not the man to make the decision, but someone here will have to," he said. "I'm not saying Arnold's right or Arnold's wrong, but something must be done to satisfy the fifteen other bodybuilders." He looked around the room at the competitors. Then he posed a question: "If we keep two classes, do we really know the best six men will be the finalists?"[63] He nodded to Boyer Coe. As Coe was the figurehead for the bodybuilders wanting one open class, he would make their case. Coe stood up, and, looking at Arnold, asked, "Arnold, why don't you give us your reasons for wanting two classes?" Arnold, who had been sitting on a small bench next to a row of lockers, now had the floor. He rose and walked to the center of the room to ensure that he had everyone's attention.

"The reason I want to keep two classes is because when the Olympia was started in 1965, we did have one class. Everybody competed against everybody else. And for years it was that way. Then the shorter men complained they weren't getting a fair chance because they had to go head-to-head with the big guys right from the start. So, in 1974 we changed to two classes to protect the small man. What's the sense in changing back? Are we going to change every time someone doesn't like the rules?"

One of the competitors (Mike thought it was Samir Bannout)[64] stated, "Not all of us can win the Olympia. So, it is important to know where we stand. Some of us would like to know how we compare."

Arnold waved him off. "We aren't here to pick second. We're here to pick first. Why change to one class?"

Now that Arnold had presented his case, Boyer intended to present his. "But Arnold . . ."

That was as far as he got.

"Excuse me, Boyer. Let's talk like adults here and let me finish, okay?" Arnold barked condescendingly. "I just don't see what the big deal is. The purpose of this contest is to pick the number one bodybuilder in the world. Not second, not third. No matter how many classes we've had, the best man has always won. All that matters is the winner."[65]

Suddenly a voice was heard:

"Besides the fact that everybody but *one guy* wants one class, it's obvious that running a contest with just one group as opposed to two is a lot faster and easier. Arnold, if there's a better, more efficient way, why not change?"[66]

All heads turned to the speaker. The voice belonged to Mike Mentzer. Arnold had assumed that there would be no pushback from any of the competitors. That he would receive opposition after he had spoken on the matter hadn't entered his mind. Mike could see it angered him.[67]

"Oh, come on Mentzer," Arnold said, by way of comeback. "We all know you lost last year's contest because of your big belly!"[68]

If Arnold thought that this irrelevant insult would back Mike off, he'd made a serious miscalculation. His words had just ignited a powder keg.

Jack Neary reported that "The room froze, save Mentzer, who rose defiantly from his seat twenty feet from his attacker. There was more on his mind than just words."[69] An icy tension now descended on the room.

"You're the one who said we should talk like adults!" Mike snapped, as he advanced towards Arnold, his eyes locked firmly on his target. "And you bring it down to this personal level."[70]

The situation had escalated so quickly that the competitors could only look on. Boyer Coe thought that he saw Mike hand close his hand into a fist and cock his arm;[71] Samir Bannout said he looked like a raging bull,[72] while Roger Walker and Tom Platz both believed that a fight was about to get underway.[73] Seeing that Mike was deadly serious, Arnold the bully suddenly gave way to Arnold the self-preservationist; he quickly turned and sat down upon a stool. Boyer Coe, Oscar State, and Bill Pearl now moved to intercept Mike.[74] Boyer recalled that "the way Arnold was sitting, if Mike would've hit him, it would've taken Arnold's head off."[75]

Mike's clenched fist now became a pointing finger which he jabbed towards Arnold's face. "Look!" he exclaimed. "Boyer said that to you as a gentleman — he didn't deserve *that*!"[76] Mike would later recall:

> On the way over I decided I wouldn't hit him. But I was surprised: Arnold Schwarzenegger *sat down*. I scared him! He went over and sat in the corner, and I continued at him. Wagging my finger at him, I told him his behavior was reprehensible; that it was not Boyer Coe who needed to grow up but him. He couldn't look me in the eye. He literally went from being a frantic hysterical adolescent to shrinking away like an injured child.[77]

At this point, several of the judges entered the room, among them the displaced Peter McCarthy. "We walked into the meeting where Mike Mentzer was just about to knock Arnold's head off," he recalled.[78] Other judges, Jacques Blommaert and Mits Kawashima, viewed the spectacle now unfolding before their eyes with an equal measure of surprise and disapproval. Ben Weider scowled. Seeing that Boyer, Oscar State, and Bill Pearl now stood between Mike and Arnold, Ben felt safe in stepping in. "Ben Weider stood between Arnold and I, and tried to assert himself," Mike said, "but it became very clear, especially later on as the day proceeded, that things weren't the way they should be."[79] By this time, Joe Weider was also on his feet and made his way over to where Arnold was sitting. "Why wreck the whole contest for everyone if the best man is going to win anyway?" he asked.[80] Arnold, still angry over what had just transpired, turned and faced the room.

"Joe just said something to me, and I agree with him. Why should I spoil it for fifteen guys? I withdraw my objection."[81]

And just like that, the issue of the weight classes was dropped.

"The IFBB is here to protect the bodybuilder," Ben Weider stated, attempting to allay any fears that his federation wasn't in control of the proceedings. "And we are here to see the rules are uniform. So, under extreme circumstances, we're making the change to one class here in the best interests of the bodybuilders."[82]

But Arnold wasn't finished yet. Sensing that cooler heads now prevailed, he stood and walked over to Ben and made a show of shaking the IFBB president's hand before announcing in a loud voice, "I want to thank you, Ben, for your support. And I want to prove one way or the other the best man will win tonight."[83]

As a diplomatic gesture to Arnold, Ben called for a round of applause. "Most hands remained still," Jack Neary recalled. "The damage had been done."[84]

The competitors looked at one another in muted disbelief as to what had just occurred. Something was definitely off about this contest, and it hadn't even started yet.

Bill Pearl asked the final question before the meeting was adjourned: did anybody have any complaints about the judges? But the bodybuilders knew nothing of the judging deviltries that had occurred behind the scenes. What they did know was that all the judges were Weider reps in their respective countries, which meant that they were the ones who booked all of the bodybuilders for seminars and exhibitions. Publicly stating that you didn't trust one of them was a surefire prescription for losing seminar money. Besides, most of the judges were familiar faces on the Olympia panel (Park and Busek had judged the event only the year before). None of the bodybuilders had any reason to suspect that the winner of the competition had already been decided. And so, they said nothing, assuming that the judges would act honorably.[85]

CHAPTER TWENTY-FIVE

THE STING

Mike Mentzer already had a bad feeling. "The atmosphere was much different," he recalled. "There was a tension there. There was a hostility, a negativity that skewed everyone's normal perception, or usual perception, and of course prevented anyone from deriving the pleasure they might have had otherwise."[1] Fellow competitor Chris Dickerson agreed: "The whole thing was a set up. It was set up like a turkey shoot."[2] But such perspectives were recorded decades after the fact. On the afternoon of October 4, 1980, none of the competitors (who were not named Arnold Schwarzenegger) knew what they were walking into.

The prejudging was set to commence at 2:00 p.m. By 1:30 p.m., all the competitors were backstage, stripped down, and starting to pump up. Looking over at Arnold, the consensus amongst the bodybuilders was that he looked thin and not ready for the competition.[3] Boyer Coe approached Mike to try and make sense out of what was going on. "Why in the world would Arnold risk his reputation when he's far from at his best?" Mike asked.[4] Boyer had no answer. Surprisingly, it was obvious to all that Arnold was strangely uneasy. "He was sweating a lot — profusely — toweling off because he seemed in doubt," Chris Dickerson recalled. "He was nervous. Had a lot to lose."[5] Arnold admitted as much during an interview with Paul Graham's camera crew:

> I was worried from the time I stepped on the stage for the first round. It's amazing how insecure you get after not being on stage for five years. I mean, I used to go out and it was my

home on stage. This time I went out and I felt very uncomfortable. . . . I had to stand out there for an hour or two and just be compared to all those different guys. And that is what I didn't like at all.[6]

Arnold also knew that he wasn't in his best shape,[7] and that many of his fellow competitors were.[8] How would that look when the telecast of the event was beamed into millions of homes around the world? He had reason to be concerned.

Oscar State, who had stepped in to replace Bill Pearl as head judge, now called out for the competitors to come out on stage. After the competitors were introduced to the audience, it was time for the first round of the competition to begin.

The first round required each bodybuilder, one at a time, to step forward and face the audience and judges from the front. Each was then requested to turn to the side, then to the back, then to turn to the other side, and finally return to facing the audience. This was the round in which a bodybuilder's overall mass, definition, proportion, and symmetry were assessed. Immediately it was clear that Arnold's legs were too small for his upper body. His proportions were out of sync. According to the contest reports that were published:

Muscle & Fitness: "The instant Arnold stepped onstage with his 15 opponents, it was apparent to this reporter that he had made a mistake. Arnold himself would tell us later, 'Look, I know I was only in 90% shape. I could look in the mirror and see that. I couldn't fool myself.' Arnold at 90% is a formidable sight indeed. The biceps are peaked and mighty, the chest full and imposing. But Arnold at 90% is 10% less than his best. And that gives breathing room to his weaknesses: slender thighs, underdeveloped triceps and deltoids, and a mediocre midsection. All of those flaws detracted from the package in a most unflattering way. And in the opinion of this reporter, Arnold's weaknesses only served to strengthen the incredible condition of the men who looked better: Chris Dickerson, Boyer Coe and Mike Mentzer. There are those who would put Frank Zane in that group."[9]

MuscleMag International: "Arnold, especially his legs, was clearly not at his best. . . . Arnold was weak in the thighs, both quadriceps and leg biceps, the middle back, and abdominals."[10]

Arnold's abdominals had always been a weak body part. Arnold's first trainer, Kurt Marnul, would tell author Nigel Andrews:

"You're supposed to have three muscles showing there, but Arnold only had two. However much he trained, he couldn't get that third muscle, so he used to stand like this when he posed." Marnul mimes holding an arm in a shielding position across his stomach.[11]

And while Arnold had decent definition in his legs, the size they required to balance the mass of his upper body simply wasn't there. Indeed, he could be said to have suffered from the same disproportion issue that fellow competitor Tom Platz did — only in reverse; Platz's lower body was far bigger than his upper body, which put his physique out of proportion. Arnold's upper body was far bigger than his lower body, which produced the same result — a physique that was out of balance.

Certain of the bodybuilders, four and five at a time, were now asked to step to the front of the stage. There, without hitting any poses, they were instructed to repeat the "standing relaxed" poses from the front, sides, and back to allow the judges to determine which competitors' physiques had better proportion, mass, symmetry, and definition than others. Perhaps hoping to distract the fans from such physique-to-physique comparison, Arnold made his move. Knowing that both Paul Graham's and the CBS cameras were rolling, he understood that he could capitalize on his celebrity and get the audience cheering for him by striking an array of poses (which was far more interesting to the crowd than watching bodybuilders merely standing in a relaxed posture on stage). Doing so also drew attention to his upper body (as he only hit upper body poses) and away from his legs. In previous Olympia appearances, Arnold had never felt the need to do this. He was, after all, a well-seasoned pro, and knew what the rules of the first round of a bodybuilding contest were. As this was a clear violation of the rules of the competition,[12] Head Judge Oscar State issued repeated warnings to Arnold to stop posing.

Vince Basile, who was taking photos of the competition that day for a variety of magazines, recalled:

> Arnold "forgot" NOT to pose in round one. He was scolded by Oscar State at the microphone and by Dennis Stallard on the platform. The damage was done though, and people like Zane, Tinerino, Dickerson, and others who obeyed the rules, were penalized in effect.[13]

This was corroborated by Norm Komich, a long-time bodybuilding fan who was present for both the inaugural Mr. Olympia contest in 1965 and the second one in 1966. Komich found himself in Sydney in October 1980 and decided to purchase a ticket to the Mr. Olympia. As he had at the previous two Olympia contests he attended, he filmed part of competition that day with his Super 8 mm camera and was witness to Arnold's on-stage antics:

> Arnold was the most recalcitrant. His attitude was and is vividly etched in my mind as he frequently did just what HE wanted to do while ignoring the requests of the directing official who I remember at one point was directing the group to stand relaxed and Arnold kept posing and posing and posing. My deepest impression of that whole scene was that Arnold acted as if he were accountable to NO one!!! He just stood there doing his thing with that infectious grin on his face, which after watching the frustrations of the director, eventually turned me off. If all or actually any of the other competitors had acted similarly, it would have been total chaos. Arnold "got away" with a great deal that day.[14]

Competitor Roger Walker recalled that Arnold "was doing exactly what he wanted and Oscar State, who was supposed to be controlling the stage, was letting him get away with doing anything he wanted. He was warned constantly, and warned about being disqualified, but obviously that was never going to happen. If I'd have done that I would have been out on my ear."[15]

Not only was Arnold not disqualified, but despite his lagging muscle development in certain body parts, his lack of proportion, and breaking the rules, the judges who it might be said were expected to vote for Arnold did so: Michael Walczak, Reg Park, Mits Kawashima, Albert Busek, and Brendan Ryan each awarded Arnold 20 points — a perfect score — for this round.[16] The two remaining judges, Jacques Blommaert and Dan Howard marked Arnold down to 18 and 19 points, respectively. Interestingly, Reserve Judge Peter McCarthy awarded Mike Mentzer a perfect score of 20, and marked Arnold down to 18. But of course, his score no longer counted.

Now that he was no longer the head judge for the event, Bill Pearl's services were secured by CBS Sports. The company originally wanted him to be the color commentator for the telecast (after Arnold decided to compete) but then thought he would be better conducting backstage interviews with the competitors. One of the competitors, Roy Duval, recalled calling out, "Why are you back *here*, Bill? I thought you were doing the commentary?"

Pearl glared at the Englishman. "I'm having nothing to do with this fiasco."

"What do you think?" Pearl asked, nodding towards Arnold, who was in the wings checking his development in a mirror.

Duval puffed out his chest. "I think Arnold's going to be a little bit disappointed!"

"No, he isn't," Pearl replied. "And that's why I'm having nothing to do with it."[17]

Shortly after his discussion with Duval, another interesting exchange occurred backstage when Pearl was preparing to interview Mike Mentzer. Just before the video cameras started up, Arnold approached the pair. He stuck out his arm and shook Mike's hand. Referring to their set-to earlier, he told Mike to "forget about it. Let's be friends."[18] When Arnold walked away, Pearl turned to Mike, and in a voice that was loud enough for Arnold to hear, said: "Mike, don't you for one minute take Arnold Schwarzenegger seriously. He has no intention of being your friend. Make no mistake about this guy!"[19]

"I had no idea what Bill was talking about at that point," Mike recalled. "The contest had barely begun. I knew what he meant later!"[20]

The judges' scoring for the first round was not shown to the bodybuilders, so they had no idea that Arnold was already comfortably ahead as they prepared to enter the second round of the competition. The second round required the competitors to strike certain compulsory poses, allowing the judges to assess the contestants' overall mass and definition as well as evaluate the development of their specific muscle groups. It also provided a means of checking for proportioned, balanced development. If, for example, a competitor flexed both of his biceps but one was considerably bigger than the other, he could be marked down for lack of symmetry. Similarly, another pose would reveal whether a competitor's upper and lower body possessed an equal level of development when flexed simultaneously. Given that the compulsory poses were, in fact, *compulsory*, every competitor had to perform them. The poses were: front double biceps, front lat spread, rear double biceps, rear lat spread, side chest, side triceps, and abdominals/thighs. Once again, all the competitors hit the poses they were told to — except Arnold. When the head judge called out for the side triceps pose, Arnold hit a biceps pose.[21] "[Arnold Schwarzenegger] never once obeyed an order by the judge's chairman," said Frank Burwash. "He posed after told not to, and even tried to push other competitors off the stage . . . indeed, if you watch the replay of the final 'posedown' closely you will see him purposely strike Australia's Roger Walker three times with an elbow jolt, trying to make him lose balance."[22]

The task of trying to enforce the rules of the competition fell to veteran IFBB stage director Dennis Stallard. Stallard was a no-nonsense Welshman who had officiated IFBB competitions for many years. He tried his best to bring Arnold in line by threatening to disqualify him from the contest if he didn't comply with the rules but with no support from the judges or Ben Weider, Stallard was on his own. Indeed, for attempting to enforce the rules of the contest, it would be Stallard who ended up being punished — at least according to Frank Zane:

> [Arnold] wasn't doing the compulsory poses. And the head judge said, "Arnold, look, do the compulsory poses or we're going to disqualify you." And Arnold just kept doing what he wanted to do. The guy's name was Dennis Stallard, I remember, from Wales, he says; "Arnold, you're disqualified. Get off the stage!" So he didn't get off the stage, and that night Stallard was fired, and they sent him back to [the UK]. That's the lesson there; when you're a favorite like that, when you're in cahoots with the organizers, you can pretty much do whatever you want.[23]

Blommaert was the only judge to mark Arnold down — and even then only to an 18 in this round. But since the judging rules stipulated that both the highest and lowest scores of each competitor were to be discarded to remove any anomalies, Blommaert's scoring didn't count in the final tally.

Once again, Walczak, Busek, Park, Ryan, and Kawashima (and, surprisingly, Howard) awarded Arnold perfect scores of 20 in this round. Later, when the judges' score cards were made available to the press, Jack Neary scratched his head. "It is a mystery to me how Arnold could command a perfect 100 score in the mandatory posing round," he said. "To score perfectly, one would have to be perfect in each pose. Regardless of the fact that Arnold neglected to do some of the compulsory poses, those he did do showed he needed another two, maybe three, weeks of training to be considered the best on that stage."[24] The remainder of the competition, if you could call it that, was more like a carnival than the premiere contest in all of professional bodybuilding:

- Judge Reg Park shouted out posing instructions to Arnold from the judges' table.[25]
- When Arnold did his posing routine during the evening show, he continued to pose after he stepped off the dais.[26]
- Franco Columbu interrupted the contest by running out on stage during the middle of the competition to wipe the sweat from Arnold's brow.[27]
- Arnold delayed the contest when everyone was ready to go on stage until a contest official located his comb so he could comb his hair first.[28]

Columbu's towel antic was more than a mere interruption of the proceedings, however. It allowed him to instruct Arnold to move to the other side of the stage, where the lighting was better, so that his muscles would stand out more impressively.[29] This was blatant interference, as none of the other competitors' friends or significant others were allowed to do this — nor would the IFBB have permitted it, lest the competition lapse into complete bedlam. Moreover, as this was supposedly the highest level of bodybuilding competition in the world, each of the competitors was assumed to be experienced enough not to require supplemental coaching from either the judges (which revealed partiality and should have been grounds for dismissal from the panel) or from their buddies in the crowd. Such sideshow activity had never taken place during a bodybuilding competition before. Boyer Coe, who had competed in over 60 bodybuilding contests in a career stretching back some 16 years (and had even competed against Arnold at the NABBA

Pro Universe in 1970),[30] was left stunned by what Arnold got away with during the prejudging:

> His antics on stage did an awful lot to disrupt the entire contest. Before the contest started there was a meeting regarding how the contest was going to be judged. Bill Pearl, head judge, stated, very strongly, that everyone would adhere to the rules completely or points would be deducted. Everyone did adhere to the rules completely, with the exception of Arnold. And there were no points deducted, nor did anyone call him down for it . . . Arnold did exactly what he wanted. It was like a showcase for Arnold, and we were the puppets being manipulated. It was like there were two sets of rules, one for Arnold, one for the rest of us.[31]

Mike Mentzer was both bewildered and angry that a man who had been the face of bodybuilding for the better part of a decade should now be willing to trample the sport underfoot for no apparent reason: "Arnold's tactics and those of his handlers were very disruptive. You had Franco Columbu coming onstage during the prejudging to give Arnold fresh oil and a towel. This is ridiculous! At one point, Arnold actually took Franco to the middle of the stage and introduced [him] and made quips and anecdotes. Can you imagine during a boxing match one of the boxers stopping the course of events to bring a friend in the ring and start making jokes just to get attention? They were also filming for the movie *Pumping Iron II*[32] with George Butler. Arnold was obviously hamming it up and the other competitors were just bit players — clowns, foils — in his act and I didn't particularly like it. [In] no other sport do you see this happen."[33]

Be that as it may, the prejudging was now in the past. There remained the final portion of the contest to prepare for, which would take place later that evening. Perhaps things would get back on track then. At least that was the hope that competitors like Boyer and Mike entertained as they left the Opera House and returned to their hotels. None of the competitors, presumably, had a clue as to how the preceding rounds had been scored. Surely with all the warnings he received, Arnold had to have been marked down. Indeed, his lack of proportion required that to be the case all on its own. Interestingly, thirty-six years later, during a talk Arnold gave on stage at his own bodybuilding contest, the Arnold Classic, Arnold would claim that Bill Pearl had pulled him aside after the prejudging to let him know that he was behind on the judges' scorecards:

> When I was competing in 1980 at the Mr. Olympia in Australia, Bill Pearl was one of the judges. . . . But he came to me in the afternoon, and he says, 'Arnold, you're in trouble.' And I said, 'why?' And he says, 'you're number three — you're in third place. So, you have to pull off some trick by the evening.' He says, 'you have to be more ripped, you have to have a better posing or something, because remember the posing round is not until the evening, so you still have a shot.'"[34]

It was a strange anecdote to relate, particularly given that Bill Pearl was not on the judging panel — and Arnold knew this. Moreover, during the prejudging, Pearl had been busy conducting interviews with the competitors backstage for CBS Sports (which Arnold also knew as he was interviewed by him). Consequently, Pearl hadn't a clue as to how the contest was being scored or where Arnold stood in the placings. Given that Pearl "wanted nothing to do with this fiasco," as he had told competitor Roy Duval, why he would he go out of his way to misrepresent his position (i.e., a judge at the contest) and lie to Arnold about the scoring? This is particularly puzzling given that Arnold related this story in 2016 and knew full well where he stood after the prejudging in 1980 as the judges' scorecards had long been a matter of public record by then. And the scorecards indicated that he wasn't in third place after the prejudging rounds, but rather in first place (with 199 points). The judging panel had seen to that. The scoring further revealed that third place was in fact occupied by Chris Dickerson (with 191 points); Frank Zane was in second (with 194 points), while Mike Mentzer was sitting in fourth place (with 186 points — 13 points behind Arnold).

The placings had actually left reserve judge Peter McCarthy in shock. He believed that Mike and other competitors had been deliberately marked down.[35] In Peter's scoring, he had Mike Mentzer and Chris Dickerson tied for first place, Frank Zane in second, and Arnold, along with Roger Walker, Boyer Coe, and Dennis Tinerino tied for fourth. But, again, McCarthy's scoring didn't count.

The final rounds of the contest that remained to be judged were the posing round (where each competitor posed individually to music) and the final posedown. In both rounds, the competitors simply performed their posing routines, which should have resulted in identical scoring as it was the same thing, the only difference being that during the former the competitors posed alone; in the latter, they posed among the top seven finalists. According to Arnold, it was during the posing round that he pulled ahead:

> Noticing how much better everyone else had gotten at posing since 1975, I realized I would have to pull out all the stops that night — play to the crowd, use all my tricks, smile, look confident. I decided not to use a set posing routine, but to go according to the mood. When I hit a shot, if I got a lot of applause, I'd stay with it; if not, I'd move right on to something else. It worked. The audience kept screaming and applauding, and I was called back three times. I did my routine, came back and did a different one, then did some poses off to the side of the posing platform. None of the other bodybuilders were called back like this. Seeing that audience reaction, I hoped I had received as good a response from the judges. Perhaps that audience response had picked up a few points for me. When I went backstage, a number of people congratulated me and said, "I think you pulled it off."[36] I pulled it off and got the extra points with my posing and won the competition, won the Olympia."[37]

Once again, however, Arnold's claims aren't supported by the facts. Arnold actually lost this round, managing no better than a tie for third place (along with Ed Corney, Boyer Coe, and Roy Callender); Chris Dickerson won this round, with Frank Zane coming in second. Judge Albert Busek's scoring was bizarre, as he awarded no less than 8 perfect scores (Arnold, Dickerson, Coe, Zane, Walker, Callender, Bannout, and Corney). Judges Jacques Blommaert and Michael Walzcak awarded a perfect score to Mike Mentzer. The scoring for this round was all over the board. Moreover, Arnold didn't change his posing routine and was also never called back for even one posing encore, let alone the three he claimed. None of the videos taken at the contest, nor any of the contest reports, reveal Arnold performing any more than one posing routine — the same as every other competitor that evening.

The judges now whittled the competitors list down to seven finalists who would then engage in a posedown (the final round) to determine the winner:

- Boyer Coe
- Arnold Schwarzenegger
- Roger Walker
- Roy Callender
- Mike Mentzer
- Frank Zane
- Chris Dickerson

The posedown began and each of the competitors hit what they believed to be their best poses. It was by no means a long and drawn-out affair, concluding approximately two minutes after it started. Peculiarly, despite rating no higher than third place during the posing round, Arnold, doing virtually the same posing routine, received first place votes from judges Albert Busek, Reg Park, Brendan Ryan, Mits Kawashima, and Michael Walzcak. The remaining two judges, Dan Howard and Jacques Blommaert, cast their votes for Chris Dickerson. This prompted *MuscleMag International* to report:

> Why they needed a posedown in a classless contest is strange indeed. During round 3 the judges awarded 25 twenty scores, demonstrating the difficulty of separating the men. Miraculously, they had no trouble in the posedown — what did they see there that they couldn't see before?[38]

The conclusion of the posedown ended the competition. It was now up to the judges to tally their scores from all four rounds and present them to Head Judge Oscar State so that he could announce the final placings.

A hush fell over the packed Sydney Opera House auditorium as Oscar received the results. He cleared his throat and made his announcements. In sixth place was Roger Walker from Australia, who many of the competitors thought would have been in the top three. Then came the bombshell: in fifth place, Mike Mentzer. "When Mentzer was called out for fifth place, the raucous crowd sat totally quiet, and unbelieving," said Frank Burwash. "During the lull, someone at the rear of the hall shouted 'bullshit!' And as

Mike appeared on stage, he waved to his cheering fans and said loudly, 'Yeah, bullshit!' which brought cheers of approval."[39] Jack Neary was stunned:

> Something started to smell when Mentzer was announced as the fifth-place finisher. How is it that the Mentzer of 1979 could score a perfect 300 and one year later, with 10 pounds more muscle and even tighter skin, score a mere 278? Fifth place? The judges had to be joking![40]

The announcement of the placings continued. In third place: the defending Mr. Olympia champion, Frank Zane. The knock against Frank in this competition was that because of his accident in August, he had entered the contest lighter than he had been when he won the Mr. Olympia title in 1979. While this was true, compared to how much lighter Arnold was in this contest compared to what he weighed at Mr. Olympia contests he had won in the past, Frank received a punishment that didn't fit the crime. After all, Frank had entered this contest weighing only (by his estimation) three to four pounds lighter than he had been the year before.[41] Arnold entered this contest weighing some 17 to 20 pounds lighter than his previous best condition. In any event, Frank Zane's three-year reign as Mr. Olympia was over.

And then there were two.

When Chris Dickerson's name was called out for second place, he wasn't surprised. Not because he didn't think he should have won, but because he suspected that the promoter, Paul Graham, had it in for him. "The promoter was a real low life, a bigot, who had a real dislike for me," he recalled. "Partly on racial grounds and partly for my sexual orientation" (Chris was Black and gay).[42] Graham, the man whom Arnold called "a great human being,"[43] had earlier been overheard telling one of the contest officials that "Chris couldn't win because he was a fag."[44]

Now faced with the reality that Arnold was the winner of the competition. the audience in the Sydney Opera House began expressing their disapproval:

- Frank Burwash: "All hell broke loose when Arnold was declared the winner. Jeers and boos erupted throughout the Opera House. Some irate fans walked out, chanting 'Rigged — rigged!' Others just sat in sheer amazement, saying to themselves, 'how can a guy with just a pair of arms win the Olympia?' And, of course, we must all agree that this is certainly not the criteria for winning any contest, much less the 'Olympic Games of Bodybuilding.'"[45]

- Jack Neary: "Arnold was declared the winner, and I'd never heard anything like this, but the crowd booed Arnold! It was a good half of the crowd jeering him and booing him. It came tumbling down from the upper parts of the balconies. And this was Arnold! The greatest bodybuilder ever! The Legend! And he just sort of grinned through it all on stage, but it was kind of a shock and I think we all realized, man, something's not right here."[46]
- Boyer Coe: "It was such an unpopular decision, as any will remember how much the crowd booed when Arnold was announced the first-place winner."[47]
- Roger Walker: "Arnold was not expecting that booing. He thought he could pull this . . . thing off. . . . The booing wouldn't stop. The crowd didn't like it. And I would say everybody in the room was booing . . . because it doesn't matter what country you're from, we can all smell bullshit."[48]

Jack Neary was dumbfounded; not only at how Arnold could have won the contest,[49] but also at how Mike could have placed so low. "Of course, he was the nemesis of Arnold, and it's no question in my mind that Arnold's friends who were on the judging panel marked Mike down to fifth. I think the whole crowd felt that."[50] As for Mike, he immediately sensed conspiracy:

> So ludicrous was the decision, that, really, all I could do was laugh. I'll tell you; somebody out there really wanted me crushed out completely. Well, that's it for me. That's the last time I'm going through that kind of training for that kind of shit decision. No one can tell me I wasn't in the best shape of my life. My bodybuilding career is over. Bodybuilding just lost what could have been its best spokesman. If only I'd been given the chance.[51]

Boyer Coe was asking anyone who wanted to listen, "Is there no justice?"[52] He recalled being approached by judge Albert Busek and being told: "I really wanted to vote for you but Arnold and I are old friends and you know how it is."[53]

Chris Dickerson felt cheated. "My personal opinion is that it was sort of presented to Arnold and it should not have happened," he said. "Everybody knows that, including Arnold, he's a professional. I'm sure he knows he wasn't in his top condition. It's like the rug was sort of picked up from under me and I'm denied the title."[54]

Bill Pearl was beside himself. "The only problem was — which we didn't realize at the time — that four of the judges we had on the panel had very strong emotional ties toward Arnold. I was probably more let down and deflated than anything I had experienced in my bodybuilding career of thirty-five years. I felt bad for the contestants. I felt bad for Arnold. . . . The physique that Arnold had — with somebody else's head — somebody let's say from Sweden, believe me, that guy would not have been in the top ten of that contest."[55] Reserve judge Peter McCarthy shared Pearl's sentiment. "Anyone who knows bodybuilding and were in the audience could see that Arnold was nowhere near the best there. The four bodybuilders who I placed ahead of him [Dickerson, Mentzer, Zane, Walker] were in pure hard, full contest shape and trained their guts out for months to get into the shape they were in. They were robbed and the crowd voiced their opinion very strongly to that effect. . . . Arnold should never have won that show, EVER!"[56] Such were the sentiments emanating from within the Sydney Opera House immediately after the contest.

Later that evening, during a post-competition banquet and cruise around Sydney Harbour, Arnold approached judge Dan Howard. Presumably, by this time he had read the judges' scorecards and noted that Dan hadn't voted for him to win the competition. The new Mr. Olympia wanted to know why. He thought that since Dan was a friend, he should have given him his full support. Dan replied that he had to judge the contest fairly, and if Arnold didn't like how he had scored him, that was his problem, not Dan's. It evidently was a problem to Arnold; he refused to speak to Dan for a year afterward.[57] Dan would later tell writer John Fair that Arnold's posing routine hadn't changed since the 1970s and was out of date[58] — and, bottom line, he wasn't in good enough shape to win.[59]

Australian bodybuilder Robert Nailon, a friend and colleague of both Arnold and Paul Graham, approached judge Reg Park for his thoughts after Arnold's victory. "All eyes were on Arnold," Reg enthused. "He was the biggest and the tallest, and, doing a side chest [pose] in a lineup, who could compare?"[60] It was an interesting statement, to be certain, as it suggested that one pose (and one body part) was what Reg was judging that day (he did not ask, for example, "Who, doing a leg pose in a lineup, could compare?" — a question that could have been answered easily with over a dozen examples), that a competitor's height counted for more than his proportion, symmetry, and definition, and, in a stunning reversal from what he had told Mike Mentzer the year before, having "big" muscles was now no longer a liability but a prerequisite for winning the top bodybuilding contest in the world. "It's interesting," Mike Mentzer noted, "at the 1980 Olympia, the only people who saw Arnold as the winner were the . . . judges [who were] his closest friends. None of the other competitors saw him as the winner; none of the audience, or very few, only those that were his friends."[61]

In an attempt to stop the growing speculation that he won the contest only because of his friends on the judging panel, Arnold told the bodybuilding press:

> I'd say the best friends of mine did not vote for me. For example, Dan Howard, one of the judges and a skiing partner of mine, voted me third, and one of my all-time friends, Blommaert, from Belgium, voted me sixth or seventh. So, here's two different guys that I've been extremely friendly with, more so than anyone else on the judging panel, and they did not vote for me.[62]

This was not only untrue but laughable. Arnold was much better friends with Albert Busek, Reg Park, Mits Kawashima, and Brendan Ryan than he was with Dan Howard and Jacques Blommaert. Evidence of this, at least in the case of the latter, is the fact that a page or two earlier in the same interview from which the above quote of Arnold's was taken, Arnold referred to his "all-time friend" Jacques Blommaert as "Julien" Blommaert.

Close friends indeed.

Perhaps more telling is the fact that six years later, when Arnold married Maria Shriver in Hyannis, Massachusetts, Busek, Kawashima, and Paul Graham were among the invited guests (Busek and Kawashima were in the wedding party).[63] These three joined in the festivities and hobnobbed with the celebrities and the political royalty that is the Kennedy family. Arnold's "best friends," Dan Howard and Jacques Blommaert, evidently didn't make the cut.

CHAPTER TWENTY-SIX

AFTERMATH

The blowback from the contest was both immediate and considerable. When word of Arnold's victory eventually made its way across the Pacific, it was greeted with shock by the bodybuilding community. What was Arnold doing in that contest? Hadn't he retired? Most surprising was the news that Arnold had been booed heavily when he was announced as the winner. It was evident that despite his victory, his legacy had taken a serious hit. Such fallout was not something Arnold had anticipated. He decided to do what he could to mitigate the damage.

Jack Neary had been home in Calgary for about a week when he received a call from the new Mr. Olympia, who informed him that he was conducting a bodybuilding seminar in Red Deer, Alberta, and perhaps he and Jack could get together, have lunch and talk.[1] Since Red Deer was only 93 miles north from where Jack lived, and being curious as to what Arnold wanted to talk to him about, the writer agreed to meet.

That Saturday Jack drove to Red Deer, and, after Arnold's seminar ended, the two men drove to a nearby restaurant for lunch. Jack recalled that, after ordering his food, Arnold got down to business.

"What did you think of the contest?"

"I don't think you deserved to win," Jack replied. "And I intend to report that."[2]

Arnold shook his head. "You know, it never does any good to be airing dirty laundry in public about controversies and stuff like that. I don't want you to write negatively of the events."[3]

Jack now understood the reason behind the luncheon invitation.

"Well, Arnold, I saw what happened, and I'm going to report what I saw. And I'm not going to sugarcoat it. I'm not going out of my way to portray you in a bad light or anyone else in a more favorable light than they deserve. But I *am* going to report how I saw it go down — and I certainly heard the booing, Arnold."

Not making any headway, Arnold made Jack a business offer.

"I'm doing an *Encyclopedia of Bodybuilding* with Bill Dobbins, but I would be happy to make you the other writer on it. You and Bill could do it together."

Arnold's previous books had been bestsellers. There was money to be made here for an ambitious writer. "He didn't directly say 'write a good piece and I'll give you this assignment,' but that was the inference," Jack recalled. At the conclusion of their lunch, Arnold pushed himself away from the table. "Why don't you think about it? We'd love to have you on the team with the *Encyclopedia*." Jack thanked Arnold for the offer and said that he would consider it and get back to him. But even as he left the restaurant that day, Jack knew he wasn't going to soft-soap his contest report in exchange for co-author status on Arnold's latest book — no matter how many copies it ended up selling:

> As soon as I got home, I said, "There's no way I'm doing it. I'm not compromising the piece. . . . He's trying to buy me and that's not happening." And so, I wrote him a letter a few days later, just turning him down, flat out. I never heard back. I can't remember if he responded. But anyway, he got the message. And then I wrote the piece I did, and I wasn't particularly negative about Arnold, but I did say he didn't deserve to win.

That was enough to put Jack in Arnold's bad books. "I think Arnold called me a whore after the report came out," Jack recalled. "We sort of had a bit of a falling-out because of that."[4]

In the immediate aftermath of the 1980 Olympia, Mike Mentzer had stated that he was done with competitive bodybuilding. But on the long flight back to Los Angeles from Australia, he thought better of his decision. The way he saw it, he could passively sit back and do nothing — and thus give Arnold and his cohorts free reign to continue to trample the sport underfoot for whatever purpose they chose in the future, or he could stand up to them to ensure that such a travesty never happened again. He chose the latter.

When word got out about Mike's intentions, a writer from *Muscle Builder* tracked him down to find out how he planned to stand up to Arnold and the bodybuilding industry:

> Mike [Mentzer] says, there was absolutely no need for the contumelious behavior that Arnold Schwarzenegger, who has contracted to co-promote the next Mr. Olympia, displayed in Australia towards the judges, fellow Mr. Olympia contenders and the entire IFBB. "He went down there with his movie crew to shoot [Paul Graham's documentary]," complained Mentzer, "and was allowed to lord it over the rest of us, as if he were some superstar actor and we were bit players. He insulted us individually and collectively by his uncalled-for remarks and in the way he flouted the strict laws that govern IFBB events all over the world. He showed complete disregard for all the rules that we had agreed to compete by." Implicit in Mike Mentzer's statement is the suggestion that if the IFBB cannot legally take the 1981 Mr. Olympia out of Arnold's hands, since contracts were signed two years ago, there is nothing to prevent the leading Mr. Olympia contenders from doing everything lawful in their power to repay Arnold for his indiscretions.[5]

Mike understood that since money was the primary thing that the IFBB and contest promoters such as Arnold and Paul Graham paid attention to, a message needed to be sent that made it clear that their collective pocketbooks would take a serious hit unless some major changes were made. Specifically, changes needed to be put into effect that forbade promoters from selecting the judges for their contests. The leverage the bodybuilders would bring to bear on the matter was the bodybuilders themselves. If the top professionals in the sport collectively refused to compete in the IFBB's most celebrated pro shows, such as the Pro Mr. Universe and the next Mr. Olympia (both were contests that were promoted by Arnold), that would negatively impact ticket sales.[6] Such a galvanized front had never occurred before in the history of bodybuilding.

Aftermath

Mike Mentzer and Boyer Coe took charge of the movement. And in no time at all, other professional bodybuilders came on board.[7] "The top professional bodybuilders have gotten together," Mike said, "and have decided that it's up to us to take control of our careers and take greater control over what's going on. We have more to lose than anybody."[8] Arnold and Jim Lorimer were promoting the IFBB Professional Mr. Universe in November of 1980, a mere one month after the Mr. Olympia, and that would be the first contest the bodybuilders would boycott. Mike already heard rumblings that Arnold had promised his friend Jusup Wilkosz the title.[9] If this was true, the nepotism had to stop — it was imperative that the bodybuilders stay away from that competition.

Not that all professional bodybuilders supported the boycott. Foremost amongst the abstainers was Roger Walker, who believed that he needed the exposure, particularly that appearing in the 1981 Mr. Olympia would provide him.[10] Tom Platz, likewise, had no interest in keeping away from professional competition. Besides, he looked upon Arnold as his hero.[11] Recognizing the power that Arnold held within the IFBB, there were other competitors who also thought it prudent to remain on Arnold's good side. Boyer Coe recalled that "Tom said, 'Well, if I don't go in, what about my career?' I said, 'If we don't stick together, *nobody's* going to have a career.'"[12]

Former Mr. Olympia Frank Zane went a step further in his protest; he not only supported the boycott of the 1981 Mr. Olympia but also refused to honor a verbal agreement he'd made with Arnold to guest pose at his Pro Mr. Universe contest. Arnold quickly sent his lawyers after him, threatening to sue. Frank ended up settling by paying Arnold's attorney fees.[13]

Former friendships were down the drain.

The Pro Mr. Universe was held on November 1, 1980, at Veterans Memorial Auditorium in Columbus, Ohio, and the bodybuilders who had opted to boycott the event looked at each other knowingly when they learned that Jusup Wilkosz was, indeed, declared the winner. Tom Platz finished in second place.[14] Certain of the holdouts were now rethinking their original decision to cast their lot with Arnold.

By the winter of 1981, CBS Sports was in a quandary about what to do with the video it had shot at the 1980 Olympia. A newspaper article in the Rochester *Democrat and Chronicle* revealed the problem:

> The 1980 Mr. Olympia turned out to be a hotly disputed contest with protests of foul. So much so that CBS Sports, taping for

a later showing, initially refused to air the show. Says Mike Delnagro of CBS public relations: "It is true we taped it and didn't air it. We initially had some concerns about the judging."[15]

This view was corroborated by Sherm Eagan, the man who produced the contest for CBS, who told the author in 1994 that the video of the competition never made it to air "because of the stink of the thing." In 2024, Eagan elaborated on the matter, stating: "That was the opinion of management in New York when I telexed the complaints being raised. It wasn't a hard decision."[16] Shortly after the production crew had returned from Australia, Eagan placed a call to Ben Weider. He wanted the IFBB president to come to the CBS studios in New York to watch the footage they'd shot and personally explain how the judges could have awarded Arnold the title. Ben was on the hook; the network had paid the IFBB a good deal of money for the exclusive broadcast rights to the Mr. Olympia for a three-year period. It had already aired the 1979 Mr. Olympia, and now, after absorbing the additional expense required to fly a production crew halfway around the world to film the second contest in their agreement, the network was left with hours of video they had no intention of airing — unless Ben could provide them with satisfactory explanations for what they interpreted as being very questionable officiating.

Ben wanted no part of this. Instead, he instructed Wayne DeMilia, who had nothing to do with the Mr. Olympia contest, to meet with Eagan and face the music as Ben's surrogate.[17] Two competitors from the 1980 contest, Boyer Coe and Chris Dickerson, happened to be in New York at the time, and so they were invited to accompany Wayne to the CBS building to view the footage.[18] Once inside, the group was met by Eagan, who ushered them into a video suite and played the tape. Even to those who had competed in the competition, the video footage was shocking. "I didn't realize what a great difference it was until you're sitting watching the thing," Boyer Coe recalled. "That's when it's really apparent that, hey, something is wrong here."[19]

Directing his attention to Wayne DeMilia, Eagan paused the tape. He inquired if a voice heard on the video calling out instructions to Arnold came from the judges' table. Wayne recognized the voice as belonging to Reg Park, who was, indeed, one of the judges at the contest.[20] When asked why a judge would be doing this, Wayne didn't have an answer. After all, he had been in New York when the contest was taking place in Australia.[21] The tape rolled again. Once again Eagan paused it. He had the judges' score sheets in front of him and now asked Wayne why Arnold received a perfect score in the compulsory posing round when he was not doing the compulsory poses.[22] Once again, Wayne had no explanation. It was getting uncomfortable.[23] Then, when Arnold was announced the winner, the booing from the crowd was heard. "It was obvious to [Eagan] that Arnold didn't deserve to win," Boyer said. "Even to the average person sitting in the audience, you realize, hey . . . this is not right."[24]

Eagan now addressed the room. "We're never going to be able to show this on TV. . . . It's just too controversial."[25]

And that was it. The network sent word to Ben Weider that not only would it not be broadcasting the 1980 Mr. Olympia footage, it also would not be attending the 1981 Mr. Olympia contest despite having already paid for the broadcast rights. The company was done with bodybuilding.[26] The bodybuilders who had trained so hard to compete for bodybuilding's biggest title were infuriated that Arnold and his antics had resulted in CBS's decision not to broadcast the footage of the competition. For some of them, it would have been the biggest exposure of their entire careers. It just didn't seem fair that they should be the ones to pay the price for the actions of Arnold and his cronies on the judging panel. "With respect to Arnold," said Roger Walker, "there was no need, his movie career would have carried on just as well. And what did he do? He made [bodybuilding] a laughingstock; the film crew that came over from America to film it put the film in the trash can. It's never seen the light of day. . . . They thought that bodybuilders were just a bunch of wankers and cheats, probably. They thought it was a joke. So, as far as I'm concerned, he sullied, he besmirched the reputation of bodybuilding for his own ego."[27] Fellow competitor Dennis Tinerino thought likewise: "It set back bodybuilding a minimum of five years. CBS has completely denounced bodybuilding. . . . We all suffer because of one individual, you know, doing his thing."[28]

There was no getting around it; bodybuilding had taken a giant leap backwards.

Compounding the matter, when the bodybuilding magazines finally came out with their reports on the contest, their headlines weren't flattering:

- "OLYMPIA REPORT: ARNOLD'S VICTORY CREATES CONTROVERSY & BITTERNESS"[29]

- "ARNOLD'S 7th OLYMPIA WIN TARNISHED BY CONTROVERSY"[30]
- "THE OLYMPIA FIASCO"[31]

Despite the negative press, however, a deal was a deal, and with *Conan the Barbarian* now in production, Joe Weider hustled together an ad featuring Arnold — in full Conan costume — endorsing Joe's "Olympians" supplements.[32] Given the lag time between layout and printing, the ad had evidently been in the works for some time. But rather than reaping the benefits, the ad gave birth to problems. First, it angered the International Olympic Committee, which eventually sued both the IFBB and Weider Health & Fitness,[33] allegedly for using both the Olympic rings and torch on the product label and ads. Second, the timing of the ad suggested to some that Joe may have had a hand in fixing the contest for Arnold to win in order to promote his new supplement line.[34] That Joe had a hand in the outcome of the contest was certainly the opinion of veteran bodybuilder Robby Robinson. He would write in his book some years later:

> Even though Arnold's physique had no business being up there, looking skinny with just biceps and a chest, he ended up winning, while Zane came in 3rd, behind a returning 40-year-old Chris Dickerson. Boyer Coe was given fourth, and Mike was put in fifth. I felt that it was Mike's year, but there was too much at stake with Weider's greatest superstar on that Olympia stage. Arnold represented Weider's high-volume training system and Mike was toting his own "HIT" (high-intensity technique) system. They couldn't let Mike win, or his system would have discredited Weider's. Arnold hadn't just entered for his ego; he was also protecting Weider's system and empire. The whole spectacle was an embarrassment to the sport.[35]

Certainly, given Arnold's controversial victory and the new Arnold-as-Conan ad, the optics weren't good, and this was potentially bad for Joe's business. After all, the success of the Weider brothers' supplement marketing depended upon the bodybuilding public believing their nutritional products — as opposed to backroom deals — were responsible for creating contest-winning physiques. In an effort to put some distance between himself and the Sydney debacle, Joe made a call to his gun-for-hire writer, Rick Wayne, giving him the task of protecting his boss from the fallout. And, in an article entitled "Arnold: Saint or Devil?" that was published in Joe's magazine, Rick did just that, pinning the blame for the 1980 Olympia solely on Arnold:

> Let us now remind Arnold that he made a fool of himself even as he was on his way to becoming Mr. Olympia for a record seventh time. Goodness knows, his reputation took a severe beating around the world as a result of his performance in Australia. He has had time enough to ponder the events of the last few months, and no doubt he is intelligent enough to know he has not been altogether "clever" throughout.[36]

That Arnold was the guilty party found support among bodybuilders. When news of Arnold's victory reached Gold's Gym in Santa Monica, the bodybuilders there concluded (according to Ken Sprague) "that the contest had been fixed with Arnold having a hand in selecting judges."[37]

Arnold was furious over Rick's article.[38] He believed Joe Weider had hung him out to dry.[39] Joe simply smirked; from his perspective, Arnold had been tinkering with explosives and had blown himself up. "If the bodybuilding world has developed ill feelings toward Arnold," he said, "that's a consequence of Arnold's own behavior. His derisive comments after the '80 Olympia made him unpopular with fans and contenders."[40] And Joe went a step further; he published an article in praise of how great Mike Mentzer looked at the 1980 Mr. Olympia,[41] imploring Mike not to quit the sport (as Mike had indicated he was going to do in Jack Neary's contest report). And then Joe took direct aim at Mike's two biggest critics — Arnold Schwarzenegger and Franco Columbu — and opened fire:

> It is upon such reflection of the astounding progress Mike has made in the three years that we have been associated, that I find it difficult to understand the spate of criticism issuing from Arnold and Franco recently regarding Mike and his physique. "Mike will never win the Mr. Olympia," Arnold stated in one magazine article. In another article he said that Mike did not possess a world caliber physique. Franco

Columbu, a protege of Arnold's, follows his mentor's lead in another article, saying he also thought Mike Mentzer would never win the Olympia and added that it was because Mike was too "stocky." I was upset by Arnold's statements, but Franco's remarks really threw me for a loop. It's beyond me how a man like Franco, who probably possesses the stockiest physique of any modern-day champ, can justify his criticism of Mike Mentzer. Let me say here that this article is not intended to defend Mike Mentzer. Besides the fact that he hardly needs a defense against such remarks. . . . How could Arnold, Franco, or anyone else say in clear conscience that Mike Mentzer doesn't possess an Olympian body? Just look back to the originators of Western civilization, the ancient Greeks. They possessed such extraordinary breadth and depth of artistic vision that their standards of beauty persist through today. Indeed, it was the ancient Greeks themselves who pointed to the Farnese Hercules as the ultimate measure of beauty and development in the male body. Mike's physique, after all, personifies the Herculean ideal. Mike Mentzer is the modern-day Hercules![42]

Such positive attention resulted in more bodybuilders looking to Mike as being the leader of the new movement to right the ship of professional bodybuilding. To that end, both Mike and Boyer Coe decided to take the pro bodybuilders intended boycott of the 1981 Mr. Olympia public. A petition was drafted and signed by all the bodybuilders who were in favor of the embargo. It was sent to all of the various muscle magazines for publication. It read:

AN OPEN LETTER FROM THE PROFESSIONAL
BODYBUILDERS OF THE I.F.B.B.

Due to present circumstances, we feel it is our responsibility to let our many fans know that we will not compete in the 1981 Mr. Olympia to be held in Columbus, Ohio, nor in the 1981 Pro Mr. Universe to be held in Sydney, Australia.

However, we wish to state publicly that we fully support the International Federation of Bodybuilders and its constitution and recognize it as the governing body in professional bodybuilding. We will compete in the I.F.B.B. Grand Prix's and other approved I.F.B.B. contests.

Signed,
Samir Bannout, Albert Beckles, Andreas Cahling, Roy Callender, Boyer Coe, Steve Davis, Chris Dickerson, Roy Duval, Tony Emmott, Bill Grant, Mike Mentzer, Ray Mentzer, Steve Michalik, Joe Nazario, Dan Padilla, Carlos Rodriguez, Don Ross, Dennis Tinerino, Ken Waller, Casey Viator, Frank Zane[43]

"We boycotted the Pro Universe last year," Mike told an interviewer. "And while we didn't get 100 percent compliance, it was successful enough to let Arnold and the rest of the world know that certain things were happening and taking place that were going to shake up the bodybuilding world. And now this year there's another boycott, this time the Olympia. And so far, we have probably 99 percent compliance. Every top bodybuilder except Wilkosz and Tom Platz has given us his promise that he will not enter and has signed a statement to that effect that will be published in every muscle magazine except *Muscle & Fitness*." When asked why Joe Weider's magazine wouldn't publish the statement, Mike replied, "I don't know why Joe and Ben don't want to do it. It's going to make them appear like they're trying to whitewash it. It's mostly Ben; he doesn't want people to think that there's a lot of dissension within the IFBB ranks. He doesn't want the world to think that it's falling apart."[44]

It didn't take long for Mike's comments to reach the ears of Ben Weider in Montreal. Despite his organization's recent legal trouble with the International Olympic Committee (IOC), Ben's ultimate dream had long been to receive recognition from that venerated institution for bodybuilding as an Olympic sport.[45] But for that to happen, the IFBB needed to be perceived as a well-structured organization that was free from taint. Mike's public comments were shining a very bright light on the federation. His outspokenness had become a problem. Ben placed a call to his brother at the Weider offices in Woodland Hills, California. He lit into Joe about what Mike was saying in his seminars regarding the officiating at the 1980 Mr. Olympia contest and how this reflected negatively on the IFBB. And when Ben learned that Mike happened to be in the building, he insisted that his sibling put him on the phone. Mike immediately received an earful from the IFBB president. This lasted for about five seconds, whereupon Mike fired back in defense of his public statements. The dialogue grew heated, and soon Mike was shouting into the receiver. Joe snatched the phone back.

"Why did you yell at my brother like that?"

Joe got another scolding from Ben. Mike wasn't sure what was being said, but he got the gist when he heard Joe ask, "What do you want me to do, Ben? Put a muzzle on the guy?" Ben made it clear that he wanted Joe to cut way back on the magazine's promotion of Mike and his views.[46] But Mike's negative comments about the 1980 Olympia were just the tip of the iceberg in terms of the problems that would soon be heading Ben Weider's way.

Mike had heard rumors that Arnold's best friend, Franco Columbu, would be coming out of his four-year retirement and had been promised victory at the 1981 Olympia.[47] This couldn't happen again, Mike thought. Not two years in a row. Bodybuilding had already lost its national audience when CBS dropped its coverage of any future contests. Another miscarriage of justice could ruin the sport forever. The Weider brothers were also concerned but for different reasons. Having already pissed off the International Olympic Committee with their supplement ads, if Mike Mentzer and Boyer Coe were successful in their effort to lead a boycott of the 1981 Olympia, it would permanently scuttle Ben Weider's chance of getting recognition for bodybuilding from the IOC. The forthcoming Olympia had to proceed successfully and without controversy. Once again, Joe reached out to writer Rick Wayne, who recalled:

> Mike Mentzer and Boyer Coe had remained rock steady in their resolve to boycott the '81 Olympia. As a direct consequence of their efforts to land Arnold with a lemon, Joe Weider assigned me the task of writing several features to counter the adverse publicity and to allay widespread fears that there'd be no Olympia contest to speak of in 1981. (Yes, I'd been made an offer too good to refuse, so there I was, on Weider's editorial staff once more.)[48]

While Rick's "Arnold: Saint or Devil?" article in the August issue of *Muscle & Fitness* saw the scribe doing his level best to place the blame for the 1980 Olympia controversy squarely at the feet of Arnold Schwarzenegger, he was now tasked with doing damage control for the forthcoming Olympia, which, by extension, required him to do damage control to its promoter. Moreover, now that *Conan the Barbarian* was officially a go, there was money to be made on the back of Arnold's cinematic efforts — and Joe wanted this to inure to the benefit of his company. But it wasn't going to happen unless Joe's magazine went someways in rehabilitating Arnold's image, an image that both Jack Neary and Rick Wayne had recently poked some gaping holes in.

Arnold certainly welcomed the support. Not only would Rick's journalistic efforts help him sell more tickets to the '81 Olympia, but they also provided him a platform from which he could lambaste those individuals who he believed had disrespected him. In the October 1981 edition of *Muscle & Fitness*, in Rick's article entitled "Mr. Olympia Is No Popularity Contest: It Has No Room for Purring Pussycats," Arnold struck out at Frank Zane, painting the former Mr. Olympia as a coward who would've dropped out of the '80 Olympia had he known Arnold was going to compete.[49] Jack Neary, who had written the damning contest report, was dismissed by Rick as an "avowed Mentzerite" (a new term concocted by the scribe).[50] And Mike Mentzer, well, where to begin? His followers were "mindless," believing he was an intellectual[51]; Mike's talk of being a premed student was "bogus"[52]; his physique didn't appeal to either bodybuilders or the general public[53]; and he would never win another contest unless he used dumbbells in his training and trained like Arnold, upping his training volume to 20 sets per body part.[54] Moreover, his jab at Mike during the competitors' meeting was made simply as a test, to see how his adversary would react under pressure. Presumably, if Mike had remained apathetic, he would've passed the test. Instead, he got angry upon being insulted, and that was his undoing.[55] Never mind that the competition was judged on stage and not during the competitors' meeting, that was beside the point. Rick also wasn't interested in getting any input from those who Arnold had attacked. He wasn't on a truth-finding mission; that wasn't the purpose of the piece.

But then the writer took a curious turn in his article. He introduced a rumor that had appeared in print nowhere else: that Arnold's antics on stage during the competition were the result of cocaine — an allegation that Arnold quickly attempted to stamp out:

> Hey . . . it's the second time this coke matter has come up in the last few hours. I was at the gym a little while ago and Ken Waller called me aside. He told me there was this fellow, a customs

official or something, who had heard a rumor that I was a heavy user of coke. Waller wanted to warn me about this fellow just in case I planned to come through LAX with the stuff anytime. I mean it's nice to know. I still have a few friends. But there's no need to worry about that. I haven't had anything to do with drugs in five years. I woke up one New Year's morning and I asked myself, what can I do to make myself a better person? Someone in full control of himself. And I said, yes, I know, I'll kick the drugs. I was no addict, you understand. It just dawned on me that there is no point to smoking marijuana and snorting coke. And I quit, just like that, five years ago. No, I was fully conscious of every move that I made in Sydney.[56]

Interestingly, during an interview with writer Peter McGough that was conducted some years later, Mike mentioned that Joe Weider himself had told him that Arnold was on cocaine during the 1980 Mr. Olympia. Hearsay, of course. But the fact that Rick Wayne felt compelled to bring it up during his interview with Arnold in 1981 suggests that other people besides Joe Weider were reporting this.

In any event, with old scores now settled and the rumors squelched, Rick set about his task of putting people's minds at ease regarding the forthcoming Mr. Olympia. Indeed, the 1981 Mr. Olympia was going to be a great success. Why, with nearly six months to go, 85 percent of the seats had already been sold and Arnold expected nothing short of a packed house come the night of the contest.[57] Playing his cards close to his vest, Arnold said he did not want to give out any names at this point, but the leading US professional bodybuilders would be competing.[58] Rick even went so far as to imply that a new bodybuilding superstar, England's Bertil Fox, would be there, and perhaps an old bodybuilding superstar, the great Sergio Oliva, as well.[59] "Obviously," Rick and Arnold assured the bodybuilding public, "there will be a Mr. Olympia contest; a great one, too."[60] The fans would have to wait until October 10, 1981, to see if what was written was true.

Despite Joe Weider's glowing article encouraging him to compete again, Mike was still uncertain about his bodybuilding future.[61] That would hinge on how the 1981 Olympia played out — and whether or not the bodybuilders who had signed his petition would honor their pledge. He decided to take part in CBS Sports' *Superstars* competition on August 13 and 14, 1981, in Key

Aftermath

Biscayne, Florida. He didn't win, but he did exceptionally well, coming in only 952 milliseconds behind NHL player Bob Nystrom in the swimming race and just failing to edge out Lou Ferrigno (who outweighed him by over 40 pounds) in the weightlifting event. Both Mike and Lou broke the previous record of 315 pounds in the overhead press (previously set by six-foot-three, 255-pound NFL player Lyle Alzado) by successfully pressing 320 pounds, but in their attempt to press 325, Mike didn't quite lock out, whereas Lou did.[62] "Even though I beat him at weightlifting, he was a good sport," Lou recalled. "I was nervous about losing. I couldn't afford to lose, you know, because I'm so much bigger than he is — but he's quite an athlete himself."[63] Harry Sneider, a man who had coached eight *Superstars* competitors in the past, including Wayne Grimditch, who had won the title in 1978, was stunned when he witnessed Mike (at a bodyweight of 219 pounds) run the 100-yard dash in 11 seconds flat during training.[64] At the end of the day, Mike finished ahead of professional athletes such as NHL player Dino Ciccarelli, professional boxers Michael Spinks and Marvis Frazier, and NBA star Otis Birdsong.[65] It made for a brief and interesting distraction from the politics of professional bodybuilding.

CHAPTER TWENTY-SEVEN

BODYBUILDING LOST

Both the IFBB and the Mr. Olympia had been knocked back on their collective heels as a result of what happened in Sydney. It should've been a wakeup call to the Weiders to get their house in order. Instead, the controversy provided an opportunity for Ben to leverage even more financial benefit to the Weider company via the IFBB and the contests that it sanctioned. Virtually all of the delegates in the IFBB were either distributors of Weider supplements or Weider publications in their respective countries, and the bulk of the judges for the contests were selected from amongst the delegates.[1] In an effort to shore up the damage that the Sydney Olympia had caused, and to at least give the appearance that the federation had taken the fallout seriously, it was announced that the IFBB, in the persons of Ben Weider and his top aide, Oscar State, would be picking the judges for the 1981 Mr. Olympia contest — not the promoters.[2] At least three of the judges deemed worthy of the privilege were distributors of Weider products. "In looking at it with honest eyes," Wayne DeMilia said, "the IFBB technically was an illegal monopoly. It violated anti-trust laws in the United States, but bodybuilding is so small, nobody cared."[3]

The new selection process didn't prevent certain individuals who were friendly with Arnold and Franco Columbu from finding their way onto the judging panel for the 1981 Olympia contest. One of the judges that slipped through the cracks was Sven-Ole Thorsen, who had been suspended from adjudicating international events after the 1980 Mr. International competition, where he was deemed to have "abused his position on the judging panel by voting with premeditated prejudice."[4] It turned out that Thorsen had voted for a competitor to win who was his friend, rather than the one who was the more deserving of the victory,[5] a familiar pattern by now with certain judges in IFBB sanctioned contests. Not that the suspension meant anything; the Dane was back in action less than a month later to judge a bodybuilding contest in London, England.[6] With Ben Weider's support, claiming that Thorsen had "redeemed himself by judging honorably and correctly [an interesting choice of words given the politics at play within the sport] in London,"[7] Thorsen was allowed onto the judging panel for the 1981 Olympia. He shouldn't have been. According to Rick Wayne, Thorsen was "close buddies" with Arnold and Franco.[8] Thorsen had appeared alongside them both in Arnold's film, *Conan the Barbarian*, and would go on to appear in 17 additional Schwarzenegger films.[9] Also finding his way onto the 1981 Mr. Olympia judging panel was Franco Fassi, the Weider distributor for Italy, who also happened to be a close friend of Franco Columbu.[10] When Roger Schwab, the man selected to be the head judge of the competition, saw who was on the panel, he hit the roof. "I wrote to Ben," Schwab recalled, "and I said you can't have the judges that you want! But it was all about the money and, you know, it was all about carrying [Weider] products and all the different nations."[11]

His appeal fell on deaf ears.

With Joe Weider blaming Arnold for the 1980 Mr. Olympia fiasco, the condemnation of that contest within the bodybuilding press, and CBS Sports refusing to air the footage of the competition, one would assume that the bodybuilders' boycott of Arnold's promotion of the 1981 Mr. Olympia contest was a *fait accompli*. However, Arnold knew bodybuilders, and he knew that, as a group, they weren't ones to stick to ethical principles when faced with the temptation of money and publicity. Boyer Coe recounts that a few months prior to the '81 Olympia, Arnold sauntered into the Rose Café, a popular eatery for bodybuilders in Santa Monica, and said, "Yeah, those bodybuilders think that they're going to boycott the Mr. Olympia, but, before it's all over they're all going to be kissing my ass and they'll be in the contest."[12] He wasn't wrong. With Mike Mentzer, Boyer Coe, and Frank Zane refusing to enter the competition, a good number of the original signatories of the petition began to realize that an opportunity for career advancement had just presented itself.[13] And when the 1981 Mr. Olympia contest finally took place that October in Columbus, Ohio, only Mike Mentzer, Boyer Coe, Frank Zane, and Albert Beckles were conspicuous by their absence.[14]

Even Chris Dickerson, who believed himself to be the uncrowned champion of the 1980 competition, and a man who had criticized Arnold's victory publicly after the contest, was competing in Arnold's contest in 1981. Three of the bodybuilders who had competed in 1980 (two of whom had signed the boycott petition) showed up in Columbus in exceptional shape — Tom Platz, Roy Callender, and Danny Padilla. Despite Tom's refusal to join in the boycott, Mike had provided him with some important dietary insights that resulted in Tom completely transforming himself. As Tom recalled:

> In the '70s, we all did what Arnold did. The meat and water diet; low-carb diet, high-fat diet. In 1980, with the influence of Mike Mentzer, I decided to go on high carbs and low fat. It was shockingly unbelievable to my system. Switching my metabolism to high-carbs, low-fat everything changed; my whole career changed. My whole body changed.[15]

Mike also invited Tom to his house in Palm Springs three days prior to the contest to get some sun and was tremendously impressed with the improvement the bodybuilder had made in his physique in 12 short months. He believed Tom to be shoo-in for the Olympia title:

> Tom trained extremely hard all year for the IFBB Mr. Olympia. He was the one guy I saw in Gold's Gym all winter long who just went to failure on every single rep. And I remember saying to my brother Ray, "This guy's serious." I had no idea what he looked like underneath his sweatsuit, because he was always covered up. In the last three days before the contest, he stayed at my home in Palm Springs to get some sun. So when I saw him by my poolside, two weeks ago, I just couldn't believe my eyes — his skin was like tissue paper! He was probably around 2 percent bodyfat. He put 12 pounds of pure muscle onto his upper body alone.[16]

But Tom wasn't the only threat to win the title that year. The rumors about Franco Columbu returning to competition proved true, and he looked to be in good shape — but for two major flaws. The first was the result of his having suffered a broken leg in 1977 while competing in the World's Strongest Man competition in Florida.[17] His leg never fully recovered, with the result that, like Arnold the year before, Franco's lower body was out of proportion with his upper body. Not only that, but his bad leg was also out of proportion to his good leg. According to author and Natural Mr. Olympia winner John Hansen, who was in the audience watching the 1981 Mr. Olympia, Franco's legs appeared puffy, with no apparent definition or muscle separation.[18] To make matters worse, said Hansen, Franco — the man who had told a Toronto audience that he had only used steroids once, in 1972 — appeared onstage that day with a very obvious case of gynecomastia;[19] that is, breast tissue growing in the nipple area of his physique, a result of taking too much synthetic testosterone.[20] These two factors should have prevented Franco from being a top contender in the competition. However, Judge Thorsen awarded Franco two perfect scores of 20 points and one score of 19 over the three rounds of the competition, while Judge Fassi couldn't have scored him higher, giving his friend perfect twenties right across the board.[21] This had evidently been enough to ensure that Franco was awarded the 1981 Mr. Olympia title.[22]

Once more, pandemonium broke out amongst the fans in attendance. As Hansen recalled:

> First of all, it was the loudest booing I've ever seen in a show. They called the top six out. They go through the posedown: Jusup Wilkosz gets sixth, and then they announced Danny Padilla in fifth, and the place erupted. Went absolutely nuts — boos, screaming. Then they go to fourth, Roy Callender gets fourth. Again, the booing never stops. . . . And then they gave Platz third and it really got bad. And then by the time they got to Dickerson and Franco, most of the audience was leaving; they're like, 'Fuck it. I don't even care who wins now!' Arnold and Joe Weider didn't even come out onstage. The people were literally going into their pockets and grabbing change and throwing it at the judges. They were throwing their programs at the judges. . . . It was insane! I never saw anything like it.[23]

Arnold's reaction to the outcome of the contest was levity. "Arnold laughed and laughed and laughed," Rick Wayne wrote. "He called the '81 Olympia 'the greatest booing contest of all time,' greater by far than that in Sydney the year before."[24] Wayne's articles in *Muscle & Fitness* leading up to the contest had assured bodybuilding fans that all was well with the sport and that the 1981 Mr. Olympia was going to be a great show. But now, even he was livid. Wayne vented his spleen in his "Flash Report" of the competition:

> Twelve months after its debut at the Sydney Opera House, the monster that many believed had since died of shame gave a wholly unexpected but far more revolting repeat performance at the 1981 Mr. Olympia Contest in Columbus. More than 4,000 stunned fans, including Joe Weider, were sick to their stomachs the night of October 9 when Oscar State announced the results of the once highly respected event. The booing and catcalling rose to a deafening volume when Franco Columbu was declared Mr. Olympia 1981, and winner of the $20,000 cash prize over an amazingly improved Tom Platz, a flawless and ripped Danny Padilla, an outrageously muscled Roy Callender. It was bodybuilding's "Good Friday," that never-to-be-forgotten Saturday night when a group of self-seekers nailed bodybuilding to the cross of disillusionment. Be sure to read the full story of the most exciting Mr. Olympia ever staged, and the regrettable finale that turned the whole event into bodybuilding's darkest hour.[25]

Backstage, competitor Roy Callender shook his head in disbelief. He had originally joined the boycott, but then, having convinced himself that this year's Mr. Olympia would be judged on the up and up, he decided to enter. Now he couldn't believe that he'd made such a mistake. "Right now, Mike Mentzer and Boyer Coe must be laughing their heads off," he said, more to himself than to anybody else.[26] But laughter wasn't the way Mike had reacted to the news. "I *wasn't* laughing," Mike recalled, "because it wasn't a 'laughing' situation. I didn't laugh last year, and I wasn't laughing this year simply because of the fact that if Tom Platz had won, he could have gone from really a nonentity, an obscure bodybuilder, to making $300,000 a year — that's serious! You're talking about a man's livelihood. Apparently, Arnold and Franco think it's a joke. In my opinion, it's a very bad joke."[27] While giving a seminar in Rexdale, Ontario, a little more than a month after the competition, Mike read Rick Wayne's flash report (cited above) aloud to all in attendance. He then fielded questions about what the result of the 1981 Mr. Olympia contest represented for the sport of bodybuilding:

> **Mike:** "So, you know a lot of the bodybuilders, including Tom Platz, sort of thought I overreacted last year when I called for a boycott to the [1981] Mr. Olympia. But now all the guys who thought I overreacted last year are just as pissed off as I was last year. Because now they were close to winning and saw it elude their grasp because of these "self-seekers," whoever they are. Think about it for a minute; think about what a win would have done for Tom Platz or Danny Padilla. But Franco won. I'm not sure what I'm saying here; I'm not sure what it all means for bodybuilding — or me."
>
> **Q.** "What's the situation now with the IFBB?"
>
> **Mike:** "The IFBB? It's a very delicate situation. The bodybuilders are more disgruntled than ever. You know, after last year's contest a lot of people were pissed off for a while, but they figured, 'Well, it was a fluke. It won't happen again.' But it's affecting more and more people now."
>
> **Audience Member:** "It goes to prove that it can be bought."
>
> **Mike:** "Well, I'm not sure it can be 'bought.' I'm not sure what's happened. I really don't know. That's one of the reasons I haven't been competing; I don't think there's a fair judge in the world."
>
> **Audience Member:** "It's a bad day for bodybuilding . . ."
>
> **Mike:** "It's very bad."
>
> **Audience Member:** "What was the role of Joe Weider in this?"
>
> **Mike:** "Well, according to what I heard, Joe Weider was just incensed over this thing and for the first time in bodybuilding history, Joe Weider refused to give out the trophy to the winner. He stormed out of the place and was heard to have said, 'Yes, I like Franco, but he and Arnold are ruining the sport,' or something like that. Of course, Joe may have been smart enough to have planned that whole scenario beforehand. That whole 'blow-up' could have been part of a staged act."
>
> **Q.** "Do you think it will happen again next year?"
>
> **Mike:** "I don't know. Next year it's going to be in London."
>
> **Q.** "I think the average person — even just looking at the

photographs — would see the corruption and would lose interest; it would leave a real bad taste in their mouths about bodybuilding."

Mike: "Yeah, very bad."

Q. "I mean, where do we go from the Olympia? The Mr. Olympia is supposed to be the top . . ."

Mike: "Yeah, if they do it to the top . . . that's exactly the thing I've been running across. Young bodybuilders from Gold's Gym run up to me and say, 'But Mike, if they're fixing the Olympia, why should I bother competing? How do I know they aren't fixing all the other contests?' I don't know what to say. It could destroy the sport."[28]

Mike had done all he could, but when the bulk of those who signed the boycott decided to kneel before Arnold and the IFBB, he knew the war was lost. None of those outraged by the judging at the 1980 Mr. Olympia, many of whom had signed on for the boycott, had raised any concerns about the judging panel at the 1981 contest. According to the contest report that appeared in *Muscle & Fitness*, Ben Weider had specifically raised the point during the competitors meeting prior to the competition:

> He invited the contenders to voice any complaints or questions they might have concerning the judges. There were no complaints and no questions. Not even after the contenders were reminded that such failure to speak up in advance of a contest had resulted in the Sydney misunderstanding. Indeed, it seemed the contenders were concerned only about the way the Olympia prize money would be awarded.[29]

With only Mike Mentzer, Boyer Coe, Albert Beckles, and Frank Zane being concerned enough about the welfare of the sport to boycott the show, the writing was on the wall. The sport was damned. It was always about the money.

While the sport of bodybuilding was descending, the business of bodybuilding was rising. The fact that Arnold won the 1980 Olympia meant that he was now back in the bodybuilding magazines in a big way. Seeing that *Conan the Barbarian* was now full steam ahead with Arnold as its star, Joe Weider knew what the smart business play was. The "Saint or Devil" articles disappeared from his publication. Instead, Joe hitched his wagon to Arnold's rising star. Henceforth, all articles about Arnold that appeared in his magazine sang Arnold's praises — and the other muscle magazine publishers followed suit. In one year (1981–82) Arnold appeared on the covers of nine bodybuilding magazines (six of them featuring him as Conan).[30] Arnold was number one again. The fans, particularly those who had recently taken up the activity, believed what they read, which, of course, was not lost on Joe. Indeed, it was precisely what had made the Weider brothers very rich men over the decades.

"Give me six months to a year," Arnold had told Rick Wayne shortly after the 1980 Mr. Olympia competition, "and they will have forgotten all the fuss — and I will still have won the Olympia seven times."[31] And so it came to pass.

"The bias of each medium of communication is far more distorting than the deliberate lie."[32] That's what Marshall McLuhan had said. And in the world of bodybuilding, at least, it proved to be true. It was just the kind of bias published in Joe's magazine that brought bodybuilders into theaters to see *Conan the Barbarian* upon its release. Joe had his new line of "Olympian" supplements, featuring Arnold as Conan in his ads, Paul Graham had his documentary, and Weider distributors in Europe, Asia, and North America had a new and heavily hyped product line to sell. The success of *Conan the Barbarian* — and Joe's new supplement line — hinged on the bodybuilding public supporting the film. And support it they did (by some estimations, one-third of the ticket buyers were bodybuilders).[33] The film launched Arnold's career as a leading man in action films and put him safely on his way to millions of dollars and, ultimately, political office. It would later come to light that Arnold owned a piece of Joe's supplement company.[34] And so, the fat cats got fatter.

The rest of bodybuilding was left behind to pick up the pieces.

CHAPTER TWENTY-EIGHT

WINDS OF CHANGE

Mike Mentzer never officially "retired" from the sport. He just never competed again. "When Franco could win a show the way he looked, then Mike was done," Danny Padilla said. "The fact that two years in a row, the sport that he loved the most, to him it was, like, denigrated. Like, 'How could they do this to bodybuilding?' It really bugged him to the point where he lost total respect for the sport."[1]

Mike, however, viewed what transpired in these two contests (the 1980 Mr. Olympia particularly) as a necessary reality check. "In some ways I'm glad the '80 Olympia turned out the way it did," he recalled many years later. "It brought into clear focus for me what the political establishment in bodybuilding was really all about. For years I was walking around in a fool's paradise; I thought everyone was as nice as guy as I was. I thought that evil was something you just read about in novels and newspapers, when, in fact, evil is something that is around all of us. This brought it all into focus and I didn't want to be involved or associated with people like that and decided to drop out."[2] But it was more than just the politics of bodybuilding that troubled him:

> I would like to do something that I consider more meaningful. Bodybuilding is obviously a self-centered pursuit, or a selfish pursuit, and after a while it gets to be too much for me. Everything is me, me, me. The common denominator is the individual. So, I'd rather do something where I'm going to help other people or be more involved with other people.

And I always thought psychiatry would give me that kind of fulfillment, but I've become disillusioned with psychiatry quite a bit over the last several years, and medicine to a degree also. But I still think I would get more fulfillment from that than competing in Grand Prix contests at the age of 40.[3]

And Mike wasn't the only Mentzer to experience competitive trouble. Ray Mentzer was unable to crack the top three in a bodybuilding contest ever again. When he entered the IFBB Canada Pro Cup in 1980, he was awarded with a ninth-place finish. He entered three contests in 1981: the IFBB California Grand Prix (where he didn't place), the IFBB New England Grand Prix (where he placed 11th) and the IFBB New York Night of Champions (where he placed ninth). He entered two more competitions in 1982, the IFBB New York Night of Champions and the IFBB World Pro Championships, where he finished tenth and seventh, respectively.[4] "Once I climbed the mountain, won my Mr. America title, from there on it was a lead wall," Ray lamented. "How do you get through a lead wall?"[5] The truth was that, unlike Mike, politics wasn't likely a factor in Ray's placings. He simply was never again able to duplicate the peak condition that he attained for the 1979 America. Nevertheless, it did seem that those competitors who dared to oppose the IFBB's political hierarchy or business interests were not winning any titles at the moment. Even Frank Zane, a three-time Mr. Olympia, and a long-time part of the bodybuilding establishment, would never win another bodybuilding competition.

In an attempt to pacify Mike and keep him in the Weider camp, Joe offered him the position of editor-in-chief of *Muscle & Fitness* magazine (rebranded from its former title of *Muscle Builder/Power*,[6] to appeal to the general public's recent interest in strength training). The title came with some input over what articles went into the publication — with Joe having the final say, of course. The salary wasn't great,[7] but it still allowed Mike to have free ad space for his mail-order business, which, apart from seminars, was now his only source of income.

Mike continued to update his mail-order products, writing new booklets, one on nutrition (*Heavy Duty Nutrition*) and another on his most recent innovations in bodybuilding training, such as the Rest-Pause protocol, and a detailed application of Dr. Hans Selye's General Adaptation Syndrome and how it applied to bodybuilding training (*Heavy Duty Journal*). In 1981, he became the first bodybuilder to break into the exercise instruction video business (a year before Jane Fonda took over the market with the *Jane Fonda's Workout* tape), when he produced his video *A Look at High-Intensity Training*.[8] He made sure to include both Cathy and Ray in the video, as Cathy's presence would allay any fears women might hold about training with weights, and with nothing happening for Ray on the professional bodybuilding front, he believed his brother might benefit from the exposure.

While video production was interesting to Mike, it didn't satisfy him. Not like his quest to build the ultimate physique had. Adding to his frustration was the fact that the editor-in-chief position had yet to materialize. While Joe wasn't specific as to when Mike would receive the honor, he had nonetheless assured him that this would be the case. In the meantime, Mike's title was upgraded to a contributing editor to the magazine, which meant he was assigned more articles to write. The downside was that apart from his "Heavy Duty" question and answer column and the odd article on his scientific approach to training, he had to write articles on other topics, such as bodybuilder profiles and training principles that ran contrary to his own. While Mike enjoyed writing, the subject matter didn't satisfy him.

Moreover, it meant being exposed to a monotonous *déjà vu* existence, with the same day repeating itself over and over again ad nauseum: a two-hour drive each morning from Palm Springs to Woodland Hills, working in the Weider building from nine to five writing and editing articles, and then another two-hour drive back to Palm Springs. The excitement and adventure he had experienced as a top bodybuilder was gone — and office life was hardly a replacement.

Mike reasoned that working in the Weider offices again might be tolerable if some of the people he had enjoyed working with in the past were working there again. He reached out to Jack Neary. "Mike lured me back to work for Weider one more time," Jack recalled. "That was in 1982. I was working in an ad agency in Calgary, and Mike called and said, 'Hey, I'd love if you'd come back, work on the staff as one of our top writers. I'm going to be hands-on with the magazine. I'll be there all the time — it'll be like old times.' I was married at the time, and I said to my wife, 'You want to go? It could it be a bit of adventure?' And we put a U-Haul trailer behind her car, we loaded it up and we moved to L.A."[9]

But Mike should never have made the offer. Not only was he not yet the editor-in-chief of *Muscle & Fitness*, but he was also dealing with a matter of a far more personal nature that consumed the lion's share of his attention. Not long after Jack arrived, Cathy Gelfo was gone from the picture. In my attempt to find out what happened, all I received were opinions from former friends of the couple. "They had grown apart," one said; "She was too religious," said another. When I attempted to contact Cathy via Facebook Messenger, there was no reply. Others who knew of such things informed me that she was married now with children of her own, and therefore not inclined to talk about the time in her life that she spent with Mike. We are left to speculate. Based on what facts we know, it appears that another woman entered the picture. And, thanks to an article Mike wrote, we know exactly when they met.

"July 17, 1982: Backstage pumping-up area." So began the profile piece Mike wrote on female bodybuilding competitor Julie McNew.[10] He had traveled to Las Vegas, along with his friend and Weider photographer, John Balik, to cover the 1982 U.S. Women's Championship. The contest was held in the Galaxy Room at Caesar's Palace, and Mike was acting as the backstage director of photography, coordinating the competitors to step before Balik's camera to be photographed. When Mike called out for competitor number 34, Julie McNew stepped forth.

Julie was 28 years old,[11] five feet, four-and-a-half-inches tall, and weighed 120 pounds — all of it muscle. She was a brunette with piercing green eyes, offset by a voice with a soft Midwestern accent, which she came by honestly, having grown up in Indianapolis, Indiana. She was a newcomer to women's bodybuilding, having only started the year before when her brother talked her into going to the gym with him.[12] Her muscles responded well to resistance training, within one month of joining a gym she placed second in her first contest. She then entered and won the 1981 Ms. Indianapolis and the Indiana Women's Championship titles.[13] Mike was transfixed; never had he seen such muscular development on a female bodybuilder before. And when he interviewed her backstage, there was an inherent shyness to her. When her emerald eyes met his, he felt as if he was in the grip of a powerful tractor beam, drawing him into her world.

Perhaps Mike saw something of himself in the young woman — her shyness was certainly relatable — and wanting to protect her from the pitfalls that he now knew to exist within bodybuilding, he felt an overwhelming desire to take her under his wing. Julie represented a new energy, a new excitement, that beckoned him out of the weary, stale, flat, and unprofitable world he now inhabited. Perhaps more significantly, if Mike's depression had returned, the increased dopamine levels that attend the excitement of a new relationship would have provided a naturally occurring stimulant to counterbalance the condition.[14] The attraction was evidently mutual, as a thinly veiled reference to their relationship appeared at the end of Mike's article: "After the Ms. America in Atlantic City [where she placed seventh in her class], Julie planned to move to California and settle down with a young man she met and fell in love with while in Las Vegas."[15]

The cryptic reference was obvious. And a mere seven weeks after first meeting, the pair were in love and Julie had moved to California. He began training her; he explained his high-intensity training method — and she adopted it. He became her Professor Henry Higgins; she, his Eliza Doolittle. The pair began to work out and take bike rides together.[16] And, with Mike at the helm of *Muscle & Fitness*, Julie began to appear in the magazine. Mike even convinced the editors of overseas muscle magazines, such as *Bodybuilding Monthly*, to run articles and question-and-answer columns "by Julie McNew" (which Mike wrote). Such exposure was exceptional for a bodybuilder who had but two amateur wins on her competitive résumé.

But the new relationship hadn't quelled Mike's pugnacious spirit. He was never more alive than when he had a battle to fight or a wrong to redress. And fighting the corruption he saw within the bodybuilding industry, exposing it, so that others didn't stumble down the same dark alleys he had, became his *raison d'être*. If it could be said to be a noble cause, it was also a foolhardy one. The dragon he had selected to do battle with was far too big and far too entrenched for any one man to slay, no matter how much science and reason one armored oneself with. Moreover, his battlefield was growing smaller by the day. Ben Weider couldn't understand why his brother allowed Mike to be involved with the magazine at all. His goal remained obtaining Olympic recognition for bodybuilding, and for this to happen it was important that the IOC believed that the IFBB had its house in order. And yet there was Mike, who had recently attempted to rally support for a boycott of the IFBB's most prestigious competition, giving seminars in which he was sounding off about what he perceived as the corrupted outcomes of the 1980 and 1981 Mr. Olympia contests. The Weiders were not First Amendment absolutists by any means, particularly if someone's right to free speech might cost them an endorsement from the IOC and the marketing opportunity that went with it.

In the fall of 1982, Arthur Jones paid an in-person visit to Mike at the latter's home in Palm Springs. Arthur told Mike that he wanted him in Florida.[17] He was creating a video production empire that would grow to be the largest supplier of all sorts of programming — from entertainment to education — in the world, and he wanted Mike to be part of it. He'd already sunk millions of dollars into creating a state-of-the-art production facility in Lake Helen, Florida:

> We own the largest television production facility in the world. It makes NBC's look like a shithouse. That's not my opinion, it's *theirs*. They've been here and left in a state of shock. I'm sure we own more video equipment, more electronics than anyone else in the world. Television is proliferating — new networks, direct-to-home satellite broadcasting, video discs and video tapes. The first thing all those developments will require is programming — massive amounts of it. So, you've got to have production facilities. There's no surplus of them in the world. Today, you may have to book a facility six months ahead. You just don't buy that kind of equipment off the shelf. Some of it you have to order years ahead, and it takes a long time to wire it up and get your people trained. By the time things really begin to happen, we'll be just about the only game in town.[18]

What Arthur was offering was an opportunity to get in on the ground floor of the industry and learn everything there was to learn about the video business — from the different types of cameras that were used and how to operate them, to producing new programs and to be part of the administration of such a burgeoning business.[19] It was an opportunity, Arthur said, "to learn!"[20] Arthur forecasted that over the next several years he expected to have no fewer than 11 studios operating 24 hours a day, seven days a week, 365 days a year, producing programming on exercise physiology, nutrition, different aspects of medicine, and entertainment.[21] He further told Mike that he wanted him to be involved with some of the ongoing research Nautilus Sports/Medical Industries was planning, and, ultimately, to be a spokesman for the company.[22]

It was a lot to unpack. Mike told Arthur he would think about his proposition.[23] In truth, by the time Arthur had left his house that day, Mike was certain he would take the entrepreneur up on his offer to come to Florida — not as an employee,[24] but to learn a technology that would soon change the world:

> Nautilus has the most sophisticated video production facility in the world and that's where my future lies. Not just my future but the future of exercise and the future period! Video will revolutionize education and people's attitudes on almost everything during the next ten years![25]

The prospect of working alongside Arthur, whom he deeply respected, and getting in on the ground floor of the video production business excited him. Arthur was a man who, in Mike's eyes, had always placed a premium on facts, truth, and knowledge. To work in an atmosphere where truth was the priority — rather than the bullshit of the bodybuilding industry — appealed strongly to Mike's ideals.[26] Besides, it was becoming increasingly apparent that such ideals were not welcome in the Weider camp. Bill Reynolds, who had been Joe's right-hand man since the magazine was known as *Muscle Builder/Power*, was still the editor-in-chief of *Muscle & Fitness*, and there was no indication that this was going to change anytime soon. It was now obvious that Joe's promise to Mike of the position had been an empty one. Moreover, as Mike was no longer competing, the magazine's attention was understandably focused on those who were, and what they were doing in their training and diet regimens. Mike still had his question-and-answer column, but it was hard to make a meaningful case for a scientific approach to training from such a modest platform.

Gradually, his seminar schedule had dried up; most of the seminars for bodybuilders were sponsored or hosted by Weider distributors who only wanted the latest stars in the industry. Mike, with his "all you need is a well-balanced diet" belief, and his outspokenness on the 1980 and 1981 Mr. Olympia contests, was not a guy that the Weiders or their representatives wanted circulating. He was bad for business.

While the IFBB may have had no use for him, Mike remained the go-to guy for bodybuilders who had training problems that needed solving. When Tom Platz tore his biceps prior to the 1982 Mr. Olympia contest, it was Mike's counsel he sought upon being given the green light by his surgeon to resume training. Mike taught him how to use the Nautilus Pullover machine, which allowed Tom to train the latissimus muscles of his upper back without involving his injured biceps muscles.[27] As a result, Tom was able to train right up until the day of the competition. Nobody but Tom and Mike knew about the injury at this point, and when Tom shared the news with Arnold, he assumed it was a confidence that would stay between friends. It didn't. Arnold made a point of telling one of the judges about the injury, and when Tom stepped onto the stage to compete, the judge called him forth and asked him to flex his injured biceps. Tom knew the contest was over for him at that point.[28] He ended up in sixth place.

Mike also found opportunity to employ his medical training. While working out in Gold's Gym, he observed a bodybuilder performing a set of vertical leg presses. After the set, the trainee staggered over to a bench and lay down, complaining that his head hurt. Mike approached and began to ask the man questions about his condition. When he asked if he had blurred vision, the man replied in the affirmative. Upon hearing this, Mike immediately checked the man's pulse, which he found to be beating rapidly, but faintly. When the man tried to stand up, he was dizzy. Mike's medical studies at the University of Maryland, as well as his years working in neurology clinics and emergency rooms, now came the fore. He suspected that the man had suffered a stroke and immediately arranged to have him taken to the nearest hospital emergency room. It turned out that the man had suffered not one but two different strokes during that set of leg presses. Had it not been for Mike's actions, the man may have attempted a third set of leg presses, which could have proved fatal.[29]

But helping bodybuilders in need wasn't paying the bills. By January 1983, Mike's income dropped so low that he could no longer afford the mortgage on his house in Palm Springs. It's not known if it was sold or repossessed. His breakup with Cathy had been a heavy hit emotionally, and now he was in a relationship with Julie McNew. In addition to his own living expenses, he was supporting Julie financially. Arthur's job offer was looking more attractive with each passing day.

While Mike grappled with personal issues, his magazine work suffered. He was now showing up at the Weider offices only sporadically, if at all. Jack

Neary was beyond frustrated. After all, Mike had told him if he moved to California, it would be like old times; they'd be working together daily and having fun. That was why Jack and his wife had made the move. But none of this was happening. "I only lasted three months," Jack recalled, "and I was hugely disappointed in Mike. Mike had said, 'I'm going to be hands-on; I'm going to be the editor-in-chief and I'm going to be involved, and we're going to do this.' But Mike hardly ever came into the office. And I was really disappointed in that. He was just preoccupied with other things. And I just realized, 'You know what? I'm getting out of here. I'm not going to hang in for this.' So I left, and Mike seemed disappointed in that."[30]

Not long after Jack had departed the scene, Mike had a chance encounter with Lou Ferrigno in the parking lot of the Rose Café. Lou informed him that Arnold was inside and had just told him that Mike had been fired from *Muscle & Fitness* because he was "irresponsible."[31] Mike was shocked at the news, because as far as he knew he was still working for Joe. Lou left, and Mike ventured inside and ordered a coffee. Arnold took notice of Mike's entry and walked over to him.

"How are you doing, Mike?"

Mike nodded but didn't say anything. He paid for his coffee and left the restaurant. Arnold followed him outside.

"Mike," Arnold called out, "let's have a glass of wine!" Mike declined the offer, which upset Arnold, who gestured as if to say, "How could you refuse?"

"Oh, what sacrilege that anyone would refuse the great Arnold Schwarzenegger's offer of a glass of wine!" Mike said sarcastically.

It would be the last time the two men ever spoke to each other.[32]

By this point, Mike was done with Joe, Arnold, and the whole bodybuilding scene. He returned to his apartment, picked up the phone, and called Arthur Jones. He told him that if there were jobs at Nautilus for Ray and Julie as well, he would accept his offer and make the move to Florida. "My bodybuilding career was going nowhere," he recalled. "I was blacklisted by the IFBB. I used to do seminars every weekend, but by 1983 I was doing hardly anything. My income went from $200,000 a year down to zero. So, joining Arthur I had nothing to lose."[33]

Bodybuilder Boyer Coe was already in Florida, having been hired by Arthur in January 1983 to oversee the development of a fitness publication that the Nautilus founder wanted published.[34] However, now that Mike, Ray, and Julie were arriving, Arthur changed his mind about the magazine. He now thought Boyer could be put to better use as a subject in a muscle-building experiment. Boyer hadn't trained since the previous October, where his return to the Mr. Olympia stage was rewarded with an 11th-place finish. For the three months prior to moving to Florida, and for the first time in decades, Boyer hadn't trained and was off steroids.[35] This was a good thing, as being off steroids was still a requirement for Nautilus Sports/Medical Industries employees.[36] Mike, of course, hadn't used steroids in some time, and saw no reason to use them in order to learn the intricacies of the video business.

Arthur's thought was to train Boyer in the new Nautilus production studio; eight cameras would film every repetition of every exercise he performed during his thrice-weekly workouts for a period of six months. Although it wasn't referenced as such, the idea, clearly, was to do a modern-day version of the Colorado Experiment. It was expected that Boyer would regain his previously held muscle size as easily as Casey Viator did, and perhaps build his body up to even bigger proportions by training in a high-intensity fashion on the new Nautilus machines. It would all be captured on state-of-the-art video that could then be edited into a marketable product for distribution to Nautilus fitness centers throughout North America.[37] However, there was a difference: In the Colorado Experiment, Casey regained his previously held muscle mass by eating up to 5,000 calories a day[38] (some would put that number at 6,100).[39] Arthur believed that Boyer could regain his muscle mass in a caloric deficit; that his body would make use of the energy liberated from the bodyfat he was burning to create additional muscle tissue. Consequently, Boyer was put on a diet of only 1,500 calories a day for the six-month period.[40]

As for Mike and Ray, their job would be to operate two of the eight cameras recording Boyer's workout sessions. Presumably, this was a step towards educating them in the use of the video technology that Arthur employed. Arthur had started the project with considerable enthusiasm, personally supervising each of Boyer's workouts. But this didn't last long. His production studio was filming multiple programs (on multiple topics) simultaneously, and Arthur wanted to be involved in overseeing each of the productions. In addition, he was still running one of the most successful exercise equipment companies in the world, and business was booming.[41] He was spending a lot of time in the design, testing, and manufacturing of a radically new leg training machine, the Nautilus Duo Squat, which delivered all the benefits of full range squats with a barbell but none of the dangers. The resistance on the machine increased as one's legs extended and diminished as one's legs returned. To match the force output of the legs as they pushed out required Arthur to create a negative cam, which, as it unwound, increased the effective resistance the leg muscles would be contracting against by roughly 2.3 times over and above the weight indicated on the machine's weight stack.[42]

Another machine Arthur was designing he considered to be a huge breakthrough, as it rehabilitated and strengthened the muscles of the lower back. The resistance was applied perpendicular to the spine, so there was no compression force brought to bear on the spinal column. This breakthrough excited him — as it did Mike Mentzer, who had been suffering from lower back problems himself for many years. "My whole spinal column is undergoing some kind of degenerative process, and it gives me problems all day long," Mike said. "I am going to use the Nautilus lower back machine which may be the best exercise machine in the history of exercise to help rehabilitate my entire spinal column."[43] Lower back problems were a huge issue, afflicting 60 to 80 percent of the population of Western countries.[44] Recognizing this represented a very big market for his new machine, Arthur devoted a good deal of what was left of his time to the field of lower back rehabilitation. Moreover, the Nautilus inventor was ultimately looking to sell his company and cash out.[45] Consequently, supervising Boyer Coe's training sessions wasn't (and couldn't be) a priority for him.

To fill the void left by Arthur's absence from the project, Mike, Ray, and Nautilus research director Ellington Darden stepped in to pick up the slack and put Boyer through his workouts. They recorded such things as the exercises he employed, the weights used, and the repetitions performed. Mike was certainly fine with this; he enjoyed his time with Boyer, and there was no shortage of wisecracks exchanged between the two during the workout sessions. When Boyer went up in repetitions on a particular exercise, Mike quipped, "You must have been imbued with the spirit of the Master Blaster!"[46] When Boyer announced that he had inadvertently swallowed a gnat that had flown into his water cup, Mike responded, "Well, your protein intake's been down anyway recently."[47]

The premise of the study was certainly a fascinating one: to determine if a workout consisting of as little as eight exercises performed for one set each, and lasting approximately 16 minutes, could stimulate the production of strength and muscle mass similar to what Boyer had displayed during his competitive bodybuilding heyday. But it was also a project that was doomed from the start.

Boyer, it must be remembered, had used steroids for over 19 years.[48] He had competed no fewer than 45 times during the previous ten years (1972–82), which included six Mr. Olympia appearances.[49] Whenever anabolic/androgenic steroids are ingested, the body's natural testosterone production slows down, and, if they are taken for prolonged periods of time, it shuts off completely.[50] By the time Boyer Coe arrived in Florida, he didn't possess the hormonal environment necessary to produce any muscle growth at all. Indeed, he was months away from having his physiology return to anything close to normal (studies have indicated that it can take anywhere from four months to two years for a man's testosterone levels to return to normal after he uses steroids for a long time).[51] And, as a further obstacle to muscle growth, Boyer was made to adhere to a diet of only 1,500 calories a day. At the end of the day, Boyer was not a good candidate for participating in a muscle-building experiment.[52]

The strange thing is that Arthur knew about the suppression of testosterone in a trainee who had been using steroids for a long period of time — he had even written an article that mentioned this phenomenon 12 years previously in *Iron Man* magazine — and yet he proceeded with the experiment.[53] Anyone who has watched the surviving footage of Boyer's training sessions from this period would conclude that his workouts were all over the board. Variables changed: exercises were added or dropped,[54] weights were randomly decreased,[55] and eventually one of his three weekly workouts was switched to a "maintenance" workout. Mike suggested in one of the videos that Boyer might need to take some time off to fully recover,[56] but this was an idea before its time and was waved off. Arthur's firm belief was that three-days-a-week training was categorically the best way to proceed. By July 1983, Boyer's hormonal system appeared to be coming back somewhat. Mike noted that Boyer's strength was starting to increase and that his size and muscle definition had started to improve. [57] But this was during month six of a six-month experiment; the previous months he hadn't shown much of any improvement at all.

The Mentzer brothers were now growing frustrated. Apart from working the video cameras and/or supervising Boyer's workouts, neither Mike nor Ray was being taught anything about the video business or its administration. This was a profound disappointment to Mike, who had sincerely believed what Arthur promised him back in Palm Springs in the fall of 1982.[58] Ellington would write in his book *The New High Intensity Training* that Mike "never came into my office to talk about training during the entire 6 months we worked together in Florida. Not once! And I never saw him train hard in Lake Helen."[59] But chatting with Ellington Darden about training or engaging in high-intensity workouts wasn't why Mike had come to Florida. Arthur had promised to teach and involve him the video business, to make him a spokesperson for the company, but it just never materialized. Seeing yet another ambition dashed, Mike felt an uneasy sense of anxiety settling in upon him. He confided to a friend, bodybuilding journalist Garry Bartlett, that he was "in the process of revaluating my goals."[60]

Working with a man like Arthur Jones presented its own unique set of challenges. While the Nautilus inventor was brilliant, he was also reportedly capable of incredible acts of violence. According to William Edgar Jones, author of *Nautilus: The Lost Empire of Arthur Jones*, when a bodybuilder came to Florida to work for Nautilus during the 1970s, he made the mistake of offering Arthur's son (Gary Jones) marijuana. When Arthur found out about it, he stormed into the factory and pulled the bodybuilder outside, where he proceeded to pistol whip the man before the startled eyes of the factory workers and anyone else who happened to be driving past Nautilus Sports/Medical Industries that day.[61] When Mike encountered the bodybuilder a week later at Gold's Gym, he noted that the man's face was a mass of welts, cuts, and bruises.

"What happened to you?" Mike asked.

"I ran into a door."

Mike raised an eyebrow.

"What? *Repeatedly?*"[62]

Knowledge of Arthur's willingness to use violence, along with the fact that he always carried a revolver, meant that his employees were terrified of doing anything that might upset him. Ray Mentzer, however, evidently didn't get the memo.

One day Arthur walked through his television facility with a group of medical men and rehabilitation specialists. He wanted to show them the benefits of the Nautilus lower back machine. They soon arrived at the set where nine Nautilus exercise machines were arranged for Boyer Coe's workout sessions. Both Mike and Ray happened to be in the studio at the time.

"Ray!" Jones bellowed as he entered the soundstage. "Get up and show these men how the lower back machine works!"

"No."

The people in the studio that day weren't sure they'd heard Ray correctly. Arthur resumed talking with his associates and, taking notice that Ray hadn't made his way to the lower back machine yet, he called out again.

"Ray! Where are you?"

"I'm right here. And I'm *not* getting up."[63]

Arthur, perhaps for the first time in his life, was speechless. Nobody who worked at Nautilus ever had the *cojones* to speak to him like that. The ball was now in Arthur's court. After a protracted period during which both men stared at each other, Arthur finally muttered something unintelligible and left the set with his associates. Mike shook his head. He knew what was coming. He had secured Ray a job at Nautilus, and Ray had just gotten both of them fired. Later that day, Ray received word from one of Arthur's underlings that his employment at Nautilus was terminated. Mike knew better than to try and reason with Arthur about allowing his brother to keep his job. And he also knew that Ray was too headstrong to walk back what had just happened.

He stewed about it for several days, and then packed his bags and returned to California.

CHAPTER TWENTY-NINE

UNMOORED

Ray Mentzer was okay with being fired from Arthur's employ. For several months prior to his termination, he had been communicating with a person who was interested in partnering up with him to open a gym in Redondo Beach. Once the finances were in place, Ray was gone from Nautilus, and a month later the gym was up and running. It looked like the timing of his insubordination to Arthur may have been more than coincidental.

Mike, on the other hand, had returned to California with nothing. Given that he had pulled strings to get Ray the job in Florida, he probably didn't know that his brother was planning on leaving. Surprisingly, some seminar and posing exhibition requests arrived from non-Weider facilities in Canada and Germany. These, along with some money for two books released that year — *Mike Mentzer's Complete Book of Weight Training* (Quill Books) and *Mike Mentzer's Spot Balancing* (Simon and Schuster) — would at least bring some money in until he decided what he was going to do next. He returned to Gold's Gym in Venice, and after a few weeks of cutting his calories back and training intensely, his physique had rebounded to decent enough shape that he felt comfortable in accepting the seminar and exhibition gigs.

It just so happened that Mike was in Germany at the same time that the 1983 Mr. Olympia contest was being held in Munich. As Samir Bannout was competing, and was said to be in exceptional shape, Mike thought he would attend the competition and cheer on his old friend.

The Mr. Olympia was promoted by Albert Busek, who invited his good friend Arnold to attend as an honored guest. *Conan the Barbarian* had been released in the United States in May 1982 to mixed reviews[1] but solid box-office receipts, and bodybuilding fans in Munich were excited at the prospect of seeing bodybuilding's premiere contest and the star of *Conan the Barbarian* together in one venue.

MuscleMag International publisher Robert Kennedy, who was there to cover the contest for his magazine, spotted Mike in the lobby of the venue. Kennedy inquired where Mike was seated and was told that he had purchased a general admission ticket. Kennedy was seated in the VIP area of the auditorium, which was much closer to the stage. As there were plenty of vacant seats in that section, he invited Mike to sit with him so they could watch the contest together.

The contest had barely gotten underway when Busek spotted Mike and sprang into action, causing Rick Wayne to write: "The promoter, a close friend of Arnold Schwarzenegger and Franco Columbu, who were both in Munich for the occasion, did add a note of excitement in evicting Mike Mentzer from his VIP seat!"[2] Despite Mike being both a Mr. America and a Mr. Universe winner, and being the only bodybuilder in history ever to receive a perfect score in both amateur and professional competition (which might qualify him as an MVP at a bodybuilding contest, one would think), Busek didn't hesitate in having him removed. These accolades had all taken place prior to the 1980 Mr. Olympia and the disrespect Mike had shown Arnold at the competitor's meeting. And since Arnold was his personal guest of honor, Busek, being the gracious host that he was, didn't want anything or anyone present that would result in Arnold being upset.[3] Mike watched the remainder of the competition from the back of the auditorium.

As for the contest, the report of Samir's condition proved to be correct, and the "Lebanese Lion" was declared Mr. Olympia for 1983. The now-traditional victory banquet for the administrators, fans, and competitors was held after the competition. Eager to celebrate with Samir, Mike attended.

As Mike stood in line for the buffet, Arnold was noticed talking with Busek. The promoter then approached Mike.

"Do you have a ticket for the banquet?"

"No, I don't, Albert."

"Then you leave. You must leave immediately."[4]

Making Mike feel persona non grata twice in one evening, both times in front of a roomful of his colleagues, was clearly a calculated move meant to be publicly embarrassing. With no shortage of food at the buffet, there was no good reason for ejecting Mike beyond appeasing Arnold.

After returning to California, Samir soon found himself in Joe Weider's bad books. The Master Blaster had agreed to give the current Mr. Olympia a full-page color ad in his magazine to market his mail-order items in exchange for Samir appearing in ads endorsing Joe's products. While the endorsement ads found their way into the magazine, the ad for Samir's products had not. This incensed Samir, who stormed into the Weider offices and demanded that Joe honor his promise. Joe told the bodybuilder that it had been a simple oversight, and to underscore his commitment to the new champion, he announced that he would fire the entire advertising department if it ever happened again. This seemed to pacify Samir, who shook Joe's hand and left the building. "The next day," Rick Wayne recalled, "all magazine personnel received their orders: No more publicity for Samir Bannout."[5]

Despite Mike's ill treatment at the recent Olympia, the experience hadn't been all bad. Robert Kennedy told him that he would publish any articles he cared to write for *MuscleMag International*. Not long after the first one appeared, Joe Weider offered Mike more money to write exclusively for his magazine.[6] It was essentially a freelance job, but the money was a little better than Kennedy was paying.

But not having a steady income was the least of Mike's problems. He was still suffering from bouts of anxiety and depression that were becoming alarmingly more frequent. He was growing concerned. The psychology and philosophy books he had been reading had done little or nothing to alleviate these conditions. He needed to find an alternative that would help him better understand what he was going through and hopefully help him to overcome it. And that's when he decided to attend a lecture given by a man named Rex Dante.

Dante referred to himself as an epistemologist,[7] a subcategory of philosophy that specializes in the mind's relation to reality and identifying and validating what can be known. He further taught his students mnemonic techniques to improve information retention and retrieval, among other cognitive skills. Mike was struck by how sharp Dante's mind was; here was a person who was clearly in full control of his brain and its relation to the world around him, which was something Mike had been grappling with ever since he was a child. After Dante's lecture, Mike approached him and introduced himself. "Upon first meeting him I recognized that he was the man of the highest mind that I had ever met," he recalled. "Very impressive. And I asked him how he got like that, and he said, 'Ayn Rand.'"[8]

The name was not unfamiliar to Mike, who had read Rand's massive novel *Atlas Shrugged* in 1977 but hadn't been particularly impressed with it or by its philosophy. "I'd read it more or less as a literary duty," he said.[9] But Dante insisted that he revisit the author's works, starting with her novel *The Fountainhead*,[10] and to do so with an eye towards seeing where epistemology came into play throughout the book. And so he did. Soon Mike had progressed to Rand's nonfiction books *The Virtue of Selfishness*, *Capitalism: The Unknown Ideal*, and *The Romantic Manifesto* (which ended up being Mike's favorite of all her books), among others.[11] Whenever Mike had an issue, Rex would tell him to go back to the Objectivist literature and reread it, and some cases re-reread it, and think about it constantly to see where and how it applied to his day-to-day situations. Over time, Mike came to understand that the study of philosophy wasn't simply a matter of studying the ideas of the great thinkers of the past but a means to help a person make decisions in the present:

> The real role of philosophy is to help man make choices, and as long as man is confronted with choices, he's going to need a philosophy, a value system. And after reading Ayn Rand's philosophy, I realized that hers was the most thoroughly reasoned, the most logical, and the most consistent. And I've adopted it and tried to live it, with lapses from time to time. But that's the responsibility of the individual over time: to consistently apply the philosophy. And that's what I'm still working on.[12]

Mike further discovered that Dante's mnemonic teachings were strengthening his memory. Within a matter of weeks, he was able to recall entire passages from books he had read, simply by attaching visual images to various passages.[13] Over a five-day period, he taught Julie McNew 100 symbols and images that, two weeks later, allowed her to memorize a 150-digit number with ease.[14]

The Objectivist concept that resonated most with Mike was referred to as "sense of life." One month before his death, Mike wrote a short story in which he revealed through autobiographical flashback why this concept was so important to him:

> I preferred to be intellectually-emotionally and morally self-sufficient. I had always been a radical. This was expressed

in my early years mainly through my "sense of life," which is the pre-conceptual, preverbal, emotional, subconsciously integrated view of man and of existence — a child's emotional, subconscious equivalent to a conscious, mature philosophy of life. In part, owing to the lack of proper, rational guidance, I was blindly rebellious and desperately sought self-assertion. As I matured, however, the blind rebelliousness progressively decreased, and I was less under the control of my subconscious, emotional sense of life, and became increasingly directed by an explicitly verbalized, conscious, rational philosophy of life. The blind rebellion had been replaced by a passionate desire to discover the dispassionate, objective truth. At the time that my maturation was reaching a pinnacle, I became thoroughly fact-centered, truth-oriented: which paced me out of step with the rest. It's not that I was a lone wolf, it was that I learned to think for myself, which I came to understand required privacy.

As a young boy, I sought to achieve an objective view of others. This was accomplished by imagining myself lifted up into space, where I could peer down and obtain a clear, unobstructed view of them. And what I observed was abject conformity and the desperate desire for the safety of will-less passivity. Not passivity of the body, but passivity of the mind. And it wasn't passivity all the way through, but beyond a certain point. They were either unwilling or unable to think beyond the confines established by the pack. The idea that achieving spiritual self-sufficiency was the goal of the process of maturation never occurred to them, something they never thought to question. They led blighted lives, bereft of any interest in science, philosophy, morality, or art. Life as they lived it was the immediately given, the not to be questioned, the stubborn adherence to tradition and the opinion of others. To me, gaining the ability to think and to judge independently was the ultimate purpose in life.[15]

He hoped to share what he was learning from Objectivism with certain of his friends in the bodybuilding world. Some were interested, but most gave up after a few months, claiming it was too demanding. "I thought that was a lame excuse," he recalled. "Life is demanding! I think the problem is daily application. It's very easy to read it and then go about your daily affairs and forget about it. If you're going to apply it, you've got to be obsessed with it for a while; you've got to think about it, and how it applies to situations in your life. At various periods when I was reading the Objectivist literature a lot, I would take every opportunity to reflect on it during the day. When I was driving down the freeway, caught in traffic snafus, or during private moments when I had time alone, I would reflect on my own life situations and see where the philosophy applied and whether I did apply it or not and resolve to apply it more consistently in the future."[16]

Julie had enthusiastically taken to Mike's training approach and was trying her best to understand his new philosophical orientation, which further deepened the Pygmalion/Galatea situation that existed between them. Mike had hoped that with his connections to the magazines, Julie's competitive bodybuilding career would be advancing, but that hadn't been the case. She took another run at the NPC USA Women's Championships but ended up in fifth place in her division.[17] The political hierarchy of bodybuilding was trying to broaden the sport's appeal by promoting women physique competitors who weren't "too muscular." Consequently, the more heavily muscled female bodybuilders, such as Julie and the Australian phenomenon Bev Francis, were passed over, while female bodybuilders like Rachel McLish (who better fit the image that the IFBB, which was made up almost entirely of men, had of what a female bodybuilder should look like), garnered the victories and the spoils. This bothered Mike, as he saw the grimy hand of politics had once again pressed its imprint into the sport. He had always believed that the women should be judged by the same standards that the men were.

Since bodybuilding wasn't rewarding her financially, Julie needed a job. Mike approached his friend Dave Mastorakis, who had recently moved to California to become the head trainer at the prestigious Matrix One fitness center in Westwood. The club was then the go-to gym for the entertainment industry's top talent; Tom Selleck, Cheryl Ladd, and Bruce Springsteen were among its many celebrity members.[18] "Mike asked me if she could train her clients in the gym," Dave recalled. "I said, 'Certainly, of course!' I believe Mike was supporting and finding clients for her."[19]

Meanwhile, Ray Mentzer's gym, Future Fitness, was doing well. It had a hard-core bodybuilding atmosphere that attracted not only serious strength athletes but also those looking to get into top shape. Word had spread quickly about his gym — and of Ray's prodigious feats of strength, such as performing two full repetitions in the barbell squat with 905 pounds across his shoulders.[20]

Things took an upward turn for Mike when entrepreneur Jim Kohls of Stewart Communications sought to capitalize on the public's growing interest in fitness by publishing a new magazine — and he hired Mike to be its associate publisher and editor-in-chief. Mike shared with the entrepreneur his vision for a soft-core bodybuilding publication that catered to *total fitness* — mental and physical — and for resistance training as its emphasis:

> Nautilus training, barbell training, per se, is the only single activity that allows you to enhance the four components of physical fitness within that one activity — not having to spread it out over a number of activities. The four components, of course, being muscular strength, cardiovascular fitness, flexibility and — one that's not mentioned very often — stress reduction.[21]

Mike's experience carried weight with the people at Stewart Communications. As he had worked as an editor and writer for the biggest magazine in the industry, in addition to authoring bestselling books on the subject, he seemed the perfect person to helm their new fitness publication. Mike enjoyed having a definite purpose present in his life once again; he likened the challenge of putting a magazine together and meeting production schedules to preparing for bodybuilding competition. "Every day for 18 months it was like I was training for the Mr. Olympia," he recalled. "I wanted to make that magazine the absolute best I could make it. I did everything I possibly could to achieve that."[22]

He wasn't exaggerating. Mike wrote the editorial for each issue, in addition to two or three articles. He selected the magazine's content and cover images, coordinated the athlete and celebrity profiles and interviews, oversaw the art department, worked with the copy editors, and dealt with the distributors. It was a job with a huge amount of responsibility, but he loved every minute of it. The name of the publication was *Workout for Fitness*, and Mike made its mission statement known in his very first editorial:

> For a publisher, the easiest part of formulating an editorial philosophy is knowing what you don't want in a magazine. For

instance, *Workout* will never exist for the aggrandizement of any individual, nor will it cater to the cult of personality. And we'll never distort the facts or slant information to push products. Our first obligation is to our readers, not our advertisers.[23]

Over the course of the next year, *Workout for Fitness* featured articles by those with PhDs (including Ellington Darden from Nautilus) in exercise and nutrition, psychology, and motivation techniques, in addition to celebrity and athlete profiles and book reviews. Mike was even able to insert some philosophy into its pages. He provided Ray with a free ad in the publication to advertise his gym and any mail-order products he wished to sell. For the moment at least, the future was looking very bright indeed.

Soon, Mike found himself invited to parties hosted by members of high society, which occasionally he felt obliged to attend. At one such event that Mike and Julie attended, the guests were mostly professional people — dentists, doctors, occupational therapists.[24] As part of the evening's entertainment, the host hired a psychic, who met with each couple and told them things about themselves: what had happened in their past and what would happen in their future. After these meetings, the couples broke into groups and compared their experiences. Evidently the psychic was convincing, as most of the guests stated how impressed they were with his clairvoyance. After Mike and Julie had met with him, they ventured back to the main room and sat down on a couch. Suddenly another couple approached.

"Oh, God!" gushed the woman. "Wasn't he *great*? Didn't he tell you neat things about what you're going to do in the future?"

"You don't really believe that, do you?" Mike asked.

"Well, of course! Didn't he impress you? Didn't he get specific about what happened to you in the past and what will happen in the future?"

"Well, he spoke in generalities. And he was very good at picking up on certain character traits. Like, he told us about our relationship based on our body language and so forth. He's very sensitive and he picked up on those things. I was quite impressed, yeah. But he has *no* psychic abilities."

Mike's reply angered the woman's husband, who now entered the conversation.

"What makes you so arrogant?"

The woman tried to calm him down, but Mike gestured that it was okay. He sometimes relished an argument — and this was one of those times.

"That's the highest compliment I've had in weeks," Mike replied. "I'm not arrogant, I'm self-confident. You failed to make the distinction, but I'll still take it as a compliment."

The husband was seething.

"They were all getting very combative," Mike recalled. "I couldn't believe it. They wanted to believe in another reality so bad. Their emotional investment in this went down to their fundamental view of reality. And once you shake that, you shake their entire belief in the core of their own being. It scares them. Their entire metaphysical view of the universe gets disturbed. And I tell you, I didn't realize what impact it would have, but I made the statement right after that, I said, 'You know what it really is about all of you? It's not that you want to believe in a *realer* reality, which is a contradiction, it's that you don't like *this* reality.' And they all gasped. And I was right, and it was true. And one guy goes, 'Well, I don't really hate this reality, but I wish I could have all my ways.'"

Mike had discovered that science and reason were as unwelcome at Hollywood cocktail parties as they were in the Master Blaster's magazines.

Over the next several months, Mike continued to work away at the magazine. His efforts were paying off, as both the newsstand sales and advertising for *Workout for Fitness* were increasing. But despite his focus, the dark clouds of mental illness had started closing in. He could sense it. He thought it might be temporary; he'd had such experiences before, and they often passed after a time. Just as he had totally given himself over to preparing for the Mr. Olympia contest, he attempted to do bring the same single-mindedness to the creation of each issue of the publication. His every waking hour was devoted to the magazine — and he extended those waking hours by once again using amphetamines.[25] It was, he thought, like when he was writing alongside Jack Neary; they'd periodically pop a Black Beauty and then spend all night working. It was no big deal. But with Jack this only happened occasionally. Now it was a continual occurrence. Often were the times that Mike would go without sleep for two to three days straight.[26] He was burning the candle at both ends, and his brain and nervous system could only take so much. And by late August of 1985, they had reached their breaking point.

Ray Mentzer was holding court in his Redondo Beach gym — and ranting. He had just returned from a seminar tour in Europe and Australia and was sharing news of what had happened to him. Among those listening to him were an off-duty police officer (a member at his gym), some bodybuilding friends, and Mike. While in Europe, Ray said, he had spoken out publicly against corruption within the bodybuilding industry.[27] He even went so far as to name names. When word got back to one of the people Ray had named, a president of one of the bodybuilding federations, he sent a thug in his employ overseas to tell Ray that he was treading on thin ice, that he had better keep his mouth shut or when he returned to California it would be in a pine box.[28] This marked the first time in either brother's experience that one of their lives had been threatened. Since Mike had been very open in his criticism of professional bodybuilding over the years and was now the associate publisher of a magazine that was in direct competition with Joe Weider's, he paid close attention to every word coming out of his brother's mouth. He attempted to reason with him.

"Ray, if this is true, it might behoove you to be quiet about it, you know? Just in case. In real life these things do happen — where you get killed by hitmen."[29]

Ray, however, did not believe that discretion was the better part of valor. "Ah, not me! Fuck it! I'm not going to let any fear of these fuckers stop me from taking it to the hilt!"

Now the off-duty police officer spoke up in an effort to calm Ray down. "You know, Ray, maybe Mike's right. Maybe you ought to just cool it for a little while until the heat dies down."

"Nah, fuck it. Not me! I'm not afraid of them!"

"He kept it up," Mike recalled. "He was obsessed about it. And I could see the cop was getting unnerved." Mike wanted to leave. However, as his car was in the shop, he asked the off-duty policeman (whom we know only by the name of Rob) if he wouldn't mind giving Mike a lift to Manhattan Beach to "get away from Ray for a while." Rob was agreeable to this, and the pair left Future Fitness, hopped in the officer's car, and headed north towards Manhattan Beach. As they drove, they continued to speak about what Ray had said back at the gym.

"You know, Mike," Rob said, "you and Ray do threaten a lot of people in bodybuilding. Maybe you ought to get him to be quiet."

"I agree, you know? But I'm not my brother."

Soon the pair arrived in Manhattan Beach, and Mike stepped out of the vehicle. Before closing the car door, Rob suggested that Mike hire some retired police officers who lived in the area for protection and promised to leave some phone numbers of ex-cops he knew at Ray's gym. Mike should give them a call. And with that, he pulled away.

Mike started walking along a sidewalk in Manhattan Beach. But he wasn't thinking straight. His amphetamine use had kept him awake for the past two nights, which had lowered his resistance to his mental illness. A powerful psychosis now descended upon him. He looked at the cars driving past him and was startled to see one of the men his brother had indicated was a hitman for one of the bodybuilding federations staring at him as he drove past. It's hard to say if what Mike saw was real, the result of his mental illness, or the result of an amphetamine-induced psychosis.[30] Whatever it was, it unsettled him further. He quickly dashed into a variety store and peered out the shop window to see if the hitman was still in the vicinity. He wasn't. Mike made his move; he dashed out of the store and ran until he came to a crosswalk. The red signal flashed at him, indicating not to proceed. While he waited impatiently for the light to change, another of the hitmen Ray mentioned drove past. Or at least that's what Mike thought. Now Mike was convinced he was being followed. Several months later he would tell the author:

> It could have been a coincidence, but I thought, "Two minutes ago, Ray told me about all this — and now I see two hitmen!" I thought, "I'm not crazy but they might be after me — who knows?" And I wasn't sure, so . . . I wasn't, like, crazed out of my mind, but I started sweating a little bit, you know? And I didn't know what to do. I thought, "Fuck it, if they are after me and they wanted to hit me they could do it very fuckin' easily, and how could I get out of here?" I thought what I should do is call the local police and have them escort me out of town. Which seemed to me to be reasonable.

It wasn't. And neither was his next move. Mike didn't wait for the crosswalk signal to change, he darted across the street and into the nearest building he could find, which happened to be a bank.

It was a decision that would prove to have disastrous consequences.

CHAPTER THIRTY

THE STORM AND THE LIGHT

U pon entering the bank, Mike looked around for a security guard. Not spotting one, he decided that he would seek out the manager. He was sweating now — and highly agitated. He periodically turned to look out through the large windows, his eyes flitting from car to car to see if the hitmen were still outside stalking him.

The bank was full of customers, the tellers were occupied. He looked on as a client stood up and shook hands with the manager. When the man exited the office, Mike drew a deep breath, tried his best to appear calm, and approached the bank manager.

"Excuse me."[1]

The manager looked up from his desk.

"Yes?"

"I'm not trying to alarm you, but I have the suspicion I'm being followed by someone out there. I could be wrong. But just in case, would you mind calling the local police to maybe have an undercover man escort me out of town?"

Certainly, it was a very odd request. Yet the manager took the news casually. The manager now stood up. "You know, curiously enough, sir, something similar happened a few weeks ago and the undercover police were very helpful."

"Great."

"Just have a seat here and I'll call them."

Mike felt his blood pressure go down about ten points. He remained seated as the manager left the office. Recognizing that he needed to have a location for the undercover officer to drop him off at, Mike pivoted the phone on the bank manager's desk around so that it was facing him and dialed the number of Rex Dante. After a few rings, Rex picked up and Mike began telling him about his predicament. "So here I am feeling relieved, you know?" Mike said. "I thought, 'I'll go home shortly and go to bed, and this will all be over.'"

It didn't work out that way.

As Mike was talking to Rex on the phone, a uniformed police officer entered the bank manager's office. He walked directly over to Mike and demanded that he leave the bank. This wasn't the plainclothes policeman Mike had requested. He stood up and told the officer he wasn't going anywhere. The policeman raised his voice, repeating that Mike had to leave the building. Rex was still on the line; he heard the exchange taking place. Things escalated incredibly fast. The officer must have been intimidated by Mike's physical size — he drew his gun and announced that Mike was under arrest. He radioed for backup on his walkie-talkie. "There I was feeling threatened already, waiting for police protection, and here a cop pulls a gun on me," Mike recalled. "I was scared; I thought he was literally going to blow my brains out! I mean, why should I suspect otherwise?" He thought that the man now standing before him might be a member of the hit squad Ray had spoken about — and there was no way he was going to let this guy put handcuffs on him. Believing his life to be in danger, Mike took the offensive. His left hand darted out, grabbing hold of the officer's arm that held the gun. With his right, Mike ripped the walkie-talkie out of the officer's hand and now started hammering him in the head with it. The officer hit the ground, whereupon Mike continued battering him.

The sound of police sirens echoed in from outside. Looking out through the bank window, Mike saw three squad cars pull up to front of the building. "Within a minute and 30 seconds, three squad cars were on the sidewalk, sirens going, lights flashing," Mike recalled. When he saw the six doors of the three cruisers fly open simultaneously, Mike knew he was in serious trouble. He ran to the front door of the bank and tried to bull his way through the police officers, but there were too many of them. Soon he was taken down to the pavement — and that's when the beatdown began:

> I was on the ground. It was three in the afternoon in front of a bank full of people. They hit me with their night sticks, poking me, kicking me. I thought I was going to die. But I resisted — not by hitting back; never once did I strike back.

I just laid there. I tensed up, you know how you tense up to protect yourself against the pain? Finally, I got so tired — it seemed like it was forever — that I said to myself, 'I was always curious about what death was like, but I sure didn't think it would come *this* soon. But now that it's happening, I really want to experience what it's like going out.' So, I totally relaxed and gave in to it. Obviously, it didn't happen, but . . . [they] beat the living piss out of me, and almost blew my brains out, I guess. One of the guys that works in the police station told me later, 'Mike, you don't know this, but they almost blew your body to bits!' They were one-tenth of a second away from killing me. It's hard to describe the experience; to have nine guys on top of you like that. And you can't see; my eyes were closed tight. All I saw was this dark greyness and this feeling of pain.

The officers slapped handcuffs on Mike and cinched them up until they cut into his wrists. "I had big chunks of meat taken out of my wrists," Mike recalled. "They put the cuffs on and squeezed them as hard as they could; any movement you make makes it go tighter. I was in agony. I couldn't believe it." The officers placed shackles on Mike's legs and jerked him to his feet. By now a crowd had gathered. "They were talking about putting me in the back of the K-9 car with the dogs. I saw 'K-9' on the car they were dragging me toward. I thought, 'Dog-gone, they're going to put me in that car and those dogs are going to chew me to bits!' I thought they were telling the truth! They put me in there and the dogs weren't there. I was scared beyond belief." Mike screamed out to the crowd that he had done nothing wrong, that he wasn't a criminal, but the crowd simply looked on in silence.

The police drove Mike to a nearby hospital to have him checked medically for injuries and also to test his blood for any drugs he might be under the influence of. Both during the examination and while waiting for the test results, Mike was strapped down on a gurney. Upon his entry to the hospital, there was a cadre of deputies awaiting his arrival, many of whom were bodybuilders. One deputy recognized him and called out, "Hey Mentzer, what the fuck are you doing here?" According to Mike:

> During the course of my being strapped down on this gurney, about an hour and a half or two hours, it's hard to tell with those

things, I was highly conscious, because I wanted to figure out what was going on here? How could this be happening to me?

After the medical checkup came the criminal charges. Evidently Mike's blood test came back negative, as he was not charged with a code 11550 (being under the influence of a controlled substance). He was, however, charged with a code 148 (resisting arrest), a code 245.B (assault with a deadly weapon other than a firearm), a code 243.C (battery on a police officer), and, thrown on top of the pile, a code V 21461.5 (pedestrian failed to obey a sign or signal, such as a crosswalk, stop sign, traffic signal). The date the charges were filed was October 10, 1985. A trial date was set for some time in the new year, and Mike was released on bail. He faced a very uncertain future.

It should be mentioned that, as Mike lay strapped down on a gurney and left unattended in the hallway of the hospital, he picked up on snippets of conversations that were going on down the hall, out of his line of sight. He was positive that he heard the voice of Arnold Schwarzenegger. But it wasn't Arnold, of course. It was the chemical disorder in his brain, along with Ray's talk of hitmen, which had left him convinced that nefarious characters were pursuing him. It was this psychosis that had caused him to ignore a simple crosswalk signal, which evidently was what had prompted the police officer to follow him into the bank in the first place.

Since there were no drugs found in his system (the blood test at the hospital and lack of charges by the police spoke to this), we are left to conclude that his erratic behavior was the result of his mental illness. There had to have been signs that his grip on reality was weakening prior to this incident. If there were, however, he had either ignored them or his altered mental state had been a process so gradual, that he hadn't detected it.

When Ray learned of Mike's arrest, he immediately phoned their father back in Ephrata and told him the news. Mike had always been Harry's favorite, and Ray saw this as an opportunity to level the playing field in terms of his father's affection. He almost delighted in pointing out that Mike was not the shining star of the Mentzer family that their father once believed him to be. The news troubled Harry, who phoned Mike to find out if what Ray had told him was true. Mike said what he could to pacify his father, but throughout the conversation he insisted that he was still being followed — by whom or to what purpose he didn't reveal. Harry didn't know what to do. He called his brother Charles and shared his concerns.[2] He wanted to be with Mike, but a gulf of 2,650 miles separated them. When he again phoned his son and offered to come to California, Mike turned him down. He was fine. Ray's talk about his erratic mental state and amphetamine use was ridiculous. Harry didn't believe him and was understandably worried that his boy was heading down a very dark road.

To make matters worse, it's highly probable that the financier of *Workout for Fitness* magazine found out about the incident. It wouldn't do to have the publication's editor-in-chief going around assaulting police officers. Moreover, while the magazine was gaining popularity, it hadn't been the out-of-the-gate success its publisher had hoped for. A *New York Times* article bearing the ominous title "Fitness Explosion: Why Many Titles May Not Last" quoted John Suhler, the president of an investment banking firm that specialized in media properties, as saying, "There's got to be some kind of shakeout coming. On the fitness side especially, there are too many of them [magazines], and they all look too much alike."[3] One of the magazines included in the photo that accompanied the article was *Workout for Fitness*.

The end came as Mike was preparing to send the tenth issue of the magazine to the printer. "I got a call one day that no more money was going to be given to *Workout* magazine, and I was left high and dry. It was a blow. I'd put 110 percent into it, and it hadn't worked out. The magazine had been the central focus of my life for a year and a half."[4] In a matter of 24 hours, Mike was out of a job and out of money — and he had nothing on the horizon save a court date that could see him sent to jail for assaulting a police officer.

At this point in the narrative the author must, as Will Durant wrote in his book *The Mansions of Philosophy*, "ask permission to be personal . . . and to use the favorite pronoun freely,"[5] as I must draw upon my direct experience with Mike in order to tell the remainder of his story.

In December 1985, I was writing articles for the British bodybuilding magazine *Bodybuilding Monthly*. The editor-in-chief of the publication was Chris Lund, who also happened to be the premier photographer in the industry. I had befriended Chris when he ran a bodybuilding supply store on Dundonald Street in downtown Toronto. Knowing that I was a university student with a keen interest in exercise physiology, he suggested that I could earn some money by writing articles for his publication. I was only too happy to oblige. Apart from training articles, he also wanted me to conduct interviews with top bodybuilders, so that he could publish photographs he had taken of them along with the articles I wrote.

I set about writing letters of request for interviews to several top bodybuilders I had long wanted to speak with, champions such as Lou Ferrigno, Arnold Schwarzenegger, Frank Zane, and Steve Reeves. However, the name at the top of my list was Mike Mentzer. To my way of thinking, he was the only bodybuilder that brought a knowledge of exercise science to bear on his training. At the two seminars of his that I attended in 1980 and 1981, he struck me as a man from whom one could learn a lot. In fact, it was an interview with Mike I read in 1981 that had sparked my interest in philosophy. He had spoken about existentialism and the writings of Nietzsche, and how existentialists believed that each person was responsible for their own life. That hooked me and inspired me to major in philosophy in university. Again, I took him to be a man that one could learn from, in terms of both mind and body. I knew nothing at this point about the mental illness Mike suffered from, nor of his misdemeanors at the bank.

In due course I received replies from everyone but Steve Reeves. Arnold's publicist at the time was Charlotte Parker, who informed me that Arnold only spoke with high-profile magazines, which *Bodybuilding Monthly* definitely wasn't. Living in Bracebridge (a small town about two hours north of Toronto), I was completely unaware of the goings-on behind the scenes in professional bodybuilding and was simply a fan who wanted to know and share whatever training tips these pros used that had resulted in their phenomenal levels of muscle growth. While steroid use was known, the extent of its use and the potency of these drugs were not, at least among lay people. While disappointed that I wouldn't get an opportunity to speak with Arnold, I received enough callbacks from the remaining bodybuilders that my schedule filled up quickly. Phone calls were exchanged, days and times for interviews arranged, and I booked a flight to Los Angeles and arranged a car rental. My training partner at the time was Stephen Langevin, who was not only a big Mike Mentzer fan but also the person who first brought Mike to my attention shortly after my parents and I had moved to Bracebridge in 1980. I asked him if he wanted to tag along with me and meet some of the bodybuilders. And so, in early January 1986, Stephen and I found ourselves on an airplane bound for California.

Upon checking into the hotel, I phoned Mike, who was then living in an apartment in West Hollywood. When he indicated that he would soon be heading to Gold's Gym for a workout, I suggested that Stephen and I swing by and pick him up and we could all go to the gym together. This would allow me to take some shots of him training that could run with the interview. Mike was agreeable to this, and so Stephen and I hopped in the rental car and headed northeast from Santa Monica to West Hollywood. It turned out to be one of the most interesting days of my life. Mike was fascinating. Not only was it fun to watch him work out, to see how he implemented the principles of his training system, but afterwards he freely shared his thoughts on the goings-on within professional bodybuilding:

- *On steroid abuse*: "Well, there are those who would contend that since it is intended for medical use, any dosage at all intended for athletic use is abuse. *Use* and *abuse* would be interchangeable. Obviously, a lot of athletes don't agree. And I certainly don't. We live in a chemical age, everything is chemical — even the food we eat. And this is not intended as a rationalization, but let's face it; even the ones who are screaming about how unethical it is to take drugs are sitting there drinking coffee and smoking a cigarette, both of which are chemicals and drugs."
- *The lure of tradition in bodybuilding*: "Almost 99 percent of all bodybuilders — in fact 99 percent of most people — do everything that they do because other people do it. They do what they do out of convention, imitation, tradition, and outright fear — fear of being different. Rather than risk disapproval or alienation from the group, they completely go along and do what they see others doing. That was always the large reason for the marathon-type training. Most bodybuilders have no interests outside of the gym, and it's one of the few areas where they feel any degree of control or efficacy. And they like the feedback, and the slapping on the back, the camaraderie that their gym-mates give them. What they've done is elevated a social need into a training method."
- *On the importance of recovery to the muscle growth process*: "There is a limited amount of recovery ability, a limited amount of growth ability, and both are connected to the body's energy systems. Whenever you have anything that exists in limited

quantities, it only makes sense to use it as economically as possible. So the ideal training routine is one that stimulates maximum muscle growth with the least amount of taxation or demand on the recovery ability, so that you have enough recovery ability and growth ability left over to grow on."

- *Why Nautilus was receiving so much negative press in Joe Weider's magazines*: "Without question because Nautilus threatens the metaphysics — the worldview — of the barbell manufacturers and the traditionalists within bodybuilding. Nautilus Enterprises and Arthur Jones were the first organization to do large-scale research. They were the first to widely disseminate information that directly opposed the prevailing worldview. The barbell manufacturers rightfully saw a real commercial threat to their once previously unthreatened market, and they wanted to try to derail this locomotive that was bearing down upon them. They did not succeed, however. They did so within the bodybuilding subculture, so to speak, but within the wider framework of the entire fitness market Nautilus has prevailed, without question."

- *On his confrontation with Arnold Schwarzenegger at the 1980 Mr. Olympia contest*: "What transpired was a heated argument, almost a physical confrontation, which arose from Arnold's behavior; from the disdain he showed to his fellow competitors. I, for one, was stunned at the unwillingness or the inability of the IFBB to control Arnold's behavior and his aggressiveness during this particular episode. He was entirely out of control. At that point, I lost a little bit of my own control. I was getting very, very psyched up and aggressive for the contest, which was imminent. I mean, we were literally moments away from the prejudging. Everybody was seething back there, waiting to tear off their sweatsuits and start pumping up so they could release some of this burgeoning energy and aggression they were harboring. Anyway, I shot out at him as though I were going to grab him. That was my first impulse. But by the time I arrived at his side — he was some 20 or 30 feet away — I had settled down. I didn't actually reach out to grab him, although Ben Weider and a few others thought I was [going to], and they were about to intercede and grab me. I made it apparent that I was not going to grab Arnold, but I put my finger right in his face and he sat back down like a little child! I forget exactly what I said to him, but it was something to the effect that he wasn't treating his fellow competitors properly, and I was not going to accept this kind of behavior. And I put my finger in his face while saying this and he refused to look at me! He was so embarrassed, which he should have been, that he couldn't look me in the eye — or anybody else!"

At this point, Julie McNew entered the gym. Mike made the introductions, and Julie struck both Stephen and me as being very fit, and very charming. Mike — clearly — was madly in love with her. He told us that he was going to downtown Los Angeles later that evening to attend a memory class taught by Rex Dante and asked if we'd be interested in tagging along. With no real plans (my next scheduled interview, with former Mr. Olympia winner Frank Zane, wouldn't take place until the next day), I informed him that our evening was free, and that we would drop by to pick him up and then head off together to the memory class.

We picked Mike up at eight o'clock. En route, I decided to interview him about philosophy, of which he possessed a surprisingly encyclopedic knowledge. During the car ride he spoke on epistemology, ethics, and the various beliefs of the different philosophic schools regarding how human beings formulate concepts. I plied him with questions from the backseat of the car (Mike was in the passenger seat, Stephen was driving) about his philosophic views. His replies were extemporaneous and (to me, at least) fascinating:

- *On Ethics*: "Ethics is a derivative branch of philosophy, the fundamentals being metaphysics and epistemology. My ethics — actually, the ethical system I subscribe to — is based on Ayn Rand's philosophy, Objectivist philosophy, and would be known as 'rational self-interest.' I believe that selfishness is a virtue, and that there are two aspects of selfishness. Part A: one must have a hierarchy of values set according to one's long-range self-interest. And Part B: one should never sacrifice a higher value for a lower value. Most people mistake selfishness with vulgar whim-worshipping. They have a vision of some brute trampling over others to get whatever it is he wants. But a genuinely selfish person knows that that kind of whim-worshipping will ultimately lead to his destruction. A genuinely selfish person wants to live long-range and be happy long-range, and so he takes time to consider what his desires and wants are. He doesn't act blindly or impulsively on them but considers their long-range effect on his survival and his happiness. That's 'rational self-interest,' or 'enlightened self-interest,' if you prefer."[6]

- *On a Supreme Being*: "The entire question to me at this point in my life is nonessential and unimportant. Even if there were a Supreme Being, which I don't think there is, it's become quite obvious to me throughout the course of my life that 'His' existence, or 'Its' existence, in no direct way, has any direct bearing or impinges upon my daily life or activities or issues, from moment to moment. Anything which I am or am not is the direct result of my own choice or abdication thereof. It's not really that important to me, at this point, again, whether or not there is a Supreme Being. I really don't think there is."
- *The ultimate grounds of knowledge*: "Its baseline or axiomatic concept is that existence exists. That's the first fact upon which all subsequent knowledge is based. Its 'ultimate grounds' are the two axiomatic concepts: 'existence exists' and 'there is a consciousness that perceives its existence.' A is A. That's the edifice upon which the rest of human knowledge is built. That's the first: axiomatics. An apple is an apple; an apple can't be an orange. There is an objective reality out there."
- *The nature of concepts*: "Before Ayn Rand, there were four basic schools of thought regarding the nature of concepts: the Platonic, the Aristotelian, the Nominalist, and the Realist. None of them were Objectivist at all. The first two, the Platonic and Aristotelian, were intrinsic; they believed that concepts revealed, somehow, through non-sensory means, the universal essence of things. That *this* was not *real* reality — even Aristotle believed that to some degree but in a lesser form than Plato. The other ones referred to are subjectivist — the Nominalist and the Realist. And they believe that consciousness

produced reality and concepts. They didn't believe in the Primacy of Existence but [in the] Primacy of Consciousness. And they believed that concepts were produced, and reality was produced, by the mind. It's so ridiculous. Ayn Rand came up with the only real nature of concepts. Concepts aren't created by the mind, nor are they revealed by the mind. They have to be gained by the mind through sensory means, and then given a definition by using a specific word for each. Denotation is a very important part of Objectivist Epistemology. The importance and nature of definitions and words — and, of course, how we get them — is through perception and reason. There is an objective reality out there, which we perceive. If there was no objective reality, if that were true, it's the "fallacy of self-exclusion"; we couldn't even be talking right now. Every single word we use has its reference in reality. The very fact that there is an independent reality allows us to communicate."

- *Animal cognition versus human cognition*: "Human cognition combines perception and concept formation. Animal cognition is purely perceptual. The thing that makes us unique is the perceptual combined with the conceptual. The important thing to say about that is the first aspect is involuntary — the perceptual — it requires no choice. But in order to engage the second part of the human mind — the conceptual — requires volition, an act of choice. Only when you do that are you really of the species 'Man.' Unless you continually make the choice to think, you are in the animal or perceptual realm. You're perceiving and reacting; you're not thinking or contextualizing; looking for similarities and differences."
- *On Man's purpose in the Universe*: "Man has no function outside of that which he creates and defines for himself. What you're asking would presuppose a 'Designer,' or a God, of which there is none."[7]

And this was all tossed out casually as we were driving along the 405 freeway on the way to Rex Dante's class! It was also en route to our destination that Mike felt comfortable enough to share what happened regarding his recent legal trouble. He had to have been comfortable, as I was a member of the bodybuilding press and could very easily have written an article about the incident that would no doubt have sold some additional copies of *Bodybuilding Monthly* and been picked up with some eagerness by Joe Weider's writers, who would have relished printing it. Instead, I sat on this information for some 40 years until writing this book. Mike was never one to pedestalize himself or to only share self-serving accounts of his life and career. If you were friends with Mike, you had better be prepared for honesty right down to the floorboards. That's what he gave of himself to friends, and what he expected his friends to give to him in return. He was interested in an honest sharing of the human experience, not a dream world portrait. Reality as it is.

After the in-car discussion, I found Rex Dante's class material to be somewhat of a letdown. In truth, I came away wondering how Mike had been so impressed by him. Mind you, it may have been Dante's approach — we all sat in classroom chairs (the ones where a small tabletop or desk is attached to the chair) and he said things like:

- "Be a progressionist not a perfectionist."
- "Applaud your mistakes because you stepped outside of your habit."

And then he had people applaud themselves when they made a mistake in accurately recollecting a series of words that he had strung together. It seemed a pointless exercise to me that I would forget as soon as I left the building, which, in fact, I did (presently, I can only recall that one of words we were to recite was *Barbasol*). Certainly, by comparison, Dante's mnemonic method for retaining information was not nearly as exciting as the dialogue Mike and I had shared during our drive to his class.

It didn't matter how simple or esoteric my question was, Mike had an answer. To have such a professorial mind encased within a champion bodybuilder's physique was an anomaly I had never encountered before or since. It made the remaining interviews I conducted that week seem remedial and flat. The big muscles these bodybuilders had, or the movie and television success certain of them enjoyed, seemed vapid when contrasted with the issues of existence that Mike and I had discussed. I was fascinated; I had come to California to learn about building bigger biceps and returned to Canada with a headful of philosophy.

The interviews I obtained proved popular with the readers of *Bodybuilding Monthly*. So popular, in fact, that Chris Lund asked me to return to California and obtain some more.

I phoned Mike to tell him I would be returning but hadn't booked a hotel at this point. "No need for that," he told me. "You can stay at my place." And so, once again, I returned to California where I ended up spending a very enjoyable week with Mike, going out for meals together, talking training, philosophy, and any other subject that popped into our heads.

After one of our discussions, Mike suggested that we head over to Julie's apartment. That was when it dawned on me that Mike and Julie were no longer a couple. They had evidently broken up but remained good friends and occasional lovers. I felt comfortable asking Mike about their relationship during the drive to her place. He seemed put off by the situation; Julie was living in an apartment that was paid for by another man she was seeing, who I gathered was an older patron of the gym she was training clients out of. Mike had told me that, given his recent unemployment, she had asked Mike what he could offer her going forward. "Just true love," he had replied. Nice though the sentiment was, she couldn't pay the rent with it, and so she went with the better offer.

After spending some time at Julie's, we decided to head out to a nearby video store. Browsing the shelves, I happened upon a documentary entitled *Bruce Lee: The Legend*. Having been a longtime fan of the martial arts icon, I purchased it and told Mike and Julie that we needed to watch it. Mike was agreeable, and we returned to Julie's apartment for an afternoon of watching videos. The documentary was well-received, and afterwards we watched *Cyrano de Bergerac* (the José Ferrer version). According to Mike, Ferrer perfectly personified the Objectivist ideal of the hero: the person who combined body and mind; an expert swordsman, poet, and philosopher, who lived his life with full fidelity to the romantic ideal of refusing to be part of the herd and completely fulfilling his human potential. Mike next popped in a video of the 21-minute W.C. Fields film *The Dentist* (1932), which was hilarious. We noted with some amusement how much the comedic actor's voice reminded us of Joe Weider's. At this point, Julie informed us that her partner would be returning to the apartment soon, and so Mike and I had to leave. All in all, it was an enjoyable afternoon.

Prior to my return to Canada, Mike presented me with three editions of *The Objectivist Forum*, a bimonthly publication containing articles on current events written by Objectivist philosophers. Each issue of the publication was well-worn and contained Mike's underlining of passages he found significant, in addition to his marginalia. The publications provided some interesting reading material for the flight home, and represented a nice memento of the many discussions Mike and I had that week.

Back in Canada, I resolved to learn more about Objectivism, as I wanted to engage with Mike about it on a higher level of understanding. Flipping through the Second Renaissance Books catalog (which Mike also gave me), I happened upon some audio courses offered for rental by Dr. Leonard Peikoff, a man who was not only Ayn Rand's intellectual and legal heir but also had a PhD in philosophy. Peikoff recorded an extensive (36-hour) audio course on "The Philosophy of Objectivism." I ended up renting the course, which took a full week to get through, but proved to be very stimulating intellectually.

Not that I ever became an Objectivist. I've never felt comfortable being a "member" of anything. I preferred reasoning things out based upon my own life experiences over simply accepting the conclusions of someone else, however brilliant that person's mind happened to be. Like most students who studied philosophy in university, I was taught that since a human being lives but a short time, perhaps 80 years, it is exceedingly difficult, if not impossible, to come to definitive conclusions on most (or any) subject matter simply because a solitary human mind lacks the total perspective required to see and understand all sides of an issue — and 80 years is simply not enough time to accumulate sufficient knowledge to make definitive statements about anything. Even Socrates was quoted by Plato as saying that he was the wisest man in Athens simply because he was the only person who knew that he knew nothing. Consequently, professors of philosophy believed (and so transmitted to their students) that, at best, we can hold tentative truths, which may be discarded should we acquire sufficient evidence to the contrary. In other words, no one can be *certain* about anything.

But what I found intriguing about Peikoff's position was that he, too, had been taught the same things. He had listened to the professors' explanations, but (unlike me) had replied, in essence: You contend that nobody can know anything, and yet you state this as a categorical fact. Therefore, we can at least know *that*. And if we can know that, then, perhaps we can know something else. And perhaps something else beyond this. In other words, we *can* be certain about things, and we can, despite our short span of 80 years, come to know an absolute truth by your very words. And if we can know one truth, why can't we know another? And isn't it worth the attempt? The Objectivist position, then, was that if we can know truth, we *can* acquire knowledge.

Expanding knowledge is what distinguishes (and advances) our species. All art, literature, music, and science are predicated on the progression or transmission of knowledge — to proceed with the knowledge that we can do or accomplish something. This is the bedrock of human progress. What the majority of philosophy professors taught was the demolition of that bedrock, or at least the attempt to demolish it. But they had to embrace a categorical statement (or ultimate truth) to deny it; in other words, they had to use it to refute it. Therefore, they were contradicting themselves. One *can* be certain, the Objectivists believed. And it was this recognition and embrace of certainty that flew in the face of what was being taught in philosophy classes throughout the world.

Any time I asked my philosophy professors about Ayn Rand's philosophy, they dismissed it out of hand. It was clear to me by their evasiveness that none of them had ever lowered themselves to read it. Moreover, Rand was not part of the old boys' academic club. In her era, the simple fact that she was a woman meant that her ideas were not taken seriously by academia. Furthermore, professional intellectuals were enraged that she challenged premises they took as axioms. An objective assessment of her philosophy could never be obtained from those who most militantly opposed it (such as philosophy professors) any more than one would expect to hear good things spoken of Republicans by Democrats or of Democrats by Republicans. It was a case of conflicting ideologies. Leonard Peikoff would tell me some years later that the pushback from those who championed the entrenched philosophy was simply the natural way of things:

> There's been a lot of people in my lifetime who have disagreed with me vigorously. But remember, part of my profession is to argue with people and to promote certain ideas. And you can't have a philosophy that challenges the whole world, and the whole history, and all the basic premises, and expect people to nod and say how wonderful you are. You're putting your

head in a buzz saw. You know if you're defying the world, the world is going to defy you.⁸

Objectivism not only took Mike's individualism to its logical end point but revealed the inherent potential in everyone to become the heroes of their own story if they consistently based their reasoning on objective reality. A "hero," by Peikoff's definition, was a person who was a "completely consistent representative of a moral code, with the connotation that therefore if a man is going to be fully consistent on any code, he stands out from the vast majority of people who are hodgepodges. He has some kind of independence, strength, courage, that the ordinary person doesn't have."⁹

Objectivism revealed to Mike Mentzer that he didn't need to win a bodybuilding contest in order to fulfill his intellectual potential and live a productive life. He simply needed to consistently use his distinguishing human trait — his mind — to its fullest rational potential.

He tried to do this. He really did. But when a mind declares war on itself, it's hard to be rational.

CHAPTER THIRTY-ONE

DESCENT INTO MADNESS

Evidently, Mike's breakup with Julie was sudden, and he took it hard. Their father had asked Ray to give Mike a job at his gym, but Ray balked at the suggestion. Mike still harbored ill will towards the police for the beating they had administered to him and treated the off-duty officers who came to the gym with derision and disdain. "Mike was nasty to the gym's police officers," Vince Basile recalled, "and was bad for business."[1]

None of the news Ray was communicating to his father was good: Mike didn't have a job. Mike was out of money. He was depressed. He was manic. He was still using amphetamines. He had nothing in his life and nothing to look forward to. Added to Mike's list of woes was the news that his father had colon cancer.[2] He was being treated for it, but the prognosis wasn't encouraging. Whatever the chemicals were that caused Mike's depression, when they washed through his mind, no amount of reason, logic, or Ayn Rand could chase them away. He could get out of bed only when he self-medicated with speed; the drug stimulated the production of norepinephrine, serotonin, and dopamine in his brain sufficiently to elevate his mood to normal levels.[3]

But if the amphetamines took the edge off Mike's depression, they also kept him awake — for days. The mental exhaustion that followed these sleepless interludes beckoned delusions and paranoia to arrive. And they did; creeping into Mike's mind, pushing reason, logic, and reality aside. He knew the risk, but given that the alternative was immobilizing depression, he opted to take it.[4]

Having finished listening to Leonard Peikoff's audiocassette course "The Philosophy of Objectivism," I forwarded the tapes to a friend in California who was into Ayn Rand. I sent them along with the request that after he had a chance to hear them he drop them off at Mike's place, as I was certain Mike would enjoy their content. I gave my friend Mike's address and left a message on Mike's answering machine that my buddy would be dropping the tapes off later that week. A week later, I called my friend to see how it went and what he thought of Mike Mentzer. His reply alarmed me.

"Is he okay?"

"What do you mean?"

"He seemed paranoid to me."

I had not expected this.

"Based on what?"

"Well, I went to his place and knocked on the door. I heard a voice from inside say, 'Who is it?' I told him my name and jokingly added, 'I'm the keeper of the Peikoff tapes.' Mike opened the door and looked at me suspiciously. I told him your name, which relaxed him a bit. He told me, 'You can't be too careful.' I thought he was joking! 'What do you need to be careful about?' I asked. He just smiled and said, 'You see that grey van parked down the street?' I looked and saw a grey van parked against the curb along with several other cars. 'Yeah,' I said. Mike smirked and said, 'Well, you're a bright guy; you figure it out.' And with that, he closed the door."

Upon hanging up, I was deflated. Instead of hooking up a couple of Ayn Rand fans to discuss philosophy, I had sent my friend to the apartment of a man who was clearly in the grip of paranoia. The calm, rational Objectivist with whom I had spent a week in January was gone, replaced by a man who believed that he was being stalked. I immediately phoned Mike. I wanted to make sure that he was okay; perhaps my buddy had misinterpreted what he'd said. Mike didn't pick up, so I left a message on his answering machine; inquiring how he was doing and asking him to call me back.

He never did.

Ray Mentzer may have been hit the hardest by Mike's mental irregularities. Mike was more than a brother to him; he was Ray's hero, a status that Mike had held in his younger brother's eyes ever since they were children. He was the person Ray had patterned his life after. To stand by and witness his hero's gradual transition from demigod to flawed mortal was confusing and painful, leaving Ray feeling abandoned and without direction. It was this frustration and concern that had been the impetus behind his frantic calls to his father. Certainly, there was an element of schadenfreude; Ray had lived his life in Mike's shadow, so the sibling rivalry element was at play. But that aside, he wanted desperately for things to go back to the way they were before; to have Mike blaze the trail, to bring celebrity to the Mentzer name, and to open doors for him. It was the hope that their father might somehow be able to reverse what was happening to Mike, and that Mike would listen to him, that had prompted Ray to make the calls. Perhaps not wanting to witness the final act in the tragedy his brother's life had become, perhaps fearing for his own life (and heeding the advice of his police officer friend from the gym), Ray decided it was time to step away from his Redondo Beach gym and away from America. He packed his bags and headed to the other side of the earth: Australia. It was a move that would change his life — for the better.

Once Ray was out of the cult of the body that permeated the very air of California, the Land Down Under provided him an environment and opportunity for intellectual growth and, surprisingly, for family. Ray had fallen in love with a woman named Kathy, whom he had first met in May 1982. And in 1986 the couple became the proud parents of a baby girl, born in Brisbane, Australia, whom they named Dagny (after the brilliant and independent heroine from Ayn Rand's novel *Atlas Shrugged*).[5] Ray was present for her birth,[6] and the experience moved him profoundly. "That's probably one of the most peak-performance elements of my life — having my little girl," he told me in 1990. "It's unbelievable. I enjoy being a father. I wouldn't pass it up for anything."[7]

Fatherhood changed him; Ray started to soften around the edges; his guard loosened up. "The World's Strongest Bodybuilder"[8] was completely won over by his little girl and realized for the first time in his life that there were far more rewarding things than bodybuilding titles or being the biggest, strongest person in the gym. Indeed, he viewed the birth of his daughter as the proudest day of his life, much preferring to be identified by the title "father" than "Mr. America." Like his brother, he was reading a lot of Ayn Rand to improve his thinking. He wanted to live "a rational, logical, pro-life type of lifestyle; laissez-faire, give and take," he said. "For the past 15 years I've read a lot of Ayn Rand. I try to follow my philosophy as best I can. I mean, we all make mistakes, but I try to stick to my philosophy. People always try to condemn you for that, but that's what I try to follow the most. What's logical and pro-life without sacrificing yourself and being altruistic in that sense. I mean, altruism, Kantian philosophy, is pretty negative, really. At its root it's very evil."[9]

Ray's studying Objectivism had resulted in a desire for more balance in his life:

> Obviously, I want to try to be as well-rounded an individual as I can — meaning studying all areas of life. You've got to have a little bit of sensitivity. You've got to understand things, like even going out and appreciating flowers. I mean, would a bodybuilder say something like that?[10]

He gave up his steroid use, noting that when he had used steroids in the past, he became unemotional, cold, and insensitive, not giving of himself to anybody.[11] He wanted no part of that going forward with his daughter.[12] He wanted to spend as much time with her as possible and for her to be the center of his universe.[13] Dagny's existence caused him to question why he had ever used the drugs in the first place.

I was still writing articles for *Bodybuilding Monthly*. Chris Lund asked me to cover the 1986 Mr. Olympia contest, held on October 11 in Columbus, Ohio. It was a welcome reprieve, as it allowed the two of us to hook up, throw back a few Guinnesses, have some laughs, and take in the competition. During our time together, Chris shared a disturbing story he had heard about Mike, which he stressed he could not verify. He had received word that Mike had stopped his car in the middle of a street in Santa Monica and took off running through the traffic. I still didn't know anything about Mike's family history of mental illness, or his amphetamine use (there had been no evidence of either when I had stayed with him in California), but it was clear to me that *something* bad that happened to him. It disturbed me to think that my friend — a man known for his mind, his knowledge of science, psychology, and philosophy, a premed student — would suddenly have lost it. Mike's being incommunicado only exacerbated my concern. Upon returning home from the contest I called Julie, but she didn't have much to tell me other than it was true that Mike was acting very strange. I asked her to tell Mike to call me the next time she saw him. She promised me she would, but no call ever came.

Life was now hammering Mike Mentzer with a vengeance, as if demanding payment for the brief highlights it had allowed him to experience during his bodybuilding heyday. It took away his competitive career, his seminar bookings, his fiancée, his home in Palm Springs, his mail-order business, his employment at Nautilus, his new magazine, his girlfriend of five years, his relationship with his brother, and, on February 1, 1987, it took away his father. Harry Mentzer died in Lancaster, Pennsylvania, after a lengthy battle with colon cancer.[14] His obituary in the *New Era* newspaper condensed his life of 63 years into a single paragraph:

> Harry E. Mentzer, 63, a retired truck driver, died Sunday afternoon at Community Hospital of Lancaster after a long illness. A resident of 48 Cedar Acres Drive, he was the husband of the late Alta Jean McCord Mentzer, who died in July 1985. Mentzer retired in January 1985 after working as a truck driver for Kenosha Auto Transport Corp. He was a member of Teamsters Chauffeurs Local Union 771. Mentzer served in the U.S. Marine Corps during World War II. Surviving are two sons, Michael J., Los Angeles, and Raymond H., Pindara, Australia; three stepchildren: Dwayne L. Markley, Lititz; and Connie L., wife of Stephen R. Schmitt, and William J. Markley, both of Lancaster; three granddaughters; three brothers: Charles W., and Robert S., both of Ephrata; and Parke G., Lebanon; and two sisters, Mary K. Bixler, Akron, and Grace E., wife of Landis Martin, Lancaster.[15]

Despite their falling out in the 1960s over Mike's choosing to embrace bodybuilding over football, Harry had moved past that. Nobody was prouder than his dad when Mike appeared on television. Whether he was competing in a bodybuilding contest or the *Superstars* competition, being interviewed on *Merv Griffin*, or lending his expertise as a color commentator to CBS Sports — that was "Harry's boy." His friends and relatives had no doubt about that. There was a bond that existed between the father and son that wasn't predicated on proximity; the two were in each other's minds constantly, despite living on different coasts. And now Harry was gone.

Harry had lived with the mental illness of Mike's mother for over two decades, and he recognized the symptoms in his son. It troubled Mike that his last communication with his father had been to assure him that he was okay. It had been a lie. He felt he had betrayed the one person whose love for him had never ceased. The reports of Mike using amphetamines had upset Harry further. Mike believed he was telling his father the truth when he denied using drugs; after all, lots of people used amphetamines, from housewives to truck drivers to college students cramming for exams. To Mike, they weren't psychosis-inducing drugs but ergogenic aids for being more productive. And yet he knew that his father didn't believe that, and that Harry's final weeks were filled with anxiety and worry about him. Harry's death sent Mike into a freefall of depression, which he sought to alleviate by taking more amphetamines, which, in turn, caused him to go without sleep and become a ready recipient of the psychosis and delusions that always followed.

With no income, Mike could no longer pay the rent in his West Hollywood apartment. He soon was evicted — and left homeless. Things became so bad that in order to eat, he lowered himself to sneaking into hotels early in the morning to eat discarded scraps from room service trays.[16] The streets of the Golden State provided very little warmth during this period. Mike's delusions became his reality. He looked at bushes, and they would suddenly morph into "benevolent bears" that would kindly wave to him, acknowledging his existence. And he would wave back.[17] This was the world Mike Mentzer was now living in.

He would later recall:

> The loss of conceptual control resulted from the very strong emotions I had associated with all my losses. That loss of conceptual control in the emotionally driven part [of my brain] was amplified by taking amphetamines. Because I was not in full conceptual control, I wasn't aware enough to have a grasp of what was going on emotionally. If you allow too strong an emotion to take over, you lose your conceptual grasp of reality. You can't monitor your own motives and thoughts. You think your actions are right and logical when, in fact, you're 180 degrees opposite to where you think you are, but you don't know it because you don't have the means to know

it. In some instances, it's a very innocent thing; the person is overwhelmed by feelings he didn't know would be around as a result of certain losses. The emotions are very strong. And at the same time you're still taking the amphetamines — which before didn't have this effect — because you *had* conceptual control. Once I lost intellectual control and got caught up in this emotional black hole, I lost awareness, and everything started spinning out of control.[18]

On occasion, Julie McNew would put him up at her apartment for the night, allowing him to sleep on a couch. It was better than a park bench or a concrete alleyway. She also gave him money to buy food. But this was no existence; there was no forward direction, and no future.[19]

Mike knew the hounds of mental illness were coming for him. They had always been coming. He had done what he could to fight them off for so long that he now no longer had the energy. He was tired of running from them and too exhausted to fight. He laid down his weapons and waited for the hounds to arrive. To devour him. He took to sleeping outside Gold's Gym, just as he used to sleep outside his girlfriend Debbie's bedroom door at her parents' house. Tom Platz recalled walking to Gold's Gym one day for a workout and seeing Mike lying in the gutter, unconscious. Tom called his name, but there was no response. Several minutes later, as Tom and his training partner were warming up in the gym, Mike entered and methodically tore down every picture of himself from the walls, much like a spurned lover might upon breaking up with someone he once believed to be his soul mate. When Gold's, his second home, no longer offered any consolation, Mike's life was over. While Platz recalled that he "felt sad for Mike," there is no indication that he tried to help him.[20]

On two occasions Mike attempted suicide. He simply didn't care anymore.[21] In both instances, he was institutionalized in a psychiatric hospital.[22] This itself was telling, as the doctors recognized that he was suffering from mental illness; they did not attribute his condition to drug use. On one of these occasions, the doctors prescribed psychiatric medication, which Mike described as "anti-mind medicine." It did nothing but deaden his brain.[23] He knew enough about clinical psychology to question the doctor's prescription, asking him: "There are over 100 chemicals in the brain — how do you know that the chemicals in this medication won't contraindicate my brain's normal function?"[24] But the doctor wasn't interested in having an intellectual debate over the merits of psychopharmacology; Mike was made to take the drugs. It galled him to be in such a position. "So much of it is just a business," he said. "You don't give a person who is sick poisons to try to make them better. The body itself has a healing mechanism and drugs just distort and slow down the body's own healing mechanism. Obviously, there are flaws in that reasoning, but modern medicine today is definitely off the track, I think, with the emphasis on drugs."[25]

After a week or two of being institutionalized, he was discharged and sent back to the streets. There he resumed his own attempts to self-medicate his depression, and the problems started all over again. "For a while I would be pursuing something in my mind, and I was convinced it was real," Mike recalled. "I would get institutionalized for it, but I would be released and think, 'Well, I'm right, they're wrong. I'm going to continue doing it even if it gets me in trouble.' I was convinced I was right."[26] It was a karmic cycle with no off-ramp.

It is during such times, when one believes one has no future and no hope, that one often finds solace in the thought of another world. A place like Heaven, where a benevolent God will take away all the pain and hurt, cleanse the soul of impurities, and reunite one's soul with those of loved ones who have passed on. At this point in his life, such a concept provided a welcome alternative to the boring, pointless, and painful world Mike was living in. However, the reasoning section of his brain (or sections, depending on the current neurophysiology) always stopped him. He knew deep down that this was merely wishful thinking on his part. But during those periods when the emotional section of his brain held sway, he looked for reasons to justify the fantasy. It was during one such interlude that my phone rang at three o'clock in the morning.

"John Little!" came the voice at the other end of the phone. Mike always led off his phone conversations with a wry salutation.[27]

"Hey, Mike!" I exclaimed, genuinely delighted to hear from him. After months of hearing nothing but worrisome news, I was relieved to have finally reestablished contact.

"How are you?" I sincerely wanted to know — and I was about to find out.

"Great! I'm working for NASA!"

"NASA?" I knew that Mike was a devout student of science; perhaps he had been hired as a health and fitness consultant?

"Yes, NASA. I'll be starting there on Saturday."

"Wow. That's awesome! In what capacity will you be working there?"

"I'm going to be heading into space — inside one of their space shuttles."

"A space shuttle?"

"Yes, me and Arthur Jones."

"Arthur Jones? The last I heard, Arthur had sold Nautilus and was working on rehabilitation equipment for the lower back?"

"Funny you should bring up Nautilus. Have you ever seen the cochlea of the ear?"

"No."

"It looks exactly like a Nautilus cam. God created the cochlea — the cam — and who is using the cam to help millions of people get better? Arthur Jones!"

I wasn't following the logic.

"Arthur Jones *is God*."

I was stunned into silence.

"It's going to be great!" he said. "Arthur is going to command the flight of the shuttle; he's taking me to Heaven, where I'll be reunited with my mom and dad."

Okay. Now I was worried.

Mike had always been an atheist. He was an Objectivist when last we spoke — a very *this-world* orientation. He had told me previously that he considered mysticism of any type abhorrent. Now he was embracing a supernatural realm and making grandiose claims about the divinity of a man who once claimed to have killed 73 men. My impulse was to ask him if he was putting me on. However, I sensed that if I told him he was talking crazy, it might push him further over the edge. I also knew he was hurting, that he felt alone and purposeless. But the fact he had attempted to draw a logical connection between images — the cochlea and the Nautilus cam — told me that there was a part of his brain that was still open to reason; that was functioning normally, making logical inferences based on empirical data. It occurred to me to try and keep his mind focused on continuing to make such logical connections; if I could keep that region of his brain engaged, the emotional region would not take over the conversation or direct his actions once we hung up the phone.

"Mike, you know you don't believe *that*. You're the one who told me you didn't believe in the supernatural — remember? You told me that was 'like believing there's a *realer* reality.' It's a contradiction and, as an Objectivist, you know that if there's a contradiction, we've made an error in our reasoning."

There was a pause. I didn't know if he was going to hang up on me. Instead, he chuckled in a way that suggested that he had momentarily stepped outside of himself and observed his space flight fantasy as being nonsensical.

We continued to speak for another three hours.

I felt like I was talking him down, as in a movie where the pilot loses consciousness, and the control tower relays instructions to a passenger on the flight as to how to land the airliner. I recall that he fell asleep on the other end of the phone. Knowing that he was now sleeping put my mind at ease. Sleep was what he needed — and so did I.

"One of the unreal concepts I got very caught up in was the idea that there was a God," Mike would later recall. "I had been a devout atheist all my life; it was only after my father died that I started thinking about God. And I went on with that one for hours and hours every day for months on end for a couple of years."[28]

More phone calls followed, always at three in the morning. I made it a point to answer each of them, knowing that if he was talking to me, he was safe — he wasn't outside, where he would be vulnerable, wandering off into bad parts of Los Angeles, speaking nonsense either to the police or to people who might do him harm. Plus getting him to focus more intensely on the thought processes that underlay what he was saying seemed to pull him out of these delusions, considerably if not entirely. By the end of our conversations, he seemed more like his old self. We'd talk about what was on his mind, and then examine his statements — pro and con — for contradictions. If there were other people he could talk to, they obviously weren't available between the hours of three and five o'clock in the morning. On one occasion, we spoke for so long that the battery in my cordless phone went dead.

Mike's calls were sporadic throughout 1988 and early 1989. I didn't realize that he considered our dialogues to have been helpful until I read a very candid profile on him that was written by Peter McGough for *Flex* magazine in 1995, in which the following quote from Mike appeared:

> John Little was one of the few who didn't approach me on the ignorant assumption that I was a "loony" or a "crazy." John understands quite a bit about the power of ideas and the way they work in the mind. He would talk with me at length, and

I remember those conversations with fondness, which causes me to think fondly of John Little. He never wrote me off.[29]

Later, when Peter gave me the recordings of his interviews with Mike, I was able to listen to the remainder of what Mike had to say about our dialogues:

> He approached it intelligently. Again, not on the assumption that I was psychotic, not knowing what psychosis even means, writing Mentzer off as a loony or a crazy. John knew that there was something going on in my soul that was very serious to me and when we spoke, it was serious. There was nothing smug, he was not laughing at me, he never thought that I was necessarily even crazy. He was actually interested in the ideas. Some of the ideas were actually quite logical, although the basic premises [laughs] were way off.[30]

When I read/heard the above quotes from Mike, I felt a strong sense of pride (one of those rare times in one's life) for having done the right thing. I was pleased that those numerous hours we spent on the phone were in some way helpful to him. The problem, however, was that I wasn't always able to get to the phone when it rang at three in the morning, and he didn't always call when the darkness descended upon him. I was shocked to discover within Peter's article that, apart from Julie and me, no one from the bodybuilding community offered any assistance during the one time in his life that Mike needed it the most:

> One thing that does disappoint me is the fact that there were so few people who seemingly made any sincere attempt to understand or extend any support. Not financially so much, just spiritually. I heard from *no one* during that period. No one wrote me a letter. No one called. No one said, "Gee, I hope you're doing all right." Then again, for some people I understand that they didn't understand it. It was beyond their comprehension at the time. But that's what disappoints me a little bit. Then again, it's a reflection of our whole society; people really don't make an effort to understand. But it's also true people have their own life dramas going on. I understand

that now. In their way, everybody every day goes through things that are traumatic, stressful. And to have to deal with what Mike Mentzer was going through I understand in several cases was just too much for them. They wanted to understand and perhaps help, but when they confronted the situation, the burden was just too much on top of everything else they were going through in their own lives.[31]

While Mike was hanging on by a thread, Arnold Schwarzenegger was riding high. By 1989, he was the biggest box office star in the world. Films such as *The Terminator* (1984), *Predator* (1987), and *Twins* (1988), among others, saw him reach a level of stardom and success that nobody could have predicted ten years earlier. Among those who took notice of Arnold's ascent was his photographer friend George Butler. During a conversation with Arnold for a book of photographs Butler had taken of him over the years, an anecdote was shared that Butler felt compelled to put into print:

> There is a bodybuilder who lives in California who spent his life dreaming about becoming Mr. Olympia. He was a giant in his time — tall, handsome, and genetically perfect. He trained like a demon, college-educated, he learned more about nutrition than any other bodybuilder. He had patrons who provided him financial freedom so he could train full-time. They advised him on his business affairs, and he became wealthy. At the peak of his career, in the best shape of his life, he competed against Arnold Schwarzenegger — once. Not only did he lose, but he was broken by the experience. Soon after, he lost his money, his wife, and his looks. He became prematurely old. Today, he wanders on the streets of Los Angeles, incoherent and homeless. Arnold did not want this to happen. But it did — such was his power over his competitors who dreamed they could beat him.[32]

Although he didn't mention Mike by name, it was obvious that Mike was the person Butler was referencing. Given that there is no evidence of Butler interviewing anyone else from the bodybuilding world in 1989, he most likely heard of Mike's dire condition directly from Arnold. If so, that both men felt obliged to put this out for public consumption is beyond the pale and makes one question what kicking a man who was down was intended to accomplish. The reader is free to draw his own conclusions on the matter. In point of fact, Butler's statement was false; neither Arnold nor the 1980 Mr. Olympia had anything to do with the inherited mental illness that had led Mike to this sad point in his life. But things were about to get even worse.

One evening in late 1989, I received a phone call. It was from Julie McNew. "Mike is in prison!"

CHAPTER THIRTY-TWO

THE GHOST IN THE MACHINE

Prison? What the hell had happened? Julie wasn't clear on the details. I assumed that it had something to do with Mike's assault charge from four years previously — but that couldn't be right. It wouldn't take four years for a criminal case to reach trial.

I wouldn't find out until years later that Mike, while in the grip of a stimulant-induced psychosis, entered a gym. His behavior was so erratic that the gym owner called the police, who shortly thereafter arrived on the scene and hauled Mike off to a nearby hospital. A blood test revealed him to be under the influence of a controlled substance. Where he obtained it (or from whom) was never discovered. Mike was charged with possession of a controlled substance for personal use as well as being under the influence of it. Charges were immediately filed with the Los Angeles Superior Court, a trial was conducted at the Beverly Hills Courthouse, and, on August 29, 1989, Mike was sentenced to six months in Chino state prison.

"Are you still there?"

"Yeah, Julie."

"I know he'd like to hear from you. Let me give you the mailing address for him at Chino."

I was numb. Mike Mentzer in prison? Part of me refused to believe it. But another part of me couldn't help but think that his recent bizarre behavior could only lead to one of two possible destinations: prison or a cemetery. For the moment, I was relieved to learn it was the former. I quickly scribbled down the address that Julie gave me, hung up the phone, and tried to deal with the punch to the solar plexus I had just received.

Chino, I would learn, is the slang term for the California Institution for Men. Its nickname derived from the fact that the institution is in the city of Chino, in San Bernardino County, California. I also learned that it had the largest Level 1 inmate population of any prison within the state of California. Mike was in with the worst of the worst — murderers, rapists, those convicted of armed robbery, and numerous other crimes.

I wrote Mike a letter, inquiring as to how he was holding up. Thinking he could use some reading material and knowing that his primary interests centered on bodybuilding and philosophy, I gathered up some bodybuilding magazines and two nonfiction books by Ayn Rand (their titles now escape me) and placed them along with the letter into a package and mailed it off to him. A few weeks later, I received a letter of reply from Mike. Its contents were alarming.

He was doing fine, he said, but it had come to his attention that his brother Ray, who was now living back in the States, had recently made a power-play of sorts behind Mike's back. Ray had gone to Joe Weider and told Joe that he was the brains behind Mike's Heavy Duty system, that Mike was done, incarcerated, and that he would now be taking over Mike's mail-order business. He wanted to barter training articles for ad space in Joe's magazine. That the brand and content that Mike had created and developed over a period of 12 years should be taken away from him, by — of all people — his brother, infuriated Mike. And that Ray would run to Joe Weider with the news of Mike's institutionalization meant that any chance Mike had to get back on his feet and earn a living from bodybuilding upon his release from prison was most likely gone. He referred to Ray as his "erstwhile brother."

For his part, Joe Weider wasn't interested in Ray or his articles. He knew that Mike created the Heavy Duty system (he was there when it happened), and that Mike was the brains, the writer, and the most decorated bodybuilder in the Mentzer family. Still, for the moment at least, any involvement Joe's company had with Mike or Heavy Duty was ancient history. As far as the Master Blaster was concerned, Ray was free to peddle his articles and his dubious pedigree to another magazine.

In fairness to Ray, we don't know what his reasoning was. Perhaps he truly wished to preserve his brother's legacy but recognized that Mike was in no condition to do it himself. Perhaps with a family to provide for, he viewed his brother's mental decline as an opportunity to earn extra money, irrespective of what that meant to his relationship with his elder sibling. It may well have been both things or neither of them. In any event, his actions drove a wedge between the brothers.

Apart from the above, Mike thanked me for thinking of him and for the reading material, indicating that the Objectivist material was most welcome, and that the magazines were a hit. Evidently there were a lot of men behind the wall who were interested in the goings-on within the bodybuilding industry and who were iron pumpers themselves. Mike got along well with these guys; being a famous bodybuilder and former Mr. Universe winner meant that he not only had status while in prison but was constantly being sought after for advice on exercise and diet, which he was happy to provide. I received periodic updates on how Mike was making out from Julie, who checked in with me from time to time after she had heard from or visited him.

Prison life, it turned out, wasn't at all bad for Mike. Indeed, it proved somewhat therapeutic. It provided the mental health care Mike required, kept him away from any mind-altering agents, provided a roof over his head and three meals a day. Perhaps more importantly, it provided him plenty of time to face the reality of his situation. "I had to wake up or it was the end of my life," he recalled. "There was something going on here that wasn't right. All that emotional trauma I had with my father dying, the magazine, the breakup with my girlfriend, along with the amphetamines, really did do something to my mind."[1]

By now he had concluded that all his years of studying psychology had yielded him nothing of benefit. Arthur Janov's primal scream, R.D. Laing's arguments to remove the stigma attached to schizophrenia, Carl Jung's interpretation of dreams, Wilhelm Reich's orgone energy, and Sigmund Freud's attempts to draw forth impact moments from childhood that had been locked away in the subconscious had not delivered him from the clutches of psychosis.[2] He knew that the problem resided in his brain, obviously, but the brain was an almost infinitely complex organ. Where to start? With psychology off the table, he once again turned to epistemology.[3] While he knew that the chemical balance within his brain periodically was upset — which would require some sort of medication — there had to be something he could do to strengthen his mind that perhaps might stave off the frequency of such occurrences. It always seemed that the onset of his psychological problems was heralded when his emotions took over. If, as Francis Bacon believed, "Nature cannot be commanded except by being obeyed," Mike understood that if he could better understand the nature of his mind, how it processed the material he absorbed, he would be in a much better position to try and assert some control over how it behaved. It was during his reading of Ayn Rand's philosophical material that he happened upon two passages that indicated how the human mind functioned (its nature) — and of a possible means of commanding or asserting some control over it:

> The loss of control over one's consciousness is the most terrifying of human experiences: a consciousness that doubts its own efficacy is in a monstrously intolerable state. Yet men abuse, subvert and starve their consciousness in a manner they would not dream of applying to their hair, toenails or stomachs. They know that these things have a specific identity and specific requirements, and, if one wishes to preserve them, one must comb one's hair, trim one's toenails and refrain from swallowing rat poison. But one's mind? Aw, it needs nothing and can swallow anything. Or so most people believe. And they go on believing it while they toss in agony on a psychologist's couch, screaming that their mind keeps them in a state of chronic terror for no reason whatever. . . . The fact [is] that man's consciousness possesses a specific nature with specific cognitive needs, that it is not infinitely malleable and cannot be twisted, like a piece of putty, to fit any private evasions or any public "conditioning."[4]

And:

> That which is merely implicit is not in men's conscious control; they can lose it by means of other implications, without knowing what it is that they are losing or when or why.[5]

The mind, in other words, had specific needs and requirements if it was to function optimally. Moreover, it could only process what one put into it; if the data being input was corrupt or false, the conclusions one reached would likewise be in error. Mike had been inputting various ideas (some good, some bad) into his cerebral computer for four years straight, but the chemical imbalance in his brain caused by his depression (and then the depression combined with amphetamines) had knocked out his filter, causing him to accept as true whatever idea happened to pop into his consciousness at any given moment. This resulted in his acting rationally or irrationally depending upon the idea. An imperfect analogy would be to liken the human brain to a computer, where the GIGO principle applies, i.e., garbage in, garbage out. But the realization that consciousness had identity meant its nature or way of operating could now be understood — this was his way out of the darkness. After all, he hadn't always been so severely afflicted; there was a considerable period of time in his life when his brain had no difficulty dealing with metaphysical reality. *That* was the state of mind he needed to return to:

> I realized that all that stuff [he had acted upon over the past four years] contradicted everything else I had believed in for a long time — and *that's* what was right! Get back to what you knew before [metaphysically], Mike Mentzer! That emotional trauma you had with your father dying and the magazine and whatever else, along with the amphetamines, really did do something to your mind. Erase all that and go back to what you did know for sure. I did that, and with that I was on to an almost immediate recovery. It was that full recognition that everything that started at a certain point in time up until that moment of reflection was literally not true. So, I acted on the conviction that none of that was true. I ripped it out of my mind. That conviction was the turning point. To be convinced about something to be true, for it to go all the way down into your soul and cause a kind of fundamental change.[6]

But like an alcoholic who must make a focused effort each and every day for the rest of his life not to take a drink, Mike understood that he would have to struggle each moment of every day to stay focused on reality and then make logical — and only logical — connections of what he perceived, integrated, and stored in his consciousness. He could not relax his mental focus for even a minute, or the creative part of his brain would take over and his problems would return. One of Mike's favorite philosophical quotes was from Arthur Koestler in the book *The Ghost in the Machine*: "The revolutions in the history of science are successful escapes from blind alleys."[7] What he was attempting would certainly be a revolutionary move in the science of how the mind functioned. Whether it would represent a successful escape from his predicament remained to be seen.

Interestingly, in the preface to that same book Koestler had cautioned:

> The creativity and pathology of the human mind are, after all, two sides of the same medal coined in the evolutionary mint. The first is responsible for the splendour of our cathedrals, the second for the gargoyles that decorate them to remind us that the world is full of monsters, devils and succubi. They reflect the streak of insanity which runs through the history of our species, and which indicates that somewhere along the line of its ascent to prominence something has gone wrong. Evolution has been compared to a labyrinth of blind alleys, and there is nothing very strange or improbable in the assumption that man's native equipment, though superior to that of any other living species, nevertheless contains some built-in error or deficiency which predisposes him towards self-destruction.[8]

Mike's mind certainly had such a built-in error that had predisposed it towards self-destruction. But by better understanding how his navigational instrument functioned, he was confident he could now be its captain, not its passenger:

> Most people have almost no understanding of the nature of their mind; how their conscious mind works in relationship to the subconscious and the emotions. I understand that very clearly now. Because I understand that very clearly, I can work more consciously to create the type of soul or character I want. I know how to intensify the positive, rational psychological processing of material, and I know how to denature or diminish the potency of the negative, irrational material. Because I understand this concept: that consciousness has *identity*. That which comes into focal awareness gets into our focal awareness for a reason. Once it's in focal awareness, the actions we take toward [that material] consciously, determine how [it will be processed] back into the subconscious. By taking a strong,

positive, conscious, affirmative stand towards certain mental content, we can be better assured that that will work in our mind for us in the future. When we find something negative in our focal awareness, we can also take an appropriate stand consciously to denature it; diminish its intensity, diminish its potency, to help ensure that that same psychological material will not work in our mind with the same kind of intensity it had in the past. This is the way that an individual creates his own soul consciously.[9]

It was a courageous undertaking, to be certain — to battle mental illness with mental strength. Certainly, whatever willpower he had had to summon for his Olympian workouts in the past would be nothing compared to the willpower he would need every day of his life going forward. It was given that there were going to be lapses from time to time from forcing such omni-vigilance upon his psyche, but if Mike restricted what he input into his mind to evidence-based reality, he might just make it through.

Much like prisoners who in their darkest moments "find" religion and follow its dictates for their salvation, Mike found the same solace in the philosophy of Objectivism. It had saved his life, he believed, and he now clung to its principles as though it they were a life raft, which, to him at least, they were.

Henceforth, he would preach its merits at every opportunity.

CHAPTER THIRTY-THREE

REDEMPTION

After his six-month sentence ended, Mike was released from Chino and headed back to Venice. As he had been incarcerated for being under the influence of a controlled substance, one of the conditions of his parole was that he submit to random urinalysis; there would be no drugs, of any kind, permitted to be found in his system. The penalty for noncompliance was an automatic return to prison.

Having little to trade on but his bodybuilding reputation, Mike thought the most practical solution would be to start a personal training business out of Gold's Gym. Julie McNew was mortified that he would venture into such a public forum, one in which there was already gossip and rumor circulating about where he had been and what he had done. However, Mike did not have time to consider the potential embarrassment:

> I can't say I was ever really embarrassed. I was down in Gold's Gym right away seeking clients. The thought of being embarrassed actually never occurred to me until Julie brought it up. She said, "How could you do that? I'd be so embarrassed." I said, "To tell you the truth, I never really thought about it." I had the idea that everybody's going through things in their life that they find hard to understand at times. A lot of people had already forgotten it to some extent. What was going on in Mike Mentzer's life wasn't the sole topic of concern or a topic for conversation. What happened to me was something people heard about; some of it was true, some of it wasn't

true. Nobody knew precisely what was true and what wasn't true — that was my stance. I knew I'd be facing people who had heard many things. And quite a few people let me know that they had heard that I was literally crazy. I heard things that weren't true, and I heard things that were true and, again, I knew that people didn't know which was true and which was false. And I went on that assumption."[1]

If anything, Mike had overestimated the gymgoers' response to his return. Not only did most not know about his past, they didn't care. Ten years had passed since Mike last competed, and bodybuilding had moved on. There were new champions on the scene who were now the center of attention. Given the weathervane nature of bodybuilding popularity, Mike was a dinosaur; a former champion who belonged to bodybuilding's past, right next to John Grimek. There was absolutely no incentive for anyone to sign up for personal training sessions with a person who was yesterday's news. It was going to take some time for his new training business to generate any meaningful income.[2] He took what little money he had and purchased a used station wagon, which he parked a block away from the gym. For the time being it would serve not only as his mode of transportation, but also his home.

Business picked up slowly but steadily, and soon Mike had enough money to rent a small apartment. In time, he had a phone installed and took out a classified ad in the *Argonaut*, a small weekly newspaper that provided news and business information for the Westside of Los Angeles:

> Attention Fitness Enthusiasts And Bodybuilders... Mr. Universe and author of the Mentzer Method to Fitness is now available for personal training. Call Mike Mentzer 453-7049.[3]

Upon learning that Mike was out of prison, I called Julie McNew, who provided me with his new phone number. After hanging up with Julie, I dialed the number and Mike picked up. It was great catching up with him. His mind was sharp; he was the same old Mike. He told me about his new personal training business. There wasn't much I could do to help promote it as the only bodybuilding magazine I wrote for was in England — over 5,000 miles away from where Mike's business operated — but I suggested I do an interview with him. That would get the word out in the bodybuilding world that he was still alive and kicking, and any publicity was good publicity, it was said. When we finally got around to doing the interview, I asked him what his future plans were. He answered honestly, as always:

> Well, right now I'm a little uncomfortable with my life because I don't have a strong goal orientation. In the past, I was always highly motivated day to day by my desire to become Mr. Olympia and a successful champion. But since that's left my life, I find that there's a bit of a void and I'm a little neurotic at times. I'm not sure about my value system, and it's very complicated and I don't want to go into it too much now. I'm still working on my writing, of course, and eventually want to make a foray into writing a novel. So there's lots of possibilities. There are business things cropping up all the time, and I always have my antenna up for those possibilities as well. So things aren't going real bad, but I just don't feel that day-to-day satisfaction with myself as I did when I was training for the Mr. Olympia. What I'm lacking is "a moral equivalent to war," as William James might have said. I love living a high-intensity lifestyle. And when you're a champion bodybuilder and you're in the limelight, you're getting a lot of attention, you're traveling, business opportunities are presenting themselves all the time, and there's very little time to sit around and "invite the devil," so to speak. "An idle mind is the devil's workshop" — that's so very true.[4]

In order to strengthen the rational part of his mind, Mike immersed himself in a study of Aristotelian logic. Learning what constituted proper reasoning, valid arguments, and common logical fallacies bolstered his thinking skills immensely. Wanting to obtain the best possible results for his training clients, he subjected his previous beliefs on training to rigorous logical analysis. "I decided to undertake a study and gain as thorough an understanding as possible of the nature of logic," he said. "I did so to improve my thinking on all important issues, including the theory of high-intensity training. I realized that if I wanted to be better able to develop my clients' muscles, I had to further develop my mind."[5]

He decided to broaden his training business by offering phone consultations to those who couldn't travel to California to train with him personally.

This was a business that also started slowly, as, apart from my interview with him in *Bodybuilding Monthly*, he had no presence at all in the bodybuilding press. That would soon change, however. When Mike's old friend, *Iron Man* magazine publisher John Balik, learned of the struggles Mike was facing, he reached out to help. "I was having a difficult time financially, and John knew about it," Mike recalled. "And out of sheer good will, he ran a series of quarter-page ads for free; ads mentioning the fact that I was starting a phone-consultation business. Once that first ad appeared, my phone started ringing immediately, and it hasn't stopped ringing since."[6] Mike began writing articles for *Iron Man*, which were so well received that Joe Weider once again took notice and asked Mike to resume his "Heavy Duty Training" column, this time for *Flex* magazine. Joe paid Mike a standard fee for each column he wrote. The money wasn't great, but the exposure was welcome, as it alerted people to his personal training business.

With the increased exposure came an increase in clients. And, given that Mike kept in-depth progress charts for each of his clients, these provided valuable data to deepen his understanding of the effects of the various training protocols he was employing in their workout sessions, and the role of full recovery between their workouts.

He quickly learned that those who did not share his genetics for muscle building, and particularly those who did not use anabolic steroids, could not make any progress at all on the routines that he had used so successfully when training for competition:

> I started out training my clients using Arthur Jones' application of 12–20 sets per workout with my clients. No one made progress, and many regressed. I knew the problem wasn't undertraining; it had to be overtraining. So, I cut the sets [per workout] back to seven to nine sets three days a week and some made minimal progress for while but hit a plateau soon thereafter. At this point, I was in a quandary. Again, I knew the problem wasn't undertraining, but how could it be that *less* training was required? It actually kind of scared me for a brief time. How could it be that I was discovering a radically different application of high intensity [training] than Jones and everyone else? At one time I actually thought Jones was infallible, that he was so incredibly smart, he had to be right.

> He was basically correct with the theory: To be productive, exercise must be intense, brief, and infrequent. Where he was wrong was on the application of the theory. I kept reducing the volume and frequency of my clients training until, finally, they were performing only two to four sets per workout once every four to seven, and in some cases every 10–14 days. The volume and frequency requirements of any given individual depend on his innate recovery ability, with individual recovery ability, like all genetic traits, being expressed across a very broad range.[7]

In other words, Mike found that each individual was different. Some recovered quickly, within 24 hours, and could train again at that point. Others, however, required a considerably longer period between workout sessions. He quickly learned that most couldn't tolerate having the training stress applied more frequently than once every four or five days if they were to recover and adapt. Mike believed that a big part of his job as a personal trainer was to precisely determine the optimal training frequency for each of his clients, which he likened to the dosing frequency in medicine:

> In medicine, the first thing the researchers had to do was identify the chemical compound that would serve as the medicine to induce the positive physical change. The next logical step, the inevitable step, was to discover how much. How much of the medication in terms of volume: how many pills a day? And [then the dosing] frequency: how often? Same thing with exercise science. Again, too, where we're looking to induce or create a positive physical change, the first thing I had to do was discover the nature of the training stress that would induce the positive physical change, and it just so happens to be a high-intensity stress. . . . There's something in medicine called the "narrow therapeutic window." That is, there's a certain amount of medication you take and you cure the symptoms. Anything beyond the narrow therapeutic window and you go into the negative; you overdose. The same is true with exercise.[8]

His approach broke new ground, moving bodybuilding training in a completely new direction. What did it matter if some trainees only exercised once every four to five days? After all, their purpose for training wasn't to win a prize for frequent appearances at the gym. Their purpose was to make progress. And if a client's genetic tolerance for exercise was such that he could not recover from seven-set workouts performed three times a week, then that was the reality the client had to deal with. While all those seeking maximal stimulation of their muscles needed to train as intensely as possible, Mike pointed out that such intense effort was a different species of exercise compared to conventional forms of resistance training. It was far more demanding, and, consequently, exposure to such a training stress had to be very brief and cautiously regulated:

> When I first started training people several years ago I had them all doing forced reps and negatives every set of every workout and almost nobody was gaining satisfactorily. That's when I came to understand much more clearly just how demanding high-intensity training really is; that the body has a strictly limited recovery ability or adaptive capacity. You've got to be very careful. I used to use the analogy that high-intensity, heavy-duty exercise is like going out into the intense August sun. I've changed that. It's more like going out into the intense August sun with the sun five million miles closer to the earth. Or, even more precise, it's like jumping into a fire. It's a very intense stress; it'll warm you up, but you've got to jump right back out.[9]

If, as the Objectivists had it, everything had a nature or identity which had to be understood or obeyed in order to then be commanded, then muscle tissue was no different. Mike believed he was onto something. But once again, the something he was onto was completely at odds with what the fitness industry was selling. With products to market, the publishers of bodybuilding magazines did not want to discourage any potential advertiser from spending their money. Consequently, it made no financial sense for them to try and crack the nut as to the best way to train; their gold was panned by remaining neutral in the matter. Given that the bodybuilding practitioners of the time were typically in the gym for hours per workout and performing several workouts per week, what Mike was saying flew in the face of their unscrutinized training habits. As both the bodybuilders and the publishers were responsible for maintaining the status quo of the industry, they did what they could to shout down Mike's heresy and protect their fiefdoms. When Mike wrote an article explaining his insights in *Flex* magazine, the editor-in-chief felt obliged to salt into the piece statements from no fewer than seven bodybuilders who trained conventionally with eight to 30 sets per body part for many days each week.[10] What did science and logic have to do with anything? Clearly, the truth always lay on the side of the majority. And if Mike quoted Ayn Rand (and he did frequently) in his articles and columns, the knives of the herd came out again. Who wanted to read about the importance of learning to think critically and independently in a bodybuilding magazine?

Evidently there were quite a few who did. Many consumers only purchased *Flex* magazine because it contained Mike's latest offerings.[11] This posed a dilemma for the editor-in-chief of *Flex*, as it was his job to feature articles that promoted Joe Weider and the methods of the Weider champions, but it was also incumbent upon him to provide content that would boost magazine sales, which, in turn, translated into more advertising revenue. Despite Mike's methods flying in the face of what was commonly promoted in the magazine, he had a following among the readers that Weider publications did not want to lose. For the time being, Mike's presence was abided in the publication, although Mike was told that there was concern about him getting too much exposure.[12]

Mike's clients, meanwhile, were obtaining phenomenal results from his radically new training approach:

- David Paul, an advanced level bodybuilder, gained seven pounds of muscle and improved his strength in the squat exercise by 185 pounds in one month.
- A client who came from France to train with Mike for one month gained 19 pounds of muscle.
- Another client from Egypt signed on with Mike for one month and gained 16 pounds of muscle, while tripling the functional ability of his legs, going from 11 repetitions to 35 repetitions with 250 pounds on the leg-extension exercise.[13]

As word spread about the success of Mike's clients, the growth of his personal training business exploded. Bodybuilders who had grown tired of spending hours per week in the gym with little to no results welcomed such a time-saving alternative. What set Mike's method apart from the rest was its logical underpinning — it simply made sense to people.

One of those who saw the sense of Mike's approach to training was the renowned martial artist and *Black Belt* magazine Hall of Famer Burton Richardson, who signed on for personal training:

> When training the Heavy Duty way, extreme motivation was imperative, especially during that last, grueling but critical rep. When Mike sensed that my resolve was waning part way through that last push or pull, he would scream out "Your mother is in a burning building! Are you going to get her out?!" Even if I knew it was coming, that one always worked. Since I trained martial arts several hours per day, Mike extended the number of days between workouts for me to ensure I had ample time for recovery and growth before lifting again. Usually one session every five days, but he would vary the frequency based on his observations of my performance. His directions were determined by what would give me the best results as opposed to a cookie cutter approach. He certainly made great choices because I made constant progress even though I trained so much outside the gym and was vegan. Mike's intuition was phenomenal.
>
> One day Mike was training me when a young man, who was not in particularly good shape, walked up to us. In a condescending voice he said to Mike, "You sure like those machines, don't you?" Instead of responding in anger to this rude comment, Mike retorted resolutely (and with a hint of sarcasm), "As a matter of fact I do like machines. A machine woke me up this morning. A machine made my coffee and I drove here in a machine. Yes, I do like machines." The young man, dumbstruck by the logic, simply walked away. Mike turned back to me and just continued with training.
>
> Mike recorded every training session, writing down both the weight used, and the number of reps achieved for each grueling set. Immediately after my last rep, he would record the numbers

then look at what I did the previous training session. If I got six reps instead of the five I did previously, he'd exclaim, "That's a twenty percent increase!" That was always motivating to hear.

Mike's breakthrough training methods meant *much* less time in the gym. Instead of the daily gym routine, the norm for me was about twenty minutes every five days. Mike said that after hearing about his radically efficient schedule, many athletes living the bodybuilder lifestyle would ask, "But what am I supposed to do if I don't go to the gym every day?" Mike would gleefully reply, "Read a book! Learn some philosophy!" That always tickled him.[14]

Soon, professional bodybuilders came to Mike for instruction — Aaron Baker, David Dearth, and, most famously, England's Dorian Yates, who would go on to win the Mr. Olympia title six years in a row. "He was coaching, I was the student," Dorian recalled. "He challenged me to, you know, to think about my training more, and made me cut back on the volume a little bit more, which I did. That was a learning experience."[15] Dorian's most ardent supporter in the North American bodybuilding press was Peter McGough, a fellow Britisher, who would later go on to be the editorial director of both *Muscle & Fitness* and *Flex* magazines.

Pleased with Mike's connection to the reigning Mr. Olympia champion, Peter asked Mike whether he ever felt unfulfilled by never having won the Mr. Olympia title himself. "It's not relevant anymore," Mike replied. "It's all behind me now. There was a time when I never thought I could say such a thing. I was obsessed by being a bodybuilder, obsessed by the thought of being Mr. Olympia. And even though during those times I never completely neglected my mind, if I could go back, I'd reverse the priority; the development of my body would be secondary to developing my intellect."[16] Peter was shocked at the reply. "Isn't there any way you're looking at Dorian's physique and seeing what you might have become? Isn't there any regret?" Again, Mike answered in the negative. "I don't have any of that stuff. I see that kind of mentality: 'I've got to fulfill my physical potential or I'm not going to be happy in life.' And that's okay, but I don't have that even slightly. There's no looking back and saying, 'Gee, I wish I had gone a little bit further.' I'm quite happy with where I'm at right now."[17]

CHAPTER THIRTY-FOUR

AGAINST THE ODDS

In the summer of 1992, I accepted a job offer to come to California to work as a writer for Joe Weider's *Flex* magazine. Part of the appeal of making the move was that I knew I would be able to spend time with Mike. I arrived a month before my wife and son did, which provided plenty of spare time for Mike and I to get together and talk training and philosophy.

I hadn't seen Mike for six years at this point, and the first thing that struck me was that his earlier desire to look normal had come true; he no longer resembled a Mr. Olympia competitor; more a retired athlete who had been taking it easy the past few years. The second thing that struck me was that he had taken up smoking, a habit which he seemed to enjoy. This, no doubt, occurred when he was in prison, where cigarettes are considered currency.

At this point in his life, Mike was excited about training again. Not the way he had been in the past, when he would learn of a new technique and then rush to the gym to try it out on himself, but in *thinking* about training. Critically analyzing the training principles and methods that were commonly employed by bodybuilders, looking for weaknesses and how the discipline might be developed into a more scientific and rational enterprise. The gym became his research lab, where he would collect data from his clients during the day and then make an in-depth analysis of it upon his return home. At this point in his life, Mike was performing such research seven days a week. His typical day looked like this:

- 7:00 a.m.: wake up.
- 7:00–8:30 a.m.: study philosophy, analyze client data.

- 8:30 a.m. (occasionally 7:30) — 12:30 p.m.: train morning clients at Gold's Gym.
- 1:00–3:30 p.m.: head home for lunch, return phone calls, conduct phone consultations, run his mail-order business, analyze more client data.
- 4:00–8:30 p.m.: return to Gold's Gym to train his afternoon and evening clients.
- 9:00–10:00 p.m.: home for dinner, analyze more client data, watch television.
- 10:00 p.m.: go to bed.[1]

"It's a very good business and I enjoy it," he said. "I enjoy it because I get to set my hours and the hours aren't all that tough. I also get to make a lot more money than most trainers because I only train my clients for 20 minutes [laughs]. I can train 20 people a day. It's not only the best way to train, but it's wonderful for business." He then laughed and added, "It's curious how reality works out when you're rational."[2] Mike told me that he wasn't living extravagantly and was saving every penny, volunteering that he had over $200,000 in the bank. "Mike, I'm proud of you," I said, "that you could come back like you have. But remember, it could all go away. You know you've got to keep focused; you don't want to go through *that* again." He nodded and told me not to worry. He was in a good place now. He even asked if I would be willing to write the foreword to his new book, a revised and updated version of his original *Heavy Duty* course. I was honored that he would ask and told him so.

At this point I was also preparing to self-publish a book on a new approach to bodybuilding that I had been working on, but when I learned how much printing costs were, I quickly realized I could not afford it; there wasn't sufficient money left over each month from my salary as a writer for *Flex* magazine. Joe Weider promised me ad space in two of his magazines, but without enough money for publication, I was all dressed up with nowhere to go. When I told Mike about my predicament, rather than rub his hands in glee that a potential rival had stalled coming out of the gate (and, make no mistake, we would have been competing for the same market), he provided me with the money to have the books printed. Without his patronage, *Power Factor Training* would not have been published. Then he went one step further: he agreed to write the foreword. This undoubtedly resulted in thousands of his fans purchasing my book solely on the strength of his endorsement alone.

He continued his research into issues such as overtraining, believing that there was no room for the arbitrary if a true science of bodybuilding training was to be established. It wasn't a case of more is better or less is better, he said, but that *precise* is best:

> If you were going to go into surgery tomorrow, you would very much want your anesthesiologist to give you the *precise* amount of anesthesia required — any more than that and you could grow toxic and die. Take that same principle from medical science and apply it to exercise science. In both cases we are dealing with a science, and, in both cases, we are dealing with the human body. In the first case the scientist, the anesthesiologist, is looking to infuse the human body with the precise amount of anesthesia required. In the second case, exercise science, we're looking to impose upon the body the requisite training stimulus in the proper, precise amount. If too little of it [in terms of intensity] is applied, no effect will be noted. If too much of it is applied, you will be overtrained.[3]

One evening Mike turned on his television to watch a network news program and was fascinated by an update on the pioneer of aerobic training, Dr. Kenneth Cooper. In 1968, Dr. Cooper minted a new word and used it as the title for a new book: *Aerobics*. It was a book that launched an industry. Tracksuits, running shoes, jogging shorts, jogging paths, bicycling, Jane Fonda, dancercize, aerobics classes, spinning, aquabics, powerwalking, and many other variants were born from Dr. Cooper's book and research. Indeed, his book proved so successful that the good doctor wrote another one, *The New Aerobics* (1970). He quit his job as a physician in the Air Force and, in 1986, looked on with pride as the word he created was added to the *Oxford English Dictionary*.[4] Soon he had his own compound, a multimillion-dollar fitness complex on a sprawling 32-acre tract of land in affluent North Dallas. There, a staff that included medical doctors would check people's health and prescribe the perfect aerobics program for them. In the mid-1990s, clients paid up to $1,200 a session for such advice.[5] It became a very big business. He created a point system for the type of activity that one engaged in, and the more one did of it, the higher the points were. Walking a round of golf, for example, earned you three points — the same as running a mile did — and running a mile five times would get you 15 points. The weekly ideal, Dr. Cooper said, was 30 points.[6] The underlying principle when it came to exercise was, in fact, that more is better. For decades this remained the belief with regard to exercise and health: You had to be active. You had to exercise every day or, at least, as often as your schedule permitted. You had to *make the time* — it was that important; you had to make exercise a daily part of your lifestyle.

But then a funny thing happened.

In 1994, Dr. Cooper came out with a new book: *The Antioxidant Revolution*. As the reader may have detected, "aerobics" was not in its title. Dr. Cooper was now selling supplements that reduced oxidative damage in the body — oxidative damage caused by aerobics, more popularly referred to these days as "cardio" — the very thing he had been preaching the virtues of to the world for decades. Now he was saying that more *wasn't* better; in fact, he said, too much exercise might be lethal.[7] He had completely reversed his position[8] — a position that had been embraced by the American public, the medical profession, and exercise scientists right across the board. Performing too much exercise led to a host of medical problems, he now claimed.[9] It started when his good friend and marathon runner Jim Fixx dropped dead from a heart attack while running.[10] And the bad news just kept on coming. According to an article published in the June 1995 edition of *Texas Monthly* magazine:

> There was the woman who spent ten hours a day teaching aerobics until she developed a melanoma on her jaw and was dead within the year. There was the super-athlete, a winner of Ironman competitions, who developed a deadly melanoma. There were the elite athletes who trained to exhaustion and came down with terminal illnesses: Fred Lebow, the founder of the New York City marathon—dead of a brain tumor; running guru George Sheehan—dead of prostate cancer; master marathoner Werner Tersago—dead of a brain tumor; world record holder Sy Mah, who had run 524 marathons—dead of cancer; Steve Scott, the first American to break a four-minute mile one hundred times—battling testicular cancer; marathoner Mark

Conover, winter of the 1988 Olympic trials—now fighting Hodgkin's disease; and Olympic runner Marty Liquori—now in the advanced stages of leukemia. Today Cooper claims to know of 150 such cases, including 94 athletes with prostate cancer who are patients at his clinic. The anecdotal evidence, he says, is overwhelming. Too much exercise can kill you.[11]

Dr. Cooper's new health and fitness counsel was that maybe you should take a brisk two-mile walk five days a week.[12] In other words, all of the running, the running shoes, the tracksuits, the lifestyle commitment, the industry — all of it — had been a giant mistake.[13] And yet to this day, people still believe you should be exercising every day and that aerobics is the method you should be employing — despite the fact that the very doctor who created the concept dropped it like a hot potato. Mike Mentzer was pleased by the doctor's admission:

> After two years of doing just about everything I could within reason to alert bodybuilders and fitness enthusiasts about the dangers of overtraining, along comes the famous Dr. Cooper stating some of the same things I have on the subject. As I have written and stated frequently, Cooper made it clear that overtraining is more than wasted effort, it is counterproductive. In fact, it is life-threatening. About eight issues ago in *Flex* I wrote in my column: "While I don't have the hard evidence, it stands to reason that chronic, gross overtraining may very well have long-range medical implications." Now here comes the well-respected Dr. Cooper stating that he has the evidence. He and his research colleagues have grown alarmed by the increasing incidence of serious diseases, including cancer and heart problems, among long-term bodybuilding and fitness enthusiasts and they ascribe it most directly to overtraining. I have no doubt that overtraining is the single most serious problem in the field of athletic training. And no one else seems to notice or care.[14]

The bodybuilding industry chose to ignore the news. As someone who worked in the industry at the time, I cannot recall any of the muscle publications covering Dr. Cooper's revelation about overtraining. Moreover, the bodybuilding publications continued to publish articles recommending high-set workouts performed up to six days a week. This incensed Mike:

> Unfortunately, too many of the self-styled experts in this field not only fail to make a nominal effort to stay apprised of the latest state-of-the-art knowledge, they actively evade such knowledge and even work diligently to suppress valid ideas that would help people to achieve greater progress, as well as to protect their health. Sheer innocent ignorance is one thing, but the conscious evasion and willful suppression of life-enhancing knowledge is another. . . . My goodness, the issue is human well-being. What does it take to make some people indignant?[15]

Recognizing that he was alone in trying to bring science and logic into bodybuilding, Mike used whatever platform he had available to him — interactions with his clients; his monthly column in *Flex* magazine — to offer an alternative for those who earnestly wished to learn facts rather than the latest advertising pitches from the industry.

Mike's method was perfect for natural, or steroid-free, trainees. He pointed out that since steroids are potent recovery-ability enhancers, those who did not take such drugs could never derive the same results from high-volume training as those who did. Indeed, the natural trainee needed to cautiously regulate both the training volume and training frequency in order to continue making progress.[16] To this end, Mike counseled that as one grew bigger and stronger, one needed to train not more but less.[17] Over time, and as the trainee reached the upper limits of his or her genetic potential (however great or modest that happened to be), they might be training with only two or three sets (total) per workout and training only once every seven days.[18] Genetics set the limit on potential growth and strength, and once it was reached, doing more exercise resulted not in more gains but in more wear and tear. Training, Mike believed, should be an adjunct to one's life, not the reason for it.[19] All around him he saw people struggling with serious life issues, none of which could be overcome by adding an inch on their arms.

A case in point was Markus Reinhardt, a 26-year-old bodybuilder who had moved to California from Stuttgart, Germany, in 1991. In fact, his hometown was only 47 miles from Hagsfeld, Karlsruhe, where Mike's fifth great grandfather on his paternal side, Johannes Jörg Meinzer, had lived prior to immigrating to America in 1790. Markus had dreams of being a great bodybuilder and, after placing third in the Light Heavyweight division of the Musclemania competition,[20] he appeared to be on his way. Markus had been training in the conventional fashion, like Arnold did, but had stopped making progress. He met Mike in 1995 and signed up for personal training in Mike's Heavy Duty system. Under Mike's watchful eye, Markus gained the better part of 25 pounds of muscle over the course of three to four months, which hooked him on the potency of the system.[21] But things took a bad turn for Markus when the young bodybuilder and his wife separated. Markus was lost, and within a matter of weeks was living on Venice Beach:

> I was actually homeless. I was living on the beach for a little bit. Mike found out about that, you know, and he asked me, "Why are you living on the beach?" I'm, like, "Well, I don't have enough money to afford a place right now, and I just want to save some money, whatever . . ." But Mike was, like, "No, man. We need to get you back on track. We're not going to have you live on the beach! You've got to be a pro bodybuilder. You've got to be the best. So, I'm going to I'm going to help you out."[22]

Mike put Markus to work helping to fulfill orders that came in for Mike's mail-order products, and in return Markus was given full use of Mike's condominium and slept on a couch in the living room. It beat the hell out of living on the beach and helped Markus reset, in terms of reassessing his goals and values. According to Markus, the kindness and counsel Mike provided saved his life:

> It was great with Mike. I mean *great*. Mike was a great host, so to speak. He really helped me out. If it hadn't had been for Mike and his advice on getting myself back on my feet and to believe in who I am, and what I can do, and what I'm capable of, especially with using my own rational mind and moving forward in the direction that I want to go, then I wouldn't be here right now. I think that just alone, that influence, really made me who I am today. I cannot express how grateful I am for this. I'm not talking about working out. I'm not talking about high-intensity training

or Heavy Duty training — sure that's all great — but it's the way he thought. He made me believe that I can believe in myself, and I can do anything I want to do if I put my mind to it.[23]

While Mike enjoyed his renaissance and success, his mental illness was always lurking just beneath the surface. During the month or so that he was living with Mike, Markus discovered that Mike suffered from vicious nightmares that caused him to awaken screaming in the night. "There was a time when I couldn't take it anymore," Markus recalled. "He would literally wake up in the middle of the night and start screaming. He was upstairs in his bedroom, and I was downstairs in the living room, and I heard him screaming — loud. And I'm, like, 'Mike! I can't sleep, man!' I didn't go up and check on him. I mean, the next day I asked him if he was having bad dreams and he said, 'No, I wasn't.' And I'm, like, 'Well I know you are.'"[24]

Maintaining his mental health was a daily challenge. Whenever Mike eased off his analysis of the content coming into his conscious awareness, the creative, emotional regions of his mind took over. He had been able to hold them off during the day, but sleep was given over entirely to his subconscious. When he felt his resistance weakening during his dreaming state, he would scream out in a last-ditch effort to keep the demons at bay. And when he awoke in the morning, sometimes they were still in control.

One morning while I was working at *Flex*, my phone rang. When I picked up, I was happy to hear Mike's voice on the other end of the line — for the first minute of the conversation, at any rate. Peter McGough recalled what happened:

> And yet, there were still occasions when the demons visited. One day in late 1994 John Little rushed to my desk and told me he had just received a call from Mike, saying he was in Las Vegas and about to fly to the moon to meet with Bill Clinton and discuss the world's problems. And Mike wasn't joking. To his credit John visited Mike and the psychotic episode was soon over.[25]

If only it went that smoothly. What Peter failed to mention in his article was that prior to rushing to his desk, I ran into the editor-in-chief's office. He was (he told us) studying to be a clinical psychologist, and some psychotherapy was exactly what I believed Mike needed at this moment. I shared with him what I had just experienced with Mike. I was terrified that he had relapsed; that all the hard work he had engaged in to get himself straight, the constant mental struggles he engaged in daily to maintain his reason, his renaissance in the bodybuilding world as a trainer, were all in danger of being swept away.

"We have to go down and see Mike!" I exclaimed.

The editor simply looked up at me lazily over his glasses.

"Why?"

"He's going through something again — like he did before! We should go *now*!"

His response was not at all what I expected.

"We'll cut his article and ads from the magazine."

"What? He needs help — not to have his livelihood cut off!"

I got that he was looking out for the interests of the magazine and the company. After all, Mike's phone number appeared both in his ads and at the end of his question-and-answer column. It was a situation that could reflect badly on the company if a reader called Mike now only to receive an earful of nonsensical rambling — or worse. However, I must admit that I wasn't looking at the big picture. From my perspective, a friend was in need of help — a friend who also happened to be a writer for our magazine — and the one person in the Weider offices who was studying to be a psychologist didn't seem to be willing to get out of his chair to lend assistance. That's when I went to speak with Peter. I told Peter that I had to leave and recognizing that time was of the essence, and that Mike might still be near his telephone/fax machine, I quickly typed, printed, and sent the following fax to Mike:

VIA FAX
Mike Mentzer
33 Reef Street
Marina del Rey, CA,
90292

July 20, 1994
Dear Mike:

I'm writing to you because the conversation we shared this morning has me very concerned.

As you're no doubt subconsciously aware, your new inclination towards theology, arguments from design, and sharing discourse with apparitions is a sign that all is not well and, in fact, that there has been a cerebral regression of sorts to the skewed perspective of five years ago.

Whether you know it or not, you're not yourself, and your conversation is not sensical. If you want help, if you want me to take you to see your doctor, let me know and I will. I don't want to see you lose everything and I want you to have help. Look at it this way, when you have an infection, you have to get some antibiotics into you. You can't reason your way out of an infection. And if you're not thinking clearly, you need some medicine that will clear up your thinking.

Mike, it bothers me to think that an unraveling of sorts is again taking place. You were able to pull yourself up by your rational faculty with a herculean act of will the last time. I'm not sure how many such pull ups one has the capacity for in a single lifetime.

Your discourse sounded to me as it did back in the late 1980's, only instead of Arthur Jones being postulated as God, you've substituted Ayn Rand. This is wrong on two counts: one, calling her a deity of any sort is to do her the ultimate disservice, as she fought her entire life against mysticism and religious perspectives. Second, Ayn Rand's teachings completely dismantle any and all reasons underpinning any purported belief in a deity. And, if as she taught, there is no "reason" for supposing or subscribing to otherworldly sources — however benevolent — then there's no reason to hold such a view.

But more to the point, Mike, as this really isn't about theology, it's about keeping touch with reality. You've worked too hard and accomplished too much to LOSE IT ALL now! The last time you spoke like this it was, in your words, owing to an addiction to amphetamines and going without sleep for several days. That causes hallucinations which, as you know, are not accurate representations of reality.

Mike, if you're back on that stuff, or if you detect that there could be a chemical imbalance, as a friend who values your friendship, well-being, and health, I implore you to get back on track before you derail completely. Your story is too noble, your contributions too great, to have them all summarily dismissed by peons and intellectual inferiors as being the "ramblings and ravings of a nut case." And, as we both know, that *is* how the jealous and the wannabes treat those who dare to use their minds in a productive fashion. And yet, if you make the effort to stay on track, the nay-sayers will fall from ear shot and, eventually, from even the footnotes of history.

You have the intellect, when you focus it properly, to achieve any goal you choose. Just look at what you've done in the past two years! You're the biggest thing in bodybuilding; you've wielded the greatest influence, and you have stated to me your goal to promote the philosophy of Objectivism and to study neurophysiology — these are attainable goals, and you should continue to aim and work at achieving them.

I've checked with Gold's, and they say they haven't seen you in three weeks and that they haven't seen Dave Mastorakis anywhere (contrary to what you told me)! That tells me that you're losing clients, which means your reputation for punctuality, efficiency and precision is being compromised and, with it, your ability to make a living. I don't want to see that happen to you as this is your livelihood.

First things first, buddy, you need some help. I'm going to be in Venice tomorrow morning. Let's get together and clear this thing up.

Sincerely,
John Little

Scrambling, I located a copy of Leonard Peikoff's book *Objectivism: The Philosophy of Ayn Rand*. I quickly flipped through it until I found some relevant passages that I hoped would keep Mike tethered to reason and reality. I photocopied two pages, and underlined the following sentences:

- "The idea of the 'supernatural' is an assault on everything man

knows about reality. It is a contradiction of every essential of a rational metaphysics."
- "Is God the creator of the universe? Not if existence has primacy over consciousness."
- "Is God the designer of the universe? Not if A is A. The alternative to 'design' is not 'chance.' It is causality."
- "Is God omnipotent? Nothing and no one can alter the metaphysically given."
- "Every argument commonly offered for the notion of God leads to a contradiction of the axiomatic concepts of philosophy. At every point, the notion clashes with the facts of reality, and with the preconditions of thought."
- "Any attempt to defend or define the supernatural must necessarily collapse in fallacies. There is no logic that will lead one from the facts of this world to a realm contradicting them; there is no concept formed by observation of nature that will serve to characterize its antithesis."[26]

I faxed Mike the letter along with the two photocopied pages from Peikoff's book and ran out of the Weider building. I got in my car and headed down to Marina del Rey to find him. I wasn't going to wait until the next morning. When I finally did locate him after several hours, he was perfectly normal; the episode had been acute but not enduring. Relieved, I told Mike to call Joe immediately, and hopefully Joe would override the editor-in-chief's decision and get Mike's article and ad reinstated for the next issue. To my relief, Joe did. The crisis had passed.

Not long afterwards, however, I received another phone call at my desk, this time from Joe's long-time personal secretary, Anneliese Leyk.

"Mr. Weider would like to meet with you in his office."

A minute or so later I was in Joe's magnificent office, looking on as the Master Blaster pored over hardcopies of articles slated for inclusion in the next issue of *Muscle & Fitness*. Evidently, someone had whispered something in his ear. It was no secret around the office that I was a good friend of Mike's, which, I had learned, put me at odds with certain of the editors on staff. I apparently needed to be brought to heel. It had been brought to Joe's attention that my new book, along with Mike's foreword, was clearly an attempt by a young upstart to undermine the Weider System. Moreover, the book was giving far too much credit to Mike and no credit at all to the Master Blaster. This needed to be nipped in the bud, and it was decided that no less a luminary than the boss himself should be the one to bring me to my senses. Joe had me wait in silence as he perused some photographs. Then, without looking up from his desk, he began.

"John. Are you happy?"

"Yeah, Joe. I'm happy."

"That's good," he replied. Now there was eye contact.

"You know, John, I like to portray the bodybuilding champions as heroes in my magazines to give bodybuilders something to look up to."

I silently acknowledged his point.

"When I have a painting done up of me as Zeus, and the other bodybuilding champions as Olympian gods, I'm not doing it because I think I'm actually God."

That much, I'm happy to relate, I had actually assumed.

Then Joe made his segue into the reason for our meeting.

"And the Weider Principles, I'm not saying I *invented* all of these different approaches to bodybuilding, but I just wanted to organize them in a manner that bodybuilders could understand and make use of — to bring them all under one umbrella."

"Okay."

"I'm telling you this because when you write a book making use of the Weider Partial Reps Principle, you should acknowledge it as a Weider Principle, and when, say, Mike Mentzer makes use of the Weider Reverse Gravity Principle, he should do likewise."

"But Joe," I countered, "I didn't learn of the concept for partial reps from you or your magazines. In fact, I've never read an article on these protocols in any of your publications. The data I gathered on that protocol came from my own research, my own training, analyzing the weight-per-unit-time factor in resistance training, and from interviewing various champion bodybuilders and strength athletes who told me that they had used the technique to increase their strength. Not one of them mentioned it as being a 'Weider Principle.' Some strength athletes, such as Paul Anderson, said he had been using it long before you wrote about it."

This didn't sit well with Joe. If it was a technique that helped a bodybuilder to gain muscle, it had to have his name on it. There was no other way. He was incapable of acknowledging that meaningful contributions to gaining muscle mass and strength could come from outside of his office in Woodland Hills. His editors at the time of course helped to bolster Joe's ego in this regard, and, unfortunately, helped to diminish Joe's legacy in such matters by doing so. In any event, Joe had communicated to me what he wanted to — that henceforth all training methodologies that I was to write about would have to be tethered to some "Weider Principle." I was dismissed without another word said.

It struck me as I left Joe's office that this was why Mike had fallen from grace within the house of Weider. He was the first professional bodybuilder (or at least among the first) to employ research in his training that had nothing to do with bodybuilding traditions. His work with Rest-Pause was a first, as was his use of Negative-Only training. Weider would later incorporate these into his "Weider Principles," but he most certainly did not originate them. Worse still, from Joe's vantage point, Mike often credited Nautilus inventor Arthur Jones as the one who had most influenced his training beliefs. This, of course, was far worse than Mike's published views that a bodybuilder didn't need protein supplements — whether Weider's or any other company's.

The pieces were now falling into place. If Mike wouldn't endorse protein supplements (and particularly Weider protein supplements) or the Weider Principles, he was viewed as more of a liability than an asset to Joe's business enterprises. Besides, big muscle men were by no means in short supply in Joe's universe, and there were plenty of impressive physiques willing to barter their integrity on such matters in return for exposure in Joe's magazines. Mike, of course, was not of this ilk, which was one of the reasons I respected him so much throughout all the years of our friendship. Nevertheless, to his detractors, Mike was a sore thumb, a person who disrupted the natural order of things. He was different from the bodybuilders who followed a very definite chain of command — Joe, Arnold Schwarzenegger, and whoever the current Mr. Olympia happened to be. This at the time was the Holy Trinity of most bodybuilding aficionados. Moreover, to the followers of this alliance, Mike seemed almost too comfortable standing apart from them, and apart from the pack of champions that endorsed Weider products, participated in daily high-volume training, and won (not surprisingly) the bulk of Joe's bodybuilding contests.

I knew the writing was on the wall for me at Weider after that meeting and, about a month later, my employment there was terminated for writing about non-Weider-related training ideas. I had finished my articles for that month's edition of *Flex* and had started researching material for another book I intended to write. The powers-that-were at Weider had tapped into my computer, and as I began to write the new (non-Weider) material, my computer shut off, and an announcement came over the PA that I was to go to a conference room on the lower floor. There sat my esteemed editor-in-chief, along with the managing editor and editor-in-chief of *Muscle & Fitness* (Joe was nowhere to be seen), who collectively informed me that I had violated their policy, and my employment was over.

It left me in a bad way for a few weeks. I had moved to California from Canada and had a wife and (by now) three children to provide for and had just lost my job. Learning of my predicament, Mike showed up at my house one day — in his station wagon — to ask if I would be willing to copy edit a manuscript for a new book he had written: *Heavy Duty II: Mind and Body*. It contained a lot of philosophy and his latest thoughts on bodybuilding exercise. Along with the manuscript, Mike handed me a check for $500. He knew I wasn't a copy editor, but he also knew that I needed money and had a family to support. How he found out about my predicament, I don't know to this day.

Fortunately, I wasn't out of work long. I was hired by Curtis Wong at CFW Enterprises as editor-in-chief of a new martial arts publication. I liked Curtis and found the work enjoyable. It certainly helped pay the bills. When December rolled around, it dawned on me that Mike would be alone at Christmas. He still wasn't speaking with Ray and didn't have a steady girlfriend. He was okay with dating occasionally but not interested in a committed relationship. "I don't think you necessarily have to be involved in a relationship to be a well-rounded individual," he'd said. "We haven't even defined what 'well-rounded' is. There are many people involved in relationships who shouldn't be. I see very few couples around me who seem to be enjoying themselves together. And it is difficult. And I'm not sure even if I found the right woman now that I'd want to be involved in a full-time relationship. As a matter of fact, I had spent most of my time in relationships and at one point I knew that there would come a time when I probably wouldn't be, and that it would be good for me. And this is the period. I'm kind of enjoying it. I like not having a relationship; it allows me more time to study and think about myself."[27]

While Mike was fine with being single, at least for the moment, that hadn't stopped certain friends from trying to set him up on dates. Markus Reinhardt, for instance, knew many beautiful women who traveled in his circle. On one occasion, he tried to match Mike up with one in the hopes that they would hit it off:

When I brought her over to Mike's place, he started talking to her and he right away gave me that look of like, 'Wow, you know, she's absolutely stunning,' right? And I left and came back later, and they were just sitting on the couch talking. I mean, not that I expected anything further than that, but there was just a lot of distance still going on with them and it looked like there was no connection and, you know, she went home. And she really liked him. Mike came up to me the next day and he said, 'She's a wonderful girl; she's beautiful, she's great, but she's not at the level that I need to have a woman in order for me to give her true love and share the value of love.' It had to be someone he connects with — his mind his brain and everything else — and then and only then he's willing to be with someone. At that point, for me, this was all new. Now I understand what he was talking about, but back then I was like, 'What the hell? Come on, bro! You know, she's hot!' — that sort of thing. But later on in life you realize that that's not all it's about; it's not all that matters. But Mike really broke it down to the point where I understood that he had to match with someone in the core of his philosophy and his belief system, for him to fall in love. And that wasn't right off the bat. There was no way he could have had that with her, not because she was dumb, but she was somewhat of a mystic. And he once said, 'I cannot be with a mystic.' He believed in reality, reason, Objectivism, and it was difficult for him to find someone [like that]. I think it really was, and you know he was so involved with his work that there wasn't that much time to really go out there and meet someone.[28]

At this stage of his life, Mike was more interested in finding a soulmate who shared his values and his philosophy. He believed that one should be able to define their values rather than merely *sense* them in order to know precisely what values or character attributes one respected and to recognize them in a potential soulmate. He once stated:

> Those who find my philosophy interesting and attractive share a certain mutuality of values with me. If not always on the level of explicit, verbalized, understanding, at least

in terms of subconscious, sense of life affinity. I have spent many years developing my philosophy, especially that aspect of most central significance: my values, which are of a positive nature. Specifically, I value reason, objectivity, logic, knowledge, science, human progress and happiness.[29]

A beautiful woman who was his polar opposite in terms of how she viewed the fundamental issues of human existence would not be a suitable long-term companion. Markus further recalled a time when he gained a deeper insight into Mike's views on romantic love:

> He used to pick me up at the gym in his car, which was quite an eyesore. It was an old station wagon, you know like the Griswold car from [the National Lampoon] *Vacation* movies with Chevy Chase — with the wood panels, that sort of car. And he picked me up in that car and I was embarrassed, you know? But he drove me back to his Playa del Rey condo, which was beautiful, by the way; it was amazing. The first time I was there, I remember he parked the car downstairs in the garage and there was a white Jaguar. All white on white, you know? Like a beautiful brand-new car. And I said, 'Whose car is that? There must be some rich people living here apparently — wow!' And he's like, 'No, Markus, that is my car. I bought this car just in case I'll meet the wonderful woman that will match me with intelligence and beauty and all the other stuff, you know? And then I will take her out to a nice romantic dinner in this car, not my shit ass car. I don't need a big car to go to Gold's Gym because I'm a big shot without a big car.' I'm like, fuck, you made you made your point.' I think it's a very wonderful romantic, old-fashioned, and intelligent way to look at love and relationship. Mike had all that and he just couldn't find someone that it was matching up with. And I think that's what this is about, you know? It's finding that ultimate soulmate.[30]

This, of course, was very much in accord with the Objectivist view of romantic love: the fires of physical attraction, or a sexual impulse, on their own, were not a viable substitute for the deep burning coals of mutual values that could be shared into old age.[31] In Mike's short story, "The Integrated Man," the protagonist, Mark Whitcraft, states Mike's belief regarding romantic love:

> This was it — the greatest pleasure life had to offer — to meet a woman with whom you fell in love, then conceptually verified this sense of life emotion by checking her personality and philosophy of life. Cindy did the same with me, as each of us had evolved philosophically far enough to understand that the emotion we call "love" is insufficient justification to form a relationship. When one falls in love, it's the other's sense of life he falls in love with. A sense of life is expressed in everything the person does — from the way they walk, talk, laugh, and move to the way they smile. . . . In addition to being attracted to each other's sense of life, Cindy and I shared an enormous mutuality of knowledge and values; and we had moved in together within several months after our first meeting each other. She was my most ardent supporter and even helped me understand things that were difficult for me.[32]

As a real-life Cindy had yet to appear in his life, and not wanting Mike to be alone on Christmas, I called him up and invited him to spend Christmas with my wife, Terri, our kids, and me in Canoga Park. I was delighted when he accepted. It turned out to be a very memorable Christmas, and Mike looked happier than I had seen him in months. After chatting for a while, I took him out to the garage and showed him a large weight training machine that had previously been owned by the late martial arts master Bruce Lee.

"I trained on a machine just like this when I was in the Air Force!" he declared with a laugh. "That, and a 45-pound dumbbell, was all they had."

We returned to the living room, and I gave Mike his gifts: two books, one on Nietzsche and the other on Ayn Rand and Objectivism, which seemed to delight him considerably.

He then gave me two gifts: a bottle of fine champagne to toast my liberation from Weider, and a copy of his new and revised *Heavy Duty* book that I had written the foreword to. When I cracked open its cover, there was an inscription inside:

To John, Thanks for everything.
To a friend of this sort . . . well, no more need be said!
Mike

It remains a treasured memento.

EPILOGUE

Shortly after our Christmas with Mike, my family and I moved to Idaho to work with the Bruce Lee estate, where I began writing a multivolume book series based upon Lee's surviving writings. I lost touch with Mike for about three years. During that time, I would occasionally check in on him via his website and was impressed to see that medical doctors and science students were contributing articles and posts in support of his methods. A huge testimonial list developed in support of his Heavy Duty program and, more uniquely for a bodybuilding website, in appreciation of his philosophy. Judging from this, he appeared to be doing well.

In 1996, Mike signed a contract with *All-Natural Muscular Development* magazine, which according to a reliable source paid him $10,000 a month. This lasted for about a year or two. During that time, he entertained the notion of getting back into competition shape. He began training hard and at one point had even started taking steroids again. But unlike in the past, the motivation wasn't there this time.[1] As Mike Tyson had announced at the end of his last fight, "I don't want to disrespect the sport that I love. My heart is not into this anymore."[2] After all the years of brutal training and near-starvation dieting for a title that now meant nothing to him, his will to train was gone. Friedrich Nietzsche and William James had left the building. Mike discontinued the workouts along with the drugs after only a few weeks.

Interestingly, Arthur Jones had experienced a similar situation. He discovered in 1972 that bodybuilding simply wasn't a priority in this life.[3] Training "just to stay in shape" was never a motivation for Mike. What had stoked the fires of his enthusiasm for training had always been the quest to build the ultimate physique, to be good enough to beat the best bodybuilders in the world in competition. And with that purpose removed, so too was removed the passion that underlay his training efforts. What lesser prize was there to train for? People telling him politely that he looked good "for his age"? Entering a "Masters Mr. Olympia" contest against former champions, who, like him, were now too old to compete onstage against the real Mr. Olympia competitors? A contract from a supplement company so he could sell more products for the bodybuilding industry? No thanks. He wasn't interested. He had clients to train and knowledge to obtain. The gym was his office, not his sanctuary.

Mike often said he wasn't put on this earth to win a popularity contest. Nor, it seemed, had he been put on earth to live an easy life. As with John Nash, the American mathematician whose life the book and film *A Beautiful Mind* were based on, Mike struggled every day to keep his mental illness at bay. This in itself was a workout sorts, which left Mike mentally exhausted until sleep put a cease to the labors of his mind. But as we've seen, sleep brought its own problems to contend with. Like Prometheus in Greek mythology, Mike spent every waking hour in an ordeal that saw the eagle of mental illness come to prey upon him. And the next day it came again and would continue to do so, if not for eternity, at least for the remainder of his time on earth. Nash, in writing about his own experience of living with mental illness, had said:

> I spent times on the order of five to eight months in hospitals in New Jersey, always on an involuntary basis and always attempting a legal argument for release. And it did happen that when I had been long enough hospitalized that I would finally renounce my delusional hypotheses and revert to thinking of myself as a human of more conventional circumstances and return to mathematical research. In these interludes of, as it were, enforced rationality, I did succeed in doing some respectable mathematical research.[4]

Nash utilized what he termed "enforced rationality" to combat the "dream-like delusional hypothesis" that often beset him. Mike, likewise, used enforced rationality to combat his own dream-like delusional hypotheses, which crept upon him whenever he let his intellectual guard down. His vigilance worked most of the time. And when it didn't, Mike was prescribed antidepressants and antianxiety medication, which he voluntarily ingested whenever he detected the power of his mental acuity diminishing.

A couple of accidents beset him and left him in a bad way. He slipped down the stairs in his condominium, which resulted in a torn triceps and leg injury that required surgery.[5] The doctors prescribed Vicodin to help with the pain — which was a big mistake. Soon an opioid dependency developed, and that, combined with an increasing use of alcohol to deaden the pain, negatively altered his personality at times and also negatively impacted his business. This was compounded when his contract with *All-Natural Muscular Development* expired. Suddenly, his forum was gone, and once again his money ran out. Mike had always been a soft touch. And certain of those around him recognized that he became a much softer touch when drugs and alcohol came into play.

Mike's primary interest in his final year of his life was in the philosophy of the mind. He had said all he wanted to say about bodybuilding training long ago, and now found that he was repeating himself to each new client, answering the same questions, employing the same analogies. It was philosophy, not bodybuilding, that had saved him from a life otherwise spent in and out of psychiatric institutions and prison. Not that bodybuilding wasn't useful, but he encouraged his clients to look deeper into what it was that was really behind their desire to build bigger muscles:

> There's a lot of self-satisfaction to be derived from recognizing that you are able to discipline yourself and use a certain amount of knowledge to take yourself from point A to point Z. To take your body from being average or below average to whatever it ultimately might be. But if you were to look deep down inside of yourself, get honest, what you're really looking for — even a businessman, somebody who wants to make a lot of money, a million dollars, they do want the money and that's fine and good — at bottom, the purpose of all goal achievement is to develop a sense of mastery, efficacy. To achieve a certain type of happiness that can only be had as a result of achieving goals. A lot of people find once they acquire the muscles they'd always dreamed of, they're not really different inside — because they don't take this philosophical approach. The idea is to gain a

sense of mastery, a sense of self-esteem, happiness, which can only be derived from achieving goals. You have to have that stated explicitly at the outset. If you think that you're going to end up having those things only as a result of having the muscles, and you don't work on developing other aspects of your life along with it, like your philosophy, then you're just going to end up with a set of muscles and be bereft of the rest. A lot of top bodybuilders have the big muscles, but they're self-arrested intellectually. They're no further ahead at the age of 30 or 40 mentally than they were ten or 15 years ago when they started. They're psychologically beset by the same conflicts, the same sense of insecurity, uncertainty, self-doubt. They've got the big muscles, but they didn't get that sense of mastery. Self-esteem can only be achieved by starting the whole process by stating explicitly, "Not only do I want big muscles, but I want self-confidence. I can only get that by enjoying the process, gaining the knowledge, and recognizing that I am a more effective person."[6]

To devote more attention to philosophy, Mike tried to get other people to train his in-the-gym clients. Dave Mastorakis recalled Mike asking him to take over at Gold's Gym for him.[7] He wanted someone else to carry on his phone consultations and tried to employ several of the people in his entourage to do this. But none of them were Mike Mentzer, and none of them had his understanding, experience, intellect, and passion for infusing philosophy into training. Phone clients didn't want to talk to an underling; they wanted to speak to Mr. Heavy Duty. A back surgery left Mike in excruciating pain. To help him convalesce, the doctors prescribed a potent drug: morphine.[8]

But Mike wasn't the only one whose body was experiencing problems; both of Ray Mentzer's kidneys gave out, a result of contracting Berger's disease, a rare kidney disorder.[9] He had to endure four-and-a-half-hour dialysis treatments three times a week.[10] It was also discovered that Ray had a rare blood clotting disorder.[11] If he didn't receive a donor kidney soon, there was a high probability that he would die. Despite their differences in the past, Ray was still Mike's little brother, and Mike offered to donate one of his kidneys to Ray. But when Mike went to the hospital for a compatibility test, the doctors discovered a rare clotting disorder in his lungs.[12] They put him on Coumadin, a potent blood thinner. Too potent, as it turned out. He sneezed, which started a nosebleed that poured forth like Niagara Falls. He was rushed back to the hospital, where he was taken off the medication and an inferior vena cava (IVC) filter was inserted into a large vein in his abdomen to block any clots making their way to his lungs.[13]

He hadn't been discharged long when he recognized something wasn't right and returned to the hospital. There, the doctors discovered that he had suffered several silent heart attacks.[14] The two packs a day of Camel cigarettes didn't help.

That's when Ray Mentzer phoned me. Or rather, he phoned my wife. The news I received was that Mike had had a heart attack and was in the West Los Angeles Veterans Affairs Medical Center. I happened to be in Los Angeles at the time, laying down the foley for a documentary I was making, *Bruce Lee: A Warrior's Journey*, when Terri called me with the news. I immediately called Ray at the number he'd left, jotted down the location of the hospital, and drove over to see Mike. When I entered the ICU, a big fellow who identified himself as a police officer barred my entrance. He said he would have to frisk me first before allowing me in the room. Apparently he was a friend of Mike's, and this was an attempt at humor on his part. To me, the situation was too serious for mirth. I shouldered my way past him and saw Mike lying on a hospital bed. I was taken aback by his appearance. He looked gaunt and frail. I was expecting to see him comatose, but it was the same old Mike. His eyes lit up and he put me at ease by informing me that the situation wasn't nearly as serious as Ray had led Terri to believe. After conversing for a while, and with the off-duty police officer staring over my shoulder the whole time, I asked Mike if he was allowed to go outside and get some air. Not a problem, he said. A nurse provided us with a wheelchair, and I pushed him out of the room, down the corridor and out into the California sunshine.

As soon as we were outside, Mike fired up a cigarette. Questions raced through my mind: Was he really okay? How was his hospitalization impacting his training business? What was his financial situation? I presumed he needed money — who knew how long his hospitalization would last — and pondered what I could do to help. His current arrangement writing articles for *Iron Man* magazine meant that only the people who purchased that magazine knew of his existence. If he was to earn money from his trade, people needed to know who he was, what he had to teach, and where to find him. That's when the idea came to me that Mike should write a new book. I had enjoyed some success in being a published author as of late and said that I knew a publisher that I believed would be willing to take on a book about Mike's unique training insights. Mike shook his head and said he didn't think he was up to writing another book. I had anticipated his response and had a ready answer to it. "But you already have. I have every article and book you've ever written. I can go through them all, collate material from your most meaningful articles and training courses, and then we can update them to reflect your current training beliefs. The book will serve as a lightning rod to attract people to your website and to your personal consultation business and other products. Consider it a mainstream business card that would appear in every bookstore and library throughout North America. That's a much larger market than the readers of a single magazine."

Mike's enthusiasm returned as a renewed sense of purpose began to take shape in his mind. After an hour or so, we said our goodbyes, and I said I would be in touch. I worked on preparing a book proposal for him to look over; if he approved it, I would send it along to the publisher. A week or so later, I sent Mike the proposal, and he was quite excited by it. He now thought our writing a book together was a great idea.[15] He was even more excited when I told him that an editor from a publishing house had told me she believed that they would pay an advance of $20,000 for the title. But a week or so later, I was disappointed when the same editor emailed to say that they had decided to pass on the project. They didn't really see the point of another fitness book, as the market was awash with them at the time. I wrote back a strongly worded email of protest, indicating the significance of Mike, the revolutionary ideas he had developed, and how he had a following that would be hungry for his latest offering. I began transcribing Mike's material and presenting it in a logically coherent structure until I had a finished book. I sent Mike the manuscript and he made what amendments he thought necessary. I then sent the final product along to the publisher to review.

While the editors reconsidered the project, I suggested to Mike that a good way for him to generate more revenue in the interim would be to create a new audio series — to read some of his best articles and essays onto tape and offer the cassettes for sale through his website. After all, he had enjoyed considerable success with an audio seminar on tape, which he released in late 1979, and with an audio series he had recorded for Twin Labs, when he worked for *All-Natural Muscular Development* magazine. But the new tapes

Epilogue

could offer something more; he could record not only his various essays on Heavy Duty training, but, even more appealing to Mike, he could record tapes on his philosophy. He became enthusiastic about the new business venture.[16] He sent me an article entitled "A Challenge to Volume Bodybuilders" that he thought would be the perfect script with which to kick off the audio series.

Bad news struck again, however, when Ray's MedX Spinal Rehabilitation clinic (which Mike had subsidized) closed, leaving Ray with no income. Mike moved into Ray's apartment to better care for his brother until a kidney became available. And then, surprise of surprises, who should ring Ray's apartment but Arnold Schwarzenegger! According to Mike:

> [Ray] received a phone call, believe it or not, from Arnold Schwarzenegger, which I found very touching, and I thank Arnold for that. Arnold called Ray and asked him how he was doing; told Ray he could call Arnold anytime he needed something or for any reason. It was a very benevolent gesture on Arnold's part, and in my eyes it raised his stature as a human being. I was shocked when the call came. I told Joe Weider many years ago, I hope Arnold really learns to mature and actualizes his full potential, because he's quite an outstanding individual.[17]

This was so bizarre, particularly given the history between Mike and Arnold, that when I caught wind of it, I called Mike and asked him if he thought Arnold's gesture was sincere. "Probably not," he said. "There's talk that Arnold is going to be running for governor of California [he would, in 2003], and he's trying to put out as many possible fires regarding his past as he can before they spread. But if he wants to help Ray out, I'm okay with that."

In May 2001, and quite out of the blue, Mike wrote a short story. It was a work of fiction, a step towards the novel he had long told me he had always wanted to write. It was an enjoyable read, and quite unlike anything he had ever written before. "A narrative tale," he called it. It was a synthesis of his bodybuilding theories with Objectivist philosophy and represented a summing-up and integration of everything he held dear in his life. It would turn out to be his final communiqué. I told him that we could use it as an appendix to the book we were working on — it could stand as his first published work of fiction. It would a great portfolio piece to have if he ever decided to write that novel. The prospect appealed to him. Mike was even more excited when I reported that the publisher had gotten back to me, and that they now wanted to proceed with the book.

But a week later his enthusiasm got the better of him; he informed me that he was going to start a new video project. This struck me as a bad idea right off the top. Number one, he was in no shape to do a training video. After all, he wasn't that long out of the hospital after having suffered multiple silent heart attacks. Surely the last thing he needed was the stress of producing a training video in which he would be in front of the camera lifting weights. Not to worry, he explained, he would only be supervising a bodybuilder (Markus Reinhardt) as he went through Mike's Heavy Duty workouts. Mike's role would be simply to explain the training concepts. As it didn't involve me, it was none of my business. I told him if he was certain his health was up to it, then he was free to do as he wished.

Over the next several weeks, he asked me to contribute an article to his website on Bruce Lee's training methods, which I did, and we shared further correspondence about our forthcoming book, his short story, the audio tape series, and certain philosophical asides. I had learned that that Friedrich Nietzsche, apart from writing philosophy, had also composed music, and that there were now CDs of his music available. Mike was pumped about this and wanted to obtain copies of them. Two new Ayn Rand books hit the market: one on nonfiction writing and another on fiction writing. Mike purchased the latter to better prepare him to write his novel. He also told me he was rereading Henry Miller for inspiration, and that he had forgotten how much he had enjoyed Miller's writing style.

Two thousand one was beginning to look like another renaissance year for Mike Mentzer.

But he had to know that he could die at any minute. In speaking with doctors afterwards, I was informed that for a man in his condition, arrhythmias would have been common, as would shortness of breath. Mike would have received such internal warnings daily, subtle reminders that each day might be his last. He had told an interviewer: "As people grow older, as I have — I'm a little bit beyond middle age — not fear of death, but concern with longevity, health, and the prospects of death become more central in one's thinking."[18] He seemed to have a premonition in this respect, which

Epilogue

may account for his flurry of activity in his final days — the new book, the audio series, the video. He was focused on getting his ideas on training out to the public one last time.

Most tellingly, in the days prior to his death Mike had made it a point to call anyone he cared for who had been a part of his life — Cathy Gelfo and Jack Neary among them — just to hear their voices and reconnect one last time. He called me from Palm Springs a week before he was to shoot the training video. He was there to get some sun, he said, to get some color back in his skin. But he was also there with his police officer friend whom I'd met at the hospital, and who now felt obliged to get on the phone and speak with me. When Mike came back on the line his voice sounded different; there was a loud, quasi-manic quality to it which made me nervous. Was he on something again?

The publishing contracts for the book arrived in Idaho on June 6. I signed them (there were three copies) and FedExed them overnight to Mike. He signed them and FedExed them on to the publisher. That was on June 7. June 10 would be his last day on earth, which he spent filming the training video at the Angel City Fitness club in Marina del Rey. The wonderful thing about Mike's video, if you can put aside the notion that he would be dead 12 hours after shooting it, is just how happy he appeared during his last day on earth. The video, book, and forthcoming audio series gave a purpose to his life that had been missing for some time. His focus and, thus his energies, were directed into something positive and productive. And having his days filled with purpose was always his raison d'être.

The famous Mentzer wit was present, as when he said wryly to Markus, who was born in Germany, "I hear you Germans are a *special breed*. Show me!" and facetiously goading Markus on in his efforts by sarcastically saying such things as "Come on, you mangy coward" and "Yes, you're very coordinated, now hurry up, goddamn it!" A "behind the scenes" video shows Mike sharing his training insights with the manager of the facility, talking with his brother while enjoying a cigarette, and respectfully flirting with the models and makeup girls for the video. At one point, with tongue planted firmly in cheek, he asks, "Do you think I look masculine enough? I'm uncertain" — this while the makeup girl brushes his hair.

The last day of his life, then, was a happy one. He knew he was filming something special. "I feel very good," he said while sitting on a seated dip machine and looking into the camcorder. "We're in the midst of making history. It is going to be the *best* exercise videotape of all time. Not just because I say so, but because we've got some great people working with us, including Markus."

"What?" Markus asked.

"I'm cheering you on," Mike replied, as the video fades to black.

The filming wrapped around 10:30 p.m. Mike, Ray, and Val Segal (who co-produced the video) headed off to get something to eat. It had been a long day. Mike was exhausted, but also invigorated. His autopsy report indicated that he had morphine in his system,[19] which suggested that at some point later that evening, the pain set in, no doubt a result of his being on his feet all day and helping to lift weights for Markus when the latter grew fatigued during the exercises. In truth, he should not have made this video, particularly being so recently out of the hospital, and still clearly recovering from his neck/back surgery. And yet who could deny him his happiness?

Upon returning to the apartment, Mike needed to decompress — but he was still excited by the day's shooting. He popped some antianxiety medication to relax, along with two antidepressants (he now recognized the need for proper medication to help keep his brain stable). But the pain continued. He reached for the bottle of morphine that had been prescribed for him upon being discharged from the hospital and took a 30-milligram tablet. He then sat down in his chair to type out some more ideas for the video.

Ray woke up shortly after midnight and came out into the living room. He noted Mike was typing away furiously on his computer. Obviously, some additional ideas for the video had come into his head. Ray told Mike to go to sleep. Mike looked up, smiled, and said he would soon. Ray returned to bed, shut out the light, and soon was fast asleep. He would be the only Mentzer brother to wake up that morning.

At 8:30 a.m., the bright sunlight streaming in through his window alerted Ray that it was time to get up. He ventured into the bathroom and from there into the living room. And that's when he saw Mike's body, crumpled on the floor beneath his computer. The chair was turned awkwardly away from him. Ray knew instantly that Mike wasn't sleeping. His brother was dead.

Ray immediately dialed 911, and within minutes, paramedics arrived and took Mike's body to the hospital, and then on to the morgue. Once word got out, the vultures descended. Mike's stereo system, along with his television, his watch, and a small amount of cash that had been left on the kitchen counter disappeared.[20] The condominium was in flux.

Epilogue

I don't remember who called to tell me the news; all I remember is the news itself: Mike was dead. I do remember that when the call came in, I was seated amongst boxes that had been packed in preparation for our family's move back to Canada. I further recall being numb upon hearing the report, but not surprised. Anger flashed: I knew Mike shouldn't have made that video! He brought this on himself! That was the defensive wall I put up, at any rate. A few hours later, Ray phoned me. He relayed his experience of finding Mike lifeless and of having just returned from the morgue where he had officially identified his brother's body. I told him to stay strong, that his brother's legacy was now in his hands. He seemed surprisingly clearheaded given what had transpired, and he agreed with me. Moreover, he said, since he would be taking over Mike's business, Mike's half of the book advance should now be made payable to him. He was, after all, Mike's next of kin. I said I'd pass the information along to the publisher, wished him well, and hung up the phone.

Later that afternoon, my family and I left for the airport and flew home to Canada. By the time we had settled into our new house and I was able to get my computer online, I noticed that numerous emails had come in. One of them was from Joanne Sharkey, Mike's secretary/business manager. Upon opening it, I was stunned to learn that Ray was dead! It was like something out of a Greek tragedy. Ray had evidently missed his dialysis appointment the morning after we had spoken, and when Joanne's husband went to Ray's apartment to do a wellness check, he discovered Ray lying in bed and cold to the touch. Just as Ray had followed his brother's lead in life, it appeared that he had also followed it into death. Both brothers had severe atherosclerotic cardiovascular disease. Mike had suffered previous heart attacks; his left main coronary artery was blocked — this factor alone could have been what triggered his fatal heart attack. Ray, similarly, had severe coronary disease and a fully occluded right main coronary artery. Both had morphine in their respective systems to help with pain management, in what was described as a "fatal concentration." But what constituted a fatal level for them given their poor health might not have been a fatal level for a healthy person. Ray further suffered from electrolyte issues resulting from his dialysis that he needed to stay on top of. Both had fluid in their lungs, which could have come prior to or after their heart attacks.[21] Their fragile condition, along with the stress of making the video (and in Mike's case, smoking) had resulted in a cardiac time bomb that could go off at any time. In any event, in a matter of two days, the Mentzer brothers were no more.

There was talk about a memorial service to be held by the bodybuilding community for the two brothers who had made such an impact on the sport. But nothing ever happened. There was no funeral. No celebration of life. No memorial. Nothing. Twenty years went by, and then Mike's ashes, along with those of Ray, were unceremoniously deposited into the Pacific Ocean by Joanne, shortly before her own death in 2021.

In contrast, those who had opposed Mike throughout his life had prospered. Ben Weider was made an Officer of the Order of Canada (OC) in 2006[22] (he had been awarded the Member of the Order of Canada, or CM, in 1975).[23] He had even been nominated for the Nobel Peace Prize in 1975.[24] In 1998, the International Olympic Committee had granted Ben and his IFBB provisional recognition of bodybuilding as a sport, thus bringing him one step closer to realizing his long-held dream.[25] While not the full recognition Ben coveted, it was no small accomplishment. In 2008, Ben passed away in his native Montreal at the age of 85.

Joe and Betty Weider were inducted into the International Sports Hall of Fame, and, in a tremendous bit of irony, the International Sports Sciences Association awarded Joe its Outstanding Lifetime Achievement Award.[26] He was a man who sold a dream, and the dreamers rewarded him with their patronage. For a man who loved money, Joe's efforts were exceedingly well compensated. He sold his magazines in 2003 for $357 million,[27] and his supplement company a year later for $14 million.[28] He would live on to the ripe old age of 93.

Arnold Schwarzenegger went on to become the biggest box office star in the world and followed the path of fame right into the Governor's Mansion of California. As he owned a piece of Weider's supplement company, he made a dollar or two on the sale of that in 2004.[29] Curiously, however, in a three-part biography on his life that was produced by Netflix (and which Arnold had creative control over), no mention was made of the 1980 Mr. Olympia contest.

And then the wheel turned.

Ben's beloved IFBB never received Olympic recognition (he lived long enough to witness the IOC withdraw its provisional recognition of bodybuilding).[30] Gradually, the IFBB's power and influence began to erode. The NPC, which had once given the IFBB and the Weiders total control over amateur bodybuilding in America, severed its ties with the federation in 2017.[31] The jewel in the crown of Joe Weider's legacy, the Mr. Olympia contest, would eventually be sold by his heirs to a man named Jake Wood.[32] The Weider legacy has already started to fade from public memory.

Epilogue

As for Arnold, his once rising star stopped rising. Even though he continued to hit the gym every day, the passage of time took away the physique that made him famous, causing him to lament in the press that "I never, ever thought . . . when I was 30 years old or 40 years old, that this is going to happen."[33] His films underperformed at the box office, while his lifelong quest for power only landed him as far as the governorship of California, where he finished out his second term with an abysmal 23 percent approval rating.[34] A far cry from Charlemagne's and Napoleon's sway, and light years' shy of Jesus's. Arnold's desire (as indicated in the documentary *Pumping Iron*) to be remembered for thousands of years now appears highly unlikely.

And yet the legacy of Mike Mentzer has witnessed a renaissance. Videos of his training methods are watched by millions, and hundreds of thousands of people have subscribed to various YouTube channels that feature his content. An online course was created about not only his bodybuilding beliefs but also his personal philosophy. As of this writing, a quarter of a century after his passing, Mike enjoys a popularity that he never experienced during his lifetime, and all signs indicate that it is growing. I suspect the reason is that, as he once said, "nothing human is foreign to me," a statement originally uttered by the Roman playwright Terence in the second century B.C. In other words, he was relatable. He lived a life that pushed the physical and mental boundaries of the human experience not only to the edge, but over it. He experienced all of the highs and lows that life had to offer. No matter what you are experiencing, Mike was a fellow human being who experienced it, too.

Not long before his death, he said, "I'm receiving more email from readers of my website who appreciate the philosophical content more than the fitness/bodybuilding/nutritional aspects."[35] Perhaps Mike's legacy will prove to be as a transmission line for philosophy rather than muscles. It certainly wouldn't be the first time that an athlete made the transition. Plato, after all, was first an athlete, a wrestler, who had been renowned for his physique (his real name was Aristocles; "Plato" is in fact his nickname, meaning "broad" as in broad-shouldered). He was said to have competed successfully at the Pythian games in Delphi, the Olympics of its day. But if he had remained in the realm of muscle, as a wrestler, we wouldn't know anything about him. But because he exalted philosophy, a means to help people make decisions in times of crisis, he is still studied 2,500 years after his passing in university classes all around the world.

"It was in the age of Classical Greece 23 centuries ago that the dictum 'a healthy mind in a healthy body' arose," Mike once said. "So, there's nothing wrong with building the body, as long as you don't miss the most crucial factor or element: the mind."[36] His philosophy of logic, science, and reason once caused the twin mists of hype and confusion that blanketed the bodybuilding world to lift. And even if this occurred only for a brief moment in time, it was enough to inspire people from various walks of life to live more authentic lives and to strengthen their minds along with their bodies.

And that, in the final analysis, may prove to be a monument to his memory far more lasting than bronze.

NOTES

PROLOGUE
1. *MuscleMag International*, March 1982.

CHAPTER ONE: BORN IN THE USA
1. R.F. Weigley et al. (eds.), *Philadelphia: A 300-Year History* (New York and London: W. W. Norton, 1982), 134.
2. National Park Service (website), "Germantown Quaker Petition Against Slavery," updated April 5, 2016.
3. History.com, "Battle of Germantown," updated June 26, 2023.
4. National Park Service (website), "Germantown White House," updated August 11, 2021.
5. Family Search (website), "Johannes Meinzer," ID: KV2D-Y6R. See also Carl Boyer, ed., *Ship Passenger Lists, Pennsylvania and Delaware (1641–1825)* (Westminster, MD: Heritage Books, [1980] 2007).
6. See note 5, Boyer.
7. See note 5, "Johannes Meinzer."
8. For Samuel Mentzer's birth, please see his draft registration card, dated June 5, 1917. For his year of death, please see his death certificate, dated September 19, 1956, Commonwealth of Pennsylvania, Department of Vital Statistics, and his obituary in the *Lancaster New Era*, September 19, 1956.
9. Samuel Mentzer's draft registration card, June 5, 1917.
10. Samuel Mentzer had written down "machinist" for "Bareville Scale Works" on his World War I draft registration card.
11. *Intelligencer Journal* (Lancaster, PA), September 20, 1956.
12. See Find a Grave (website), "Kathryn 'Katie' Coldren Mentzer," Memorial ID: 92580675. See also *Sunday News* (Lancaster County, PA) May 24, 1959.
13. 1940 United States Federal Census.
14. U.S. World War II Draft Cards Young Men, 1940–47.
15. Samuel and Kathryn ("Katie") Mentzer had six children: Charles Walter, born April 6, 1916 (U.S. World War II Draft Cards Young Men, 1940–47, registration date: October 16, 1940); Mary Kathryn, July 8, 1917 (U.S. Social Security Applications and Claims Index,

1936–2007); Grace Etta, August 13, 1919 (U.S. Social Security Applications and Claims Index, 1936–2007); Robert Samuel, November 23, 1921 (U.S. Social Security Applications and Claims Index, 1936–2007); Harry Earl, July 12, 1923 (U.S. Veterans Burial Card); Parke Geist, February 2, 1930 (U.S. Social Security Applications and Claims Index, 1936–2007).

16. U.S. Federal Naturalization Records, December 1, 1943.
17. U.S. Federal Naturalization Records, June 15, 1929.
18. U.S. Federal Naturalization Record for Anna De Stefano, District Court, Eastern District, Pennsylvania, Petition Number: 121281, November 14, 1935.
19. See note 18.
20. U.S. Veterans Burial Card, Commonwealth of Pennsylvania Department of Military Affairs.
21. Ray Mentzer interview, Australia, 1985.
22. Uno E. Mantyla in the 1940 United States Federal Census; Minnesota, U.S., Births and Christenings Index, 1840–1980.
23. Virginia, U.S., Birth Records, 1912–2015, Delayed Birth Records, 1721–1920.
24. *Philadelphia Inquirer*, June 18, 1940.
25. See Find a Grave (website), "Elmer Mantyla Jr." Memorial ID: 204734831.
26. *Minneapolis Star*, September 10, 1949.
27. 1950 United States Federal Census.
28. See note 27.
29. Mike Mentzer's interview with Irene Hause, 1981.
30. *Intelligencer Journal*, April 29, 1972.
31. U.S. Social Security Death Index, 1935–2014; Mike Mentzer's interview with Peter McGough, 1993.
32. U.S. Social Security Applications and Claims Index, 1936–2007; Mike Mentzer, McGough interview, 1993.
33. See note 29.
34. Henry Gannett, *The Origin of Certain Place Names in the United States* (Washington Government Printing Office, 1905), 120.
35. Charles Coulombe, "Heretic of the Week: Conrad Beissel." *Catholic Herald* (website). November 21, 2019.
36. See note 33. See also Sid Mentzer interview, emailed to the author on July 19, 2023.
37. See note 33.
38. See note 33.
39. Mike Mentzer quoted from Twin Labs, audiocassette series, 1996, tape 4: "Mike Mentzer: The Man and the Controversy."
40. See note 33.
41. See note 39.
42. See note 33.
43. See note 33.
44. Sid Mentzer interview.
45. See note 44.
46. *New Era* (Lancaster, PA), February 2, 1987.
47. See note 29.
48. See note 33.

49. *Ephrata Review*, July 2, 1964, and June 29, 1967.
50. See note 33.
51. *Muscle Builder/Power*, August 1979.
52. See note 51.
53. See note 39.
54. *Intelligencer Journal*, August 3, 1962.
55. See note 39.
56. *Ephrata Review*, May 21, 1964.
57. *Ephrata Review*, October 1, 1964. See also *Ephrata Review*, October 29, 1964.
58. See note 39.
59. See note 51.
60. See note 33.
61. "He [Mike Mentzer] did tell me once that his mother suffered from depression, but that's all he said. Mike himself told me he also tended to suffer from depression and thought it might be a genetic tendency inherited from his mother." Facebook message from Jerry Brainum on July 3, 2023.
62. In conducting research for this book, the author uncovered at least five instances in Mike Mentzer's life where he was beset by a strong depression, at times so overwhelming that he couldn't get out of bed.
63. Mike Mentzer, interview with the author, 1986.
64. See note 33.

CHAPTER TWO: BRAVE NEW WORLD

1. *New Era*, November 10, 1978.
2. *Sun Magazine* (Baltimore, MD), June 19, 1977.
3. Steve Reeves, John Little, and Bob Wolff, *Building the Classic Physique: The Natural Way* (Calabasas, CA: Little-Wolff Creative Group, 1995), 147.
4. George Snyder and Rick Wayne, *Three More Reps* (Pennsylvania: Olympus Health & Recreation, 1978), 139.
5. Mike Mentzer, McGough interview.
6. See note 5.
7. See note 5.
8. Mike Mentzer, interview with the author, 1990.
9. See note 5.
10. *Ephrata Review*, June 20, 2001.
11. Mike Mentzer, interview with the author, 1986. See also Mike Mentzer and John Little, *High-Intensity Training the Mike Mentzer Way* (New York: McGraw Hill, 2003), 24.
12. See note 11.
13. Mike Mentzer quoted from Mike Mentzer and Ardy Friedberg, *The Mentzer Method to Fitness* (New York: William Morrow, 1980), 19.
14. *Muscle Builder/Power*, August 1979.
15. *Ephrata Review*, November 7, 2007. See also Mike Mentzer, McGough interview. And: *Ephrata Review*, October 12, 2016.
16. *Tucson Daily Citizen*, February 7, 1976.
17. Cyberpump (site discontinued), "The Steel Spiel! With Mike Mentzer," October 8, 2001.
18. *Muscle & Fitness*, February 1981.

19. *Ephrata Review*, February 17, 1972.
20. USA Strength & Conditioning Coaches Hall of Fame (website), "Robert C. Hoffman."
21. Twin Labs, tape 4: "Mike Mentzer: The Man and the Controversy."
22. Encyclopedia.com, "Grimek, John (1910–1998)," March 18, 2024.
23. *Health and Strength*, July 19, 1956.
24. David Chapman, "John Grimek: The Glow That Never Failed," MuscleMemory (online database).
25. John Grimek, interview with the author, 1992.
26. IOC (website). "Berlin 1936 Weightlifting 82.5 Kg Heavyweight Men Results."
27. See note 25.
28. See note 21.
29. Heavy Duty College, "John Grimek (Mr. America): 'I Made My Best Gains Ever on a One Set Per Exercise Program,'" YouTube video, July 29, 2023.
30. Randy Roach, *Muscle, Smoke & Mirrors, Volume I* (Bloomington, IN: AuthorHouse, 2008), 145.
31. Dan Lurie and David Robson, *Heart of Steel: The Dan Lurie Story* (Bloomington, IN: AuthorHouse, 2009), 56. See also *Los Angeles Times*, March 2, 1989.
32. *Montreal Gazette*, September 23, 2008.
33. Roach, *Volume I*, 146. See also Ben and Joe Weider, *Brothers of Iron* (Champaign, IL: Sports Publishing, 2006), 104.
34. *Classic Physique Builder* (blog), "*Your Physique*: Joe Weider's First Bodybuilding Magazine," September 1, 2007.
35. Dan Lurie (archived official website), "Dan Lurie Barbell Company."
36. Roach, *Volume I*, 275.
37. Weider and Weider, *Brothers of Iron*, 104. See also note 35.
38. Roach, *Volume I*, 146.
39. M&F Editors, "Joe Weider: The Master Blaster," *Muscle & Fitness* (website).
40. To wit: "Bob Birdsong's Zappy Leg Routine," "My Whack-The-Back Program for Instant Growth," "Bombing Arnold's Forearms with the Double Split," *Muscle Builder/Power*, January 1975.
41. *Sports Illustrated*, April 6, 1970.
42. IFBB (website), "The Founding Fathers, Ben and Joe Weider."
43. *Sports Illustrated*, April 9, 1962.
44. *Strength and Health*, September 1948.
45. MuscleMemory (online database), "Larry Scott."
46. See note 5. See also Old School Labs (website), "Mr. Olympia 1965: The First-Ever Mr. Olympia."
47. *Muscle Builder/Power*, January 1966.
48. Greg Merritt, "The 1965 Mr. Olympia," TheBarbell.com, September 27, 2022.
49. See note 5.
50. See note 47.
51. See note 47.
52. *Muscle Builder/Power*, May 1978.
53. See note 47.
54. Rick Wayne, *Muscle Wars* (New Jersey: BookBaby, 2013), 186.

55. Tony DeFrancisco, "How Larry Scott trained to win the Mr. Universe and Mr. Olympia Titles," LinkedIn, May 24, 2017.
56. Larry Scott, *Loaded Guns* (North Salt Lake, UT: Larry Scott & Associates, 1991), 1.
57. See note 47.
58. See note 47.
59. See note 47.
60. Wayne, *Muscle Wars*, 725.
61. Wayne, *Muscle Wars*, 736.
62. See note 5.
63. See note 5.

CHAPTER THREE: THE DREAM MERCHANTS

1. Larry Scott, interview with the author, 1992.
2. Roach, *Volume I*, 330.
3. Roach, *Volume I*, 397. See also Golden Era Bookworm, "Evidence of Testosterone in the Silver Era," YouTube video, March 18, 2023.
4. Wayne, *Muscle Wars*, 1338–43.
5. Roach, *Volume I*, 336–37, citing Bill Pearl, *Getting Stronger* (Bolinas, CA: Shelter Publications Inc., 1986), 405.
6. J.M. Beiner et al., "The Effect of Anabolic Steroids and Corticosteroids on Healing of Muscle Contusion Injury," *American Journal of Sports Medicine* 27, no. 1 (1999). See also Kire Stojkovski and Daniel Boyer, "How Do Steroids Work?" *Charlotte Observer* (website), January 10, 2023.
7. Shalender Bhasin et al., "The Effects of Supraphysiologic Doses of Testosterone on Muscle Size and Strength in Normal Men," *New England Journal of Medicine* 335, no. 1 (July 4, 1996): 1–7.
8. Doug McGuff, "Enhanced vs Unenhanced Training Results," YouTube video, January 15, 2024.
9. Mark Bowden, *Killing Pablo: The Hunt for the World's Greatest Outlaw* (New York: Atlantic Monthly Press, 2001), 34.
10. Conor Heffernan, "Old Time Selling — Eugen Sandow and the Business of Supplements," Physical Culture Study (website), October 4, 2023.
11. The coupon that appears in and on the back cover of the November 1947 edition of Joe Weider's *Muscle Power* magazine states: "Dear Joe: I want a strong body . . . fast! Rush me, quick, my complete Weider Superior Bodybuilding Gym, PLUS the famous Weider System of Instruction." The gym was either a 235-pound or 335-pound barbell set (the reader's choice for either $38 or $48 respectively) that consisted of a barbell, two dumbbells, swing bell handle, two kettle bell handles, iron boots, headstrap, wrist roller, collars and barbell plates. This was one of 15 ads that appeared in the publication for training equipment — there is not one supplement ad to be found.
12. In the January 1965 edition of *Mr. America* magazine, there appear 28 ads promoting Joe Weider's supplements. Interestingly, one can trace the profitability of supplement sales versus equipment sales via the ads that appeared for both in the magazines. The August 1965 edition of *Mr. America* magazine (which would feature the first ad for the 1965 Mr. Olympia contest), contained 74 ads for training equipment and 29 ads for supplements. By March 1979, *Muscle Builder* featured 39 supplement ads and 47

ads for equipment. By November 1994, Weider's *Flex* magazine boasted 55 supplement ads and only 36 for equipment.
13. *Mr. America* magazine, December 1959, 37.
14. See note 12.
15. *U.S. Postal Service v. Joseph Weider*, October 29, 1975.
16. *Muscle Builder/Power*, March 1968.
17. *Your Physique*, December 1951.
18. Randy Roach, *Muscle, Smoke & Mirrors, Volume II* (Bloomington, IN: AuthorHouse, 2011), 7–8.
19. Roach, *Volume II*, 9.
20. Heavy Duty College, "Mike Mentzer: Nutrition for Bodybuilding," YouTube video, May 8, 2023.
21. Mike Mentzer, *Heavy Duty Nutrition* (Los Angeles, CA: self-published course, 1979), 1.
22. Roach, *Volume II*, 623.
23. *U.S. Postal Service v. Joseph Weider*, October 29, 1975.
24. Conor Heffernan, "Soy, Science and Selling: Bob Hoffman's Hi-Proteen Powder," Physical Culture Study (website), July 18, 2023.
25. See note 23.
26. See note 23.
27. Roach, *Volume I*, 202–3.
28. *Strength and Health* magazine, March 1962, 5.
29. See note 19.
30. Conor Heffernan, "Supplements Bodybuilding Forgot: Bob Hoffman's Fish Protein Powder," Physical Culture Study (website), July 14, 2023.
31. Mentzer and Little, *High-Intensity Training*, 23.
32. Clarence Bass (website), "Beyond the Universe: The Bill Pearl Story," 2006.
33. Bill Pearl Enterprises (archived website), "Bill's Career."
34. Rodney A. Labbe, "1999 Bill Pearl Interview," *The Tight Tan Slacks of Dezso Ban* (blog), March 2, 2020.
35. Mentzer and Little, *High-Intensity Training*, 128.
36. Flex Staff, "Pearl's Wisdom," *Muscle & Fitness* (website).
37. *Muscle Builder/Power*, October 1979.
38. Heavy Duty College, "Mike Mentzer: Bodybuilding Training," YouTube video, August 14, 2023.
39. Mike Mentzer, interview with the author, 1996.
40. Peter McGough, "Dan Lurie: 1923–2013," *Muscular Development* (website), November 7, 2013.
41. *Iron Man* (website), "Dave Mastorakis, 59, Strives to Get His Contest Body Back," January 11, 2011. See also *Muscle Builder/Power*, January 1966.
42. Dave Mastorakis, interview with the author, July 9, 2023.
43. *Strength and Health*, December 1965.
44. Dave Mastorakis, email to the author, August 16, 2023. See also *Iron Man* magazine, "Dave Mastorakis" (online article).
45. See note 41.
46. Dave Mastorakis, email to the author, July 25, 2023.
47. See note 42.

Notes

CHAPTER FOUR: FAMILY ISSUES

1. *Atlanta Journal and Constitution*, February 13, 1972. The Ephrata newspapers cease mention of Mike playing football after 1964. His yearbook from 1968 indicates that he was still on the Ephrata Track and Field team.
2. *Sun Magazine*, June 19, 1977. See also *Ephrata Review*, February 17, 1972.
3. *Ephrata Review*, June 20, 2001.
4. *Atlanta Journal and Constitution*, February 13, 1972.
5. Mike Mentzer, McGough interview.
6. *Advocate*, June 12, 1980.
7. *New Era*, November 10, 1978. Mike's views on homosexuality remained liberal throughout his life. When interviewed by a reporter from the gay and lesbian publication the *Advocate*, he said: "I'm heterosexual and I'm not turned on sexually by male bodies. . . . I've never been approached by another top bodybuilder, but I have been approached by people who train in gyms. Many of them don't look like they even lift weights. Some of them are obviously there to procure sexual partners. Which is all right. I mean, heterosexuals go anywhere they want to pick up women. I don't particularly like it in the gym because this is where I work, this is my office. I've been here [in California] two and a half years now and the word has gotten around that Mentzer doesn't deal. It doesn't appall me that certain bodybuilders make a living doing that sort of thing. To me, life is a big adventure and diversity is what makes it an adventure." *Advocate*, June 12, 1980.
8. *Muscle Builder/Power*, October 1977. See also *Sun Magazine*, June 19, 1977. And: Mentzer, *Heavy Duty Nutrition*.
9. Mike Mentzer, "The Psychology of a Competitive Bodybuilder: A Narrative Tale," unpublished, 2001, property of the author.
10. Mentzer, *Heavy Duty Nutrition*.
11. *Muscle Builder/Power*, October 1977. See also *Pittsburgh Post-Gazette*, April 3, 1979. And: *Atlanta Journal and Constitution*, February 13, 1972.
12. Dave Mastorakis, interview with the author, July 9, 2023.
13. See note 12.
14. See note 12.
15. See note 12.
16. See note 12.
17. See note 12.
18. See note 12.
19. Dave Mastorakis, email to the author, August 16, 2023.
20. See note 12.
21. See note 12.
22. See note 12.
23. See note 12.
24. See note 12.
25. Dave Mastorakis, email to the author, July 24, 2023.
26. *Intelligencer Journal*, August 28, 1969.
27. See note 3.
28. Ray Mentzer's football successes as indicated in the Ephrata High School Yearbook (1969).

29. *Ephrata Review*, December 1, 1969.
30. *Ephrata Review*, March 2, 2011.
31. *Intelligencer Journal*, September 20, 1969. See also *Intelligencer Journal*, August 28, 1969, and *Ephrata Review*, December 1, 1969.
32. *Muscle Builder/Power*, August 1979.
33. *New Era*, June 4, 1971. It was evident that Mike had been training there for a while by this time.
34. Joe Weider, *The IFBB Album of Bodybuilding All-Stars* (New York: Elsevier-Dutton, 1979), 228.
35. *Wichita Falls Times*, November 5, 1976.
36. *Rochester Democrat and Chronicle*, February 1, 1978. See also *Charlotte Observer*, January 25, 1976, and *Sunday Courier & Press* (Evansville, IN), February 20, 1972. And: *GQ*, February 1980, 159.
37. *GQ*, February 1980.
38. *Wichita Falls Times*, November 5, 1976. See also *Ephrata Review*, February 17, 1972.
39. *Sunday Courier & Press*, February 20, 1972.
40. Roger Schwab, interview with the author, July 17, 2023.
41. See note 39.
42. *Sun Magazine*, June 19, 1977.
43. Cyberpump (site discontinued), "The Steel Spiel! With Mike Mentzer." See also Mentzer, McGough interview. And: *New Era*, June 13, 2010.
44. See note 4.
45. See note 2.
46. Mike Mentzer, Hause interview.
47. *MuscleMag International Annual 3*, 1978–79.
48. See note 47.
49. *Ephrata Review*, November 21, 1968.
50. See note 2.
51. Mike Mentzer, interview with the author, 1986.
52. Vince Basile, interview with the author, July 17, 2023.
53. Commonwealth of Virginia, Department of Health — Bureau of Vital Records and Health Statistics. Marriage Return; marriage certificate between Harry Earl Mentzer and Alta Jean Markley — maiden name: McCord, June 6, 1972.
54. Sid Mentzer interview.
55. See note 46.

CHAPTER FIVE: THE WILL TO POWER

1. MuscleMemory (online database), "Arnold Schwarzenegger." See also: Arnold Schwarzenegger (official website), "Bio."
2. *Flex*, May 2005.
3. Greg Merritt, "Joe Weider's Story: Bodybuilding, Magazines, and Arnold Schwarzenegger," *Muscle & Fitness* (website).
4. MuscleMemory (online database), "Arnold Schwarzenegger."
5. See note 4.
6. Laurence Leamer, *Fantastic: The Life of Arnold Schwarzenegger* (New York: St. Martin's Press, 2005), 12.

Notes

7. Leamer, 17.
8. Arnold Schwarzenegger with Peter Petre, *Total Recall: My Unbelievably True Life Story* (New York: Simon and Schuster, 2012), 17.
9. Jack Beresford, "Fact Check: Was Arnold Schwarzenegger's Dad a Nazi Sergeant?" *Newsweek* (website), August 21, 2021.
10. "I was born with a father that was a Nazi." Arnold Schwarzenegger quoted from CNN, "Schwarzenegger says his dad was 'sucked into a hate system.'" YouTube video short, April 27, 2023. See also: "After a two-month investigation, in which Simon Wiesenthal was involved, the verdict was in: Gustav Schwarzenegger was indeed a member of the Nazi party; he voluntarily applied for membership in 1938." *Los Angeles Times*, August 14, 2003. See also: "Millions of Austrians in the thirties believed that Hitler would bring order and discipline to the world, but only a minority of them joined the Nazi Party, as Gustav did in 1938, four months after the annexation of Austria. As a police officer, he surely found it advantageous to carry a party card." Leamer, 16.
11. See note 8.
12. Nola Ojomu, "'He Could Go Crazy at Any Time': Arnold Schwarzenegger Brands His Nazi Father 'a TYRANT' as He Recalls the 'Brutal' Abuse and Beatings He Suffered at His Hands as a Child," *Daily Mail* (website), June 6, 2023.
13. Mark Leibovich, "Arnold Schwarzenegger's Last Act: What Happens When the Terminator Turns 75," *Atlantic* (website), March 8, 2023.
14. See note 12.
15. Leamer, *Fantastic*, 48. See also: Betsy Morris et al. "Arnold Power: He Accumulates It. He Wields It. He Wins Over Voters with It. But Is the Governator's Star Power Enough to Win the War of Wills with His California Opponents?" *Fortune*, August 9, 2004.
16. Arnold Schwarzenegger with Douglas Kent Hall, *Arnold: The Education of a Bodybuilder* (New York: Simon & Schuster, 1977), 19.
17. Wendy Leigh, *Arnold: An Unauthorized Biography* (Chicago: Congdon & Weed, 1990), 26.
18. Nigel Andrews, *True Myths: The Life and Times of Arnold Schwarzenegger* (Secaucus, NJ: Birch Lane Press, 1996), 20.
19. Golden Era Bookworm, "Arnold's Trainer Reveals Arnold's First Cycle & Training Program! Kurt Marnul Interview 2," YouTube video, September 19, 2021.
20. See note 19.
21. See note 19.
22. See note 19. This works out to (oral steroids)10 mg × 3 per day = 30 mg a day × 7 days = 210 + 100 mg (injectable steroid) = 310 mg per week. For Arnold starting bodybuilding training at age 15, see Schwarzenegger and Hall, *Arnold*, 13.
23. *Iron Man* magazine, July 1967. See also note 19.
24. Leigh, *Arnold*, 27 and 46.
25. Wayne, *Muscle Wars*, 1394–99. See also Leigh, 67.
26. Schwarzenegger and Petre, 65.
27. Leigh, 29.
28. *Iron Man* magazine, July 1967.
29. See note 28.
30. *Pumping Iron*, directed by George Butler and Robert Fiore (Holderness, NH: White Mountain Films, 1977).

31. Roach, *Volume II*, 23–24. See also Leamer, *Fantastic*, 52.
32. John Fair, "The Intangible Arnold: The Controversial Mr. Olympia Contest of 1980." *Iron Game History* 11, no. 1 (September 2009). See also Leamer, 45.
33. Leamer, 48–49.
34. Leamer, 49.
35. Leamer, 20–21.
36. "Altruism was not Welder's primary motive. He said that the circulation of his magazines was declining, as was the sport itself in terms of popularity. If he could make Arnold Schwarzenegger the greatest bodybuilder of his time, not only would Weider have his greatest achievement as a kingmaker, but his magazines and business empire would benefit immeasurably." Leamer, 55.
37. Scott, *Loaded Guns*, 38.
38. Cuban Studies Institute, "Oliva, Sergio," CubansinAmerica.us.
39. Wayne, *Muscle Wars*, 1881.
40. Leamer, 56.
41. *Muscle Builder/Power*, September 1969, 32.
42. See note 41.
43. Andy Richardson, "Bodybuilder 'The Chemist' Who Beat Arnold Schwarzenegger Still Pumping Iron at 80," *Daily Star* (website), July 30, 2022. Author Rick Wayne put the weight differential between Schwarzenegger and Zane at 70 pounds: "Mr. America, Frank Zane, who was some 70 pounds lighter than Arnold but displayed deep cuts, ridges, and aesthetic curves all over." Wayne, *Muscle Wars*,1546.
44. "I thought the competition was fixed because he [Frank Zane] was just not big enough to win against me. Even though I lacked the definition, he was a scrawny little guy." Schwarzenegger and Petre, 75. See also Rachel Dobkin, "Needs Work: I'm a 3-Time Mr. Olympia & Crushed Arnold Schwarzenegger's Mr Universe Dreams — His 'Balloon Belly' Was a Major Mistake," *US Sun* (website), July 5, 2003.
45. Wayne, *Muscle Wars*, 1546.
46. Daniel Figueroa, "Vince Gironda Talks About Arnold Training at His Gym," YouTube video, July 6, 2019.
47. T.C. Luoma, "1993 Vince Gironda Interview," *The Tight Tan Slacks of Dezso Ban* (blog), October 15, 2023.
48. See note 46.
49. Kim "Kong" Farrison, "Mits Kawashima Interview (Part 1 of 6)," YouTube video, February 11, 2009. See also *Iron Man* magazine, "Arnold Schwarzenegger and Franco Columbu remember Mits Kawashima," YouTube video, July 5, 2012; Schwarzenegger and Petre, 96–97, and *Honolulu Star-Bulletin & Advertiser*, February 2, 1969, which contains an advertisement for the "1969 International Health Spectacular" to be held on Saturday, February 8, 1969, at McKinley High School auditorium. The ad features an image of Arnold Schwarzenegger, his name, and his titles "1967 Amateur Mr. Universe, 1968 Professional Mr. Universe" and states that tickets to the event can be purchased at "Mit's Health Studio."
50. For Paul Graham being a bodybuilder, strongman, crocodile wrestler, and professional wrestler, see Brad Forrest's article, "Like Father, Like Son — Not Horsing Around with Dude," *St George & Sutherland Shire Leader* (website), February 16, 2013. See also Online World of Wrestling (website), "Paul Graham." And: *Honolulu Star-Bulletin*,

January 30, 1969. For some reason, in his autobiography, *Total Recall*, Arnold does not refer to Paul Graham by name, instead identifying him as "one of my brand-new gym friends, an Australian strongman and crocodile wrestler." Schwarzenegger and Petre, 79.
51. Leamer, 56.
52. Tsantens, "Paul Graham and Arnold Schwarzenegger: A Partnership Forged in Iron," JoinArnold.com, August 4, 2023.
53. Roach, *Volume II*, 22 and 24.
54. Schwarzenegger and Petre, 96.
55. See note 54.
56. Leamer, 56–57.
57. *San Francisco Examiner*, December 4, 1968.
58. *Honolulu Star-Bulletin*, January 30, 1969. See also *Honolulu Advertiser*, January 30, 1969.
59. *Honolulu Star-Bulletin*, February 10, 1969.
60. Fair, "The Intangible Arnold."
61. "And although the FBI has no jurisdiction over local car thefts, it can move in when a stolen auto is put aboard a ship and becomes an article in foreign commerce." *San Francisco Examiner*, December 4, 1968.
62. "Just as Joe Weider had promised, I got a car; a secondhand white Volkswagen Beetle which made me feel at home." Schwarzenegger and Petre, 85.
63. Leamer, 66 (referencing *Mr. America*, March 1969).
64. Leamer, 64.

CHAPTER SIX: MIND AND BODY
1. National Museum of the United States Air Force (website), "Lt. Gen. Frank M. Andrews."
2. PCSing.com, "Andrews Air Force Base."
3. *Sun Magazine*, June 19, 1977.
4. Heavy Duty College, "The Mike Mentzer Story," YouTube video, May 3, 2023.
5. *Muscle Builder* magazine, October 1979.
6. See note 5.
7. *Ephrata Review*, February 17, 1972.
8. Mike Mentzer, conversation with the author, December 25, 1995.
9. Mike Mentzer, McGough interview.
10. See note 7.
11. *Charlotte Observer*, January 25, 1976. See also note 3.
12. Xenophon, *Memorabilia*, trans. Amy L. Bonnette (Ithaca, NY: Cornell University Press, 1994), 106.
13. See note 9.
14. *Intelligencer Journal*, January 14, 1971.
15. Joe Weider, *The World's Leading Bodybuilders Answer Your Questions* (Chicago: Contemporary Books, 1981), 78. See also *Miami News*, February 2, 1979.
16. *Sunday News*, January 24, 1971.
17. See note 9.
18. *New Era*, June 4, 1971.
19. *New Era*, July 21, 1971.
20. Mike Mentzer, Hause interview.
21. *New Era*, Lancaster, May 29, 1979.

22. *New Era*, April 28, 1972 (Harry was 48; Marie 47).
23. Cooper Family Law (website), "Fault Divorce Grounds in Pennsylvania."
24. *New Era*, October 5, 1976.
25. *Intelligencer Journal*, November 12, 1971. See also *Ephrata Review*, August 20, 1970; September 7, 1970; and July 29, 1971.
26. *New Era*, February 19, 1970; *Ephrata Review*, December 31, 1970, and December 30, 1971.
27. *Ephrata Review*, March 2, 2011.
28. Cyberpump (site discontinued), "The Steel Spiel! With Mike Mentzer."
29. *Muscle & Fitness*, August 1982.
30. Bob Burns, "Mike Mentzer — Bodybuilder, Writer, and Philosopher," Attitude Adjustment (Luke Setzer's website).
31. See note 28.
32. Heavy Duty College, "Mike Mentzer: 'Nothing Human is Foreign to Me.'" YouTube video, October 11, 2021.
33. Mentzer and Friedberg, *The Mentzer Method to Fitness*, 17.
34. See note 9.
35. Mentzer and Friedberg, *The Mentzer Method to Fitness*, 22.
36. Yukio Mishima, *Sun and Steel* (Tokyo, Kodansha International, 1970), 22–23.
37. *Muscle & Fitness*, September 1980.
38. Mike Mentzer and Ardy Friedberg, *Mike Mentzer's Complete Book of Weight Training* (New York: Quill Books, 1983), 34–35.
39. See note 28. See also note 9.
40. See note 28.
41. Mentzer and Friedberg, *The Mentzer Method to Fitness*, 78–79.
42. B. Senf, "Wilhelm Reich: Discoverer of Acupuncture Energy?" *American Journal of Acupuncture* 2, no. 7 (April–June 1979): 109–18. See also L. Southgate, *Chinese Medicine and Wilhelm Reich: An Analysis of Chinese Medical and Reichian Theories of Life Force, and Experimental Orgone-Acupuncture Study* (London: Lambert, 2009).
43. Zawn Villines, "What Are Chakras and How Do They Affect Health?" Medical News Today (website), updated November 20, 2023. See also Osho, "Nobody Listened to Wilhelm Reich," *Osho News* (website), September 26, 2013.
44. Encyclopedia Nomadica (website), "Reich-Einstein Experiment."
45. Myron Sharaf, *Fury on Earth: A Biography of Wilhelm Reich* (Boston: Da Capo Press, 1994), 460–61.
46. *Encyclopaedia Britannica*, "Wilhelm Reich" (archived webpage), November 22, 2022.
47. Webster Schott, "Wilhelm Reich: A Prisoner of Sex," *Washington Post* (website), February 5, 1983.
48. Jack Neary, interview with the author, August 27, 2023.
49. Roger Schwab, interview with the author, August 13, 2023.
50. Mentzer and Friedberg, *The Mentzer Method to Fitness*, 79.
51. *Miami News*, February 2, 1979.
52. See note 50.
53. See note 49.
54. See note 9.
55. *Intelligencer Journal*, July 20, 1971.
56. See note 9.

57. Mike Mentzer, interview with the author, 1987.
58. Mentzer and Friedberg, *The Mentzer Method to Fitness*, 17.
59. *Muscular Development*, September 1971.
60. See note 59.
61. John Wood, "The Arm of Casey Viator," *Oldtime Strongman* (blog), January 28, 2014.
62. See note 9.
63. See note 59.
64. See note 59.
65. See note 59.
66. See note 59.
67. See note 59.
68. The Sandwich, "Mike Mentzer: Words of Tribute From his Friends, Colleagues and Those He Inspired," *Iron Man* magazine (website), November 1, 2001.
69. Mike Mentzer, interview with the author, 1990.
70. See note 68.

CHAPTER SEVEN: NAUTILUS EMERGES

1. Arthur Jones (official website), "And God Laughs . . ."
2. See note 1.
3. See note 1.
4. See note 1.
5. *Sports Illustrated*, April 1975.
6. See note 5.
7. See note 5. See also *MuscleMag International*, September 1981.
8. Patricia Sullivan, "Arthur Jones, Eccentric Reshaped the Exercise World, Dies at 80," *Seattle Times* (website), September 2, 2007.
9. *New York Times*, July 25, 1982.
10. See note 1.
11. Elephant Database (website), "Jumbolair (Arthur Jones) Elephants in United States," updated December 9, 2020.
12. See note 11.
13. *New York Times*, August 30, 2007.
14. See note 13.
15. Herman L. Masin, "A Beautiful Mind: Arthur Jones, the Man Who Invented the Nautilus Machine and Revolutionized Strength Training. (Person to Person)," *Coach and Athletic Director*, Scholastic Inc., May 1, 2002. The Free Library by Farlex (website).
16. William Zucker, "Keeping Up with Arthur Jones," 2000, Arthur Jones (official website).
17. Arthur Jones and Dr. Elliott Plese, "The Colorado Experiment," Arthur Jones (official website).
18. Dr. James A. Peterson, "Total Conditioning: A Case Study," *Athletic Journal*, September 1975.
19. Arthur Jones (official website), "The Most Important Area of the Body: Featuring the Lower Back Machine."
20. Kirk Semple, "The Rise of the Machines," *New York Times* (website), October 11, 2008. See also *Time* magazine, June 10, 1985.

21. See note 5.
22. See note 20.
23. See note 1.
24. Brian D. Johnston, "An Interview with Arthur Jones," Arthur Jones (official website).
25. Mike Mentzer, McGough interview.
26. Mike Mentzer, interview with the author, 1996.
27. See note 25.
28. Mike Mentzer, Hause interview.
29. See note 25.
30. See note 28.
31. Old School Labs (website), "Mr. Olympia 1970 — The Arnold & Sergio Rematch." See also *Muscular Development*, September 1971. And: Arthur Jones (official website), "My First Half-Century in the Iron Game," chapter 11.
32. MuscleMemory (online database), "Franco Columbu."
33. See note 32.
34. Schwarzenegger and Petre, 107.
35. See note 34. See also Sagnik Bagchi, "'I Really Missed Him': Despite Arnold Schwarzenegger Making Tons of Money for Joe Weider, He Sidelined His One Request for a Long Time," EssentiallySports (website).
36. Schwarzenegger and Petre, 106–7.
37. LeDuff, "Ethnic Issues in Recall" (archived webpage).
38. *Iron Man* magazine, September 1971.
39. The Barbell Team, "Howard Stern Interviews Arnold: 5 Things We Learned," TheBarbell.com, November 4, 2019.
40. See note 38.
41. Ian Webster, "Value of $25,000 from 1970 to 2024," In2013Dollars.com.
42. "In my opinion, Arnold, in his prime, had one of the two best physiques in history; it would be difficult for me to decide just which was best, Arnold's physique or that of Sergio." Arthur Jones (official website), "My First Half-Century in the Iron Game," chapter 11.
43. "During his earlier visit to Florida, Arnold told me that Joe Weider was paying him $125.00 a week, then about half an hour later he said it was $175.00 a week. But what really bothered me was the fact that while working for Joe he went to great lengths in the direction of knocking both Joe and his wife; if Joe had heard Arnold's stories about Joe's wife he probably would have shot Arnold. I have never been an admirer of Joe myself, but I cannot respect a man who tells the kind of stories about his employer that Arnold did." Arthur Jones (official website), "My First Half-Century in the Iron Game," chapter 11.
44. Ellington Darden, *The New High Intensity Training* (Emmaus, PA: Rodale, 2004), 41.
45. WebMD, "Ellington Darden."
46. Darden, *New High Intensity Training*, 41–42.
47. See note 9. See also *MuscleMag International*, September 1981.
48. Arnold Schwarzenegger and Bill Dobbins, *Encyclopedia of Modern Bodybuilding* (New York: Simon & Schuster, 1985), 118.
49. Darden, *New High Intensity Training*, 45.
50. See note 49.

51. *Muscle Builder/Power*, January 1975. See also Brian D. Johnston, "Sergio Oliva Interview," Muscle and Brawn (website).
52. Arnold, in his mail-order course *Arnold Strong Photo Album* ("Strong" was the surname Arnold was using at the time, Weider believing that "Schwarzenegger" was too hard for people to pronounce, which would be a problem for advertising) lists his arm size as "21½-inches." Arnold Strong, *Arnold Strong Photo Album* (self-published, 1975), 1. Recall also that Albert Busek, in an effort to promote Arnold in North America had claimed "[Arnold's] Upper arm 20½ . . . (measurements taken before training, cold.)" *Iron Man* magazine, July 1967.
53. Arthur Jones (official website), "Nautilus Bulletin #2," chapter 36.

CHAPTER EIGHT: AUTHORITIES BY PROXY

1. Mike Mentzer, McGough Interview.
2. Greatest Physiques (website), "Casey Viator." See also Chris Lund, "Looking Back: Casey Viator," *Flex*, August 2013.
3. See note 2, Lund. See also *Iron Man*, September 1970.
4. The February 1972 edition of *Muscle Builder/Power* magazine features both Arnold Schwarzenegger and Franco Columbu on the cover with the following captions under their respective images: "Arnold Schwarzenegger, Mr. Olympia. . . . A Weider Pupil" and "Franco Columbu, Mr. Universe. . . . A Weider Pupil." See also "Weider Student, Arnold Schwarzenegger, Changes Name to Arnold Strong," *Sports Illustrated*, April 6, 1970.
5. *Muscle Builder/Power*, April 1972.
6. See note 5.
7. Old School Labs (website), "Mr. Olympia 1971: A Controversial Year."
8. Kevin Grech, "Arnold Schwarzenegger Risked Suspension from the IFBB in 1971," EvolutionOfBodybuilding.net, March 31, 2023.
9. David Robson, "An Interview with the Myth: The One and Only Sergio Oliva!" Bodybuilding.com (webpage discontinued).
10. See note 5.
11. See note 7.
12. See note 5.
13. Darden, *New High Intensity Training*, 44.
14. *Iron Man*, February 1971.
15. See note 13.
16. *Atlanta Journal and Constitution*, February 13, 1972.
17. Mike Mentzer, Hause interview.
18. *Miami News*, February 2, 1979.
19. See note 17.
20. See note 1.
21. *Sunday Courier & Press*, February 20, 1972.
22. *Intelligencer Journal*, April 25, 1972.
23. See note 13.
24. See note 13.
25. *Advocate*, June 12, 1980.
26. *New Era*, April 28, 1972, and *Intelligencer Journal*, April 29, 1972.

27. *Muscle Builder/Power*, August 1979.
28. Commonwealth of Virginia, Department of Health — Bureau of Vital Records and Health Statistics. Marriage Return; marriage certificate between Harry Earl Mentzer and Alta Jean Markley — maiden name: McCord, June 6, 1972.
29. See note 27.
30. See note 27.
31. Dave Mastorakis interview with the author, July 9, 2023.
32. See note 27.

CHAPTER NINE: THE CUBAN MUSCLE CRISIS

1. Randy Roach, email to the author, September 25, 2023.
2. Ken Sprague, email to the author, September 21, 2023.
3. Brian D. Johnston, "Sergio Oliva Interview" (online article).
4. Leamer, *Fantastic*, 93 and 94. See also John Hansen, "Sergio Oliva 'The Myth' — R.I.P.," *Iron Man* magazine (website), November 17, 2012.
5. Sagnik Bagchi, "Sergio Was Better Than Arnold: Bodybuilding Legend Who Defeated Arnold Schwarzenegger Disclosed the Unknown Details About 1972 Mr. Olympia," EssentiallySports (website), March 23, 2023.
6. John Hansen, "Arnold vs Sergio — Part 3," RxMuscle (website), July 24, 2013.
7. See note 6.
8. John Hansen, "Sergio Oliva Should have won the 72 Olympia," YouTube video, January 18, 2019. See also note 5. See also note 4, Hansen.
9. Leamer, 94.
10. Wayne, *Muscle Wars*, 1955.
11. *Arnold*, season 1, episode 1, "Part 1: Athlete," directed by Lesley Chilcott, featuring Arnold Schwarzenegger, aired June 7, 2023, on Netflix. TV Show Transcripts (online database).
12. To wit, Joe Weider's first attack on Nautilus occurred in the October 1973 edition of *Muscle Builder/Power*, and the final one in the January 1975 edition of the magazine.
13. *Muscle Builder/Power*, October 1974.
14. Wayne, *Muscle Wars*, 1988.
15. See note 14.
16. See note 13.
17. See note 13.
18. Wayne, *Muscle Wars*, 1982.
19. *Muscle Builder/Power*, October 1973. Arnold's alleged statement here is a direct contradiction to what he had written in *Iron Man* magazine in 1971.
20. Fitness Volt Editorial Team, "Arthur Jones — Complete Profile: Height, Workout and Diet," Fitness Volt (website), updated December 30, 2023.
21. See note 20.
22. See note 20. Interesting to note, Frank Zane would in fact later purchase a Nautilus pullover machine for use in his home gym in Palm Springs. See his Instagram account, @therealfrankzane, July 20, 2019, https://www.instagram.com/p/BoJTdjChDNy/.
23. See note 20.
24. *Muscle Builder/Power*, January 1975.
25. See note 24.

26. See note 24.
27. See note 24.
28. Darden, *New High Intensity Training*, 37.
29. Jack Neary interview with the author, August 27, 2023.
30. See note 11.
31. Leamer, 91.
32. Arthur Jones, "My First Half-Century in the Iron Game 44-b."
33. Darden, *New High Intensity Training*, 34.
34. Arthur Jones (official website), "Nautilus Bulletin #2," chapter 24.
35. Arthur Jones (official website), "The Colorado Experiment, Part 3: Conduct of the Experiment."
36. *Iron Man*, September 1973.
37. Jones and Plese, "The Colorado Experiment" (online article).
38. Ellington Darden, "Old-School Muscle: How Jones Trained Viator for the 1971 Mr. America," T Nation (website), April 6, 2006.
39. See note 36.
40. See note 37.
41. See note 36.
42. See note 36.
43. See note 36.
44. In 2003, author John Szimanski published a book on Arthur Jones entitled *Younger Women, Faster Airplanes, Bigger Crocodiles* (Mauldin, SC: PDA Press). In his research for the book, he was able to access the handwritten records of the Colorado Experiment, including the workout sheets that listed the workout sessions, along with the exercises performed, the sets, weights, and repetitions. He listed the exercises and workout sessions in his book but did not include much if any of the other information. Szimanski offered the documents for sale online. I reviewed the workout sheets he took photos of online and jotted down the particulars, such as the weights each subject used, which is how I have the data regarding the workout sessions.
45. See note 36.
46. See note 36.
47. John Hansen, "The Tijuana Incident," RxMuscle (website), February 9, 2014.
48. Roach, *Volume II*, 125.
49. *Muscle Builder/Power*, October 1973.
50. See note 48.
51. Wayne, *Muscle Wars*, 1955, 1973–77.
52. Roach, *Volume II*, 125.
53. See note 47.
54. *Muscle Builder/Power*, January 1974. See also Leamer, 94–95.
55. See note 47.
56. See note 49.
57. See note 49.
58. *Muscle Builder/Power*, January 1974.
59. See note 58.
60. See note 58. See also Roach, *Volume II*, 124.
61. See note 47.

62. Roach, *Volume II*, 124.
63. See note 58.
64. See note 58.
65. See note 47.

CHAPTER TEN: A NEW APPROACH
1. *Sun Magazine*, June 19, 1977.
2. *Ephrata Review*, October 7, 1976.
3. Mike Mentzer, Hause interview.
4. Mike Mentzer, letter to Dave Mastorakis, April 12, 1974.
5. Mike Mentzer, McGough interview.
6. *Charlotte Observer*, January 25, 1976.
7. See note 6.
8. See note 1.
9. See note 5.
10. See note 6.
11. See note 6.
12. Roger Schwab, interview with the author, August 13, 2023.
13. See note 12. See also *Miami News*, February 2, 1979.
14. *Sunday Courier & Press*, February 20, 1972.
15. See note 4.
16. *Muscle Builder/Power*, March 1979.
17. See note 5.
18. See note 5.
19. Mike Mentzer, letter to Dave Mastorakis, March 1974.
20. Roger Schwab's handwritten notes from his telephone conversation with Mike Mentzer on April 2, 1974, emailed to the author on August 17, 2023.
21. See note 4.
22. See note 2.
23. Mike Mentzer, letter to Dave Mastorakis, June 1974.
24. See note 5.
25. See note 5.
26. Michael Levenson, interview with the author via Facebook Messenger, August 20, 2023.

CHAPTER ELEVEN: RELATIONSHIPS
1. Unless otherwise indicated, all information on or quotes from Cathy Gelfo are drawn from Cathy Gelfo and Mike Mentzer, *Heavy Duty for Women* (Los Angeles, CA: self-published, 1979).
2. See also: "After the Air Force, I went to Prince Georges Community College for a while, which is where I met Cathy by the way in a philosophy class." Mike Mentzer, Hause interview.
3. Heavy Duty College, "Ray Mentzer: The Truth About Bodybuilding," YouTube video, October 9, 2023.
4. *Muscle Builder/Power*, August 1979.
5. Mentzer, McGough interview.
6. See note 4.

Notes

7. *New Era*, October 5, 1976.
8. See note 1.
9. *Muscle Builder/Power*, November 1975.
10. *Sports Illustrated*, October 1974
11. Obviously in reference to Weider's ongoing attacks on Sergio Oliva, who had recently started promoting Dan Lurie's products.
12. See note 10.
13. Old School Labs (website), "Mr. Olympia 1974: The Final Showdown of Arnold & Lou."
14. See note 13. See also *Muscle Builder/Power*, March 1975.
15. See note 13. See also MuscleMemory (online database), "1974 Olympia — IFBB."
16. See note 13.
17. See note 13. See also *Muscle Builder/Power*, March 1975.
18. *Muscle Builder/Power*, March 1975.
19. See note 18.
20. *Muscle Builder/Power*, March 1975: "*Miss Americana* 1974 is a dollie named April Davis with two nifties, Sandra Milstead and Natalie Rebozo runners-up. However, this event featured the female equivalent of Arnold Schwarzenegger in unbelievable Kelly [*sic*] Everts and it is beyond comprehension why she didn't win. Kelly [*sic*] is a Vargas *Playboy* drawing of a fantastic super-bunny *in reality*. Aside from a super face she possesses the biggest knockers outside of a barnyard, great legs and everything else — yessir, the works! At no point did the audience spend a moment looking at another chick when Kelly [*sic*] was onstage, and several entrants would not return after pre-judging due to the one-sided adulation. The judges gave her only *Most Shapely* but at 4 in the morning I know who they wish they were sacked out with. Hypocrites, you guys. Next year, vote for sex . . . not Miss Americana apple pie."
21. *Muscle Builder/Power*, March 1975: "After pre-judging, one of New York's famous Shopping Bag Ladies gets on Birdsong's case. Shopping Bag Ladies are withered sixty-year-old hags who keep all their belongings in shopping bags, wear sneakers, live in the street and sleep in doorways. This particular hag was musclecrazy and bugged 'Bird' for an autograph. She said she saw him at the 1973 show and figured he'd win in 74. Bird signed and split quick. Is she one of his letter-writing fans we mentioned in earlier gossip columns?"
22. *Muscle Builder/Power*, March 1975: "An amusing footnote to all this muscular mayhem is that Arnold and the bronzed West Coast gods went to a LaLanne gym for a suntan (lamp style). Leaving Santa Monica and going to NY for a tan is like a Jew emigrating to Germany in 1938. But on with the show."
23. Leamer, *Fantastic*, 80.
24. IMDb (online database), "*Hercules in New York*: Trivia."
25. See note 24.
26. Leamer, 81.
27. Michael Hiltzik, "A True 'Hot Property': Elliott Gould's 'Long Goodbye' Apartment Is for Rent!" *Los Angeles Times* (website), December 3, 2014.
28. IMDb (online database), "*Happy Anniversary and Goodbye*."
29. Leamer, 101.
30. Shawn Perine, "Pumping Iron: The George Butler Interview," TheBarbell.com, August 8, 2021.

31. Leamer, 106.
32. Ron Harris, "The Story Behind Arnold Schwarzenegger & Pumping Iron," *Muscular Development* (website), January 18, 2016. See also Leamer, 104.
33. Leamer, 104. See also Roach, *Volume II*, 76.
34. Roach, *Volume II*, 76.
35. U.S. Department of State Archive, "The End of Apartheid," 2001-2009.state.gov.
36. Ajani Husbands, "Timeline of Apartheid," Stanford University (website), updated September 19, 2004.
37. Tim Ferriss (blog), "Arnold Schwarzenegger on The Tim Ferriss Show — Transcript," episode 60, February 2, 2015.
38. Wayne, *Muscle Wars*, 2046–51.
39. Leigh, *Arnold*, 68.
40. *Muscle Builder/Power*, August/September 1976.
41. Leamer, 47 and 50.
42. Schwarzenegger and Hall, *Arnold*, 82.
43. Leigh, 131. See also Wayne, *Muscle Wars*, 2041.
44. Wayne, *Muscle Wars*, 2041–46.
45. *Muscle Builder/Power*, July 1974.
46. Roach, *Volume II*, 89.
47. See note 46.
48. Roach, *Volume II*, 90.
49. See note 48.
50. Matt Weik, "An Interview with Six-Time World Champion Bodybuilder Serge Nubret!" Bodybuilding.com (webpage discontinued).
51. Leigh, 131.
52. See note 51.
53. See note 51.
54. Arnold Schwarzenegger (official website), "This is a Long One (But It's Worth It)."
55. See note 54.
56. Arnold began training 101 days out from the 1975 Mr. Olympia, which was scheduled to take place November 8, 1975 (per the info on the board behind the front desk at Gold's Gym which appears at the 6:33 mark of the documentary *Pumping Iron*). This would put the date of the start of his contest training on August 1, 1975, giving him four months to the day to get into competition shape.
57. *Playboy*, January 1988. See also: "'I took them under a doctor's supervision once a year, six or eight weeks before competition,' he told *Playboy* magazine in 1988. Schwarzenegger said he began taking steroids when he arrived in the U.S. at age 20 because 'all you want to do is be a champion and you take what anyone else is taking.'" Mark Arax, "An Ethos Developed in the Gym," *Los Angeles Times* (website), September 29, 2003.
58. Golden Era Bookworm, "Steroids, Paco Arce & Super Responders in the Golden Era with Jerry Brainum," YouTube video, January 27, 2022.
59. Schwarzenegger and Dobbins, *Encyclopedia of Modern Bodybuilding*, 186.
60. Schwarzenegger and Dobbins, 695.
61. There is some conflict as to what Arnold weighed at the 1975 Mr. Olympia contest. His fellow competitor Serge Nubret recalled: "When Arnold competed against me in the 1975 Mr. Olympia, I was 200 lbs. and Arnold was 220 lbs." Weik, "An Interview

Notes

with . . . Serge Nubret" (online article). However, Armand Tanny, who covered the contest for Joe Weider's magazine reported: "He [Arnold] weighed 225 to Nubret's 200½ pounds." *Muscle Builder/Power*, July 1976. What both reports indicate is that Arnold did not weigh the 237 pounds that he had previously weighed at the 1974 Mr. Olympia contest.

62. Lonnie Teper, "Lou Ferrigno," *Iron Man* magazine (website), April 27, 2009.
63. Conor Heffernan, "The Real Story Behind the 1975 Mr. Olympia Is Far More Fascinating Than 'Pumping Iron' Ever Portrayed," BarBend (website), November 18, 2023.
64. Wayne, *Muscle Wars*, 2041–46 and 2321.
65. Wayne, *Muscle Wars*, 2041–46 and 2126.

CHAPTER TWELVE: A MAN OF SCIENCE

1. *Muscle Builder/Power*, May 1975.
2. Michael Levenson, Facebook message to the author, August 31, 2023.
3. Mike Mentzer, interview with the author, 1986.
4. Solace Treatment Center (website), "What Is Steroid Induced Psychosis?"
5. Mike Mentzer, Hause interview.
6. Schwarzenegger and Hall, *Arnold*, 28.
7. "It was a low set principle done on a three day a week routine. I worked the whole body each workout. I started with legs and then worked down to the smallest muscle group, the arms. I did 5 sets per bodypart. The workout took just about one hour. I stuck to that for about a year, got great results. As a matter of fact, when I competed in the [1975] IFBB Mr. America contest two years ago, I was on this type of training exclusively. . . . I was training that way up to the day of the contest." *Muscle Builder/Power*, March 1978.
8. "The 1975 Mr. America contest was scheduled for July in Los Angeles, but I began training (three days a week, one hour per workout) and dieting in January just to make sure I'd be in my best condition." Mentzer and Friedberg, *Mentzer Method to Fitness*, 21–22.
9. Heavy Duty College, "The Mike Mentzer Story" (YouTube video).
10. *Muscle Builder/Power*, January 1976.
11. See note 9.
12. See note 9.
13. The Bodybuilding Archive (website), "The Story of Gold's Gym: The Mecca of Bodybuilding," July 15, 2022.
14. Roger Schwab, interview with the author, August 13, 2023.
15. While Mike won the Junior Mr. America contest, it is by no means clear when and where it was held. Mike would recollect that he won it in Holyoke, Massachusetts, prior to coming to Los Angeles (Mike Mentzer, McGough interview), while *Muscle Builder/Power* magazine stated that he won the contest *after* his third-place finish at the Mr. America contest in 1975 (*Muscle Builder/Power*, December/January 1976). For Mike's third place finish at the Mr. USA, see *Muscle Builder/Power*, February 1976.
16. *Ephrata Review*, January 1, 1976. See also Mentzer and Little, *High-Intensity Training*, 67. And: *Muscle & Fitness*, July 1980.
17. Bill Starr, "Doc Ziegler," Starting Strength (website), September 15, 2011.

18. See note 17.
19. "Ziegler was something of a pioneer in sports medicine; he had been the physician for the American Olympic weightlifting team, had trained champion weightlifters and bodybuilders such as Bill March and Vern Weaver, and even had a hand in helping to develop the anabolic steroid Dianabol. Ziegler, in fact, is often cited as the person responsible for introducing anabolic steroids to the American sports scene — something I'm sure he considered a rather dubious distinction." Mentzer and Little, *High-Intensity Training*, 67. See also: ". . . but I wish to God now I'd never done it [created Dianabol]. I'd like to go back and take that whole chapter out of my life." John Ziegler quoted from John Fair, "Isometrics or Steroids? Exploring New Frontiers of Strength in the Early 1960s." *Journal of Sport History* 20, no. 1 (Spring 1993).
20. *Muscle Training Illustrated*, January 1980.
21. Mentzer and Little, *High-Intensity Training*, 98.
22. *Ephrata Review*, January 1, 1976.
23. See note 3.
24. Mentzer and Friedberg, *Mike Mentzer's Complete Book of Weight Training*, 47–48.
25. *New Era*, October 5, 1976.
26. Erik Gregersen, "History of Technology Timeline," *Encyclopaedia Britannica* (website), January 15, 2019. See also David R. Williams, "Apollo Lunar Landings (1969–1972)," NSSDCA (website), updated March 6, 2017.
27. See note 21.
28. See note 21.
29. See note 21.
30. Mentzer and Little, *High-Intensity Training*, Chapter 9.
31. Joe Weider, *The World's Leading Bodybuilders Answer Your Questions*, 53.
32. Arthur H. Steinhaus, *Toward an Understanding of Health and Physical Education* (Dubuque, IA: Wm. C. Brown, 1963), 85.
33. See note 32.
34. Steinhaus, *Toward an Understanding of Health*, 322.
35. Ronald M. Deutsch, *Realities of Nutrition* (Palo Alto, CA: Bull, 1975), 1–2.
36. See note 3.
37. Mentzer and Friedberg, *Mentzer Method to Fitness*, 21–22.
38. Per-Olof Åstrand and Kåre Rodahl, *Textbook of Work Physiology: Physiological Bases of Exercise* (New York: McGraw Hill, 1977), 93.
39. Peterson, "Total Conditioning: A Case Study" (online article).
40. *Oakland Tribune*, July 14, 1980.
41. Paul A. DeVore and Mike Mentzer, *Mr. America's Total Physical Fitness Weight Control Program* (Washington, D.C.: DMS Associates, 1977), ix.

CHAPTER THIRTEEN: MUSCLES, MASCULINITY, AND Mr. AMERICA

1. *Muscle & Fitness*, October 1982.
2. *Muscle & Fitness*, October 1982: "Type A males involve themselves in a chronic struggle to achieve more and more in less and less time. These men are very prone to a hostile attitude. Probably the outstanding characteristic of the Type A male personality is a slavish commitment to the 'numbers game' — the number of business

successes he's had, the number of contests he's won, the number of dollars he earns each year. His self-esteem is based on the sheer number of his accomplishments, the sheer number of his possessions — rather than by how much innate satisfaction these things offer. So, no matter how many contests this individual may win, his hunger for success remains unsated. No matter how much money he earns, it is never enough. His need to dominate others grows until it dominates him. The lust for power springs from a fundamental insecurity in facing the world and is expressed in the way he compulsively manipulates friends and family in power plays and constantly practices one-upmanship on everyone he encounters."

3. See note 1.
4. See note 1.
5. *MuscleMag International Annual 3*, 1978–79.
6. *Muscle Builder/Power*, January 1978.
7. DeVore and Mentzer, *Mr. America*, x–xi.
8. *Muscle Builder/Power*, October 1979.
9. Mike Mentzer, McGough interview.
10. See note 9.
11. See note 8.
12. "Next year I'll look as good as Arnold." Mike Mentzer quoted in *Muscle Builder/Power*, April 1976.
13. See note 8.
14. MuscleMemory (online database), "1971 Teen Mr America — AAU."
15. *Muscle & Fitness*, July 1980.
16. *Muscle Builder/Power*, May 1980.
17. *Sun Magazine*, June 19, 1977.
18. Mike Mentzer, Hause interview.
19. Maxwell Maltz, *Psycho-Cybernetics* (New York: Pocket Books, 1960), xii.
20. *Flex*, October 1990.
21. *Wichita Falls Times*, November 5, 1976.
22. See note 8.
23. See note 8.
24. *Muscle Builder/Power*, August/September 1976.
25. Brian Cautillo, "Madison Square Garden," *History of New York City* (TLTC blog).
26. See note 24.
27. Old School Labs (website), "Mr. Olympia 1976: An Absent Arnold Provides Opportunity."
28. *Muscle Builder/Power*, September/October 1976.
29. See note 27.
30. *Muscle Builder/Power*, December 1976.
31. MuscleMemory (online database), "1975 Mr World — IFBB."
32. Unless otherwise indicated, all dialogue from the competitors' room is drawn from *Muscle Builder/Power*, January 1977.
33. See note 8.
34. *Intelligencer Journal*, October 6, 1976.
35. *Iron Man*, January 11, 2011.
36. See note 8.

37. All dialogue regarding Jack Neary's interaction with the fan and Cathy Gelfo's comments is taken from *Muscle Builder/Power*, October 1979.
38. Jack Neary, interview with the author, August 27, 2023.
39. *Muscle Builder/Power*, January 1977.
40. See note 39.
41. See note 39.
42. See note 9.
43. Heavy Duty College, "The Mike Mentzer Story" (YouTube video).
44. See note 39. "Arnold Schwarzenegger was one of nine judges. Before long his natural leadership tendencies began taking over and it was apparent the rest of the panel were looking to him as the voting trendsetter."
45. Snyder and Wayne, *Three More Reps*, 148.
46. See note 45.
47. See note 39.
48. See note 39.
49. See note 43.

CHAPTER FOURTEEN: DESTINY BECKONS

1. *Muscle Builder/Power*, October 1979.
2. Jack Neary, interview with the author, August 27, 2023.
3. *Muscle Builder/Power*, January 1977.
4. Mike Mentzer, McGough interview.
5. DeVore and Mentzer, *Mr. America*, xi–xii.
6. Mike Mentzer, interview with the author, 1986.
7. See note 5.
8. DeVore and Mentzer, xii.
9. *Wichita Falls Times*, November 5, 1976.
10. Some of the newspapers that carried the story of Mike's win during this time were *New Era* (October 5, 1976), *Intelligencer Journal* (October 6, 1976), *Ephrata Review* (October 7, 1976, November 11, 1976, and December 30, 1976), *Wichita Falls Times* (November 5, 1976), *New York Daily News* (January 19, 1977), *Sun-Democrat* (Paducah, KY, March 21, 1977), and *Sun Magazine* (June 19, 1977).
11. *Sun Magazine*, June 19, 1977.
12. Shelly Mentzer Sweigart, email to the author, July 19, 2023.
13. Waymarking.com, "Centre Claude-Robillard (Montreal 1976)."
14. *Montreal Gazette*, November 6, 1976.
15. Retro Muscle, "1976 IFBB Mr. Universe," YouTube video, May 3, 2020.
16. See note 15.
17. *Montreal Gazette*, November 4, 1976.
18. IFBB (website), "1976 World Bodybuilding Championships and International Congress."
19. See note 18.
20. See note 15.
21. See note 4.
22. Robby Robinson had appeared on the cover of *Muscle Builder/Power* twice by the time of the World Championships (January 1976 and December 1976). The captions

Notes

beneath his image on each edition read "Robin Robinson: Another Star Weider Pupil" and "Robby Robinson Mr. America — Weider Pupil," respectively.

23. See note 4.
24. See note 14.
25. See note 15.
26. MuscleMemory (online database), "Robby Robinson."
27. Robby Robinson, *The Black Prince: My Life in Bodybuilding: Muscle vs. Hustle* (Los Angeles, CA: self-published, 2011), 225–26.
28. Generation Iron, "Robby Robinson Tells All on Experiencing Racism in Pro Bodybuilding," YouTube video, July 20, 2020.
29. Robinson, *Black Prince*, 502.
30. Robinson, *Black Prince*, 360–62.
31. *Ephrata Review*, October 7, 1976.
32. *Wichita Falls Times*, November 5, 1976. For the conversion of a 3.7 GPA score to 92 percent, see GPACalculator.net, "3.7 GPA."
33. Cyberpump (site discontinued), "The Steel Spiel! With Mike Mentzer."
34. See note 6.
35. *Sports History Weekly* (website), "'Pumping Iron' Goes Mainstream," March 17, 2019. See also AFI Catalog (website), "Pumping Iron (1977)."
36. *Muscle Builder/Power*, August/September 1976.
37. Katharine Lowry, "The Shadow of Muscles at the Whitney Was Vitiated by Academic Flabbiness," *Sports Illustrated*, June 7, 1976.
38. See note 37.
39. *Daily News*, January 19, 1977.
40. See note 4.
41. *Sports Illustrated*, April 6, 1970.
42. See note 4.
43. See note 4.
44. See note 2.
45. See note 2.
46. MuscleMemory (online database), "Ray Mentzer."
47. "*The New York Times* calls him for an interview." From *Sun Magazine*, June 19, 1977.
48. *Ephrata Review*, January 1, 1976.
49. Mike Mentzer quotes are drawn from the article "Mike Mentzer, Mr. America: In Pursuit of the 'Perfect Physique'" by Eric Siegel, *Sun Magazine* (Baltimore, MD), June 19, 1977.
50. See note 11.
51. See note 11.
52. *Rolling Stone*, June 3, 1976.
53. *The Canadian Encyclopedia* (website), "Queen Elizabeth Theatre," February 1, 2010.
54. Heavy Duty College, "Mike Mentzer: Mr. North America 1977," YouTube video, October 9, 2021. See also *Looking Good*, September 1977.
55. *Looking Good*, September 1977.
56. See note 55.
57. See note 11.
58. *Muscle Builder/Power*, March 1979.

CHAPTER FIFTEEN: A PEEK BEHIND THE CURTAIN

1. Mike Mentzer, McGough interview.
2. See note 1.
3. Ken Sprague, email to the author, September 21, 2023. See also note 1.
4. See note 3.
5. See note 1.
6. See note 1. See also Jack Neary, interview with the author, August 27, 2023.
7. Jack Neary, interview with the author, August 27, 2023.
8. *Wichita Falls Times*, November 5, 1976.
9. See note 1.
10. *Muscle Builder/Power*, October 1979.
11. See note 10.
12. See note 1.
13. See note 1.
14. See note 3.
15. Mike's covers bookended the year 1977; in the January 1977 edition of *Muscle Builder/Power*, Joe captioned Mike's photo with "Mike Mentzer, Mr. America — Weider Pupil," while the December 1977 edition of the magazine featured an image of Mike performing a seated dumbbell concentration curl under the heading: "Will Mike Mentzer Be Our Next Mr. Olympia?"
16. See note 7.
17. See note 1. See also *New Era*, November 10, 1978.
18. Jonathan Black, "Charles Atlas: Muscle Man," *Smithsonian Magazine* (website), August 2009.
19. Tanmay Roy, "While Other Bodybuilders Failed, Mastermind Arnold Schwarzenegger Made Millions in Mail-Order Business Back in the Days," Essentially Sports (website), March 18, 2023.
20. "Schwarzenegger's income now ranges between $40,000 and $60,000 a year, chiefly from' endorsements, a mail-order instruction business and posing exhibitions. Only he and Franco Columbu have been able to support themselves professionally in the sport." From the article "The Men and the Myth" by Richard W. Johnston, *Sports Illustrated*, October 1974.
21. Leamer, *Fantastic*, 78.
22. Baker, *Arnold and Me*, 75–76.
23. Leamer, 79: "When Arnold came home to his apartment, he went through the stack of mail, holding each envelope up to the light to see if there was a check or cash. If there was money, he put the letter in a stack on the table. If it appeared to be nothing but fan mail, several of Arnold's friends say that he dumped the letter into the wastebasket. Photographer George Butler says Arnold not only threw the letters away but bragged about it. It was not a scene that fit into the hagiographic image Weider was creating for Arnold, but it was a realistic, if cynical, appraisal of Arnold's own reality."
24. Leamer, 78–79.
25. Kathleen Elk, "The Way Arnold Schwarzenegger Made His First Million Had Nothing to Do with Acting," CNBC (website), February 6, 2017. See also Tanmay Roy, "Decades Later, Arnold Schwarzenegger Discloses How He Made Millions

Notes

While America Was Witnessing One of the Biggest Inflations in the 70s," *Essentially Sports* (website), June 7, 2023.
26. *Muscle Builder/Power*, November 1979.
27. See note 1.
28. Mike Mentzer, Hause interview.
29. See note 1.
30. See note 1.
31. See note 3.
32. *Muscle Builder/Power*, January 1978.
33. John Hansen, "Bodybuilding Legends Podcast #251 — Rick Wayne, Part Three." YouTube video, December 29, 2022.
34. See note 32.
35. See note 32.
36. See note 32.
37. See note 32.
38. See note 32.
39. See note 32.
40. See note 32.
41. See note 32.
42. Schwarzenegger and Hall, *Arnold*, 203. See also Schwarzenegger and Dobbins, *Encyclopedia of Modern Bodybuilding*, 484–85.
43. See note 32.
44. See note 32.
45. *Muscle Training Illustrated*, July 1979.
46. See note 45.
47. See note 32.
48. Roger Lockridge, "Becoming a Legend: Frank Zane's Top 10 Training Tips," *Muscle & Fitness* (website). Some reports put Zane's competition weight at only 185 pounds: see Muscle & Strength (website), "Interview with Mr. Olympia Frank Zane." See also MuscleMemory (online database), "Frank Zane."
49. "Mike, with a chest structure similar to his idol, Reeves, reverently seems to have held his chest development to like proportions. Reeves had flat, but defined, rectangular pecs, that in some quarters are still considered the ideal." *Muscle Builder/Power*, December/January 1976.
50. MuscleMemory (online database), "Kalman Szkalak."
51. Greatest Physiques (website), "Kalman Szkalak." See also note 50.
52. *Muscle Builder/Power*, December 1976.
53. See note 52.
54. See note 52.
55. "The resemblance between Kal and Arnold when the former strikes his side chest pose is uncanny." *Muscle Builder/Power*, November 1976. Also, the very first cover mention of Kal Szkalak in *Muscle Builder/Power* (October 1976) indicated: "Kal Szkalak, AAU Mr. America 1976. Is He the Man to Make Arnold Think Again?"
56. Yegor Khzokhlachev, "Kal Szkalak Gallery 2," Built Report (website), September 27, 2022.
57. *Muscle Builder/Power*, November 1976.

58. *Muscle Builder/Power*, November 1976: "Ironically enough, Kal's one fault at this time centers on the legs. Just as Arnold's main problem when he came to California to train under Joe Weider was under-developed legs."
59. Roach, *Volume II*, 194. See also note 57.
60. See note 57.
61. Nîmes Tourisme (website), "Nîmes across the Centuries."
62. *Encyclopaedia Britannica* (website).
63. See note 7.
64. *Muscle Builder/Power*, March 1978.
65. See note 64.
66. *Muscle Builder/Power*, March 1978: "What Neary had been unaware of was that the evening posedown was judged, that it would be the final round. Neary was under the impression that it was merely for show, that the contest had already been decided." See also: "Oscar State would suggest that the audience was doing the judging and not the finest judges the IFBB has. Writes State in the Congressional IFBB report, 'Szkalak seemed to have a bigger following among the audience who yelled and screamed his name during the exciting posedown. This must have had some influence on at least two of the judges because four of them placed Szkalak first and only three voted for Mentzer.'" Oscar State and Kal Szkalak quoted in Muscle Digest, May/June 1978. See also: "The heavy weight class (over 90 kg./198 lb.) was between Kal Szkalak and Mike Mentzer, with Paul Grant third. This class pointed out a heretofore unrecognized absurdity, an evening posedown among the top places in a class. The result: Mike outscores Kal 279-269 during a gruelling, meticulous 3 hours of prejudging, only to lose 11 points to 10 at the evening pose off. The much vaunted IFBB Judging System needs a closer look. Why 3 hours at prejudging if a 5 minute posedown overrides it?" *MuscleMag International Annual* 3, 1978–79.
67. Oscar State, the Secretary of the IFBB Judges Committee, had written in the October 1976 edition of *Muscle Builder/Power* that, "The posedown is used mainly for the benefit of the public."
68. See note 64.
69. See note 64.
70. See note 64.
71. See note 64.
72. See note 64.
73. See note 7.
74. See note 7.
75. See note 64.

CHAPTER SIXTEEN: THE CHALLENGE TO THE THRONE

1. All dialogue between Jack Neary and Mike Mentzer drawn from *Muscle Builder/Power*, March 1978.
2. Kal Szkalak and Jack Neary conversation quoted from *Muscle Builder/Power*, March 1978.
3. Jack Neary interview with the author, August 27, 2023.
4. *Muscle Builder/Power*, October 1979.
5. John Little, *The Mike Mentzer Question and Answer Book* (Northern River, 2023), 9–10.

6. See note 5.
7. Unless otherwise noted, the dialogue between Mike Mentzer and Jack Neary is drawn from *Muscle Builder/Power*, October 1979.
8. Little, *Mike Mentzer Question*, 12–13.
9. Jack Neary interview with the author, August 27, 2023: "In one month, I gained 20 pounds, certainly not all muscle, but a good deal more than I've ever gained before in such a short time. After eight weeks my weight went from 143 to 175, and my strength increased proportionately. We didn't have a workout longer than one hour — the average being about 40 minutes. That's with two people. One man on his own would be half that time. The Mentzer Heavy Duty System is difficult to master. It is of an intensity I've never experienced in other training routines, but it's certainly worth it."
10. See note 3.
11. *Pittsburgh Post-Gazette*, April 3, 1979.
12. *Sun Magazine*, June 19, 1977.
13. Mike Mentzer seminar in Rexdale, Ontario, November 15, 1981, and Heavy Duty College, "Mike Mentzer: How to Gain 10 Pounds of Muscle," YouTube video, August 7, 2023.
14. *Muscle Builder/Power*, October 1978.
15. Mike Mentzer, McGough interview.
16. Roach, *Volume II*, 161.
17. Leamer, *Fantastic*, 109.
18. Roach, *Volume II*, 162.
19. See note 18.
20. See note 18.
21. *Muscle Builder/Power*, November 1976.
22. See note 16.
23. Roach, *Volume II*, 162.
24. Roach, *Volume II*, 160.
25. Roach, *Volume II*, 168.
26. See note 25.
27. Roach, *Volume II*, 169.
28. *Joe Gold's Gym, Inc. v. Arnold Schwarzenegger* lawsuit, Los Angeles, 18.
29. Roach, *Volume II*, 190.
30. See note 27. See also the poster for the contest: "Tickets: $50 first five rows main floor center and first three rows in loge. Other reserved seats, $20 and $10. Prejudging $5 (first come)."
31. See note 27.
32. Set For Set, "Every Olympia Winner & Prize Money," email newsletter, December 7, 2022.
33. See note 27.
34. Joe Weider quoted from his sworn statement on July 20, 1978, in the *Joe Gold's Gym, Inc. v. Arnold Schwarzenegger* lawsuit, Los Angeles, 8.
35. Charles Feldman, "Man Who Dreamed of Being 'King of the Earth.'" CNN (website), August 12, 2003.
36. Joe Weider quoted from his sworn statement on July 20, 1978, in the *Joe Gold's Gym, Inc. v. Arnold Schwarzenegger* lawsuit, Los Angeles, 6.

> Q. "When did the old contract [with Arnold Schwarzenegger] expire approximately if you can remember?"
> A. "I don't know. About a year or so ago."
> Q. "That would be about July of '77?"
> A. "I can't be sure, but if it is necessary I can get you the date."

37. "Well, when the contract expired, we were going to renew another agreement... We were going to go into a new agreement with him. At that point I told him it would maybe be a year or maybe less before it materialized, and we left it at that." Joe Weider quoted from his sworn statement on July 20, 1978, in the *Joe Gold's Gym, Inc. v. Arnold Schwarzenegger* lawsuit, Los Angeles, 4–5.
38. Joe Weider quoted from his sworn statement on July 20, 1978, in the *Joe Gold's Gym, Inc. v. Arnold Schwarzenegger* lawsuit, Los Angeles, 24.

> Q. "Did you ever have a contract with Szkalak?"
> A. "Yes."
> Q. "When did that terminate or did it?"
> A. "It terminated just before the contest that was held last year. I think that was in November. I think it terminated around September."

See also: "Upon returning to California, Kal was contracted by Joe Weider. Joe offered Kal the opportunity to do exercise photos and articles — for $50 a week; not enough to cover Kal's weekly food bill.... To go along with the deal, Weider wanted Kal to enter the 1976 Universe. That was out of the question — Kal knew exactly who he could beat at the time, and he wasn't ready for Robby Robinson. He also had no intention of taking a second place. To anyone. With his sights set on Nimes and 1977, Kal trained through the next year." From the article "Kal Szkalak: Bodybuilding's Undefeated Superstar," *Muscle Digest*, July/August 1978.

39. "He [Arnold] said, 'Okay,' [to waiting for Joe to renew his contract] as long as I kept giving him the ads and I thought everything was satisfactory." Joe Weider quoted from his sworn statement on July 20, 1978, in the *Joe Gold's Gym, Inc. v. Arnold Schwarzenegger* lawsuit, Los Angeles, 5.
40. Joe Weider quoted from his sworn statement on July 20, 1978, in the *Joe Gold's Gym, Inc. v. Arnold Schwarzenegger* lawsuit, Los Angeles, 22.

> Q. "I guess a few more questions about *Muscle Digest*. Do you know if there is any financial arrangement between Arnold and *Muscle Digest*?"
> A. "Well, Arnold told me that he had an arrangement with *Muscle Digest* in the end of this year. How true it is, like anything else, I don't know. You see, when I see his articles in *Muscle Digest*, I didn't even know his article is in there. I called him up and I said, 'Look, you are writing for *Muscle Digest*. If you are, you are not going to get any ads in my magazine, and that's it, you are finished. You can't write for them and be with me.' There were a couple of them who wrote for *Muscle Digest*. They all dropped them except Arnold." Arnold said, 'I couldn't do anything about it. I have a contract till the end of the year.'"
> Q. "By 'the end of the year,' do you mean December '78?"

A. "Yes."

41. "I think he can control *Muscle Digest* to utilize him as the kingpin. In other words, he must think from what I can gather that he will use *Muscle Digest*, *Muscle Digest* will promote World Gym as we promoted Gold's Gym. This way he figures he can dominate Gold's Gym and he can dominate *Muscle Digest*. . . . Most likely he wants to be like me so that he can have work with World Gym like I work with Gold's Gym. He figures we have *Muscle Builder*, that he would work with [*Muscle Digest*] magazine. In other words, he is trying to run bodybuilding." Joe Weider quoted from his sworn statement on July 20, 1978, in the *Joe Gold's Gym, Inc. v. Arnold Schwarzenegger* lawsuit, Los Angeles, 9 and 10.

42. Joe Weider and Ken Sprague quoted from Joe Weider's deposition on July 20, 1978, in the *Joe Gold's Gym, Inc. v. Arnold Schwarzenegger* lawsuit, Los Angeles, 7–8.

> Q. "I believe you stated that Arnold trained at Gold's Gym?"
> A. "Yes."
> Q. "Does he still train at Gold's Gym?"
> A. "No, not that I know of."
> Q. "Do you know when he stopped training at Gold's Gym?"
> A. "I think about a year ago."
> Q. "That would be approximately July of 1977? Would that be correct?"
> Mr. Sprague: "Yes, a little longer than that."
> A: "Maybe a year and a half."
> Mr. Sprague: "Yes."
> Q. "Do you know why he [Arnold] left Gold's Gym?"
> A. "Well, I would think he was jealous of Ken Sprague's success, and that he did not want to glorify Ken and Gold's Gym anymore."

43. Roach, *Volume II*, 190.
44. Roach, *Volume II*, 191.
45. See note 44. Note: While Arnold may or may not have had a financial stake in World Gym when it first opened, he certainly did help finance it at various times throughout his life. See: "So, he decided to open a bigger and better gym and call it World Gym. . . . This actually sufficed and the gym opened up on Main Street in Santa Monica. . . . Joe moved the gym in Santa Monica over to Venice in another huge building that he made by hand and it was tri-level. It was a very unusual shape but lacked the charisma of his other gyms. Arnold gave a hand in some of the financing and it stayed there for a few years." Rick Drasin, "The Birth of World Gym," *HuffPost*, July 6, 2016. See also: "Earlier this year, Gold stepped down as chairman of World Gym and World Gym Licensing, passing the reins to Schwarzenegger. Close-mouthed about the specific financial arrangements, Gold says only that he is now a consultant for World Gym Licensing and the no-frills gym located at Main Street and Abbot Kinney Boulevard." Kathleen Kelleher, "Men of Steel: For Arnold Schwarzenegger, It's No Sweat Taking Over for Joe Gold," *Los Angeles Times*, May 3, 1992.
46. Joe Weider quoted from his sworn statement on July 20, 1978, in the *Joe Gold's Gym, Inc. v. Arnold Schwarzenegger* lawsuit, Los Angeles, 15.

> Q. "Does Arnold try and dissuade people from training at Gold's Gym?"
> A. "Yes."
> Q. "Does he try to shepherd them to World Gym?"
> A. "That's right."

47. "Kal came back to California [from Nîmes, France] and continued his training at the World Gym.... With the 1978 Mr. Olympia contest approaching, Kal now trains twice a day, six days a week.... Training friends like Schwarzenegger, [Joe] Gold, [Denny] Gable, [Roger] Callard, [Lou] Ferrigno, [Franco] Columbu and [Ed] Giuliani backing him up, Kalman Szkalak has the momentum building toward that September night of the 23rd." *Muscle Digest*, July/August 1978. See also: "However, Arnold was, in fact, in control of the Mr. Olympia event and many of the top pros felt obligated to follow Arnold to World Gym." Roach, *Volume II*, 91.
48. Ken Sprague, interview with the author, email, September 30, 2023.
49. "There had been other clashes. For instance, during an interview filmed for *Pumping Iron*, someone had suggested to Arnold that Franco was on the verge of toppling him from his Olympia perch. Arnold had retorted with a contemptuous 'What! Franco is a baby. He comes to me for advices.' The line had greatly angered Franco, although not nearly as much as it upset his wife, Anita. But then Arnold and Anita had never been bosom buddies. According to persons who ought to know, Anita had rescued Franco from Arnold's bullying clutches when the two men shared a Santa Monica apartment." Wayne, *Muscle Wars*, 2326.
50. Hansen, "Bodybuilding Legends Podcast #251" (YouTube video). See also Joe Weider quoted from his sworn statement on July 20, 1978, in the *Joe Gold's Gym, Inc. v. Arnold Schwarzenegger* lawsuit, Los Angeles, 9–10:

> Q. "Is he [Arnold Schwarzenegger] using anybody else, any other bodybuilder?"
> A. "I think he is using Kalman Szkalak as a front person."
> Q. "What is Szkalak doing?"
> A. "Well, I think he is the president of the professional bodybuilder's federation that they are trying to form. From what I gather, they are all the bodybuilders who went to the meeting that Arnold is behind, and he is using Kal."
> Q. "Is that organization that you mentioned, does that exist now or is that a planned organization?"
> A. "I don't know if it is existing or in the planning stage."
> Q. "Is it supposed to be like a union?"
> A. "It is kind of a union."
> Q. "Of professional bodybuilders?"
> A. "Of professional bodybuilders."
> Q. "Have you learned what their basic demands are?"
> A. "Well, they are floundering around, but they are trying, I guess, to organize to make certain demands of promoters which I think, you know, is silly. It is not going to work. You know, you organize against enemies, you don't organize against a friend, and the promoters are their friends. They are friends, they are not against them. It is not going to work. In

other words, I think that the formula that we have, the I.F.B.B. is an organization for the bodybuilders. I figure if he makes his union, it will be like the I.F.B.B. he figures. Most likely he wants to be like me so that he can have work with World Gym like I work with Gold's Gym. He figures we have *Muscle Builder*, that he would work with [*Muscle Digest*] magazine. In, other words, he is trying to run bodybuilding."

See also: "Joe wasn't alone in his thinking when he disclosed in the above court deposition that he believed Arnold was manipulating matters behind the scenes. In a discussion before an emergency meeting that Ben Weider had called in August of 1978 regarding the union matter, Ben had also told Wayne DeMilia that he felt Arnold was behind the movement." Roach, *Volume II*, 194–95. And: "First, it was Arnold who wanted the union. Arnold had all of those guys complaining that they weren't getting enough money for the Olympia and all this." Rick Wayne quoted from Hansen, "Bodybuilding Legends Podcast #251." (YouTube video).

51. Wayne, *Muscle Wars*, 2177–82.
52. "Several West Coast muscle stars promised their support, evidently figuring that with Schwarzenegger's muscle on their side they had what it took to stand up to the IFBB plutocracy." Wayne, *Muscle Wars*, 2182.
53. *Daytona Beach Morning Journal*, March 25, 1978.

CHAPTER SEVENTEEN: BETRAYALS

1. The address of the Chung and Tinberg law office is indicated on the title page of Joe Weider's sworn statement on July 20, 1978, in the *Joe Gold's Gym, Inc. v. Arnold Schwarzenegger* lawsuit, Los Angeles.
2. *Los Angeles Times*, March 2, 1989.
3. All questions and answers are excerpted from Joe Weider's sworn statement on July 20, 1978, in the *Joe Gold's Gym, Inc. v. Arnold Schwarzenegger* lawsuit, Los Angeles. Provided to the author with permission by Ken Sprague.
4. *Muscle Builder/Power*, December 1978.
5. The phrase "The Greatest Bodybuilding Contest in History" and the various contests to be held that day are indicated in the promotional posters for the competition as seen in Gold's Gym and published in *Muscle Builder/Power* in 1978.
6. *Muscle Builder/Power*, October 1977.
7. See note 4.
8. Mike Mentzer, McGough interview.
9. See note 8.
10. All information about the first meeting between Kal Szkalak, Arnold Schwarzenegger, and the bodybuilders at World Gym is drawn from *Muscle Builder/Power*, December 1978.
11. See note 4.
12. See note 4 and Roach, *Volume II*, 195.
13. Wayne, *Muscle Wars*, 2187.
14. See note 4.
15. See note 4.
16. See note 4.

17. Wayne, 2187–96.
18. See note 4.
19. See note 4.
20. Robinson, *Black Prince*, 272. See also: "Arnold, when seeing the meeting was not going in favor of the bodybuilders, got up, went over to Ben Weider, whispered in his ear then left." Roach, *Volume II*, 195.
21. See note 4.
22. See Roach, *Volume II*, 195: "[Wayne] DeMilia stated that when he had asked Ben for himself what Arnold had said, Ben told him that Arnold mentioned he had a meeting to run to and that he fully supported the IFBB. He then mentioned to Wayne that he did not trust Arnold at all."
23. "That was classic Joe; promising the moon to him, as he did to everyone. He even did it to me. Joe once said to me, 'If you'll keep training hard, I'll put you on the cover and give you $50,000.' *Please*. Come on, like, you know, let's get real here. He would say stuff like that just because Joe wanted to be liked, to be accepted and liked by the guys. And [because] Joe had tremendous power and influence, of course, with the magazines, he started making promises: 'We'll put you in an ad, and we'll make money, and we'll do this.' But, you know, no one would be surprised to know Joe overpromised and then under-delivered. And Kal was the kind of guy that if you said you were going to do this, that's what he wanted. He was the kind of guy who was a bit of a hothead." Jack Neary, interview with the author, August 27, 2023.
24. Neary, interview with the author, August 27, 2023.
25. Neary, Facebook message to the author, November 13, 2023.
26. See note 24.
27. See note 24. That a lawsuit was filed, see: "Kal Szkalak, once Mr. America and Mr. Universe, recently filed a $102 million suit against Mr. Weider for breach of contract. He said that he had signed a contract with Mr. Weider for a salary in return for endorsements and writing some articles and that Mr. Weider did not come through with the money." *New York Times*, "(Body) Building an Empire," November 28, 1981.
28. Noah Zucker, "Power Shift: I was a Mr. Olympia finalist mentored by Arnold Schwarzenegger — I'm Unrecognizable after Switching to Another Sport," *US Sun* (website), July 11, 2023.
29. *Muscle Builder/Power*, April 1979.
30. See note 29.
31. See note 29.
32. See note 29.
33. See note 29.
34. See note 24.
35. See note 29.
36. Albert Busek's comment on Bill Pearl's posted Facebook photo of Kalman Szkalak, August 4, 2019.

CHAPTER EIGHTEEN: PERFECTION IN ACAPULCO

1. *Muscle & Fitness*, November 1981.
2. "For Acapulco I trained four days a week, working out by myself, and my workouts

lasted only about 30–45 minutes. I did back, legs and abs one day, with chest, delts and arms the next." *Muscle Builder/Power*, March 1979.
3. Mike Mentzer seminar in Rexdale, Ontario.
4. "My back workout was typical of what I did for the entire body. I would do predominantly Nautilus. . . . The Nautilus pullover and pulldown were the heart of my workout, along with the behind-neck and rowing machines. I'd do a maximum of six sets, usually less, and within each set did positive reps to failure, forced reps, and finally negatives." *Muscle Builder/Power*, March 1979.
5. "My poundages also gradually went up until I was very, very strong. In the past I've squatted 505 for 15 reps, and on most of the Nautilus machines I was using the entire stack of weights. On the leg extension machine, I got up to using the whole weight stack, plus 150 pounds of plates. With little rest between exercises this type of weight becomes even heavier than it seems." *Muscle Builder/Power*, March 1979.
6. *Muscle Builder/Power*, March 1979.
7. "Someone else asked him [Franco Columbu] about using steroid drugs to stimulate muscle growth. Mr. Columbu said he tried them in 1972, but hasn't used them since. Later, at a press conference, Mr. Schwarzenegger said he'd tried the drugs several times, though not for competitions, but he wouldn't recommend anyone using them. 'The name of this sport is bodybuilding,' he said. 'Drugs destroy the body.'" *Globe and Mail*, April 28, 1980.
8. "Then he [Mike Mentzer] switched to a diet of mostly beef and protein supplements, popping steroids — the synthetic male hormone he says all top bodybuilders use — as well as pumping iron." *Sun Magazine*, June 19, 1977.
9. Mike Mentzer, interview with the author, 1990.
10. House of Representatives, Anabolic Steroid Control Act of 2004, GovInfo (website), April 2, 2004.
11. *Muscle Builder/Power*, June 1979.
12. *Muscle Builder/Power*, January/February 1979.
13. See note 12.
14. See note 6
15. Mike Mentzer, interview with the author, 1986.
16. See note 6
17. William James, *The Energies of Men* (New York: Moffat, Yard, 1914), 14.
18. James, *Energies of Men*, 16.
19. *Muscle & Fitness*, February 1990.
20. See note 6
21. *Ephrata Review*, December 28, 1978.
22. See note 6
23. See note 6.
24. See note 6.
25. See note 6.
26. *New Era*, November 10, 1978.
27. See note 6
28. See note 6.
29. See note 6.
30. Mentzer and Friedberg, *Mentzer Method to Fitness*, 13. See also note 7.

31. Mentzer and Friedberg, *Mentzer Method to Fitness*, 13.
32. Mentzer and Friedberg, *Mentzer Method to Fitness*, 14. See also *Intelligencer Journal*, November 8, 1978. And: *Oakland Tribune*, April 3, 1979.
33. *Muscle Builder/Power*, January/February 1979. See also note 6.

CHAPTER NINETEEN: TURNING PRO

1. "The night before my Mr. Universe victory in Acapulco in 1978, Cathy and I had dinner with Joe and Betty Weider at a very nice restaurant. The fare for the evening revolved around seafood, which contains a certain amount of salt, and the appetizer, as I recalled sometime later, was particularly laden with salt. Of course, salt makes you thirsty, and our waiter made sure our glasses were always filled with the vital fluid. Needless to say, I woke up on the morning of the biggest contest of my life (to that point) waterlogged and devoid of most of the deep cuts and blinding striations I had had just the day before." Mike Mentzer, *Heavy Duty Journal*, (Los Angeles, CA: self-published), 34.
2. *Muscle Builder/Power*, March 1979.
3. See note 1.
4. See note 1.
5. See Chapter One, note 61.
6. See note 1.
7. Mike Mentzer, McGough interview.
8. *Muscle Builder/Power*, May 1979.
9. The dates and locations of these contests are taken from their promotional posters.
10. See note 1.
11. *Sunday Courier & Press*, February 20, 1972. See also *Sun Magazine*, June 19, 1977.
12. *Muscle Builder/Power*, June 1979.
13. IOC (website), "Anthony Michael Garcy."
14. Pre-exhaustion method: "Muscle growth is stimulated by intense exercise. Maximum progress can only be achieved by maximum exertion, that is, 100 percent of your momentary ability must be expended on every single exercise. This isn't always possible in many conventional exercises because of muscular 'weak links.' When doing incline presses, for example, the work of the pectoral muscles is limited because of the involvement of the smaller and weaker triceps. The point of failure in the incline press will be reached when the triceps (the weak links) fail. This is long before the bigger and stronger pectorals are exhausted. A similar problem exists when the latissimus dorsi muscles are worked with such conventional exercises as rows, chins, or pull-downs on the lat machine. The biceps (the weak links), worked along with the lats in these exercises, fail before the lats become fatigued. But you can work around these weak links by using an isolation exercise for the stronger muscles before performing the compound exercise. Dumbbell flyes, cable crossovers, or Nautilus chest are ideal isolation exercises for the pecs, and when carried to total failure will "pre-exhaust" the pecs while preserving the strength of the triceps. This isolation exercise must be followed immediately with absolutely no rest by a compound exercise — dips or incline presses — that allows the fresh triceps to serve the exhausted pecs. The triceps now have a temporary strength advantage over the pecs and this forces the pecs to continue to contract closer to 100 percent of the momentary strength. If you delay as little as three seconds in moving from the isolation to the compound exercise, the primary muscle group (in this case

the pecs) will regain up to 50 percent of its original strength, thus making the auxiliary muscle the weak link again. When the isolation-compound cycle has been completed, it's all right to rest for as long as necessary before moving ahead in your workout." Mentzer and Friedberg, *Mentzer Method to Fitness*, 167–168.
15. See note 11.
16. D.W. Edington and V.R. Edgerton, *The Biology of Physical Activity* (Boston: Houghton Mifflin, 1976), 142–44.
17. Mentzer and Little, *High-Intensity Training*, 94–95.
18. See note 11.
19. *Ephrata Review*, December 28, 1978.
20. *Muscle & Fitness*, October 1987.
21. See note 7.
22. Robinson, *Black Prince*, 27–28.
23. Robinson, 380–89.
24. *Muscle Builder/Power*, April 1979.
25. See note 7.
26. See note 6.
27. See note 7.
28. See note 7.
29. See note 7.
30. See note 7.
31. See note 7.
32. See note 6.
33. See note 7.
34. See note 7.
35. Robinson, 389–40.
36. See note 7.
37. See note 7.

CHAPTER TWENTY: THE BLOWS OF FATE

1. Unless otherwise indicated, all information about the party at the apartment and dialogue with Ray Mentzer is drawn from *Muscle Builder/Power*, June 1979.
2. "Ray was out of his mind. Ray could get violent. All you had to do was look at Ray the wrong way. I mean, I was fairly close to both of them. Much closer to Mike than to Ray. I judged a contest once in Atlantic City that Ray was in. And, you know, Ray liked me and we were friends, but he was pissed off that I didn't place him higher. Not only was he pissed but the look in his eye! Like an animal. I mean, he was violent. He had a violent temper." Roger Schwab, interview with author, August 13, 2023.
3. See note 1.
4. Mike Mentzer, Hause interview.
5. Jack Neary, interview with the author, August 27, 2023.
6. See note 1.
7. See note 1.
8. See note 1.
9. See note 1.
10. See note 1.

11. *Pittsburgh Post-Gazette*, April 3, 1979.
12. *Muscle & Fitness*, November 1987.
13. *Muscle Builder/Power*, August/September 1979.
14. See note 13.
15. As quoted in *Muscle & Fitness*, March 1980.
16. See note 13.
17. See note 13.
18. *Sun Magazine*, June 19, 1977.
19. *Wichita Falls Times*, November 5, 1976.
20. Mike Mentzer, interview with the author, 1986.
21. "When asked what a friend was, Aristotle replied 'one soul dwelling in two bodies.'" Attributed to Aristotle in Diogenes Laërtius, *Lives and Opinions of Eminent Philosophers*, book 5, sec. 11, ed. James Miller, trans. Pamela Mensch (Oxford, UK: Oxford University Press, 2018), 221.
22. See note 13.
23. See note 4.
24. See note 4.
25. Gulzar Haider, "Making a Space for Everyday Ritual and Practice," in *Making Muslim Space in North America and Europe*, ed. Barbara Daly Metcalf (Berkeley: University of California Press), 1996.
26. Mike Mentzer, McGough interview.
27. *Muscle Builder/Power*, July 1979.
28. See note 26.
29. See note 27.
30. See note 27.
31. Mike Mentzer, "The Psychology of a Competitive Bodybuilder."
32. See note 26.
33. *Honolulu Star-Bulletin*, April 15, 1979.
34. *Muscle Builder/Power*, October 1979.
35. See note 5.
36. See note 26.
37. *New Era*, May 29, 1979.
38. See note 26.
39. See note 26.
40. See note 26.
41. See note 12.
42. See note 34.
43. See note 26.
44. See note 12.
45. See note 12.
46. The Sandwich, "Mike Mentzer's Last Interview," *Iron Man* magazine (website), October 1, 2001.

CHAPTER TWENTY-ONE: PLAYING WITH FIRE

1. *Muscle & Fitness*, November 1987.
2. See note 1.

3. See note 1.
4. For Ray duplicating Mike, see: "Looking back at my journal for the nine months leading up to this year's America, I can see a very positive upward trend in training intensity"; "It was very beneficial to be reunited with Mike, because we'd been training partners before he moved West. We're very close in strength level, have equally strong motivation, and we're both used to how the other trains. When I need forced reps, I can count on Mike to know precisely when to kick in that little nudge of assistance on the weight, and I can depend on him giving me precisely the amount of help I need. Other partners I've had just didn't mesh as well in my system of training"; "My diet consisted of about 1500–2000 calories per day, with most of them in the morning and early afternoon. At night I'd try to taper off. I ate primarily fruit, fish, chicken, and turkey, so the fat content of my diet was very low. I've only had about five steaks in the last two years, because my body doesn't react well to fats. I eat vegetables only in the off-season, and prior to a contest prefer low-calorie fruits like strawberries and cantaloupe"; "A typical workout day was very heavy in aerobic activities, which I find to be excellent for burning off fat"; "I'd get a craving for fats and just have to eat some ice cream, but I was still losing a lot of body fat every day"; "I'd get up around 5 a.m. and begin to get psyched up for my workout. I'd really get into deep mental states by listening to certain dramatic classical music, reading Nietzsche, and concentrating totally on an image of me being the absolute best." *Muscle Builder/Power*, January 1980.
5. *Muscle Builder/Power*, January 1980.
6. See note 5. See also note 1.
7. Mike Mentzer, McGough interview.
8. Vermont Department of Health, "A Brief History of Methamphetamine — Methamphetamine Prevention in Vermont" (archived webpage).
9. Nicolas Rasmussen, "Medical Science and the Military: The Allies' Use of Amphetamine during World War II," *Journal of Interdisciplinary History* 42, no. 2 (2011): 205–33. See also Peter Andreas, "How Methamphetamine Became a Key Part of Nazi Military Strategy," *Time* (website), January 7, 2020. And: *Bulletin of Anesthesia History* 29, no. 2, April 2011, 21–24, 32.
10. See note 8.
11. Leslie, L. Iversen, *Speed, Ecstasy, Ritalin: The Science of Amphetamines* (Oxford, UK: Oxford University Press, 2008), 17.
12. Carmen Pope, "'Black Beauties' capsules in the 1970's — What Drug Was That?" Drugs.com, updated September 5, 2022.
13. Jack Neary, interview with the author, August 27, 2023.
14. Joe Weider, *The Best of Joe Weider's Muscle & Fitness: More Training Tips and Routines* (Chicago, Contemporary Books, 1982), 33.
15. Journal entry was published in *Flex*, March 1994.
16. Journal entry was published in *Muscle & Fitness*, November 1981.
17. See note 15.
18. Mentzer and Little, *High-Intensity Training*, 196.
19. See note 5.
20. WorthPoint (website), "AAU Mr America Contest Sept 8, 1979 Bodybuilding Program Frank Zane Cover."
21. *Muscular Development*, December 1979.

22. *Fort Lauderdale News*, May 30, 1980.
23. Although the exact cause of Nietzsche's mental illness has been the subject of some debate in academic circles, that he suffered from mental illness is indisputable.
24. *Selected Letters of Friedrich Nietzsche*, ed. and trans. Christopher Middleton (Indianapolis / Cambridge, UK: Hackett, 1996), 335.
25. Lesley Chamberlain, *Nietzsche in Turin* (New York: Picador, 1996), 205.
26. *Selected Letters of Friedrich Nietzsche*, 327.
27. Mentzer and Little, *High-Intensity Training*, 196.
28. Mayo Clinic (website), "Bipolar Disorder," December 13, 2022.
29. *Muscle Builder/Power*, May 1980.
30. John Hansen, "Bodybuilding Legends Podcast #194 — Danny Padilla, Part Two." YouTube video, May 11, 2021.
31. *Pro Bodybuilding Weekly* (talk radio), "PBW: Remembering Mike Mentzer," episode 191, hosted by Dan Solomon and Bob Cicherillo, May 24, 2010.
32. Unless otherwise indicated, all information leading up to and including the 1979 Mr. Olympia contest is drawn from *Muscle Builder/Power*, February 1980.
33. Frank Zane (official website), "1979 My Greatest Mr. Olympia Win," October 18, 2021.
34. MuscleMemory (online database), "Frank Zane."
35. See note 34.
36. See note 34.
37. See note 33.
38. James Sadek, "An Interview with Mr. Universe Roger Walker!" Bodybuilding.com (webpage discontinued).
39. John Hansen, "The Bodybuilding Legends Show #19 — Roger Walker Interview," YouTube video, November 10, 2016.
40. See note 15.
41. See note 15.
42. *MuscleMag International*, March 1980.
43. See note 16.
44. See note 42.
45. See note 7.
46. See note 32: "Arnold told me I should hit a lot more poses, and that's what I tried to do."
47. See note 42.
48. Peter McGough, "Hey Frank! I Have a Secret!" *Muscular Development* (website), September 10, 2013.
49. *MuscleMag International Annual*, 1981. See also: "In 1979 I was convinced I was the winner, and I was given two reasons why I lost. I asked Paul Graham, one of Arnold's best friends, who was a contest promoter, why I lost, and he said that I posed too fast in the posedown, which is ludicrous. That was obviously a rationalization of sorts. Even if I did pose a little bit too fast, why would that wipe out the rest of (what I accomplished at) the competition? Then I walked over to Reg Park, and I said, 'Reg, how can I possibly have lost this contest?' With another ludicrous excuse, he said, 'Mike, you're ahead of your time. The crowd literally couldn't comprehend what they were seeing. When you do that first pose, where your arms open up and you spread your lats, you took up the whole stage. You're just too much. They want more of the Zane-type of physique.' I replied, 'Reg, I just find that hard to believe coming from

you, a man who had a great bodybuilding career out of being large. In fact, you were Arnold's hero precisely because of your tremendous mass, and now you're telling me it's a vice, not a virtue?'" Mike Mentzer's interview, *Iron Man*, December 2000.
50. *Muscle Builder/Power*, October 1979.
51. See note 13.
52. Joe Weider had attacked machines (and by extension Arthur Jones) in the January 1980 edition of *Muscle Builder/Power*, as the cover of the issue featured the headline "Machines: The Deceptive Selling of an Idea" and contained an article criticizing machine training by George H. Elder entitled "Machines & Deceptive Claims." An editorial written by Joe and published in the February 1980 edition of his magazine was entitled "Free Weights vs. Machines" and stated that "you can't produce a superstar weightlifter or bodybuilder with machines alone" (this coming two pages after an ad for Joe's barbell set that proclaimed, "The Joe Weider Big 16 Can Make You a Champion!").
53. See note 50.
54. Frank Zane, *Symmetry* (La Mesa, CA: Zananda, 2012), 12.
55. Ken Sprague, email to the author, December 13, 2023.
56. Brian D. Johnston, "Sergio Oliva Interview" (online article).

CHAPTER TWENTY-TWO: LEVERAGE

1. *Muscle Builder/Power*, May 1980.
2. See note 1.
3. See note 1.
4. Jack Neary, interview with the author, August 27, 2023.
5. See note 1.
6. See note 1.
7. See note 1.
8. Greg Merritt, "Chris Dickerson (1939–2021): The Life of the 1982 Mr. Olympia," TheBarbell.com, December 24, 2021.
9. Mike Mentzer, McGough interview.
10. Mike Mentzer, Garry Bartlett interview, 1983.
11. See note 9.
12. "Mike Mentzer was a Weider favorite through the late 1970s, often touted in Weider's magazines as a future champion. He felt assured of the 1979 title; all the experts gave it to him beforehand. According to Mentzer, he and Weider sat down to renegotiate his contract not long before the competition, and they could not come to terms. Mentzer finished second in the Olympia title competition that year . . ." *Rochester Democrat and Chronicle*, April 15, 1984.
13. The two articles were "Special Section: Columbus Diary" by Bill Dobbins, *Muscle Builder/Power*, February 1980, and "In Defense of Zane" by Garry Bartlett, *Muscle Builder/Power*, May 1980.
14. *Muscle & Fitness*, June 1981.
15. *Muscle Builder/Power*, February 1980.
16. See note 15.
17. See note 15.
18. *Muscle Builder/Power*, May 1980.
19. See note 18.

20. Garry Bartlett, "The Lost Mike Mentzer Interview," unpublished, sent to the author via email, April 15, 2001.
21. *Fort Lauderdale News*, May 30, 1980. See also *Daily News*, January 17, 1980.
22. *MuscleMag International*, March 1982.
23. IMDb (online database), "*The Mike Douglas Show*, Episode #19.161."
24. *Sun Magazine*, October 19, 1980.
25. See note 9.
26. *Ephrata Review*, December 28, 1978.
27. *Pottsville Republican*, May 3, 1980.
28. To wit, Weider scribe Jeff Everson's description of the "Weider Instinctive Principle": "How you decide to mix and match exercises, sets, reps and bodyparts falls right into the Instinctive Training Principle. Basically, you follow your own instinct in designing your training and, from day to day, you simply choose those principles that seem best, without being forced into a given training convention." From the article "Laws of Physiques: How the Weider Principles Can Turn Training Into a Science" by Jeff Everson, *Muscle & Fitness*, July 1999. See also Arnold Schwarzenegger's published response to a reader's question from the "Ask Arnold" column, *Muscle Builder/Power*, January 1975:

> Q. "Is it true that Joe Weider makes up all of your exercise programs, or do you devise your own routines?"
>
> A. "After mastering the Weider System and all of its techniques, I have been applying the Weider Instinctive Training Principle by adjusting my workouts to best suit my needs at each time and place. Therefore, for the past two years, I have been designing all of my own training programs and new exercise innovations which are all based on Weider techniques. What I do is figure out the exercises and the routines that I think will work the best, then I go to Joe — who I think is the greatest trainer of champions ever — and we discuss my plans. Since Joe's more than thirty years of experience is better than my ten years, I listen carefully to all of his suggestions. Also, Joe sees my weak points and offers his advice on how to correct them. After talking things over, we may decide to throw out a couple of exercises and add some new ones. However, after taking Joe's ideas into consideration, I am the one who makes the final decision when it comes to my training programs."

Mike's view on the above matter was succinct: "A human being is not a cat, a dog, a bird, a horse; we are not instinctual creatures whose knowledge is hardwired into the nervous system. There is no 'Instinctive Principle' to guide us in our training efforts, as many people seem to believe." Mike Mentzer, phone consultation, 1994.
29. *Muscle Builder/Power*, January 1978.
30. Joe Weider had claimed that he created the Weider System thusly: "I had the opportunity to train and be with many of the emerging bodybuilding stars. . . . I studied their methods and found that they were instinctively doing things in their workouts that they were unaware of, little cheats and turns that expedited the movement of weights." Joe Weider and Bill Reynolds, *Joe Weider's Ultimate Body Building: The Master Blaster's Principles of Training and Nutrition* (Chicago: Contemporary Books, 1989), xi.

31. *Muscle Builder/Power*, January 1978.
32. See note 31.
33. "The US post office considers you a catalog if you don't have a certain percentage of outside advertising. To have a second-class mailing permit was a great asset to a publisher because he could deliver a magazine to a subscriber at a very reasonable cost. Until Weider started to take substantial (early 1980s) outside advertising, the percentage escapes me, he could only sell on the newsstand — very few subscribers." John Balik, email to the author, December 3, 2023.
34. "Weider's flagship magazine, *Muscle & Fitness* [the rebrand of *Muscle Builder/Power*] just surpassed 600,000 in monthly circulation, a sevenfold increase in 10 years. Foreign-language editions are now sold in France, Germany, Italy, Spain and Japan." *Los Angeles Times*, March 2, 1989.
35. "Joe Weider is not my coach." Arnold Schwarzenegger quoted from the article "The Men and the Myth" by Richard W. Johnston, *Sports Illustrated*, October 14, 1974. See also David Robson, "An Interview with Three-time Mr. Olympia Frank Zane," Bodybuilding.com (webpage discontinued):

    > Q. "Would you have considered yourself a Weider athlete?"
    > A. "I wouldn't say that. Basically, I contributed to the Weider magazines and wrote articles and took photos and stuff in exchange for advertising. That was pretty much the deal."
    > Q. "Did Joe Weider oversee your training at any point?"
    > A. "No."

    See also Robinson, *Black Prince*, 365: "Rick Wayne, a former competitor from Barbados, had been editor of the magazine and a great sportswriter for some time and was supportive of me, or so I thought. I felt I could trust him more than other writers not to credit Weider for my development, though at times he came close."
36. Dr. Ken Leistner, "York, Weider, and Jackson," Titan Support Systems (website), June 17, 2014. See also Jack Neary, interview with the author, August 27, 2023.
37. "Chiropractor and strength coach Ken Leistner had a business rapport with Joe Weider over the years and commented on how effective Weider could be at playing both sides of the fence. Leister recalled asking Weider at one point why, as a teenager, when he bought all the supplements Weider recommended to get big and muscular, he didn't get the results as advertised. Leistner paraphrased Weider: 'My job was to pull as many young boys off the street and into the gym as I could using the advertising that I did. By the time you realized it was bullshit, I already had you hooked into a healthier lifestyle of working out and eating better.' Leistner admits that it was a pretty good comeback by Weider and it caught him off guard. Nevertheless, Joe failed to mention just how much cash came floating in from said 'bullshit.'" Roach, *Volume I*, 388–89.
38. "'My goal,' said Mentzer, 'is to make as much money as I can in the next three years and then get out. Four years from now I want to be lying on a beach in the Bahamas. At that point I could very possibly be a millionaire.'" *Ephrata Review*, December 28, 1978.
39. *Oakland Tribune*, July 14, 1980.
40. "His [Joe Weider's] ego is herculean: A single recent issue of Weider's *Muscle & Fitness* magazine contains at least 80 photos or likenesses of Weider — mostly on advertised Weider products — and more than 110 mentions of Weider's name. At 67, Weider

claims credit for producing every muscle-building champion of the last 40 years." David Ferrell, "Body Building: Joe Weider's Iron Grip on an Empire," *Los Angeles Times* (website), March 2, 1989.
41. The paintings of Rick Wayne, Arnold Schwarzenegger, and Larry Scott, along with the bronze bust of Joe Weider, can be seen in one of the photographs accompanying the *Los Angeles Times*' online obituary for Joe: "Joe Weider dies at 93; bodybuilding pioneer and publisher," March 23, 2013.
42. Robinson, 317–21.
43. *Muscle Builder/Power*, December 1979.
44. Philip Berk, "Tomorrow's Stars Yesterday: Arnold Schwarzenegger, 1977," Golden Globes (official website), March 8, 2021.
45. Ian Farrington (blog), "The Streets of San Francisco: Dead Lift (1977, Michael Preece)," September 13, 2020.
46. IMDb (online database), "*The San Pedro Beach Bums* (1977)."
47. El blog de kalidor, "Arnold Schwarzenegger Interview from the North Delta Fitness Centre 1981," YouTube video, March 2, 2021.
48. *Muscle & Fitness*, February 1981.
49. John Hansen, "The Bodybuilding Legends Show #19 — Roger Walker Interview," YouTube video, November 10, 2016.
50. "Arnold — A Unique, Honest Insight into Arnold Schwarzenegger: His Thoughts, Goals, and Desires for the Future . . ." *Muscle Digest*, May/June 1978:

    Q: "When you will you begin filming the Conan series?"
    Arnold: "Probably in the summer."

    This would prove to be a projection that was off by a margin of three and a half years. Abhimanyu Das, "Everything You Never Knew About the Making of *Conan the Barbarian*," Gizmodo (website), February 17, 2015: "The first scene to be filmed (on January 7, 1981) was of Conan fighting off a pack of wolves, and also included the first of the tumultuous shoot's many accidents."
51. Schwarzenegger and Petre, 232. See also: "De Laurentiis liked the script (despite thinking it was too violent) and, after an extended period of negotiations, bought it and took over control of financing and production." Das, "Making of *Conan the Barbarian*." (online article).
52. "He looked at me and said, 'You havva an accent. I cannot use-a you.'" Schwarzenegger and Petre, 201. See also: "De Laurentiis still despised me. . . . Even though I was under contract, he wanted to get rid of me." Schwarzenegger and Petre, 233. And: "Dino De Laurentiis bought the project to produce it for Universal Studios. He tried to get me off the project." Fred Topel, "Beyond Fest: Arnold Schwarzenegger and Bill Duke Q&A," We Live Entertainment (website), October 7, 2017. Note: There is some confusion as to when this meeting took place and what movie it was about. Arnold maintains that it was for the movie *Flash Gordon* and that it took place in 1977. John Milius, the director of *Conan the Barbarian*, claims it was for *Conan* and took place closer to 1979 — and that he was present during the meeting. "I remember bringing Arnold in, and Dino had this great desk at the end of this long room. And Arnold walks in and says, 'What does such a little man like you need with such a big desk?' You know, typical Arnold. And, of course, that freaked Dino out." Cyber Chaos

Notes

Crew, "Conan Unchained — The Making of Conan the Barbarian," YouTube video, May 4, 2020. This would only make sense, as Milius had nothing to do with *Flash Gordon* and wouldn't have been present at a meeting for that production. Moreover, one of the producers of *Conan*, Buzz Feitshans, also claimed to have been present at the meeting (or at one immediately afterward in which De Laurentiis expressed his concern about Arnold Schwarzenegger being the leading man). As Feitshans also had nothing to do with *Flash Gordon*, it's more likely that Arnold is mistaken in his recollection and the meeting involved the star, director, and producers of *Conan*. See: "Dino thought no one could understand him [Arnold]." Cyber Chaos Crew, "Conan Unchained" (YouTube video).

53. "That was the end. They escorted me out." Fred Topel, "Beyond Fest: Arnold Schwarzenegger and Bill Duke Q&A" (online article).
54. "In the fall of 1977 we agreed on a deal for me to star in *Conan the Warrior* and four sequels. The money was all laid out: $250,000 for the first film, $1 million for the next, $2 million for the next, and so on, plus 5 percent of the profits. All five movies would be worth $10 million over ten years. I thought, 'This is fantastic! I'm way beyond my goal.'" Schwarzenegger and Petre, *Total Recall*, 229–30.
55. Schwarzenegger and Petre, 231–32. For Rotten Tomatoes' score, see https://www.rottentomatoes.com/m/jayne_mansfield_a_symbol_of_the_50s.
56. *Biography*, "Arnold Schwarzenegger," hosted by Jack Perkins, aired on February 28, 1997, on A&E.
57. "He [Arnold Schwarzenegger] decided that it would help promote his movie if he competed and won the 1980 Mr. Olympia." Leamer, *Fantastic*, 133.
58. "Arnold brought something else that most Hollywood film studios had not yet fully grasped: the significance of the worldwide market. Arnold was famous in much of the world as a bodybuilder, and De Laurentiis envisioned *Conan the Barbarian* as a movie that would make its profit by being successful in scores of countries. De Laurentiis was going through one of his periodic downtimes, and he needed to sell those foreign rights if he was going to get the film into production." Leamer, 130.
59. *Muscle & Fitness*, February 1981.
60. "The thing that bothers me most about all of this . . . was what Arnold reportedly told a magazine writer shortly after the contest in Australia. He said he had entered the Olympia only because he thought Mike Mentzer and I needed to be taught a lesson. Now I really don't know much about his relationship with Mike, but I had always thought of him as a friend, with the added understanding that we held each other in high regard. For him to suggest I had done him some injustice in the past that merited revenge — well, that's the part that hurts most." Boyer Coe quoted in *Muscle & Fitness*, August 1981.
61. Joe Weider's message to Mike via his sidebar critique in the October 1979 edition of *Muscle Builder/Power* evidently hadn't registered. In 1980, Mike was still talking up Nautilus in the press. He did so because he believed in the superiority of the equipment; he never received a penny from Arthur Jones or his company. Examples of Mike's comments that were taken up by newspapers are: "Ideally, the weight training program Mentzer outlines should include access to dumbbells and barbells, equipment the average person doesn't own. Continuous-resistance Nautilus equipment, which many health clubs now feature, is even better, says Mentzer." *Oakland Tribune*,

July 14, 1980. See also: "In his book, he writes, 'Weight training could be the fitness mode of the '80s.' 'The interest is tremendous and it's getting bigger all the time,' he elaborated. 'One thing that has helped is the Nautilus machine. In California, "Nautilus" is a household word.'" *Sun Magazine*, October 19, 1980.

62. "I mentioned the idea to Joe Weider just to see what he would say, and he told me, 'Arnold, you're a champion. If you can get in shape and want to enter the contest, go ahead; it's open to all top-class bodybuilders.'" *Muscle & Fitness*, February 1981.

63. *Muscle Digest*, December 1980.

CHAPTER TWENTY-THREE: PREPARING FOR WAR

1. John Hansen, "Bodybuilding Legends Podcast #132 — Frank Zane," YouTube video, February 12, 2020.

2. A letter sent to Ben Weider from Neil S. Mallard (sports editor, Visnews Ltd., London, England) read as follows:

   > Dear Ben,
   >
   > The Mr. Olympia contest went to 50 TV networks via our film print service.
   >   But the name of the game now is satellites. This meant that the contest went on our Pacific satellite, which downlegs into Hong Kong, Tokyo, Singapore, Sydney and Auckland, then fans out via a cassette service from Hong Kong. It also went through the afternoon satellite to all the Gulf Arab networks.
   >   I would estimate a world viewing audience of 100 million for your contest. Congratulations!

   The letter was published along with the Mr. Olympia contest report in *Muscle Builder/Power*, February 1980.

3. "I was appointed to the position at the 1979 Congress in Columbus that took place in November." Wayne DeMilia quoted from email to Randy Roach, December 11, 2023, shared with the author with permission from both parties.

4. "Ben wanted to keep control over the Olympia." Wayne DeMilia quoted from email to Randy Roach, December 11, 2023, shared with the author with permission from both parties. See also: "Whether there was a professional committee or not, those promoting a professional IFBB event were dealing directly with Ben Weider anyway." Roach, *Muscle, Smoke & Mirrors, Volume III*, 12.

5. This would have been a legitimate cause for concern. Indeed, at least one bodybuilding journalist, writing after the 1980 Mr. Olympia took place and not knowing that Arnold had stepped down, questioned the ethics of Arnold competing while still holding an executive position in the IFBB: "The ethical question is . . . seeing Arnold is a member of the 'Mr. Olympia' organising committee, and as he has actually promoted the contest in recent years, and as he will no doubt have a hand in promoting it in the future, how was he permitted to enter in the first case?" *Muscle Digest*, April 1981.

6. *Globe and Mail*, April 28, 1980.

7. "'I was never a fanatic about diet. It was Frank Zane and Franco Colombu who put

my vitamins together. And then we would experiment with steroids . . . Everybody in the bodybuilding field who is up there on the top is taking steroids. Maybe five percent of my progress is from the steroids.' Schwarzenegger continues: 'I had doctors' supervision. You stayed with a very strict rule of doing it four months a year before a competition, and then lay off.'" Jess Hardiman, "Arnold Schwarzenegger Reveals How Much of His Bodybuilding Progress Was Down to Steroids," UNILAD (website), June 6, 2023.

8. I was surprised, 21 years later, that Mike had remembered our initial meeting. He would write the following as in introduction to an article I had contributed to his website: "I first met John Little at [Simpsons] department store in Toronto where Arnold, Franco, and I had made an appearance for Weider and the IFBB, in [1980]. We hit it off immediately, as John was philosophically oriented, along with having a passionate interest in bodybuilding." Mike Mentzer's introduction to John Little's article, "'Warm Marble': The Lethal Physique of Bruce Lee" on Mentzer's archived official website, May 24, 2001.

9. Heavy Duty College, "Mike Mentzer: Infitonic & Omni Contraction Training," YouTube video, August 28, 2023.

10. This was the body part sequencing that Mike had been following since his World Championships victory in 1978: "For Acapulco I trained four days a week . . . I did back, legs and abs one day, with chest, delts and arms the next." *Muscle Builder/Power*, March 1979.

11. Mike Mentzer, interview with the author, 1986.

12. *Flex*, May 1988.

13. Mentzer, interview with the author, 1990.

14. Vince Basile's Facebook message to the author, December 10, 2023, and his reply (#93) to the Getbig forum, "Topic: Robby Robinson is a national treasure (maybe not)," January 4, 2023.

15. *Muscle Digest*, April 1981.

16. Roach, *Volume III*, 62.

17. Ken Sprague, email to the author, December 13, 2023.

18. Wayne DeMilia's email to Randy Roach, February 21, 2024. Shared with the author with permission from both parties.

> Roach: "I could have sworn that I published your statement about Paul Graham believing George Butler made a fortune on *Pumping Iron*. John would like a reference, so do you mind responding to this email and affirming that you in fact did share that Graham believed *Pumping Iron* to be extremely financially lucrative?"
>
> DeMilia: "I have always said it did not turn a profit. Paul did not believe me."

19. Author Randy Roach pointed out that "Regardless of how much competitive fire Arnold Schwarzenegger had left in his belly in 1980, his rapidly expanding career in business, promotion and movies all served to ask the obvious question: why move backwards? His actions suggested hesitancy so much that it is reasonable to ask whether Arnold even wanted to compete at all. Was Paul Graham's desire for Arnold to compete one more time and star in his movie enough to tip the scales in favour of a Schwarzenegger return to bodybuilding? Could Paul Graham actually persuade Arnold

in such a manner? . . . Authors Arnold Schwarzenegger, Laurence Leamer and John D. Fair have all written on a specific incident that took place shortly after Arnold's arrival in the United States. From former to latter, each writer expanded the context of this occurrence to the point that it may bear significance to the subject at hand, Arnold's return to bodybuilding." Roach, *Volume III*, 92. The "occurrence" alluded to is Paul Graham's incarceration, and the extent that Arnold may or may not have been involved and shielded from the illegalities of it.

20. According to writer John Fair, "The cards had already been stacked in Schwarzenegger's favor. Although the Weider brothers and their chief facilitator Oscar State had the final say, it is the contest director and President of the Australian Bodybuilding Federation, Paul Graham, who is the leading suspect in the selection of judges so favorably disposed to Arnold." Fair, "The Intangible Arnold" (journal article). Fair's take on the situation was seconded by competitor Boyer Coe: "Arnold picked who he wanted as judges, well in advance and had Paul invite them and set it long beforehand." Boyer Coe quoted from Fair, "The Intangible Arnold" (journal article).
21. *Pro Bodybuilding Weekly* (talk radio), "PBW: Remembering Mike Mentzer Part 4," YouTube video, episode 191, hosted by Dan Solomon and Bob Cicherillo, May 24, 2010.
22. *Muscle Digest*, December 1980.
23. Roach, *Volume III*, 87.
24. *MuscleMag International*, May 1980.
25. Frank Zane (official website), "1980 Mr. Olympia," October 12, 2022.
26. See note 24.
27. *Muscle & Fitness*, February 1981.
28. See note 24.
29. See note 24.
30. See note 24.
31. See note 1.
32. "I'm no purist, but I said, 'there's *no injectables*. I don't want you to have needles in my house' — and he didn't." Roger Schwab, interview with the author, August 13, 2023.
33. Schwab interview, August 17, 2023.
34. *New Era*, November 10, 1978.
35. Schwab interview, August 13, 2023.
36. See note 26.
37. *Muscle & Fitness*, May 1983.
38. John Hansen, "The Bodybuilding Legends Show #9 — Boyer Coe Interview, Part Two," YouTube video, March 30, 2015.
39. See note 37.
40. See note 37. See also *Pro Bodybuilding Weekly*, "PBW: Remembering Mike Mentzer PART 4," YouTube video.
41. *Pro Bodybuilding Weekly*, "PBW: Remembering Mike Mentzer Part 4" (YouTube video).
42. See note 24.
43. See note 24.
44. Wayne DeMilia quoted from email to Randy Roach, December 11, 2023, shared with the author with permission from both parties.
45. The secrecy was probably a good thing, as Arnold was having trouble keeping his

story straight regarding why he was back in the gym training and why he would be flying to Australia along with the other bodybuilders for the Mr. Olympia contest. He had said that he was training to build up muscle for *Conan*: "It was one of those fortunate things. I was training very hard throughout the whole summer, and so I was training for my next film [*Conan*] where I have to be . . . we have to gain like 15 pounds of bodyweight. And so, I was already almost in competition shape when I then decided I that might as well just slip into the competition . . ." Gary Kasmar, "Arnold Schwarzenegger Interview — North Delta Fitness Centre — 1981," YouTube video, March 23, 2019.

See also: "After three years of political in-fighting among the studio bosses, production for the long awaited $15-million film *Conan the Barbarian* was underway. The film's star was needed in the kind of condition that brought him his ego-soothing string of six Olympia titles. Within a few weeks, Arnold's body was firming up and growing at an alarming rate. It was almost changing its form before the very eyes of the men who trained around him every morning." *Muscle & Fitness*, February 1981. He was simply holding the muscle he built from training for the role of Mickey Hargitay in *The Jayne Mansfield Story*: "Arnold admitted that he'd been taking regular workouts at World Gym in Santa Monica, but that was only because his role as Mickey Hargitay, Jayne Mansfield's Hungarian Mr. Universe husband, required him to look like a champion. He'd continued to work out after completing the Mansfield project because movie director John Milius wanted him in contest condition for *Conan the Barbarian*, which was scheduled to go before the cameras in November or December in Spain." Wayne, *Muscle Wars*, 2216. He was going to Australia to do color commentary for CBS Sports' coverage of the contest: see note 46.

See also: "'I'll be there doing the TV commentary for CBS' he told me." Frank Zane (official website), "1980 Mr. Olympia." He was going there to cover the contest for CBS News: "Arnold had flown to Sydney as a CBS News commentator for the contest." George Butler, *Arnold Schwarzenegger: A Portrait* (New York: Simon and Schuster, 1990), 142. He was going to Australia to MC the contest: "Nobody knew that Arnold was competing in 1980 until the last minute. He was supposed to be MC at the show . . ." Robert Nailon, "Arnold Schwarzenegger Q & A Interview," The Arnold Collection (website). He was going to be a judge at the competition: "I went to Australia being . . . I was invited to be a judge in Australia at the Mr. Olympia contest." Kasmar, "Arnold Schwarzenegger Interview — North Delta Fitness Centre — 1981" (YouTube video).

46. "He said he'd be in Australia on the date of the 1980 Olympia (to be held at the Sydney Opera House), but he swore he wouldn't be among the expected fifteen or sixteen contenders. He'd be there because he'd been contracted by CBS Television to do color commentary on the contest." Wayne, *Muscle Wars*, 2222.

47. "I originally had intended around eight weeks ago, to start training very hard with the objective in mind to get in my best possible shape for a film I am going to do, which is *Conan the Barbarian*. And we're going to start shooting the first few scenes in October, and so I really wanted to be muscular, because the idea was that Conan was a very muscular, heroic-looking guy, and that I should be in top shape. . . . And, around . . . two weeks ago, I decided, 'Well, I think it would be kind of an interesting challenge really to do something in eight weeks that most of the guys do in preparing

a year or two years in advance.'" Arnold Schwarzenegger quoted from Kit Laughlin's 1980 documentary *The Comeback*, YouTube video, September 14, 2014. See also: "One day, just a few weeks before the contest, I woke up and the idea of competing was fixed firmly in my mind. . . . With only three weeks to attain contest perfection, I wasn't positive I could do it. So, I asked Franco and other friends not to talk about my entering the Olympia." *Muscle & Fitness*, February 1981.

48. Arnold had been hitting the gym hard to regain his physique for some months prior to when *Conan the Barbarian* was scheduled to start shooting. However, the start of principal photography was delayed, which meant that Arnold had to continue his training for a longer period. Raffaella De Laurentiis, a producer on *Conan the Barbarian*, was scouting locations in Yugoslavia throughout the early part of 1980: "We went to former Yugoslavia and we started pre-production on the movie there. And we worked there for three or four months, and then we started getting a little bit concerned about the political situation. And we decided it was probably safer to move the picture out of Yugoslavia. We moved to Spain, and so we postponed the picture by six months." Cyber Chaos Crew, "Conan Unchained — The Making of Conan the Barbarian [HD]," YouTube video, May 4, 2020. This is corroborated by the American Film Institute (AFI): ". . . production was to commence in Yugoslavia, Spain and England by the end of 1980. A May 12, 1980, *LAT* new items noted that political turmoil resulting from the death of the president of Yugoslavia, as well as various production problems, caused the start of shooting to be delayed to Jan 1981. A January 28, 1981, HR production item notes that shooting began that month exclusively in Spain." AFI Catalog (website), "Conan the Barbarian (1982)." In a 2007 interview, Arnold revealed: "I was training for the *Conan* movie. And the *Conan* movie was supposed to start [at the] end of the summer/beginning of fall [1980]. And then, all of a sudden, they postponed the movie. And I felt like they were, ah . . . you know, I've been training now for six months really hard for this movie, now they postpone it again. Who knows if it goes to spring?" Roach and Tascs, "Arnold's Reasons for His 1980 Comeback" (podcast audio). See also note 45: Kasmar, "Arnold Schwarzenegger Interview." Arnold's statements, then, indicate that he had been in hard training for six months prior to the postponement, and then continued throughout that summer and into September. This would have put his total training time at ten months (December 1979 to October 1980).
49. *MuscleMag International*, August/September 1980.
50. See note 26.
51. "When Arnold decided to upset everyone by entering and winning the Mr. Olympia unannounced, he would hang up signs in the gym declaring 'Mentzer is Coming' in order to psych himself up to train harder." John Hansen, "The Most Controversial Olympia — Part 1," RxMuscle (website), August 6, 2011. An image of this appears on page 136 of George Butler's book *Arnold Schwarzenegger — A Portrait* (New York: Simon and Schuster), 1990.
52. Butler, *Arnold Schwarzenegger*, 138.
53. Butler, *Arnold Schwarzenegger*, 141.
54. Roach, *Volume III*, 37.
55. Wayne, *Muscle Wars*, 2245.
56. Leamer, *Fantastic*, 134–35.

Notes

57. See note 27.
58. Butler, *Arnold Schwarzenegger*, 138.
59. Butler, *Arnold Schwarzenegger*, 138.
60. "Reg [Park] was one of a small group of people in my life who was always there to support me. Whether it was winning bodybuilding competitions, starring in a new film or becoming Governor, there was always a note and kind words from Reg. That pumped me up and helped inspire me for my next goal. As a young man, I lived and trained with Reg in South Africa." Arnold Schwarzenegger, "Arnold Schwarzenegger Remembers Reg Park," *Iron Game History* 10, no. 2 (April/May 2008): 5. In Arnold's book, *Arnold: The Education of a Bodybuilder*, Reg Park was singled out as being his inspiration. Arnold also promoted him whenever possible; Park was the MC for the 1975 Mr. Olympia contest in South Africa, had joined him on the original panel of the IFBB Professional Division, and Arnold had Park guest pose at the 1979 Mr. Olympia contest in Columbus, Ohio. Without Arnold's ongoing support and promotion, it's doubtful that many bodybuilders would have remembered the former three-time NABBA Mr. Universe winner (1951, 1958, and 1965) any more than they remembered Bruce Randall (who won it in 1959) or Henry Downs (who won it in 1960). No other contemporary bodybuilder did more to promote Reg Park than Arnold Schwarzenegger. Arnold had further looked after Reg and Maryeon Park's son Jon Jon for a year and half when Jon Jon moved to Long Beach, California. "I spent a great deal of time with him on weekends in the spare bedroom. He'd sometimes drive down and take me for dinners, pick me up, bring me back to L.A. You know, he treated me kind of like a kid brother." Jon Jon Park quoted from John Fair's "The Intangible Arnold" (journal article). According to bodybuilder Bill Pearl, who knew both Arnold and Park well, "Reg and Arnold were as tight as ticks." Bill Pearl also quoted from Fair's "The Intangible Arnold."
61. "Although only 23, Busek was already editor of a German bodybuilding magazine when he co-produced the Jr. Mr. Europe in Stuttgart, Germany, on Oct. 31, 1965, and met the Austrian phenom. Busek has been championing his friend's career for 50 years." Greg Merritt, "Arnold Schwarzenegger's 12 Secrets to Success," *Muscle & Fitness* (website). See also: "Kellie got to know Albert Busek, one of the best friends of Arnold, in London. He sat across from her at dinner, banging the table with his fist, arguing with an English guy about Arnold. The Englishman said that Arnold had a flaw . . . 'What flaw! . . . Arnold is perfect!,' mad Busek proclaimed." Kellie Everts (official website), "The Arnold & Kellie Affair." It would be impossible indeed to vote anything less than first place for a friend who was "perfect."
62. Starting in 1979, Arnold was the co-promoter of Kawashima's "Hawaiian Islands" bodybuilding contest. "Known by all who met him as 'Mits,' Kawashima popularized bodybuilding in Hawaii in the 1980s as promoter of the Hawaiian Islands contest, an event that he co-promoted with his longtime friend Arnold Schwarzenegger. Kawashima and his late wife, Dot, ran the event from 1979 to 2007, with emerging Hollywood star Schwarzenegger emceeing the first seven contests before large crowds at the Blaisdell Concert Hall." *Honolulu Star Advertiser*, February 19, 2012. See also: "As the years went by, the connection between Arnold and Mits deepened and evolved . . . to a prosperous business partnership. Over the course of approximately three decades, they joined forces to co-produce bodybuilding competitions in Hawaii." Yegor Khzokhlachev, "Arnold

Schwarzenegger in Hawaii," Built Report (website), January 18, 2015. It is highly unlikely that Mits Kawashima would vote against Arnold for obvious business reasons.
63. Fair, "The Intangible Arnold" (journal article).

CHAPTER TWENTY-FOUR: FLASH POINT DOWN UNDER
1. Mike Mentzer, interview with the author, 1990.
2. Mentzer, McGough interview. See also Mike Mentzer seminar in Rexdale, Ontario.
3. Mike Mentzer seminar in Rexdale, Ontario.
4. Mike Mentzer, McGough interview.
5. Golden Era Bookworm, "The Gold's Gym Steroid Doctors with Jerry Brainum," YouTube video, September 14, 2022.
6. See note 4.
7. Maggie Watkinson and Julie Jenks, "Minimising the risks of amphetamine use for young adults with diabetes," Primary Care Diabetes Society (website), December 9, 1998. See also Mike Mentzer, interview with the author, 1986.
8. See note 4.
9. See note 4.
10. See note 4.
11. See note 4.
12. See note 4.
13. Jack Neary, interview with the author, August 27, 2023.
14. *Muscle & Fitness*, February 1981.
15. See note 14.
16. See note 14.
17. See note 14.
18. See note 14.
19. *Pro Bodybuilding Weekly* (talk radio), "PBW: Remembering Mike Mentzer," aired May 24, 2010.
20. See note 4.
21. See note 14.
22. See note 3.
23. "There were rumors that Arnold's body weight at almost 6'2" (188 cm) was between 217 and 220 pounds (98.6–100 kg) which if true put him almost 20 pounds (9.09 kg) lighter than his biggest Olympia showing in 1974." Roach, *Volume III*, 42.
24. According to Arnold's training partner Roger Callard, "Well, he didn't have big legs. His legs were not big. He had a good cut in them, but he didn't have great legs, and he didn't have wide shoulders. He had thick deltoids, but they weren't wide, and huge arms and huge back and huge chest. But if you analyze his body, he didn't have great forearms, he didn't have great calves, I can tell you that. . . . He had them done in Mexico." John Hansen, "Bodybuilding Legends Podcast #2 — Season 1, Episode 2 Roger Callard," YouTube video, December 13, 2017. Rick Drasin, another training partner of Arnold's, said, "A while back when he would go on back to Austria for to visit his family. He went one year, four to three months, and he came back with his huge calves. Rumor had it he had implants. I don't know if it is or I don't know but it isn't, I can't say either way. But I know they were really big, much bigger than before he left." Rick Drasin, "Arnold and the Boys Leg Training," YouTube video, February

Notes

4, 2010. This was a view shared by Gold's Gym owner, Ken Sprague, in whose gym Arnold was training at the time: "I have always suspected that Arnold's calves were not 'natural' — my recollection is my surprise that his calves looked structurally different before and after his trip to Germany. If anything, rather than implants, the 'lumps' looked more like the result of silicone. But without having been present at a medical 'procedure,' I cannot go beyond suspicion to a point of certainty (An aside: Heidi, sitting topless on Arnold's shoulders in PI [*Pumping Iron*] book, traveled to Germany for breast implants during that same period)." Email from Ken Sprague to the author, September 21, 2023. All these men were gym mates of Arnold at the time the alleged procedure took place during the 1970s. Years later, bodybuilder Mike Quinn stated that Joe Weider also knew about it: "My arms were the biggest. Weider loved big arms. He virtually pulled me offstage and said, 'I'll do for you what I did for Arnold . . .' He wanted to send me for calf implants. Said he'd send me to Arnold's doctor. I kid you not. I decided against that." Michael Dusa, "Conversation with Mr. Universe, Mighty Mike Quinn," Bodybuilding Mauritius & South Africa (blog), February 25, 2015. If there had been only one hearsay source for this, the author would not have felt obliged to report the allegation. That it has been indicated by four separate sources (two of which were Arnold's training partners) indicates a fair degree of smoke, which may indicate the reality of fire.

25. See note 14.
26. See note 14.
27. Mike Mentzer seminar in Rexdale, Ontario.
28. See note 14.
29. Vince Basile, Facebook post, March 18, 2016.
30. Roach, *Volume III*, 61.
31. Fair, "The Intangible Arnold" (journal article).
32. "It was a very poor judges' panel. We were told there weren't enough judges, so they had to choose from individuals present. Just one of the many ridiculous things that took place and cast a black eye upon the sport." Mike Mentzer quoted in *Muscle Digest*, December 1980.
33. "They didn't have as many qualified judges as they wanted, so Bill Pearl . . . asked me to be a judge. I went there in case they needed help. There is only one way to help bodybuilding and that is to get involved, so you make your services available. I had judged the California Grand Prix this year, so I felt that I could contribute." Dan Howard quoted in *Muscle Digest*, December 1980. See also: "I picked Dan Howard as a last-minute judge, because I knew he couldn't be bought, that he is an honest man." Bill Pearl quoted in *Muscle Digest*, December 1980.
34. "Dr. Michael Walczak . . . was Arnold's doctor; the NPC had isolated him from judging AAU/NPC in the mid-late '70s shows because of his reputation of placing his patients higher than obviously deserved." Ken Sprague, email to the author, December 13, 2023. Arnold Schwarzenegger's former girlfriend, Barbara Outland Baker, referred to Dr. Walzcak in her book as "our normally calm friend." She indicates that Walczak might have been Arnold's doctor at the time: "The consciousness training seminar may not have taught Arnold anything directly, but Michael [Walczak] did toss him an unexpected threat one day at his doctor's office saying, 'If you don't take it, she could leave you.'" Baker, *Arnold and Me*, 146.

35. "According to [Boyer] Coe, who otherwise knew 'nothing about him,' Ryan managed the gym operated by Olympia director Paul Graham, and because of that connection Boyer was 'sure he did what he was told to do.'" Fair, "The Intangible Arnold" (journal article).
36. "I did not know as yet whether he was actually going to enter the contest, but he asked me to step outside the little gym where he was working out and did some poses for me. I told him, 'Arnold, you're not ready.'" Dan Howard quoted from Fair, "The Intangible Arnold" (journal article).
37. "I remember most clearly meeting with Jacques Blommaert the day before the show at Paul Graham's gym. He was concerned that his friend Arnold was going to destroy his legend. He told me that, in fact, Arnold had told him he was going to go in the show and how he tried to talk him out of it." Mike Mentzer, McGough interview.
38. See note 14.
39. See note 4.
40. IFBB (website), "IFBB Rules for Bodybuilding and Fitness," 2021 edition.
41. "The only problem was — which [I] didn't realize at the time — that four of the judges we had on the panel had very strong emotional ties toward Arnold." Bill Pearl, quoted in *Muscle Digest*, December 1980.
42. Roach, *Volume III*, 46.
43. See note 13.
44. See note 14.
45. See note 14.
46. See note 13.
47. "Believe it or not, [Peter McCarthy] arrived at the Opera House an hour late for the judges meeting. He claims he was told 1 p.m. instead of the real time of 12 p.m." Vince Basile, Facebook post, March 18, 2016. See also: "The judges and competitors meeting at the 80 Olympia was held at the same time. Peter was given the wrong time so was chatting with Frank and myself when someone came up and told him the meeting was on. He swore and ran off only to be told he was late, so he was not allowed to be one of the official judges." Vince Basile, Facebook message to the author, December 9, 2023. And: "On the day of the contest, Vince Basile was speaking with Peter McCarthy and Frank Burwash when Peter was informed that the judges meeting had already begun. Basile recalled McCarthy swearing out loud and running off to the meeting. It was Graham, promoter of the 1980 Mr. Olympia, who gave McCarthy the wrong time for the judges meeting. Peter had planned to arrive 30 minutes before the meeting but ended up 30 minutes late due to the late time Graham gave him." Roach, *Volume III*, 62.
48. "He [Paul Graham] then told me I had been replaced and made a reserve judge." Peter McCarthy quoted from Randy Roach, *Volume III*, 62.
49. "I always believed I was replaced by Brendan Ryan." Peter McCarthy quoted from Roach, *Volume III*, 62.
50. Roach, *Volume III*, 62.
51. *Muscle Digest*, April 1981.
52. See note 38.
53. Mike Mentzer, Bartlett interview.

Notes

54. "... Brendan and his wife, Audra. How surprised I was to realize that the handsome blond Australian was another old contact from the seventies. He joined in our chatter and drove me back in time." Baker, *Arnold and Me*, 286. And: "Our Australian friend, Brendan Ryan, expanded on this theme." Baker, *Arnold and Me*, 73.
55. "For one thing, I might change my mind when October came around. Also, I was concerned for Paul Graham, the promoter of the Mr. Olympia contest. I thought that if it were generally known that I was going to compete, a number of the other bodybuilders might decide not to enter, and this would be bad for the contest and the fans." Arnold Schwarzenegger quoted in *Muscle & Fitness*, February 1981 (this evidently had not crossed Paul Graham's mind at all, as he had told Vince Basile about Arnold competing in the contest a month previous to it: see *Muscle Digest*, December 1980).
56. "I know that Arnold did not enter the contest until he knew who was on the judging panel." Bill Pearl quoted from Fair, "The Intangible Arnold" (journal article). Interestingly, Ken Sprague, who was a successful promoter of bodybuilding contests, knew that this was exactly the way to ensure a victory for Arnold: "The issue's focus is, one; who selected the panel? And two, how were they connected to Arnold? From personal experience, I knew the result of a contest could be manipulated by the choice of judges. Even without an outright 'fix,' knowing the personal taste preferences and relationships to contestants eviscerated any concept of fair competition." Ken Sprague, email to the author, December 13, 2023.
57. *Muscle Digest*, April 1981. See also note 14.
58. Retro Muscle, "1980 IFBB Mr. Olympia," YouTube video, November 30, 2020.
59. See note 4.
60. Roach, *Volume III*, 44–45.
61. Roach, *Volume III*, 39.
62. See note 14.
63. See note 14.
64. See note 4.
65. See note 14.
66. See note 14.
67. See note 4.
68. See note 4.
69. See note 14.
70. See note 14.
71. John Hansen, "Bodybuilding Legends Podcast #154 — 1980 Mr. Olympia Interviews," YouTube video, July 11, 2020.
72. See note 71.
73. For Roger Walker, see note 71; for Tom Platz, see Rep One, "Legendary Tom Platz Seminar: David Gym Zurich," YouTube video, September 27, 2018.
74. John Hansen, "Bodybuilding Legends Podcast #186 — Jack Neary, Part Two," YouTube video, March 6, 2021. See also note 53.
75. See note 71.
76. See note 4.
77. See note 4.
78. Peter McCarthy, email to the author and Randy Roach, May 17, 2024.

79. Heavy Duty College, "Mike Mentzer: The Interview That Blew People's Minds," YouTube video, January 30, 2023.
80. See note 14.
81. See note 14.
82. See note 14.
83. See note 14.
84. See note 14.
85. See note 14.

CHAPTER TWENTY-FIVE: THE STING

1. Mike Mentzer, McGough interview.
2. John Hansen, "Bodybuilding Legends Podcast #154," (YouTube video).
3. Witness for example, the following statements from Arnold's fellow competitors: Roger Walker: "I'd seen Arnold [at his best]. The first time I saw Arnold was in '72 and I thought, 'Wow.' And I don't say that very often . . . but 'Wow.' But I didn't say that then [1980]. He was human then." Chris Dickerson: "I sort of felt, here's a great champion, and he's not ready for this"; Samir Bannout: "I wasn't impressed with Arnold backstage in Sydney . . . I looked at Arnold, when he took his shirt off and [I thought,] 'He's not the same guy I saw in Santa Monica.' He was really off; he was depleted."; Roy Duval: "I grew up with him, and . . . he was like an idol. I was quite sad to see him compete looking the way he did because he wasn't the old Arnold. . . . He looked much, much smaller."; Boyer Coe: "I remember sitting back there at the prejudging. And Mike Mentzer and I were sitting there talking. And we see Arnold, and the best way I can describe him, he looks thin . . . Arnold was — by far — not in his best shape." All quotes are from John Hansen, "Bodybuilding Legends Podcast #154," (YouTube video). See also: "Throughout that [competitor's] meeting Arnold had on a tight-knit sweater and I knew what his concerned friends meant: he looked skinny! I was curious to see what he looked like once he'd stripped down. When he did strip down, I remember looking at him and thinking, 'Not only am I going to win this contest but I'm going to beat Arnold Schwarzenegger!'" Mike Mentzer, McGough interview.
4. *Pro Bodybuilding Weekly* (talk radio), "PBW: Remembering Mike Mentzer Part 4" (YouTube video).
5. Hansen, "Bodybuilding Legends Podcast #154," (YouTube video). See also: "And even though he knew the outcome ahead of time, he [Arnold Schwarzenegger] was still visibly nervous at the prejudging." Boyer Coe from the video "PBW: Remembering Mike Mentzer Part 4" (YouTube video).
6. Arnold Schwarzenegger quoted from Laughlin's, *The Comeback* (YouTube video).
7. "I thought I was near 90%." *Muscle Digest*, December 1980.
8. *Pro Bodybuilding Weekly* (talk radio), "PBW: Remembering Mike Mentzer Part 4" (YouTube video):

> **Joe Gold:** "I've never seen so many guys come in [top] shape."
> **Arnold Schwarzenegger:** "That's right. It's a dangerous situation."

9. *Muscle & Fitness*, February 1981.
10. *MuscleMag International Annual*, 1981.

Notes

11. Andrews, *True Myths*, 21. See also: "Arnold's waistline was small, but he did not have great abdominal tone." Frank Zane quoted from Leamer, 99.
12. IFBB, "IFBB Rules for Bodybuilding and Fitness" (online article).
13. *Muscle Digest*, April 1981.
14. Roach, *Volume III*, 49.
15. Hansen, "Bodybuilding Legends Podcast #154" (YouTube video).
16. All judging scores of the competitors from the 1980 Mr. Olympia contest are from Roach, *Volume III*, 185–91.
17. See note 15.
18. Mike Mentzer, McGough interview.
19. See note 18.
20. See note 18.
21. Roach, *Volume III*, 53.
22. See note 13.
23. See note 15. See also Roach, *Volume III*, 55.
24. See note 9.
25. See note 18. See also Roach, *Volume III*, 48.
26. This is evident in the documentary *The Comeback* after Arnold completes his posing routine during the evening finals.
27. Leigh, *Arnold*, 185.
28. Roach, *Volume III*, 48.
29. Leamer, *Fantastic*, 137.
30. MuscleMemory (online database), "Boyer Coe."
31. *Muscle Digest*, December 1980.
32. There was a belief among certain of the competitors (most notably Mike Mentzer) that George Butler was involved in the documentary that was being filmed (Paul Graham's *The Comeback*). Since Butler was involved in the producing the documentary *Pumping Iron*, along with the fact that, everywhere Arnold went — to Paul Graham's gym, backstage before, during and after the competition — Butler and the documentary crew were present, some competitors assumed that Butler was involved with the new documentary. Also, Butler, when asked, said he was in Australia because he was working on a new version of *Pumping Iron* (not specifying that it was the book he was referring to), which only added to the confusion. When the reporter for *Muscle Digest* asked Mike if he was sure they were filming *Pumping Iron II*, Mike replied "Oh yeah, George Butler was there, and he told everybody what he was there for." *Muscle Digest*, December 1980.
33. *Muscle Digest*, December 1980.
34. Supersetman, "Arnold FINALLY Admits He Was NOT the BEST at Mr. Olympia 1980," (YouTube video).
35. "Mentzer and the others were definitely marked down." Peter McCarthy email to the author and Randy Roach, May 24, 2024.
36. *Muscle & Fitness*, February 1981.
37. See note 34.
38. *MuscleMag International Annual*, 1981.
39. See note 13.
40. See note 9.

41. *Muscle Digest*, December 1980.

> *Muscle Digest:* "Contrary to what people said your weight was this year — as opposed to last year's 190 — what did you really weigh?"
> **Frank Zane:** "About 186. 187, right in that area, a few pounds less."

42. Fair, "The Intangible Arnold" (journal article).
43. Leamer, *Fantastic*, 57.
44. See note 42.
45. See note 13.
46. Hansen, "Bodybuilding Legends Podcast #186" (YouTube video).
47. Boyer Coe quoted from *Pro Bodybuilding Weekly* (talk radio), "PBW Remembers Mike Mentzer," aired May 24, 2010.
48. See note 15.
49. See note 36.
50. Hansen, "Bodybuilding Legends Podcast #186" (YouTube video).
51. See note 36.
52. See note 36.
53. Roach, *Volume III*, 79.
54. *Muscle Digest*, December 1980.
55. See note 54.
56. Roach, *Volume III*, 78.
57. "After the contest, during a cruise in Sydney harbor, Howard told Arnold that he had to judge the contest fairly and that Schwarzenegger's fourth place finish was 'his problem, not my problem.' Arnold seemed incredulous, pointing out that 'they were friends, after all,' and he could not believe Dan did not place him first. According to Howard, Arnold refused to talk to him for a year." Fair, "The Intangible Arnold" (journal article). See also Dan Howard quoted from *Muscle Digest*, December 1980: "In my eyes he wasn't up to what he used to be when he was winning it, so, you know, he shouldn't have won. That's the way I voted and that's what I stand by, whether Arnold's upset with me or not."
58. "'In the contest Arnold posed the way he always had, and it was out of date,' he [Dan Howard] says. This was a view shared by Jack Neary who wrote: "His [Arnold Schwarzenegger's] posing had the leonine grace and power, but it seemed uninspired and old hat." Fair, "The Intangible Arnold" (journal article). See also note 36.
59. Dan Howard: "'I had no doubt that if he had six more weeks, he would have been in proper shape to win. I don't think Arnold should have won." Fair, "The Intangible Arnold" (journal article).
60. Reg Park quoted by Robert Nailon. Fair, "The Intangible Arnold" (journal article).
61. Heavy Duty College, "Mike Mentzer: The Interview That Blew People's Minds," (YouTube video).
62. See note 54.
63. "Kawashima, along with Busek, also served as an usher for Schwarzenegger's wedding in 1986." Fair, "The Intangible Arnold" (journal article). See also Leamer, *Fantastic*, 37: "Graham left the United States and returned to Australia, where he became the top executive in the bodybuilding federation controlled by the Weiders. Arnold invited the Australian to his wedding and was best man at Graham's."

CHAPTER TWENTY-SIX: AFTERMATH

1. Hansen, "Bodybuilding Legends Podcast #186" (YouTube video).
2. See note 1.
3. Unless otherwise indicated, the remainder of the discussion Jack Neary and Arnold Schwarzenegger had over lunch in Red Deer is drawn from Jack Neary, interview with the author, August 27, 2023.
4. See note 1.
5. *Muscle Builder/Power*, August 1981.
6. Mike Mentzer, Hause interview.
7. Retro Muscle, "1980 IFBB Mr. Olympia" (YouTube video).
8. See note 6.
9. Wayne, *Muscle Wars*, 2280–85.
10. Hansen, "The Bodybuilding Legends Show #19" (YouTube video).
11. Peter McGough, "When Platz Met Schwarzenegger," *Muscular Development* (website), April 3, 2013. See also John Hansen, "Remembering the 1981 Mr. Olympia — Part 1," *Iron Man* magazine (website), May 6, 2012.
12. Hansen, "Bodybuilding Legends Podcast #154" (YouTube video).
13. Leamer, *Fantastic*, 138. See also: "I had agreed to pose in Columbus Ohio for his Mr. World [Pro Mr. Universe] contest but after the Australia fiasco I refused. Since Arnold had MCed a contest Christine and I ran that summer, I owed him this posing exhibition and when I didn't do it letters from his attorney began arriving threatening a lawsuit. 'Just pay my attorney costs and we'll call it even' he told me, so I did." Frank Zane (official website), "1980 Mr. Olympia Part II," January 6, 2022.
14. "Afterward, Tom [Platz] had refused to support the proposed boycott of the succeeding Universe and Olympia events. In fact, he went to Columbus fully expecting to win the Universe. When the winner's check went to Germany's Jusup Wilkosz instead—exactly as had been predicted by Arnold's detractors—Tom was shattered." Wayne, *Muscle Wars*, 2393. For Tom Platz finishing second, see MuscleMemory (online database), "1980 Universe — Pro — IFBB."
15. *Rochester Democrat and Chronicle*, April 15, 1984.
16. Sherman Eagan, interview with the author, 1994, and email to the author, February 23, 2024.
17. Roach, *Volume III*, 14.
18. Roach, *Volume III*, 14–15.
19. Hansen, "Bodybuilding Legends Podcast #154," (YouTube video).
20. Roach, *Volume III*, 48.
21. Roach, *Volume III*, 15.
22. Roach, *Volume III*, 48.
23. Roach, *Volume III*, 15.
24. See note 19.
25. See note 19.
26. See note 19.
27. See note 19.
28. Heavy Duty College, "Aftermath: The 1980 & 1981 Mr. Olympia Disasters," YouTube video, February 26, 2024.
29. *Muscle & Fitness*, February 1981.

30. *Muscle Digest*, December 1980.
31. *Muscle Australia Magazine*, reprinted in *Muscle Digest*, April 1981.
32. The Arnold/Conan ad appeared in the same issue as the report of the 1980 Mr. Olympia contest (*Muscle & Fitness*, February 1981).
33. The International Olympic Committee named both the IFBB and Weider Health & Fitness in its lawsuit (see *U.S. Olympic Committee v. International Federation of Body Builders and Weider Health & Fitness, Inc*, May 14, 1984).
34. The allegations of Joe Weider fixing contests were still in effect three years later in 1984, when the *Democrat and Chronicle* newspaper contacted him and received the following quote: "There's more than a half dozen other magazines at every major competition, taking pictures and writing on the event. Don't you think they'd cry foul against me if I tried to rig something? Look, there's nine judges from all over the world, six to seven thousand people in the audience, television and movie cameras rolling . . . how am I going to rig? I've spent 36 years building this sport and my business. I'm not so stupid as to harm that . . . for what, to pick the winner? What do I care who wins? They all use my products anyway. My magazines pay the best rates for photos and stories and we have, by far, the largest circulation. So if you win, don't you want to make the most money? Have your name reaching the most people? That's my influence; nothing to do with any shenanigans." From the article "Danny Padilla: The Giant Killer" by Ken Tesoriere, *Democrat and Chronicle*, April 15, 1984.
35. Robinson, *Black Prince*, 414–15.
36. *Muscle & Fitness*, August 1981.
37. "The inside buzz was more of a roar that the contest had been fixed w/ Arnold having a hand in selecting judges." Ken Sprague, email to author, September 21, 2023.
38. John Hansen, "Bodybuilding Legends Podcast #250 — Rick Wayne, Part Two," YouTube video, November 6, 2022.
39. Wayne, 2749–56.
40. Wayne, 2769–75.
41. *Muscle & Fitness*, April 1981.
42. See note 41.
43. See note 7.
44. See note 6.
45. *Ottawa Citizen*, March 25, 1972.
46. Mike Mentzer, McGough interview.
47. "All year long, everybody was telling me, 'Franco Columbu's going to win, obviously, Arnold's his buddy.' And I said, 'No. No way they're going to do it two years in a row. It would be a slap in the face.'" Mike Mentzer, seminar in Rexdale, Ontario. See also: "Casey Viator . . . stated that Arnold just laughed over the whole 1980 Mr. Olympia event and when he was finished laughing, he told Casey, 'And, next year, Franco is going to win!'" Roach, *Volume III*, 100. Also see Wayne, *Muscle Wars*, 2341–46.
48. Wayne, 2372–77.
49. "I didn't want anyone pulling out on my account. I couldn't risk that. I know Frank Zane, for one, would have ducked out the minute he knew for certain that I planned to compete. All he needed was a good excuse." Arnold Schwarzenegger quoted from *Muscle & Fitness*, October 1981.
50. "Jack Neary, an avowed Mentzerite, if not the best advertisement for Heavy Duty,

Notes

offered for reward his own vitriolic account of the Sydney Fiasco via the pages of this magazine." Rick Wayne quoted from *Muscle & Fitness*, October 1981.

51. "Arnold said Mentzer had somehow given mindless bodybuilders the erroneous impression that he is something of a genius, an intellectual giant." Rick Wayne quoted from *Muscle & Fitness*, October 1981.
52. "He [Arnold] said Mentzer had passed himself off as a future doctor of medicine with a lot of bogus talk about pre-med school." Rick Wayne quoted from *Muscle & Fitness*, October 1981.
53. "Mentzer should realize that his physique is not attractive, not to bodybuilding fans and not to the general public." Arnold Schwarzenegger quoted from *Muscle & Fitness*, October 1981.
54. "He's [Mike Mentzer's] got to make radical changes in his physique if he wants to win. And to accomplish that he has to train the way Sergio trains, the way Franco trains, the way I have always trained. He's got to start doing 20 sets a bodypart, he's got to include more dumbbell work in his programs." Arnold Schwarzenegger quoted from *Muscle & Fitness*, October 1981.
55. "I had tested him and, instead of maintaining his cool, Mentzer had exposed his insecurity." Arnold Schwarzenegger quoted from *Muscle & Fitness*, October 1981.
56. Arnold Schwarzenegger quoted from *Muscle & Fitness*, October 1981.
57. ". . . he [Arnold] had been informed by his business colleagues that ticket sales were as good as ever. With nearly six months to go before the contest, a whopping 85% of the seats had already been sold. He fully expected a packed house." Rick Wayne quoted from *Muscle & Fitness*, October 1981.
58. "As far as the Mr. Olympia contestants were concerned, well, he [Arnold] did not want to give out names at this point, since he didn't want to cause anyone unnecessary embarrassment. But he could say the leading US professionals would be in Columbus." Rick Wayne quoted from *Muscle & Fitness*, October 1981.
59. "Already the forecast is that we're in for a very hotly contested 1981 Mr. Olympia, with even more formidable contenders than were present at the Sydney Opera House last November [Rick was a month late in his reporting of the date of the Sydney Olympia, which took place on October 4, 1980]. Look out for Bertil Fox. And if the rumors are correct, Sergio Oliva too." Rick Wayne quoted from the article "Mr. Olympia Revisited," *Muscle & Fitness*, October 1981.
60. Rick Wayne quoted from *Muscle & Fitness*, October 1981.
61. *Muscle & Fitness*, August 1981.
62. *Miami Herald*, August 14, 1981:

    EVENTS: Swimming, Weightlifting, Tennis, Rowing, Golf, Bowling.

    Lou (The Incredible Hulk) Ferrigno broke Lyle Alzado's 1979 record with a lift of 225. Bodybuilder Mike Mentzer also broke the record with a lift of 220 but failed at 225.

    Men's Preliminary:
    Swimming (50 yards) — Nystrom, 26:53 seconds; 2. Mentzer, 27:05; 3. Mahre, 28:50; 4. Liquori 28:53; Birdsong, 31:41.

Rowing (100 yards) 1. Ferrigno 37:23; 2. Liquori 38:37; Ciccarelli 42:33; Nystrom 40:90, Mentzer 41:40.

63. Lou Ferrigno, interview with the author, 1996.
64. "In training he [Mike Mentzer] had shocked coach Harry with a time of 11.0 seconds." *Muscle & Fitness*, May 1982.
65. "Standings: 1. (tie) Nystrom and Liquori 33; 2. Ferrigno 20, 3. Mahre 16; 4. Mentzer 15; Ciccarelli 9; 5. Spinks 7; 6. M. Frazier 3; Birdsong 2." *Miami Herald*, August 14, 1981.

CHAPTER TWENTY-SEVEN: BODYBUILDING LOST

1. Roach, *Volume III*, 146.
2. *Muscle & Fitness*, February 1982. See also *Muscle & Fitness*, March 1982.
3. See note 1. See also: "In October 1988 *California Business* summed up the magnitude of Weider's current operation: 'Weider and his brother Ben, president of the International Federation of Body Builders, the worldwide professional bodybuilding organization, almost completely control the bodybuilding game. It's as if Walter O'Malley owned not only the Dodgers, but also Chavez Ravine, NBC Sports, *Sports Illustrated* — and most of the players.'" Wendy Leigh, *Arnold: An Unauthorized Biography*, 83.
4. *Muscle & Fitness*, March 1982.
5. See note 4.
6. See note 4.
7. See note 4.
8. "Arnold, Franco and Thorsen are close buddies." *Muscle & Fitness*, March 1982.
9. IMDb (online database), "Sven-Ole Thorsen."
10. Roach, *Volume III*, 109.
11. Roger Schwab, interview with author, August 13, 2023.
12. Hansen, "Bodybuilding Legends Podcast #54," (YouTube video).
13. See note 12.
14. See note 12.
15. AEG Fitness, "Switching Metabolism Benefits: Tom Platz & Mike Mentzer," YouTube video, August 23, 2023.
16. Mike Mentzer seminar in Rexdale, Ontario.
17. *New York Times*, September 5, 2019.
18. RxMuscle, "The TRUE Story of the 1980–1981 Mr Olympia!" YouTube video, September 7, 2019.
19. John Hansen, "1981 Mr. Olympia Report — Part 2," *Iron Man* magazine (website), January 11, 2013.
20. Dr. Babak Dadvand (website), "Gynecomastia and Steroid Use."
21. Judges' scorecards from Roach, *Volume III*, 191–95.
22. "Had Sven Ole-Thorsen and Franco Fassi been removed from the judging panel due to their relationship to Columbu, then Dickerson or Platz would probably have been Mr. Olympia for 1981." Roach, *Volume III*, 171.
23. See note 18.
24. Wayne, 2706.
25. *Muscle & Fitness*, January 1982.
26. Wayne, 2716.

27. See note 16.
28. See note 16.
29. See note 4.
30. MuscleMemory (online database), "Arnold Schwarzenegger."
31. Leigh, 187.
32. Marshall McLuhan, *Counterblast* (Toronto: McClelland & Stewart, 1969), 119.
33. "When this film was released, audiences filled up three auditoriums; a third of the audience were made up of bodybuilders. People lined up around the block in 16 cities for up to eight hours to see it." IMDb (online database), "*Conan the Barbarian*: Trivia."
34. "Weider Nutrition International, a public company that grossed $280 million last year and includes Schiff vitamins. Schwarzenegger, who for many years was a spokesperson for Weider products, holds a stake in Weider Nutrition." Ann Louise Bardach, "The Hush-Hush Deal That Made Arnold Schwarzenegger Governor," *Los Angeles Magazine* (website), September 1, 2004.

CHAPTER TWENTY-EIGHT: WINDS OF CHANGE

1. *Pro Bodybuilding Weekly* (talk radio), "PBW: Remembering Mike Mentzer," aired May 24, 2010.
2. Heavy Duty College, "The Mike Mentzer Story" (YouTube video).
3. Mike Mentzer, Hause interview.
4. MuscleMemory (online database), "Ray Mentzer."
5. Heavy Duty College, "Ray Mentzer: The Truth About Bodybuilding" (YouTube video).
6. Jack Neary, interview with the author, August 27, 2023.
7. Dave Mastorakis, email to the author, January 1, 2024.
8. Heavy Duty College, "Mike Mentzer: In-Depth Phone Interview (By John Little, February 1990)." YouTube video, December 19, 2021.
9. See note 6.
10. *Muscle & Fitness*, May 1983.
11. MuscleMemory (online database), "Julie McNew."
12. *Soldiers: The Official U.S. Army Magazine*, July 1982, 51.
13. See note 10.
14. "Being love-struck also releases high levels of dopamine, a chemical that 'gets the reward system going,' said [Jacqueline] Olds. Dopamine activates the reward circuit, helping to make love a pleasurable experience similar to the euphoria associated with use of cocaine or alcohol." Scott Edwards, "Love and the Brain," *On the Brain*, Spring 2015.
15. See note 10.
16. See note 7.
17. Mike Mentzer, McGough interview.
18. *Playboy*, March 1983.
19. *MuscleMag International*, February 1984.
20. See note 19.
21. Mike Mentzer, Bartlett interview.
22. Mike Mentzer, interview with the author, 1986.
23. See note 17.
24. See note 21.

25. See note 19.
26. See note 19.
27. RepOne, "Legendary TOM PLATZ Seminar" (YouTube video).
28. See note 26.
29. John Little with Joanne Sharkey, *The Wisdom of Mike Mentzer* (New York: McGraw Hill, 2005), 166.
30. See note 6.
31. See note 17.
32. See note 17.
33. See note 17.
34. Ellington Darden, *The Nautilus Advanced Bodybuilding Book* (New York: Fireside Books, 1984), 93.
35. See note 8. See also note 21.
36. Darden, *New High Intensity Training*, 22.
37. Darden, *Nautilus Advanced Bodybuilding*, 96.
38. Lund, "Looking Back" (online article).
39. Roach, *Volume II*, 429.
40. See note 19.
41. *Los Angeles Times*, September 1, 2007.
42. "So we designed the negative cams in the new squat machine with this limitation clearly in mind . . . the result being that the maximum force, using the entire weight of 510 pounds, is approximately 1,174 pounds as you reach the finishing position of the squat; which is approximately equal to doing the last part of a barbell squat with 1,000 pounds." Arthur Jones (official website), "From Here to Infinity . . . or very close."
43. See note 21.
44. Rebecca Gordon and Saul Bloxham, "A Systematic Review of the Effects of Exercise and Physical Activity on Non-Specific Chronic Low Back Pain," *Healthcare* 4, no. 2 (June 2016): 22.
45. USA Strength & Conditioning Coaches Hall of Fame (website), "Arthur Jones."
46. Heavy Duty College, "Mike Mentzer: Laughs in the Gym with Boyer Coe," YouTube video, May 19, 2022.
47. Heavy Duty College, "Once That Gnat Hits Your Bloodstream," YouTube video, May 26, 2023.
48. Hansen, "The Bodybuilding Legends Show #9" (YouTube video); Boyer Coe also self-published a 52-page book on steroid use in 1979 entitled *Steroids: An Adjunctive Aid to Training*.
49. MuscleMemory (online database), "Boyer Coe."
50. Parviz K. Kavoussi, "Anabolic Steroids Long Term Effect," Austin Men's Health (website), November 18, 2014.
51. Better Health Channel (website), "Anabolic Steroids," December 8, 2022. See also Jon Jarløv Rasmussen et al., "Former Abusers of Anabolic Androgenic Steroids Exhibit Decreased Testosterone Levels and Hypogonadal Symptoms Years after Cessation: A Case-Control Study," *pLoS One* 11, no. 8. (2016): e0161208.
52. As an aside, the problem that Boyer brought to the experiment proved to be a lesson that would be forgotten at Nautilus Sports/Medical Industries. Several years later, hoping to repeat the success Arthur had enjoyed when training Casey Viator in preparation

for the 1971 Mr. America contest, Ellington Darden found another young bodybuilder with exceptional genetics, Eddie Robinson. The thought was to train Eddie for the Mr. America contest using a high-intensity training program and, from this experience, craft a book on bodybuilding program he used. Like Boyer, Eddie was instructed to go off steroids. But when Ellington had Eddie's testosterone level checked prior to starting the training program, he was shocked startled to discover that it was lower than that of a prepubescent girl. The project was subsequently abandoned. Nate Green, "HIT, Spit, and Bullshit: An Interview with Ellington Darden," T Nation (website), October 2008.
53. Arthur Jones (official website), "The Next Step."
54. In Boyer Coe's "A" workout on June 17, 1983, he was using the ten-degree chest machine. In his "A" workout on July 20, 1983, the ten-degree chest machine had been replaced by the 40-degree chest machine.
55. In Boyer Coe's "B" workout of June 20, 1983, he was using 350 pounds on the calf raise exercise for 15 repetitions. In his "B" workout of July 18, 1983, he was only using 275 pounds on the same exercise for 16 repetitions. In his "A" workout from June 17, 1983, he was using 460 pounds for 18 repetitions (nine repetitions per leg) on the Duo Squat machine; but in his "A" workout on July 20, 1983, it was down to 410 pounds for 26 repetitions (13 per leg).
56. Mike Mentzer quoted from the video of Boyer Coe's 52nd workout, on May 31, 1983:

> **Mike:** "You are down two reps thought from the last [workout]. I'm just wondering . . . Have you talked to Arthur about changing the routine in a more dramatic fashion or perhaps taking a layoff?"
> **Boyer:** "I don't know. We're going to discuss it when he gets back."
> **Mike:** "You've been training, what? Almost four months now nonstop."
> **Boyer:** "Yeah. But there's so little time in the workout itself."
> **Mike:** "Yeah. Well, sometimes just for psychological reasons, a week off will give you a chance to recoup.

57. See note 22.
58. See note 22. See also: "Jones had a habit of painting pictures of the future that were grandiose and motivating. But the many small steps that were necessary to get from here to there were left to his employees. Those employees, however, often found it tough to move forward without Jones's direction. The boss was involved in so many different projects at once that you never knew when he was going to give you feedback on your assignment." Darden, *New High Intensity Training*, 72.
59. Darden, *New High Intensity Training*, 75.
60. See note 21.
61. William Edgar Jones, *Nautilus: The Lost Empire of Arthur Jones* (self-published, 2019), 17.
62. See note 22.
63. Darden, *New High Intensity Training*, 74–75.

CHAPTER TWENTY-NINE: UNMOORED

1. Jack Kroll of *Newsweek* referred to Schwarzenegger's performance as that of "a dull clod with a sharp sword, a human collage of pectorals and latissimi who's got less style and wit than Lassie." *Newsweek*, May 17, 1982.
2. Wayne, *Muscle Wars*, 3072–77.

3. Greg Zulak, a writer for Robert Kennedy, recalled his boss returning from Munich and telling him that he and Mike had been seated in the VIP section when Arnold arrived and sat down next to Kennedy. Arnold leaned over to Robert, and nodding in Mike's direction, whispered, "What is *this* asshole doing here?" It was shortly thereafter that Mike was asked to leave his seat by one of Albert Busek's staff members. Greg Zulak, email to Randy Roach, January 4, 2024, shared with the author by permission from both parties.
4. Greg Zulak quoted from his email to Randy Roach, January 6, 2024, shared with the author by permission from both parties.
5. Wayne, *Muscle Wars*, 3240.
6. Mike Mentzer, McGough interview.
7. Mike Mentzer, interview with the author, 1986.
8. Heavy Duty College, "Mike Mentzer: Radio Interview on Ayn Rand, Philosophy and Bodybuilding," YouTube video, July 23, 2023.
9. See note 8.
10. See note 8.
11. See note 8.
12. Mike Mentzer, interview with the author, 1990.
13. See note 7.
14. See note 7.
15. Mike Mentzer, "The Psychology of a Competitive Bodybuilder."
16. See note 12.
17. MuscleMemory (online database), "Julie McNew."
18. *Los Angeles Times*, September 15, 1987.
19. Dave Mastorakis, email to the author, January 1, 2024.
20. Heavy Duty College, "Ray Mentzer: High-Intensity Training the Ray Mentzer Way," YouTube video, April 4, 2022.
21. Heavy Duty College, "Champions Mike Mentzer, Ray Mentzer and Boyer Coe Talk Bodybuilding," YouTube video, October 17, 2023.
22. See note 6.
23. *Workout for Fitness*, December 1984.
24. All information and dialogue from the party are taken from Mike Mentzer, interview with the author, 1986.
25. See note 6.
26. See note 6.
27. An interview conducted with Ray in Australia during this time reveals the substance of what he was saying on this topic during his seminars: "Bodybuilding as a sport isn't a good sport. It's a very illicit sport. It's a very crude sport. The idealism of it is very good, but the actuality of it is very bad. Now, bodybuilding and training are two different things. The training part of it is growing immensely. The bodybuilding [competition] side of it is at the lowest it's ever been since 1899. . . . It's run by thieves, stealers, bilkers — people who are robbing the system. . . . They're just taking it for everything it's worth and it's going down the tubes rapidly. And I'm here to expose that and make people aware." Heavy Duty College, "Ray Mentzer: The Truth About Bodybuilding" (YouTube video).
28. See note 27: "They'll kill me. They've threatened my life already."
29. Unless otherwise indicated, all dialogue from Ray Mentzer's gym is drawn from Mike Mentzer, interview with the author, 1986.

30. Jørgen G. Bramness et al., "Amphetamine-Induced Psychosis — A Separate Diagnostic Entity or Primary Psychosis Triggered in the Vulnerable?" *BMC Psychiatry* 12, no. 221 (2012). See also Jeff M. Mullen et al., "Amphetamine-Related Psychiatric Disorders," *StatPearls* (Treasure Island, FL: StatPearls; online publication, updated June 8, 2023).

CHAPTER THIRTY: THE STORM AND THE LIGHT

1. Unless otherwise indicated, all dialogue and action from Mike's interaction with the bank manager and police in Manhattan Beach are from Mike Mentzer, interview with the author, 1986.
2. "Harry [Mike's dad] was concerned for Mike with the emotional issues. Mike feared that people were following him." Shelly Mentzer Sweigart, email to the author, July 19, 2023.
3. *New York Times*, June 15, 1985.
4. Mike Mentzer, McGough interview.
5. Will Durant, *The Mansions of Philosophy* (New York: Simon and Schuster, 1929), 235.
6. See Heavy Duty College's YouTube videos "Philosophy in a Car," April 22, 2022, and "Philosophy in a Car (Part 2)," February 11, 2023.
7. Mike Mentzer, interview with the author, 1987.
8. Dr. Leonard Peikoff, interview with the author, February 2006.
9. See note 8.

CHAPTER THIRTY-ONE: DESCENT INTO MADNESS

1. Vince Basile, Facebook message to the author, July 18, 2023.
2. Shelly Mentzer Sweigart, email to the author, July 19, 2023. See also *Intelligencer Journal*, February 4, 1987.
3. Dustin Martin and Jacqueline K. Le, "Amphetamine," *StatPearls* (Treasure Island, FL: StatPearls; online publication, updated July 31, 2023).
4. "I had read the literature on amphetamines. I had never heard of any long-term physical damage, but I did know it could possibly result in acute episodes of psychosis, without a doubt. I had studied that years ago as part of my interest in the mind and psychiatry." Mike Mentzer, McGough interview.
5. Jennika Allen, Facebook message to the author, January 15, 2024.
6. Ray Mentzer, interview with the author, 1990.
7. See note 6.
8. The title "The World's Strongest Bodybuilder" appeared in Ray Mentzer's ad for Ray Mentzer's Future Fitness: "Maximize your potential with Ray Mentzer, the 'Mastodon,' 'Mr. America,' the world's strongest bodybuilder . . ." *Workout for Fitness*, October 1985, 66.
9. See note 6.
10. See note 6.
11. See note 6.
12. See note 6.
13. See note 6.
14. Shelly Mentzer Sweigart, email to the author, July 19, 2023.
15. *New Era*, February 2, 1987.
16. Mike Mentzer, interview with the author, 1995.

17. See note 16.
18. Mike Mentzer, McGough interview.
19. See note 18.
20. Dorian Yates Nutrition, "Tom Platz: A Life of Innovation and Inspiration in Fitness," YouTube video, January 31, 2024.
21. See note 18.
22. See note 18.
23. See note 18.
24. See note 16. Mike had other arguments up his sleeve if need be. He had written: "Actually, it is very difficult — nearly impossible, in fact — to accurately assess mental states and the factors that influence them. Because we exist in a time continuum, our state of being — both physical and mental — is dynamic and never the same from moment to moment. Although we may appear clinically 'normal' in one instance, exposure to another set of circumstances might cause us to be diagnosed as psychotic or deranged." *Muscle Builder/Power*, May 1980.
25. Mike Mentzer, Hause interview.
26. See note 18.
27. The author recollects the content of this phone conversation vividly, as it was the first time I had ever spoken with somebody in the throes of psychosis.
28. See note 18.
29. *Flex*, February 1995.
30. See note 18.
31. See note 18.
32. Butler, *Arnold Schwarzenegger*, 49.

CHAPTER THIRTY-TWO: THE GHOST IN THE MACHINE

1. Mike Mentzer, McGough interview.
2. See note 1.
3. See note 1.
4. Ayn Rand, *The Voice of Reason: Essays in Objectivist Thought*, ed. Leonard Peikoff (New York: Meridian, 1989), 93.
5. Ayn Rand, *For the New Intellectual* (New York: Signet, 1961), 101.
6. See note 1.
7. Koestler, Arthur. *The Ghost in the Machine* (New York: Random House, 1982), 168.
8. Koestler, *Ghost in the Machine*, xi.
9. See note 1.

CHAPTER THIRTY-THREE: REDEMPTION

1. Mike Mentzer, McGough interview.
2. "I was quite surprised that it [his personal training business] did start out very slow. I thought that with my visibility and name recognition I'd move into that business, and it would be a spectacular success right from the outset, but it was not. The first four or five months, I only had a few clients." Heavy Duty College, "Mike Mentzer: The Interview That Blew People's Minds," (YouTube video).
3. *Argonaut*, May 2, 1991.
4. Mike Mentzer, interview with the author, 1990.

5. Twin Labs, tape 1: "The Logical Path to Successful Bodybuilding."
6. The Sandwich, "Mike Mentzer's Last Interview" (online article).
7. John Stamatopoulos, "Mike Mentzer Exclusive Interview! A Bodybuilding Legend," Bodybuilding.com (webpage discontinued).
8. Heavy Duty College, "Mike Mentzer: Radio Interview on Ayn Rand, Philosophy and Bodybuilding" (YouTube video).
9. See note 2.
10. *Flex*, October 1992.
11. Heavy Duty College, "Mike Mentzer: The Interview That Blew People's Minds" (YouTube video).
12. See note 11.
13. Heavy Duty College, "Mike Mentzer: What's Possible with High Intensity Training?" YouTube video, November 5, 2022.
14. Burton Richardson, Facebook Message to the author, October 20, 2023.
15. Mike Thurston, "Training Legs with Dorian Yates," YouTube video, September 6, 2022.
16. *Flex*, February 1995.
17. See note 11.

CHAPTER THIRTY-FOUR: AGAINST THE ODDS

1. Mike Mentzer, McGough interview.
2. See note 1.
3. Heavy Duty College, "Mike Mentzer: The Heavy Duty Training System (High-Intensity Training — Theory and Application," YouTube video, March 21, 2022.
4. The Cooper Institute (blog), "Legendary 'Father of Aerobics' Dr. Kenneth H. Cooper Turned 90," May 12, 2021.
5. Helen Thompson, "Walk, Don't Run," *Texas Monthly* (website), June 1995.
6. See note 5.
7. Kenneth Cooper, *Dr. Kenneth H. Cooper's Antioxidant Revolution* (Nashville, TN: Thomas Nelson Publishers, 1997) 3–4 and 8.
8. Cooper, *Antioxidant Revolution*, 7.
9. Cooper, *Antioxidant Revolution*, xii.
10. See note 5.
11. See note 5.
12. See note 5.
13. See note 5.
14. Heavy Duty College, "Mike Mentzer: Overtraining Can Be Life-Threatening," YouTube video, July 3, 2023.
15. Heavy Duty College, "Mike Mentzer: The Poison Flies of the Marketplace," YouTube video, August 22, 2022.
16. Mentzer and Little, *High-Intensity Training*, 52.
17. Mentzer and Little, *High-Intensity Training*, 157–62.
18. Mike Mentzer, interview with the author, 1993.
19. Mike Mentzer, interview with the author, 1986.
20. MuscleMemory (online database), "Markus Reinhardt."
21. Markus Reinhardt High Intensity Trainer, "How I Trained before Mike Mentzer's Duty Training/High Intensity Training," YouTube video, June 6, 2024.

22. Markus Reinhardt High Intensity Trainer, "How I Lived with Mike Mentzer 1," YouTube video, June 12, 2024.
23. See note 22.
24. Markus Reinhardt, interview with the author, August 8, 2023.
25. Peter McGough, "Mike Mentzer: The Untold Story of the Journey to his Final Days," *Muscular Development* (website), November 5, 2017.
26. Leonard Peikoff, *Objectivism: The Philosophy of Ayn Rand* (New York: Meridian, 1993), 31–32.
27. See note 1.
28. Markus Reinhardt High Intensity Trainer, "Was Mike Mentzer Gay?" YouTube video, July 2, 2024.
29. Twin Labs, tape 1: "The Logical Path to Successful Bodybuilding."
30. See note 28.
31. "Objectivism contends that love is actually our response to those few people we meet toward whom we feel the highest respect, admiration, and attraction. It is not a blank check granted to random passersby, but instead the result of our careful examination and approval of another's character. Granting unconditional love is like appraising a piece of property without examining its size, quality, or location: one is likely to grant unearned love to the unworthy and withhold love from those who deserve it most. Before you can really grant love to those you value, you must be in tune with your own values and character and know what it is you believe to be the right and the good, what qualities you are looking for in other people." Andrew Bissel, "Love," The Atlas Society (website). January 26, 2011.
32. Mentzer, Mike. "The Integrated Man," 2001. As a side note, Mike believed in the Objectivist value of romantic love deeply. In fact, internet dating was still in its infancy in the early 2000s, so Mike had asked me to send an image of him to an online dating service (he wasn't tech savvy) that Mike had signed up for to hopefully connect with a woman who shared his values. Sadly, this was only two weeks prior to his passing, so I'm unaware if he had made a connection or not.

EPILOGUE

1. Shelly Andrens, interview with the author, August 4, 2023.
2. Dan Rafael, "No 'Guts,' No Glory for Tyson in Defeat," *ESPN* (website), June 11, 2005.
3. *Muscle Training Illustrated*, March 1972.
4. Nobel Prize (official website), "John F. Nash Jr. Biographical."
5. County of Los Angeles, Department of Coroner Investigator's Narrative, Case Number: 2001-04287.
6. Heavy Duty College, "The Mike Mentzer Story" (YouTube video).
7. Dave Mastorakis, interview with the author, 2023.
8. See note 5. See also The Sandwich, "Mike Mentzer's Last Interview" (online article).
9. County of Los Angeles, Department of Coroner Investigator's Narrative, Case Number: 2001-04262.
10. See note 8, Sandwich.
11. See note 10.
12. See note 10.

Notes

13. See note 5.
14. See note 5.
15. Mike Mentzer, email to the author, November 20, 2000.
16. Mike Mentzer (archived official website), "The Best Within Us," May 29, 2001.
17. See note 10.
18. Heavy Duty College, "Mike Mentzer: Radio Interview on Ayn Rand, Philosophy and Bodybuilding" (YouTube video).
19. See note 5.
20. This information was communicated by Mike Mentzer's secretary/business manager, Joanne Sharkey, in her email to the author on the day of Ray Mentzer's death.
21. See notes 5 and 9.
22. The Canadian Press, "Ben Weider among New Inductees to Order of Canada," CBC (website), February 20, 2007.
23. The Governor General of Canada (website), "Mr. Ben Weider."
24. Bernard Bujold, "Ben Weider," LeStudio1 (webpage discontinued).
25. Mike Rowbottom, "President Rafael Santonja — Building a Body of Opinion to take IFBB towards the Olympics," Inside the Games (website), March 18, 2018.
26. Joe Weider (official website), "Awards."
27. Adam Tanner, "Legendary Promoter Says Steroids Widespread in Sports," Reuters, August 9, 2007.
28. Natural Products Insider (website), "Weider Sells Active Nutrition Brands," May 23, 2005.
29. Bardach, "Hush-Hush Deal" (online article).
30. See note 22.
31. Desmond Butler and John Sullivan, "Rigged: The Undoing of America's Premier Bodybuilding Leagues," *Washington Post* (website), December 16, 2022.
32. Jonathan Salmon, "Breaking: Mr. Olympia Has Been Sold by American Media Inc," Generation Iron (website), February 14, 2020.
33. Philip Ellis, "Arnold Schwarzenegger Says It 'Sucks' Not Having His Mr. Olympia Body," *Men's Health* (website), October 20, 2023.
34. Christian Toto, "How Arnold Schwarzenegger Became Box Office Poison," Hollywood in Toto (website), November 5, 2019.
35. See note 18.
36. Heavy Duty College, "Mike Mentzer: 'My Philosophy!'" YouTube video, December 23, 2023.

BIBLIOGRAPHY

INTERVIEWS
Andrens, Shelly, with the author, 2023.
Basile, Vince, with the author, 2023.
Eagan, Sherman, with the author, 1994 and 2024.
Ferrigno, Lou, with the author, 1986.
Grimek, John, with the author, 1992.
Mastorakis, Dave, with the author, 2023.
Mentzer, Mike, with Irene Hause, 1981.
Mentzer, Mike, with Garry Bartlett, 1983.
Mentzer, Mike, with Peter McGough, 1993.
Mentzer, Mike, with the author, 1986.
Mentzer, Mike, with the author, 1987.
Mentzer, Mike, with the author, 1990.
Mentzer, Mike, with the author, 1993.
Mentzer, Mike, with the author, 1995.
Mentzer, Ray, Australia, 1985.
Mentzer, Ray, with the author, 1990.
Neary, Jack, with the author, 2023.
Reinhardt, Markus, with the author, 2023.
Schwab, Roger, with the author, 2023.
Peikoff, Leonard, with the author, 2006.
Scott, Larry, with the author, 1992.
Zane, Frank, with the author, 1986.

LETTERS
Mentzer, Mike, to Dave Mastorakis, March 1974.
Mentzer, Mike, to Dave Mastorakis, April 12, 1974.
Mentzer, Mike, to Dave Mastorakis, June 1974.

Bibliography

EMAILS

Balik, John, to the author, December 3, 2023.
DeMilia, Wayne, to Randy Roach, December 11, 2023.
Mastorakis, Dave, to the author, July 9, 2023.
Mastorakis, Dave, to the author, July 24, 2023.
Mastorakis, Dave, to the author, August 16, 2023.
Mastorakis, Dave, to the author, January 1, 2024.
McCarthy, Peter, to the author and Randy Roach, May 17, 2024.
McCarthy, Peter, to the author and Randy Roach, May 24, 2024.
Mentzer, Sid (via his daughter Shelly Mentzer Sweigart), to the author, interview, July 19, 2023.
Mentzer, Mike, to the author, November 20, 2000.
Poljak, Tamala, to the author, August 15, 2021.
Roach, Randy, to the author September 25, 2023.
Schwab, Roger, to the author, August 17, 2023.
Sprague, Ken, to the author, September 21, 2023.
Sprague, Ken, to the author, September 30, 2023.
Sprague, Ken, to the author, December 13, 2023
Zulak, Greg, to Randy Roach, January 4, 2024.
Zulak, Greg, to Randy Roach, January 6, 2024.

SEMINARS/CONSULTS

Mentzer, Mike, seminar at Simpson's department store, 1980.
Mentzer, Mike, seminar in Rexdale, Ontario, November 15, 1981.
Mentzer, Mike, phone consultation, 1994.

FACEBOOK MESSAGES

Allen, Jennika, to the author, January 15, 2024.
Basile, Vince, to the author, July 18, 2023.
Basile, Vince, to the author, December 10, 2023.
Brainum, Jerry, to the author, July 3, 2023.
Levenson, Michael, to the author, August 20, 2023.
Levenson, Michael, to the author, August 31, 2023.
Neary, Jack, to the author, November 13, 2023.
Parr, John, to the author, December 30, 2023.
Richardson, Burton, to the author, October 20, 2023.

FACEBOOK POSTS

Busek, Albert. Comment on Bill Pearl's photo of Kalman Szkalak, August 4, 2019. https://www.facebook.com/116733248412758/photos/a.758901990862544/1482088755210527.

FORUM POSTS

Basile, Vince. "Topic: Robby Robinson is a national treasure (maybe not)," reply #93, January 4, 2023. https://www.getbig.com/boards/index.php?topic=682468.75.

INSTAGRAM POSTS

Yates, Dorian. "Biceps with Mike Mentzer in my 1992 off season," May 7, 2023. https://www.instagram.com/thedorianyates/p/Cr79aKksHys/.

MAGAZINES

Advocate, June 12, 1980.
Flex, May 1988.
Flex, October 1990.
Flex, October 1992.
Flex, March 1994.
Flex, November 1994.
Flex, February 1995.
Flex, May 2005.
Health and Strength, July 19, 1956.
Iron Man, July 1967.
Iron Man, September 1970.
Iron Man, February 1971.
Iron Man, September 1971.
Iron Man, September 1973.
Iron Man, December 2000.
Looking Good, September 1977.
Mr. America, December 1959.
Mr. America, September 1961.
Mr. America, February 1962.
Mr. America, October 1962.
Mr. America, March 1964.
Mr. America, November 1964.
Mr. America, January 1965.
Mr. America, April 1965.
Mr. America, August 1965.
Muscle Builder/Power, November 1960.
Muscle Builder/Power, December 1962.
Muscle Builder/Power, June 1963.
Muscle Builder/Power, June 1964.
Muscle Builder/Power, December 1964.
Muscle Builder/Power, March 1965.
Muscle Builder/Power, January 1966.
Muscle Builder/Power, March 1968.
Muscle Builder/Power, September 1969.
Muscle Builder/Power, February 1972.
Muscle Builder/Power, April 1972.
Muscle Builder/Power, October 1973.
Muscle Builder/Power, January 1974.
Muscle Builder/Power, July 1974.
Muscle Builder/Power, October 1974.
Muscle Builder/Power, January 1975.

Muscle Builder/Power, March 1975.
Muscle Builder/Power, May 1975.
Muscle Builder/Power, November 1975.
Muscle Builder/Power, January 1976.
Muscle Builder/Power, February 1976.
Muscle Builder/Power, April 1976.
Muscle Builder/Power, July 1976.
Muscle Builder/Power, August 1976.
Muscle Builder/Power, September 1976.
Muscle Builder/Power, October 1976.
Muscle Builder/Power, November 1976.
Muscle Builder/Power, December 1976.
Muscle Builder/Power, January 1977.
Muscle Builder/Power, October 1977.
Muscle Builder/Power, December 1977.
Muscle Builder/Power, January 1978.
Muscle Builder/Power, March 1978.
Muscle Builder/Power, May 1978.
Muscle Builder/Power, October 1978.
Muscle Builder/Power, December 1978.
Muscle Builder/Power, January/February 1979.
Muscle Builder/Power, March 1979.
Muscle Builder/Power, April 1979.
Muscle Builder/Power, May 1979.
Muscle Builder/Power, June 1979.
Muscle Builder/Power, July 1979.
Muscle Builder/Power, August 1979.
Muscle Builder/Power, August/September 1979.
Muscle Builder/Power, October 1979.
Muscle Builder/Power, November 1979.
Muscle Builder/Power, January 1980.
Muscle Builder/Power, February 1980.
Muscle Builder/Power, May 1980.
Muscular Development, October 1964.
Muscular Development, September 1971.
Muscular Development, December 1979.
Muscle Digest, May/June 1978.
Muscle Digest, December 1980.
Muscle Digest, April 1981.
Muscle & Fitness, March 1980.
Muscle & Fitness, July 1980.
Muscle & Fitness, September 1980.
Muscle & Fitness, February 1981.
Muscle & Fitness, April 1981.
Muscle & Fitness, June 1981.
Muscle & Fitness, August 1981.

Muscle & Fitness, October 1981.
Muscle & Fitness, November 1981.
Muscle & Fitness, January 1982.
Muscle & Fitness, May 1982.
Muscle & Fitness, August 1982.
Muscle & Fitness, October 1982.
Muscle & Fitness, May 1983.
Muscle & Fitness, October 1987.
Muscle & Fitness, November 1987.
Muscle & Fitness, February 1990.
Muscle & Fitness, July 1999.
MuscleMag International Annual 3, 1978–79.
MuscleMag International, March 1980.
MuscleMag International, May 1980.
MuscleMag International, August/September 1980.
MuscleMag International, September 1981.
MuscleMag International Annual, 1981.
MuscleMag International, March 1982.
MuscleMag International, February 1984.
MuscleMag International, May 1985.
Muscle Power, November 1947.
Muscle Training Illustrated, March 1972.
Muscle Training Illustrated, July 1979.
Muscle Training Illustrated, January 1980.
Newsweek, May 17, 1982.
Playboy, March 1983.
Rolling Stone, June 3, 1976.
Soldiers: The Official U.S. Army Magazine, July 1982.
Sports Illustrated, April 9, 1962.
Sports Illustrated, April 6, 1970.
Sports Illustrated, October 1974.
Sports Illustrated, April 1975.
Strength and Health, September 1948.
Strength and Health, December 1965.
Strength and Health, March 1962.
Texas Monthly, June 1995.
Time, June 10, 1985.
Workout for Fitness, December 1984.
Workout for Fitness, October 1985.
Your Physique, December 1951.

COURT DOCUMENTS

Joe Weider's sworn statement, *Joe Gold's Gym, Inc. v. Arnold Schwarzenegger* lawsuit, Los Angeles, 1978.

U.S. Olympic Committee v. International Federation of Body Builders and Weider Health &

Bibliography

Fitness, Inc, May 14, 1984. U.S. Court of Appeals for the District of Columbia Circuit, 735 F.2d 618. https://law.justia.com/cases/federal/appellate-courts/F2/735/618/212344/.

U.S. Postal Service v. Joseph Weider, October 29, 1975. https://about.usps.com/who-we-are/judicial/admin-decisions/1975/2-81.htm.

CORONER'S REPORT

County of Los Angeles, Department of Coroner Investigator's Narrative, Case Number: 2001-04287.

NEWSPAPERS

Argonaut (Los Angeles), May 2, 1991.
Atlanta Journal and Constitution, February 13, 1972.
Charlotte Observer, January 25, 1976.
Daytona Beach Morning Journal, March 25, 1978.
Democrat and Chronicle (Rochester, NY), April 15, 1984.
Democrat and Chronicle, February 1, 1978.
Ephrata Review, May 21, 1964.
Ephrata Review, July 2, 1964.
Ephrata Review, October 1, 1964.
Ephrata Review, October 29, 1964.
Ephrata Review, June 29, 1967.
Ephrata Review, November 21, 1968.
Ephrata Review, December 1, 1969.
Ephrata Review, September 7, 1970.
Ephrata Review, December 31, 1970.
Ephrata Review, July 29, 1971.
Ephrata Review, December 30, 1971.
Ephrata Review, February 17, 1972.
Ephrata Review, January 1, 1976.
Ephrata Review, October 7, 1976.
Ephrata Review, November 11, 1976.
Ephrata Review, December 30, 1976.
Ephrata Review, December 28, 1978.
Ephrata Review, June 20, 2001.
Ephrata Review, November 7, 2007.
Ephrata Review, March 2, 2011.
Ephrata Review, October 12, 2016.
Fort Lauderdale News, May 30, 1980.
Globe and Mail, April 28, 1980.
Honolulu Advertiser, January 30, 1969.
Honolulu Star Advertiser, February 19, 2012.
Honolulu Star-Bulletin, January 30, 1969.
Honolulu Star-Bulletin & Advertiser, February 2, 1969.
Honolulu Star-Bulletin, February 10, 1969.
Honolulu Star-Bulletin, April 15, 1979.

Intelligencer Journal (Lancaster, PA), September 20, 1956.
Intelligencer Journal, August 3, 1962.
Intelligencer Journal, August 28, 1969.
Intelligencer Journal, September 20, 1969.
Intelligencer Journal, January 14, 1971.
Intelligencer Journal, July 20, 1971.
Intelligencer Journal, November 12, 1971.
Intelligencer Journal, April 25, 1972.
Intelligencer Journal, April 29, 1972.
Intelligencer Journal, October 6, 1976.
Intelligencer Journal, November 8, 1978.
Intelligencer Journal, February 4, 1987.
Lafayette Advertiser, July 17, 1980.
Los Angeles Times, September 15, 1987.
Los Angeles Times, March 2, 1989.
Los Angeles Times, May 3, 1992.
Los Angeles Times, August 14, 2003.
Los Angeles Times, September 1, 2007.
Miami Herald, August 14, 1981.
Miami News, February 2, 1979.
Minneapolis Star, September 10, 1949.
Montreal Gazette, November 4, 1976.
Montreal Gazette, November 6, 1976.
Montreal Gazette, September 23, 2008.
New Era (Lancaster, PA), September 19, 1956.
New Era, February 19, 1970.
New Era, June 4, 1971.
New Era, July 21, 1971.
New Era, April 28, 1972.
New Era, October 5, 1976.
New Era, November 10, 1978.
New Era, May 29, 1979.
New Era, February 2, 1987.
New Era, June 13, 2010.
New York Daily News, January 17, 1980.
New York Daily News, January 19, 1977.
New York Times, Nov. 28, 1981.
New York Times, July 25, 1982.
New York Times, June 15, 1985.
New York Times, October 3, 2003.
New York Times, August 30, 2007.
New York Times, September 5, 2019.
Oakland Tribune, April 3, 1979
Oakland Tribune, July 14, 1980.
Ottawa Citizen, March 25, 1972.

Philadelphia Inquirer, June 18, 1940.
Pittsburgh Post-Gazette, April 3, 1979.
Pottsville Republican, May 3, 1980.
San Francisco Examiner, December 4, 1968.
Sun-Democrat (Paducah, KY), March 21, 1977.
Sun Magazine (Baltimore, MD), June 19, 1977.
Sunday Courier & Press (Evansville, IN), February 20, 1972.
Sunday News (Lancaster County, PA), September 7, 1969.
Sunday News, January 24, 1971.
Tucson Daily Citizen, February 7, 1976.
Wichita Falls Times, November 5, 1976.

YEARBOOKS
Ephrata High School, 1968.
Ephrata High School, 1969.

BOOKS
Aeschylus. *Agamemnon*. Translated by Herbert Weir Smyth. London: Loeb Classical Library, 1963.
Andrews, Nigel. *True Myths: The Life and Times of Arnold Schwarzenegger*. Secaucus, NJ: Birch Lane Press, 1996.
Åstrand, Per-Olof, and Kåre Rodahl. *Textbook of Work Physiology: Physiological Bases of Exercise*. New York: McGraw Hill, 1977.
Baker, Barbara Outland. *Arnold and Me: In the Shadow of the Austrian Oak*. Bloomington, IN: AuthorHouse, 2006.
Bowden, Mark. *Killing Pablo: The Hunt for the World's Greatest Outlaw*. New York: Atlantic Monthly Press, 2001.
Butler, George. *Arnold Schwarzenegger: A Portrait*. New York: Simon and Schuster, 1990.
Chamberlain, Lesley. *Nietzsche in Turin*. New York: Picador, 1996.
Cooper, Kenneth. *Aerobics*. New York: Bantam Books, 1968.
Cooper, Kenneth. *Dr. Kenneth H. Cooper's Antioxidant Revolution*. Nashville, TN: Thomas Nelson Publishers, 1997.
Darden, Ellington. *The Nautilus Advanced Bodybuilding Book*. New York: Fireside Books, 1984.
Darden, Ellington. *The New High-Intensity Training*. Emmaus, PA: Rodale Inc., 2004.
Deutsch, Ronald M. *Realities of Nutrition*. Palo Alto, CA: Bull, 1975.
DeVore, Paul A., and Mike Mentzer. *Mr. America's Total Physical Fitness Weight Control Program*. Washington, DC: DMS Associates, 1977.
Diogenes Laërtius. *Lives and Opinions of Eminent Philosophers*. Edited by James Miller. Translated by Pamela Mensch. Oxford, UK: Oxford University Press, 2018.
Durant, Will. *The Mansions of Philosophy*. New York: Simon and Schuster, 1929.
Edington, D.W., and V.R. Edgerton. *The Biology of Physical Activity*. Boston: Houghton Mifflin, 1976.
Fair, John D. *Mr. America: The Tragic History of a Bodybuilding Icon*. Austin: University of Texas Press, 2015.
Gelfo, Cathy, and Mike Mentzer. *Heavy Duty for Women*. Los Angeles, CA: self-published, 1979.

Haider, Gulzar. "Making a Space for Everyday Ritual and Practice." *Making Muslim Space in North America and Europe*. Edited by Barbara Daly Metcalf. Berkeley: University of California, 1996. http://ark.cdlib.org/ark:/13030/ft2s2004p0/.

Homer. *The Odyssey*. Translated by Robert Fagles. New York: Penguin, 1996.

Iversen, Leslie L. *Speed, Ecstasy, Ritalin: The Science of Amphetamines*. Oxford, UK: Oxford University Press, 2008.

James, William. *The Energies of Men*. New York: Moffat, Yard, 1914.

Jones, William Edgar. *Nautilus: The Lost Empire of Arthur Jones*. Self-published, 2019.

Koestler, Arthur. *The Ghost in the Machine*. New York: Random House, 1982.

Leamer, Laurence. *Fantastic: The Life of Arnold Schwarzenegger*. New York: St. Martin's Press, 2005.

Leigh, Wendy. *Arnold: An Unauthorized Biography*. Chicago: Congdon & Weed, 1990.

Little, John, and Joanne Sharkey. *The Wisdom of Mike Mentzer*. New York: McGraw Hill, 2005.

Little, John. *The Mike Mentzer Question and Answer Book*. Bracebridge, ON: Northern River Publishing, 2023.

Lurie, Dan, and David Robson. *Heart of Steel: The Dan Lurie Story*. Bloomington, IN: AuthorHouse, 2009.

Maltz, Maxwell. *Psycho-Cybernetics*. New York: Pocket Books, 1960.

Martin, Dustin, and Jacqueline K. Le. "Amphetamine." *StatPearls*. Treasure Island, FL: StatPearls Publishing. Updated July 31, 2023. https://www.ncbi.nlm.nih.gov/books/NBK556103/.

McLuhan, Marshall. *Counterblast*. Toronto: McClelland & Stewart, 1969.

McGuff, Doug, and John Little. *Body by Science*. New York: McGraw Hill, 2009.

Mentzer, Mike, and Ardy Friedberg. *The Mentzer Method to Fitness*. New York: William Morrow, 1980.

Mentzer, Mike, and Ardy Friedberg. *Mike Mentzer's Complete Book of Weight Training*. New York: Quill Books, 1983.

Mentzer, Mike, and John Little. *High-Intensity Training the Mike Mentzer Way*. New York: McGraw Hill, 2003.

Mentzer, Mike. *Heavy Duty Journal*. Los Angeles, CA: self-published, 1980.

Mentzer, Mike. *Heavy Duty Nutrition*. Los Angeles, CA: self-published course, 1979.

Mentzer, Mike. *Heavy Duty II: Mind and Body*. Los Angeles, CA: self-published, 1996.

Nietzsche, Friedrich. *Selected Letters of Friedrich Nietzsche*. Edited and translated by Christopher Middleton. Indianapolis / Cambridge, UK: Hackett, 1996.

Mishima, Yukio. *Sun and Steel*. Tokyo: Kodansha International, 1970.

Mullen, Jeff M., et al. "Amphetamine-Related Psychiatric Disorders." *StatPearls*. Treasure Island, FL: StatPearls Publishing. Updated June 8, 2023. https://www.ncbi.nlm.nih.gov/books/NBK482368/.

Pearl, Bill. *Getting Stronger*. Bolinas, CA: Shelter Publications Inc., 1986.

Peikoff, Leonard. *Objectivism: The Philosophy of Ayn Rand*. New York: Meridian, 1993.

Rand, Ayn. *For the New Intellectual*. New York: Signet, 1961.

Rand, Ayn. *The Voice of Reason: Essays in Objectivist Thought*. Edited by Leonard Peikoff. New York: Meridian, 1989.

Reeves, Steve, John Little, and Bob Wolff. *Building the Classic Physique the Natural Way*. Calabasas, CA: Little-Wolff Creative Group, 1995.

Roach, Randy. *Muscle, Smoke & Mirrors Volume I*. Bloomington, IN: AuthorHouse, 2008.

Bibliography

Roach, Randy. *Muscle, Smoke & Mirrors Volume II*. Bloomington, IN: AuthorHouse, 2011.
Roach, Randy. *Muscle, Smoke & Mirrors Volume III, Book I*. Toronto: Primal Synergy, 2015.
Robinson, Robby. *The Black Prince: My Life in Bodybuilding: Muscle vs. Hustle*. Los Angeles, CA: self-published, 2011.
Schwarzenegger, Arnold, and Bill Dobbins. *Encyclopedia of Modern Bodybuilding*. New York: Simon & Schuster, 1985.
Schwarzenegger, Arnold, and Douglas Kent Hall. *Arnold: The Education of a Bodybuilder*. New York: Fireside Books, 1977.
Schwarzenegger, Arnold, with Peter Petre. *Total Recall: My Unbelievably True Life Story*. New York: Simon and Schuster, 2012.
Scott, Larry. *Loaded Guns*. North Salt Lake, UT: Larry Scott & Associates, 1991.
Sharaf, Myron. *Fury on Earth: A Biography of Wilhelm Reich*. Boston: Da Capo Press, 1994.
Snyder, George, and Rick Wayne. *Three More Reps*. Pennsylvania: Olympus Health & Recreation, 1978.
Southgate, L. *Chinese Medicine and Wilhelm Reich: An Analysis of Chinese Medical and Reichian Theories of Life Force, and Experimental Orgone-Acupuncture Study*. London: Lambert, 2009.
Steinhaus, Arthur H. *Toward an Understanding of Health and Physical Education*. Dubuque, IA: Wm. C. Brown, 1963.
Szimanski, John. *Younger Women, Faster Airplanes, Bigger Crocodiles*. Mauldin, SC: PDA Press, self-published, 2003.
Wayne, Rick. *Muscle Wars*. New Jersey: BookBaby, 2013. Kindle.
Weider, Ben, and Joe Weider. *Brothers of Iron*. Champaign, IL: Sports Publishing, 2006.
Weider, Joe, and Bill Reynolds. *Joe Weider's Ultimate Body Building: The Master Blaster's Principles of Training and Nutrition*. Chicago: Contemporary Books, 1989.
Weider, Joe. *The Best of Joe Weider's Muscle & Fitness: More Training Tips and Routines*. Chicago: Contemporary Books, 1982.
Weider, Joe. *The IFBB Album of Bodybuilding All-Stars*. New York: Elsevier-Dutton, 1979.
Weider, Joe. *The World's Leading Bodybuilders Answer Your Questions*. Chicago: Contemporary Books, 1981.
Weigley, R.F., et al., eds. *Philadelphia: A 300-Year History*. New York and London: W.W. Norton, 1982.
Xenophon. *Memorabilia*. Translated by Amy L. Bonnette. Ithaca, NY: Cornell University Press, 1994.
Zane, Frank. *Symmetry*. La Mesa, CA: Zananda, 2012.

UNPUBLISHED WORKS
Mentzer, Mike. "The Integrated Man," 2001. Property of the author.

JOURNAL ARTICLES
Bhasin Shalender, et al. "The Effects of Supraphysiologic Doses of Testosterone on Muscle Size and Strength in Normal Men." *New England Journal of Medicine* 335, no. 1 (July 4, 1996). https://www.nejm.org/doi/full/10.1056/NEJM199607043350101.
Beiner, J.M., et al. "The Effect of Anabolic Steroids and Corticosteroids on Healing of Muscle Contusion Injury." *American Journal of Sports Medicine* 27, no. 1 (1999). https://pubmed.ncbi.nlm.nih.gov/9934411/.

Bramness, Jørgen G., et al. "Amphetamine-Induced Psychosis — A Separate Diagnostic Entity or Primary Psychosis Triggered in the Vulnerable?" *BMC Psychiatry* 12, no. 221 (2012). https://doi.org/10.1186/1471-244X-12-221.

Defalque, Ray J., and Amos J. Wright, M.L.S., "Methamphetamine for Hitler's Germany: 1937–1945." *Bulletin of Anesthesia History* 29, no. 2 (April 2011).

Edwards, Scott. "Love and the Brain." *On the Brain* (Spring 2015). https://hms.harvard.edu/news-events/publications-archive/brain/love-brain.

Fair, John. "The Intangible Arnold: The Controversial Mr. Olympia Contest of 1980." *Iron Game History* 11, no. 1 (September 2009). https://starkcenter.org/igh/igh-vII/igh-vII-n1/igh1101p04.pdf.

Fair, John. "Isometrics or Steroids? Exploring New Frontiers of Strength in the Early 1960s." *Journal of Sport History* 20, no. 1 (Spring 1993). https://web.archive.org/web/20090227084608/http://www.la84foundation.org/SportsLibrary/JSH/JSH1993/JSH2001/jsh2001b.pdf.

Gordon, Rebecca, and Saul Bloxham. "A Systematic Review of the Effects of Exercise and Physical Activity on Non-Specific Chronic Low Back Pain." *Healthcare* 4, no. 2 (June 2016).

Quattrocelli, Mattia, et al. "Intermittent Glucocorticoid Steroid Dosing Enhances Muscle Repair without Eliciting Muscle Atrophy." *Journal of Clinical Investigation* 127, no. 6 (June 1, 2017). https://www.ncbi.nlm.nih.gov/pmc/articles/PMC5451235/.

Rasmussen, Jon Jarløv, et al. "Former Abusers of Anabolic Androgenic Steroids Exhibit Decreased Testosterone Levels and Hypogonadal Symptoms Years after Cessation: A Case-Control Study." *pLoS One* 11, no. 8. (2016). https://www.ncbi.nlm.nih.gov/pmc/articles/PMC4988681/.

Rasmussen, Nicolas. "Medical Science and the Military: The Allies' Use of Amphetamine During World War II." *Journal of Interdisciplinary History* 42, no. 2 (2011).

Schwarzenegger, Arnold. "Arnold Schwarzenegger Remembers Reg Park." Governor's press release, November 22, 2007. *Iron Game History* 10, no. 2 (April/May 2008). https://starkcenter.org/igh/igh-v10/igh-v10-n2/igh1002p05.pdf.

Senf, B. "Wilhelm Reich: Discoverer of Acupuncture Energy?" *American Journal of Acupuncture* 2, no. 7 (April–June 1979).

Todd, Terry. "The Myth of the Muscle-Bound Lifter." *National Strength and Conditioning Association Journal* 7, no. 3 (June 1985).

Wade, Nicholas. "Anabolic Steroids: Doctors Denounce Them, but Athletes Aren't Listening." *Science* 176, no. 4042 (June 30, 1972).

AUDIO

Roach, Randy, and Tamas Acs. "Arnold's Reasons for His 1980 Comeback." *The World of Muscle*. Podcast, episode 29. https://www.theworldofmuscle.com/029-arnold-speaks-1980-comeback/.

Twin Labs. Audiocassette series, 1996, tape 1: "The Logical Path to Successful Bodybuilding."

Twin Labs. Audiocassette series, 1996, tape 2: "Fundamentals of Muscular Development."

Twin Labs. Audiocassette series, 1996, tape 4: "Mike Mentzer: The Man and the Controversy."

Bibliography

VIDEOS

AEG Fitness. "Switching Metabolism Benefits: Tom Platz & Mike Mentzer." August 23, 2023. https://www.youtube.com/watch?v=kXhpSpTuH0s.

Butler, George, and Robert Fiore, dir. *Pumping Iron*. Holderness, NH: White Mountain Films, 1977.

Chilcott, Lesley, dir. *Arnold*. Season 1, episode 1, "Part 1: Athlete." Aired June 7, 2023, on Netflix. https://tvshowtranscripts.ourboard.org/viewtopic.php?f=1885&t=63519.

CNN. "Schwarzenegger says his dad was 'sucked into a hate system.'" April 27, 2023. https://www.youtube.com/shorts/xfLvq-LBdA0.

Cyber Chaos Crew. "Conan Unchained — The Making of Conan the Barbarian [HD]." May 4, 2020. https://www.youtube.com/watch?v=jiQ9rUgQcXI.

Dorian Yates Nutrition. "Tom Platz: A Life of Innovation and Inspiration in Fitness." January 31, 2024. https://www.youtube.com/watch?v=evQVaHimZz0.

Iron Man magazine. "Arnold Schwarzenegger and Franco Columbu remember Mits Kawashima." July 5, 2012. https://www.youtube.com/watch?v=Ktst44lK2zE.

El blog de kalidor. "Arnold Schwarzenegger interview from the North Delta Fitness Centre 1981." March 2, 2021. https://www.youtube.com/watch?v=GayIRfDMbow&t=57s.

Farrison, Kim "Kong." "Mits Kawashima Interview (Part 1 of 6)." February 11, 2009. https://www.youtube.com/watch?v=YdNSKgCuJuo.

Figueroa, Daniel. "Vince Gironda Talks About Arnold Training at His Gym." July 6, 2019. https://www.youtube.com/watch?v=3yehXODBmI4.

Generation Iron. "Robby Robinson Tells All on Experiencing Racism in Pro Bodybuilding." July 2, 2020. https://www.youtube.com/watch?v=r0VK-JKqJDE.

Golden Era Bookworm. "Arnold's Trainer Reveals Arnold's First Cycle & Training Program! Kurt Marnul Interview 2." September 19, 2021. https://www.youtube.com/watch?v=A098zfffVQA.

Golden Era Bookworm. "Evidence of Testosterone in the Silver Era." March 18, 2023. https://www.youtube.com/watch?v=7QGH_HggjqQ.

Golden Era Bookworm. "The Gold's Gym Steroid Scene — Interview with Ken Sprague." July 8, 2023. https://www.youtube.com/watch?v=XxHzf8_Gtxc.

Golden Era Bookworm. "The Gold's Gym Steroid Doctors with Jerry Brainum!" September 14, 2022. https://www.youtube.com/watch?v=GMrl-pC4e5c.

Golden Era Bookworm. "Steroids, Paco Arce & Super Responders in the Golden Era with Jerry Brainum." January 22, 2022. https://www.youtube.com/watch?v=Dant_PM8S5k.

Hansen, John. "Bodybuilding Legends Podcast #132 — Frank Zane." February 12, 2020. https://www.youtube.com/watch?v=zEhFppuzVFk.

Hansen, John. "Bodybuilding Legends Podcast #154 — 1980 Mr. Olympia Interviews." July 11, 2020. https://www.youtube.com/watch?v=OnqlFUq_QWI.

Hansen, John. "Bodybuilding Legends Podcast #186 — Jack Neary, Part Two." March 6, 2021. https://www.youtube.com/watch?v=ivrobP-PJZw.

Hansen, John. "Bodybuilding Legends Podcast #194 — Danny Padilla, Part Two." May 11, 2021. https://www.youtube.com/watch?v=-EjpEwGRSn8.

Hansen, John. "Bodybuilding Legends Podcast #2 — Season 1, Episode 2 Roger Callard." December 13, 2017. https://www.youtube.com/watch?v=OIBGxZmcn8o.

Hansen, John. "Bodybuilding Legends Podcast #250 — Rick Wayne, Part Two." November 6, 2022. https://www.youtube.com/watch?v=F2aFFdmNQOw.

Hansen, John. "Bodybuilding Legends Podcast #251 — Rick Wayne, Part Three." December 29, 2022. https://www.youtube.com/watch?v=ollboF29OnE.

Hansen, John. "The Bodybuilding Legends Show #19 — Roger Walker." November 10, 2016. https://www.youtube.com/watch?v=rgcy_egaDsc.

Hansen, John. "The Bodybuilding Legends Show #9 — Boyer Coe Interview, Part Two." March 30, 2015. https://www.youtube.com/watch?v=1PcJoX2G9PA.

Hansen, John. "Sergio Oliva Should Have Won the 72 Olympia." January 18, 2019. https://www.youtube.com/watch?v=uLBe3TdOEPg.

Heavy Duty College. "Aftermath: The 1980 & 1981 Mr. Olympia Disasters." February 26, 2024. https://www.youtube.com/watch?v=PPBhg-7qQxs.

Heavy Duty College. "Champions Mike Mentzer, Ray Mentzer and Boyer Coe Talk Bodybuilding Exercise." October 17, 2023. https://www.youtube.com/watch?v=IytizKffQFs.

Heavy Duty College. "John Grimek (Mr. America): 'I Made My Best Gains Ever on a One Set Per Exercise Program.'" July 29, 2023. https://www.youtube.com/watch?v=G5RqbQooE-8.

Heavy Duty College. "The Mike Mentzer Story." May 3, 2023. https://www.youtube.com/watch?v=Qq4_1U1XrkA.

Heavy Duty College. "Mike Mentzer: Bodybuilding Training (1990). August 14, 2023. https://youtube.com/watch?v=Fqeohe4cSdw.

Heavy Duty College. "Mike Mentzer: The Complete Interview (1991)." November 21, 2022. https://www.youtube.com/watch?v=zNjhzdvAEUI.

Heavy Duty College. "Mike Mentzer: Genetics (Determining Your Potential for Building Muscle)." February 21, 2023. https://youtube.com/watch?v=71aEEnHVims.

Heavy Duty College. "Mike Mentzer: The Heavy Duty Training System (High-Intensity Training — Theory and Application)." March 21, 2022. https://www.youtube.com/watch?v=Bpuo59KoycM.

Heavy Duty College. "Mike Mentzer: How to Gain 10 Pounds of Muscle." August 7, 2023. https://www.youtube.com/watch?v=rHd8sp81lwU.

Heavy Duty College. "Mike Mentzer: In-Depth Phone Interview (by John Little, February 1990)." December 19, 2021. https://youtube.com/watch?v=XVAElcOMp8A.

Heavy Duty College. "Mike Mentzer: Infitonic & Omni-Contraction Training." August 28, 2023. https://youtube.com/watch?v=Nger4XdvGUk.

Heavy Duty College. "Mike Mentzer: The Interview That Blew People's Minds." January 30, 2023. https://www.youtube.com/watch?v=4jQ_XtZil6E.

Heavy Duty College. "Mike Mentzer: Mr. North America 1977." October 9, 2021. https://www.youtube.com/watch?v=2VpN8v8fKzU.

Heavy Duty College. "Mike Mentzer: 'My Philosophy!'" December 23, 2023. https://www.youtube.com/watch?v=VU4PiyPSu9k.

Heavy Duty College. "Mike Mentzer: 'Nothing Human Is Foreign to Me.'" October 11, 2021. https://youtube.com/watch?v=pyC8_NE_oLQ.

Heavy Duty College. "Mike Mentzer: Nutrition for Bodybuilding." May 8, 2023. https://www.youtube.com/watch?v=wVsMz-yVVTs.

Heavy Duty College. "Mike Mentzer: 'Overtraining Can Be Life-Threatening.'" July 3, 2023. https://www.youtube.com/watch?v=qmAbtCxcDuo.

Heavy Duty College. "Mike Mentzer: Philosophy in a Car (Part 2)." February 11, 2023. https://www.youtube.com/watch?v=cp_aDsrT9vg.

Bibliography

Heavy Duty College. "Mike Mentzer: Philosophy in a Car (Stereo)." April 22, 2022. https://youtube.com/watch?v=/HfUoES_IwNU.

Heavy Duty College. "Mike Mentzer: The Poison Flies of the Marketplace." August 22, 2022. https://www.youtube.com/watch?v=l7nWv4K-TCg.

Heavy Duty College. "Mike Mentzer: Radio Interview on Ayn Rand, Philosophy and Bodybuilding." July 23, 2023. https://youtube.com/watch?v=tUPfp2Ur8wg.

Heavy Duty College. "Mike Mentzer: 'Realize Your Muscular Potential in One Year or Less!'" January 1, 2024. https://www.youtube.com/watch?v=lovwBagKyoM.

Heavy Duty College. "Mike Mentzer: What's Possible with High Intensity Training?" November 5, 2022. https://www.youtube.com/watch?v=odJTnR8FveU.

Heavy Duty College. "Ray Mentzer: High-Intensity Training with the Ray Mentzer Way." April 4, 2022. https://www.youtube.com/watch?v=d_-aNUqNreE.

Heavy Duty College. "Ray Mentzer: The Truth About Bodybuilding." October 9, 2023. https://www.youtube.com/watch?v=v1G8mJw9Rvw.

Kasmar, Gary. "Arnold Schwarzenegger interview — North Delta Fitness Centre — 1981." March 23, 2019. https://www.youtube.com/watch?v=KS9AqscrZCQ.

Laughlin, Kit, dir. *The Comeback* (a.k.a. *Total Rebuild*). 1980. Produced by Paul Graham and Geoff Bennett. https://www.youtube.com/watch?v=DgHQHLAepMg.

Markus Reinhardt High Intensity Trainer. "How I Lived with Mike Mentzer 1." June 12, 2024. https://www.youtube.com/watch?v=umSgNm83y5M.

Markus Reinhardt High Intensity Trainer. "How I Trained before Mike Mentzer's Duty Training/High Intensity Training." June 6, 2024. https://www.youtube.com/watch?v=LOdiVDoVTLQ&t=1s.

Markus Reinhardt High Intensity Trainer. "Was Mike Mentzer Gay?" July 2, 2024. https://www.youtube.com/watch?v=G1k2VWoVqmw.

McGuff, Doug. "Enhanced vs Unenhanced Training Results." January 15, 2024. https://www.youtube.com/watch?v=bj8Iumo7JwQ.

Perkins, Jack, host. *Biography*. "Arnold Schwarzenegger." Aired February 28, 1997, on A&E. https://www.youtube.com/watch?v=EypYuyBZnpc.

Pro Bodybuilding Weekly (talk radio). "PBW: Remembering Mike Mentzer Part 4." Episode 191. Hosted by Dan Solomon and Bob Chicherillo, May 24, 2010. See YouTube channel for more parts. https://www.youtube.com/watch?v=pUH8dQ28yuo.

RepOne. "Legendary Tom Platz Seminar: David Gym Zurich." September 27, 2018. https://youtube.com/watch?v=D8kPImEouHE.

Retro Muscle. "1976 IFBB Mr. Universe." May 3, 2020. https://www.youtube.com/watch?v=rtKMQeslaXw.

Retro Muscle. "1980 IFBB Mr. Olympia." November 30, 2020. https://www.youtube.com/watch?v=ot93yeQjYYo.

RxMuscle. "The TRUE Story of the 1980–1981 Mr Olympia!" September 7, 2019. https://www.youtube.com/watch?v=lAo8T__LLtQ.

Supersetman. "Arnold FINALLY Admits He Was NOT the BEST at Mr. Olympia 1980." March 12, 2023. https://www.youtube.com/watch?v=R6QWNdALGgo.

Thurston, Mike. "Training Legs with Dorian Yates." September 6, 2022. https://www.youtube.com/watch?v=a2nUmEQLKyw.

ONLINE ARTICLES

AFI Catalog. "Conan the Barbarian (1982)." https://catalog.afi.com/Catalog/moviedetails/56748.

AFI Catalog. "Pumping Iron (1977)." https://catalog.afi.com/Catalog/moviedetails/55925.

Andreas, Peter. "How Methamphetamine Became a Key Part of Nazi Military Strategy." *Time*. January 7, 2020. https://time.com/5752114/nazi-military-drugs/.

Arax, Mark. "An Ethos Developed in the Gym." *Los Angeles Times*. September 29, 2003. https://www.latimes.com/archives/la-xpm-2003-sep-29-fi-arnold29-story.html.

Arnold Schwarzenegger. "Bio." http://www.schwarzenegger.com/bio.

Bagchi, Sagnik. "'I Really Missed Him': Despite Arnold Schwarzenegger Making Tons of Money for Joe Weider, He Sidelined His One Request for a Long Time." EssentiallySports. June 14, 2023. https://www.essentiallysports.com/bodybuildinng-news-i-really-missed-him-despite-arnold-schwarzenegger-making-tons-of-money-for-joe-weider-he-sidelined-his-one-request-for-a-long-time/.

Bagchi, Sagnik. "Sergio Was Better Than Arnold: Bodybuilding Legend Who Defeated Arnold Schwarzenegger Disclosed the Unknown Details About 1972 Mr. Olympia." March 23, 2023. https://www.essentiallysports.com/us-sports-news-bodtbuilding-news-sergio-was-better-than-arnold-bodybuilding-legend-who-defeated-arnold-schwarzenegger-disclosed-the-unknown-details-about-mr-olympia/.

The Barbell Team. "Howard Stern Interviews Arnold: 5 Things We Learned." November 4, 2019. https://www.thebarbell.com/howard-stern-interviews-arnold-5-things-we-learned/.

Bardach, Ann Louise. "The Hush-Hush Deal That Made Arnold Schwarzenegger Governor." *Los Angeles Magazine*. September 1, 2004. https://lamag.com/news/the-hush-hush-deal-that-made-arnold-schwarzenegger-governor.

Bass, Clarence. "Beyond the Universe: The Bill Pearl Story." 2006. https://www.cbass.com/BillPearl.htm.

Beresford, Jack. "Fact Check: Was Arnold Schwarzenegger's Dad a Nazi Sergeant?" *Newsweek*. August 21, 2021. https://www.newsweek.com/fact-check-was-arnold-schwarzeneggers-dad-nazi-sergeant-1618664.

Berk, Philip. "Tomorrow's Stars Yesterday: Arnold Schwarzenegger, 1977." Golden Globes. March 8, 2021. https://goldenglobes.com/articles/tomorrows-stars-yesterday-arnold-schwarzenegger-1977/.

Better Health Channel. "Anabolic Steroids." December 8, 2022. https://www.betterhealth.vic.gov.au/health/healthyliving/steroids.

Bill Pearl Enterprises. "Bill's Career." https://web.archive.org/web/20120128094628/http://www.billpearl.com/career.asp.

Black, Jonathan. "Charles Atlas: Muscle Man." *Smithsonian Magazine*. August 2009. https://www.smithsonianmag.com/history/charles-atlas-muscle-man-34626921/.

Bissell, Andrew. "Love." The Atlas Society. January 26, 2011. https://www.atlassociety.org/post/love.

The Bodybuilding Archive. "The Story of Gold's Gym: The Mecca of Bodybuilding." July 15, 2022. https://thebodybuildingarchive.com/the-story-of-golds-gym-the-mecca-of-bodybuilding/.

BrightQuest. "Amphetamine-Induced Psychosis." https://www.brightquest.com/drug-induced-psychosis/amphetamine-induced-psychosis/.

Bibliography

Bujold, Bernard. "Ben Weider." https://www.lestudio1.com/BiographyBenWeider.html (webpage discontinued).

Burns, Bob. "Mike Mentzer — Bodybuilder, Writer, and Philosopher." https://attitudeadjustment.tripod.com/Speeches/SI-02-01.pdf.

Butler, Desmond, and John Sullivan. "Rigged: The Undoing of America's Premier Bodybuilding Leagues." *Washington Post*. December 16, 2022. https://www.washingtonpost.com/investigations/interactive/2022/manion-bodybuilding-competition-npc-subversion/#.

The Canadian Encyclopedia. "Queen Elizabeth Theatre." February 1, 2010. https://www.thecanadianencyclopedia.ca/en/article/queen-elizabeth-theatre-emc.

Cautillo, Brian. "Madison Square Garden." *History of New York City* (TLTC blog). https://blogs.shu.edu/nyc-history/msg-2/.

Canadian Press. "Ben Weider among New Inductees to Order of Canada." February 20, 2007. https://www.cbc.ca/news/canada/montreal/ben-weider-among-new-inductees-to-order-of-canada-1.658966.

Chapman, David. "John Grimek: The Glow That Never Failed." https://www.musclememory.com/articles/Grimek.html.

Classic Physique Builder (blog). "*Your Physique*: Joe Weider's First Bodybuilding Magazine." September 1, 2007. http://classicphysiquebuilder.blogspot.com/2007/09/your-physique-joe-weiders-first.html?m=1.

Cooper Family Law. "Fault Divorce Grounds in Pennsylvania." https://cooperfamilylawfirm.com/resources/grounds-divorce-pennsylvania/.

The Cooper Institute (blog). "Legendary "Father of Aerobics" Dr. Kenneth H. Cooper Turned 90." May 12, 2021. https://www.cooperinstitute.org/blog/legendary-father-of-aerobics-dr-kenneth-h-cooper-turned-90.

Coulombe, Charles. "Heretic of the Week: Conrad Beissel." *Catholic Herald*. November 21, 2019. https://catholicherald.co.uk/heretic-of-the-week-conrad-beissel/.

Cuban Studies Institute. "Oliva, Sergio." https://cubansinamerica.us/prominent-cuban-americans/sports/sergio-oliva/.

Cyberpump. "The Steel Spiel! With Mike Mentzer." October 28, 2001. http://www.cyberpump.com/features/interviews/interview015.html (site discontinued).

Dadvand, Babak. "Gynecomastia and Steroid Use." https://losangelesgynecomastia.org/blog/gynecomastia-and-steroid-use/.

Darden, Ellington. "Old-School Muscle: How Jones Trained Viator for the 1971 Mr. America." April 6, 2006. https://www.t-nation.com/training/old-school-muscle/.

Das, Abhimanyu. "Everything You Never Knew About the Making of *Conan the Barbarian*." Gizmodo. February 17, 2015. https://gizmodo.com/everything-you-never-knew-about-the-making-of-conan-the-1686337892.

DeFrancisco, Tony. "How Larry Scott Trained to Win the Mr. Universe and Mr. Olympia titles." May 24, 2017. https://www.linkedin.com/pulse/how-larry-scott-trained-win-mr-universe-olympia-tony-tony-defrancisco.

Dobkin, Rachel. "Needs Work: I'm a 3-Time Mr. Olympia & Crushed Arnold Schwarzenegger's Mr Universe Dreams — His 'Balloon Belly' Was a Major Mistake." *US Sun*. July 5, 2003. https://www.the-sun.com/news/8531469/bodybuilder-frank-zane-beat-arnold-schwarzeneggers-mr-universe/.

Drasin, Rick. "The Birth of World Gym." *HuffPost*. July 26, 2016. https://www.huffpost.com /entry/the-birth-of-world-gym_b_11172306.

Dusa, Michael. "Conversation with Mr. Universe, Mighty Mike Quinn." *Bodybuilding Mauritius & South Africa* (blog). February 25, 2015. https://bodybuilding-mauritius. blogspot.com/2015/02/conversation-with-mr-universe-mighty.html.

Elephant Database. "Jumbolair (Arthur Jones) Elephants in United States." Updated December 9, 2020. https://www.elephant.se/location2.php?location_id=914.

Elk, Kathleen. "The Way Arnold Schwarzenegger Made His First Million Had Nothing to Do with Acting." CNBC. February 6, 2017. https://www.cnbc.com/2017/02/06/the -way-arnold-schwarzenegger-made-his-first-million.html.

Ellis, Philip. "Arnold Schwarzenegger Says It 'Sucks' Not Having His Mr. Olympia Body." *Men's Health*. October 10, 2023. https://www.menshealth.com/uk/fitness/a45508341 /arnold-schwarzenegger-aging-body-image-physique/.

Encyclopaedia Britannica. "Eugen Sandow, German Athlete." Updated March 29, 2024. https://www.britannica.com/biography/Eugen-Sandow.

Encyclopaedia Britannica. "Nîmes." https://www.britannica.com/place/Nimes.

Encyclopaedia Britannica. "The 20th and 21st Centuries." https://www.britannica.com /technology/history-of-technology/The-20th-and-21st-centuries.

Encyclopaedia Britannica. "Wilhelm Reich." November 22, 2022. http://www.britannica .com/biography/Wilhelm-Reich.

Encyclopedia.com. "Grimek, John (1910–1998)." *St. James Encyclopedia of Popular Culture*. March 18, 2024. https://www.encyclopedia.com/media/encyclopedias-almanacs -transcripts-and-maps/grimek-john-1910-1998.

Encyclopedia.com. "The 1970s Medicine and Health: Chronology." *U-X-L American Decades*. March 18, 2024. https://www.encyclopedia.com/social-sciences/culture -magazines/1970s-medicine-and-health-chronology.

Encyclopedia Nomadica. "Reich-Einstein Experiment." https://encyclopedianomadica .org/index.html.

Everts, Kellie. "The Arnold & Kellie Affair." http://kellieevertsistripforgod.com /arnoldkellieaffair.php.

Family Search. "Johannes Meinzer (ID: KV2D-Y6R)." https://ancestors.familysearch.org /KV2D-Y6R/johannes-meinzer-1701-1781.

Farrington, Ian (blog). "The Streets of San Francisco: Dead Lift (1977, Michael Preece)." September 13, 2020. https://ianfarrington.wordpress.com/2020/09/13/the-streets-of -san-francisco-dead-lift-1977-michael-preece/.

Ferrell, David. "Body Building: Joe Weider's Iron Grip on an Empire." *Los Angeles Times*. March 2, 1989. https://www.latimes.com/archives/la-xpm-1989-03-02-mn-254-story.html.

Feldman, Charles. "Man Who Dreamed of Being 'King of the Earth.'" CNN. August 12, 2003. http://www.cnn.com/2003/ALLPOLITICS/08/12/schwarzeneger.ambition/.

Ferriss, Tim (blog). "Arnold Schwarzenegger on *The Tim Ferriss Show* — Transcript." Episode 60, February 2, 2015. https://tim.blog/arnold-schwarzenegger-transcript/.

Find a Grave. "Elmer Mantyla Jr." Memorial ID: 204734831. https://www.findagrave.com /memorial/204734831/elmer-mantyla.

Find a Grave. "Kathryn 'Katie' Coldren Mentzer." Memorial ID: 92580675. https://www .findagrave.com/memorial/92580675/kathryn-mentzer.

Bibliography

Fitness Volt Editorial Team. "Arthur Jones — Complete Profile: Height, Workout and Diet." Updated December 30, 2023. https://fitnessvolt.com/15785/arthur-jones/.

Flex Staff. "Pearl's Wisdom." *Muscle & Fitness*. https://www.muscleandfitness.com/flexonline/flex-news/pearls-wisdom/.

Forrest, Brad. "Like Father, Like Son — Not Horsing Around with Dude." *St George & Sutherland Shire Leader*. February 16, 2013. https://www.theleader.com.au/story/1299457/like-father-like-son-not-horsing-around-with-dude/.

Gallagher, Marty. "Muscle Myths." April 17, 2022. https://www.ironcompany.com/blog/muscle-myths.

The Governor General of Canada. "Mr. Ben Weider." https://www.gg.ca/en/honours/recipients/146-13149.

GPACalculator.net. "3.7 GPA." https://gpacalculator.net/gpa-scale/3-7-gpa/.

Gregersen, Erik. "History of Technology Timeline." *Encyclopaedia Britannica*. January 15, 2019. https://www.britannica.com/story/history-of-technology-timeline.

Greatest Physiques. "Casey Viator." https://www.greatestphysiques.com/male-physiques/casey-viator/.

Greatest Physiques. "Kalman Szkalak." https://www.greatestphysiques.com/male-physiques/kalman-szkalak/.

Grech, Kevin. "Arnold Schwarzenegger Risked Suspension from the IFBB in 1971." March 31, 2023. https://www.evolutionofbodybuilding.net/arnold-schwarzenegger-risked-suspension-in-1971-from-the-ifbb/.

Green, Nate. "HIT, Spit, and Bullshit: An Interview with Ellington Darden." T Nation. October 2008. https://forums.t-nation.com/t/hit-spit-and-bullshit/284518.

Hansen, John. "Arnold vs. Sergio — Part 3." July 24, 2013. http://rxmuscle.com/articles/john-hansen/8867-arnold-vs-sergio-part-3.html.

Hansen, John. "The Most Controversial Olympia — Part 1." August 6, 2011. http://www.rxmuscle.com/index.php/articles/john-hansen/3854-the-most-controversial-mr-olympia-part-1.html.

Hansen, John. "1981 Mr. Olympia Report — Part 2." *Iron Man*. January 11, 2013. https://www.ironmanmagazine.com/1981-mr-olympia-report-part-2/.

Hansen, John. "Remembering the 1981 Mr. Olympia — Part 1." *Iron Man*. May 6, 2012. https://www.ironmanmagazine.com/remembering-the-1981-mr-olympia-part-1/.

Hansen, John. "Sergio Oliva 'The Myth' — R.I.P." *Iron Man*. November 17, 2012. https://www.ironmanmagazine.com/741/.

Hansen, John. "The Tijuana Incident." February 9, 2014. https://www.rxmuscle.com/index.php/articles/john-hansen/10155-the-tijuana-incident.html.

Hardiman, Jess. "Arnold Schwarzenegger Reveals How Much of His Bodybuilding Progress Was Down to Steroids." UNILAD. June 6, 2023. https://www.unilad.com/film-and-tv/did-arnold-schwarzenegger-use-steroids-netflix-documentary-792970-20230606.

Harris, Ron. "The Story Behind Arnold Schwarzenegger & *Pumping Iron*: Exclusive Interview with George Butler." *Muscular Development*. January 18, 2016. https://www.musculardevelopment.com/news/bodybuilding-news/14866-the-story-behind-arnold-schwarzenegger-pumping-iron-exclusive-interview-with-george-butler.html.

Heffernan, Conor. "Old Time Selling — Eugen Sandow and the Business of Supplements."

https://physicalculturestudy.com/2015/05/12/old-time-selling-eugen-sandow-and-the-business-of-supplements/.

Heffernan, Conor. "The Real Story Behind the 1975 Mr. Olympia Is Far More Fascinating Than 'Pumping Iron' Ever Portrayed." Updated September 15, 2023. https://barbend.com/1975-mr-olympia/.

Heffernan, Conor. "Soy, Science and Selling: Bob Hoffman's Hi-Proteen Powder." Physical Culture Study. June 15, 2016. https://physicalculturestudy.com/2016/06/15/soy-science-and-selling-bob-hoffmans-hi-proteen-powder/.

Heffernan, Conor. "Supplements Bodybuilding Forgot: Bob Hoffman's Fish Protein Powder." Physical Culture Study. May 12, 2016. https://physicalculturestudy.com/2016/05/12/supplements-bodybuilding-forgot-bob-hoffmans-fish-protein-powder/.

Hiltzik, Michael. "A True 'Hot Property': Elliott Gould's 'Long Goodbye' Apartment Is for Rent!" *Los Angeles Times*. December 3, 2014. https://www.latimes.com/business/hiltzik/la-fi-mh-goulds-long-goodbye-apartment-20141203-column.html.

History.com. "Battle of Germantown." Updated June 26, 2023. https://www.history.com/topics/american-revolution/battle-of-germantown.

Husbands, Ajani. "Timeline of Apartheid." Updated September 19, 2004. https://web.stanford.edu/~jbaugh/saw/Ajani_Apartheid.html.

IFBB (International Fitness and Bodybuilding Federation). "The Founding Fathers, Ben and Joe Weider." https://ifbb.com/the-founding-fathers-ben-and-joe-weider/.

IFBB. "IFBB Rules for Bodybuilding and Fitness." 2021 edition. https://ifbb.com/wp-content/uploads/2021/04/01-IFBB-General-Rules-2021-edition-F.pdf.

IFBB. "1976 World Bodybuilding Championships and International Congress." https://www.rbimba.lt/faktai/1976congress.html.

IOC (International Olympic Committee). "Anthony Michael Garcy." https://olympics.com/en/athletes/anthony-michael-garcy.

IOC. "Berlin 1936 Weightlifting 82.5 KG Heavyweight Men." https://olympics.com/en/olympic-games/berlin-1936/results/weightlifting/825kg-heavyweight-men.

IMDb. "*Conan the Barbarian*: Trivia." https://m.imdb.com/title/tt0082198/trivia/?ref_=tt_trv_trv.

IMDb. "*Happy Anniversary and Goodbye*." https://m.imdb.com/title/tt0438076/.

IMDb. "*Hercules in New York*: Trivia." https://m.imdb.com/title/tt0065832/trivia/.

IMDb. "*The Mike Douglas Show*, Episode #19.161" https://www.imdb.com/title/tt4590324/.

IMDb. "*The San Pedro Beach Bums* (1977)." https://www.imdb.com/title/tt0075575/characters/nm0000216.

IMDb. "Sven-Ole Thorsen." https://www.imdb.com/name/nm0861752/.

Iron Man magazine. "Dave Mastorakis, 59, Strives to Get His Contest Body Back." January 11, 2011. https://www.ironmanmagazine.com/dave-mastorakis-59-strives-to-get-his-contest-body-back/.

Johnston, Brian D. "An Interview with Arthur Jones." http://arthurjonesexercise.com/Extras/Interview1.PDF.

Johnston, Brian D. "Sergio Oliva Interview." https://muscleandbrawn.com/workouts/sergio-oliva-training-routine/.

Jones, Arthur. "And God Laughs . . ." http://arthurjonesexercise.com/GodLaughs/2.PDF.

Jones, Arthur. "The Colorado Experiment." http://arthurjonesexercise.com/Iron Man/Colorado.PDF.

Bibliography

Jones, Arthur. "From Here to Infinity . . . or very close." http://arthurjonesexercise.com/Athletic/DuoSquat.PDF.

Jones, Arthur. "My First Half-Century in the Iron Game," chapter 11. http://arthurjonesexercise.com/First_Half/11.PDF.

Jones, Arthur. "The Most Important Area of the Body Featuring the Lower Back Machine." http://arthurjonesexercise.com/Athletic/MostImportant.PDF.

Jones, Arthur. "Nautilus Bulletin #2," chapter 23. http://arthurjonesexercise.com/Bulletin2/23.PDF.

Jones, Arthur. "Nautilus Bulletin #2," chapter 24. http://arthurjonesexercise.com/Bulletin2/24.PDF.

Jones, Arthur. "Nautilus Bulletin #2," chapter 36. http://arthurjonesexercise.com/Bulletin2/36.PDF.

Jones, Arthur. "The Next Step." *Iron Man*, July 1971. http://arthurjonesexercise.com/Ironman/NextStep.PDF.

Jones, Arthur, and Dr. Elliott Plese. "The Colorado Experiment." http://arthurjonesexercise.com/Unpublished/Colorado.pdf.

Kavoussi, Parviz K. "Anabolic Steroids Long Term Effect." November 18, 2014. https://austinmenshealth.com/anabolic-steroids-long-term-effect/.

Khzokhlachev, Yegor. "Arnold Schwarzenegger in Hawaii." January 18, 2015. https://www.builtreport.com/arnold-schwarzenegger-in-hawaii/.

Khzokhlachev, Yegor. "Kal Szkalak Gallery 2." September 27, 2022. https://www.builtreport.com/kal-szkalak-gallery-2/.

Labbe, Rodney A. "1999 Bill Pearl Interview." March 2, 2020. *The Tight Tan Slacks of Dezso Ban* (blog). http://ditillo2.blogspot.com/2020/03/1999-bill-pearl-interview-rodney-labbe.html.

LeDuff, Charlie. "Ethnic Issues in Recall Play Out at Latino Parade." *New York Times*. September 8, 2003. https://web.archive.org/web/20140309092800/http://www.nytimes.com/2003/09/08/national/08ARNO.html?hp.

Leibovich, Mark. "Arnold Schwarzenegger's Last Act: What happens when the Terminator turns 75." *The Atlantic*. March 8, 2023. https://www.theatlantic.com/magazine/archive/2023/04/arnold-schwarzenegger-ukraine-covid-speech/673089/.

Leistner, Ken. "York, Weider, and Jackson." June 17, 2014. https://titansupport.com/history-of-powerlifting-weightlifting-and-strength-training-part-9/.

Little, John. "'Warm Marble' The Lethal Physique of Bruce Lee." Introduction by Mike Mentzer. May 24, 2001. See "Articles" tab in the navigational menu. https://web.archive.org/web/20010708014936/http://www.mikementzer.com/.

Lockridge, Roger. "Becoming a Legend: Frank Zane's Top 10 Training Tips." *Muscle & Fitness*. https://www.muscleandfitness.com/athletes-celebrities/pro-tips/becoming-legend-frank-zane-s-top-10-training-tips/.

Los Angeles Times. "Joe Weider Dies at 93; Bodybuilding Pioneer and Publisher." March 23, 2013. https://www.latimes.com/local/obituaries/la-me-0324-joe-weider-20130324-story.html.

Lowry, Katharine. "The Show of Muscles at the Whitney Was Vitiated by Academic Flabbiness." *Sports Illustrated*. June 7, 1976. https://vault.si.com/vault/1976/06/07/the-show-of-muscles-at-the-whitney-was-vitiated-by-academic-flabbiness.

Lund, Chris. "Looking Back: Casey Viator." *Flex*. August 2013. https://www.caseyviator.com/flexarticle.pdf.

Luoma, T.C. "1993 Vince Gironda Interview." *The Tight Tan Slacks of Dezso Ban* (blog). October 15, 2023. http://ditillo2.blogspot.com/2013/10/1993-vince-gironda-interview-tc-luoma.html.

Lurie, Dan. "Dan Lurie Barbell Company." See "Business" tab in the navigational menu. https://web.archive.org/web/20211201025455/http://danlurie.com/.

Masin, Herman L. "A Beautiful Mind: Arthur Jones, the Man Who Invented the Nautilus Machine and Revolutionized Strength Training. (Person to Person)." *Coach and Athletic Director*. Scholastic Inc. May 1, 2002. https://www.thefreelibrary.com/A+beautiful+mind%3A+Arthur+Jones%2C+the+man+who+invented+thwith theautilus...-a086040249.

Mayo Clinic Staff. "Bipolar Disorder." December 13, 2022. https://www.mayoclinic.org/diseases-conditions/bipolar-disorder/symptoms-causes/syc-20355955.

McGough, Peter. "Dan Lurie: 1923–2013." *Muscular Development*. November 7, 2013. https://www.musculardevelopment.com/news/bodybuilding-news/12334-dan-lurie-1923-2013.html#.UvszWnz-Cf8.

McGough, Peter. "Dorian & Mentzer: Was It a Pupil-Mentor Relationship?" *Muscular Development*. April 24, 2013. https://www.musculardevelopment.com/news/the-mcgough-report/5582-dorian-mentzer-was-it-a-pupil-mentor-relationship.html.

McGough, Peter. "Hey Frank! I Have a Secret!" *Muscular Development*. September 10, 2013. https://www.musculardevelopment.com/news/the-mcgough-report/12079-hey-frank-i-have-a-secret.html.

McGough, Peter. "Mike Mentzer: The Untold Story of the Journey to his Final Days." *Muscular Development*. November 5, 2017. https://www.musculardevelopment.com/news/the-mcgough-report/13217-mike-mentzer-the-untold-story-muscular-development.html.

McGough, Peter. "Tom & Arnold: When Platz Met Schwarzenegger." *Muscular Development*. April 3, 2013. https://musculardevelopment.com/news/the-mcgough-report/5492-when-platz-met-schwarzenegger-by-peter-mcgough.html.

M&F Editors. "Joe Weider: The Master Blaster." *Muscle & Fitness*. https://www.muscleandfitness.com/athletes-celebrities/news/joe-weider-master-blaster/.

Mentzer, Mike. "The Best Within Us." May 29, 2001. See "Welcome" tab in the navigational menu. https://web.archive.org/web/20010708014936/http://www.mikementzer.com/.

Merritt, Greg. "Arnold Schwarzenegger's 12 Secrets to Success." *Muscle & Fitness*. https://www.muscleandfitness.com/athletes-celebrities/pro-tips/arnolds-12-secrets-success/.

Merritt, Greg. "Chris Dickerson (1939–2021): The Life of the 1982 Mr. Olympia." December 24, 2021. https://thebarbell.com/chris-dickerson-life-of-1982-mr-olympia/.

Merritt, Greg. "Joe Weider's Story: Bodybuilding, Magazines, and Arnold Schwarzenegger." *Muscle & Fitness*. https://www.muscleandfitness.com/athletes-celebrities/news/joe-weiders-story-bodybuilding-magazines-and-arnold-schwarzenegger/.

Merritt, Greg. "The 1965 Mr. Olympia." September 27, 2022. https://www.thebarbell.com/first-mr-olympia/.

Morris, Betsy, et al. "Arnold Power: He Accumulates It. He Wields It. He Wins Over Voters with It. But Is the Governator's Star Power Enough to Win the War of Wills with His California Opponents?" *Fortune*, August 9, 2004. https://money.cnn.com/magazines/fortune/fortune_archive/2004/08/09/377908/.

MuscleMemory. "Arnold Schwarzenegger." http://www.musclememory.com/show.php?s=Arnold+Schwarzenegger&g=M.

Bibliography

MuscleMemory. "Boyer Coe." http://musclememory.com/show.php?s=Boyer+coe&g=M.
MuscleMemory. "Franco Columbu." http://musclememory.com/show.php?a=Columbu,+Franco.
MuscleMemory. "Frank Zane." http://musclememory.com/show.php?a=Zane,+Frank.
MuscleMemory. "Julie McNew." https://musclememory.com/show.php?a=McNew,+Julie&g=1.
MuscleMemory. "Kalman Szkalak." http://musclememory.com/show.php?a=Szkalak,+Kalman.
MuscleMemory. "Larry Scott." https://musclememory.com/show.php?a=Scott,+Larry.
MuscleMemory. "Ray Mentzer." http://musclememory.com/show.php?a=Mentzer,+Ray.
MuscleMemory. "Robby Robinson." http://musclememory.com/show.php?a=Robinson,+Robby.
MuscleMemory. "1971 Teen Mr America — AAU." http://musclememory.com/show.php?c=Teen+Mr+America+-+AAU&y=1971.
MuscleMemory. "1975 Mr USA — IFBB." http://musclememory.com/show.php?c=Mr+USA+-+IFBB&y=1975.
MuscleMemory. "1975 Mr World — IFBB." https://www.musclememory.com/show.php?c=Mr+World+-+IFBB&y=1975.
MuscleMemory. "1980 Universe — Pro — IFBB." http://musclememory.com/show.php?c=Universe+-+Pro+-+IFBB&y=1980.
Muscle & Strength. "Interview with Mr. Olympia Frank Zane." https://www.muscleandstrength.com/articles/interview-with-mr-olympia-frank-zane.html.
Nailon, Robert. "Arnold Schwarzenegger Q & A Interview." https://thearnoldcollection.com/schwarzenegger-blog/arnold-schwarzenegger-q-a-interview-robert-nailon/.
National Museum of the United States Air Force. "Lt. Gen. Frank M. Andrews." https://www.nationalmuseum.af.mil/Visit/Museum-Exhibits/Fact-Sheets/Display/Article/196933/lt-gen-frank-m-andrews/.
National Park Service. "Germantown Quaker Petition Against Slavery." Updated April 5, 2016. https://www.nps.gov/articles/quakerpetition.htm.
National Park Service. "Germantown White House." Updated August 11, 2021. https://www.nps.gov/inde/learn/historyculture/places-germantownwhitehouse.htm.
Natural Products Insider. "Weider Sells Active Nutrition Brands." May 23, 2005. https://www.naturalproductsinsider.com/market-trends-analysis/weider-sells-active-nutrition-brands.
Nîmes Tourisme. "Nîmes across the Centuries." https://www.nimes-tourisme.com/experience/en/.
The Nobel Prize. "John F. Nash Jr. Biographical." https://www.nobelprize.org/prizes/economic-sciences/1994/nash/biographical/.
Ojomu, Nola. "'He could go crazy at any time': Arnold Schwarzenegger Brands His Nazi Father 'a TYRANT' as He Recalls the 'Brutal' Abuse and Beatings He Suffered at His Hands as a Child." *Daily Mail*. June 6, 2023. https://www.dailymail.co.uk/tvshowbiz/article-12165575/Arnold-Netflix-Schwarzenegger-opens-abusive-childhood-Nazi-father.html.
Old School Labs. "Mr. Olympia 1965: The First-Ever Mr. Olympia." https://www.oldschoollabs.com/mr-olympia-1965/.
Old School Labs. "Mr. Olympia 1970 — The Arnold & Sergio Rematch." https://www.oldschoollabs.com/mr-olympia-1970/.

Old School Labs. "Mr. Olympia 1971: A Controversial Year." https://www.oldschoollabs.com/mr-olympia-1971/.

Old School Labs. "Mr. Olympia 1974: The Final Showdown of Arnold & Lou." https://www.oldschoollabs.com/mr-olympia-1974/.

Old School Labs. "Mr. Olympia 1976: An Absent Arnold Provides Opportunity." https://www.oldschoollabs.com/mr-olympia-1976/.

Online World of Wrestling. "Paul Graham." https://www.onlineworldofwrestling.com/profile/paul-graham/.

Osho. "Nobody Listened to Wilhelm Reich" September 26, 2013. https://www.oshonews.com/2013/09/26/osho-on-wilhelm-reich/.

PCSing.com. "Andrews Air Force Base." https://pcsing.com/base/andrews-air-force-base.

Perine, Shawn. "Pumping Iron: The George Butler Interview." August 8, 2021. https://thebarbell.com/pumping-iron-the-george-butler-interview/.

Peters, Justin. "The Man Behind the Juice: Fifty Years Ago, a Doctor Brought Steroids to America." February 18, 2005. https://slate.com/culture/2005/02/the-doctor-who-brought-steroids-to-america.html.

Peterson, James A. "Total Conditioning: A Case Study." *Athletic Journal*. September 1975. http://arthurjonesexercise.com/Athletic/Total.PDF.

Pope, Carmen. "'Black Beauties' capsules in the 1970's — What drug was that?" Updated September 5, 2022. https://www.drugs.com/medical-answers/remember-taking-black-capsule-1970s-called-black-2367873/.

Rafael, Dan. "No 'Guts', No Glory for Tyson in Defeat." ESPN. June 11, 2005. https://www.espn.com/sports/boxing/news/story?id=2083271.

Richardson, Andy. "Bodybuilder 'The Chemist' Who Beat Arnold Schwarzenegger Still Pumping Iron at 80." *Daily Star*. July 30, 2022. https://www.dailystar.co.uk/diet-fitness/bodybuilder-the-chemist-who-beat-27589101.

Robson, David. "An Interview with the Myth: The One and Only Sergio Oliva!" https://www.bodybuilding.com/fun/drobson331.htm (webpage discontinued).

Robson, David. "An Interview with Three-time Mr. Olympia Frank Zane." https://www.bodybuilding.com/fun/drobson294.htm (webpage discontinued).

Rotten Tomatoes. "The Jayne Mansfield Story." https://www.rottentomatoes.com/m/jayne_mansfield_a_symbol_of_the_50s.

Rowbottom, Mike. "President Rafael Santonja — Building a Body of Opinion to take IFBB towards the Olympics." March 18, 2018. https://www.insidethegames.biz/articles/1062811/president-rafael-santonja-building-a-body-of-opinion-to-take-ifbb-towards-the-olympics.

Roy, Tanmay. "Decades Later, Arnold Schwarzenegger Discloses How He Made Millions While America Was Witnessing One of the Biggest Inflations in the 70s." June 7, 2023. https://www.essentiallysports.com/bodybuilding-news-mr-olympia-news-decades-later-arnold-schwarzenegger-discloses-how-he-made-millions-while-america-was-witnessing-one-of-the-biggest-inflations-in-the/.

Roy, Tanmay. "While Other Bodybuilders Failed, Mastermind Arnold Schwarzenegger Made Millions in Mail-Order Business Back in the Days." March 18, 2023. https://www.essentiallysports.com/us-sports-news-bodybuilding-news-mr-olympia-news-while-other-bodybuilders-failed-mastermind-arnold-schwarzenegger-made-millions-in-mail-order-business/.

Bibliography

Sadek, James. "An Interview with Mr. Universe Roger Walker!" https://www.bodybuilding.com/fun/teen-james48.htm (webpage discontinued).

Salmon, Jonathan. "Breaking: Mr. Olympia Has Been Sold by American Media Inc." February 14, 2020. https://generationiron.com/olympia-muscle-fitness-sold/.

The Sandwich. "Mike Mentzer's Last Interview." *Iron Man* magazine. October 1, 2001. https://www.ironmanmagazine.com/mike-mentzers-last-interview/.

The Sandwich. "Mike Mentzer: Words of Tribute From his Friends, Colleagues and Those He Inspired." *Iron Man* magazine. November 1, 2001. https://www.ironmanmagazine.com/mike-mentzer/.

Saunders, Doug. "Schwarzenegger's views on Hitler examined." *Globe and Mail*. October 4, 2003. https://www.theglobeandmail.com/news/world/schwarzeneggers-views-on-hitler-examined/article18432068/.

Schwarzenegger, Arnold. "This is a Long One (But It's Worth It)." http://www.schwarzenegger.com/newsletter/post/this-is-a-long-one-but-its-worth-it.

Semple, Kirk. "The Rise of the Machines." *New York Times*. October 11, 2008. https://www.nytimes.com/2007/09/02/weekinreview/02semple.html.

Set For Set. "Every Olympia Winner & Prize Money." Email newsletter. December 7, 2022. https://deal.town/set-for-set/every-olympia-winner-and-prize-money-FKT4BQJT8.

Schott, Webster. "Wilhelm Reich: A Prisoner of Sex." *Washington Post*. February 5, 1983. https://www.washingtonpost.com/archive/entertainment/books/1983/02/06/wilhelm-reich-a-prisoner-of-sex/10e319e7-fab3-4e69-9ce4-5b93b1e91f8c/.

Solace Treatment Center. "What Is Steroid Induced Psychosis?" https://solacetreatmentcenter.com/steroid-induced-psychosis/.

Sports History Weekly. "'Pumping Iron' Goes Mainstream." March 17, 2019. https://www.sportshistoryweekly.com/stories/arnold-schwarzenegger-pumping-iron-bodybuilding-lou-ferrigno,691.

Stamatopoulos, John. "Mike Mentzer Exclusive Interview! A Bodybuilding Legend." https://www.bodybuilding.com/fun/mminter.htm (webpage discontinued).

Starr, Bill. "Doc Ziegler." September 15, 2011. https://startingstrength.com/article/doc_ziegler.

Stojkovski, Kire, and Daniel Boyer. "How Do Steroids Work?" *Charlotte Observer*. January 10, 2023. https://www.charlotteobserver.com/health-wellness/article267495348.html.

Sullivan, Patricia. "Arthur Jones, Eccentric Reshaped the Exercise World, Dies at 80." *Seattle Times*. September 2, 2007. https://www.seattletimes.com/nation-world/arthur-jones-eccentric-reshaped-the-exercise-world-dies-at-80/.

Tanner, Adam. "Legendary Promoter Says Steroids Widespread in Sports." Reuters. August 9, 2007. https://www.reuters.com/article/idUSN09328725/.

Teper, Lonnie. "Lou Ferrigno." *Iron Man* magazine. April 27, 2009. https://www.ironmanmagazine.com/lou-ferrigno/.

Thompson, Helen. "Walk, Don't Run." *Texas Monthly*. June 1995. https://www.texasmonthly.com/news-politics/walk-dont-run/.

Thornton, Philip. "Phentermine." Updated November 9, 2023. https://www.drugs.com/phentermine.html.

Topel, Fred. "Beyond Fest: Arnold Schwarzenegger and Bill Duke Q&A." October 7, 2017. https://weliveentertainment.com/welivefilm/beyond-fest-arnold-schwarzenegger-bill-duke-qa/.

Toto, Christian. "How Arnold Schwarzenegger Became Box Office Poison." November 5, 2019. https://www.hollywoodintoto.com/schwarzenegger-box-office-poison/.

Tsantens. "Paul Graham and Arnold Schwarzenegger: A Partnership Forged in Iron." August 4, 2023. https://joinarnold.com/paul-graham/.

USA Strength & Conditioning Coaches Hall of Fame. "Arthur Jones." https://www.usastrengthcoacheshf.com/member/arthur-jones.

USA Strength & Conditioning Coaches Hall of Fame. "Robert C. Hoffman." https://www.usastrengthcoacheshf.com/member/robert-c-hoffman.

U.S. Department of State — Bureau of Consular Affairs. "Visitor Visa." https://travel.state.gov/content/travel/en/us-visas/tourism-visit/visitor.html.

U.S. Department of State Archive. "The End of Apartheid." https://2001-2009.state.gov/r/pa/ho/time/pcw/98678.htm.

Vermont Department of Health. "A Brief History of Methamphetamine — Methamphetamine Prevention in Vermont." https://web.archive.org/web/20120419175754/http://healthvermont.gov/adap/meth/brief_history.aspx.

Villines, Zawn. "What are Chakras and How Do They Affect Health?" Updated November 20, 2023. https://www.medicalnewstoday.com/articles/what-are-chakras-concept-origins-and-effect-on-health.

Watkinson, Maggie, and Julie Jenks. "Minimizing the Risks of Amphetamine Use for Young Adults with Diabetes." December 9, 1998. https://www.pcdsociety.org/resources/details/minimising-the-risks-of-amphetamine-use-for-young-adults-with-diabetes.

Waymarking.com. "Centre Claude-Robillard (Montreal 1976)." https://www.waymarking.com/waymarks/WMYN0D_Centre_Claude_Robillard_Montreal_1976.

WebMD. "Ellington Darden." https://www.webmd.com/ellington-darden.

Webster, Ian. "Value of $25,000 from 1970 to 2024." https://www.in2013dollars.com/us/inflation/1970?amount=25000.

Wieder, Joe. "Awards." https://www.joeweider.com/photos/awards/.

Weik, Matt. "An Interview with Six-Time World Champion Bodybuilder Serge Nubret!" https://www.bodybuilding.com/fun/weik79.htm (webpage discontinued).

Williams, David R. "Apollo Lunar Landings (1969–1972)." NSSDCA (NASA Space Science Data Coordinated Archive). Updated March 6, 2017. https://nssdc.gsfc.nasa.gov/planetary/lunar/apolloland.html.

Wood, John. "The Arm of Casey Viator." January 28, 2014. *Oldtime Strongman* (blog). https://www.oldtimestrongman.com/blog/2014/01/28/the-arm-of-casey-viator/.

WorthPoint. "AAU Mr America Contest Sept 8, 1979 Bodybuilding Program Frank Zane Cover." https://www.worthpoint.com/worthopedia/aau-mr-america-contest-sept-1979-2008921197.

Zane, Frank. "1979 My Greatest Mr. Olympia Win." October 18, 2021. https://frankzane.com/1979-my-greatest-mr-olympia-win/.

Zane, Frank. "1980 Mr. Olympia." October 12, 2022. https://frankzane.com/1980-mr-olympia/.

Zane, Frank. "1980 Mr. Olympia Part II." January 6, 2022. https://frankzane.com/1980-mr-olympia-part-ii/.

Zucker, Noah. "Power Shift: I was a Mr. Olympia Finalist Mentored by Arnold Schwarzenegger — I'm Unrecognizable after Switching to Another Sport." *US Sun*. July 11, 2023. https://www.the-sun.com/news/8575120/kalman-szkalak-bodybuilder-switch-cycling-sports-athlete/amp/.

Bibliography

Zucker, William. "Keeping Up with Arthur Jones." Interview, 2000. http://arthurjones exercise.com/Extras/Interview2.PDF.

GOVERNMENT DOCUMENTS

Alberta Municipal Affairs. "1980 Population." http://municipalaffairs.gov.ab.ca/documents /ms/1980population.pdf.

Boyer, Carl, ed. *Ship Passenger Lists, Pennsylvania and Delaware (1641–1825)*. Westminster, MD: Heritage Books, (1980) 2007.

Commonwealth of Virginia, Department of Health — Bureau of Vital Records and Health Statistics. Delayed Birth Records, 1721–1920.

Gannett, Henry. *The Origin of Certain Place Names in the United States*. Washington Government Printing Office, 1905.

House of Representatives. "Anabolic Steroid Control Act of 2004." 108th Congress, 2nd Session, Report 108-461, April 2, 2004. https://www.govinfo.gov/content/pkg/CRPT -108hrpt461/html/CRPT-108hrpt461-pt1.htm.

Minnesota, U.S. Births and Christenings Index, 1840–1980.

1940 United States Federal Census.

1950 United States Federal Census.

The Origin of Certain Place Names in the United States. Washington Government Printing Office, 1905.

U.S. and Canada, Passenger and Immigration Lists Index, 1500s–1900s.

U.S. Federal Naturalization Record for Anna De Stefano, District Court, Eastern District, Pennsylvania, Petition Number: 121281.

U.S. Federal Naturalization Records, December 1, 1943.

U.S. Federal Naturalization Records, June 15, 1929.

U.S. Social Security Applications and Claims Index, 1936–2007.

U.S. Social Security Death Index, 1935–2014.

U.S. Veterans Burial Card, Commonwealth of Pennsylvania Department of Military Affairs.

U.S. World War II Draft Cards Young Men, 1940–47.

Virginia, U.S., Birth Records, 1912–2015

ACKNOWLEDGMENTS

The author is indebted to many people who assisted him in the writing of this book. First and foremost, an enormous debt of thanks is owed Randy Roach, the most knowledgeable person on the planet when it comes to the history of bodybuilding. Randy kindly took the time to answer my questions, provide materials, and fact-check the manuscript at different stages of its evolution to ensure that my take on the various bodybuilding contests referenced throughout the text was accurate. He further allowed me to "borrow" from his considerable research as presented in his three-volume book series *Muscle, Smoke & Mirrors*. I am beholden to Randy both for his acumen and for his friendship. Other individuals who assisted in the research were John Hansen, who laboriously complied with my repeated requests for articles from the muscle magazines that came out during the 1970s, and Ken Sprague, who provided some fascinating insights and startling material from his legal files. I further need to acknowledge Jack Neary, a fabulous Canuck who revealed through his writings the many facets of Mike and who had the courage and intellectual integrity to write the truth when temptation beckoned him to do otherwise. Thanks to the late, great Roger Schwab (who I wish had been a judge at the 1980 Mr. Olympia) and David Mastorakis (who kept the fires of Mike's youthful bodybuilding ambition stoked). These men gave freely of their time and provided vital information about Mike during the periods of time that they knew him. Dave further gifted me three letters Mike wrote to him from Nautilus headquarters in 1974, which I shall treasure for the rest of my life. A huge thank you goes out to Chris Lund, who provided the photo he took of Mike and me together

Acknowledgments

and was also the man who formally introduced me to Mike. Thanks are also extended to John Balik, not just for his incredible photographs of Mike that he permitted to be included in this publication, but for the kindness he showed to Mike when he was coming out of his dark period. John was the one publisher who was always fair and honest, both in his personal and his business dealings. I know he had Mike's respect, and he most certainly has mine. Thanks also to ace lensman, Garry Bartlett, for providing three images he shot of Mike, one of which I have long held to be the best contest shot ever taken of Mike. Garry became a good friend of Mike's and allowed me access to an interview he recorded with him while in Florida in 1983. I am further grateful to Gail Gardener for the wonderful shot her husband Bob took of Mike that graces the cover. Everyone I interviewed provided a vital piece of the puzzle of Mike's life, and their sharing this information with me resulted in a much better book than it would have been otherwise. I further would like to thank Simon Shawcross (who hosted me and my son in Greece, in an effort to share with us the philosophical landmarks where Mike Mentzer's philosophy arose), Mike Levensen, Markus Reinhardt, Dr. Doug McGuff, Jennika Allen, James Bishop, Jeremy Hymers (who has assisted me in training clients in Mike's methods for over 16 years), Irene Hause, and Peter McGough for their contributions. And, of course, my family — Terri, Riley, Taylor, Brandon, and Ben.

And finally, to Mike Mentzer himself, a man whose company I miss every day, and whose example impacted my life (positively) more than any friend I've ever had.

Γιατί ένας φίλος με καρδιά κατανόησης δεν αξίζει λιγότερο από έναν αδερφό.

For a friend with an understanding heart is worth no less than a brother.

ABOUT THE AUTHOR

JOHN LITTLE is the bestselling author of *Who Killed Tom Thomson?*, *The Donnellys*, and *Wrath of the Dragon*. He was a close friend of Mike Mentzer's for 21 years and the co-author with Mentzer on his final book, *High-Intensity Training the Mike Mentzer Way*. Little's articles have been published in the world's leading health and fitness publications and he has been featured in the *Toronto Star*, the *Globe and Mail*, the *Wall Street Journal*, CNN, A&E's *Biography*, *Unsolved Mysteries*, The Family Channel, NPR, BBC, Global News, *Variety*, and the *Hollywood Reporter*. He resides with his wife, Terri, in Bracebridge, Ontario. He hosts the YouTube channel Heavy Duty College and is the co-creator with Simon Shawcross of the official website for Mike Mentzer, both of which are devoted to the teachings and legacy of Mike Mentzer.

HEAVY DUTY COLLEGE
https://www.youtube.com/channel/UCfQ4gtZm_kUdnxmLIZ5VE6A

THE OFFICIAL WEBSITE FOR MIKE MENTZER
www.mikementzer.org

Entertainment. Writing. Culture.

ECW is a proudly independent, Canadian-owned book publisher. We know great writing can improve people's lives, and we're passionate about sharing original, exciting, and insightful writing across genres.

Thanks for reading along!

We want our books not just to sustain our imaginations, but to help construct a healthier, more just world, and so we've become a certified B Corporation, meaning we meet a high standard of social and environmental responsibility — and we're going to keep aiming higher. We believe books can drive change, but the way we make them can too.

Being a B Corp means that the act of publishing this book should be a force for good — for the planet, for our communities, and for the people that worked to make this book. For example, everyone who worked on this book was paid at least a living wage. You can learn more at the Ontario Living Wage Network.

This book is also available as a Global Certified Accessible™ (GCA) ebook. ECW Press's ebooks are screen reader friendly and are built to meet the needs of those who are unable to read standard print due to blindness, low vision, dyslexia, or a physical disability.

This book is printed on FSC®-certified paper. It contains recycled materials, and other controlled sources, is processed chlorine free, and is manufactured using biogas energy.

ECW's office is situated on land that was the traditional territory of many nations, including the Wendat, the Anishinaabeg, Haudenosaunee, Chippewa, Métis, and current treaty holders the Mississaugas of the Credit. In the 1880s, the land was developed as part of a growing community around St. Matthew's Anglican and other churches. Starting in the 1950s, our neighbourhood was transformed by immigrants fleeing the Vietnam War and Chinese Canadians dispossessed by the building of Nathan Phillips Square and the subsequent rise in real estate value in other Chinatowns. We are grateful to those who cared for the land before us and are proud to be working amidst this mix of cultures.

ecwpress.com